Lecture Notes in Computer Science 1499

Edited by G. Goos, J. Hartmanis and J. van Leeuwen

T0241022

Springer

Berlin
Heidelberg
New York
Barcelona
Budapest
Hong Kong
London
Milan
Paris
Singapore
Tokyo

Shay Kutten (Ed.)

Distributed Computing

12th International Symposium, DISC'98
Andros, Greece, September 24-26, 1998
Proceedings

Springer

Series Editors

Gerhard Goos, Karlsruhe University, Germany
Juris Hartmanis, Cornell University, NY, USA
Jan van Leeuwen, Utrecht University, The Netherlands

Volume Editor

Shay Kutten
IBM T.J. Watson Research Center
P.O. Box 704, Yorktown Heights, NY 10598, USA
and
Faculty of Industrial Engineering and Management
The Technion
Haifa 32000, Israel
E-mail: kutten@ie.technion.ac.il

Cataloging-in-Publication data applied for

Die Deutsche Bibliothek - CIP-Einheitsaufnahme

Distributed computing : 12th international symposium ;
proceedings / DISC '98, Andros, Greece, September 24 - 26, 1998.
Shay Kutten (ed.). - Berlin ; Heidelberg ; New York ; Barcelona ;
Budapest ; Hong Kong ; London ; Milan ; Paris ; Singapore ; Tokyo :
Springer, 1998
  (Lecture notes in computer science ; Vol. 1499)
  ISBN 3-540-65066-0

CR Subject Classification (1991): C.2.4, C.2.2, F.2.2, D.1.3, F.1, D.4.4-5

ISSN 0302-9743
ISBN 3-540-65066-0 Springer-Verlag Berlin Heidelberg New York

Typesetting: Camera-ready by author
SPIN 10638936   06/3142 – 5 4 3 2 1 0   Printed on acid-free paper

Preface

The name of WDAG was changed to DISC (The International Symposium on DIStributed Computing) to reflect the expansion from a workshop to a symposium, as well as the expansion of the area of interest. DISC'98 builds on, and expands, the tradition of WDAG as a truly international symposium on all aspects of distributed computing. It aims to reflect the exciting and rapid developments in this field, and to help lead its continued exploration, by serving as a meeting point for researchers from various sub-fields.

Following 11 WDAGs, DISC'98 is the 12th in the series. This volume of DISC'98 contains the 28 extended abstracts presented at the symposium, held on September 24-26, 1998, in Andros, Greece. Opening the volume are three extended abstracts based on three keynote lectures given at the symposium by Yoram Moses, Nicola Santoro, and Santosh Shrivastava.

The contributed papers were selected from 87 submissions, at a meeting of the program committee held in Athens, following an on-line discussion. The papers were read and evaluated by the program committee members, with the additional very helpful assistance of external reviewers when needed. It is expected that papers based on most of these extended abstracts will appear in scientific journals.

The program committee consisted of: Yair Amir (Johns Hopkins University), Tushar Chandra (IBM T.J. Watson Research Center), Bernadette Charron-Bost (CNRS, Ecole Polytechnique), Alfredo de Santis (University of Salerno), Faith Fich (University of Toronto), Ajei Gopal (IBM, Pervasive Computing), Yuh-Jzer Joung (National University of Taiwan), Shay Kutten – Chair (IBM T.J. Watson Research Center and Technion), Marios Mavronicolas (University of Cyprus), Louise Moser (University of California, Santa Barbara), Noam Nisan (Hebrew University and IDC), Boaz Patt-Shamir (Tel Aviv University), Peter Ruzicka (Comenius University), Nicola Santoro (Carleton University), Marc Shapiro (INRIA), Alex Shvartsman (University of Connecticut), and Paul Spirakis (Patras University and Computer Technology Institute).

The local arrangements (both for the committee meeting, and for the conference) were made by a team headed by Paul Spirakis (local arrangements chair) and Panagiota Fatourou (local arrangements co-chair) from the Computer Technology Institute in Greece. They also took care of advertising the symposium, and the program committee chair would like to thank them for a wonderful job.

We would like to thank all the authors who submitted extended abstracts. There were interesting papers among those we could not accept, and their authors also contributed towards enhancing DISC. We hope to see the continuing support of the next DISC, by everybody. We would also like to thank the invited speakers for joining us in Andros. The program chair would like to thank the program committee members who invested a lot of work and thought in the symposium.

We would like to thank ACM SIGACT for letting us use its automated submission server and its program committee server at sigact.acm.org, and Springer-Verlag for following the tradition and publishing our proceedings. It is a special pleasure to thank

Esther Jennings and Rinat Regev for helping with operating the SIGACT server and Dana Fruchter for her help in putting together the final proceedings.

DISC thanks the following for their generous support: The Greek Ministry of Education, the Greek General Secretary of Research and Technology, the University of Patras, Greek PTT (OTE), Intracom, and Intrasoft.

Continuation of the DISC events is supervised by the DISC Steering Committee, which, for 1998, consists of: Özalp Babağlu (U. Bologna), Bernadette Charron-Bost (E. Polytechnique), Vassos Hadzilacos (U. Toronto), Shay Kutten (IBM and Technion), Marios Mavronicolas (U. Cyprus), Sam Toueg (Cornell) – Chair, and Shmuel Zaks (Technion) - Vice Chair.

July 1998   Shay Kutten
                                            DISC'98 Program Committee Chair

External Reviewers

The Program Committee wishes to thank the following persons, who acted as referees for DISC'98:

Y. Afek
D. Agrawal
M. Aguilera
A. Allist
J. H. Anderson
A. Baggio
G. Banavar
C. Bastarrica
A. Basu
Y. Ben-Asher
K. Berket
X. Blondel
P. Boldi
R. Borgstrom
S. Chari
O. Cheiner
M. S. Chen
P. Dasgupta
A. K. Datta
S. Dandamudi
O. Dedieu
C. Delporte-Gallet
S. Demurjian
S. Dolev
N. Dorta
T. Eilam
B. Englert
O. Etzion
H. Fauconnier
P. Flocchini
B. Folliot
C. Fournet
P. Fraigniaud
J. A. Garay
C. Gavoille

M. Greenwald
R. Guerraoui
M. Herlihy
L. Higham
G. Hunt
J. James
E. Jennings
M. Kalantar
V. Kalogeraki
D. Kaminsky
S. Katz
I. Keidar
C. Khoury
R. R. Koch
E. Kushilevitz
F. Le Fessant
C. L. Lei
G. Le Lann
S. Leonardi
G. Lindstrom
T. J. Liu
D. Malkhi
B. Mans
C. Mascolo
F. Mattern
P. M. Melliar-Smith
M. Moir
B. Mukherjee
P. Narasimhan
L. Narayanan
G. Neiger
R. Netzer
S. Onn
J. Parameswaran
D. Peleg

J. Pershing
F. Petit
G. Pierre
K. Potter-Kihlstrom
S. Rajsbaum
A. Roncato
E. M. Royer
E. Santos
A. Schiper
H. Shachnai
D. Shaw
G. Singh
J. Stanton
R. Strom
D. Sturman
R. B. Tan
G. Taubenfeld
G. Tel
L. A. Tewksbury
S. Toueg
D. Touitou
Y. K. Tsay
G. Tsudik
M. Tuttle
R. VanRenesse
V. Villain
D. W. Wang
F. Wang
M. J. Ward
S. Weiss
A. Wool
D. Wu
L. C. Wuu
S. Zaks

Table of Contents

Keynote Lectures

Contributed Papers

Sense of Direction in Distributed Computing

Paola Flocchini[1], Bernard Mans[2], Nicola Santoro[3]

[1] Département d'Informatique Université du Quebec à Hull
(flocchini@uqah.uquebec.ca)
[2] Department of Computing, School of MPCE, Macquarie University, Sydney,
(bmans@mpce.mq.edu.au)
[3] School of Computer Science, Carleton University, Ottawa
(santoro@scs.carleton.ca)

1 Introduction

1.1 Distributed Model

There are numerous models for distributed systems, differing from one another on a large number of important factors and parameters. We shall restrict ourselves to systems based on the point-to-point message-passing model: there is no common memory, and a node may communicate directly only with its direct neighbors by exchanging messages. The communication topology of the system can be described by an edge labeled graph where nodes correspond to entities and edges correspond to direct communication links between entities [32]. Let $G = (V, E)$ be the graph; let $E(x)$ denote the set of edges incident to node $x \in V$, and $d(x) = |E(x)|$ the degree of x. Each node has a local label (port number) associated to each of its incident edges. Given a set Σ of labels, a *local orientation* of $x \in V$ is any injective function $\lambda_x : E(x) \to \Sigma$ which associates a distinct label $l \in \Sigma$ to each edge $e \in E(x)$. The set $\lambda = \{\lambda_x : x \in V\}$ of local labeling functions will be called a *labeling* of G, and by (G, λ) we shall denote the corresponding *(edge-)labeled graph*.

Any property of the labeling λ can be exploited to improve the performance of the system, e.g., by reducing the amount of communication required to perform some distributed tasks. The most basic property is *Local Orientation*: the capacity at each node to distinguish between the incident links; by definition, we only consider labelings having this property. Another interesting property is *Edge Symmetry*: there exists a bijection $\psi : \Sigma \to \Sigma$ such that for each $\langle x, y \rangle \in E$, $\lambda_y(\langle y, x \rangle) = \psi(\lambda_x(\langle x, y \rangle))$; ψ will be called the edge-symmetry function. The particular case of edge symmetry called *Coloring* where the edge-symmetry function is the identity (i.e., the labels on the two sides of each edge are the same) is also of interest. For specific labelings in specific topologies, some other properties have been extensively studied; e.g., *Orientation* in ring networks with "left-right" labeling or in tori with the compass labeling.

Without any doubt, the property of labeled graphs which has been shown to have a definite impact on computability and complexity, and whose applicability ranges from the analysis of graph classes to distributed object systems, is *Sense of Direction*. In the rest of the paper, we will provide some introduction and pointers to the relevant results and literature.

1.2 Sense of Direction

Informally, in a labeled a graph (G, λ). the labeling is a (weak) sense of direction if it is possible to understand, from the labels associated to the edges, whether different walks from a given node x end in the same node or in different nodes. A *walk* π in G is a sequence of edges in which the endpoint of one edge is the starting point of the next edge. Let $P[x]$ denote the set of all the walks starting from $x \in V$, $P[x, y]$ the set of walks starting from $x \in V$ and ending in $y \in V$. Let $\Lambda_x : P[x] \to \Sigma^+$ and $\Lambda = \{\Lambda_x : x \in V\}$ denote the extension of λ_x and λ, respectively, from edges to walks; let $\Lambda[x] = \{\Lambda_x(\pi) : \pi \in P[x]\}$, and $\Lambda[x, y] = \{\Lambda_x(\pi) : \pi \in P[x, y]\}$.

A *coding function* f of a graph (G, λ) be any function such that: $\forall x, y, z \in V$, $\forall \pi_1 \in P[x, y]$, $\pi_2 \in P[x, z]$ $f(\Lambda_x(\pi_1)) = f(\Lambda_x(\pi_2))$ iff $y = z$.

Definition 1 *[15]* - Weak Sense of Direction
A system (G, λ), has weak sense of direction *iff there exists a coding function f.*

A *decoding function* h for f is a function that, given a label and a coding of a string (sequence of labels), returns the coding of the concatenation of the label and the string. More precisely, given a coding function f, a decoding function h for f is such that $\forall x, y, z \in V$, such that $\langle x, y \rangle \in E(x)$ and $\pi \in P[y, z]$, $h(\lambda_x(\langle x, y \rangle), f(\Lambda_y(\pi)) = f(\lambda_x(\langle x, y \rangle) \circ \Lambda_y(\pi))$, where $\circ$ is the concatenation operator. We can now define sense of direction:

Definition 2 *[15]* - Sense of Direction
A system (G, λ), has a sense of direction *(SD) iff the following conditions hold:*
1) there exists a coding function f,
2) there exists a decoding function h for f.

We shall also say that (f, h) is a sense of direction in (G, λ).

Several instances of sense of direction (*contracted, chordal, neighboring, cartographic*) have been described in [15]; a class of sense of direction called *group SD* that comprises contracted, chordal, and cartographic SDs has been defined in [48].

It has been shown that WSD does not imply SD; in fact there are labeled graphs which have WSD but do not have any SD [4].

1.3 Sense of Direction and Local Names

The definition of both coding and decoding (and, thus, of sense of direction) can be restated in terms of "translation" capability of local names.

Each node x refers to the other nodes using local names from a finite set $\mathcal{N}$ called name space; let $\beta_x(y)$ be the name associated by x to y. Let us stress that these local names are *not* necessarily identities (i.e., unique global identifiers); in fact, the system could be *anonymous*. The family of injective functions $\beta = \{\beta_x : V \to \mathcal{N} : x \in V\}$ will be called a *local naming* of G.

Let us restate the definition of coding function: a *coding function* f of a graph (G, λ) endowed with local naming β is any function such that: $\forall x, y \in V$,

$\forall \pi \in P[x,y]$, $f(\Lambda_x(\pi)) = \beta_x(y)$. In other words, a coding function translates the sequence of labels of a path from x to y into the local name that x gives to y. Note that while the resulting name is *local* (i.e. x and z might choose different local names for the same node y), the coding function is *global* (i.e., the same for all the nodes).

Let us restate the definition of decoding in terms of local naming. Given a coding function f, a decoding function h for f is any map such that $\forall x, y, z \in V$, with $\langle x, y \rangle \in E(x)$, $h(\lambda_x(\langle x, y \rangle), \beta_y(z)) = \beta(x(z)$. To understand the capabilities of the decoding function in terms of names, consider the situation of node y sending to its neighbor x a message containing information about a node z (see Figure 1. Node z is known at y as $\beta_y(z)$, thus, the message sent by y will contain

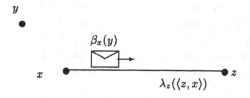

Fig. 1. Communication of information about node y from node x to z.

information about a node called "$\beta_y(z)$". The decoding function allows x to "translate" such a name into its own local name for z $\beta_x(z)$, knowing only the label of the link $\lambda_x(\langle x, y \rangle)$ on which the message is received.

1.4 Sense of Direction and Structural Knowledge

The study of sense of direction is part of the larger investigation on structural knowledge. Informally, the term "structural knowledge" refers to any knowledge about the structure of the system; in general we can distinguish between four distinct types, depending on whether the knowledge is about: 1. the communication topology (T); 2. the labeling (L); 3. the (input) data (D); 4. the status of the entities and of the system (S).

Clearly, sense of direction is of type L. In most cases, its impact, existence and properties will be strongly affected also by the other forms of structural information available in the system. It is thus important to both distinguish among different types and within each type.

Examples of type-T knowledge are: *metric information (TM)*: "numeric" information about the network; e.g., size of the network (exact or approximate), number of edges, maximum degree, length of the diameter, girth, etc. *topological properties (TP)*: knowledge of some properties of the topology; e.g., the fact that the topology of the network is a regular graphs, a Cayley graph, a (edge-, vertex-, cycle-) symmetric graph, etc. *topological classes (TC)*: information about the "class" to which the topology belongs; for example, the fact that the topology is a ring, a tree, a mesh, a tori,etc. *topological awareness* (TA): a knowledge equivalent to the knowledge of the adjacency matrix that describes the topology. *complete knowledge of the topology* (TK): each node knows the adjacency matrix and its position in it (this knowledge is partial when truncated at distance d)

Examples of type-D knowledge are: *unique identifiers*: all input values are distinct; *anonymous network*: all input values are identical; *size*: number of distinct values.

Examples of type-S knowledge are: *system with leader*: there is a unique entity in state "leader"; *reset* all nodes are in the same state.

2 Impact of Sense of Direction on Computability

A large amount of research has been devoted to the study of computability in anonymous systems; i.e., the study of what problems can be solved when there are no distinct identifiers associated to the nodes (e.g., [2, 29, 30, 51]). Clearly, which problems can be solved depend on many factors including the structural properties of the system as well as the amount and type of structural knowledge available to the system entities (the nodes).

The computational power of sense of direction in anonymous systems has been studied in [19] and shown to be linked to the notion of surrounding introduced in [18]. The *surrounding* $N(u)$ of a node u in (G, λ) is a labeled graph isomorphic to (G, λ) where the isomorphism maps each node $v \in V$ to the set $\Lambda[u, v]$ of strings corresponding to all walks from u to v. It has been proven in [19] that, in anonymous distributed systems with sense of direction, the surrounding of a node represents the maximum information that an entity can obtain by message transmissions. Moreover, what is computable in such systems depends on the number of distinct surroundings as well as on their multiplicity (i.e., how many nodes have a given surrounding) [19]. It also depends on the amount of type-T knowledge available.

Let $\mathcal{W}_K(P)$ denote the set of graphs with sense of direction where, in presence of type-T knowledge K, problem P can be solved. In [19] it has been shown that, with weak sense of direction, for every type-T knowledge K and for every problem P, $\mathcal{W}_K(P) \supseteq \mathcal{W}_{TK}(P)$. Since $\mathcal{W}_K(P)$ do not depend on K we will denote it as $\mathcal{W}(P)$.

A powerful implication of this result is the formal proof that, *with sense of direction, it is possible to do shortest path routing even in anonymous networks*.

This result also implies that the obvious knowledge-computability hierarchy

$$\mathcal{W}_{ni}(P) \subseteq \mathcal{W}_{ub}(P) \subseteq \mathcal{W}_{size}(P) \subseteq \mathcal{W}_{TA}(P) \subseteq \mathcal{W}_{TK}(P)$$

collapses, where ni, ub, $size$, TA, TK denote no knowledge, knowledge of an upper bound on the size of the network, knowledge of the exact size, topological awareness, and complete knowledge of the topology, respectively.

Another interesting result is about the relationship between the strongest type-T knowledge and the lowest with sense of direction (i.e., $\mathcal{W}(P)$). Let $D_K(P)$

denote the set of graphs with just local orientation where, in presence of type-T knowledge K, problem P can be solved; clearly, $\mathcal{D}_K(P) \subseteq \mathcal{W}_K(P)$ for every type-T knowledge K. In [19] it has been shown that sense of direction and complete knowledge of the topology have the same computational power; in fact $\mathcal{W}(P) = \mathcal{D}_{TK}(P)$ for every problem P.

The relation between *topological awareness* and sense of direction has been studied with respect to several problems including leader and edge election, and spanning tree construction. It has been shown that, for each of these problems, there exist graphs in which they are not solvable with topological awareness (TA); on the other hand, they can be solved with *any* weak sense of direction; that is, *sense of direction is strictly more powerful than topological awareness.*

3 Impact of Sense of Direction on Complexity

The evidence of the impact that specific sense of direction have on the communication complexity of several problems in particular network topologies has been accumulating in the recent years. Most of the distributed algorithms presented in the literature assume and exploit specific, and mostly implicit, instances of sense of direction within their pre-defined set of assumptions on the structural knowledge (held by the entities) and the attributes of the network. Techniques developed for most of the existing applications are *ad hoc*, network- or application-specific; they do not provide seamless mechanisms for allowing processors to inter-operate with all intended assumptions on knowledge.

A large amount of investigations has been dedicated to the study of a small but typical set that recur in most applications: broadcast ($\mathcal{B}$), depth-first traversal ($\mathcal{DFT}$), spanning tree construction ($\mathcal{SPT}$), minimum finding ($\mathcal{MF}$), election (or leader finding)($\mathcal{LF}$). The next sections provide a schematic view of the most important results.

3.1 Arbitrary Network

A network topology is said to be arbitrary if it is unknown to the entities. This can be understood as a lack of topological awareness. The results on the impact of sense of direction in arbitrary networks are listed below.

Arbitrary Networks

	Broadcast Depth First Traversal	Election Spanning Tree Min Finding
local orientation	$\Theta(e)$	$\Theta(e + n \log n)$ [24, 43]
neighboring $\mathcal{SD}$	$\Theta(\min(e, n^{1+\Theta(1)}))$ [3, 24] Theta(n)	$O(e + n \log n)$
chordal $\mathcal{SD}$	$\Theta(n)$ [36]	$O(e + n \log n)$
any $\mathcal{SD}$	$2n - 2$ [17]	$3n \log n + O(n)$ [17, 36, 35]

Here and in the following n denotes the number of nodes of the network and e the number of edges.

Note that Depth First Traversal can be performed in $O(n)$ with *any sense of direction* even if the graph is *anonymous*. In arbitrarily labeled graphs, this problem requires $\Omega(e)$ messages even if the system is not anonymous; this bound can be easily achieved (e.g., [7]). An improvement in the communication complexity has been shown to exist if each entity has a distinct identity *and* knows the identities of all its neighbors; in this case, this problem can be solved with $O(n)$ messages [44]. This result implies that, in presence of neighboring sense of direction, $\mathcal{DFT}$ can be performed in $O(n)$ messages. Recall that graphs with neighboring labelings are *not* anonymous. A similar reduction has been shown to exist in the presence of chordal sense of direction [16]. It has been proven in [3] that a similar complexity can be obtained for broadcasting without sense of direction only if the size of messages is unbounded.

3.2   Regular Networks

Complete Networks

	Broadcast	Depth First Traversal	Election
local orientation	$(n-1)$	$O(n^2)$	$\Theta(n^2)$ [24]
local orientation with topological awareness	$(n-1)$	$O(n^2)$	$\Theta(n \log n)$ [28]
chordal $\mathcal{SD}$	$(n-1)$	$(n-1)$	$\Theta(n)$ [31, 37, 45]

The results for the Leader Election problem show explicitly that, despite maximum connectivity, there are strict (reachable) lower bounds on what optimal solutions can achieve. A strict and proper classification of the structural information can be deduced. In complete networks also the problem of fault-tolerant leader election has been studied with chordal $\mathcal{SD}$ [35, 38].

Hypercube Network

	Broadcast	Election
local orientation	$O(n)$ [9, 11]	$O(n \log \log n)$ [12]
local orientation and Hamming node-labeling	$O(n)$ [41]	$O(n \log \log n)$
neighboring $\mathcal{SD}$	$O(n)$ [3]	$O(n \log \log n)$
dimensional $\mathcal{SD}$	$O(n)$ (Folklore)	$\Theta(n)$ [14, 42, 47, 50]
chordal $\mathcal{SD}$	$O(n)$ (Folklore)	$O(1)$ [14]

Note that for both Broadcast and Election, a similar complexity can be obtained in all cases (beside neighboring) even if the graph is *anonymous*.

All solutions provided in [14, 47, 42, 50] exploit the implicit region partitioning of the topology and an efficient and implicit scheme to compute and represent shortest paths. Recently, several Broadcast algorithms succeed to exploit the highly symmetric topology without considering processor or link names. Nevertheless, in this case, the best known message complexity for the Election problem is $O(n \log \log n)$ (for large Hypercubes and with a large asymptotic constant) [12].

Chordal Rings

	Broadcast	Election
$\langle 1, 2, .., k \rangle_n$ local orientation chordal $\mathcal{SD}$	$O(n)$ [34] $n-1$ (Folklore)	$O(n \log n)$ $O(n \log n)$
$\langle S \rangle_n \ |S| < \log n$ local orientation chordal $\mathcal{SD}$	$O(|S|n)$ $n-1$ (Folklore)	$O(n \log n)$ $O(n)$ [1]
$\langle S \rangle_n \ |S| < \log \log n$ local orientation chordal $\mathcal{SD}$	$O(|S|n)$ $n-1$ (Folklore)	$O(n \log n)$ $O(n)$ [27]
$\langle S \rangle_n \ |S| < \log^* n$ local orientation chordal $\mathcal{SD}$	$O(|S|n)$ $n-1$ (Folklore)	$O(n \log n)$ $O(n \log^* n)$ [40]

The results on chordal rings give information on the situation of a complete graph where, at each node, the chordal labeling is known only for a subset (S) of the edges. In this view must also be interpreted the result on double loop [33].

Wake-up

	Time × Bits
local orientation	$\Theta(n^2)$ [17]
chordal $\mathcal{SD}$	$O(n \log^2 n)$ [25]

In all previous results, the communication complexity is measured in terms of number of messages. In the case of synchronous systems, the complexity measure is the trade-off between completion time and amount of transmitted information. A strong example of impact of sense of direction in synchronous systems is the *wake-up* (or, *weak unison*) problem in complete graphs:

3.3 Open Problems

The interplay between symmetry of the graph and consistency of the labels is an important open question. As illustrated in the previous results, there is an empirical evidence that highly regular topologies are difficult to exploit efficiently when the edges are not labeled with consistent structural information.

4 Constructing and Testing Sense of Direction

4.1 Deciding and Testing Sense of Direction

Given a labeled graph (G, λ), how can we verify (decide) whether there is sense of direction?

In [4], the authors have shown that there exist polynomial algorithms for deciding both $\mathcal{WSD}$ and $\mathcal{SD}$. Furthermore, they have shown that deciding weak sense of direction can be done very efficiently in parallel. In fact, considering as model of computation a CRCW PRAM, weak sense of direction is in AC^1 for all graphs, where AC^1 denotes the class of problems which are solvable in time $O(\log n)$ using a polynomial number of processors (in this case n^6 processors). This result is based on a characterization of weak sense of direction in purely combinatorial terms. In fact weak sense of direction is shown to be equivalent to a combinatorial condition on the labeling of a graph called *uniformity*, and checking such a condition has then been proved to be in AC^1. Deciding sense of direction is not as efficient in parallel, in fact it is in AC^1 only for some classes of graphs (k-reducible graphs).

4.2 Constructing Sense of Direction

Since Sense of Direction is known to improve the communication complexity of distributed algorithms, computing $\mathcal{SD}$ as a preprocessing phase in unlabeled topology has been studied in [46, 48] showing that any algorithm computing the common sense of direction for cliques, hypercubes, arbitrary graphs, or tori, exchanges at least $\Omega(e - \frac{1}{2}n)$ messages in a network with n nodes and e edges.

This result is not attractive for these dense topologies (e.g., $\Omega(n^2)$ for cliques and $\Omega(n \log n)$ for the hypercube); although natural algorithms matching the lower bounds have been proposed [46], most of the solutions proposed cannot avoid a complete flooding of the communication links in the network.

The interest is more relevant for topologies with a linear number of edges such as tori or chordal rings of constant degree, as shown in the following table presenting the known message complexity.

	Cost	Type of $\mathcal{SD}$
Complete graph	$\Theta(n^2)$ [46]	chordal $\mathcal{SD}$
Hypercube	$\Theta(n \log n)$ [46]	dimensional $\mathcal{SD}$
Torus ($\sqrt{n} \times \sqrt{n}$)	$\Theta(n)$ [33]	compass SD
Double Loop $\langle 1, \sqrt{n} \rangle_n$	$\Theta(n)$ [33]	chordal $\mathcal{SD}$

Interesting constructions of sense of direction have been given in [5], where the authors have concentrated on the problem of constructing senses of direction that use a small number of labels. Such a number always lies between the maximum degree of the graph (in that case it is minimum) and the number of vertices. By exploiting compositional, algebraic and geometrical techniques, they have shown some constructions of large graphs with sense of direction using few labels; the idea of their constructions is to build large networks by appropriately connecting smaller ones. The authors show that with their approach they obtain minimal senses of direction in Cayley graphs. Their result is a first attempt of developing a set of techniques for constructing sense of direction in graphs by using primitive constructions.

4.3 Coping with Lack of Sense of Direction

The results on constructing sense of direction suggested that it may be more efficient to cope with the lack of sense of direction than to use a pre-processing phase which constructs it. Indeed, some problems in unlabeled networks require only a partial orientation to achieve an optimal solution. In tori and chordal rings, the *handrail* technique, introduced in [33], uses the complete knowledge of the topology truncated at distance 2 (or 2-surrounding) to provide any node with the ability to pass a message in the same dimension or to make the message "turn" in the same consistent direction. In the torus, the message-passing scheme will be consistent (clockwise, or counter-wise, squares) in the world according to the leader.

For hypercubes, the *mask* paradigm, introduced in [11], allows a source node to build a small dominating set; the mask coverage is built by including consistently (according to the source) appropriate nodes in each layer of the hypercube. Such a set, once available, can be used efficiently to solve problems such as broadcasting even when the traditional dimensional SD is not available.

4.4 Open Problems

The problem of constructing graphs have a sense of direction with the minimum number of labels has been extensively studied in regular graphs (e.g., [6, 13, 18]), but still very little is known in the general case. This problem will be discussed in more details in Section 5.

The paradigms of handrail and mask could be exploited for other topologies with relevant partial structural properties. Both schemes demonstrate that a *local* information of a distance-2 surrounding (although, combined with non-trivial algorithms) may be sufficient to solve particular problems optimally. This raises the interesting and more general question of characterizing the minimal structural properties that a network must possess to solve particular classes of problems within a specific message complexity range (see also [10]).

5 Minimal Sense of Direction in Regular Graphs

In this Section we consider labeled graphs (G, λ) where λ is minimal; i.e., it uses $d(G) = max\{d(x) : x \in V\}$ labels. In particular, we focus on d-regular graphs. If λ is minimal and there is (weak) sense of direction, (G, λ) is said to have *minimal (weak) sense of direction*.

5.1 Minimal SD and Cycle Symmetry

A graph has *cycle symmetry* if each node belongs to the same number of cycles of the same length [13].

In [13], the author has shown that cycle symmetry is a *necessary condition* for having a minimal sense of direction in a regular graph. For example, the graph of Figure 2 *b*) does not have a minimal SD since it is not cycle symmetric. On the other hand, figure 2 *a*) shows a graph with cycle symmetry where there exists a minimal SD. Such a condition, however, is *not sufficient*; for example, Peterson's graph has cycle symmetry but it cannot have minimal sense of direction [13].

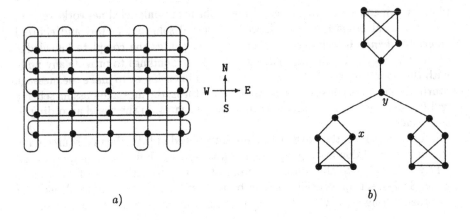

Fig. 2. Regular graphs for which *a)* there exists a minimal $\mathcal{SD}$, *b)* there exists no minimal $\mathcal{SD}$.

5.2 Minimal $\mathcal{SD}$ with Symmetric Labeling

A labeling λ is *symmetric* if there exists a bijection $\psi : \Sigma \to \Sigma$ such that for each $\langle x, y \rangle \in E$, $\lambda_y(\langle y, x \rangle) = \psi(\lambda_x(\langle x, y \rangle))$; ψ will be called the edge-symmetry function.

In the case of symmetric labelings, minimality is linked to the notion of surrounding (discussed in section 2). A labeled graph is *surrounding symmetric* (*S*-symmetric) when every node has the same surrounding.

A necessary and sufficient condition has been given in [18] where the authors have shown that a regular graph with symmetric labeling has a minimal $\mathcal{SD}$ iff it is surrounding symmetric.

Hence, we have a characterization of minimal $\mathcal{SD}$ in terms of Cayley graphs: a regular graph has a minimal $\mathcal{SD}$ iff it is a Cayley graph with a Cayley labeling [6, 18]. Note that in [6] the theorem is more general since it holds for directed graphs.

5.3 Minimal $\mathcal{SD}$ with non-Symmetric Labeling

Given a regular graph with a non-symmetric labeling (G, λ), a necessary and sufficient condition for (G, λ) to have minimal sense of direction has been given in [23]. A regular graph has a minimal $\mathcal{SD}$ iff it is the graph of a semi-group which the direct product of a group and a left-zero semi-group.

5.4 Open Problems

Cycle symmetry is not yet perfectly understood; in fact, its relationship with other well known notions of symmetries (e.g., vertex symmetry) is not always clear. For example, it is evident that a vertex symmetric graph is also cycle symmetric, but it is not known whether a cycle symmetric graph is always vertex symmetric.

The general characterization of minimal sense of direction in arbitrary graphs is still completely open.

An other interesting problem is the following: given a topology which does not have minimal sense of direction, what is the minimum number of labels necessary for having a sense of direction in that topology ? If it cannot be done with $d(G)$ labels (where $d(G)$ is the maximum degree) is it always possible to do it with $d(G) + 1$ labels ?

Also the problem: given a graph G and an integer k, can G have a sense of direction using at most k labels ? is still open and suspected to be NP-complete.

6 Topological Constraints for Sense of Direction

The interplay between topology of the system and the properties that a labeling must satisfy for having sense of direction have been studied in [21, 22, 20].

In some graphs, all the labelings with the same simple properties have sense of direction. It is clearly important to identify which property for which graphs.

The authors have considered the following question: *Given a system (G, λ), where the labeling λ has certain properties, under what topological conditions (G, λ) has sense of direction ?*

In particular, they have considered a hierarchy of labelings: *local orientation*, local orientations with *edge symmetry* , and *colorings*. For each class, it has been shown for what graphs every labeling has a sense of direction (*feasible graphs*) and for what other graphs the property of the labeling does not suffice for having sense of direction (they contain *forbidden subgraphs*). This characterization is *complete*: in fact it has been shown that every graph is either feasible or contains a forbidden subgraph.

Local orientation suffices for having sense of direction only in trees and in some trivial graphs; the simultaneous presence of local orientation and edge symmetry guarantees sense of direction in a larger class of graphs which, in addition to trees, includes rings and particular types of "spiked rings"; finally, a coloring suffices for having sense of direction in a even larger class of graphs (some of them are shown in Figure 3).

7 An Application: Object Naming

Sense of direction has been used to implement an efficient naming scheme in systems of distributed objects [49].

An object system consists of a collection of objects and their relations; each object has a state (e.g., local variables) and a behavior (set of actions it may execute) and the global behavior of a system is described in terms of interactions between its objects.

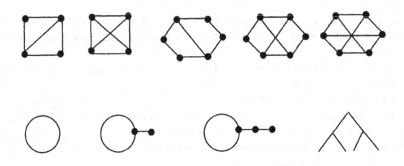

Fig. 3. Some feasible graphs for colorings.

A *naming scheme* is a mechanism used for naming objects and manipulating objects through their names. In object systems, some of the main objectives of a naming scheme are: to *designate* an object, to distinguish between objects *independently of their state*; to *communicate* to other objects the knowledge about some objects. Furthermore, a naming scheme should be *stable* and *reliable*, that is, names must remain valid, and keep denoting the same objects when the system changes its state.

In order to achieve these goals, the existing naming schemes (e.g., [26, 39, 8]) either use an approach based on *global* names (e.g., each object uses as its name an intrinsic property which distinguishes it from the other objects) or they use *hierarchical* names often based on the location of the objects (e.g., email addresses). On the other hand, locality of names and independence on the location are two very desirable characteristics of a naming scheme.

In [49], a naming scheme in which a name of an object does not depend neither on its state nor to its characteristics, nor to its location has been proposed based on sense of direction. A distributed object system is here described by a labeled graph (G, λ) where nodes are objects, links represent references between objects and the labeling λ is chosen in such a way that the system has sense of direction. The name that an object uses to refer to another object is either the label of the link between them (if there is such a direct link), or the coding of a (arbitrarily chosen) sequence of labels leading to it. More precisely,

Given a coding function f, the local object naming scheme β_x for x is constructed as follows: $\forall x, y$,

$$\beta_x(y) = \begin{cases} \lambda_x(x, y) & \text{if } y \in E(x) \\ f(\alpha) & \text{otherwise} \end{cases}$$

where α is the sequence of labels corresponding to an arbitrary path between

x and y. The collection of all local object naming schemes $\beta = \{\beta_x : x \in V\}$ constitutes the (global) *object naming scheme*.

This approach based on sense of direction constitutes the first naming scheme that uses *local names*, provides *mechanisms for the correct communication* of names and is *location independent*.

Acknowledgements. This work has been partially supported by NSERC and FCAR.

References

1. H. Attiya, J. van Leeuwen, N. Santoro, and S. Zaks. Efficient elections in chordal ring networks. *Algorithmica*, 4:437–446, 1989.
2. H. Attiya, M. Snir, and M.K. Warmuth. Computing on an anonymous ring. *Journal of the A.C.M.*, 35(4):845–875, 1988.
3. B. Awerbuch, O. Goldreich, D. Peleg, and R. Vainish. A trade-off between information and communication in broadcast protocols. *Journal of the A.C.M.*, 37(2):238–256, April 1990.
4. P. Boldi and S. Vigna. On the complexity of deciding sense of direction. In *Proc. of 2nd Colloquium on Structural Information and Communication Complexity*, pages 39–52, Olympia, 1995.
5. P. Boldi and S. Vigna. Good fibrations and other constructions which preserve sense of direction. In *3rd International Colloquium on Structural Information and Communication Complexity*, number 6, pages 47–58, Siena, 1996.
6. P. Boldi and S. Vigna. Minimal sense of direction and decision problems for Cayley graphs. *Information Processing Letters*, 64:299–303, 1997.
7. T.Y. Cheung. Graph traversal techniques and the maximum flow problem in distributed computation. *I.E.E.E. Transactions on Software Engineering*, 9:504–512, 1983.
8. DCE. Guide to writing distributed computing environement applications, digital equipment corporation, 1994.
9. K. Diks, S. Dobrev, E. Kranakis, A. Pelc, and P. Ružička. Broadcasting in unlabeled hypercubes with linear number of messages. *Information Processing Letters*. to appear.
10. S. Dobrev. An alternative view on structural information. In *5th International Colloquium on Structural Information and Communication Complexity*, Amalfi, 1998. to appear.
11. S. Dobrev, P. Ružička, and G. Tel. Time and bit optimal broadcasting in anonymous unoriented hypercubes. In *Proc. of 5th Colloquium on Structural Information and Communication Complexity*, Amalfi, 1998. to appear.
12. S. Dobrev and P. Ruzicka. Linear broadcasting and $n \log \log n$ election in unoriented hypercubes. In *Proc. of the 4th International Colloquium on Structural Information and Communication Complexity*, pages 53–68, 1997.
13. P. Flocchini. Minimal sense of direction in regular networks. *Information Processing Letters*, 61:331–338, 1997.
14. P. Flocchini and B. Mans. Optimal election in labeled hypercubes. *Journal of Parallel and Distributed Computing*, 33(1):76–83, 1996.

15. P. Flocchini, B. Mans, and N. Santoro. Sense of direction: definition, properties and classes. *Networks*. To appear. Preliminary version in *Proc. of 1st Colloquium on Structural Information and Communication Complexity*, 9-34,1994.

16. P. Flocchini, B. Mans, and N. Santoro. Distributed traversal and broadcasting in arbitrary network with distance sense of direction. In *Proc. of 9th International Symposium on Computer and Information Sciences*, pages 196–203, 1994.

17. P. Flocchini, B. Mans, and N. Santoro. On the impact of sense of direction on message complexity. *Information Processing Letters*, 63(1):23–31, 1997.

18. P. Flocchini, A. Roncato, and N. Santoro. Complete symmetries and minimal sense of direction in labeled graphs. *Discrete Applied Mathematics*. to appear. Preliminary version in *Proc. of 27th SE Conference on Combinatorics, Graph Theory and Computing*; Congressus Numerantium 121, 3-18, 1996.

19. P. Flocchini, A. Roncato, and N. Santoro. Computing on anonymous networks with sense of direction. *Theoretical Computer Science*. To appear. (Preliminary version in *Proc. of 3rd Colloquium on Structural Information and Communication Complexity*, 32–46, 1996).

20. P. Flocchini and N. Santoro. Proper coloring and sense of direction. Submitted.

21. P. Flocchini and N. Santoro. Topological constraints for sense of direction. *International Journal on Foundations of Computer Science*. To appear. Preliminary version in *Proc. of 2nd Colloquium on Structural Information and Communication Complexity*, 27-38, 1995.

22. P. Flocchini and N. Santoro. Topological constraints for sense of direction. In *Proc. of 2nd Colloquium on Structural Information and Communication Complexity*, pages 27–38, Olympia, 1995.

23. S. Foldes. Personal communication.

24. R.G. Gallager, P.A. Humblet, and P.M. Spira. A distributed algorithm for minimum spanning tree. *A.C.M. Transactions on Programming Languages and Systems*, 5(1):66–77, 1983.

25. A. Israeli, E. Kranakis, D. Krizanc, and N. Santoro. Time-message trade-offs for the weak unison problem. *Nordic Journal of Computing*, 4:317–329, 1997.

26. ISO/IEC JTC1. Information technology - open distributed processing - naming framework, iso/iec dis147771, july 1997.

27. T.Z. Kalamboukis and S.L. Mantzaris. Towards optimal distributed election on chordal rings. *Information Processing Letters*, 38:265–270, 1991.

28. E. Korach, S. Moran, and S. Zaks. Tight lower and upper bounds for a class of distributed algorithms for a complete network of processors. In *Proc. of 3rd Symposium on Principles of Distributed Computing*, pages 199–207, Vancouver, 1984.

29. E. Kranakis and D. Krizanc. Distributed computing on anonymous hypercubes. *Journal of Algorithms*, 23:32–50, 1997.

30. E. Kranakis and N. Santoro. Distributed computing on anonymous hypercubes with faulty components. In *Proc. of 6th Int. Workshop of Distributed Algorithms*, Lecture Notes in Computer Science 647, pages 253–263. Springer-Verlag, 1992.

31. M.C. Loui, T.A. Matsushita, and D.B. West. Election in complete networks with a sense of direction. *Information Processing Letters*, 22:185–187, 1986. see also Information Processing Letters, vol.28, p.327, 1988.

32. N. Lynch. *Distributed Algorithms*. Morgan-Kaufmann, 1995.

33. B. Mans. Optimal distributed algorithms in unlabeled tori and chordal rings. *Journal on Parallel and Distributed Computing*, 1997. To appear. Preliminary version

in *Proc. of the 3rd International Colloquium on Structural Information and Communication Complexity*, 17-31,1996.

34. B. Mans and D. Peleg. Broadcasting in unlabelled chordal rings, 1997. Personal Communication.

35. B. Mans and N. Santoro. Optimal fault-tolerant leader election in chordal rings. *IEEE Transactions on Computers*. To appear.

36. B. Mans and N. Santoro. On the impact of sense of direction in arbitrary networks. In *Proc. of 14th International Conference on Distributed Computing Systems*, pages 258-265, Poznan, 1994.

37. G.H. Masapati and H. Ural. Effect of preprocessing on election in a complete network with a sense of direction. In *Proc. of I.E.E.E. International Conference on Systems, Man and Cybernetics*, volume 3, pages 1627-1632, 1991.

38. T. Masuzawa, N. Nishikawa, K. Hagihara, and N. Tokura. A fault-tolerant algorithm for election in complete networks with a sense of direction. *Systems and Computers in Japan*, 22(12):11-22, 1991.

39. OMG. Naming service specification clause 3, corba services, omg, march 199.

40. Yi Pan. A near-optimal multi-stage distributed algorithm for finding leaders in clustered chordal rings. *Information Sciences*, 76(1-2):131-140, 1994.

41. D. Peleg. Message-optimal broadcast on a hypercubes with no neighbour knowledge, 1997. Personal Communication.

42. S. Robbins and K.A. Robbins. Choosing a leader on a hypercube. In *Proc. of International Conference on Databases, Parallel Architectures and their Applications*, pages 469-471, Miami Beach, 1990.

43. N. Santoro. Sense of direction, topological awareness and communication complexity. *SIGACT NEWS*, 2(16):50-56, Summer 1984.

44. M.B. Sharma, S.S. Iyengar, and N.K. Mandyam. An efficient distributed depth-first-search algorithm. *Information Processing Letters*, 32:183-186, September 1989. see also Information Processing Letters, vol.35, p.55, 1990.

45. G. Singh. Efficient leader election using sense of direction. *Distributed Computing*, 10:159-165, 1997.

46. G. Tel. Network orientation. *International Journal of Foundations of Computer Science*, 5(1):1-41, 1994.

47. G. Tel. Linear election in hypercubes. *Parallel Processing Letters*, 5(1):357-366, 1995.

48. G. Tel. Sense of direction in processor networks. In *Proc. of Conference on Theory and Practice of Informatics*, Lecture Notes in Computer Science 1012, pages 50-82. Springer-Verlag, 1995.

49. G. v. Bochmann, P. Flocchini, and D. Ramazani. Distributed objects with sense of direction. In *1st Workshop on Distributed Data and Structures*, Orlando. To appear.

50. A.M. Verweij. Linear-message election in hypercubes. Manuscript.

51. M. Yamashita and T. Kameda. Computing on anonymous networks, part I: characterizing the solvable cases. *IEEE Transaction on Parallel and Distributed Computing*, 7(1):69-89, 1996.

Top-Down Considerations
on Distributed Computing*

Ron van der Meyden[1] and Yoram Moses[2]

[1] University of Technology Sydney, P.O.Box 123 Broadway, NSW 2007 Australia
[2] Faculty of Electrical Engineering, The Technion, Haifa 3200 Israel

Distributed programs and systems are notoriously complex to design and prove correct. Even very short and seemingly intuitive distributed programs have been shown to behave in unexpected ways. As a result, the literature on distributed algorithms has tended to concentrate on solving specific problems in isolation. While this is an effective way of dealing with the complexity of distributed computing, the solutions obtained for manageable subproblems must eventually be composed to form more complex systems.

We are currently engaged in a research project concerned with developing a methodology for the top-down design of distributed programs. The purpose of the talk is to discuss some issues related to compositionality that arise in this work, and that may be relevant more broadly. This abstract presents in an informal manner a few of the points that will be discussed in the talk.

Sequential Composition: A very common practice in problem solving is to *divide and conquer*. Break a problem into simpler subproblems, solve each of them, and combine the solutions to a solution of the original problem. We could, for example, want to design a protocol for voting by breaking it into three parts: (a) Compute a minimum spanning tree (MST) of the network; (b) elect a leader using the MST; and (c) coordinate the vote through the leader. Clearly, these operations should be performed in sequence. Solutions to the abovementioned subproblems are typically assumed to start operating at a well-defined initial global state. But solutions to the MST problem or to leader election are not guaranteed to terminate at a well-defined global state [2]. How, then, do we compose the solutions? It is possible to overcome this problem by performing a synchronization step at the end of the intermediate steps, say in the form of termination detection. The cost of synchronizing the processes in the network can be high, however, and should be incurred only if needed. In our particular example this should not be necessary.

Extending the intuitions underlying the work on communication-closed layers [3, 1, 6, 7], we prefer to view distributed programs as operating between *cuts*, where a cut specifies an instant on the time-line of each of the processes. Intuitively this means that, as far as sequential composition is concerned, cuts constitute a distributed analogue of states of a sequential computation. With this view, it is possible to sequentially compose terminating programs such as those in our voting example.

---

* this work is supported by a grant from the Australian Research Council

The seemingly small move of viewing distributed programs as operating between cuts has considerable repercussions. For example, we now need to consider much more carefully what assumptions must be made about the *initial cut* of a given program, to ensure the program behaves in the desirable fashion. In some cases, the initial cut needs to be fairly tightly synchronized, perhaps a global state or something very close to it such as a consistent cut. In other cases, we can make do with much less. For example, in many cases it suffices that a message that is sent by process i in the course of executing its portion of the distributed program P and is received by j before j is ready to execute its part of P, will be presented again to j after j starts executing its portion of P. Properly formalized, such a condition is all that is needed to solve our voting example in a reliable asynchronous model, without needing to perform costly synchronization between the three layers of the computation. A characterization of distributed problems and solutions according to the degree of synchronization they require and those they provide is an important open problem.

High-level programs: It is possible to extend the discussion of properties and assumptions on initial cuts one step further. Informally, let us define a *cut formula* to be a formula that is interpreted over cuts. For every cut formula φ there will be a set of pairs r, c where r is a run and c is a cut, at which φ will be considered true. Cut formulas can be treated just like state formulas in a sequential computation. In fact, they enable the definition of branching and iteration at the level of distributed programs. If P and Q are distributed programs and φ is a cut formula, we can define

$$\textbf{if } \varphi \textbf{ then } P \textbf{ else } Q \quad \text{and} \quad \textbf{while } \varphi \textbf{ do } P$$

as *high-level* distributed programs. High-level programs of this nature resemble structured programs in sequential computing. But there is an important difference between the two. Whereas in the sequential case the tests in **if** and **while** statements are usually executable and can be accepted by the compiler as such, the corresponding tests on cut formulas are not directly executable in general. Nevertheless, such high-level constructs of distributed programming can serve as rigorous *descriptions* of the desired behavior. This, in turn, can be helpful in the process of designing a distributed program, when the designer wishes to transform a specification of a desired program into a concrete implementation. For example, we might decide to implement a program for computing the MST of a network in an incremental fashion by repeatedly adding an MST edge to the forest under construction. This will correspond to executing a loop of the form **while** φ **do** P, where φ is the cut formula stating that the MST is not completed yet, and P is a distributed program that adds one edge to the MST.

Termination: We have argued that considering programs as operating between cuts provides us with an improved facility for handling sequential composition of distributed programs. We need to assume, of course, that each participant in a distributed program ultimately terminates its participation in the program, before it can go on to performing the next program. This is taken for granted when dealing with sequential programs, where a nonterminating computation amounts to an outright failure and is usually totally undesirable. When we deal with distributed programs, there are common settings in which it is provable that desirable tasks cannot be solved by terminating distributed programs. For example, the work of Koo and Toueg [5] shows that in a setting in which messages may be lost but communication channels are *fair*, every protocol that requires the successful delivery of at least one message in each run, must have executions in which one or more of the processes cannot terminate. This appears to be an issue if we are after sequential composition of programs in this model.

An example of a nonterminating program in this context is the standard protocol for sending a single bit between a sender S and a receiver R. The sender's program is to send the bit repeatedly until it receives an acknowledgement. The receiver, in turn, sends one acknowledgement for each message it receives. A close analysis shows that the receiver must forever be ready to send one more acknowledgement in case it receives another copy of the bit. This example indicates that while the receiver cannot safely reach a terminating state with respect to the bit transmission program, the situation is not similar to the divergence of a sequential program. Despite not reaching a terminating state, the receiver should not be expected to abstain from taking part in further activities, provided that the receipt of a new copy of the bit will prompt the sending of an additional acknowledgement.

Inspired by the work of Havelund and Larsen [4], we subscribe to an approach by which part of the activity of a process can be considered as taking place "in the background." We call a program that operates in the background a *forked* program, and have an explicit **fork**(P) operator to capture this in our framework. The distinction between foreground and background activities has to do with how the compose with later programs. A forked activity takes place concurrent with whatever comes next, it need not terminate, and and if it does, its termination need not cause another activity to start. In the bit transmission problem, for example, we can view the receiver having a *top-level* or "foreground" activity consisting of waiting for the sender's message, and consuming it, or making use of the information therein once it arrives. The "background" activity, which the receiver would happily delegate to an assistant or, say, the mail system, involves sending the acknowledgements. Once the message is obtained by the receiver, the receiver can proceed to its next task. A similar distinction between aspects of distributed programs can be applied to a variety of well-known protocols and problems.

A separation of concerns between foreground and background activities allows the designer of a program to make fine-grained distinctions in specifying the control structure of the program. It enables mixing terminating programs with nonterminating programs and makes sequential composition of programs possible again even in models or for problems where termination is not a simple matter.

In summary, we feel that the concerns about composition of distributed programs raised above should receive more attention than they have in the past. We believe that they could give rise to new problems and techniques in the field of distributed algorithms. In our work, the observations made in this abstract form the basis of a refinement calculus for the top-down development of distributed programs from specifications. A detailed description of that work will be the subject of future papers.

References

1. Chou, C., Gafni, E.: Understanding and verifying distributed algorithms using stratified decomposition. Proc. 7th ACM PODC (1988) 44–65
2. Gallager, R., Humblet, P., Spira, P.: A distributed algorithm for minimum-weight spanning trees. ACM Trans. on Prog. Lang. and Syst., 5(1) (1983) 66–77
3. Elrad, T., Francez, N.: Decomposition of distributed programs into communication-closed layers. Sci. Comp. Prog., 2(3) (1982) 155-173
4. Havelund, K., Larsen, K.G.: The fork calculus. Proc. 20th ICALP, LNCS 700 (1993) 544–557
5. Koo, R., Toueg, S.: Effects of message loss on termination of distributed protocols. Inf. Proc, Letters, 27 (1988) 181–188
6. Stomp, F., de Roever, W.P.: A principle for sequential reasoning about distributed systems. Form. Asp. Comp., 6(6) (1994) 716–737
7. Zweirs, J., Janssen, W.: Partial-order based design of concurrent systems. Proc. REX Symp. "A decade of concurrency", J. de Bakker, W. P. de Roever, G. Rozenberg eds., LNCS 803 (1994) 622-684

Inter-task Co-ordination
in Long-Lived Distributed Applications

Santosh K. Shrivastava

Department of Computing Science, Newcastle University,
Newcastle upon Tyne, NE1 7RU, England.
Santosh.shrivastava@ncl.ac.uk

Abstract

We will discuss issues in the design of a fault-tolerant application composition and execution environment for distributed applications whose executions could span arbitrarily large durations. We are particularly interested in the domain of electronic commerce applications in the Internet/Web environment. The Internet frequently suffers from failures which can affect both the performance and consistency of applications run over it. A number of factors need to be taken into account in order to make these applications fault-tolerant. First, most such applications are rarely built from scratch; rather they are constructed by composing them out of existing applications and protocols. It should therefore be possible to compose an application out of component applications in a uniform manner, irrespective of the languages in which the component applications have been written and the operating systems of the host platforms. Application composition however must take into account individual site autonomy and privacy requirements. Second, the resulting applications can be very complex in structure, containing many temporal and data-flow dependencies between their constituent applications. However, constituent applications must be scheduled to run respecting these dependencies, despite the possibility of intervening processor and network failures. Third, the execution of such an application may take a long time to complete, and may contain long periods of inactivity (minutes, hours, days, weeks etc.), often due to the constituent applications requiring user interactions. It should be possible therefore to reconfigure an application dynamically because, for example, machines may fail, services may be moved or withdrawn and user requirements may change. Fourth, facilities are required for examining the application's execution history (e.g., to be able to settle disputes). So, a durable 'audit trail' recording the interactions between component applications needs to be maintained. Taken together, these are challenging requirements to meet!

Our approach has been to implement the application composition and execution environment as a *transactional workflow system* that enables sets of inter-related tasks to be carried out and supervised in a dependable manner [1,2]. Workflows are rule based management software that direct, co-ordinate and monitor execution of tasks arranged to form *workflow applications* representing business processes. *Tasks (activities)* are application specific units of work. A *Workflow schema (workflow script)* is used explicitly to represent the structure of an application in terms of tasks and temporal dependencies between tasks. An application is executed by *instantiating* the corresponding workflow schema.

We will describe how our system provides a uniform way of composing a complex task out of transactional and non-transactional tasks. This has been made possible because the system supports a simple yet powerful *task model* permitting a task to perform application specific input selection (e.g., obtain a given input from one of several sources) and terminate in one of several outcomes, producing distinct outputs. The system has been structured to provide dependability at *application level* and *system level*. Support for application level dependability has been provided through flexible task composition mentioned above that enables an application builder to incorporate alternative tasks, compensating tasks, replacement tasks etc., within an application to deal with a variety of exceptional situations. The system provides support for system level dependability by recording inter-task dependencies in transactional shared objects and by using transactions to implement the delivery of task outputs such that destination tasks receive their inputs despite finite number of intervening machine crashes and temporary network related failures; this also provides a durable audit trail of task interactions.

Our system architecture is decentralized and open: it has been designed and implemented as a set of CORBA services to run on top of a given ORB. Wide-spread acceptance of CORBA and Java middleware technologies make our system ideally suited to building Internet applications.

Acknowledgements

Stuart Wheater and Frederic Ranno have played key roles in the design and implementation of the workflow system. This work has been supported in part by grants from Nortel Technology, Engineering and Physical Sciences Research Council, ESPRIT LTR Project C3DS (Project No. 24962) and ESPRIT project MultiPLECX (Project No. 26810).

References

[1] Nortel & University of Newcastle upon Tyne, "Workflow Management Facility Specification", OMG document bom/98-01-11, Updated submission for the OMG Business Object Domain Task Force (BODTF): Workflow Management Facility.

[2] S. M. Wheater, S. K. Shrivastava and F. Ranno, "A CORBA Compliant Transactional Workflow System for Internet Applications", Proc. of IFIP Middleware 98, September 1998.

Seamlessly Selecting the Best Copy from Internet-Wide Replicated Web Servers

Yair Amir, Alec Peterson, and David Shaw

Department of Computer Science
Johns Hopkins University
{yairamir, chuckie, dshaw}@cs.jhu.edu

Abstract. The explosion of the web has led to a situation where a majority of the traffic on the Internet is web related. Today, practically all of the popular web sites are served from single locations. This necessitates frequent long distance network transfers of data (potentially repeatedly) which results in a high response time for users, and is wasteful of the available network bandwidth. Moreover, it commonly creates a single point of failure between the web site and its Internet provider. This paper presents a new approach to web replication, where each of the replicas resides in a different part of the network, and the browser is automatically and transparently directed to the "best" server. Implementing this architecture for popular web sites will result in a better response-time and a higher availability of these sites. Equally important, this architecture will potentially cut down a significant fraction of the traffic on the Internet, freeing bandwidth for other uses.

1. Introduction

The explosion of the web has led to a situation where a majority of the traffic on the Internet is web related. In fact, in the beginning of 1995, web traffic became the single largest load on the Internet [1]. Today, practically all of the popular web sites are served from single locations. This necessitates frequent long distance network transfers of data (potentially repeatedly) which results in a high response time for users, and is wasteful of the available network bandwidth. Moreover, it commonly creates a single point of failure between the web site and its Internet service provider.

We present a new approach that uses web replication where each of the replicas resides in a different part of the network. The key contribution of this paper is how to have the client – the web browser – automatically and transparently contact the *best* replica, taking into account:

- Network topology: which replica is "closest" to the client, network-wise.
- Server availability: which servers are currently active.
- Server load: which server is currently able to return the most rapid response.

Most of the existing web replication architectures involve a cluster of servers that reside at the same site. These architectures improve performance by sharing the load between the different replicas, and improve availability by having more than one server. However, they cannot address the performance and availability problems embedded in the network.

Our architecture, in contrast, incorporates wide-area replication and automatic server selection to adequately address the above issues. Moreover, the architecture can be used in conjunction with both caching and cluster replication. The architecture includes three alternative methods to automatically direct the user's browser to the best replica.

- *The HTTP redirect method*: This method is implemented using web server-side programming at the application level.
- *The DNS round trip times method*: This method is implemented at the Domain Name Service (DNS) level, using the standard properties of DNS.
- *The shared IP address method*: This method is implemented at the network routing level, using the standard Internet routing.

Implementing this architecture for popular web sites will result in a better response-time and higher availability for these sites. Equally important, this architecture will potentially cut down a significant fraction of the traffic on the Internet, freeing bandwidth for other uses.

The reminder of the paper is organized as follows: The next section describes current web caching and replication methods. We then describe the alternative methods that automatically direct the web browser to the best replica. The next section describes our experience with the different methods. We then analyze and compare the methods, and draw our conclusions.

Due to lack of space, we will not detail a replication protocol to keep the consistency of the web server replicas. Several primary-backup [2], active replication [3], or lazy replication [4] techniques may be adequate.

2. Current web caching and replication methods

The two most common methods used to alleviate slow web response problems today are *caching* and *replication* (sometimes referred to as mirroring). In caching, we still have one main web server. On demand, pieces of the data are cached closer to the client. Subsequent requests for the same data are served from the cache rather than necessitating an access to the main web server.

Practically, web caching uses a special proxy on either the client or server side. This proxy acts as the go-between between the web browser and web server. Client side caching is when a client makes all requests through the proxy. The proxy then makes the actual request and caches the response for other clients (who are presumably at the same site as the original client). Many browsers (including Netscape's and Microsoft's) support this capability internally and perform client side caching on a per-user basis. This per-user caching is independent of any other caching done at the server or client side. Some caches used on a per-site basis include the Squid [5], Harvest [6], and Apache [7] caches.

In server-side caching, there are one or more caching servers that are front ends to the main server. When a document is requested, the caching server attempts to serve the document from its own cache, or from that of another caching server, before resorting to retrieving the document from the main web server. Frequently accessed documents will therefore be quickly cached, and thus the load for serving them will not fall onto the main web server. These caching methods do not conflict, and any or all of them may be used together as needed.

An intrinsic limitation for caching arises where the client is sending information to the server and asking for more than a static page (e.g. CGI scripts, or other server-side programming). Since the server's response to the request is dependent on the parameters sent along with the request, the response cannot be cached.

Another caching limitation is in the freshness of data. Given a particular document, it may be found in any (or all) of numerous caches between the client and the server. This creates a consistency problem as there is no to way guarantee the validity of any particular cache. No cache can guarantee complete freshness of data without the immediate expiration of cache data and the subsequent refresh from the master server. This clearly defeats the purpose of a cache, as every request will need to be served (however indirectly) by the master server.

In HTTP 1.0 [8] the cache management abilities were poor. This has been rectified in HTTP 1.1 [9], and authors now have the ability to exercise considerable control over the caching (or non-caching) of their documents, but this is not universally supported yet.

Web *replication* duplicates the web server, including its data and any ancillary abilities. A user can access any of the replicas, as any of them will provide a valid response. Replication addresses some of the limitations of caching as certain types of responses cannot be cached. These include responses to requests that require client-server interaction such as CGI scripts, database lookups, and server-generated pages.

Moreover, replication correctly handles situations such as advertising, where an accurate count of requests needs to be kept. For these situations, caching must be disabled: since the caches may not be under the web server's control, there is no way to count the number of actual hits (for more information, see [10]).

There is a problem that arises in both caching and replication: There is no way for the client to determine which is the "best" server to connect to. This paper examines a few possible methods that address this problem. These methods are applicable to both replicated and cached servers, as the benefits for connecting a client to the "best" replica are similar (though not identical) to those for connecting the client to the best cache.

3. Automatically locating the best replica

All of these methods involve the concept of the "best" server. This is a relative term, dependent on where the client is located on the network, and which of the collection of replicated servers is most able to answer the clients' request. Weighting is also a factor – in the extreme case, server load may be more significant than network topology, as it is probably a better decision for the client to be sent to a more distant server than to one that is extremely overloaded, but closer.

Once the best server is determined, there are several possible ways to get the client there.

The HTTP redirect method

This is clearly the simplest method, but is the most limited as well.

The HTTP protocol since version 1.0 [8] has supported an "HTTP redirect", where the client seeking a particular resource is told to go elsewhere for it. In combination with an intelligent server, this capability can be used to send the client to the proper place. Once this transfer of control takes place, the client will continue to communicate with the second server for the rest of the session.

As the HTTP redirect method works without any knowledge of the network topology and the location of the client within it, the HTTP redirect method is only really useful for connecting a client to the best server *overall*, rather than the best server for that particular client. This is significant, as it only addresses part of the problem. For example, even given a very fast and unloaded server, and a slower and heavily loaded server, the faster server may well not be the best choice for the client, if that client happens to be on the same network as the slower server.

There is also a major disadvantage in the HTTP redirect method in that there has to be a "central" server to accept the HTTP query and pass it off onto another server. This model has a single point of failure – a failure at this central server can immobilize the entire system. This problem can be partially addressed by using multiple central servers, but this leads to other problems.

The final problem with this method is that the user can inadvertently or otherwise defeat it. A user that notes down ("bookmarks") the address of a web site after the redirection has taken place may get the wrong address noted down – that of one of the "children" rather than the central redirection server. Each further access would then go to that child directly, bypassing and defeating any optimization that is applied at the central server.

All is not negative for this method, and in fact there is one optimization that is possible here, but not with other methods – one where the actual content of the request is taken into account before the best server is determined. It can be determined that certain servers are better at serving some sorts of requests (for example, a server optimized for running CGI scripts, and another server optimized for serving static text). While both servers may be identical replicas data-wise, they still differ in their underlying capabilities.

The DNS round trip times method

This method utilizes the domain name system (DNS) [11], [12] to help determine which server is closest to the client. To explain this, a brief review of how a name-to-IP address lookup is done may be helpful:

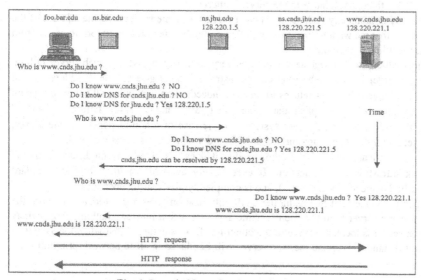

Fig. 1. Domain Name Service Resolution

Every server on the Internet has a fully qualified domain name (FQDN). FQDN are usually read from left to right, and each segment is rooted in the segment after it. www.cnds.jhu.edu is a machine known as "www" located in the Center for Networking and Distributed Systems, which is part of the Johns Hopkins University, which is an educational institution in the US. There is an assumed dot (".") at the end of each FQDN, which stands for the root domain at the top of the domain name tree. Barring any information cached on a local name server, a query for www.cnds.jhu.edu is sent to one of the root (".") name servers. This server (which due to the enormous size of the entirety of the domain name system cannot know every address), returns a list of name servers for "edu.", and the process is repeated, with one of the "edu." servers returning a list of name servers for "jhu.edu.", and one of the "jhu.edu." servers returning a list of servers for "cnds.jhu.edu.", one of which then returns the requested IP address(es) for "www.cnds.jhu.edu". Caching is used to reduce the difficulty of the problem. If at any stage, a server has the address requested (or the address of a name server authoritative for that domain) cached, it will return it directly, short-cutting the above process.

This method takes advantage of the fact that each local server, when querying a remote server, keeps track of the round trip time (RTT) of packets to that server. This is done for optimization reasons, as over time the local server will try and favor those servers that respond faster. Given otherwise similar servers, this usually indicates a server that is closer network-wise.

This optimization can be leveraged for the problem being discussed by changing one concept in the DNS – normally, all servers for a particular domain (called a "zone" in DNS terms) carry the same data, but this is *not* a requirement. From the perspective of a querying server all that is significant is whether the remote server is in the chain of authority for the domain we are querying.

Thus, if we have many name servers, each serving an *authoritative, but different* IP address for www.cnds.jhu.edu, the web server the client is directed to is dependent on which name server the client's local name server happens to ask. Since, as already established, the client's local name server tends to favor those remote name servers that are closest to it, an excellent system for adding the last missing piece of information – that of "where is the client relative to the server" emerges.

Thus, by dynamically updating [13] each particular name server with the address of the web server that we want to direct users in that particular area of the network to, users from that area will tend to go there.

This method handles web server failures very well. In the case of a web server failure, the name server for that web server can be instructed to not give out the IP address of that server until that web server returns to service. Indeed, simply stopping all name service on that machine will accomplish the same thing, as a name server failure is handled automatically by the name server system – in the case of a non-responsive name server, other servers for that zone are queried in RTT-order until an answer is received.

A major advantage of this method is that it does not entail *any* modification of the network infrastructure to function. It uses readily available building blocks (standard unmodified name and web servers), and is completely platform-independent.

It can be pointed out that using the DNS optimization gives a good idea how close the chosen name server is to the client's name server, but that may say nothing about where the web server is located relative to the client itself. It is assumed that when the system is set up, the name server and the web server will be placed in close network proximity. In addition, the local name server the client is querying is expected to be in close network proximity to the client, as is the usual setup on the Internet today.

The RTT method the DNS uses to determine the best name server for a particular zone is not necessarily optimal, but over time is a reasonable approximation. The time it takes to establish this reasonable approximation is the chief problem with this method. In order for the local name server to query the fastest responding name server, it needs to try them all. Thus, until all servers for the remote zone are queried at least once, the local server may query a server that is very far away network-wise, and thus get the IP address of a web server that is very far away from the client. The local server is unlikely to repeat its error, as this distant name server will likely have a larger RTT value than the other servers in the list will, but for this one connection the harm has already been done.

Due to the necessity for the client's local name server to cycle through and establish timings for all of the name servers for the zone in question, the web server must receive a fairly large quantity of hits from a relatively concentrated area (generally one institution such as an ISP or a university) for this method to work. Thus this method is fairly unlikely to work in the short term. It *will*, however, work in the long term.

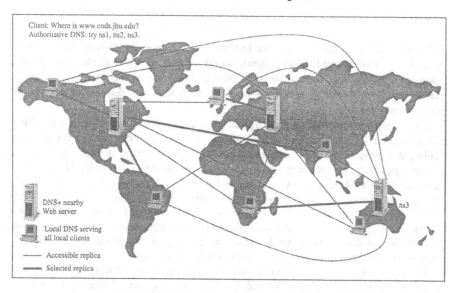

Fig. 2. DNS Round Trip Times method in action

The DNS Round Trip Times method is illustrated in figure 2. The server www.cnds.jhu.edu is replicated in three places, and has an accompanying name server in each place. Clients that want to query this server ask their local name server to resolve the name. The local name server will (eventually) try all three of the possible name servers that are authoritative for www.cnds.jhu.edu. Eventually, the local name server learns which remote name server is closest and concentrates on the web server that is pointed to by this name server.

To help the process along a bit, another concept from DNS can be used. Each name-to-number mapping can have a variable time-to-live (TTL) value. This number specifies a time, after which the address returned should be regarded as invalid, and not used again. By setting a lower than usual TTL on the address record of the web server, we can force the name to be re-requested with greater frequency. Of course, this can be a disadvantage as well, as each request causes extra traffic and occasionally a perceptible delay to the client, as the name is re-resolved.

Using this system, one connection (defined as one or more connections to the web server within a certain TTL) has a *1/n* chance of getting the "correct" server, where *n* is defined as the number of name servers serving that zone. Therefore, given the characteristics of the zone, one can estimate the optimal number of name servers for that zone. For example, a very popular site that gets continual connections from around the world (e.g., Yahoo) could have many more name servers than a site that gets a slower stream of connections. The larger number of connections that a busy site will receive can more quickly get past the disadvantage of being forced to try all of the name servers for a zone before optimizing on the best one. The TTL value may also be "tuned" to give the best results in the particular environment it is used in. Note that this time period is timed relative to the local name server, and not the client or the web server — if several clients that share a local name server all request a document from the same web server within the time period, that still counts as one "connection".

The shared IP address method

Typically, any given machine on the Internet has a unique IP address. While this is necessary for most things to work properly on the network, it is possible to have multiple machines share an IP address. If this configuration is implemented properly on a network that spreads over a wide geographic area, some very intelligent distribution of network load becomes possible.

If an autonomous network (such as Sprint, MCI, or any other Internet Service Provider) has data centers in San Francisco and Washington DC, for example, the network operator could put servers in each of those locations that have the same IP address. Since all networks nowadays practice what is known as "closest exit routing" this kind of approach can work very well. Closest exit routing is based on the premise that the destination network will know how to find a specific host better than the host, so it should be handed to the destination network as quickly as possible. With external routing protocols, many addresses are aggregated into one announcement to help keep the size of the global routing table down. The destination network that makes those aggregated announcements has the required knowledge to find the specific address that a packet is destined for.

The protocols that carry this more specific information are capable of dealing with multiple instances of the same IP address. The vast majority of these protocols use Dijkstra's Shortest Path First algorithm, which can deal with duplicate addresses. This is done by simply importing the closest instance of the IP address into the router forwarding table. When the destination network gets the packet from the source network, it will send the packet to the closest instance of the shared IP address from its own point of view.

In effect, this creates the illusion that one logical machine is connected in several places of the network via an extremely fast connection. The true situation, of course, is that behind each connection there is a different replica.

Once the servers with the shared IP address are placed throughout a network, one must still implement the higher-level services (HTTP, FTP, etc) on them. An intuitive way to approach the problem is to assign the web server the shared IP address, so that the requests will be sent directly to the "closest" web server. This naïve approach may work in a completely stable network environment, but if the network topology changes during a TCP/IP session, then the client connection with the "closest" web server will immediately break.

We solve this problem by assigning the shared IP address to the DNS servers rather to the web servers we wish to replicate. Each of the DNS servers is configured with the unique IP address of the web server that is "closest" to it. Since DNS requests are stateless, we will not run into the problem stated above, because all stateful communications are done with a unique IP address. As in the DNS Round Trip Times method above, DNS dynamic update can be used to ensure the proper addresses are given to the clients, taking into account the load on the servers and their current availability.

4. Experience and Analysis

We ran a number of tests to confirm the feasibility of all three approaches.

- The HTTP redirect method can easily be implemented using the CGI functionality built into all modern web servers. Some servers can even do this internally without using an external process at all. As previously discussed, this method has no intrinsic ability to incorporate network distance to select the most suitable server. It has, however, the ability to base its decision on the actual request made by the client.

- To verify the DNS Round Trip Times method, we set up seven authoritative name servers around the world. There is one each in Austria, Israel, and Australia, and four in the United States: one in Maryland (at Johns Hopkins), and three in Colorado. Each of these DNS servers responds with a different IP address for the same name of the undergraduate web server on the Department of Computer Science, The Johns Hopkins University, which is a fairly busy server. On the server at Hopkins, we used a special web server configuration using multiple IP addresses, so we could log the address of the client as well as which web server replica it used. In this way we were able to identify the DNS server that was contacted by the user's name server.

  - We have found that over the period of several days, clients sharing a remote name server did indeed tend to converge on the name server closest to them. The results presented in Table 1 show, for example, that over a short period of time (approximately 15 days, including the convergence period) 53% of all hits from Australia (as selected by hostnames that end in ".au") went to the IP address given out by the name server in Australia. If the local name server effect (see below) is discounted, we estimate that this figure may rise as high as 80%. Note that this time period includes the convergence period, for which this method is inaccurate. The effectiveness of this method will rise even further over time after the convergence is completed. Therefore, we expect longer tests to show even better behavior.

  - This is not an ideal test, as some clients do not have reverse DNS, nor are all Australian clients in a ".au" domain, but it is illustrative of the concept. For a similar reason, it is very difficult to determine the location of clients in the ".com" and ".edu" (and other three-letter) domains.

  - We have found that the system convergence time goes up linearly with the number of replicas. However, the law of diminishing returns dictates that the benefit derived from each additional replica decreases. Since the system is not effective until it converges, we feel that using a smaller number of replicas will provide the best overall performance.

- A small change in the way DNS works can remedy the above problem: If the DNS will check the round trip time for all of the remote name servers when it first resolves the name, this method will converge after the first access. This does not seem to be a major change in DNS, and does not seem to create too much extraneous load on the network, but it gives a huge benefit to the current DNS round trip time heuristics.

- One limitation that we discovered is that the name server that delegates to the multiple authoritative name servers should not also be used as a local name server for users. If this is done, that name server would soon learn which of the replicas is the best for its own users, and will return that answer to any remote name server. This distorting effect will last until the TTL of the web server's address expires. This effect explains the skew of the results presented in Table 1 towards the Baltimore server, because the jhu.edu primary name server also serves local clients on the Johns Hopkins campus.

- To test the Shared IP method, we used the Erols Internet network. Erols is an Internet Service Provider servicing all major markets on the East Coast of the US, from Boston MA to Norfolk VA, with about 340,000 users. The Erols network contains about eighty routers running the OSPF routing protocol.

  - We have assigned the same IP address to machines on two different routers: one in New York City, and one in Vienna, Virginia. We have observed that accesses for this shared IP address from New Jersey arrived at the New York City machine. Accesses from Washington DC, in contrast, arrived at the Vienna machine, as expected.

  - We have observed that the network converges to the correct address within about forty seconds after a change to the network, such as one of these machines crashing, occurs. In that case, all of the traffic is directed to the remaining machine after the network converges.

  - It is interesting to note that accessing this IP address from Baltimore, which is, coincidentally, exactly half way between New York's and Vienna's routers according to the network metric, we managed to observe some of the traffic going to the New York machine and some going to the Vienna machine. This confirmed the fact that there will be a problem if the shared IP address is assigned to the web server itself. However, this has no adverse effect when the shared IP address is assigned to the DNS server, thanks to the stateless single-packet nature of most DNS.

Table 1. DNS Round Trip Times Method Results

Location	Accesses from Australia	Accesses from Israel	Accesses from Austria
Baltimore	2192	635	174
Austria	279	233	88
Colorado 1	72	24	5
Colorado 2	56	18	2
Colorado 3	78	4	13
Israel	325	841	132
Australia	3439	236	42

To analyze the relative merits and drawbacks of the three methods, we have identified five important criteria that allow us to compare the different methods:

- *Long-term effectiveness*: How effective and accurate is the method? What factors can be considered?
- *Convergence speed*: How fast can the method converge to the best replica?
- *Setup complexity*: What is required from the web site manager in order to implement such a solution?
- *Extensibility to other services*: How general is this method?
- *Special requirements*: Are there any special requirements?

Table 2 compares the different methods according to the above criteria.

Table 2. Comparing the different location methods.

Property	HTTP redirect	DNS round trip times	Shared IP address
Long- term effectiveness	Not able to consider network distance internally. Can incorporate server load and current availability. The only method that can consider request content in the decision.	Uses round trip times to approximate network distance. Can consider server load and current availability.	Accurately incorporates network distance. Can incorporate server load and current availability.
Convergence speed	Method is in effect only after the first access. Fully effective after that.	Convergence is linear with the number of replicas. Convergence is done per source DNS. All of the remote name servers must be accessed at least once before convergence is achieved. Usually, it is slow (hours to days).	Method is always in effect. Convergence is immediate when there is a network change (about 30 seconds).
Setup complexity	Programming CGI scripts that may re-direct to another replica.	Set up a number of secondary DNS servers that are close to the web server replicas	Set up a shared IP address for the primary DNS servers.

Extensibility to other services	Limited only to the web and HTTP.	The same method works for any name based service (ftp, e-mail, etc.)	The same method works for any name based service (ftp, e-mail, etc.)
Special requirements	None	None	All DNS (and probably all web replicas) have to be on the **same** autonomous network. *i.e.* have the same Internet provider (such as MCI, Sprint, BBN, Erols).

5. Conclusions

We have presented a new approach that uses web replication where each of the replicas resides in a different part of the network. We showed three different methods to seamlessly direct the client to the best replica taking into account the network topology and the server availability and load.

In cases where it is possible to implement the shared IP address method for DNS, we recommend using this method because of the fast convergence time. However, there can be cases where this is not possible, such as when the replicas span different continents and there is no access provider that can route a shared IP address solution (cheaply enough). In these cases, we recommend using the DNS round trip times method with a small number of widely separated replicas.

Preliminary tests show that using either method, our approach may yield significant benefit, both for the client (fast response time, higher availability), and for the network (lower overall traffic).

References

1. NSFNET Backbone Traffic Distribution by Service report. ftp://ftp.merit.edu/nsfnet/statistics/1995/nsf-9503.ports.gz
2. Trigdell, A., Mackerras, P.: The Rsync Algorithm. Technical Report TR-CS-96-05, The Australian National University. Available at ftp://samba.anu.edu.au/pub/rsync/
3. Amir, Y.: Replication Using Group Communication over a Partitioned Network, Ph.D. Thesis, Institute of Computer Science, The Hebrew University of Jerusalem, Israel (1995). Available at http://www.cs.jhu.edu/~yairamir/
4. Ladin, R., Liskov, B., Shrira, L., Ghemawat, S.: Providing Availability Using Lazy Replication ACM Transactions on Computer Systems, 10(4), pages 360-391.
5. Squid Internet Object Cache. http://squid.nlanr.net/Squid/

6. Chankhunthod, A., Danzig, P. B., Neerdaels, C., Schwartz, M. F., Worrell, K. J.: A Hierarchical Internet Object Cache. Technical Report 95-611, Computer Science Department, University of Southern California, Los Angeles, California, (1995).

7. The Apache HTTP Server Project. http://www.apache.org/

8. Berners-Lee, T., Fielding, R., Frystyk, H.: RFC-1945: Hypertext Transfer Protocol – HTTP/1.0. (1996).

9. Fielding, R., Gettys, J., Mogul, J., Frystyk, H., Berners-Lee, T.: RFC-2068: Hypertext Transfer Protocol – HTTP/1.1. (1997).

10. On Interpreting Access Statistics. http://www.cranfield.ac.uk/docs/stats/

11. Mockapetris, P.: RFC-1034: Domain Names – Concepts and Facilities. (1987).

12. Mockapetris, P.: RFC-1035: Domain Names – Implementation and Specification. (1987).

13. Vixie, P. (ed), Thompson, S., Rekhter, Y., Bound, J.: RFC-2136: Dynamic Updates in the Domain Name System (DNS UPDATE). (1997).

Wait-Free Synchronization in Quantum-Based Multiprogrammed Systems* (Extended Abstract)

James H. Anderson, Rohit Jain, and David Ott

Department of Computer Science
University of North Carolina at Chapel Hill

Abstract. We consider wait-free synchronization in multiprogrammed uniprocessor and multiprocessor systems in which the processes bound to each processor are scheduled for execution using a scheduling quantum. We show that, in such systems, any object with consensus number P in Herlihy's wait-free hierarchy is universal for any number of processes executing on P processors, provided the scheduling quantum is of a certain size. We give an asymptotically tight characterization of how large the scheduling quantum must be for this result to hold.

1 Introduction

This paper is concerned with wait-free synchronization in multiprogrammed systems. In such systems, several processes may be bound to the same processor. In related previous work, Ramamurthy, Moir, and Anderson considered wait-free synchronization in multiprogrammed systems in which processes on the same processor are scheduled by priority [4]. For such systems, Ramamurthy et al. showed that any object with consensus number P in Herlihy's wait-free hierarchy [2] is universal for any number of processes executing on P processors, i.e., universality is a function of the number of *processors* in a system, not the number of *processes*. An object has *consensus number* C iff it can be used to solve C-process consensus, but not $(C+1)$-process consensus, in an asynchronous system in a wait-free manner. An object is *universal* in a system if it can be used to implement any other object in that system in a wait-free manner.

In this paper, we establish similar results for multiprogrammed systems in which quantum-based scheduling is used. Under quantum-based scheduling, each processor is allocated to its assigned processes in discrete time units called *quanta*. When a processor is allocated to some process, that process is guaranteed to execute without preemption for Q time units, where Q is the length of the quantum, or until it terminates, whichever comes first. In this paper, we show that quantum-based systems are similar to priority-based systems with regard

* Work supported by NSF grants CCR 9510156 and CCR 9732916, and by a Young Investigator Award from the U.S. Army Research Office, grant number DAAH04-95-1-0323. The first author was also supported by an Alfred P. Sloan Research Fellowship.

to universality. In particular, we show that any object with consensus number P in Herlihy's wait-free hierarchy is universal in a quantum-based system for any number of processes executing on P processors, *provided* the scheduling quantum is of a certain size. We give an asymptotically tight characterization of how large the scheduling quantum must be for this result to hold.

Our results are summarized in Table 1. This table gives conditions under which an object with consensus number C is universal in a P-processor quantum-based system. In this table, T_{max} (T_{min}) denotes the maximum (minimum) time required to perform any atomic operation, Q is the length of the scheduling quantum, and c is a constant that follows from the algorithms we present. Obviously, if $C < P$, then universal algorithms are impossible [2]. If $P \leq C \leq 2P$, then the smallest value of Q that suffices is a value proportional to $(2P + 1 - C)T_{max}$. If $2P \leq C < \infty$, then the smallest value of Q that suffices is a value proportional to $2T_{max}$. If $C = \infty$, then Q (obviously) can be any value [2].

An important special case of our main result is that reads and writes are universal in quantum-based uniprocessor systems ($P = 1$). In this case, the scheduling quantum must be large enough to encompass the execution of eight high-level language instructions (see Theorem 1). In any practical system, the scheduling quantum would be much larger than this. Thus, in practice, Herlihy's wait-free hierarchy collapses in multithreaded uniprocessor applications in which quantum-based scheduling is used.

It is important to note that the results of this paper do *not* follow from the previous results of Ramamurthy et al. concerning priority-based systems, because priority-based and quantum-based execution models are fundamentally incomparable. In a priority-based system, if a process p is preempted during an object invocation by another process q that invokes the same object, then p "knows" that q's invocation must be completed by the time p resumes execution. This is because q has higher priority and will not relinquish the processor until it completes. Thus, operations of higher priority processes "automatically" appear to be atomic to lower priority processes executing on the same processor. This is the fundamental insight behind the results of Ramamurthy et al.

In contrast, in a quantum-based system, if a process is ever preempted while accessing some object, then there are no guarantees that the process preempting it will complete any pending object invocation before relinquishing the processor. On the other hand, if a process can ever detect that it has "crossed" a quantum boundary, then it can be sure that the next few instructions it executes will be performed without preemption. Several of the algorithms presented in this paper employ such a detection mechanism. This kind of detection mechanism would be ill-suited for use in a priority-based system, because a process in such a system can never be "sure" that it won't be preempted by a higher-priority process.

Our quantum-based execution model is based on two key assumptions:

(i) If a process is preempted during an object invocation, then the first such preemption may happen at any point in time after the invocation begins.

(ii) When a process resumes execution after having been preempted, it cannot be preempted again until after Q time units have elapsed.

consensus number C	universal if:	not universal if:
P	$Q \geq c(P+1)T_{max}$	$Q \leq PT_{min}$
$P+1$	$Q \geq cPT_{max}$	$Q \leq (P-1)T_{min}$
$\vdots$	$\vdots$	$\vdots$
n, where $P \leq n < 2P$	$Q \geq c(2P+1-n)T_{max}$	$Q \leq (2P-n)T_{min}$
$\vdots$	$\vdots$	$\vdots$
$2P-2$	$Q \geq c3T_{max}$	$Q \leq 2T_{min}$
$2P-1$	$Q \geq c2T_{max}$	$Q \leq T_{min}$
$2P$	$Q \geq c2T_{max}$	$Q \leq T_{min}$
$2P+1$	$Q \geq c2T_{max}$	$Q \leq T_{min}$
$\vdots$	$\vdots$	$\vdots$
∞	$Q \geq 0$	—

Table 1. Conditions under which an object with consensus number C is universal for any number of processes in a P-processor quantum-based system.

Note in particular that we do not assume that each object invocation starts at the beginning of a quantum. This is because the objects we implement might be used in other algorithms, in which case it might be impossible to ensure that each invocation of an object begins execution at a quantum boundary. We also make no assumptions regarding how the next process to run is selected on a processor. Indeed, the process currently running on a processor may be allocated several quanta in succession before the processor is allocated to a different process — in fact, the processor may *never* be allocated to another process.

These assumptions rule out certain trivial solutions to the problems we address. For example, the above-mentioned result about the universality of reads and writes in quantum-based uniprocessors is obtained by presenting a wait-free implementation of a consensus object that uses only reads and writes. It may seem that such an implementation is trivial to obtain: simply define the quantum to be large enough so that any consensus invocation fits within a single quantum! However, our model precludes such a solution, because we do not assume that each object invocation starts at the beginning of a quantum.

It is similarly fruitless to implement a uniprocessor consensus object by requiring each process to repeatedly test some condition (i.e., by busy waiting) until a quantum boundary has been crossed, and to then perform the consensus invocation (safely) within the new quantum. This is because, for a process to detect that a quantum boundary has been crossed, it must eventually be preempted by another process. Such a preemption may never occur. Even if we were able to assume that such a preemption would eventually occur (e.g., because round-robin scheduling was being used), the proposed solution should still be rejected. This is because it forces operations (on consensus objects, in this case) to be performed at the rate the processor is switched between processes. This defeats one of the main attractions of the quantum-based execution model:

in most quantum-based systems, the scheduling quantum is large enough to allow many operations to be performed safely inside a single quantum without any fear of interferences, i.e., the rate at which operations potentially could be performed is *much* higher than the rate of process switches.

The remainder of this paper is organized as follows. In Sect. 2, we present definitions and notation that will be used in the remainder of the paper. Then, in Sect. 3, we present our results for quantum-based uniprocessor systems. We begin by presenting a wait-free, constant-time implementation of a consensus object that uses only reads and writes and a quantum of constant size. This implementation proves that reads and writes are universal in quantum-based uniprocessor systems [2]. Object implementations of practical interest are usually based on synchronization primitives such as *compare-and-swap* (C&S), not consensus objects. We show that, given a quantum of constant size and using only reads and writes, C&S can be implemented in a quantum-based uniprocessor system in constant time. We also show that any read-modify-write primitive can be implemented in constant time as well. In Sect. 4, we present our results for quantum-based multiprocessor systems. Our goal in this section is to establish universality results for objects with consensus number C, where $C \geq P$. We do this by showing how to use such objects to implement a wait-free consensus object for any number of processes running on P processors. As C varies, the quantum required for this consensus implementation to work correctly is as given in Table 1. In the full paper, we prove that our characterization of the required quantum is asymptotically tight [1]. This proof is omitted here due to space limitations. We end the paper with concluding remarks in Sect. 5.

2 Definitions and Notation

A *quantum-based system* consists of a set a processes and a set of processors. In most ways, quantum-based systems are similar to shared-memory concurrent systems as defined elsewhere. For brevity, we focus here on the important differences. In a quantum-based system, each process is assigned to a distinct processor. Associated with any quantum-based system is a *scheduling quantum* (or *quantum* for short), which is a nonnegative integer value. In an actual quantum-based system, the quantum would be given in time units. In this paper, we find it convenient to more abstractly view a quantum as specifying a statement count. This allows us to avoid having to incorporate time explicitly into our model. Informally, when a processor is allocated to some process, that process is guaranteed to execute without preemption for at least Q atomic statements, where Q is the value of the quantum, or until it terminates.

Our programming notation should be self explanatory; as an example of this notation, see Fig. 1. In this and subsequent figures, each numbered statement is assumed to be atomic. When considering a given object implementation, we consider only statement executions that arise when processes perform operations on the given object, i.e., we abstract away from the other activities of these processes outside of object accesses. For "long-lived" objects that may be invoked repeatedly, we assume that when a process completes some operation on the object, that process's program counter is updated to point to the first statement of some nondeterministically-selected operation of the object.

We define a program's semantics by a set of histories. A *history* of a program is a sequence $t_0 \xrightarrow{s_0} t_1 \xrightarrow{s_1} \cdots$, where t_0 is an initial state and $t_i \xrightarrow{s_i} t_{i+1}$ denotes that state t_{i+1} is reached from state t_i via the execution of statement s_i; unless stated otherwise, a history is assumed to be a maximal such sequence. Consider the history $t_0 \xrightarrow{s_0} t_1 \xrightarrow{s_1} \cdots t_i \xrightarrow{s_i} t_{i+1} \cdots t_j \xrightarrow{s_j} t_{j+1} \cdots$, where s_i and s_j are successive statement executions by some process p. We say that p *is preempted before* s_j in this history iff some other process on p's processor executes a statement between states t_{i+1} and t_j. A history $h = t_0 \xrightarrow{s_0} t_1 \xrightarrow{s_1} \cdots$ is *well-formed* iff it satisfies the following condition: for any statement execution s_j in h by any process p, if p is preempted before s_j, then no process on p's processor other than p executes a statement after state t_{j+1} until either (i) p executes at least Q statements or (ii) p's object invocation that includes s_j terminates. We henceforth assume all histories are well-formed. We define program properties using invariants and stable assertions. An assertion is *stable* in a history iff it holds from some state onward. An assertion is an *invariant* in a history iff it is stable and initially true.

Notational Conventions: The number of processes and processors in the system are denoted N and P, respectively. Processors are labeled from 1 to P. M denotes the maximum number of processes on any processor. Q denotes the value of the quantum, and C will be used to refer to a given object's consensus number (see Sect. 1). Unless stated otherwise, p, q, and r are assumed to be universally quantified over process identifiers. The predicate $running(p)$ holds at a state iff process p is the currently-running process on its processor at that state. The predicate $p@s$ holds iff statement s is the next statement to be executed by process p. We use $p@S$ as shorthand for $(\exists s : s \in S :: p@s)$, $p.s$ to denote statement number s of process p, $p.v$ to denote p's local variable v, and $pr(p)$ to denote process p's processor. *valtype* denotes an arbitrary type. □

3 Uniprocessor Systems

In this section, we present constant-time implementations of a consensus object (Sect. 3.1), a C&S object (Sect. 3.2), and a read-modify-write object (Sect. 3.3) for quantum-based uniprocessor systems. Each of these implementations uses only reads and writes and requires a quantum of constant size.

3.1 Consensus

Our uniprocessor consensus algorithm is shown in Fig. 1. Here Q is assumed to be eight atomic statements. In lines 1-14 of the algorithm, the worst-case execution sequence consists of nine atomic statements (in particular, lines 1-8 and 14). Thus, with $Q = 8$, a process can be preempted at most once while executing within lines 1-14. Note that each process p both begins and ends this

shared variable $Dec1$, $Dec2$: $valtype \cup \perp$ **initially** $\perp$;
$\qquad\qquad\quad Run$: $1..N$

procedure $decide(in: valtype)$ **returns** $valtype$
private variable val: $valtype \cup \perp$ $\qquad$ /* local to process p, the invoking process */

```
1:      Run := p;
2:      if Dec2 = ⊥ then
3:          Dec1 := in;
4:          if Run ≠ p then
5:              val := Dec2;          /* statements 5-9 execute without preemption */
6:              if val = ⊥ then
7:                  Dec1 := in;
8:                  Dec2 := in
                else
9:                  Dec1 := val
                fi
            else
10:             Dec2 := in;
11:             if Run ≠ p then
12:                 val := Dec1;      /* statements 12-13 execute without preemption */
13:                 Dec2 := val
                fi
            fi
        fi;
14:     Run := p;
15:     return Dec2
```

Fig. 1. Uniprocessor consensus using reads and writes.

code sequence by assigning $Run := p$. Thus, if any process p is preempted while executing within lines 1-14 by another process q that also executes within lines 1-14, then $Run \neq p$ holds by the time p resumes execution. This is because q's execution of lines 1-14 can itself be preempted at most once, and thus if q executes any of these statements within a quantum, then it must execute $q.1$ or $q.14$ or both within that quantum. This handshaking mechanism is typical of those employed in the algorithms in this paper to enable a process to detect if it has been preempted.

Having explained the manner in which preemptions are detected, we can now describe the rest of the algorithm. Two shared "decision" variables are employed, $Dec1$ and $Dec2$. Both are initially $\perp$, and it is assumed that no process's input value is $\perp$. All processes return the value assigned to $Dec2$. Before returning, each process attempts to assign its input value to both $Dec1$ and $Dec2$ in sequence.

To understand how the algorithm works, suppose that a process p is preempted just before executing the assignment to $Dec1$ at line 3. If, while p is preempted, another process q executes within lines 1-14, then p will detect this when it resumes execution and then execute lines 5-9. When p resumes execution, it will immediately perform the assignment at line 3. Note that p may be assigning $Dec1$ here very "late", i.e., well after other processes have reached a decision and terminated. However, the algorithm ensures that p's late assignment does not cause some process to return an erroneous value. To see this, note that because p has already been preempted once during lines 1-14, it executes lines 5-9 without preemption. Thus, it can safely deal with its late assignment without any fear of interferences due to further preemptions. The late assignment is dealt with as follows. If a decision has not yet been reached, then p assigns its own input value to both $Dec1$ and $Dec2$ (lines 7 and 8). Otherwise, p "undoes" its late assignment to $Dec1$ by copying to $Dec1$ the current value within $Dec2$ (line 9). The need to "undo" late assignments is the main reason why the algorithm uses two decision variables — to restore the value of one variable, another variable is needed.

A process p potentially could also be preempted just before performing the assignment to $Dec2$ at line 10. If, while p is preempted, another process q executes within lines 1-14, then p will detect this when it resumes execution and then execute lines 12 and 13 without preemption. These lines "undo" p's potentially "late" assignment to $Dec2$ by copying to $Dec2$ the current value of $Dec1$.

The correctness of this algorithm follows from the following three lemmas, which due to space limitations are stated here without proof.

Lemma 1: $p@15 \Rightarrow (\exists q :: Dec2 = q.in)$ *is an invariant.* □

Lemma 2: $Dec2 \neq \bot \Rightarrow ((Dec1 = Dec2) \vee (\exists p :: running(p) \wedge p@\{4..9, 11..13\}))$ *is an invariant.* □

Lemma 3: $(\forall v : v \neq \bot :: (Dec1 = v \wedge Dec2 = v) \vee (\exists p :: running(p) \wedge p@\{4..9\} \wedge Dec2 = v) \vee (\exists p :: running(p) \wedge p@\{11..13\} \wedge Dec1 = v))$ *is stable.* □

Theorem 1: *In a quantum-based uniprocessor system with $Q \geq 8$, consensus can be implemented in constant time using only reads and writes.* □

3.2 Compare-and-Swap

Our uniprocessor **C&S** implementation is shown in Fig. 2. The most important shared variables in the implementation are $X1$ and $X2$. Each of these variables has three fields, *val*, *proc*, and *alt*. $X2.val$ gives the "current" value of the implemented object at all times. It can be seen by inspecting lines 25-48 that the way in which $X1$ and $X2$ are assigned is very reminiscent of the way $Dec1$ and $Dec2$ were assigned in our consensus algorithm. After each is assigned, a check is made to see if a preemption has occurred, in which case the assignment is undone if necessary. Assuming Q is defined to be large enough so that each **C&S** invocation is preempted at most once, this "undo code" cannot be preempted.

In our consensus algorithm, undoing a late assignment was relatively simple because a consensus object is accessed only once by each process. For the sake of comparison, consider what happens when a process p detects that $Run \neq p$ at line 11 in Fig. 1. For $Run \neq p$ to be detected, p must have been preempted

type
  X-type = **record** *val: valtype*; *proc*: 1..*N*; *alt*: 0..1 **end** /* stored in one word */

shared variable
  Seen1, Seen2: **array** [1..*N*, 0..1] **boolean**;
  Run: 1..*N*;
  *X*1, *X*2: *X-type* **initially** $(v, (1, 0))$, where v is object's initial value

procedure C&S(*old, new: valtype*)
                returns boolean
private variable
  /* p denotes the invoking process */
  v: *X-type*;
  b: **boolean**

```
1:   if old = new then
2:     return X2.val = old
     fi;
3:   Run := p;
4:   v := X2;
5:   Seen1[v.proc, v.alt] := true;
6:   if Run ≠ p then
       /* lines 7-11 nonpreemptable */
7:     b := Seen2[v.proc, v.alt];
8:     Seen1[v.proc, v.alt] := b;
9:     v := X2;
10:    Seen1[v.proc, v.alt] := true;
11:    Seen2[v.proc, v.alt] := true
     else
12:    Seen2[v.proc, v.alt] := true;
13:    if Run ≠ p then
       /* lines 14-18 nonpreemptable */
14:      b := Seen1[v.proc, v.alt];
15:      Seen2[v.proc, v.alt] := b;
16:      v := X2;
17:      Seen1[v.proc, v.alt] := true;
18:      Seen2[v.proc, v.alt] := true
       fi
     fi;
19:  if v.val ≠ old then
20:    Run := p;
21:    return false
     fi;
22:  alt := 1 − alt;
23:  Seen1[p, alt] := false;
24:  Seen2[p, alt] := false;
```

```
25:  X1 := (new, p, alt);
26:  if Run ≠ p then
       /* lines 27-35 nonpreemptable */
27:    v := X2;
28:    X1 := v;
29:    Seen1[v.proc, v.alt] := true;
30:    Seen2[v.proc, v.alt] := true;
31:    if ¬Seen2[p, alt] then
32:      if X2.val = old then
33:        X1 := (new, p, alt);
34:        X2 := (new, p, alt);
35:        Seen2[p, alt] := true
         fi
       fi
     else
36:    X2 := (new, p, alt);
37:    if Run ≠ p then
       /* lines 38-46 nonpreemptable */
38:      v := X1;
39:      X2 := v;
40:      Seen1[v.proc, v.alt] := true;
41:      Seen2[v.proc, v.alt] := true;
42:      if ¬Seen2[p, alt] then
43:        if X2.val = old then
44:          X1 := (new, p, alt);
45:          X2 := (new, p, alt);
46:          Seen2[p, alt] := true
           fi
         fi
       else
47:      Seen2[p, alt] := true
       fi
     fi;
48:  Run := p;
49:  return Seen2[p, alt]
```

Fig. 2. Uniprocessor C&S implementation. For simplicity, the object being accessed is left implicit. To be precise, the object's address should be passed as a parameter to the C&S procedure. The object can be read by reading *X*2.*val*.

either before or after its assignment to $Dec2$ at line 10. If it was preempted after assigning $Dec2$, then it assigned both $Dec1$ and $Dec2$ (lines 3 and 10) without preemption, in which case copying the value of $Dec1$ to $Dec2$ in lines 12 and 13 has no effect. (The value copied from $Dec1$ must equal that assigned to $Dec1$ by p: another process q can alter $Dec1$ only if it executes lines 2 and 3 without preemption and detects $Dec2 = \bot$ at line 2.) On the other hand, if p was preempted before assigning $Dec2$, then this is a potentially late assignment that may have overwritten a previously agreed upon decision value. In this case, copying the value of $Dec1$ to $Dec2$ in lines 12 and 13 undoes the overwrite.

Undoing a late assignment in our C&S implementation is much more complicated, because each process can perform repeated C&S operations. Some of the subtleties involved can be seen by considering what happens when a process p detects that $Run \neq p$ upon executing line 37 in Fig. 2 (the counterpart to the situation considered above for our consensus algorithm). By our handshaking mechanism, this implies that p was preempted either before or after its assignment to $X2$ at line 36. The question is: Should this assignment to $X2$ be undone? Given that $X2.val$ defines the current state of the implemented object, the answer to this question depends on whether the value assigned to $X2$ by p has been "seen" by another process. If p's value has been seen, then its assignment to $X2$ *cannot* be undone. There is no way for p to infer that its value has been seen by inspecting the value of $X2$ (or $X1$, for that matter), so an additional mechanism is needed. In our implementation, the $Seen$ flags provide the needed mechanism. There are two pairs of such flags for each process p, $Seen1[p, 0]/Seen2[p, 0]$ and $Seen1[p, 1]/Seen2[p, 1]$. p alternates between these pairs from one C&S to the next. The current pair is given by p's alt variable. If p detects that $Seen2[p, alt]$ holds, then it knows that a value it has assigned to $X1$ or $X2$ has been seen by another process. Two pairs of $Seen$ flags are needed to distinguish values assigned by p in consecutive C&S operations. Two $Seen$ flags per pair are needed to be able to undo late assignments to these flags after preemptions. The $proc$ and alt fields in $X1$ and $X2$ allow a process to detect which $Seen$ flags to use.

Given the above description of the shared variables that are used, it is possible to understand the basic structure of the code. Trivial C&S operations for which $old = new$ are handled in lines 1 and 2. Lines 3-49 are executed to perform a nontrivial C&S. In lines 3-18, the current value of the implemented object is read and the process that wrote that value is informed that its value has been seen by updating that process's $Seen$ flags. The code sequence that is used here is similar to that employed in our consensus algorithm to update $Dec1$ and $Dec2$. In lines 19-21, a check is made to see if the current value of the object matches the specified old value. If they do match, then lines 22-49 are executed to attempt to update the object to hold the specified new value. In lines 23 and 24, the invoking process's $Seen$ flags are initialized. The rest of the algorithm is as described above. First $X1$ is written, and a preemption check is performed. If a preemption occurs, then the assignment to $X1$ is undone if necessary. After writing $X1$, $X2$ is written. Once again, a preemption check is performed and the assignment is undone if necessary. Note that a process may update another

```
procedure RMW (Addr: pointer to valtype; f: function) returns valtype
private variable old, new: valtype
1:    old := *Addr;
2:    new := f(old);
3:    if C&S(Addr, old, new) = false then
4:        old := *Addr;   /* statements 4 and 5 execute without preemption */
5:        *Addr := f(old)
      fi;
6:    return old
```

Fig. 3. Uniprocessor read-modify-write implementation.

process's *Seen* flags in lines 29 and 30 and in lines 40 and 41. Because these lines are each within a code fragment that is executed without preemption, the *Seen* flags can be updated here without resorting to a more complicated code sequence like in lines 5-18.

The formal correctness proof of our C&S implementation is not hard, but it is quite long, so due to space limitations, we defer it to the full paper. The correctness proof hinges upon the assumption that a process can be preempted at most once while executing within lines 3-48. A C&S invocation completes after at most 26 atomic statement executions. The worst case occurs when the following statements are executed in order: 1, 3-6, 12, 13, 19, 22-26, 36-46, 48, 49. Thus, lines 3-48 give rise to at most 24 statement executions. It follows that if $Q \geq 23$, then our preemption requirement is met. This gives us the following theorem.

Theorem 2: *In a quantum-based uniprocessor system with $Q \geq 23$, any object that is accessed only by means of read and C&S operations can be implemented in constant time using only reads and writes.*   □

3.3   Other Read-Modify-Write Operations

A RMW operation on a variable X is characterized by specifying a function f. Informally, such an operation is equivalent to the atomic code fragment $\langle x := X;$ $X := f(x);$ **return** $x \rangle$. Example RMW operations include fetch-and-increment (F&I), fetch-and-store, and test-and-set. RMW operations can be implemented on a uniprocessor as shown in Fig. 3. If the C&S at line 3 succeeds, then the RMW operation atomically takes effect when the C&S is performed. If the C&S fails, then the invoking process must have been preempted between lines 1 and 3. Provided Q is defined to be large enough so that lines 1-5 can be preempted at most once, lines 4 and 5 execute without preemption. If we implement C&S as in Fig. 2, then the C&S invocation consists of at most 26 statement executions. Thus, a value of $Q \geq 26 + 3$ suffices. This gives us the following theorem.

Theorem 3: *In a quantum-based uniprocessor system with $Q \geq 29$, any object accessed only by means of read, write, and read-modify-writes can be implemented in constant time using only reads and writes.*   □

4 Multiprocessor Systems

In this section, we show that wait-free consensus can be implemented for any number of processes in a P-processor quantum-based system using C-consensus objects (i.e., objects that implement consensus for C processes), where $C \geq P$, provided Q is as specified in Table 1. For simplicity, we assume here that $C \leq 2P$, because for larger values of C, the implementation we give for $C = 2P$ can be applied to obtain the results of Table 1. The consensus implementation we present to establish the results in this table is shown in Fig. 4. In addition to C-consensus objects, a number of uniprocessor C&S and F&I objects are used in the implementation. Recall from Sect. 3 that these uniprocessor objects can be implemented in constant time using only reads and writes. We use "local-C&S" and "local-F&I" in Fig. 4 to emphasize that these are uniprocessor objects.

In our implementation, processes choose a decision value by participating in a series of "consensus levels". There are L consensus levels, as illustrated in Fig. 5. L is a function of M and P, as described below. Each consensus level consists of a C-consensus object, where $C = P + K$, $0 \leq K \leq P$. Also associated with each consensus level l is a collection of shared variables $Outval[l, i]$, where $1 \leq i \leq P$. $Outval[l, i]$ is used by processes on processor i to record the decision value from level l (see line 17 in Fig. 4). When a process assigns a value to $Outval[l, i]$, we say that it "publishes" the result of level l. The requirement that at most C processes can access a C-consensus object is enforced by defining $P + K$ "ports" per consensus level. Processors 1 through K have two ports per object, and processors $K + 1$ through P have one port. A process can access a C-consensus object only by first claiming one of the ports allocated to its processor. A process claims a port by executing lines 4-12. One can think of all ports across all consensus levels as being numbered in sequence, starting at 1. Ports can be claimed on each processor i by simply performing a F&I operation on a counter $Port[i]$ that is local to processor i, with one special case as an exception. This special case arises when a process p executing without preemption on a processor $i \leq K$ (which has two ports per level) accesses the first of processor i's ports at some level l. In this case, if p simply increments $Port[i]$, then it is then positioned to access the second port of level l, which is pointless because a decision has already been reached at that level. To correct this, $Port[i]$ is updated in such a case using a C&S operation in line 8.

The consensus levels are organized into a sequence of blocks as shown in Fig. 5. The significance of these blocks is explained below. Each process attempts to participate in each consensus level in the order depicted in Fig. 5, skipping over levels for which a decision value has already been published. When a process accesses some level, the input value it uses is either the output of the highest-numbered consensus level for which there is a published value on its processor, or its own input value, if no previously-published value exists (see lines 2, 13, and 14). So that an input value for a level can be determined in constant time, a counter $Lastpub[i]$ is used on each processor i to point to the highest-numbered level that has a published value on processor i. Due to preemptions, $Lastpub[i]$ may need to be incremented to skip over an arbitrary number of levels. It is

constant $L = (M(P - K)^2 + 1)(KM + 1)$
/* total number of consensus levels for $C = P + K$, where $0 \leq K \leq P$ */

shared variable
  Lastpub: array[1..P] of 0..L initially 0;
    /* latest level on a processor for which there is a published consensus value */
  Outval: array[1..L, 1..P] of *valtype*;
      /* $Outval[l, i]$ is the consensus value for level l on processor i */
  Port: array[1..P] of 1..2L + M initially 1 /* next available port on processor */

procedure *decide(val : valtype)* **returns** *valtype*
private variable   /* local to process p */
  input, output: *valtype*;   /* input/output value for a level */
  level, last_level: 0..L + M;   /* current (last) level accessed by p */
  numports: 1..2;   /* number of ports per consensus object on processor $pr(p)$ */
  port, newport: 1..2L + M;   /* port numbers */
  publevel: 0..L /* last level for which there is published value on processor $pr(p)$ */

```
1:   if pr(p) ≤ K then numports := 2 else numports := 1 fl;
2:   input, last_level, level := val, 0, 0;
3:   while level ≤ L do
4:       port := Port[pr(p)];                              /* determine port and level */
5:       level := ((port − 1) div numports) + 1;
6:       if last_level = level then        /* if level didn't change, make correction */
7:           newport := port + numports;
8:           if local-C&S(&Port[pr(p)], port, newport + 1) then port := newport
9:           else port :=local-F&I(Port[pr(p)])
10:          fl
         else
11:          port :=local-F&I(Port[pr(p)])
         fl;
12:      level := ((port − 1) div numports) + 1;
13:      publevel := Lastpub[pr(p)];                  /* determine input for next level */
14:      if publevel ≠ 0 then input := Outval[publevel, pr(p)] fl;
15:      if level ≤ L then    /* necessary because F&I may overshoot the last level */
16:          output := C-consensus(level, input);  /* invoke the C-consensus object */
17:          Outval[level, pr(p)] := output;                  /* publish the result */
18:          local-C&S(&Lastpub[pr(p)], publevel, level)
         fl
19:      last_level := level;
     od;
20:  publevel := Lastpub[pr(p)];
21:  return(Outval[publevel, pr(p)])
```

Fig. 4. Multiprocessor consensus implementation.

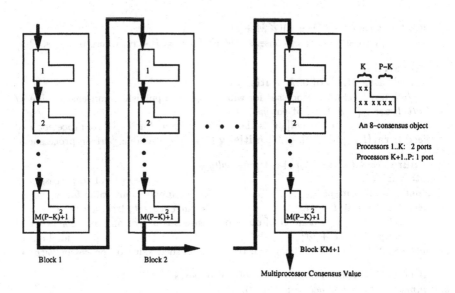

Fig. 5. Organization of the consensus levels in the implementation in Fig. 4.

therefore updated using a C&S operation instead of F&I (see line 18). Each process on processor i completes by returning the output value from level $Lastpub[i]$.

When a process p attempts to determine an input value for a level, there may be a number of previous levels that are inaccessible to p (because all available ports have been claimed) yet no decision value has been published. This can happen for a previous level l only if the process(es) on p's processor that accessed level l were preempted before publishing an output value for that level. We say that the preempted process(es) at level l *cause an access failure at level l*.

Obviously, there is a correlation between the number of access failures that can occur on a processor and the number of preemptions that can occur on that processor. The latter in turn depends on the size of the scheduling quantum Q. We show below that with a suitable choice of Q, the number of levels for which an access failure occurs on each processor is limited to a fraction of all the levels. Using a pigeon-hole argument, it is possible to show that, in any history, there exists some level for which no process on any processor experiences an access failure. We call such a level a *deciding level*. A simple inductive argument shows that at all levels below a deciding level l, the output value of level l is used by *every* process on *every* processor when accessing any level below l, even if access failures occur when accessing levels lower than l.

We now state some lemmas about the number of access failures that may occur in a history. We first consider the two extremes $C = 2P$ and $C = P$ and then the general case (proofs of Lemmas 4 and 5 can be found in [1]).

Lemma 4: *Suppose that $C = 2P$ and that Q is large enough to ensure that each process can be preempted at most once while accessing any two consensus levels in succession (the two levels don't have to be consecutive). If processes p and q on processor i cause an access failure at level l, then at least one of p and q does not cause an access failure at any level less than l.* □

Corollary 1: *If C and Q are as defined in Lemma 4, and if there are at most M processes per processor, then there can be at most M access failures on any processor. Furthermore, there exists a deciding level among any $MP + 1$ levels.* □

Lemma 5: *Suppose that $C = P$ and that Q is large enough to ensure that each process can be preempted at most once while accessing any $P + 1$ consensus levels in succession (these levels don't have to be consecutive). If there are at most M processes on any processor, then there exists a deciding level within any consecutive $MP^2 + 1$ consensus levels.* □

Lemma 6: *Suppose that $C = P + K$, where $0 \leq K \leq P$, and that Q is large enough to ensure that each process can be preempted at most once while accessing any $P - K + 1$ consensus levels in succession (these levels don't have to be consecutive). If there are at most M processes on any processor, then there exists a deciding level in any consecutive $(M \cdot (P - K)^2 + 1) \cdot (KM + 1)$ levels.*

Proof: For processors $K + 1$ through P, we know from Lemma 5 that there exists a deciding level among any consecutive $M \cdot (P - K)^2 + 1$ levels. If we have $KM + 1$ groups of $M \cdot (P - K)^2 + 1)$ levels each, then processors $K + 1$ through P have at least one deciding level in each group. Also, by Corollary 1, processors 1 through K can experience at most KM access failures in total. Thus, there exists at least one level that is a deciding level for the whole system. □

The proof of Lemma 6 reveals the insight as to why we group the levels into $KM + 1$ blocks as depicted in Fig. 5. It is easy to see that each consensus level is accessed in constant time (recall that our uniprocessor C&S and F&I algorithms take constant time). Thus, letting c denote the worst-case number of statement executions per level, we have the following (it can be shown that $c = 96$ suffices).

Theorem 4: *In a P-processor, quantum-based system, consensus can be implemented in a wait-free manner in polynomial space and time for any number of processes using read/write registers and C-consensus objects if $C \geq P$ and $Q \geq \max(2c, c(2P + 1 - C))$.* □

In the full paper, we prove the following theorem, showing that the quantum used in the implementation above is asymptotically tight [1].

Theorem 5: *In a P-processor, quantum-based system, consensus cannot be implemented in a wait-free manner for any number of processes using read/write registers and C-consensus objects if $C \geq P$ and $Q \leq \max(1, 2P - C)$.* □

If we were to add time to our model, then we could easily incorporate the T_{max} and T_{min} terms given in Table 1 in the bounds on Q given above.

```
shared variable P: array[1..3] of valtype ∪ ⊥ initially ⊥
procedure decide(val: valtype) returns valtype
private variable v, w: valtype
1:  v := val;
2:  for i := 1 to 3 do
3:      w := P[i];
4:      if w ≠ ⊥ then
5:          v := w
        else
6:          P[i] := v
        fi
    od;
7:  return P[3]
```

Fig. 6. Moir and Ramamurthy's uniprocessor consensus algorithm.

5 Concluding Remarks

Our work was partially inspired by a read/write consensus algorithm for quantum-based uniprocessor systems due to Moir and Ramamurthy [3]. Actually, their goal was to design wait-free algorithms for multiprocessor systems in which the processor-to-memory bus is allocated to processors using quantum-based scheduling. Their consensus algorithm, which is shown in Fig. 6, is also correct in a quantum-based uniprocessor system. This algorithm is correct if $Q = 8$ (this requires first replacing the **for** loop by straight-line code), just like our uniprocessor consensus algorithm. However, their algorithm requires fewer references to shared memory. The algorithm employs three shared variables, $P[1]$, $P[2]$, and $P[3]$. The idea is to attempt to copy a value from $P[1]$ to $P[2]$, and then to $P[3]$. We found our mechanism of detecting preemptions to be much easier to employ when implementing other objects.

References

1. J. Anderson, R. Jain, and D. Ott. Wait-free synchronization in quantum-based multiprogrammed systems, May 1998. Available at http://www.cs.unc.edu/~anderson/papers.html.
2. M. Herlihy. Wait-free synchronization. *ACM Transactions on Programming Languages and Systems*, 13(1):124–149, 1991.
3. M. Moir and S. Ramamurthy. Private communication. 1998.
4. S. Ramamurthy, M. Moir, and J. Anderson. Real-time object sharing with minimal support. *Proceedings of the 15th Annual ACM Symposium on Principles of Distributed Computing*, pp. 233–242. 1996.

Computing in Totally Anonymous Asynchronous Shared Memory Systems
(Extended Abstract)

Hagit Attiya* Alla Gorbach** and Shlomo Moran***

Department of Computer Science, The Technion

Abstract. In the *totally anonymous* shared memory model of asynchronous distributed computing, processes have no id's and run identical programs. Moreover, processes have identical interface to the shared memory, and in particular, there are no *single-writer* registers. This paper assumes that processes do not fail, and the shared memory consists only of read/write registers, which are initialized to some default value. A complete characterization of the functions and relations that can be computed within this model is presented. The consensus problem is an important relation which can be computed. Unlike functions, which can be computed with two registers, the consensus protocol uses a linear number of shared registers and rounds.

The paper proves logarithmic lower bounds on the number of registers and rounds needed for solving consensus in this model, indicating the difficulty of computing relations in this model.

1 Introduction

In this work, we study the *totally anonymous shared memory* model of asynchronous distributed computing. Like in previous works that studied computations by identical processes, e.g., [3, 4], we assume that processes have no id's and run identical programs. We also assume that the means by which processes access the shared memory are identical to all processes. This implies, for example, that a process cannot have a private register to which only this process may write and all other processes can read, as is usually assumed. In this work we study only the case where processes do not fail, and the shared memory consists only of read/write shared registers, which are initialized to some default value. In some cases, we also assume that the number of processes that execute a given task is unknown.

This model is related to an environment where an unknown set of processes execute a common task using a "public" server, in which the communication

---

* Email: `hagit@cs.technion.ac.il`.
** Email: `allag@msil.sps.mot.com`.
*** Email: `moran@cs.technion.ac.il`. Research supported by the Bernard Elkin Chair for Computer Science. Part of the work was done while this author was at the University of Arizona, supported by US-Israel BSF grant 95-00238.

media cannot distinguish between different processes. This models an environment where the communication route connecting a process to the shared server can be dynamically replaced by an alternative one.

We will be mainly interested in the computation power of this model, namely, what kind of distributed tasks [14] can be computed by it. We restrict our attention to consensus-like tasks, in which each process has a private input, and processes have to agree on the same output. Such a task defines a *relation* between input vectors and possible output values. This relation is a *function* if the corresponding output is uniquely determined by the processes inputs (e.g., the AND function); note that the standard consensus task [15] is not a function.

First we give a complete characterization of the functions that can be computed within this model, and show that if a function can be computed, then it can be computed with only two shared registers. It turns out that the class of functions that can be computed is quite limited (for instance, the AND or OR functions cannot be computed); in view of this, it is a little surprising that consensus is computable in this model. We will provide a (fault-free) consensus protocol in which both the number of shared registers and the number of rounds is linear in the number of processes. Using this protocol, we then give a complete characterization of the relations that can be computed.

One can ask whether consensus can be solved in the totally anonymous model with a smaller number of shared registers, and/or smaller number of rounds. We give a partial answer to this question by showing that these figures cannot be bounded by a constant independent of the number of processes. Specifically, we prove logarithmic lower bounds on the number of shared registers and the number of rounds needed for solving consensus.

Our lower bound proofs combine two seemingly unrelated techniques:

The first one is of "covering" registers, which is similar to the technique used by Burns and Lynch [6] to prove that any protocol for mutual exclusion among N processes needs N shared registers. Different variants of this technique appear in the "hiding lemma" used by Moran and Taubenfeld [13] to prove impossibility of wait-free counting, and in the "reconstruction lemma" used in the context of public data structures by Brit and Moran [5].

The other tool we use in our lower bound proofs is the existence of bivalent states, introduced by Fischer, Lynch and Paterson [8] to prove the impossibility of asynchronous consensus in the presence of one faulty process. This tool was used extensively afterwards, e.g., [7, 10, 12], mainly in the context of impossibility results in fault tolerant computations. Thus, our results demonstrate a certain connection between faulty models with distinct processes, and non-faulty models with totally anonymous processes.

Many works on shared memory systems studied models with faults [1, 2, 10, 12]. These papers assume that processes are not anonymous, and may run different protocols.

Jayanti and Toueg [11] studied anonymous read/write shared memory models. They considered two models: In the first model, the processes have no names but the shared registers are single writer (each process has its "own" register).

The second model is similar to ours, but the shared memory is not initialized to a known state. In the first model, the *wakeup* problem [9] and the consensus problem can be solved, but the leader election problem cannot be solved; in the second model, all these problems, and in particular, consensus, cannot be solved.

2 Outline of the Model

We consider a standard asynchronous system of $N \geq 2$ anonymous non-faulty processes which communicate via read/write shared registers. For ease of exposition, we refer to the processes by the unique names $p_1, p_2, \ldots, p_N$, but the names are not available to the processes. Every process can read from or write to any shared register.

Each process has an *internal state*, including *input* and *output* registers and an unbounded amount of internal storage. Each process acts according to a *transition function*, determining for each internal state, the new internal state and the next action—whether this is a read or a write, to which register and what is the value written.

An *initial state* prescribes starting values to the input register and the internal storage, and the *empty* value to the output register. A process is in a *terminated state* if its output register is not empty.

A *protocol* specifies for each process the initial value of the internal storage and a transition function; we assume these are the same for all processes. We assume that the protocol is *uniform* and the total number of processes in the system is unknown, unless stated otherwise.

A *configuration* consists of the internal states of all processes, together with the values of the shared registers. An *initial configuration* of a protocol $\mathcal{P}$ requires every process to be in the initial state prescribed by $\mathcal{P}$ and the shared registers to contain default values.

The computation proceeds by *steps*, each by a single process, taking one configuration to a successive configuration; a step is a read or a write from a single register, or a *nop*. Read and write steps can be taken only if the process is not in a terminated state; nop steps can be taken only if the process is in a terminated state. If p is a process and C is a configuration, then $p(C)$ denotes the configuration obtained after p takes a step in C according to the transition function of a specific protocol $\mathcal{P}$.

A *schedule* is a sequence of process names. If $\sigma = p_{i_1}, p_{i_2}, \ldots, p_{i_n}$ is a finite schedule and C is a configuration, then $\sigma(C)$ denotes $p_{i_n}(p_{i_{n-1}}(\ldots p_{i_1}(C) \ldots))$.

An *execution* of a protocol $\mathcal{P}$ is a (finite or infinite) sequence of the form

$$C_0, p_{i_1}, C_1, p_{i_2}, C_2, p_{i_3}, \ldots,$$

where C_0 is an initial configuration and for every $k \geq 1$, C_k is a configuration, p_{i_k} is a process, and C_k is $p_{i_k}(C_{k-1})$. If α is a finite execution, then $C_{end}(\alpha)$ is the last configuration in α.

Given a schedule σ, a configuration C and a protocol $\mathcal{P}$, the execution segment that results from applying steps of processes according to σ to the configuration C is denoted (C, σ).

An infinite schedule σ is *fair* if every process occurs infinitely many times in σ. An infinite execution α is *fair* if the corresponding schedule is fair.

A *task* is a set of pairs, each containing an input vector and a set of output vectors that are allowable for this input vector.

We restrict our attention to *relations* which are tasks in which all processes have to agree on the same output value; in this case, all entries of an output vector are equal. A vector is a *legal input vector* for a relation R if it appears in the left-hand side of some pair in R; the *domain* of R, denoted $\mathcal{D}_R$, contains the legal input vectors for R.

A typical relation is *k-valued consensus*; the inputs are vectors of integers from $\{0, \ldots, k-1\}$, and the allowable output values for an input vector $\overline{X}$ are all the values in $\overline{X}$.

A protocol $\mathcal{P}$ *computes* a relation R if for every legal input vector $\overline{X} = (x_1, x_2, \ldots, x_N)$ and for every fair execution α of $\mathcal{P}$ in which process p_i has an input x_i, every process eventually writes the same *decision value* $d \in R[\overline{X}]$ into its local output register.

3 Basic Properties

A basic property of our model is that a single process can be replaced by a group of processes where each process has the same input, and vice versa. In this section, we define notions of *multiplication* and *equivalence*, capturing this property. The impossibility results and lower bounds presented later rely on these notions.

Given a finite execution α, let the *view* of process p after α, denoted $\alpha|p$, be the vector containing the internal state of p and the values of the shared registers in $C_{end}(\alpha)$. If α and β are finite executions and p and q are processes appearing in α and β, respectively, then we write $(\alpha, p) \sim (\beta, q)$, if $\alpha|p = \beta|q$.

A finite execution α of $p_1, \ldots, p_k$ *hides* a finite execution β of $q_1, \ldots, q_n$, denoted $\alpha \preceq \beta$, if for every p_i there exists q_j such that $(\alpha, p_i) \sim (\beta, q_j)$. If $\alpha \preceq \beta$ and $\beta \preceq \alpha$, i.e., they hide each other, then α and β are *equivalent*, denoted $\alpha \approx \beta$. This notion extends to infinite executions if it holds after infinitely many finite prefixes of them.

Let σ be a schedule of $q_1, \ldots, q_n$, and let $\{P_1, \ldots, P_n\}$ be a set of groups of processes, where $P_i = \{p_i^1, p_i^2, \ldots, p_i^{l(i)}\}$, for every i, $1 \leq i \leq n$. The *multiplication* of σ by $\{P_1, \ldots, P_n\}$ is the schedule obtained from σ by substituting every appearance of q_i in σ with the sequence $p_i^1, p_i^2, \ldots, p_i^{l(i)}$. Let α be an execution whose schedule is σ, such that q_i has an input x_i in α. The *multiplication* of α by $\{P_1, \ldots, P_n\}$ is the execution obtained by letting each process in P_i start with input x_i and applying the multiplication of σ.

Lemma 1. *Let α be an execution of $q_1, \ldots, q_n$. If β is the multiplication of α by $\{P_1, \ldots, P_n\}$, then $(\alpha, q_i) \sim (\beta, p)$, for every i, $1 \leq i \leq n$, and for every $p \in P_i$.*

Corollary 2. *Let α be an execution of $q_1, \ldots, q_n$. If β is a multiplication of α, then $\alpha \approx \beta$.*

Note that if $\alpha \approx \beta$, then the same set of shared registers is accessed in α and in β.

Since the model is anonymous, neither the order of values in the input vector nor the multiplicity of a value are significant. The following definition and lemma formalize this property.

If $\overline{X} = (x_1, x_2, \ldots, x_N)$ is an input vector, then let $set(\overline{X})$ be the set of distinct values in $\overline{X}$. The next lemma shows that for any input vector $\overline{X}$, if we run processes with a single appearance of each input value then processes have to decide on a value in $R[\overline{X}]$.

Lemma 3. *Let R be a relation, let $\mathcal{P}$ be a protocol that computes R, and let $\overline{X}$ be an N-entry input vector of R with n distinct values. If $\overline{Z}$ is an n-entry vector such that $set(\overline{Z}) = set(\overline{X})$, then in every fair execution of n processes with input vector $\overline{Z}$ all processes decide on $y \in R[\overline{X}]$.*

4 Computability Results

4.1 Functions

We start with a characterization of the functions that can be computed in our model. A relation R is a *function* if a single output value is allowed for every legal input vector.

Theorem 4. *A function f can be computed in the totally anonymous model if and only if for every pair of input vectors $\overline{X}, \overline{Y} \in \mathcal{D}_f$ such that $set(\overline{X}) \subseteq set(\overline{Y})$ it holds that $f[\overline{X}] = f[\overline{Y}]$.*

An example is computing the minimum of N input values where exactly k values are different (for some known constant k). Note that the multiplicity of values in the input vector does not affect the function's value, and thus the characterization only refers to the input sets.

To prove that the condition is sufficient, consider a function f satisfying the assumption of Theorem 4.

A set $Z = \{z_1, \ldots, z_k\}$ is *determining* for f if there exists an output value $val(Z)$ such that for every input vector $\overline{X} \in \mathcal{D}_f$, if $Z \subseteq set(\overline{X})$ then $f[\overline{X}] = val(Z)$.

Intuitively, the idea is to find a determining set that allows to compute the function. A simple protocol uses an unbounded number of Boolean registers, one for each possible input value,[4] initialized to *false*. A process announces its input by setting the appropriate register to *true*, and then repeatedly reads the

---

[4] The protocol assumes that the set of possible input values is enumerable and, for simplicity, refers to them as integers.

registers (each time more and more registers), until it obtains a determining set Z, and outputs $val(Z)$.

It is not guaranteed that all processes see the same determining set, but if a process sees a determining set, then processes obtaining a later determining set will have the same output value. Moreover, this value must be $f(\overline{X})$, where $\overline{X}$ is the input vector. Processes halt when all input values have been written (at the latest), since $set(\overline{X})$ is a determining set.

The protocol can be modified to use only two registers. One register is used to collect all the input values known so far, while the other is used to announce a decision value. As long as no decision value is announced, a process makes sure that the other register contains all input values it knows of. The detailed code and correctness proof of this protocol are omitted.

In the full version, we also prove that there are functions which cannot be computed with a single register.

To prove that the condition is necessary, consider some function f, for which there is a pair of input vector $\overline{X}, \overline{Y}$ such that $set(\overline{X}) \subseteq set(\overline{Y})$ and $f[\overline{X}] \neq f[\overline{Y}]$. Let $set(\overline{X}) = \{x_1, \ldots, x_k\}$ and let $\overline{Y} = (x_1, \ldots, x_k, x_{k+1}, \ldots, x_r)$.

Suppose for contradiction that there is a protocol for computing f.

Informally, we let k processes with inputs $x_1, \ldots, x_k$ run on their own; by Lemma 3, eventually they decide on $f[\overline{X}]$. Then we let the processes with inputs $x_{k+1}, \ldots, x_r$ run on their own; they have to decide on $f[\overline{Y}] \neq f[\overline{X}]$. Therefore, the decision of the first k processes is incorrect. The formal arguments are left to the full version.

4.2 Consensus

We outline how consensus can be solved in our model, starting with the binary case.

The protocol for binary consensus employs a procedure **ReduceOne** that reduces the "disagreement" in processes' inputs. The procedure uses two binary shared registers, awake[0] and awake[1], both initially *false*. A process with input x writes *true* to awake[x] and reads the other register. If the other register is *false*, the procedure returns x; if the other register is *true* and $x = 0$, the procedure returns $\perp$; if the other register is *true* and $x = 1$, then the procedure returns 0. **ReduceOne** guarantees the following properties:

- The output of at least one process is not $\perp$.
- If the output of p_i is $v \neq \perp$, then there exists some process whose input is v.
- If processes output both 0 and 1, then the number of processes with output 1 is strictly less than the number of processes with input 1.

When the number of processes, N, is known, **ReduceOne** can be used to solve consensus in the following simple way.

Take $N - 1$ copies of procedure **ReduceOne**. Each process starts the first copy of **ReduceOne** with its input; if it gets $\perp$, then it waits to read a non-empty value from a separate decision register; otherwise, it starts the next copy of

ReduceOne with the output from the current copy, and follows the same rules. When a process gets a non-$\perp$ output in the $(N-1)$-st copy of ReduceOne, it writes this value to the decision register and decides on it; a process waiting for a non-empty value in the decision register, decides upon reading this value.

It is guaranteed that at least one process participates in every copy of ReduceOne; in particular, at least one process performs the $(N-1)$-st copy; moreover, the inputs to all copies of ReduceOne are valid, and all processes have the same output in the $N-1$-st copy of ReduceOne.

If N is not known, then we modify the protocol so that each process checks, before starting the i-th copy, whether a process with an opposite value already participated in this copy; if so, it waits to read a non-empty value from the decision register. Moreover, a process proceeds to the $(i+1)$-st copy only if some other process performed the $(i-1)$-st copy with an opposite input; otherwise, the processor writes its current output to the decision register and terminates with this value. The detailed code and precise correctness proof for the protocol, which are based on the above ideas, are omitted.

There are N copies of ReduceOne, each requiring two shared registers; thus, the protocol requires $O(N)$ shared registers.

Non-binary consensus is achieved by agreeing (using binary consensus) on each bit of the output. Once again, the details are omitted.

4.3 Relations

Finally, we characterize which relations can be computed in our model.

Theorem 5. *A relation R can be computed in the totally anonymous model if and only if for every input vector $\overline{X}$ it holds that $\bigcap\{R[\overline{Y}] \mid \overline{Y} \in \mathcal{D}_R$ and $set(\overline{Y}) \supseteq set(\overline{X})\} \neq \Phi$.*

The consensus problem satisfies this condition and, indeed, it can be computed. The characterization for functions (Theorem 4) is a special case of Theorem 5.

To prove that the condition is sufficient, consider a relation R satisfying the assumption of Theorem 5.

The *tower* of $set(\overline{X})$ is $\{set(\overline{Y} \mid \overline{Y} \in \mathcal{D}_R$ and $set(\overline{Y} \supseteq set(\overline{X})\}$. Every input set is in some tower, and the union of the towers is the input domain of the relation. Note that the towers do not depend on the output values.

By the assumption on R, each tower has an output value that is legal for all inputs in the tower. Thus, if processes agree on a tower that the input vector belongs to, they can compute R; it suffices to agree on some set in the tower.

The idea is to reach consensus on some subset of the input set. If the subset includes the input set of some legal input vector, this determines the output value, otherwise there are values that can be added to the subset.

The protocol works in iterations; in each iteration, the protocol of the previous section is used to solve consensus. Each process starts the first iteration with its input; if the decision in the j-th consensus protocol is x, then processes with input x do not participate in later iterations; if the decisions after j iterations are $set(\overline{Z})$, for some valid input vector $\overline{Z}$, then a process that participates in the j-th iteration writes the set to the decision register; a process that stops participating at some stage, reads the decision register until it finds a non-empty value.

The detailed code and correctness proof for the protocol are omitted.

To prove that the condition is necessary, consider a relation R, with an input vector $\overline{X}$ such that $\bigcap\{R[\overline{Y}] \mid \overline{Y} \in \mathcal{D}_R \text{ and } set(\overline{Y}) \supseteq set(\overline{X})\} \neq \Phi$, and let $set(\overline{X})$ be $\{x_1, x_2, \ldots, x_k\}$.

Suppose for contradiction that there is a protocol computing R.

We let k processes with inputs $x_1, \ldots, x_k$ run on their own; by Lemma 3, they eventually decide on $z \in R[\overline{X}]$.

By the assumption on $\overline{X}$, there exists $\overline{Y} \in \mathcal{D}_R$ such that $set(\overline{Y}) \supseteq set(\overline{X})$ and $z \notin R[\overline{Y}]$; otherwise, z is in the intersection, which violates the assumption on $\overline{X}$. Without loss of generality, $\overline{Y} = (x_1, x_2, \ldots, x_k, x_{k+1}, \ldots, x_r)$.

Now, let processes with inputs $x_{k+1}, \ldots, x_r$ run, extending the execution of the first k processes. They have to decide on some value from $R[\overline{Y}]$, but the first k processes decide on $z \notin R[\overline{Y}]$, which is a contradiction. The details appear in the full version.

5 Lower Bounds for Consensus

5.1 Lower Bound on the Number of Registers

Following Fischer, Lynch and Paterson [8], a configuration C is *0-valent* if only 0 is decided in executions from C; similarly, C is *1-valent* if only 1 is decided in executions from C. C is *univalent* if it is either 0-valent or 1-valent, and is *bivalent* otherwise. Although processes do not fail, we can prove the following lemma:

Lemma 6. *There is an initial configuration with two processes which is bivalent.*

Proof. Consider an initial configuration, C_0, with two processes—p_0 with an input 0 and p_1 with an input 1. $\overline{X} = (0, \ldots, 0)$ is an N-entry input vector for consensus; by Lemma 3, p_0 decides 0 in an infinite p_0-only execution from C_0. Similarly, $\overline{Y} = (1, \ldots, 1)$ is an N-entry input vector for consensus; by Lemma 3, p_1 decides on 1 in an infinite p_1-only execution from C_0. Therefore, C_0 is bivalent. □

Following Burns and Lynch [6], we say that a process p *covers* a register r in a configuration C if the step of p from C is a write to r. In order to prove the lower bound on the number of registers, we construct an execution in which "many" registers are covered. The construction is iterative; in each iteration, one more register is covered.

In each iteration a process can be *active*, i.e., take steps in the current iteration, or *waiting*, i.e., take no steps in the current iteration. At each iteration, waiting processes cover all registers written in all previous iterations. Thus, if no new register is written, waiting processes may overwrite all registers and continue as if the current iteration never happened. That is, a "new" register must be written, and the execution can be extended with one more covered register.

The next lemma is the inductive step of the lower bound proof.

Lemma 7. *Let α be a finite execution of $n \leq N/2$ processes, that ends with a bivalent configuration in which k registers are covered, and all writes in α are to covered registers. Then there exists a finite execution β of $2n$ processes, that ends with a bivalent configuration in which $k+1$ registers are covered, and all writes in β are to covered registers.*

Proof. Let α be a finite execution of $q_1, \ldots, q_n$ satisfying the conditions of the lemma. Let α' be the multiplication of α by $\{\{p_1, p_1'\}, \ldots, \{p_n, p_n'\}\}$. Assume α ends in configuration C and α' ends in configuration C'.

By Corollary 2, $\alpha \approx \alpha'$, and thus all writes in α' are to the k covered registers, denoted $r_1, \ldots, r_k$. By Lemma 1, $(\alpha, q_i) \sim (\alpha', p_i')$ and thus there are k processes $p_{i_1}', \ldots, p_{i_k}'$ that cover $r_1, \ldots, r_k$ in C'.

Consider a $\{p_1', \ldots, p_n'\}$-only schedule σ starting with the sequence $p_{i_1}' \cdot p_{i_2}' \cdots p_{i_k}'$ (each of the covering processes takes one step). Since in every $\{q_1, \ldots, q_n\}$-only fair execution all processes eventually decide, in every $\{p_1', \ldots, p_n'\}$-only fair execution all processes eventually decide. Without loss of generality, assume that the decision in (C', σ) is 0.

Since C is bivalent, there is a $\{q_1, \ldots, q_n\}$-only schedule ρ such that the decision in (C, ρ) is 1. Since $(\alpha, q_i) \sim (\alpha', p_i)$ for all i, there is a $\{p_1, \ldots, p_n\}$-only schedule τ such that the decision in (C', τ) is 1.

Assume there is a prefix τ' of τ such that $\tau'(C')$ is univalent and the only writes in (C', τ') are to $r_1, \ldots, r_k$. Since the decision in (C', τ) is 1, $\tau'(C')$ must be 1-valent. Consider the execution $(\tau'(C'), \sigma)$. Since all writes in (C', τ') are to $r_1, \ldots, r_k$, after the k writes to the registers $r_1, \ldots, r_k$, the memory state is the same as in the execution from C' and the states of $p_1', \ldots, p_n'$ are the same. Therefore, the decision in $(\tau'(C'), \sigma)$ is also 0, contradicting fact that $\tau'(C')$ is 1-valent. (See Figure 1.)

Therefore, there must be a write to a register other than $r_1, \ldots, r_k$ in (C', τ) and the configuration before the first such write is bivalent. Let τ'' be the longest prefix of τ that do not include the first write to $r_{k+1} \notin \{r_1, \ldots, r_k\}$. Let β be the execution extending α' with the schedule τ''.

In β, $2n$ processes participate; β ends with a bivalent configuration; $k+1$ registers are covered after β: $r_1, \ldots, r_k$ are covered by $p_{i_1}', \ldots, p_{i_k}'$ and r_{k+1} is covered by the construction; all writes in β are to $r_1, \ldots, r_{k+1}$, by construction. Thus, β is the required execution. $\qquad\square$

By careful induction on k, in which Lemma 6 provides the base case, and Lemma 7 provides the inductive step, we can prove that for every k, $0 \leq k < \log N$, there exists an execution α_k of 2^{k+1} processes ending with a bivalent configuration, such that k registers are covered after α_k. Taking $k = \log N - 1$, we get:

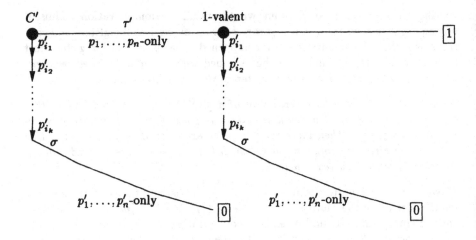

Fig. 1. Illustration for the proof of Lemma 7.

Theorem 8. *In the totally anonymous model, a protocol solving consensus among N processes requires $\Omega(\log N)$ shared registers.*

5.2 Lower Bound on the Round Complexity

Given a schedule σ of $p_1, \ldots, p_n$, a *round* in σ is a minimal segment (consecutive subsequence) of σ in which each process appears at least once. The *number of rounds* in a schedule σ is the maximal k such that σ includes k disjoint rounds. If σ includes k rounds, then it can be written as a concatenation $\sigma_1, \ldots, \sigma_k \sigma'$, where the (possibly empty) schedule σ' is not a round. If σ' is not empty, then we refer to it as the $(k+1)$-st *incomplete* round of σ; otherwise, we say that the final (k-th) round of σ is *complete*.

The *round complexity of an execution* α is the number of rounds in the schedule corresponding to the maximal finite prefix of α in which no process decides; the rounds of an execution are induced in a natural way from the rounds of the corresponding schedule. The *round complexity of a protocol* is the maximal round complexity, over all the executions of the protocol. It can be verified that the round complexity of the binary consensus protocol presented in Section 4.2 is $O(N)$.

Let $\mathcal{P}$ be a binary consensus protocol for N processes.

For a schedule σ of $p_1, \ldots, p_n$ with k rounds, $NY_{k+1}(\sigma)$ ("not yet" in round $k+1$ of σ) denotes the set of processes that do not appear in the incomplete round of σ; if the last round of σ is complete, then $NY_{k+1}(\sigma) = \{p_1, \ldots, p_n\}$. The next simple lemma, whose proof is omitted, shows that multiplication (defined in Section 3) preserves the number of rounds and the sets NY.

Lemma 9. *Let σ be a schedule of $q_1, q_2, \ldots, q_n$ with k rounds and let τ be the multiplication of σ by $\{P_1, \ldots, P_n\}$. Then τ has k rounds (of $\cup_{i=1}^{n} P_i$). Moreover, if some process $p \in P_i$ is in $NY_{k+1}(\tau)$ then q_i is in $NY_{k+1}(\sigma)$.*

A configuration C is *critical* if there are two processes p and q such that a step of p in C leads to a v-valent configuration and the pair of steps q and then p leads to a $\bar{v}$-valent configuration. We say that p is a *critical leader* in C. The following lemma is from [8].

Lemma 10. *Let C be a bivalent configuration and let p be a process. Then there is a finite schedule σ such that either a step of p from $\sigma(C)$ leads to a bivalent configuration or p is a critical leader in $\sigma(C)$.*

Given a protocol solving consensus, we construct, in iterations, an execution that includes "many" rounds. In each iteration, the execution contains one more round; all executions end with a bivalent configuration.

Lemma 11. *Let α be an execution of $n < N$ processes with k rounds that ends with a bivalent configuration. Then there exists an execution β of at most $n + 1$ processes with k rounds that ends with a bivalent configuration, such that $|NY_{k+1}(\beta)| < |NY_{k+1}(\alpha)|$.*

Proof. Let D be the final configuration in α. Since D is bivalent and α includes exactly k rounds, $NY_{k+1}(\alpha)$ is not empty. Let p_i be a process from $NY_{k+1}(\alpha)$. By Lemma 10, there is a finite schedule τ such that either a step of p_i in $\tau(D)$ leads to a bivalent configuration or $\tau(D)$ is a critical configuration and p_i is a critical leader in $\tau(D)$.

Let γ be the execution that extends α with schedule τ and assume it ends with the configuration C.

If a step of p_i from C leads to a bivalent configuration, then let β be the extension of γ with a step of p_i. All requirements hold: n processes participate in β; β ends with a bivalent configuration, by assumption; β is an extension of α and therefore includes k complete rounds; $NY_{k+1}(\beta)$ includes at least one process less than $NY_{k+1}(\alpha)$, that is, p_i. Therefore, β is the required execution.

Otherwise, p_i is a critical leader in $C = C_{end}(\gamma)$; let p_j be the other process that takes part in the "critical" extension.

Consider the steps of p_i and p_j from C. Simple arguments, which are omitted, show that $i \neq j$, that p_i and p_j access the same register r and that at least one of them writes to r.

If p_i writes to r, then consider an execution γ', ending with a configuration C', that is the multiplication of γ by $\{\{p_1\}, \ldots, \{p_i\}, \ldots, \{p_j, p'_j\}, \ldots, \{p_n\}\}$. By Corollary 2, $\gamma' \approx \gamma$.

Consider the schedule $\pi = p_j \cdot p_i$ (see Figure 2).

Since $(\gamma', p_i) \sim (\gamma, p_i)$, $(\gamma', p_j) \sim (\gamma, p_j)$, $(\gamma', p'_j) \sim (\gamma, p_j)$, the step of p_i is a write to r and p_j also accesses r, $(C, p_j \cdot p_i) \preceq (C', p_j \cdot p_i)$. Since $p_j \cdot p_i(C)$ is 1-valent, for every p'_j-free schedule σ', the decision in $(\pi(C'), \sigma')$ is 1.

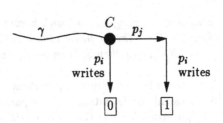

Fig. 2. p_i writes to r.

Similarly, $(C, p_i) \preceq (C', p_j \cdot p_i)$. Since $p_i(C)$ is 0-valent, for every p_j-free schedule σ'', the decision in $(\pi(C'), \sigma'')$ is 0.

Therefore, $\pi(C')$ is bivalent (see Figure 3).

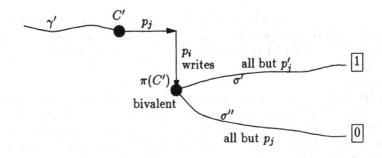

Fig. 3. The contradiction when p_i writes to r.

Let β be the execution extending γ' with the schedule π; $n + 1$ processes participate in β; β ends with a bivalent configuration. Since γ includes k rounds, γ' also includes k complete rounds (by Lemma 9). Therefore, $p_i, p_j \notin NY_{k+1}(\beta)$. For every process $p \neq p_i, p_j, p'_j$, by Lemma 9, if $p \in NY_{k+1}(\gamma')$ then $p \in NY_{k+1}(\gamma)$ and thus $p \in NY_{k+1}(\alpha)$.

If $p_j \notin NY_{k+1}(\alpha)$ then $p'_j \notin NY_{k+1}(\beta)$ and thus, since $p_i \in NY_{k+1}(\alpha)$, $|NY_{k+1}(\beta)| < |NY_{k+1}(\alpha)|$. If $p_j \in NY_{k+1}(\alpha)$, then it is possible that $p'_j \in NY_{k+1}(\beta)$; but since $p_i \in NY_{k+1}(\alpha)$, $|NY_{k+1}(\beta)| < |NY_{k+1}(\alpha)|$.

The other case, when p_i reads from r (and p_j writes to r), follows by similar arguments, multiplying p_i and taking $\pi = p_i \cdot p_j \cdot p'_i$. □

Lemma 11 can be used (within an induction) to prove the next lemma:

Lemma 12. *Let α be an execution of $n \leq N/2$ processes with k rounds that ends with a bivalent configuration. Then there exists an execution β of $\leq 2n$ processes with $k + 1$ rounds that ends with a bivalent configuration.*

This lemma, in turn, can be used (within an induction) to prove that for every k, $0 \leq k \leq \log N - 1$, there exists an execution of 2^{k+1} processes with k rounds and ending with a bivalent configuration. Taking $k = \log N - 1$ we get the desired lower bound:

Theorem 13. *In the totally anonymous model, the round complexity of a protocol solving binary consensus among N processes is $\Omega(\log N)$.*

References

1. K. Abrahamson. On achieving consensus using a shared memory. In *Proceedings of the 7th Annual ACM Symposium on Principles of Distributed Computing*, pages 291–302. ACM, 1988.
2. Y. Afek, H. Attiya, D. Dolev, E. Gafni, M. Merritt, and N. Shavit. Atomic snapshots of shared memory. *J. ACM*, 40(4):873–890, Sept. 1993.
3. D. Angluin. Local and global properties in networks of processors. In *Proceedings of the 12th ACM Symposium on Theory of Computing*, pages 82–93, 1980.
4. H. Attiya, M. Snir, and M. Warmuth. Computing on an anonymous ring. *J. ACM*, 35(4):845–876, Oct. 1988.
5. H. Brit and S. Moran. Wait-freedom vs. bounded wait-freedom in public data structures. *Universal Journal of Computer Science*, pages 2–19, Jan. 1996.
6. J. E. Burns and N. A. Lynch. Bounds on shared memory for mutual exclusion. *Information and Computation*, 107(2):171–184, Dec. 1993.
7. D. Dolev, C. Dwork, and L. Stockmeyer. On the minimal synchronism needed for distributed consensus. *J. ACM*, 34(1):77–97, Jan. 1987.
8. M. J. Fischer, N. A. Lynch, and M. S. Paterson. Impossibility of distributed consensus with one faulty processor. *J. ACM*, 32(2):374–382, Apr. 1985.
9. M. J. Fischer, S. Moran, S. Rudich, and G. Taubenfeld. The wakeup problem. *SIAM J. Comput.*, 25(6):1332–1357, Dec. 1996.
10. M. P. Herlihy. Wait-free synchronization. *ACM Trans. Prog. Lang. Syst.*, 13(1):124–149, Jan. 1991.
11. P. Jayanti and S. Toueg. Wakeup under read/write atomicity. In J. van Leeuwen and N. Santoro, editors, *Proceedings of the 4th International Workshop on Distributed Algorithms*, volume 486 of *Lecture Notes in Computer Science*, pages 277–288. Springer-Verlag, 1990.
12. M. C. Loui and H. H. Abu-Amara. Memory requirements for agreement among unreliable asynchronous processes. In *Advances in Computing Research, Vol. 4*, pages 163–183. JAI Press, Inc., 1987.
13. S. Moran and G. Taubenfeld. A lower bound on wait-free counting. *Journal of Algorithms*, 24:1–19, 1997.
14. S. Moran and Y. Wolfsthal. An extended impossibility result for asynchronous complete networks. *Inf. Process. Lett.*, 26:141–151, 1987.
15. M. Pease, R. Shostak, and L. Lamport. Reaching agreement in the presence of faults. *J. ACM*, 27(2):228–234, Apr. 1980.

Transient Fault Detectors

(Extended Abstract)

Joffroy Beauquier[1]   Sylvie Delaët[1]   Shlomi Dolev[2]*   Sébastien Tixeuil[1]

[1] Laboratoire de Recherche en Informatique, Bâtiment 490, Université de Paris Sud,
F91405 Orsay Cedex, France. Email: {jb, delaet, tixeuil}@lri.fr.
[2] Department of Mathematics and Computer Science, Ben-Gurion University,
Beer-Sheva, 84105, Israel. Email: dolev@cs.bgu.ac.il.

Abstract. In this paper we present failure detectors that detect transient failures, i.e. corruption of the system state without corrupting the program of the processors. We distinguish *task* which is the problem to solve, from *implementation* which is the algorithm that solve the problem. A task is specified as a desired output of the distributed system. The mechanism used to produce this output is not a concern of the task but a concern of the implementation.

In addition we are able to classify both the *distance locality* and the *history locality* property of tasks. The distance locality is related to the diameter of the system configuration that a failure detector has to maintain in order to detect a transient fault. The history locality is related to the number of consecutive system configurations that a failure detector has to maintain in order to detect a transient fault.

1 Introduction

In a system that may experience transient faults it is impossible for the processors to "know" that the system is currently in a consistent state: assume that every processor has a boolean variable that is true whenever the processor knows that the system is in a consistent state and is false otherwise. The value of this variable may not reflect the situation of the system since it is a subject for transient faults. This is the reason that the processors in self-stabilizing systems must continue the execution of the algorithm forever and never know for sure that the system is stabilized.

In this paper we propose a tool for identifying the inconsistency of a system, namely a transient failure detector. The requirement that every processor will know whether the system is in a consistent state is relaxed, instead we require that at least one processor identifies the occurrence of a fault when the system is in an inconsistent state. Moreover, the transient failure detector is unreliable since it can detect inconsistent state as a result of a transient fault that corrupt the state of the failure detector itself. The only guarantees we have is that when

---

* Part of this research was done while visiting the Laboratoire de Recherche en Informatique, Bâtiment 490, Université de Paris Sud. Partly supported by the Israeli ministry of science and arts grant #6756195.

the system is not in a consistent sate a failure is detected, and when both the system and the failure detectors are in a consistent state no failure is detected.

Our focus in this paper is in the implementation of failure detectors and not in the operations invoked as a result of detecting a fault; we just mention two such possible operations, namely: resetting (e.g., [4]) and repairing (e.g., [8, 13, 1, 16]).

In this paper we present failure detectors that detect transient failures, i.e. corruption of the system state without corrupting the program of the processors. We distinguish *task* which is the problem to solve, from *implementation* which is the algorithm that solves the problem. A task is specified as a desired output of the distributed system. The mechanism used to produce this output is not a concern of the task but a concern of the implementation. We study transient fault detectors for tasks and for implementations, separately. Designing failure detectors for tasks (and not for a specific implementation) gives the implementation designers the flexibility of changing the implementation without modifying the failure detector.

In addition we are able to classify both the *distance locality* and the *history locality* property of tasks. The distance locality is related to the diameter of the system configuration that a processor has to maintain in order to detect a transient fault. The history locality is related to the number of consecutive system configurations that a processor has to maintain in order to detect a transient fault. Both the distance and the history locality of a task may give the implementation designer hints concerning the techniques and resources that are required for implementing the task.

Then we turn to investigate failure detectors for a specific implementation — specific algorithm. Obviously, one may use a failure detector for the task of the algorithm without considering the data structure and techniques used by the algorithm. However, we are able to show that in many cases the amount of resources required is dramatically reduced when we use failure detector for a specific implementation and not a failure detector for the task.

Related work: The term failure detector was introduced in a different context in [5], where an abstract failure detector is used for coping with asynchrony and solving consensus. In the context of self-stabilizing systems checking the consistency of a distributed system was used in [15] where a snapshot of the system is repeatedly collected. Failure detectors, called observers, that are initialized correctly and are not subject to state corruption are used in [17]. Monitoring consistency *locally* for a restricted set of *algorithms* has been suggested in e.g., [3, 2]. A local monitoring scheme for every on-line and off-line algorithm has been presented in [1]. The local monitoring technique of [1] is a general technique that monitors the consistency of any *algorithm*. The method of [1] uses pyramids of snapshots and therefore the memory requirement of each processor is related to the size of the system. In this work we present a hierarchy of failure detectors for *tasks* and *algorithms* that is based on the amount of information used by the failure detector.

The rest of the paper is organized as follows: The system is described in Section 2, failure detectors for asynchronous silent tasks are considered in Section 3 and for synchronous non silent tasks in Section 4, respectively. Failure detectors for implementation (algorithms) are presented in Section 5. Implementation details of transient failure detectors appear in Section 6 and concluding remarks are presented in Section 7. Most of the proofs are omitted from this extended abstract.

2   The System

Distributed system: Our system settings is similar to the one presented in [10]. We consider an asynchronous system of n processors, each processor resides on a distinct node of the system's *communication graph* $G(V, E)$, where V is the set of *vertices* and E is the set of *edges*. Two processors that are connected by an edge of G are *neighbors*. Communication among neighboring processors is carried out by *communication registers*. In the sequel we use the term registers for communication registers. An edge (i, j) of G stands for two registers $r_{i,j}$ and $r_{j,i}$. P_i (P_j) can write in $r_{i,j}$ ($r_{j,i}$, respectively) and both processors can read both registers. The registers in which a processor P_i writes are the registers of P_i.

Configurations and runs: Each processor is a finite state machine whose program is composed of *steps*. Processors have unique identifiers. The *state* of a processor consists of the values of its internal variables. A *configuration*, $c \in (S_1 \times S_2 \times \cdots \times R_1 \times R_2 \times \cdots \times R_m)$ is a vector of the states of all the processors and the values of all the registers.

An *asynchronous run* of the system is a finite or infinite sequence of configurations $R = (c_1, c_2, \cdots)$ such that c_{i+1} is reached from c_i by a step of one processor. In such a step, a processor may execute internal computations followed by a read or write operation. This scheduling policy is known as the *read-write* atomicity model. We use the *round complexity* (See [11, 8, 7]) to measure time in asynchronous system. The first round of a run is the minimal prefix of the run in which each processors reads the registers of all its neighbors and writes to its registers[3]. The second round is the first round of the rest of the run, and so on.

A *synchronous run* of the system is a finite or infinite sequence of configurations $R = (c_1, c_2, \cdots)$ such that c_{i+1} is reached from c_i by the following steps of the processors: first every processor reads the register of its neighbors, once every processor finishes reading, the processors change state and write into their registers.

Specifications and failure detectors: An *abstract run* is a run in which only the values of a subset of the state variables, called the *output variables* are shown

---

[3] The round complexity is sometime defined by the execution of a single step of every processor, note that $O(\Delta)$ such rounds are equivalent to our definition, where Δ is the maximal degree of a node.

in each configuration. The *specification* P of a task T for a given system S is a (possibly infinite) set of abstract runs of S. For example, the mutual execution task is defined by a set of abstract runs, such that in each run in this set at most one processor executes the critical section at a time and every processor executes the critical section infinitely often — it is assumed that an output boolean variable that indicates whether the processor is executing the critical section exists.

S is *self-stabilizing* (in fact *pseudo self-stabilizing* [14]) with relation to P if and only if each of its runs has a non empty suffix in P. The aim of a *failure detector* is to check if a particular run of the system S matches the specification P. More precisely, a failure detector is assimilated to a boolean variable that obtains the value *false* if the specification is not satisfied and *true* otherwise. We use the convention in which once a failure is detected i.e., a failure detector returns *false*, the output of the failure detector is not changed until an external process resets the operation of the failure detector.

We assume that each processor P_i maintains a variable $V_i^d[1..s]$ for some s, called the *array of views* of P_i. $V_i^d[j]$, is the view of P_i on every component of the system up to distance d from itself, the view $V_i^d[j]$ is related to time j. In more details, the variable $V_i^d[j]$, $1 \leq j \leq s$, contains the communication graph description up to distance d from P_i and a portion of the state of each processor in this graph description. Note that since we are interested in tasks, the portion of the state that we are interested in, is the portion that defines the output of the system. At this stage we do not concern ourselves with the way each processor obtains and maintains the value of the variables in $V_i^d[1..s]$, later in Section 6 we present ways to implement failure detectors.

It turned out that the fault detection capabilities of a failure detector is related to the amount of information it stores. We distinguish two parameters that are related to the storage used by a failure detector:

- Distance — the distance d of $V_i^d[1..s]$, where d is in between 0 and $r+1$, and r is the radius of the system.
- History — the number s of views in the array $V_i^d[1..s]$.

A *failure detector at a processor* P_i is a process executed by P_i that we denote $\mathcal{FD}_d^s(P_i)$. $\mathcal{FD}_d^s(P_i)$ is responsible to repeatedly communicate to every neighbor P_j of P_i the portion of $V_i^d[1..s]$ *that is shared with* $V_j^d[1..s]$. $\mathcal{FD}_d^s(P_i)$ is also responsible to check whether the shared portions of $V_i^d[1..s]$ and $V_j^d[1..s]$ agree and satisfy a certain predicate.

A failure detector of the system is the combination of the failure detectors of all the processors in the system, denoted $\mathcal{FD}_d^s$.

A task is (d, s)-*local* if and only if the following conditions are satisfied:

1. For each run R of the system S and for all $1 \leq i \leq n$ $\mathcal{FD}_d^s(P_i)$ returns *true* if R is correct (i.e. matches the task specification), and there exists an index $1 \leq i \leq n$ such that $\mathcal{FD}_d^s(P_i)$ returns *false* if R is incorrect (i.e. does not match its specification).

2. There exists a run R that is correct (i.e. matches the task specification) and index i such that $\mathcal{FD}_{d-1}^{s}(P_i)$ returns *false* or there exists an incorrect run R' in which for every $1 \leq i \leq n$ $\mathcal{FD}_{d-1}^{s}(P_i)$ returns *true*.

3. There exists a run R that is correct (i.e. matches the task specification) and index i such that $\mathcal{FD}_{d}^{s-1}(P_i)$ returns *false* or there exists an incorrect run R' in which for every $1 \leq i \leq n$ $\mathcal{FD}_{d}^{s-1}(P_i)$ returns *true*.

Roughly speaking, if only the state of one process is needed, the specification is a *pure local* specification, since failure detectors need not check P_i's neighbors to detect a transient failure; if $d = 1$, the specification is *local*, and if $d = r+1$ the specification is *global*. In addition, one can identify task specification for which only a single view is needed as a *safety* specification, and the related task as a *silent* task. In contrast, *liveness* specification may require unbounded number of consecutive views.

3 Failure Detectors for Silent Tasks

In this section we study failure detectors for silent tasks ([9]) where the communication between the processors is fixed from some point of the run. In our model, registers are used for communication between processors. A system solving a silent task has the property that the contents of the communication registers is not changed. Since silent tasks are 1-history local, in the following, we assume that the locality property only refers to distance locality. Thus, there is no need for the variable that stores the views information to be an array; we use $\mathcal{V}_i^d$ to denote the view of P_i. Similarly, we use $\mathcal{FD}_d$ instead of $\mathcal{FD}_d^1$.

We now list several silent tasks, present their specification, and identify the minimal distance required for their failure detectors. We start with three tasks, maximum independent set, coloring and topology update that are 1-distance local.

3.1 Maximum Independent Set, Coloring and Topology Update

Maximum independent set, task specification: Each processor P_i maintains a local boolean variable $\mathcal{IS}_i$. No two neighbors may have their variable set to *true*. In addition every processor P_i with $\mathcal{IS}_i = false$ has at least one neighbor P_j with $\mathcal{IS}_j = true$.

Lemma 1. *The maximum independent set task is 1-distance local.*

Proof. The proof is by presenting a failure detector in the set of $\mathcal{FD}_1$ and proving impossibility result for the existence of a failure detector for this task in $\mathcal{FD}_0$.

By the definition of 1-distance local every processor P_i repeatedly sends the portion of its view $\mathcal{V}_i^1$ that is shared with the portion of the view $\mathcal{V}_j^1$ of its neighbor P_j. In other words each processor P_i repeatedly sends the value of $\mathcal{IS}_i$ to every of its neighbors P_j. Thus, a processor knows the value of $\mathcal{IS}_j$ of every of its neighbors. P_i can verify that: if $\mathcal{IS}_i = true$, then $\forall j \in Neighbors_i$, $\mathcal{IS}_i \neq \mathcal{IS}_j$, and if $\mathcal{IS}_i = false$, then $\exists j \in Neighbors_i$, $\mathcal{IS}_i \neq \mathcal{IS}_j$.

The failure detector at P_i will indicate the occurrence of a fault in case any of the above properties doesn't hold. The above test ensures that the value of all the $\mathcal{IS}$ variables constructs a maximum independent set.

By the definition of 0-distance local no information is communicated. Thus, no fault is detected in a configuration in which the $\mathcal{IS}_i$ variable of every processor P_i holds *true*. $\quad\square$

A similar proof holds for the coloring task that we now present.

Coloring, task specification: Each processor P_i maintains a variable C_i representing its color. In addition for every two neighboring processors P_i and P_j it holds that $C_i \neq C_j$.

Lemma 2. *The coloring task is 1-distance local.*

Topology update, task specification: Each processor P_i maintains a local variable T_i, containing the representation of the communication graph, say by using neighboring matrix or the list of the communication graph edges.

Lemma 3. *The topology update task is 1-distance local.*

Proof. The proof is by presenting a failure detector in the set of $\mathcal{FD}_1$ and proving the (obvious) impossibility result for the existence of a failure detector for this task in $\mathcal{FD}_0$.

By the definition of 1-distance local every processor P_i repeatedly sends the portion of its view $\mathcal{V}_i^1$ that is shared with the portion of the view $\mathcal{V}_j^1$ of its neighbor P_j. In other words each processor P_i repeatedly sends the value of the output variable T_i to every of its neighbors P_j. Thus, a processor knows the value of the variables T_j of every of its neighbors. Therefore, P_i can verify that $T_i = T_j$ for every neighboring processor P_j. The failure detector at P_i will notify the occurrence of a fault in case there exists a neighbor for which the above equality does not hold. The above test ensures that if no processor detects a fault then the value of all the T variables is the same. In addition the failure detector at P_i checks whether the local topology of P_i appears correctly in T_i. [4] This test ensures that the (common identical) value of T is correct, since every processor identified its local topology in T.

By the definition of 0-distance local no communication take place. Thus, no fault is detected in a configuration in which the T_i variable of every processor P_i holds the local topology of P_i i.e. P_i and its neighbors without the rest (non empty portion) of the system. $\quad\square$

3.2 Rooted Tree Construction

In this subsection we present the rooted tree construction task that is $\lceil n/4 \rceil$-distance local.

---

[4] It is assumed that every processor knows the identity of its neighbors.

Rooted tree construction, task specification: Each processor P_i maintains two boolean variables $\mathcal{P}_{ij}$ and $\mathcal{C}_{ij}$ for each of its neighbors, P_j. The value of $\mathcal{P}_{ij}$ is true if P_i chooses P_j to be its parent in the tree. The value $\mathcal{C}_{ij}$ is true if P_i considers P_j to be one of its children in the tree. A single processor in the system, P_r which we call the *root*, has an hardwired false value in every $\mathcal{P}_{rj}$, while the value of the variables of the other processors define a tree rooted at P_r.

Lemma 4. *The rooted tree construction task is* $\lceil n/4 \rceil$*-distance local.*

Proof. The proof is by presenting a failure detector in the set of $\mathcal{FD}_{\lceil n/4 \rceil}$ and proving impossibility result for the existence of a failure detector for this task that is in $\mathcal{FD}_{\lceil n/4 \rceil - 1}$.

First we describe a failure detector that is in $\mathcal{FD}_{\lceil n/4 \rceil}$. The failure detector of every non root processor, P_i, checks that the value of exactly one $\mathcal{P}_{ij}$ is true. In addition every processor will verify that the value of each variable $\mathcal{C}_{ij}$ is equal to the value of $\mathcal{P}_{ji}$. The failure detector in every non-root processor will check whether a cycle exists or there is an evidence that the tree that is connected to the root does not include all the processors: The view includes all the processors in the above tree (i.e. each processor in the view does not have a child outside the tree) but there exists at least one additional processor in the view. The failure detector of the root will check whether there is an evidence that the subtree connected to it does not include all the processors.

Obviously, no failure is detected when the system encodes a tree rooted at P_r. If a processor which is not the root has no parent, this is detected immediately by the processor itself. Then only the case in which a partial tree is rooted at the root and where the other nodes belong to a cycle has to be considered. Consider a system in which no error is detected. In this system, the root does not belong to a cycle and each processor different from the root has a parent. If the output does not encode a rooted tree, then it is composed of a rooted subtree and of one or more cycles. But every cycle of $\lceil n/2 \rceil$ or less processors is detected by the processors in the cycle. Thus, if no cycle is detected it must be of length greater than $\lceil n/2 \rceil$ processors. Hence, the number of processor connected to the subtree of the root is less than $\lfloor n/2 \rfloor$. The diameter of this subtree is no more than the number of the processors in it. Thus, there exists a processor with a view on the entire subtree and at least one additional neighboring processor that does not belong to the tree, this processor identifies that there exists a processor that is not in the tree.

To prove that the task is not $(\lceil n/4 \rceil - 1) - local$ we assume that in a configuration c in which a chain of $\lceil n/2 \rceil$ processors are connected to the root and the rest of the processors are in a cycle, some processor indicates a fault and we prove that every such possible processor will indicate a fault in a configuration that encodes a tree.

Assume that the communication graph of the system in which a cycle exists includes in addition to the above chain and cycle a (non-tree) edge between the processor at the end of the chain and a processor in the cycle (thus it is possible to have a tree spanning the graph).

Assume that a processor P_i in the cycle identifies a fault in c then there exists at least one processors P_j in the cycle that is not included in V_i^d (where $d = (\lceil n/4 \rceil - 1)$. There exists a configuration c', that includes an additional edge from P_j to the root, P_j may have chosen this edge to be a tree edge and therefore no cycle exists in c', but P_i will still have the same view V_i^d in c' and therefore will indicate a fault in c'.

If the processor that indicates a fault is on the chain that is connected to the root, then there is at least one processor, P_j, on the chain and one processor P_k on the cycle that are not included in V_i^d. Thus, P_i will indicate a fault when the system is in another configuration, one in which there are no cycles since P_j and P_k are connected by an edge and P_k chooses P_j as its parent.

□

3.3 $(x, \delta x)$−Graph Partition

$(x, \delta x)$−**Graph Partition, task specification:** Each processor P_i maintains a boolean variable $\mathcal{B}_{ij}$ for every of its attached links (i, j). If the edges with $\mathcal{B} = true$ which are called the *border* edges are disconnected then the graph is partition into connected component of at least x processors and no more than δx processors, where δ is the maximal degree of a node in the communication graph and x is a positive integer smaller than n (See [12] for such a partition). In the full paper we show that a graph partition task such as the $(x, \delta x)$−Graph Partition task is $O(\delta x)$−*distance local*.

3.4 Leader Election and Center Determination

In Sections 3.1, 3.2 and 3.3 we have presented silent task that requires failure detectors with larger and larger views in order to detect inconsistency. In this Section we present a class of tasks that requires that at least one processor will have a view on the entire system. We start with the leader election task.

Leader election, task specification: Each processor P_i maintains a local boolean variable $\mathcal{L}_i$ that is set to *true* if the node is elected and *false* otherwise. There is exactly one node P_l with local variable $\mathcal{L}_l$ set to *true*.

Lemma 5. *The leader election task is* $(r + 1)$−*distance local.*

Proof. The proof is by proving impossibility result for the existence of a failure detector for this task in $\mathcal{FD}_r$ and presenting a failure detector in the set of $\mathcal{FD}_{r+1}$ for the task.

By the definition of r−distance local every processor P_i knows the portion of the configuration that includes itself and its neighbors at distance r.

Consider the system S_1 of radius r with $(4r - 2)$ processors represented in Figure 3.4.

Consider a configuration of this system in which all variables $\mathcal{L}_i$ are set to false. Every processor knows the portion of the configuration including itself, its neighbors at distance r and all the outgoing channels (but not necessarily the

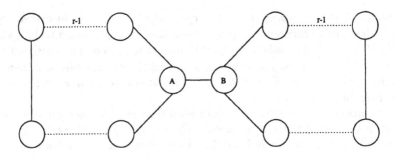

Fig.1. Leader election (1/2)

processors at their extremities). At least one processor must trigger an error and it is easy to see that, because all other processors have a partial view of the system, only A and B can possibly do that. Now consider a second system S_2, of $4r$ processors and with the same radius r, represented in Figure 3.4.

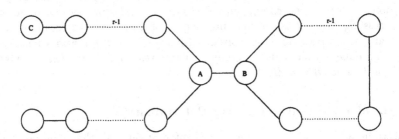

Fig.2. Leader election (2/2)

In S_2, all variables $\mathcal{L}_i$ are set to *false*, but the variable of C, which is set to *true* (so that a unique leader is elected). In both systems, the views at distance r of B are identical. Thus, in both systems, B must decide the same. Because in system S_2, B does not detect a failure, it does not detect a failure either in S_1. By considering a dual system, one can conclude that, in S_1, A cannot detect a failure as well.

The contradiction is complete since, in S_1, no processors triggers an error. Hence, there exists no failure detector in $\mathcal{FD}_r$ for the leader election task.

We now present a failure detector in the set $\mathcal{FD}_{r+1}$ for the leader election task. By the definition of $(r+1)$−distance local every processor P_i knows the part of configuration including itself and its neighbors at distance $(r+1)$. Thus P_i can check whether it knows the entire system, that is whether or not it is a center. If P_i is not a center, it never triggers an error. If P_i is a center, it checks in its $(r+1)$-view whether there is exactly one processor with its variable $\mathcal{L}_i$ set to true. It triggers an error if and only if this test is negative. □

Remark. Note that each time that the specification of a task is a predicate on the global system configuration, there is a failure detector in $\mathcal{FD}_{r+1}$ for this task. As above, the centers check whether the global predicate is true on their $(r+1)$-views and the other processors do nothing. The next, center determination task has a similar property.

Center determination, task specification: Each processor P_i maintains a local boolean variable $\mathcal{I}_i$ which is true if and only if the processor is a center of the system.

Lemma 6. *The center determination task is* $(r+1)-distance\ local.$

4 Failure Detectors for Non-silent Tasks

In this section we consider the set of non-silent tasks. Unlike the previous section that consider failure detectors for asynchronous (as well as synchronous) systems, we consider in this section failure detector for synchronous systems. We present tasks that are s-history local, with $s > 1$. Here, s defines the size of the array $\mathcal{V}_i^d[1..s]$ that is maintained by each processor P_i. The system is synchronous and each view in $\mathcal{V}_i^d[1..s]$ is correlated to a different time. This array is thereafter referred as the *local history* of processor P_i. Each $\mathcal{V}_i^d$ is a view on every component of the system up to distance d from P_i.

We now list several non-silent tasks, present their specification, and identify the minimal history required for their failure detectors. We start with the trivial bounded privilege task. In fact this task does not require any communication among the processors.

4.1 Bounded Privilege

Bounded privilege, task specification: Each processor P_i maintains a local boolean variable $\mathcal{P}riv_i$. For each processor P_i $\mathcal{P}riv_i$ is set to true exactly once (another variant is at least once) in every c synchronous steps ($c \geq 2$). It is easy to show that the bounded privilege task is 0-distance local, c-history local.

Lemma 7. *The bounded privilege task is 0-distance local, c-history local.*

Proof. A local history of $c-1$ views, such that in each view the output variable $\mathcal{P}riv_i$ is false does not give an indication on task violation. On the other hand it is clear that a local history of c views is sufficient for fault detection. □

4.2 Bounded Privilege Dining Philosophers

Bounded privilege dining philosophers, task specification: Each processor P_i maintains a local boolean variable $\mathcal{P}riv_i$. For each processor P_i $\mathcal{P}riv_i$ is set to true at least once in every c synchronous steps ($c \geq 2$). In addition for every two neighboring processors P_i and P_j if $\mathcal{P}riv_i = true$ then $\mathcal{P}riv_j = false$. It is easy to show that the bounded privilege dining philosophers task is 1-distance local, c-history local.

Lemma 8. *The bounded privilege dining philosophers task is 1-distance local, c-history local.*

4.3 Deterministic Non-interactive Tasks

In a synchronous run of a non-randomized, non-interactive, bounded space algorithm a configuration must be reached more than once, and thus the system must repeat its actions infinitely often, in every infinite run. Therefore, there is a bounded *repetition pattern* that can be identified, where the actions of the processors repeat themselves.

Each processor can have a local history that includes all the views of the repetition pattern in the order they should be repeated. The processor repeatedly send to their neighbors their local history and detect inconsistency if two views that are related to the same time do not agree, or the current value of the output variables are not correct. The distance of the views is a function of the task. Note that in fact, when the distance of views is equal to the diameter of the system, the above failure detectors may serve as an implementation of the task — there is no need for an algorithm.

5   Failure Detectors for Algorithms

Unlike the case of failure detectors for tasks the failure detectors for algorithms (implementation of tasks) may use the entire state of the processors (and not only the output that is defined by the task). For example, in an implementation of the spanning tree construction in which every processor has a variable with the distance from the root the failure detector may use the distance variable to detect inconsistency: if every processor has a distance that is one greater than its parent distance, and the root has no parent then the system is in a consistent state.

A monitoring technique that can be used as a failure detector is presented in [1]. The monitoring technique can detect inconsistency of every on-line or off-line *algorithm*. Since the monitoring technique is universal it is possible to design a more efficient (in terms of memory) failure detectors for specific sets of algorithms.

Hierarchy for failure detectors of algorithms can be defined analogously to the definition of the failure detectors for tasks. The choice of the algorithm that implement a task influences the fitting failure detector. For instance, one may suggest to use a topology update algorithm to implement the above silent tasks. A topology update algorithm provides each processor with the information concerning the entire system, thus every processor may perform *local* computations using this information to elect a leader, to elect an identifier, or to count the nodes in the system. Clearly, the above choice of implementation results in using much more memory than other possible implementations. On the other hand, it is possible to monitor the consistency of this particular implementation by a failure detector in $\mathcal{FD}_1$.

6 Implementing Transient Fault Detectors

In this section, we give a possible implementation for using and maintaining the local variables of the failure detectors, namely the local view (for silent algorithms) and the local history (for non-silent algorithms) variables.

As we have already stated, each processor P_i repeatedly communicates to every of its neighbors, P_j the portion of $\mathcal{V}_i^d$ that is shared with $\mathcal{V}_j^d$. In other words P_i does not communicate to P_j the view on the system components that are of distance $d + 1$ from P_j (according to the communication graph portion in $\mathcal{V}_i^d$). When P_i receives the view $\mathcal{V}_j^d$ from its neighbor P_j, P_i checks whether the shared portions of $\mathcal{V}_i^d$ and $\mathcal{V}_j^d$ agree. P_i outputs a failure indication if these portions do not agree.

It is easy to see that the above test ensures that every processor has the right view on the components up to distance d from itself. Assume that the view of P_i is not correct concerning the variable of some processor P_k. Let $P_i, P_{j1}, P_{j2}, \cdots, P_k$ be the processors along a shortest path (of length not greater than d) from P_i to P_k. Let P_{jl} be the first processor in this path for which $\mathcal{V}_{jl}$ and $\mathcal{V}_i$ hold non equal values for a variable of P_k. Note that there must exists such a processor since P_i and P_k holds different values for the variables of P_k. Clearly, P_{jl} and $P_{j(l-1)}$ identify the inconsistency.

The updating policy of the array is the following: in each synchronous step the last view $\mathcal{V}_i^d[s]$ becomes the first view, each other view $\mathcal{V}_i^d[j]$ is copied into $\mathcal{V}_i^d[j + 1]$, $1 \leq j < s$.

The last issue in implementing the failure detector is the action taken upon inconsistency detection. Although it is out of the scope of the paper, we mention the reset (e.g., [15], [4]) and the repair operations (e.g, [1], [16]), both should result in a consistent state of the system and the failure detector.

7 Concluding remarks

In this paper, we investigated the resources required for implementing transient fault detectors for tasks and algorithms. We have presented hierarchy of transient fault detectors that detect the occurrence of transient faults in a *single* asynchronous round (in an asynchronous system) or a single synchronous step (in a synchronous system). We propose a measure for identifying the *locality* of tasks and algorithms, which is the amount of information needed to implement a transient failure detector.

References

1. Y. Afek, and S. Dolev, "Local Stabilizer," *Proc. of the 5th Israeli Symposium on Theory of Computing and Systems*, pp. 74-84, 1997. Brief announcement in *Proc. of the 16th Annual ACM Symp. on Principles of Distributed Computing*, pp. 287, 1997.
2. Y. Afek, S. Kutten, and M. Yung, "Memory efficient self-stabilization on general networks", *Proc. 4th Workshop on Distributed Algorithms*, pp. 15-28, 1990.
3. B. Awerbuch, B. Patt-Shamir and G. Varghese, "Self-stabilization by local checking and correction," *Proc. 32nd IEEE Symp. on Foundations of Computer Science*, pp. 268-277, 1991.
4. B. Awerbuch, B. Patt-Shamir, G. Varghese, and S. Dolev, "Self-Stabilization by Local Checking and Global Reset," *Proc. of the 8th International Workshop on Distributed Algorithms*, pp. 226-239, 1994.
5. T. Chandra and S. Toueg, "Unreliable failure detectors for asynchronous systems," *Journal of the ACM*, 43(2):225-267, March 1996.
6. E. W. Dijkstra, "Self-Stabilizing Systems in Spite of Distributed Control", *Communications of the ACM 17,11* (1974), pp. 643-644.
7. S. Dolev, "Self-Stabilizing Routing and Related Protocols," *Journal of Parallel and Distributed Computing*, 42, 122-127, 1997.
8. S. Dolev, T. Herman, "SuperStabilizing protocols for dynamic distributed systems," *Proceedings of the Second Workshop on Self-Stabilizing Systems*, 1995.
9. S. Dolev, G. Gouda, and M. Schneider, "Memory Requirements for Silent Stabilization," *Proc. of the 15th Annual ACM Symp. on Principles of Distributed Computing*, pp. 27-34, 1996.
10. S. Dolev, A. Israeli and S. Moran, "Self Stabilization of Dynamic Systems Assuming Only Read/Write Atomicity", *Distributed Computing*, Vol. 7, pp. 3-16, 1993. *Proc. of the Ninth Annual ACM Symposium on Principles of Distributed Computation*, Montreal, August 1990, pp. 103-117. *Proc. of the first Workshop on Self-Stabilizing Systems*, 1989.
11. S. Dolev, A. Israeli, and S. Moran. "Analyzing expected time by scheduler-luck games", *IEEE Transactions on Software Engineering*, Vol. 21, pp. 429–439, 1995.
12. S. Dolev, E. Kranakis, D. Krizanc and D. Peleg. "Bubbles: Adaptive Routing Scheme for High-Speed Dynamic Networks", *Proc. of the 27th Annual ACM Symposium on the Theory of Computing*, pp. 528-536, 1995. To appear in *SIAM Journal on Computing*.
13. S. Ghosh, A. Gupta, T. Herman and S. V. Pemmaraju, "Fault-Containing Self-Stabilizing Algorithms", *Proc. of the Fifteenth Annual ACM Symposium on Principles of Distributed Computation*, Philadelphia, May 1996, pp. 45-54.
14. J. E Burns, M. G Gouda, and R. E Miller. "Stabilization and pseudo-stabilization", *Distributed Computing*, Vol. 7, pp. 35–42, 1993.
15. S. Katz and K. J. Perry, "Self-stabilizing extensions for message-passing systems", *Distributed Computing*, Vol. 7, pp. 17-26, 1993. *Proc. of the Ninth Annual ACM Symposium on Principles of Distributed Computation*, Montreal, August 1990, pp. 91-101. *Proc. of the first Workshop on Self-Stabilizing Systems*, 1989.
16. S. Kutten and B. P. Shamir, "Time-Adaptive Self Stabilization", *Proc. of the Sixteenth Annual ACM Symposium on Principles of Distributed Computing* pp. 149-158, 1997.
17. C. Lin and J. Simon, "Observing self-stabilization," *Proc. of the Eleventh Annual ACM Symposium on Principles of Distributed Computing* pp. 113-123, 1992.

Directed Virtual Path Layouts in ATM Networks[*]
(Extended Abstract)

Jean-Claude Bermond, Nausica Marlin [**], David Peleg [***],, and
Stéphane Perennes[**]

Abstract. This article investigates the problem of designing virtual di-paths (VPs) in a directed ATM model, in which the flow of information in the two directions of a link are not identical. On top of a given physical network we construct directed VPs. Routing in the physical network is done using these VPs. Given the capacity of each physical link (the maximum number of VPs that can pass through the link) the problem consists in defining a set of VPs to minimize the diameter of the virtual network formed by these VPs (the maximum number of VPs traversed by any single message). For the most popular types of simple networks, namely the path, the cycle, the grid, the tori, the complete k-ary tree, and the general tree, we present optimal or near optimal lower and upper bounds on the virtual diameter as a function of the capacity.
Keywords : ATM, Virtual path layout, diameter, Embedding,

1 Introduction

The advent of fiber optic media has changed the classical views on the role and struc-ture of digital communication networks. Specifically, the sharp distinction between tele-phone networks, cable television networks, and computer networks has been replaced by a unified approach. The most prevalent solution for this new network challenge is *Asynchronous Transfer Mode* (ATM for short), which is thoroughly described in the literature [6, 15]. The transfer of data in ATM is based on packets of fixed length, termed *cells*. Each cell is routed independently, based on two routing fields at the cell header, called *virtual channel identifier* (VCI) and *virtual path identifier* (VPI). This method effectively creates two types of predetermined simple routes in the network, namely, routes which are based on VPIs (called *virtual paths* or VPs) and routes based on VCIs and VPIs (called *virtual channels* or VCs). VCs are used for connecting net-work users (e.g., a telephone call); VPs are used for simplifying network management - routing of VCs in particular. Thus the route of a VC may be viewed as a concatenation of complete VPs.

[*] This work has been supported by the French-Israeli cooperation "AFIRST"

[**] I3S Université de Nice, SLOOP joint project CNRS-UNSA-INRIA, 2004 route des Lucioles, BP93, F-06902 Sophia-Antipolis, France. ({Jean-Claude.Bermond, Nausica.Marlin, Stephane.Perennes}@sophia.inria.fr)

[***] Department of Applied Mathematics and Computer Science, The Weizmann Insti-tute, Rehovot 76100, Israel. (peleg@wisdom.weizmann.ac.il)

A major problem in this framework is the one of defining the set of VPs in such a way that some good properties are achieved.

1. A capacity (or bandwidth) is assigned to each VP. The sum of the capacities of the VPs that share a physical link constitutes the *load* of this link. Naturally, this load must not exceed the link's capacity, namely, the amount of data it can carry. The sum of the capacities of all the physical links is a major component in the cost of the network, and should be kept as low as possible.

2. The maximum number of VPs in a virtual channel, termed *hop count* in the literature, should also be kept as low as possible so as to guarantee low set up times for the virtual channels and high data transfer rates.

In its most general formulation, the *Virtual Path Layout (VPL)* problem is an optimization problem in which, given a certain communication demand between pairs of nodes and constraints on the maximum load and hop count, it is first required to design a system of virtual paths satisfying the constraints and then minimizing some given function of the load and hop count.

We employ a restricted model similar to the one presented by Cidon, Gerstel and Zaks in [12]. In particular, we assume that all VPs have equal capacities, normalized to 1. Hence the load of a physical link is simply the number of VPs that share this link.

Although links based on optical fibers and cables are directed, traditional research uses an undirected model. Indeed, this model imposes the requirement that if there exists a VP from u to v then there exists also a VP from v to u. In fact, that is the way ATM networks are implemented at the present time. However, the two VPs (the one from u to v and the one in the other direction) do not need to have the same capacity. Indeed, in many applications the flows on the VPs are not equal. For example, in a video application where u is a server and v a consumer there is a VP from u to v using a large capacity (transmission of video data) and a VP from v to u used only for control or acknowledgments with a very small capacity which can be considered as negligible. Therefore, it seems more reasonable to use a directed model like the one introduced by Chanas and Goldschmidt in [5]. This would allow us to model the situation described above by a single VP of capacity 1 in the main direction.

We focus on the all-to-all problem (all pairs of nodes are equally likely to communicate). Thus, the resulting maximum hop count can be viewed as the *diameter* of the graph induced by the VPs.

More formally, given a communication network, the VPs form a virtual directed graph on the top of the physical one, with the same set of vertices but with a different set of arcs. (Specifically, a VP from u to v is represented by an arc from u to v in the virtual digraph.) This virtual digraph provides a *directed virtual path layout (DVPL)* for the physical graph. Each VC can be viewed as a simple dipath in the virtual digraph. Therefore, a central problem is to find a tradeoff between the maximum load and the virtual diameter. In this article, we consider the following problem:

Given a capacity on each physical arc, minimize the diameter of an admissible virtual graph (a virtual digraph that doesn't load an arc more than its capacity)

Related Work The problem has been considered in the undirected case, for example, in [12, 11, 20, 10, 16, 8]. The problem of minimizing the maximum load over all VPL with bounded hop-count is studied in [9, 1], and minimizing also the average load is considered in [11]. The one-to-many problem is handled in [9, 11], where the focus is on minimizing the eccentricity of the virtual graph from a special point called the root (this problem is the *rooted virtual path layout problem*) rather than minimizing the diameter of the virtual graph. A duality in the chain network between the problem of minimizing the hop-count knowing the maximum load, and the one of minimizing the load, knowing the maximum hop-count, is established in [9]. The reader can find an excellent survey of the results in the undirected model in [21].

The techniques involved in our constructions bear a certain resemblance to various embedding techniques used previously in the context of parallel computing, in order to implement a useful virtual architecture on a given practical machine topology (cf. [18, 14]). The parameters of interest in such embeddings are the number of virtual processors mapped onto any physical processor, the load on the physical links, and the dilation of the embedding, namely, the maximum length of the physical path corresponding to a given virtual link. The relevant concerns in our context are somewhat different, as dilation is of no consequence, and on the other hand, we have the freedom of designing the virtual topology as desired, in order to optimize its diameter.

Our Results The following table summarizes the results, giving lower and upper bounds on the virtual diameter (the minimum diameter of an admissible virtual digraph) as a function of the number of vertices n in the physical graph, its diameter D_G, its maximum in- and out-degree d, and the capacity c considered as a constant. Some of the proofs are omitted and will appear in the full version, and other proofs are included in the appendix. The results mentioned in the table for the path in the special case of $c = 1$ are due to [4, 3].

Graph G	Capacity	Lower Bound	Upper Bound
General Graph	$c = \mathcal{O}(1)$	$\frac{\log n}{\log(cd)} - 1$	D_G
Path P_n	$c = 1$	$\frac{n}{2} + \log n$	$\frac{n}{2} + \log n + \mathcal{O}(1)$
	$c = \mathcal{O}(1)$	$\Omega(n^{\frac{1}{2c-1}})$	$\mathcal{O}(c \cdot n^{\frac{1}{2c-1}})$
Cycle C_n	$c = 1$	$2\sqrt{2n} + \mathcal{O}(1)$	$2\sqrt{2n} + \mathcal{O}(1)$
	$c = \mathcal{O}(1)$	$\Omega(n^{\frac{1}{2c}})$	$\mathcal{O}(c \cdot n^{\frac{1}{2c}})$
Torus $TM(a,b), a \le b$	$c = \mathcal{O}(1)$	$\Omega((a \cdot b)^{1/2ac})$	$\mathcal{O}(a \cdot b^{1/2ac})$
Mesh $M(a,b), \log b \le a \le b$	$c = \mathcal{O}(1)$	$\Omega(\log n)$	$\mathcal{O}(\log n)$
Arbitrary Tree T	$c = 2$	$1/2 \cdot n^{1/3}$	$\tilde{D}(P_{D_T}, c)$ $32 \cdot n^{1/3}$ $D_G^{1/3} \cdot \log n$
	$c = \mathcal{O}(1)$	$\Omega(D_G^{1/(2c-1)})$	$8c \cdot n^{1/(2c-1)}$ $D_G^{1/(2c-1)} \cdot \log n$
Complete k-ary Tree T	$c = 2, k = 2$	$D_G/2 - 1$	$D_G/2 + 2$
	$c = \mathcal{O}(1)$	$2\left\lfloor \frac{h-1}{\lfloor \log_k c \rfloor + 1} \right\rfloor + 1$	

2 The model

The physical network is represented by a strongly connected weighted digraph $G = (V, E, c)$. The number of vertices is denoted by $n = |V|$. The vertex set V represents the network switches and end-users, and the arc set E represents the set of physical directed links. The parameter c is the capacity (or weight) function, assigning to each arc e its capacity $c(e)$. For simplicity, given $c_0 \in N^+$, we denote by c_0 the constant capacity function in which $c(e) = c_0$ for all e.

The network formed by the VPs is represented by a strongly connected digraph $H = (V, E')$ and a function P assigning to each arc $e' = (x, y) \in E'$ a simple dipath $P(e')$ connecting x to y in G. In our terminology, the pair (H, P) is a *virtual digraph on* G, an arc of H is a *virtual arc*, and the dipath $P(e')$ in G associated with a virtual arc e' is a *virtual dipath* (*VP*). To a dipath $Q = (e'_1, \ldots, e'_l)$ in H is associated a *route* in G consisting of the concatenation of $P(e'_1), \ldots, P(e_l)$.

The *load* of an arc e of G is the number of dipaths $P(e')$ of G associated to an arc e' of H (or virtual dipaths) that contain the arc e, that is, $l(e) = |\{e' \in E' \ s.t. \ e \in P(e')\}|$ A virtual digraph (H, P) satisfying the requirement $\forall e \in E$, $l(e) \leq c(e)$ is referred as a *c-admissible directed virtual paths layout of* G, shortly denoted *c-DVPL of* G. The aim is to design *c-DVPL* of G with minimum hop-count. This corresponds to minimizing the diameter of the virtual digraph. For any digraph F, $d_F(x, y)$ denotes the distance from x to y in F, and D_F denotes F's diameter. The *virtual diameter*, $\tilde{D}(G, c)$, of the digraph G with respect to the capacity c, is the minimum of D_H over all the *c-DVPL* H of G.

Note that both problems are NP-hard. (Indeed, deciding the question of whether $\tilde{D}(G, c_0) = 1$ is equivalent to determining the arc-forwarding index of G, which is known to be NP-hard, see also [4].)

3 General Bounds

For most digraphs it turns out that $\tilde{D}(G, c_0)$ is logarithmic even for $c_0 = 1$. Hence the ratio $\frac{\tilde{D}(G, c_0)}{\log n}$ is of importance. For d-bounded degree digraphs[1], a classical result states that $\frac{\log n}{\log(c_0 d)} - 1 \leq \tilde{D}(G, c_0)$. It is obtained by applying the Moore bound to the virtual digraph with n nodes, degree at most $c_0 d$, and diameter $\tilde{D}(G, c_0)$ (see [16, 20]). Note also that $\tilde{D}(G, 1) \leq D_G$.

Here we derive a tighter bound related to the expansion-congestion parameters of G. First we recall three standard definitions: A *routing* for G is a mapping associating to each pair of vertices (x, y) a *route* (i.e. a dipath in G) from x to y; the *congestion* of a routing is the maximal *load* of an arc of G (i.e., the maximum number of routes going through an arc); the *arc-forwarding index of* G, denoted $\pi(G)$, is the minimum congestion of a routing.

The parameter $\pi(G)$ has been extensively studied and many relations exist between π and other parameters like bisection or expansion, see [17, 19, 13]. There are strong relationships between $\pi(G)$ and the DVPL issue. A routing for G is a DVPL of G where H is the complete digraph, and so $\pi(G)$ is the smallest integer c_0 such that $\tilde{D}(G, c_0) = 1$.

Proposition 1. *Let G be a d-bounded digraph, then*

$$\frac{\log \pi(G)}{\log(c_0 d)} - 1 + O(\log \tilde{D}) \ \leq \ \tilde{D}(G, c_0) \ .$$

---

[1] where both the in- and out- degrees are upper-bounded by d

Proof. With every c_0-DVPL H of G one can associate a routing for G as follows. Note that for any ordered pair of vertices (x, y) there exists at least one dipath in H from x to y with length smaller than D_H. We select one such dipath and choose the associated real dipath as the route from x to y. Due to the capacity constraint, at most $c_0 d$ virtual dipaths enter (resp., leave) any given vertex of G; one can easily check that the number of dipaths in H of length k that use an arc is at most $k c_0 (c_0 d)^{k-1}$. Hence the congestion of our routing is upper-bounded by $M = c_0 + 2 c_0 (c_0 d) + 3 c_0 (c_0 d)^2 + \ldots + D_H c_0 (c_0 d)^{D_H - 1}$.

By definition, $\pi \leq M$; as $M \leq c_0 \frac{D_H (c_0 d)^{D_H}}{c_0 d - 1}$, taking the logarithm we obtain the result.

Remark 1. The lower bound of proposition 1 is quite similar to the one derived on the gossip time of a network under WDM or wormhole models [7, 2]. In both cases one must construct a route between any pair of vertices: for gossip problems the route is built along T time steps, whereas in the context of VPL design it is constructed by using $\tilde{D}(G, c)$ jumps.

The following proposition indicates that for *bounded* c_0, one can expect $\tilde{D}(G, c_0)$ to be logarithmic only if D_G is not too large. The result is valid for (distance-) symmetric digraphs (namely, such that $d(x, y) = d(y, x)$).

Proposition 2. *Let G be a symmetric bounded degree digraph with $\log D_G = \Omega(\log n)$.*

$$\text{If } \tilde{D}(G, c_0) = \Theta(\log n), \text{ then } c_0 = \Omega\left(\frac{D_G \log n}{n}\right).$$

In particular, if c_0 is constant and $\tilde{D}(G, c_0) = \Theta(\log n)$ then $D_G = O(\frac{n}{\log n})$.

We will see in proposition 8 that the above lower bound is tight in some sense.

Proof. The idea is that the design of an efficient DVPL is prevented by the existence of a long geodesic dipath contained in G. Let us first formalize the notion that a digraph "contains" some bad sub-structure.

Define a *retraction* of a digraph G as a digraph G' such that there exist a mapping f from $V(G)$ onto $V(G')$ satisfying a *contraction* condition: $d_G(x, y) \geq d_{G'}(f(x), f(y))$. Define the *total load* of G for virtual diameter D_0 as : $\mathcal{L}(G, D_0) = \min(\sum_{e \in E} l(e))$ where the minimum is taken on all DVPL such that $D_H \leq D_0$.

Due to the contraction condition, for any retraction G' of G we have $\mathcal{L}(G, D_0) \geq \mathcal{L}(G', D_0)$. Moreover, denoting the number of arcs of G by $|E|$, the maximum load is greater than or equal to the average load. Hence we have proven the following.

Lemma 1. *If G' is a retraction of G then $\pi(G, D_0) \geq \frac{\mathcal{L}(G, D_0)}{|E|} \geq \frac{\mathcal{L}(G', D_0)}{|E|}$.*

First, we claim that the path P_{D_G} of length D_G is a retraction of G. To prove this, consider the following mapping. Label the vertices of P_{D_G} by $0, 1, \ldots, D_G$, and choose a pair of vertices (x, y) of G such that $d(x, y) = d(y, x) = D$; then map any vertex at distance i from x onto vertex i of the path. Due to the triangle inequality, and to symmetry, the mapping is contracting.

Now, suppose that we are given a bounded degree digraph G with $\log D_G = \Theta(\log n)$, and the capacity function c_0 Consider any DVPL with diameter $D_H = \Theta(\log n)$. By lemma 1 we have $c_0 \geq \frac{\mathcal{L}(L_{D_G}, D_H)}{|E|}$. we also know that if $D_0 \sim \log D_G$ then $\mathcal{P}(L_{D_G}, D_0) \sim D_G \log D_G$ [21]; it follows that $c_0 \geq \frac{D_G \log D_G}{|E|}$. As $|E| \leq nd$, we obtain $c_0 \geq \frac{D_G \log n}{dn}$.

4 The Cycle C_n

In this section the physical digraph G is C_n, the symmetric directed cycle of length n. We choose arbitrarily a sense of direction on C_n. For concreteness, consider as positive, or forward (resp., negative or backward) the clockwise (resp., counterclockwise) direction. We assume that $\forall e \in E$, $c(e) = c^+$ if e is a forward arc and $c(e) = c^-$ if e is a backward arc.

It turns out that our bounds can be expressed as functions of $\sigma = c^+ + c^-$. It is then convenient to define $ubc(n, \sigma)$ (resp., $lbc(n, \sigma)$) as an upper bound (resp., lower bound) on $\tilde{D}(C_n, c)$ valid if c satisfies $c^+ + c^- = \sigma$. By the definition, $lbc(n, \sigma) \leq \tilde{D}(C_n, c) \leq ubc(n, \sigma)$.

Proposition 3.

$$\frac{n^{\frac{1}{\sigma}}}{2} \leq \tilde{D}(C_n, c) < 2\sigma \left(\frac{n}{2}\right)^{\frac{1}{\sigma}} + 1 .$$

In particular, if $c = c_0$ then

$$\frac{n^{\frac{1}{2c_0}}}{2} \leq \tilde{D}(C_n, c_0) < 4c_0 \left(\frac{n}{2}\right)^{\frac{1}{2c_0}} + 1 .$$

Upper and lower bounds are both proved by induction from the next two lemmas (to be proved later):

Lemma 2. $lbc(n, \sigma) \geq \min_{p \in N^+}\{\max(\frac{n}{2p}, lbc(p, \sigma - 1))\}$.

Lemma 3. $ubc(n, \sigma) \leq \min_{p \in N^+}\{2(p - 1) + ubc(\lceil \frac{n}{p} \rceil, \sigma - 1)\}$

Proof (proposition 3). First we consider the lower bound. We prove by induction on σ that $lbc(n, \sigma) \geq \frac{1}{2}n^{\frac{1}{\sigma}}$. For the initial case we have $lbc(n, 1) = n - 1 \geq \frac{n}{2}$. Now to go from $\sigma - 1$ to σ we use lemma 2 which states that $lbc(n, \sigma) \geq \min_{p \in N^+} \max(\frac{n}{2p}, \frac{1}{2}p^{\frac{1}{\sigma-1}})$. An elementary analysis shows that $\max(\frac{n}{2p}, \frac{1}{2}p^{\frac{1}{\sigma-1}}) \geq \frac{1}{2}n^{\frac{1}{\sigma}}$. Hence $lbc(n, \sigma) \geq \frac{1}{2}n^{\frac{1}{\sigma}}$ and the proof is completed.

Now, we prove the upper bound. First we show by induction on σ that for $n = 2a^\sigma, a \in N$, $ubc(n, \sigma) \leq 2\sigma \left(\frac{n}{2}\right)^{1/\sigma} - 2\sigma + 1 = 2\sigma a - 2\sigma + 1$. For $\sigma = 1$, $ubc(n, 1) \leq n - 1$. For the inductive step from $\sigma - 1$ to σ, we apply lemma 3 with $p = a$, getting $ubc(n, \sigma) \leq 2(a - 1) + ubc(2a^{\sigma-1}, \sigma - 1)$. By induction, $ubc(2a^{\sigma-1}, \sigma - 1) = 2(\sigma - 1)a - 2(\sigma - 1) + 1$; so we get the expected result.

For other values of n, the claim is proved as follows. Let a be such that $2(a - 1)^\sigma < n \leq 2a^\sigma$, that is $a - 1 < \left(\frac{n}{2}\right)^{1/\sigma} \leq a$. By applying lemma 3 with $x = a$ for σ times, we obtain $ubc(n, \sigma) \leq 2\sigma a - 2\sigma + 1$. As $a \leq \left(\frac{n}{2}\right)^{\frac{1}{\sigma}} + 1$, this implies $ubc(n, \sigma) < 2\sigma \left(\frac{n}{2}\right)^{\frac{1}{\sigma}} + 1$.

Proof (lemma 2). Let H be an optimal c-DVPL of C_n and let $[x_1, y_1]$ be the dipath consisting of all the vertices of C_n between x_1 and y_1 in the positive direction. Let $d(x_1, y_1)$ denote the number of arcs in $[x_1, y_1]$. We say that $[x_1, y_1]$ is *covered* by H if (the VP corresponding to) some virtual arc contains $[x_1, y_1]$.

First we prove that if $[x_1, y_1]$ is covered then $D_H \geq lbc(d(x_1, y_1), \sigma - 1)$. For this, we shorten the cycle by identifying all the nodes in $[y_1, x_1]$ with x_1, obtaining a cycle C'

of length $d(x_1, y_1)$. Virtual arcs are just transformed according to this graph quotient. As example a virtual arc from $x \in [x_1, y_1]$ to $y \in [x_1, y_1]$ is left unchanged; and a virtual arc from $x \in [x_1, y_1]$ to $y \in [y_1, x_1]$ is transformed into the arc (x, x_1). Note that the virtual arc containing the positive arcs of $[x_1, y_1]$ (see figure 1) is transformed into a loop. We also remove loops or multiple virtual dipaths in order to get a simple DVPL on C'.

Note that our transformation does not increase the load of any arc; furthermore the virtual arc from x_1 to y_1 disappears, so the congestion of any positive arc decreases. Moreover, our transformation does not increase the virtual diameter.

Consequently, we obtain a c'-DVPL of C' (a cycle of length $d(x_1, y_1)$) with $c'^+ + c'^- = \sigma - 1$, and diameter at most D_H. It follows that

$$D_H \geq lb_C(d(x_1, y_1), \sigma - 1) \tag{1}$$

Now we argue that there exist vertices u and v with large $d(u, v)$ such that $[u, v]$ is covered. Let $\mathcal{P}$ be the shortest dipath in H from 0 to $n/2$, and assume w.l.o.g. that $\mathcal{P}$ contains the arcs of $[0, n/2]$. Let $\mathcal{S}$ denote the set of vertices of $\mathcal{P}$ between x and y in the positive direction. Then $|\mathcal{S}| \leq D_H + 1$, and therefore there exist vertices u and v such that $[u, v]$ is covered and with

$$d(u, v) \geq \frac{n}{2 D_H} . \tag{2}$$

Let $p = \max\{d(u, v) \mid [u, v] \text{ is covered}\}$. From (2) we have $D_H \geq \frac{n}{2p}$, and from (1) it follows that $D_H \geq lb_C(p, \sigma - 1)$.

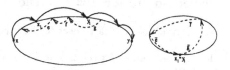

Fig. 1. Collapsing a cycle

Proof (lemma3). Let us construct a c-DVPL on C_n. Without lost of generality suppose that $c^+ \geq c^-$, so $c^+ \neq 0$. Let $p \in N^+$, we proceed as follows.

- Use n virtual arcs $(i, i+1)_{i \in [0..n-1]}$ of dilation 1 in the positive direction.
- Let S be the set of vertices $\{0, p, 2p, \ldots, (\lceil \frac{n}{p} \rceil - 1)p\}$, and note that vertices of S form a cycle $C_{\lceil \frac{n}{p} \rceil}$.
- Use an optimal c'-DVPL for $C_{\lceil \frac{n}{p} \rceil}$ with $c'^+ = c^+ - 1$, and $c'^- = c^-$, that is $c'^+ + c'^- = \sigma - 1$.

By construction, the diameter $\Delta(S)$ of the set S (i.e., the maximal distance of two vertices in S) is at most $ub_C(\lceil \frac{n}{p} \rceil, \sigma - 1)$; moreover, for any vertex x, we have $d(S, x) \leq p - 1$ and $d(x, S) \leq p - 1$. Hence $d(x, y) \leq d(S, x) + d(y, S) + \Delta(S) \leq 2(p-1) + ub_C(\lceil \frac{n}{p} \rceil, \sigma - 1)$.

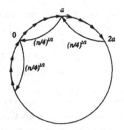

Fig. 2. C_n for $c = 1$ $(\sigma = 2)$

In the case of capacity $c_0 = 1$ we have been able to determine $\tilde{D}(C_n, c)$ quite exactly.

Proposition 4. $2\sqrt{2n} - \Theta(1) \leq \tilde{D}(C_n, 1) \leq 2\sqrt{2n} + 1$.

The upper bound is the one given for the general case, We conjecture that $\tilde{D}(C_n, 1) = 2\sqrt{2n} - 3$, and wish for simpler argument that would extend to greater capcaities. Note also that using lemma 2 from the starting condition $lb_C(n, 2) \geq 2\sqrt{n} + \Theta(1))$ would slightly improve the lower bound on $lb_C(n, \sigma)$. the lower bound proof requires some care so the next section is devoted to its exposure.

4.1 Proof of the lower bound for $c = 1$ in the cycle

Let H be an optimal virtual digraph on G with respect to the capacity 1.

Definition 1. $-$ *The* forward successor *of a vertex x is denoted x^+,*
- $P_{C_n}^+(x, y)$ *denotes the dipath from x to y in C_n in the positive direction,*
- *a path $Q = (e_1', \dots e_q')$ from x to y in H is said to be of type $+$ if $P_{C_n}^+(x, y) \subset W(Q)$.*

Definitions are given for the positive direction, but similar notions apply for the negative direction as well.

Definition 2. *A* circuit-bracelet *of size n is a digraph A constructed as follows (see figure 3):*

- *The digraph is made of a set of cycles $C_i, i \in I$ directed in a clockwise manner.*
- *For any i, C_i and $C_{i+1 \bmod I}$ share a unique vertex $v_{i+1 \bmod I}$.*
- *The length of the dipath in C_i from v_{i-1} to v_i is denoted p_i and is called the* positive length *of C_i; similarly, the length of the dipath in C_i from v_{i-1} to v_i is denoted n_i and is called the* negative length *of C_i.*

Denote by $f(n)$ the minimal value of D_A, where A is any circuit-bracelet of size n. In the remaining of the section indices are taken modulo I.

Lemma 4. $f(n) = \tilde{D}(C_n, 1)$

Proof. Notice that if an arc e of G is not used by a virtual dipath $P(e')$ with $e' \in E'$, we add a virtual arc e' such that $P(e') = (e)$. This transformation can only decrease the diameter of H, which is of no consequence since we only look for a lower bound on the virtual diameter. Using this manipulation, we know that $\forall e \in E, \exists e' \in E'$ s.t. $e \in P(e')$. This implies

$$\sum_{e' \text{ arc of type } -} w(e') = \sum_{e' \text{ arc of type } +} w(e') = n . \tag{3}$$

Now, we show that : *If $e' = (x,y) \in E'$ is an arc of type $+$ of weight $w(e') > 3$ then all the arcs of type $-$ between y^- and x^+ are of weight 1.*

Since the capacity of any arc of G is 1, and there is already a virtual arc of type $+$ between x and y, there is no virtual arc of type $+$ ending at any vertex between x^+ and y^-. Since $H = (V, E')$ is strongly connected, there is at least one arc ending at each one of these vertices. These arcs are of type -. For the same reasons of capacity and connectivity, these virtual arcs are of weight 1. Due to this property it is easy to see that there exists a digraph isomorphism from H to a circuit-bracelet of size n (see figure 3).

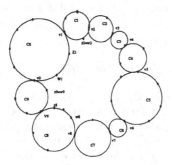

Fig. 3. A circuit-bracelet

We first prove the result for the special case of a *regular circuit-bracelet*, namely, a circuit-bracelet satisfying $p_i = 1$ for every i. Let $g(n)$ denote the minimal value of D_A where A is any regular circuit-bracelet of size n.

Lemma 5. $g(n) = 2\sqrt{2n} + \Theta(1)$.

Proof. We know from the construction of lemma 3 that there exists a regular circuit-bracelet with diameter $D \leq \sqrt{2n} + O(1) = \Theta(\sqrt{n})$, and prove that $D \geq 2\sqrt{2n} + \Theta(1)$. We assume that n is sufficiently large, and fix a positive integer p. Note that the circuits of a regular circuit-bracelet all consist of a single arc in the positive direction. Call a circuit *large* if its size is greater than $\frac{D}{p}$. Note that the size of any circuit is at most $D + 1 = O(\sqrt{n})$, hence there is at least $\Omega(\sqrt{n})$ circuits. Moreover the total number of circuits is $O(\sqrt{n})$, otherwise the distance between two antipodal vertices would be greater than D. As $n \leq s\frac{D}{p} + bD$ with $s + b = \Theta(\sqrt{n})$ it follows that :

$$\text{For sufficiently large } p : b = \Theta(\sqrt{n}) \tag{4}$$

Suppose that large circuits are ordered cyclically according to the circuit-bracelet structure: $C_{i_0}, C_{i_1}, \ldots C_{i_{b-1}}$, and that there are s small circuits. Let δ denote the number of vertices in the small circuits. We denote the ancestor of v_i in C_i by w_i, and the successor of v_{i+1} in C_i by z_i. Let $k \in \{0, 1, \ldots b-1\}$ and consider dipaths from z_{i_k} to $w_{i_{k-p}}$; in the negative direction the cost is exactly $d_1 = \sum_{j \in [k-p,k]} n_{i_j} - 2$; as these circuits are large, $n_{i_j} \geq \frac{D}{p}$ and hence $d_1 \geq \frac{p+1}{p}D - 2$. So we must use the positive direction. The length is $d_k = n_{i_k} + n_{i_{k-p}} + b + s - \#$ circuits in $[i_{k-p}, i_k]$. Summing on all the k's, each circuit is counted $b-p$ times; moreover, all the vertices in large circuits are counted twice. Hence we have $\sum_{k=0}^{k=b-1} d_k = 2(n - \delta) + b(b+s) - p(b+s) \leq bD$. So $\frac{2(n-\delta)}{b} + b + s - p - p\frac{s}{b} \leq D$. Note now that $\delta \leq s \cdot \frac{D}{p}$, so :

$$\frac{2n}{b} + b - \frac{2sD}{pb} + s - p - p\frac{s}{b} \leq D$$
$$\frac{2n}{b} + b + s(1 - \frac{2D}{bp} - \frac{p}{b}) - p \leq D \tag{5}$$

In (5) the left member is greater than $\frac{2n}{b} + b - p$ when the factor with s is positive, that is : $b \geq \frac{D}{p} + p$. Due to claim (4) it is verified if p has been choosen large enough. The minimum of the left member in (5) is then $2\sqrt{2n} + \Theta(1)$ and is achieved for $s = 0, b = \sqrt{2n}$. So we have $g(n) = 2\sqrt{2n} + \Theta(1)$.

Proposition 5. $\tilde{D}(C_n, 1) = f(n) = 2\sqrt{2n} + \Theta(1)$.

Proof. Recall that $D = \Theta(\sqrt{n})$. Consider a circuit-bracelet, and note that $n_i + p_i \leq D+2$, so that we can find an integer k such that $C_1, C_2, \ldots C_k$ contains $x \geq 2D+2, x = \Theta(\sqrt{n})$ vertices. Consider the shortest dipath from v_1 to v_{k+1} and suppose that it uses the positive direction, so that $\sum_{i \in [1,k]} p_i \leq D$. It follows that $\sum_{i \in [1,k]} n_i > D$. So, the dipath from v_k to v_1 cannot use the negative direction, and must use the positive one. It follws that $\sum_{i \notin [1,k]} p_i \leq D$. Globally, $\sum p_i \leq 2D = \Theta(\sqrt{n})$. If we remove this $\Theta(\sqrt{n})$ vertices we obtain a regular circuit-bracelet with lesser diameter. It follows that $f(n) \geq g(n - \Theta(\sqrt{n})) = 2\sqrt{2n} + \Theta(1)$.

5 The Path P_n

In this section the physical digraph G is the n-vertex path P_n. Our bounds are valid for any capacity function c such that positive (resp., negative) arcs have capacity c^+ (resp., c^-), with $c^+ + c^- = \sigma \geq 2$, and the additional requirement $c^+ \geq 1, c^- \geq 1$.

Proposition 6.

$$\frac{n^{\frac{1}{\sigma-1}}}{2} \leq \tilde{D}(P_n, c) \leq (2(\sigma - 1)) \left(\frac{n-1}{2}\right)^{\frac{1}{\sigma-1}} + 2 .$$

Proof. Will appear in the full version

6 Grids and Toroidal Meshes

First the physical digraph G is the toroidal mesh of dimensions $a \times b$, $TM(a, b)$. Recall that $TM(a, b) = C_a \square C_b$, the Cartesian sum (also called product) of two cycles.

Proposition 7.

$$\tilde{D}(TM(a, b), c_0) \leq 2(4c_0) \cdot \left(\frac{a}{2}\right)^{1/2c-1} + 2a + 1 + (4ac_0 - 1)\left(\frac{b}{2}\right)^{1/2ac_0} .$$

Note that in order to get a graph G such that $\tilde{D}(G, c_0) \sim \log n$ with c_0 bounded we can use a toroidal mesh $T(\log n \frac{n}{\log n})$. Hence we have the following.

Proposition 8. *There exists an infinite family of digraphs with n vertices and diameter $n/\log n$, such that with bounded capacity c_0, $\tilde{D}(G, c_0) = \Theta(\log n)$.*

Note that this is the counterpart of proposition 2 .
For $\lceil \log_2 b \rceil \leq a \leq b$ we have :

Proposition 9. $\tilde{D}(T(a, b), 1) = \Omega(\log n)$.

Results for the grid $M(a, b) = P_a \square P_b$ are similar and will be detailed in the full version.

7 The Complete Symmetric k-ary Tree $T(k, h)$

Let us recall that in a complete k-ary tree, each vertex that is not a leaf has exactly k children. The *depth* of a vertex is its distance from the root. The depth of the tree is the maximum depth of its vertices. In this section the physical digraph G is $T(k, h)$, the directed symmetric complete k-ary tree of depth h rooted in r_0, the only vertex of degree k. $T(k, h)$ has $\frac{k^{h+1}-1}{k-1}$ vertices and diameter $2h$. For a vertex x of the graph $T(k, h)$, let $f(x)$ denote its parent; vertex y is said to be *below* x if $\exists i \geq 0$ s.t. $f^i(y) = x$. Note that x is below itself.

7.1 Lower Bound

Proposition 10. $\tilde{D}(T(k, h), c) \geq 2\left\lfloor \frac{h-1}{\lfloor \log_k c \rfloor + 1} \right\rfloor + 1$.

Proof. Let H be an c-DVPL of $T(k, h)$. Let $\gamma = \lfloor \log_k c \rfloor + 1$. Let r be a vertex of depth d, $1 \leq d \leq h - \gamma$; Let $B(\gamma, r)$ denote the complete k-ary subtree of $T(k, h)$ of depth γ rooted in r. A leaf x of $B(\gamma, r)$ is said to be *upward-bad for r* if there doesn't exist any virtual arc e' that starts below x and ends not below r. If there doesn't exist any virtual arc e' that starts not below r and ends below x then x is said to be *downward-bad for r*. We claim the following: *For any vertex r of depth d, $1 \leq d \leq h - \gamma$ there exist an upward-bad vertex and a downward-bad vertex for r.*

Indeed, suppose that all the k^γ leaves of $B(\gamma, r)$ are not upward-bad. There exists a virtual arc that starts below each leaf and ends not below r. Then the load of the arc $(r, f(r))$ is at least k^γ. Since the capacity of this arc is $c < k^{\lfloor \log_k c \rfloor + 1}$, there exists at least one leaf that is upward-bad for r. The same argument considering the load of arc $(f(r), r)$ completes the proof of the claim.

Now we prove that $D_H \geq 2(\lfloor \frac{h-1}{\gamma} \rfloor) + 1$. Let $i_0 = \lfloor (h-1)/\gamma \rfloor + 1$. Define two sequences of vertices $(l_i)_{i=1..i_0}$ and $(r_i)_{i=1..i_0}$ as follows. Let l_1 and r_1 be the leftmost and the rightmost neighbors of the root of $T(k, h)$, respectively. If $i \leq i_0 - 1$, choose for l_{i+1} an upward-bad vertex for l_i. By induction, the depth of l_i is $1 + \gamma(i-1)$ and if $i \leq i_0 - 1$ it is less than $h - \gamma$ so, from the claim, l_{i+1} exists. Symmetrically, we define the sequence $(r_i)_{i=1..i_0}$ by choosing r_{i+1} as one of the downward-bad vertices for r_i.

Let us now consider the shortest path $\mathcal{P}$ in H from l_{i_0} to r_{i_0}. Let y be the first vertex of $\mathcal{P}$ not below l_1. By construction, $\mathcal{P}$ uses at least i_0 virtual arcs from l_{i_0} to y. Also x, the predecessor of y in $\mathcal{P}$, is below l_1 and thus not below r_1. Hence, $\mathcal{P}$ uses at least i_0 virtual arcs from x to r_{i_0}. In summary, $\mathcal{P}$ uses at least $2i_0 - 1$ virtual arcs. So $D_G \geq 2i_0 - 1$ that is $2(\lfloor (h-1)/\gamma \rfloor) + 1$.

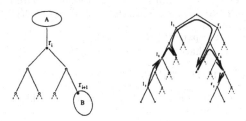

Fig. 4. $k = 2$, $c = 2$ or 3, $\gamma = 2$, there exist no arcs from A to B; (on the right) $k = 2$, $\gamma = 2$, $h = 6$, one cannot do better than 5 from l_3 to r_3

7.2 Upper Bound for $k = 2$, $c = 2$

Proposition 11. $\tilde{D}(T(2, h), 2) \leq D/2 + 1$.

Proof. The construction of an admissible virtual graph H on $D(T(2, h))$ is undirected. In other words, for each VP from x to y, there is a VP from y to x using the opposite path. Place a VP of dilation 2 between each vertex of even depth and its grandparent and a VP of dilation 1 between each vertex of even depth and its parent. If h is odd then add a VP of dilation 1 between each leaf and its parent. This construction gives the upper bound.

8 Arbitrary Trees

In this section, the graph at hand is an arbitrary tree T. The lower bound follows from our bound for the n-vertex path P_n, upon noting the following.

Proposition 12. $\tilde{D}(T, c) \geq \tilde{D}(P_{D_T}, c)$.

One natural upper bound follows by embedding a cycle around the tree. Consider a cycle C_{2n-2} embedded around the tree T in a depth-first fashion. Let $c^+ = \lceil c/2 \rceil$ and $c^- = \lfloor c/2 \rfloor$. An admissible graph H on C_{2n-2} with respect to c^+ on positive arcs and c^- on negative ones gives us an admissible virtual graph on T. Thus, $\tilde{D}(T, c) \leq \tilde{D}(C_{2n-2}, c/2) \leq 2c(n-1)^{1/c} + 1$.

Another upper bound is derived by a recursive construction.

Proposition 13. *There exists a constant such that* $\tilde{D}(T,c) \leq 8c.n^{\frac{1}{2c-1}}$.

Proposition 14. $\tilde{D}(T,c) \leq \tilde{D}(P_{D_T}, c) \cdot \log n$.

9 Open problems and directions

Some of our bounds are not tight, and the remaining gaps may be narrowed. Establishing upper and lower bounds on $\tilde{D}$ for other families of graphs may also be interesting and useful.

Looking for the minimum diameter is reasonable when all the connections may be requested with roughly the same probability, which is also not always realistic. In case of non-uniform traffic, instead of studying $\tilde{D}$, one may try to optimize its weighted counterpart, $\sum r(i,j) \cdot d_H(i,j)$, where $r(i,j)$ denotes the traffic requirements between i and j; such a target function may make it desirable to place the VPs between the node pairs which communicate the most.

Finally, there may be other parameters of the directed ATM model worth studying. One may also consider variations on the model with variable capacity of the VPs.

Acknowledgments

The authors would like to thank Amotz Bar-Noy, Bruno Beauquier, Pascal Chanas, Michele Flammini, Cyril Gavoille and Daniel Kofman for helpful discussions.

References

1. L. Becchetti, P. Bertolazzi, C. Gaibisso, and G. Gambosi. On the design of efficient ATM routing schemes. manuscript, 1997.
2. J.-C. Bermond, L. Gargano, S. Perennes, A. Rescigno, and U. Vaccaro. Effective collective communication in optical networks. In *Proceedings of ICALP 96*, volume 1099 of *Lectures Notes In Computer Science*, pages 574–585. Springer Verlag, July 1996.
3. M. Burlet, P. Chanas, and O. Goldschmidt. Optimization of VP layout in ATM networks. In preparation, 1998.
4. P. Chanas. *Dimensionnement de réseaux ATM*. PhD thesis, CNET Sophia, Sept. 1998. In preparation.
5. P. Chanas and O. Goldschmidt. Conception de réseau de VP de diamètre minimum pour les réseaux ATM. In *Road-f'98*, pages 38–40, 1998.
6. M. De Pricker. *Asynchronous Transfer Mode, Solution for Broadband ISDN*. Prentice Hall, August 1995. 3rd edition 332p.
7. O. Delmas and S. Perennes. Circuit-Switched Gossiping in 3-Dimensional Torus Networks. In *Proc. Euro-Par'96 Parallel Processing / 2nd Int. EURO-PAR Conference*, volume 1123 of *Lecture Notes in Computer Science*, pages 370–373, Lyon, France, Aug. 1996. Springer Verlag.
8. T. Eilam, M. Flammini, and S. Zaks. A complete characterization of the path layout construction problem for ATM networks with given hop count and load. In *24th International Colloquium on Automata, Languages and Programming (ICALP)*, volume 1256 of *Lecture Notes in Computer Science*, pages 527–537. Springer-Verlag, 1997.

9. M. Feighlstein and S. Zaks. Duality in chain ATM virtual path layouts. In *4th International Colloquium on Structural Information and Communication Complexity (SIROCCO)*, Monte Verita, Ascona, Switzerland, July 1997.

10. O. Gerstel, I. Cidon, and S. Zaks. The layout of virtual paths in ATM networks. *IEEE/ACM Transactions on Networking*, 4(6):873–884, 1996.

11. O. Gerstel, A. Wool, and S. Zaks. Optimal layouts on a chain ATM network. In *3rd Annual European Symposium on Algorithms*, volume LNCS 979, pages 508–522. Springer Verlag, 1995.

12. O. Gerstel and S. Zaks. The virtual path layout problem in fast networks. In *Symposium on Principles of Distributed Computing (PODC '94)*, pages 235–243, New York, USA, Aug. 1994. ACM Press.

13. M.-C. Heydemann, J.-C. Meyer, and D. Sotteau. On forwarding indices of networks. *Discrete Appl. Math.*, 23:103–123, 1989.

14. J.-W. Hong, K. Mehlhorn, and A. Rosenberg. Cost trade-offs in graph embeddings, with applications. *J. ACM*, 30:709–728, 1983.

15. D. Kofman and M. Gagnaire. *Réseaux Haut Débit, réseaux ATM, réseaux locaux et réseaux tout-optiques*. InterEditions-Masson, 1998. 2eme édition.

16. E. Kranakis, D. Krizanc, and A. Pelc. Hop-congestion trade-offs for high-speed networks. *International Journal of Foundations of Computer Science*, 8:117–126, 1997.

17. Y. Manoussakis and Z. Tuza. The forwarding index of directed networks. *Discrete Appl. Math.*, 68:279–291, 1996.

18. A. Rosenberg. Issues in the study of graph embeddings. In *Graph-Theoretic concepts in computer science*. Springer, 1980.

19. P. Solé. Expanding and forwarding. *Discrete Appl. Math.*, 58:67–78, 1995.

20. L. Stacho and I. Vrt'o. Virtual path layouts for some bounded degree networks. In *Structure, Information and Communication Complexity, 3rd Colloquium, SIROCCO*, pages 269–278. Carleton University Press, 1996.

21. S. Zaks. Path layout in ATM networks - a survey. In *The DIMACS Workshop on Networks in Distributed Computing, DIMACS Center, Rutgers University*, Oct. 1997. manuscript.

A Decision-Theoretic Approach to Reliable Message Delivery*

Francis Chu and Joseph Halpern

Department of Computer Science
Upson Hall, Cornell University
Ithaca, NY 14853-7501, USA
{fcc,halpern}@cs.cornell.edu

Abstract. We argue that the tools of decision theory need to be taken more seriously in the specification and analysis of systems. We illustrate this by considering a simple problem involving reliable communication, showing how considerations of utility and probability can be used to decide when it is worth sending heartbeat messages and, if they are sent, how often they should be sent.

1   Introduction

In designing and running systems, decisions must always be made: When should we garbage collect? Which transactions should be aborted? How big should the page table be? How often should we resend a message that is not acknowledged? Currently, these decisions seem to be made based on intuition and experience. However, studies suggest that decisions made in this way are prone to inconsistencies and other pitfalls. (See [RS89] for some common mistakes people make when making decisions.) Just as we would like to formally verify critical programs in order to avoid bugs, we would like to apply formal methods when making important decisions in order to avoid making suboptimal decisions. Mathematical logic has given us the tools to verify programs, among other things. There are also standard mathematical tools for making decisions, which come from *decision theory* [Res87]. We believe that these tools need to be taken more seriously in systems design. This paper can be viewed as a first step towards showing how this can be done and the benefits of so doing.

Before we delve into the technical details, let us consider a motivating example. Suppose Alice made an appointment with Bob and the two are supposed to meet at five. Alice shows up at five on the dot but Bob is nowhere in sight. At 5:20, Alice is getting restless. Should she stay or leave? That depends. Clearly, if Bob is an important business client and they are about to close a deal she might be willing to wait longer. On the other hand, if Bob is an in-law she never liked, she might be happy to have an excuse to leave. At a more abstract level,

---

* This work was supported in part by NSF grant IRI-96-25901 and by the Air Force Office of Scientific Research grant F49620-96-1-0323.

the *utility* of actually having the meeting is (or, at least, should be) an important ingredient in Alice's calculations. But there is another important ingredient: likelihood. If Alice meets Bob frequently, she may know something about how prompt he is. Does he typically arrive more or less on time (in which case the fact that he is twenty minutes late might indicate that he is unlikely to come at all) or is he someone who quite often shows up half an hour late? Not surprisingly, utilities and probabilities (as measures of likelihood) are the two key ingredients in decision theory.

While this example may seem far removed from computer systems, it can actually be viewed as capturing part of *atomic commitment* [SKS97]. To see this, suppose there is a coordinator p_c and two other processes p_a and p_b working on a transaction. To commit the transaction, the coordinator must get a YES vote from both p_a and p_b. Suppose the coordinator gets a YES from p_a, but hears nothing from p_b. Should it continue to wait or should it abort the transaction? The type of information we need to make this decision is precisely that considered in the Alice-Bob example above: probabilities and utilities. While it is obvious the amount of time Alice should wait depends on the situation, atomic commit protocols do not seem to take the importance of the transaction or the cost of waiting into account when deciding how long to wait. Instead, they typically have a fixed timeout period; if p_c has not heard from a process by this time, then the process is declared faulty and the transaction is aborted.

Although it is not done in atomic commit protocols, there certainly is an awareness that we need to take utilities or costs into account elsewhere in the database literature. For example, when a deadlock is detected in a database system, some transaction(s) must be rolled back to break the deadlock. How do we decide which ones? The textbook response [SKS97, p. 497] is that "[we] should roll back those transactions that will incur the minimum cost. Unfortunately, the term minimum cost is not a precise one." Typically, costs have been quantified in this context by considering things like how long the transaction has been running and how much longer it is likely to run, how many data items it has used, and how many transactions will be involved in a rollback. This is precisely the type of analysis to which the tools of decision theory can be applied. Ultimately we are interested in when each transaction of interest will complete its task. However, some transactions may be more important than others. Thus, ideally, we would like to attach a utility to each vector of completion times. Of course, we may be uncertain about the exact outcome (e.g., the exact running time of a transaction). This is one place where likelihood enters into the picture. Thus, in general, we will need both probabilities and utilities to decide which are the most appropriate transactions to abort.

Of course, obtaining the probabilities and utilities may in practice be difficult. Nevertheless, we may often be able to get reasonable estimates of them (see Section 6 for further discussion of this issue), and use them to guide our actions.

In this paper, we illustrate how decision theory can be used and some of the subtleties that arise in using it. We focus on one simple problem involving reliable communication. For ease of exposition, we make numerous simplifying assumption in our analysis. Despite these simplifying assumptions, we believe our results show that decision theory can be used in the specification and design of systems.

We are not the first to attempt to apply decision theory in computer science. Shenker and his colleagues [BBS98, BS98], for example, have used ideas from decision theory to analyze various network protocols; Microsoft has a Decision Theory and Adaptive Systems group that has successfully used decision theory in a number of applications, including troubleshooting problems with printers and intelligent user interfaces in Office '97 (for further details, see http://www.microsoft.com/research/dtg). However, our focus on writing specifications in terms of utility, and the subtleties involved with the particular application we consider here—reliable communication—make the thrust of this paper quite different from others in the literature.

The rest of this paper is organized as follows. We first give a brief review of briefly review some decision-theoretic concepts in Section 2. In Section 3 we describe the basic model and introduce the communication problem that serves as our running example. We show that the expected cost of even a single attempt at reliable communication is infinite if there is uncertainty about process failures. We then show in Section 4 how we can achieve reliable communication with finite expected cost by augmenting our system with *heartbeat* messages, in the spirit of [ACT97]. However, the heartbeat messages themselves come at a cost; this cost is investigated in Section 5. We offer some conclusions in Section 6.

2 A Brief Decision Theory Primer

The aim of decision theory is to help agents make rational decisions. There are a number of equivalent ways of formalizing the decision process. Here, we assume that (a) we have a set $\mathcal{O}$ of possible states of the world or *outcomes*, (b) the agent can assign a real-valued *utility* to each outcomes in $\mathcal{O}$, and (c) each action or choice a of the agent can be associated with a subset $\mathcal{O}_a$ of $\mathcal{O}$ and a probability distribution on $\mathcal{O}_a$. Roughly speaking, the utility associated with an outcome measures how happy the agent would be if that outcome occurred. Thus, utilities quantify the preferences of the agent. The agent prefers outcome o_1 to outcome o_2 iff the utility of o_1 is higher than that of o_2. The set $\mathcal{O}_a$ of outcomes associated with an action or choice a are the outcomes that might arise if a is performed or chosen; the probability distribution on $\mathcal{O}_a$ represents how likely each outcome is if a is performed. These are highly nontrivial assumptions, particularly the last two. We discuss them (and to what extent they are attainable in practice) in Section 6. For now though, we just focus on their consequences.

Recall that a random variable on the set $\mathcal{O}$ of outcomes is a function from $\mathcal{O}$ to the reals. Given a random variable X and a probability distribution Pr on the outcomes, the expected value of X with respect to Pr, denoted $\mathbf{E}_{\mathrm{Pr}}(X)$, is $\sum_{o \in \mathcal{O}} \mathrm{Pr}(o)X(o)$. (We drop the subscript Pr if it is clear from the context.) Note that utility is just a random variable on outcomes. Thus, with each action or choice, we have an associated expected utility, where the expectation is taken with respect to the probability distribution associated with the choice. The "rational choice" is then typically taken to be the one that maximizes expected utility. While other notions of rationality are clearly possible, for the purposes of this paper, we focus on expected utility maximization. Again, see Section 6 for further discussion of this issue.

We can now apply these notions to the Alice-Bob example from the introduction. One way of characterizing the possible outcomes is as pairs (m_a, m_b), where m_a is the number of minutes that Alice is prepared to wait and m_b is the time that Bob actually arrives. (If Bob does not arrive at all, we take $m_b = \infty$.) Thus, if $m_a \geq m_b$, then Alice and Bob meet at time m_b in the outcome (m_a, m_b). If $m_a < m_b$, then Alice leaves before Bob arrives. What is the utility of the outcome (m_a, m_b)? Alice and Bob may well assign different utilities to these outcomes. Since we are interested in Alice's decision, we consider Alice's utilities. A very simple assumption is that there is a fixed positive benefit **meet-Bob** to Alice if she actually meets Bob and a cost of **c-wait** for each minute she waits, and that these utilities are additive. Under this assumption, the utility of the outcome (m_a, m_b) is **meet-Bob** $+ m_b$**c-wait** if $m_a \geq m_b$ and m_a**c-wait** if $m_a < m_b$.

Of course, in practice, the utilities might be much more complicated and need not be additive. If Alice has a magazine to read, waiting for the first fifteen minutes might be relatively painless, but after that, she might get increasingly frustrated and the cost of waiting might increase exponentially, not linearly. The benefit to meeting Bob may also depend on the time they meet, independent of Alice's frustration. For example, if they have a dinner reservation for 6 PM at a restaurant half an hour away, the utility of meeting Bob may drop drastically after 5:30. Finally, the utility of (m_a, m_b) might depend on m_b even if $m_a < m_b$. For example, Alice might feel happier leaving at 5:15 if she knew that Bob would arrive at 6:30 than if she knew he would arrive at 5:16.

Once Alice has decided on a utility function, she has to decide what action to take. The only choice that Alice has is how long to wait. With each choice m_a, the set of possible outcomes consists of those of the form (m_a, m_b), for all possible choices of m_b. Thus, to compute the expected utility of the choice m_a, she needs a probability distribution over this set of outcomes, which effectively means a probability distribution over Bob's possible arrival times.

This approach of deciding at the beginning how long to wait may seem far removed from actual practice, but suppose instead Alice sent her assistant Cindy to meet Bob. Knowing something about Bob's timeliness (and lack thereof), she may well want to give Cindy instructions for how long to wait. Taking the cost of waiting to be linear in the amount of time that Cindy waits is now not so unreasonable, since while Cindy is tied up waiting for Bob, she is not able to help Alice in other ways. If Cindy goes to meet Bob frequently for Alice, it may make more sense for Alice just to tell Cindy her utility function, and let Cindy decide how long to wait based on the information she acquires regarding the likelihood of Bob arriving. Of course, once we think in terms of Alice sending an assistant, it is but a small step to think of Alice running an application, and giving the application instructions to help it decide how to act.

3 Reliable Communication

We now consider a problem that will serve as a running example throughout the rest of the paper. Consider a system S_0 consisting of a sender p and a receiver q connected by an unreliable bidirectional link, which drops messages with probability $0 < \gamma < 1$. If a message is not dropped, the transmission delay is τ. A process is *correct* if it never crashes. Let $x \in \{p, q\}$ and let α_x be the probability that x is correct. That is, if we select a run (uniformly) at random, the probability that x is correct in that run is α_x. In runs in which x is not correct, x crashes in each time unit with probability $\beta_x > 0$. We assume that events of p being correct or of crashing if it is not correct are both independent of the corresponding events for q.

We remark that the assumption that $\alpha_p = \alpha_q = 0$ is the one that seems most reasonable to us in practice—there is always a positive probability that a process will crash in any given round.[2] We allow the possibility that $\alpha_x \neq 0$ to facilitate comparison to most of the literature, which does not make probabilistic assumptions about failure. It also may be a useful way of modeling that processes stay up forever "for all practical purposes" (for example, if the system is replaced before the process crashes).

We want to implement a reliable link on top of the unreliable one. More precisely, suppose we use send/receive to denote the (unreliable) send and receive provided by the link. We want to implement reliable high-level SEND/RECEIVE actions as a sequence of send/receive events. What specification should SEND and RECEIVE satisfy? Clearly we do not want them to create messages out of whole cloth. Thus, we certainly want the following requirement:

S_0 If p SENDs m then p must also send m (possibly at some earlier time); if q RECEIVEs m from p, then q must also receive m from p and at some earlier time q must SEND m to q.

We shall implicitly assume S_0 without further comment throughout the paper.

The more interesting question is what reliability requirements should we impose on SEND/RECEIVE. Perhaps the most obvious requirement is

S_1. If p and q are correct and p SENDs m then q eventually RECEIVEs m.

Although S_1 is very much in the spirit of typical specifications, which only focuses on what happens if processes are correct, we would argue that it is rather uninteresting, for two reasons (which apply equally well to many other similar specifications). The first shows that it is too weak: If $\alpha_p = \alpha_q = 0$, then p and q are correct (i.e., never crash) with probability 0. Thus, specification S_1 is rather uninteresting in this case; it is saying something about a set of runs with vanishingly small likelihood. The second problem shows that S_1 is too strong: In runs where p and q are correct, there is a chance (albeit a small one) that p sends the message m infinitely often, yet q never RECEIVEs it. In this case S_1 is not satisfied.

---

[2] We assume that *round* k takes place between time $k - 1$ and k.

Of course, both of these problems are well known. The standard way to strengthen S_1 to deal with the first problem is to require only that p and q be correct for "sufficiently long", but then we need to quantify this; it is far from clear how to do so. The standard way to deal with the second problem is to restrict attention to *fair* runs, according to some notion of fairness [Fra86], and require only that q RECEIVE the message in fair runs. Fairness is a useful abstraction for helping us characterize conditions necessary to prove certain properties. However, what makes fairness of practical interest is that, under reasonable probabilistic assumptions, it holds with probability 1.

Our interest here, as should be evident from the introduction, is to make more explicit use of probability in writing a specification. For example, we can write a probabilistic specification like the following:

S_2. $\lim\limits_{t \to \infty} \Pr(q$ RECEIVEs m by time $t \mid p$ SENDs m at time 0 and p and q do not crash up to time $t) = 1$.

Requirement S_2 avoids the two problems we saw with S_1. It says, in a precise sense, that if p and q are up for sufficiently long, then q will RECEIVE m (where now "sufficiently long" is quantified probabilistically). Moreover, by making only a probabilistic statement, we do not have to worry about unfair runs; they occur with probability 0.

While we believe S_2 is a better specification of what is desired than S_1, it is is still not good enough for our purposes, since it does not take costs into account. For example, it is possible to satisfy S_2 using an algorithm that has p sending its Nth message only at time 2^N. This does not seem so reasonable. As a first step to thinking in terms of costs, consider the following specification:

S_3. The expected cost of a SEND is finite.

As stated, S_3 is not well defined, since we have not specified the cost model. We now consider a particularly simple cost model, much in the spirit of the Alice-Bob example discussed in Section 2. Suppose we have a protocol that implements SEND and RECEIVE. Its outcomes are just the possible *runs* or *executions*. We want to associate with each run its utility. There are two types of costs we will take into account: sending messages and waiting. The intuition is that each attempt to send a message consumes some system resources and each time unit spent waiting costs the user. The total cost is a weighted sum of the two; the utility of a run is its negative cost.

More precisely, let c-send and c-wait be constants representing the cost of sending a message and of waiting one time unit, respectively. Given a run r, let $n_{send}(r)$ be the number of invocations of send made by the protocol during run r. If one of the processes crashes in run r before q RECEIVEs m, let $t_{wait}(r)$ be the time of the crash. Otherwise, if q eventually RECEIVEs m in r, let $t_{wait}(r)$ be the time q RECEIVEs m. Let $t_{wait}(r) = \infty$ if both processes are correct and q never RECEIVEs m in r. The cost of waiting in run r is then $t_{wait}(r)$c-wait. (Implicitly, we assume here that p starts out wanting to SEND m to q at time 0.) Intuitively, $t_{wait}(r)$ measures the amount of time q has to wait until it RECEIVEs m. There is a subtle issue of how to define $t_{wait}(r)$ if one of the processes crashes before q RECEIVEs m. If q crashes first, then it seems reasonable to stop penalizing the protocol at this point; after all, after q has crashed, it is no longer waiting for the message. It is not so obvious what to do if p crashes first. For definiteness, we have taken an approach that is consistent with specifications like S_1 and have decided that the protocol has no further obligation when p crashes; we capture this by not charging for waiting time from that point on. While this choice suffices for our purposes, it is clearly not the only reasonable choice that could have been made. This just emphasizes some of the subtleties involved in defining a cost model.

We take the cost of run r to be c-SEND$(r) = n_{send}(r)$c-send$+t_{wait}(r)$c-wait. Note that c-SEND is a random variable on runs; S_3 says that we want $\mathbf{E}($c-SEND$)$ to be finite.

In this cost model, S_2 and S_3 are incomparable. Consider a protocol where p sends m to q in every round until it receives an ACK message, and q sends its kth ACK message N^k rounds after receiving m for the kth time, where $N\gamma > 1$. It is easy to see that this protocol satisfies S_2 but not S_3. On the other hand, suppose $\alpha_p = \alpha_q = 0$. Then it is easy to see that the trivial protocol (where no messages are sent at all) satisfies S_3. One of p or q will crash with probability $\beta_p + \beta_q - \beta_p\beta_q$, so one of them is expected to crash by time $1/(\beta_p + \beta_q - \beta_p\beta_q)$. Thus, $\mathbf{E}($c-SEND$) = $ c-wait$/(\beta_p + \beta_q - \beta_p\beta_q)$ for the trivial protocol, so the trivial protocol satisfies S_3, although it clearly does not satisfy S_2.

The following theorem characterizes when S_3 is implementable, using the cost model above. Moreover, it shows that with this cost model, when S_3 is satisfiable, there are in fact protocols that satisfy S_3 and S_2 simultaneously.

Theorem 1. *If* c-SEND *characterizes the cost of a run, then* S_3 *is implementable in* S_0 *iff* $\alpha_p = 0$ *or* $\alpha_q = 0$ *or* $\alpha_q = 1$ *or* $\alpha_p = 1$. *Moreover, if* $\alpha_p = 0$ *or* $\alpha_q = 0$ *or* $\alpha_q = 1$ *or* $\alpha_p = 1$, *then there is a protocol that satisfies both* S_2 *and* S_3.

Proof: Suppose $\alpha_q = 1$ or $\alpha_p = 0$. Consider the protocol in which p SENDs m by sending m to q at every round it gets ACK(m) from q and q sends ACK(m) whenever it receives m. Thus, the SEND starts when p first sends m and ends when p receives the first ACK(m) from q; the RECEIVE starts and ends the first time q receives m. To see that this works, first consider the case that $\alpha_q = 1$. Let C_p be the set of runs in which p receives an ACK(m) from q before crashing. Clearly the probability that p sends a message m which is received by q is $1 - \gamma$; the probability that both m is received by q and the corresponding ACK(m) is received by p is $(1 - \gamma)^2$. Suppose the N_1th copy of m is the one first received by q and the N_2th copy is the one whose acknowledgement is first received by p. We expect N_1 to be $\frac{1}{(1-\gamma)}$ in runs of C_p and N_2 to be $\frac{1}{(1-\gamma)^2}$. Since a message takes τ to arrive and messages are sent in every round, it follows that $\mathbf{E}(t_{wait}|C_p) = \frac{1}{(1-\gamma)}+\tau$. Moreover, since p stops sending when it receives ACK(m) from q, it will stop 2τ rounds after sending the N_2th copy of m. Thus, p expects to send $\frac{1}{(1-\gamma)^2} + 2\tau - 1$ messages in runs of C_p. We expect q to receive $1 - \gamma$ of these messages and then send an ACK(m) in response to each of them. Thus, q

expects to send $\frac{1}{(1-\gamma)} + (2\tau - 1)(1 - \gamma)$ messages in runs of C_p. We conclude that $\mathbf{E}(n_{\text{send}}|C_p) = \frac{1}{(1-\gamma)} + \frac{1}{(1-\gamma)^2} + (2\tau - 1)(2 - \gamma)$.

It is easy to see that $\mathbf{E}(t_{wait}|\overline{C_p}) \leq \mathbf{E}(t_{wait}|C_p)$, since in runs of $\overline{C_p}$, p crashes before it receives an ACK(m) from q. Similarly, $\mathbf{E}(n_{\text{send}}|\overline{C_p}) \leq \mathbf{E}(n_{\text{send}}|C_p)$. It follows that $\mathbf{E}(\text{c-SEND}) \leq (\frac{1}{(1-\gamma)} + \frac{1}{(1-\gamma)^2} + (2\tau - 1)(2 - \gamma))\text{c-send} + (\frac{1}{(1-\gamma)} + \tau)\text{c-wait}$. Thus, this protocol satisfies $\mathbf{S}_3$.

For $\mathbf{S}_2$, note that for $t \geq \tau$, the probability that q does not RECEIVE m by time t given that both p and q are still up, is $\gamma^{t-\tau}$. Thus $\mathbf{S}_2$ is also satisfied.

Now consider the case that $\alpha_p = 0$. Note that in this case, p is expected to crash at time $1/\beta_p$. Thus, $\mathbf{E}(t_{wait}) \leq 1/\beta_p$ and $\mathbf{E}(n_{\text{send}}) \leq 2/\beta_p$ (since each time unit p is up it sends m exactly once and q will send at most one ACK(m) in response), regardless of whether q is correct. Thus $\mathbf{E}(\text{c-SEND})$ is again finite. The argument that $\mathbf{S}_2$ is satisfied is the same as before.

Now suppose $\alpha_p = 1$ or $\alpha_q = 0$. These cases are somewhat analogous to the ones above, except we need a "receiver-driven" protocol. Consider a protocol in which q continually queries p until it gets a message from p. More precisely, if we want to SEND/RECEIVE a number of messages, we assume that each query is numbered. The kth SEND starts when p gets the first query numbered k from q and ends with the send event just prior to when p receives the first query numbered $k+1$ from q. (Note that this means that p does not know that the kth SEND has ended until the $(k + 1)$th begins.) The kth RECEIVE starts when q sends the first query numbered k to p and ends when q receives the kth message from p. By reasoning similar to the previous cases, we can show that $\mathbf{E}(n_{\text{send}})$ and $\mathbf{E}(t_{wait})$ are both finite and that $\mathbf{S}_2$ is satisfied.

We now turn to the negative result. We show that c-SEND $= \infty$ with some probability $\varepsilon > 0$. (Note that this is stronger than we need.) Suppose $0 < \alpha_p < 1$ and $0 < \alpha_q < 1$. Let P be a protocol. Let $R_1 = \{r : q \text{ crashes at time } 0 \text{ and } p \text{ is correct in } r\}$. Note that p will do the same thing in all runs in R_1. Either p stops sending messages after some time t or p never stops sending messages. If p never stops, then $n_{\text{send}} = \infty$ for each $r \in R_1$ and we can take ε to be $\alpha_p(1 - \alpha_q)\beta_q$, the probability of R_1. Now suppose p stops after time t. Let $R_2 = \{r : p \text{ crashes at time } 0 \text{ and } q \text{ is correct in } r\}$. Note that q will do the same thing in all runs of R_2. Either q stops sending messages after some time t' or q never stops sending messages. If q never stops, the same reasoning as above works. So suppose q stops after time t'. Let $t'' \geq t, t'$. Consider $R_3 = \{r : \text{both processes are correct and all messages up to time } t'' \text{ are lost in } r\}$. Let n_p be the number of messages sent by p and n_q be the number of messages sent by q. Then $t_{wait} = \infty$ for all $r \in R_3$ and we can take ε to be $\alpha_p\alpha_q\gamma^{n_p+n_q}$. ∎

Of course, once we think in terms of utility-based specifications like $\mathbf{S}_3$, we do not want to know just whether a protocol implements $\mathbf{S}_3$. We are in a position to compare the performance of different protocols that implement $\mathbf{S}_3$ (or of variants of one protocol that all implement $\mathbf{S}_3$) by considering their expected utility. Let $\mathbf{P}_s^\delta$ and $\mathbf{P}_r^\delta$ be generalizations (in the sense that they send messages every δ rounds where δ need not be 1) of the sender-driven and receiver-driven protocols from

Theorem 1, respectively. Let P_{tr} denote the trivial (i.e., "do nothing") protocol. We use $\mathbf{E}^P$ to denote the expectation operator determined by the probability measure on runs induced by using protocol P. Thus, for example, $\mathbf{E}^{P_s^\delta}(n_{\text{send}})$ is the expected number of messages sent by P_s^δ. If $\alpha_p = \alpha_q = 0$, then P_s^δ, P_r^δ, and P_{tr} all satisfy $\mathbf{S_3}$ (although P_{tr} does not satisfy $\mathbf{S_2}$). Which is better?

In practice, process failures and link failures are very unlikely events. So we assume, for the rest of the paper, that β_p, β_q, and γ are all very small, so that we can ignore sums of products of these terms (with coefficients like $2\tau^2$, δ, etc.).[3] (Informally, products involving α_p, α_q, and γ are $O(\varepsilon)$ terms and $2\tau^2$, δ, etc., are $O(1)$ terms.) We write $t_1 \approx t_2$ if t_1 and t_2 differ by an expression that is the sum of products involving (at least) one of β_p, β_q or γ. Note that we do not assume expressions like β_p/β_q and β_q/β_p are small.

Proposition 2. *If $\alpha_p = \alpha_q = 0$, then*

$$\mathbf{E}^{P_{tr}}(t_{wait}) \approx \tfrac{1}{\beta_p + \beta_q} \quad \mathbf{E}^{P_s^\delta}(t_{wait}) \approx \tau \qquad \mathbf{E}^{P_r^\delta}(t_{wait}) \approx 2\tau$$

$$\mathbf{E}^{P_{tr}}(n_{\text{send}}) = 0 \quad \mathbf{E}^{P_s^\delta}(n_{\text{send}}) \approx \tfrac{\tau\beta_q}{\delta\beta_p} + 2\left\lceil\tfrac{2\tau}{\delta}\right\rceil \quad \mathbf{E}^{P_r^\delta}(n_{\text{send}}) \approx \tfrac{\tau\beta_p}{\delta\beta_q} + 2\left\lceil\tfrac{2\tau}{\delta}\right\rceil.$$

Proof: See the full paper. ∎

Note that the expected cost of messages for P_s^δ is the same as that for P_r^δ, except that the roles of β_p and β_q are reversed. The expected time cost of P_r^δ is roughly τ higher than that of P_s^δ, because q cannot RECEIVE m before time 2τ with a receiver-driven protocol, whereas q may RECEIVE m as early as τ with a sender-driven protocol. This says that the choice between the sender-driven and receiver-driven protocol should be based largely on the relative probability of failure of p and q. It also suggests that we should take δ very large to minimize costs. (Intuitively, the larger δ, the lower the message costs in the case that q crashes before acknowledging p's message.) This conclusion (which may not seem so reasonable) is essentially due to the fact that we are examining a single SEND/RECEIVE in isolation, As we shall see in Section 5, this conclusion is no longer justified once we consider repeated invocations of SENDs/RECEIVEs. Finally, note that if the cost of messages is high, waiting is cheap, and q is quite likely to fail (relative to p), then p is better off (according to this cost measure) not sending any messages at all (i.e., using P_{tr}) than sending them in the hope of getting a response for q.

Thus, as far as $\mathbf{S_3}$ is concerned, there are times when P_{tr} is better than P_s^δ or P_r^δ. How much of a problem is it that P_{tr} does not satisfy $\mathbf{S_2}$? Our claim is that if this desideratum (i.e., $\mathbf{S_2}$) is important, then it should be reflected in the cost measure. While the cost measure we have chosen does does take into account waiting time, it does not penalize it sufficiently to give us $\mathbf{S_2}$. It is not too hard to find a cost measure that captures $\mathbf{S_2}$. For example, suppose we take c-SEND$^*(r) = N^{t_{wait}}$, where $N(1 - \beta_p - \beta_q + \beta_p\beta_q) > 1$.[4]

---

[3] Of course, with a little more effort, we can do more exact calculations, but doing this yields no further insight and results in unwieldy expressions.

[4] Note that $\mathbf{S_3}$ may be unsatisfiable for certain values of N.

Proposition 3. *If* c-SEND* *characterizes the cost of a run, then* S_3 *implies* S_2.

Proof: See the full paper. ∎

The moral here is that S_3 gives us the flexibility to specify what really matters in a protocol, by appropriately describing the cost measure.

4 Using Heartbeats

We saw in Section 3 that S_3 is not implementable if we are not certain about the correctness of the processes (i.e., if the probability that they are correct is strictly between 0 and 1). Aguilera, Chen, and Toueg [ACT97] (ACT from now on) suggest an approach that avoids this problem, using *heartbeat* messages.[5] Informally, a heartbeat from process i is a message sent by i to all other processes to tell them that it is still alive. ACT show that there is a protocol using heartbeats that achieves *quiescent* reliable communication; i.e., in every run of the protocol, only finitely many messages are required to achieve reliable communication (not counting the heartbeats). Moreover, they show that, in a precise sense, quiescent reliable communication is not possible if processes may not crash and communication is unreliable, a result much in the spirit of the negative part of Theorem 1.[6] In this section, we show that (using the linear cost model of the previous section) we can use heartbeats to implement S_3 for all values of α_p and α_q.

For the purposes of this paper, assume that processes send a message we call HBMSG to each other every δ time units. Protocol RC in Figure 1 is a protocol for reliable communication based on ACT's protocol. (It is not as general as theirs, but it retains all the features relevant to us.) Briefly, what happens according to this protocol is that the failure detector layer of q sends HBMSG to the corresponding layer of p periodically. If p wants to SEND m, p checks to see if any (new) HBMSG has arrived; if so p sends m to q, provided it has not already received an ACK from q; q sends ACK(m) every time it receives m. Note that according to this protocol, q does not send any HBMSGs. That is the job of the failure detection layer, not the job of the protocol. We assume that the protocol is built on top of a failure detection mechanism. By using the cost measure of the previous section, we actually do not count the cost of HBMSGs. It is also worth noting that this is a sender-driven protocol, quite like that given in the proof of Theorem 1. It is straightforward to also design a receiver-driven protocol using heartbeats.

---

[5] The heartbeat messages are used to implement what they call a *heartbeat failure detector*, which is a distributed oracle.

[6] ACT actually show that their impossibility result holds even if there is only one process failure, only finitely many messages can be lost, and the processes have access to a *strong* failure detector, which means that eventually every faulty process is permanently suspected and at least one correct process is never suspected. The model used by ACT is somewhat different from the one we are considering, but we can easily modify their results to fit our model.

The sender's protocol:	The receiver's protocol:
1. **while** ¬receive(ACK(m)) **do**	1. **while true do**
2. **if** receive(HBMSG) **then**	2. **if** receive(m) **then**
3. send(m)	3. send(ACK(m))
4. **fi**	4. **fi**
5. **od**	5. **od**

Fig. 1. Protocol RC

We now want to show that RC implements S_3 and get a good estimate of the actual cost.

Theorem 4. *If c-SEND characterizes the cost of a run, then Protocol RC implements S_3 in S_0. Moreover,* $\mathbf{E}(t_{wait}) \approx 2\tau$ *and* $\mathbf{E}(n_{send}) \approx 2\left\lceil \frac{2\tau}{\delta} \right\rceil$, *so that* $\mathbf{E}(\text{c-SEND}) \approx 2\tau\mathbf{c\text{-}wait} + 2\left\lceil \frac{2\tau}{\delta} \right\rceil \mathbf{c\text{-}send}$.

Proof: See the full paper. ∎

The analysis of RC is much like that of P_s^δ in Proposition 2. Indeed, in the case that $\alpha_p = \alpha_q = 0$, the two protocols are almost identical. The waiting time is roughly τ more in RC, since p does not start sending until it receives the first HBMSG from q. On the other hand, we are better off using RC if q crashes before acknowledging p's message. In this case, with P_s^δ, p continues to send until it crashes, while with RC, it stops sending (since it does not get any HBMSGs from q). This leads to an obvious question: Is it really worth sending heartbeats? Of course, if both α_p and α_q are between 0 and 1, we need heartbeats or something like them to get around the impossibility result of Theorem 1. But if $\alpha_p = \alpha_q = 0$, then we need to look carefully at the relative size of **c-send** and **c-wait** to decide which protocol has the lower expected cost.

This suggests that the decision of whether to implement a heartbeat layer must take probabilities and utilities seriously, even if we do not count either the overhead of building such a layer or the cost of heartbeats. What happens if we take the cost of heartbeats into account? This is the subject of the next section.

5 The Cost of Heartbeats

In the last section we showed that S_3 is achievable with the help of heartbeats. When we computed the expected costs, however, we were not counting the HBMSGs because the heartbeats were not sent by the protocol. This cost model is appropriate if we consider the heartbeat layer as given, and are just interesting in designing a protocol that takes advantage of it. But it is not appropriate if we are trying to decide whether to use a heartbeat protocol at all or how frequently heartbeats should be sent.

As evidence of this, note that it is immediate from Theorem 4 that under the cost model we have been using, the choice of δ that minimizes the expected cost is clearly at most $2\tau + 1$. Intuitively, if we do not charge for heartbeats, there is no incentive to space them out. On the other hand, if we do charge for heartbeats, then typically we will be charging for heartbeats that are sent long after a given invocation of RC has completed.

The whole point of heartbeat messages is that they are meant to be used, not just by one invocation of a protocol, but by multiple invocations of (possibly) many protocols. We would expect that the optimal frequency of heartbeats should depend in part on how often the protocols that use them are invoked. The picture we have is that the RC protocol is invoked from time to time, by different processes in the system. It may well be that various invocations of it are running simultaneously. All these invocations share the heartbeat messages, so their cost can be spread over all of them. If invocations occur often, then there will be few "wasted" heartbeats between invocations, and the analysis of the previous subsection gives a reasonably accurate reading of the costs involved. On the other hand, if δ is small and invocations are infrequent, then there will be many "wasted" heartbeats. We would expect that if there are infrequent invocations, then heartbeats should be spaced further apart.

We now consider a setting that takes this into account. For simplicity, we continue to assume that there are only two processes, p and q, but we now allow both p and q to invoke RC. (It is possible to do this with n processes, but the two-process case suffices to illustrate the main point, which is that the optimal δ should depend on how often RC is invoked.) We assume that each process, while it is running, invokes RC with probability σ at each time unit. Thus, informally, at every round, each running process tosses a coin with probability of σ of landing heads. If it lands heads, the process then invokes RC with the other as the recipient.

Roughly speaking, in computing the cost of a run, we consider the cost of each invocation of RC together with the cost of all the heartbeat messages sent in the run. Our interest will then be in the cost *per invocation of* RC. Thus, we apportion the cost of the heartbeat messages among the invocations of RC. If there are relatively few invocations of RC, then there will be many "wasted" heartbeat messages, whose cost will need to be shared among them.

For simplicity, let us assume that each time RC is invoked, a different message is sent. (For example, messages could be numbered and include the name of the sender and recipient.) We say RC(m) *is invoked at time* t_1 *in* r if at time t_1 some process x first executes line 1 of the code of the sender with message m. This invocation of RC *completes* at time t_2 if the last message associated with the invocation (either a copy of m or a copy of ACK(m)) is sent at time t_2. If the receiver crashed before x invokes RC(m), we take $t_2 = t_1$ (that is, the invocation completes as soon as it starts in this case).

The processes will (eventually) stop sending m or ACK(m) if either process crashes or if x stops sending m because it received ACK(m). Thus, with probability 1, all invocations of RC will eventually complete. (Note that we are still not counting heartbeat messages.) Let $\mathbf{cmp}(r, T)$ be the number of invocations of RC that have completed by time T in r; let $\mathbf{c\text{-}SEND}(r, T)$ be the cost of these invocations. Let $c\text{-hb}(r, T)$ be the cost of the HBMSGs up to time T in r. This is simply the number of HBMSGs sent up to time T (which we denote by $n\text{-hb}(r, T)$) multiplied by $c\text{-send}$. Let $t\text{-cst}(r, T) = c\text{-SEND}(r, T) + c\text{-hb}(r, T)$. Finally, let $c\text{-SEND}'(r) = \limsup_{T \to \infty} t\text{-cst}(r, T)/(\text{cmp}(r, T) + 1)$, where $\limsup$ denotes the limit of the supremum, that is, $\lim_{T' \to \infty} \sup_{0 \leq T \leq T'} t\text{-cst}(r, T)/(\text{cmp}(r, T) + 1)$.[7] Thus $c\text{-SEND}'(r)$ is essentially the average cost per invocation of RC, taking heartbeats into account. We write $\limsup$ instead of $\lim$ since the limit may not exist in general. (However, the proof of the next theorem shows that in fact, with probability 1, the limit does exist.)

For the following result, we assume that $\sqrt{\beta_p}$ and $\sqrt{\beta_q}$ are also $O(\varepsilon)$.

Theorem 5. $E(c\text{-SEND}') \approx ((1 - \alpha_p)(1 - \alpha_q)\lambda + \alpha_p\alpha_q)\left(2\left\lceil\frac{2\tau}{\delta}\right\rceil c\text{-send} + (2\tau + \frac{\delta}{2})c\text{-wait}\right) + \frac{1}{\delta\sigma}c\text{-send}$, where $0 < \lambda < 1$ is a constant that depends only on β_p and β_q.[8]

Proof: See the full paper. ∎

Note that with this cost model, we have a real decision to make in terms of how frequently to send heartbeats. As before, there is some benefit to making $\delta > 2\tau$, to minimize the number of useless messages sent when RC is invoked (that is, messages sent by the sender before receiving the receiver's acknowledgement). Also, by making δ larger we will send fewer heartbeat messages between invocations of RC. On the other hand, if we make δ too large, then the sender may have to wait a long time after invoking RC before it can send a message to the receiver (since messages are only sent upon receipt of a heartbeat). Intuitively, the greater $c\text{-wait}$ is relative to $c\text{-send}$, the smaller we should make δ. Clearly we can find an optimal choice for δ by standard calculus.

In the model just presented, if $c\text{-wait}$ is large enough relative to $c\text{-send}$, we will take δ to be 1. Taking δ this small is clearly inappropriate once we consider a more refined model, where there are buffers that may overflow. In this case, both the probability of message loss and the time for message delivery will depend on the number of messages in transit. The basic notions of utility still apply, of course, although the calculations become more complicated. This just emphasizes the obvious point is that in deciding what value (or values) δ should have, we need to carefully look at the actual system and the cost model.

6 Discussion

We have tried to argue here for the use of decision theory both in the specification and the design of systems. Our (admittedly rather simple) analysis already shows both how decision theory can help guide the decision made and how much

---

[7] By adding 1 to the denominator, we guarantee it is never 0; adding 1 also simplifies one of the technical calculations needed in the proof of Theorem 5.

[8] Intuitively, λ depends on the probability that both p and q are up relative to the probability that one is up and the other down.

the decision depends on the cost model. None of our results are deep; the cost model just makes precise what could already have been seen from an intuitive calculation. But this is precisely the point. By writing our specification in terms of costs, we can make the intuitive calculations precise. Moreover, the specification forces us to make clear exactly what the cost model is and encourages the elicitation of utilities from users. We believe these are both important features. It is important for the user (and system designer) to spend time thinking about what the important attributes of the system are and to decide on preferences between various tradeoffs.

A possible future direction is to study standard problems in the literature (e.g., Consensus, Byzantine Agreement, Atomic Broadcast, etc.) and recast the specifications in utility-theoretic terms. One way to do this is to replace a liveness requirement by an unbounded increasing cost function (which is essentially the "cost of waiting") and replace a safety requirement by a large penalty. Once we do this, we can analyze the algorithms that have been used to solve these problems, and see to what extent they are optimal given reasonable assumptions about probabilities and utilities.

While we believe that there is a great deal of benefit to be gained from analyzing systems in terms of utility, it is quite often a nontrivial matter. Among the most significant difficulties are the following:

1. Where are the utilities coming from? It is far from clear that a user can or is willing to assign a real-valued utility to all possible outcomes in practice. There may be computational issues (for example, the set of outcomes can be enormous) as well as psychological issues. While the agent may be prepared to assign qualitative utilities like "good", "fair", or "bad", he may not be prepared to assign .7. While to some extent the system can convert qualitative utilities to a numerical representation, this conversion may not precisely captures the user's intent. There are also nontrivial user-interface issues involved in eliciting utilities from users. In light of this, we need to be very careful if results depend in sensitive ways on the details of the utilities.

2. Where are the probabilities coming from? We do not expect users to be experts at probability. Rather, we expect the system to be gathering statistics and using them to estimate the probabilities. Of course, someone still has to tell the system what statistics to gather. Moreover, our statistics may be so sparse that we cannot easily obtain a reliable estimate of the probability.

3. Why is it even appropriate to maximize expected utility? There are times when it is far from clear that this is the best thing to do, especially if our estimates of the probability and utility are suspect. For example, suppose one action has a guaranteed utility of 100 (on some appropriate scale), while another has an expected utility of 101, but has a nontrivial probability of having utility 0. If the probabilities and utilities that were used to calculate the expectation are reliable, and we anticipate performing these actions frequently, then there is a good case to be made for taking the action with the higher expected utility. On the other hand, if the underlying numbers are suspect, then the action with the guaranteed utility might well be preferable.

We see these difficulties not as ones that should prevent us from using decision theory, but rather as directions for further research. It may be possible in many cases to learn a user's utility. Moreover, we expect that in many applications, except for a small region of doubt, the choice of which decision to make will be quite robust, in that perturbations to the probability and utility will not change the decision. Even in cases where perturbations do change the decision, both decisions will have roughly equal expected utility. Thus, as long as we can get somewhat reasonable estimates of the probability and utility, decision theory may have something to offer.

Clearly another important direction for research is to consider *qualitative decision theory*, where both our measures of utility and probability and more qualitative, and not necessarily real numbers. This is, in fact, an active area of current research, as the bibliography of 290 papers at http://walrus.stanford.edu/diglib /csbibliography/Ai/qualitative.decision.theory.html attests. Note that once we use more qualitative notions, then we may not be able to compute expected utilities at all (since utilities may not be numeric) let alone take the action with maximum expected utility, so we will have to consider other decision rules.

Finally, we might consider what would be an appropriate language to specify and reason about utilities, both for the user and the system designer.

While it is clear that there is still a great deal of work to be done in order to use decision-theoretic techniques in systems design and specification, we hope that this discussion has convinced the reader of the promise of the approach.

Acknowledgements

We thank Sam Toueg for numerous discussions regarding heartbeats and Jim Gray for giving us some insight on costs in database computations and for pointing out the use of costs in deadlock detection.

References

[ACT97] M. K. Aguilera, W. Chen, and S. Toueg. Heartbeat: a timeout-free failure detector for quiescent reliable communication. In *Proc. 11th Int. Workshop on Distributed Algorithms*, pages 126–140. Springer-Verlag, 1997. A full version is available as Cornell University Technical Report 97-1631, 1997.

[BBS98] S. Bajaj, L. Breslau, and S. Shenker. Uniform versus priority dropping for layered video. Submitted for publication, 1998.

[BS98] L. Breslau and S. Shenker. Best-effort versus reservations: A simple comparative analysis. Submitted for publication, 1998.

[Fra86] N. Francez. *Fairness*. Springer-Verlag, Berlin/New York, 1986.

[Res87] M. D. Resnik. *Choices: An Introduction to Decision Theory*. University of Minnesota Press, 1987.

[RS89] J. E. Russo and P. J. H. Schoemaker. *Decision Traps: Ten Barriers to Brilliant Decision-Making and How to Overcome Them*. Doubleday, 1989.

[SKS97] A. Silberschatz, H. Korth, and S. Sudarshan. *Database System Concepts*. McGraw-Hill, third edition, 1997.

Propagation and Leader Election in a Multihop Broadcast Environment

Israel Cidon and Osnat Mokryn

Department of Electrical Engineering
Technion - Israel Institute of Technology
cidon@tera.technion.ac.il, osnaty@tx.technion.ac.il

Abstract. The paper addresses the problem of solving classic distributed algorithmic problems under the practical model of Broadcast Communication Networks. Our main result is a new Leader Election algorithm, with $O(n)$ time complexity and $O(n \cdot \lg(n))$ message transmission complexity. Our distributed solution uses a special form of the propagation of information with feedback (PIF) building block tuned to the broadcast media, and a special *counting and joining* approach for the election procedure phase. The latter is required for achieving the linear time.

It is demonstrated that the broadcast model requires solutions which are different from the classic point to point model.

Keywords: Broadcast networks, distributed, leader election.

1 Introduction

Broadcast networks are often used in modern communication systems. A common broadcast network is a single hop shared media system where a transmitted message is heard by all nodes. Such networks include local area networks like Ethernet and token-ring, as well as satellite and radio networks. In this paper we consider a more complex environment, in which a transmitted message is heard only by a group of neighboring nodes. Such environments include: Multihop packet radio networks, discussed for example in [7], [5]; Multichannel networks, in which nodes may communicate via several non-interfering communication channels at different bands [11]; and a wireless multistation backbone system for mobile communication [3].

Since such networks are very important in the emerging area of backbone and wireless networks, it is important to design efficient algorithms for such environments. We address here the problem of finding efficient algorithms for classic network problems such as propagation of information and leader election in the new models.

In the classic model of network communication, the problem of leader election is reducible to the problem of finding a spanning tree. The classic model is a graph of n nodes and m edges, with the nodes representing computers that communicate via the edges which represent point-to-point bidirectional links. Gallager, Humblet and Spira introduced in their pioneering work [9] a distributed minimum weight spanning tree (MST) algorithm, with $O(n \cdot \lg(n))$ time and $O(n \cdot \lg(n) + 2 \cdot m)$ message complexity. This algorithm is based on election phases in which the number of leadership candidates (each represents a fragment) is at least halved. Gallager et al. ensured a lower bound on a fragments level. In a later work, Chin and Ting [4] improved Gallager's algorithm to $O(n \cdot lg^*(n))$ time, estimating the fragment's size and updating its level accordingly, thus making a fragment's level dependent upon its estimated size. In [1], Awerbuch proposed an optimal $O(n)$ time and $O(n \cdot lg(n) + 2 \cdot m)$ message complexity algorithm, constructed in three phases. In the first phase, the number of nodes in the graph is established. In the second phase, a MST is built according to Gallager's algorithm, until the fragments reach the size of $n/lg(n)$. Finally, a second MST phase is performed, in which waiting fragments can upgrade their level, thus addressing a problem of long chains that existed in [9], [4]. A later article by Faloutsos and Molle ([8]) addressed potential problems in Awerbuch's algorithm. In a recent work Garay, Kutten and Peleg ([10]) suggested an algorithm for leader election in $O(D)$ time, where D is the diameter of the graph. In order to achieve the $O(D)$ time, they use two phases. The first is a controlled version of the GHS algorithm. The second phase uses a centralized algorithm, which concentrates on eliminating candidate edges in a pipelined approach. The message complexity of the algorithm is $O(m + n \cdot \sqrt{n})$.

It is clear that all of the above election algorithms are based on the fact that sending different messages to distinct neighbors is as costly a sending them the same message, which is not the case in our model. Our model enables us to take advantage of the broadcast topology, thus reducing the number of sent messages and increasing parallelism in the execution. Note, that while we can use distinct transmissions to neighbors it increases our message count due to unnecessary reception at all neighbors.

Algorithms that are based on the GHS algorithm, chose a leader via constructing a MST in the graph. First these algorithms distinguish between internal and external fragment edges, and between MST-chosen and rejected edges. An agreement on a minimal edge between adjacent fragments is done jointly by the two fragments, while other adjacent fragments may wait until they join and increase in level. In this paper it is seen that the broadcast environment requires a different approach, that will increase parallelism in the graph.

Our main goal is to develop efficient distributed algorithms for the new model. We approach this goal in steps. First, we present an algorithm for the basic task of Propagation of Information with Feedback (PIF) [12] with $O(n)$ time and message transmission complexity. In the classic point-to-point model the PIF is an expensive building block due to its message complexity. The native broadcast enables us to devise a message efficient *fragment-PIF* algorithm, which provides a fast communication between clusters. Next, using the *fragment-PIF* as a building block, we present a new distributed algorithm for Leader Election, with $O(n)$ time and $O(n \cdot lg(n))$ message transmission complexity. In order to prove correctness and establish the time and message complexity, we define and use an equivalent high level algorithm for fragments, presented as a state machine.

The paper is constructed as follows: Section 2 defines the the model. Section 3 presents a PIF algorithm suited for the model. Section 4 introduces a distributed

Leader Election algorithm for this model and shows and proves properties of the algorithm. We conclude with a summary of open issues.

2   The Model

A broadcast network can be viewed as a connected graph $G(V, E)$, where V is the set of nodes. Nodes communicate by transmitting messages. If two nodes are able to hear each other's transmissions, we define this capability by connecting them with an edge. A transmitted message is heard only by a group of neighboring nodes. In this paper we use the terms message and message transmission interchangeably. E is the set of edges. All edges are bidirectional. In the case of radio networks, we assume equal transmission capacity on both sides.

Our model assumes that every node knows the number of its neighbors. The originator of a received message is known either by the form of communication, or by indication in the message's header.

In the model, a transmitted message arrives in arbitrary final time to all the sender's neighbors. Consecutive transmissions of a node arrive to all its neighbors in the same order they were originated, and without errors. We further assume that there are no link or node failures, and additions.

It should be noted, that we assume that the media access and data link problems, which are part of OSI layer 2 are already solved. The algorithms presented here are at higher layers, and therefore assume the presence of a reliable data link protocol which delivers messages reliably and in order. Bar-Yehuda, Goldreich and Itai ([2]) have addressed a lower level model of a multihop radio environment even with no *collision detection* mechanism. In their model, concurrent receptions at a node are lost. We assume models which are derived from conflict free allocation networks such as TDMA, FDMA or CDMA cellular networks, which maintain a concurrent broadcast environment with no losses.

3   Basic Propagation of Information Algorithms in our Model

The problem introduced here is of an arbitrary node that has a message it wants to transmit to all the nodes in the graph. The solution for this problem for the classic model of communication networks was introduced by [12], and is called Propagation of Information (PI). The initiating node is ensured that after it has sent the message to its neighbors, all the nodes in the network will receive the message in finite time. An important addition to the PI algorithm is to provide the initiator node with knowledge of the propagation termination, i.e., when it is ensured that all the nodes in the network have received the message. This is done with a feedback process, also described in [12] and added to the PI protocol. We describe a Propagation of Information with Feedback (PIF) algorithm for broadcast networks. Because of the unique character of broadcast networks, it is very easy to develop a PI algorithm for this environment. When a node gets a message for the first time it simply sends it once to all neighbors, and then ignores any additional messages. In the feedback process messages are sent backwards over a virtual spanned tree in the broadcast network, to the initiator node.

3.1 Algorithm Description

We describe here the Propagation of Information with Feedback. A message in this algorithm is of the form: *MSG(target, l, parent)*, where *target* specifies the target node or nodes. A null value in the *target* header field indicates a broadcast to all neighboring nodes, and is used when broadcasting the message. The *parent* field specifies the identity of the parent of the node that sends the message. It is important to note that a node receives a message only when addressed in the *target* header field by its *identification* number or when this field is null. The *l* field determines the sender's identity. The initiator, called the *source* node, broadcasts a message, thus starting the propagation. Each node, upon receiving the message for the first time, stores the *identity* of the sender from which it got the message, which originated at the *source*, and broadcasts the message. The feedback process starts at the *leaf* nodes, which are childless nodes on the virtual tree spanned by the PIF algorithm. A *leaf* node that is participating in the propagation from the *source*, and has received the message from all of its neighboring nodes, sends back an acknowledgment message, called a feedback message, which is directed to its *parent* node. A node that got feedback messages from all of its child nodes, and has received the broadcasted message from all of its neighboring nodes sends the feedback message to its parent. The algorithm terminates when the *source* node gets broadcast messages from all of its neighboring nodes, and feedback messages from all of its child neighboring nodes.

Formal description of the algorithm can be found in [6].

3.2 Properties of the Algorithm

We define here the properties of the PIF algorithm in a broadcast network. Because of the similarity to the classic model, the time and message complexity is $O(n)$.

Theorem 1. *Suppose a* source *node i initiates a propagation of a message at time $t = \tau$. Then, we can say the following:*

- *All nodes j connected to i will receive the message in finite time.*
- *Each node in the network sends one message during the propagation, and one message during the acknowledgment, to the total of two messages.*
- *The* source *node i will get the last feedback message at no later than $\tau + 2 \cdot n$ time units.*
- *The set of nodes formed by the set $\{parent_s \cup i\}$ nodes spans a virtual tree of fastest routes, from the* source *node, on the graph.*

The proof is similar to [12].

4 Leader Election

The leader election algorithm goal is to mark a single node in the graph as a leader and to provide its identity to all other nodes.

4.1 The Algorithm

During the operation of the algorithm the nodes are partitioned into *fragments*. Each fragment is a collection of nodes, consisting of a *candidate* node and its domain of supportive nodes. When the algorithm starts all the candidates in the graph are *active*. During the course of the algorithm, a candidate may become *inactive*, in which case its fragment joins an active candidate's fragment and no longer exists as an independent fragment. The algorithm terminates when there is only one candidate in the graph, and its domain includes all of the nodes. First, we present a higher level algorithm that operates at the fragment level. We term this algorithm the general algorithm. We then present the actual distributed algorithm by elaborating upon the specific action of individual nodes. In order to establish our complexity and time bounds we prove correctness of the general algorithm, and then prove that the general and distributed leader election algorithms are equivalent. We do so by proving that every execution of the general algorithm, specifically the distributed one, behaves in the same manner. We conclude by proving the properties and correctness of the algorithm.

The General Algorithm for a Fragment in the graph We define for each fragment an *identity*, denoted by $id(F)$, and a *state*. The identity of a fragment consists of the size of the fragment, denoted by *id.size* and the candidate's identification number, denoted by *id(F).identity*. The state of the fragment is either *work*, *wait* or *leader*. We associate two variables with each edge in the graph, its current state and its current direction. An edge can be either in the state *internal*, in which case it connects two nodes that belong to the same fragment, or in the state *external*, when it connects two nodes that belong to different fragments. External edges will be directed in the following manner: Let e be an external edge that connects two different fragments $F1$ and $F2$. The algorithm follows these definitions for directing an edge in the graph:

Definition 1. *The lexicographical relation $id(F1) > id(F2)$ holds if:*
$id(F1).size > id(F2).size$ *or*
if $[id(F1).size = id(F2).size$ and $id(F1).identity > id(F2).identity]$.

Definition 2. *Let e be the directed edge $(F1, F2)$ if $id(F1) > id(F2)$ as defined by definition 1*

If the relation above holds, e is considered an *outgoing* edge for fragment $F1$ and an *incoming* edge for fragment $F2$, and fragments $F1$ and $F2$ are considered neighboring fragments. We assume that when an edge changes its direction, it does so in zero time.

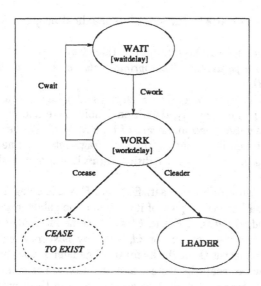

Fig. 1. *A Fragment State Machine*

When the algorithm starts, each node is an active candidate, with a fragment size of 1. We describe the algorithm for every fragment in the graph by a state machine as shown in Figure 1. A fragment may be in one of the following states: *wait, work* or *leader*. A Fragment is in the virtual state *cease-to-exist* when it joins another candidate's fragment. The initial state for all fragments is *wait*, and the algorithm terminates when there is a fragment in the *leader* state. During the course of the algorithm, a fragment may move between states only when it satisfies the transition condition, as specified by the state machine.

The delays within the states are defined as follows: *waitdelay* - A delay a fragment suffers while in the *wait* state, while waiting for other fragments to inform of their *identity*. *workdelay* - This is a delay each fragment suffers while in the *work* state. Both delays are arbitrary limited, positive delays. The transition conditions are: *Cwait* which is defined by rule 2(b)i below, *Cleader* which is defined by rule 3 below, *Ccease* which is defined by rule 2(b)ii below and *Cwork* which is defined by rule 1 below. None of the transition conditions can cause any delay in time.

The State Machine Formal Description:

1. A fragment F enters the *wait* state when it has at least one *outgoing* edge (*Cwait* condition definition).
2. A Fragment F transfers to the *work* state from the *wait* state (*Cwork* condition definition) when all its external edges are *incoming* edges. In the *work* state, the fragment will incur a delay named *workdelay*, while it performs the following:
   (a) Count the new number of nodes in its current domain. The new size is kept in the variable *new_size*. We define the delay caused by the counting process by *countdelay*.

(b) Compare its *new_size* to the size of its maximal neighbor fragment, F'.[1]

    i. If $new\_size(F) > X \cdot id(F').size$ then fragment F remains active. *(X > 1, a parameter. The optimal value of X is calculated in Section 4.3).*
Let $id(F).size \leftarrow new\_size$. F changes all of its external edges to the *outgoing* state. (clearly, definition 2 holds here and at this step, all of its neighbors become aware of its new size.) We define the delay caused by notifying the neighboring fragments of its new size by *innerdelay*. At this stage, condition *Cwait* is satisfied, and F transfers to the *wait* state.

    ii. Else, condition *Ccease* is satisfied, and F ceases being an active fragment and becomes a part of its maximal neighbor fragment F'. External edges between F and F' will become internal edges of F'. F' does not change its *size* or *id*, but may have new external edges, which connect it through the former fragment F to other fragments. The new external edges' state and direction are calculated according to the current size of F'. It is clear that all of them will be *outgoing* edges at this stage. We define the delay caused by notifying all of the fragment's nodes of the new candidate id *innerdelay*.

3. A Fragment that has no external edges is in the *leader* state. (*Cleader* condition definition).

The Distributed Algorithm for Nodes in the Graph We describe here the distributed algorithm for finding a leader in the graph. In Theorem 3 we prove that this algorithm is equivalent to the general algorithm presented above.

When the algorithm starts, each node in the graph is an active *candidate*. During the course of the algorithm, the nodes are partitioned into fragments, supporting the fragment's *candidate*. Each node always belong to a certain fragment. Candidates may become *inactive* and instruct their fragment to join other fragments in support of another *candidate*. A fragment in the *work* state may remain active if it is X times bigger than its maximal neighbor. The information within the fragment is transfered in PIF cycles, originating at the *candidate* node. The feedback process within each fragment starts at nodes called *edge* nodes. An *edge* node in a fragment is either a *leaf* node in the spanned PIF tree within the fragment, or has neighboring nodes that belong to other fragments. The algorithm terminates when there is one fragment that spans all the nodes in the graph.

Definition 3. *Let us define a PIF in a fragment, called a* fragment-PIF, *in the following manner:*

− *The* source *node is usually the* candidate *node. All nodes in the fragment recognize the candidate's identity. When a fragment decides to join another fragment, the* source *node is one of the* edge *nodes, which has neighbor nodes in the joined fragment (the winning fragment).*

---

[1] Note, that before the action, $id(F') > id(F)$. Therefore, F' stays at its current size.

- *All the nodes that belong to the same fragment broadcast the fragment-PIF message which originated at their* candidate's *node, and no other fragment-PIF message.*
- *An* edge *node, which has no child nodes in its fragment, initiates a feedback message in the fragment-PIF when it has received broadcast messages from all of its neighbors, either in its own fragment or from neighboring fragments.*

Algorithm Description

The algorithm begins with an initialization phase, in which every node, which is a fragment of size 1, broadcasts its identity. During the course of the algorithm, a fragment that all of its *edge* nodes have heard PIF messages from all their neighbors enter state *work*. The fragment's nodes report back to the *candidate* node the number of nodes in the fragment, and the identity of the maximal neighbor. During the report, the nodes also store a path to the edge node which is adjacent to the maximal neighbor. The *candidate* node, at this stage also the *source* node, compares the newly counted fragment size to the maximal known neighbor fragment size. If the newly counted size is *not* at least X times bigger than the size of the maximal neighbor fragment, then the fragment becomes *inactive* and joins its maximal neighbor. It is done in the following manner: The *candidate* node sends a message, on the stored path, to the fragment's edge node. This edge node becomes the fragment's *source* node. It broadcasts the new fragment identity, which is the joined fragment identity. At this stage, neighboring nodes of the joined fragment disregard this message, thus the maximal neighbor fragment will not enter state *work*. The *source* node chooses one of its maximal fragment neighbor nodes as its parent node, and later on will report to that node. From this point, the joining fragment broadcasts the new identity to all other neighbors. In case the newly counted size was at least X times that of the maximal neighboring fragment, the *candidate* updates the fragment's identity accordingly, and broadcasts it. (Note, this is actually the beginning of a new *fragment-PIF* cycle.) The algorithm terminates when a *candidate* node learns that it has no neighbors.

[6] contains a more detailed description, a mapping between the general algorithm and the distributed algorithm and simulation results of the algorithm.

4.2 Properties of the Algorithm

In this section we prove that a single candidate is elected in every execution of the algorithm. Throughout this section we refer to the high level algorithm, and then prove consistency between the versions. All proofs of lemmas and theorems in this section appear in Appendix A.

Theorem 2. *If a nonempty set of candidates start the leader election algorithm, then the algorithm eventually terminates and exactly one candidate is known as the leader.*

Theorem 3. *If all the nodes in the graph are given different identities, then the sequence of events in the algorithm does not depend on state transition delays.*

Corollary 1. *If all the nodes in the graph are given different identities, then the identity of the leader node will be uniquely defined by the high level algorithm.*

4.3 Time and Message Complexity

We prove in this section, that the time complexity of the algorithm is $O(n)$. It is further shown, that for $X = 3$ the time bound is the minimal, and is $9 \cdot n$. We also prove that the message complexity is $O(n \cdot lg(n))$.

In order to prove the time complexity, we omit an initialization phase, in which each node broadcasts one message. This stage is bounded by n time units. (Note, that a specific node is delayed by no more than 2 time units - its message transmission, followed by its neighbors immediate response.)

Let us define a *winning* fragment at time t during the execution of the algorithm to be a fragment which remained active after being in the *work* state. Thus, excluding the initialization phase, we can say the following:

Property 1. From the definitions and properties defined in [6], it is clear that the delay *workdelay* for a fragment is bounded in time as follows: (a) For a fragment that remains *active*, the delay is the sum of *countdelay* and *innerdelay*. (b) For a fragment that becomes *inactive*, it is the sum: *countdelay* $+2 \cdot$ *innerdelay*.

Theorem 4. *Let t_i^j be the time measured from the start, in which a winning fragment F_j completed the work state at size k_i. Then, assuming that $workdelay_i^j \leq 3 \cdot k_i$, and that $countdelay_i^j \leq k_i$, we get that:*

$$t_i^j \leq \frac{X^2 + 3 \cdot X}{X - 1} \cdot k_i$$

Proof of Theorem 4 We prove by induction on all times in which fragments in the graph enter state *work*, denoted $\{t_i^j\}$.

t_1: The minimum over t_i^j for all j. It is clear that the lemma holds.

Let us assume correctness for time t_i^j, and prove for time $t_i^j + workdelay_i^j$, for any j.

From lemma 4 we deduct that $k_i > X^2 \cdot k_{i-1}$. Therefore, according to the induction assumption, F_j entered state *work* for the $i - 1$ time in time: $t_{i-1}^j \leq \frac{X^2 + 3 \cdot X}{X - 1} \cdot k_{i-1}$. Let us now examine the time it took F_j to grow from its size at time t_{i-1}^j to size k_i: $t_i^j - t_{i-1}^j$. Since F_j is a winning fragment at time t_i^j, it is at least X times the size of any of its neighboring fragments. In the worst case, the fragment has to wait for a total of size $(X - 1) \cdot \frac{k_i}{X}$ that joins it. Note, that the induction assumption holds for all of F_j's neighbors.

$$t_i^j \leq \frac{X^2+3 \cdot X}{X-1} \cdot k_{i-1} + workdelay_{i-1}^j + \frac{X^2+3 \cdot X}{X-1} \cdot (X - 1) \cdot \frac{1}{X} \cdot k_i + countdelay_i^j$$

$$\leq \frac{X^2+3 \cdot X}{X-1} \cdot \frac{1}{X^2} \cdot k_i + 3 \cdot \frac{1}{X} \cdot k_i + \frac{X^2+3 \cdot X}{X-1} \cdot (X - 1) \cdot \frac{1}{X} \cdot k_i + k_i$$

$$= \frac{X^2+3 \cdot X}{X-1} \cdot k_i$$

Corollary 2. *From property 1 it is obtained that the delay* workdelay *for every fragment of size k is indeed bounded by* $3 \cdot k$, *and that the delay* countdelay *is bounded by k. Therefore, from Theorem 4 the time it takes the distributed algorithm to finish is also bounded by*

$$t_i^j \leq \frac{X^2 + 3 \cdot X}{X - 1} \cdot n$$

where n is the number of nodes in the graph, and therefore is $O(n)$.

Corollary 3. *When* $X = 3$ *the algorithm time bound is at its minimum:* $t_i^j \leq 9 \cdot n$.

Theorem 5. *The number of messages sent during the execution of the algorithm is bounded by:*

$$(\frac{lg(n) - lg(1 + X)}{lg(\frac{X+1}{X})} + 1) \cdot 3 \cdot n \; ; \quad X > 1$$

The proof of Theorem 5 is in Appendix A.

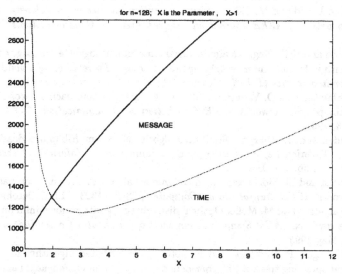

Fig. 2. *Time and Message Complexity as a factor of X*

5 Summary

We presented new distributed algorithms for emerging modern broadcast communication systems. Under the new model we introduced algorithms for PIF and Leader Election. The algorithms are optimal in time and message complexity.

By using the *fragment-PIF* approach our leader election algorithm enables a fragment to affect all of its neighbors concurrently, thus increasing parallelism in the graph. This new approach may be used for all fragments based decision algorithms in a broadcast environment.

There are several more problems to investigate under this model, such as other basic algorithms (e.g. DFS), failure detection and recovery. Other environments, such as a multicast environment, may require different approaches. Extensions of the model might also be viewed. Broadcast LANs are often connected via bridges. This leads to a more general model that includes both point to point edges and a broadcast group of edges connected to each node. For such a general model, the design of specific algorithms is required as well.

References

1. B. Awerbuch. Optimal distributed algorithms for minimum weight spanning tree, counting, leader election and related problems. *Proc. 19th Symp. on Theory of Computing*, pages 230 – 240, May 1987.
2. R. Bar-Yehuda, O. Goldreich, and A. Itai. On the time-complexity of broadcast in multi-hop radio networks: An exponential gap between determinism and randomization. *Journal on Computer and System Sciences*, 45:104–126, 1992.
3. A. Ben-David and M. Sidi. Collision resolution algorithms in multi-station packet radio network. *IEEE Journal on Selected Areas in Communications*, November 1983.
4. F. Chin and H.F. Ting. An almost linear time and o(vlogv + e) message distributed algorithm for minimum weight spanning trees. *Proceedings of Foundations Of Computer Science (FOCS)*, October 1985.
5. I. Chlamtac and O. Weinstein. The wave expansion approach to broadcasting in multihop radio networks. *IEEE Transaction on Communications*, COM-39(3):426 – 433, 1991.
6. I. Cidon and O. Mokryn. Distributed algorithms in a multihop broadcast environment. *Technical Report - Center for Communication and Information Technologies, Technion*, no. 241, 1998.
7. I. Cidon and M. Sidi. Distributed assignment algorithm for multihop packet radio networks. *IEEE Transaction on Computers*, 38(10):1353 – 1361, October 1989.
8. M. Faloutsos and M. Molle. Optimal distributed algorithms for minimum spanning trees revisited. *ACM Symp. on Principles of Distributed Computing*, pages 231 – 237, May 1995.
9. R. Gallager, P. Humblet, and P. Spira. A distributed algorithm for minimum weight spanning trees. *ACM Transactions on Programming languages and Systems*, 4(1):66 – 77, January 1983.
10. J.A. Garay, S. Kutten, and D. Peleg. A sub-linear time distributed algorithm for minimum-weight spanning trees. *SIAM Journal on Computing*, pages 302–316, 1998.
11. M.A. Marsen and D. Roffinella. Multichannel local area network protocols. *IEEE Journal on Selected Areas in Communications*, SAC-1(5):885 – 897, November 1983.
12. A. Segall. Distributed network protocols. *IEEE Transaction on Information Theory*, IT-29(1):23 – 35, January 1983.

Appendix A

Proof of Theorem 2 In order to proof the Theorem, we will state some Properties and Lemmas.

Property 2. When an active fragment changes its state from *work* to *wait*, all of its external edges are outgoing edges.

Lemma 1. *During every execution of the algorithm, at least one active candidate exists.*

Proof of Lemma 1 By definition, an active candidate exists in the graph either in the *work, wait* or *leader* state. A candidate becomes inactive according to the algorithm if it discovers, while in the *work* state, an active neighbor fragment of bigger size, as can be seen in 2(b)ii. By this definition it is clear that a candidate may cease to exist only if it encountered another active candidate of at least half its size. Therefore, during the execution of the algorithm, there will always be at least one active candidate.

Property 3. When an active fragment changes its state from *work* to *wait*, all of its external edges are outgoing edges.

Lemma 2. *During the execution of the algorithm, there is always a fragment in the* work *or leader states.*

Proof of Lemma 2 A fragment will be in the *work* state if it has the minimal *id* among all its neighbors. Definition 1 determines that the fragment's *id* consists of its size and identity number. If there exists a fragment of minimal size, then it is the fragment with the minimal *id*. Otherwise, there are at least two fragments in the graph that have the same minimal size. As defined, the fragment with the lower identity number has the lower *id*. It is clear then, that at any stage of the algorithm there exists a fragment with a minimal *id*, and therefore there will always be a fragment in the *work* or *leader* state.

Lemma 3. *If a fragment F was in the* work *state and remained active in* wait *state, it will enter the* work *state again only after each and every one of its neighboring fragments has been in the* work *state as well.*

Proof of Lemma 3 According to Property 3, when F entered the *wait* state, all of its edges are in the *outgoing* state. In order to enter the *work* state again, all of F's *external* edges have to be *incoming* edges. While in the *wait* state, F does nothing. Its neighbor activity is the only cause for a change in the edges' state or direction. An *outgoing* edge may change its state to *internal*, if the neighbor fragment enters the *work* state and becomes a supporter of F or changes its direction to *incoming*, according to Definition 2, as a result of a neighbor fragment changing its *size*. Hence, all F's neighboring fragments must be in the *work* state before F may enter it again.

Corollary 4. *A fragment F in the* wait *state which has a neighbor fragment F'
in the* work *state may enter the* work *state only after F' has changed its state
to the* wait *state.*

Lemma 4. *Let us consider a fragment, F, that entered the* work *state for two
consecutive times, i and i+1 and remained active. Let t_i be the time it entered
the* work *state for the i-th time, and let t_{i+1} be the i+1 time. Let us define by
k_i its known size at time t_i, and by size k_{i+1} its size at time t_{i+1} + countdelay.
Then, $k_{i+1} \geq X^2 \cdot k_i$.*

Proof of Lemma 4 If F enters the *work* state for the *i-th* time at time t_i, then
according to Lemma 3 all of its neighbor fragments will be in the *work* state
before time t_{i+1}. We know that at time t_i F is of known size k_i. According to
rules 2(b)ii and 2(b)i, if it stayed active, it has enlarged its size by a factor of X at
least. (Note, $X > 1$). Since F reentered the *work* state, any of its new neighboring
fragments is at least as big as F, i.e. at size of at least $X \cdot k_i$. We know that F
remains active after completing both *work* states. Therefore, following the same
rules [2(b)ii and 2(b)i], at time t_{i+1}+countdelay, its size, k_{i+1}, must be at least
X times the size of its maximal neighbor. It follows directly that $k_{i+1} \geq X^2 \cdot k_i$.

Corollary 5. *The maximal number of periods that an active candidate will be
in the* work *state is $\lg_X n$.*

Now we can proceed with the Theorem:
From Lemma 1 and Lemma 2 it is clear that the algorithm does not deadlock,
and that the set of active candidates is non-empty throughout the course of the
algorithm. Property 5 limits the number of times a candidate may enter the
work state. Since at any time there is a candidate in the *work* state, there always
exists a candidate that enlarges its domain. It follows that there exists a stage
in the algorithm where there will be only one candidate, and its domain will
include all the nodes in the graph.

Proof of Theorem 3 Let U be the set of fragments in the *work* state at any
arbitrary time during the execution of the general algorithm. If we view the
times before a fragment in the graph enters the *leader* state, then by lemma 2
and corollary 4 we can conclude that:

1. U is non-empty until a leader is elected
2. Fragments in U cannot be neighbors
3. All the neighboring fragments of a fragment $F \subseteq U$ cannot change their *size*
   until F is no longer in U (i.e., F completes the *work* state and changes its
   state to *wait*).

At every moment during the execution of the algorithm, the graph is acyclic
and the edges' directions determine uniquely which fragments are in the *work*
state. Let us examine the state of the graph at an arbitrary time, before any
fragment enters the *leader* state. The conclusions above imply that there is a
predetermined order in which fragments enter the *work* state. The time it takes

a fragment to enter the *work* state from the *wait* state is determined by the *Cwork* condition. Excluding initialization, a fragment can reenter the *work* state after each of its neighboring fragments completed a period in the *work* state. The duration within the *work* state for a fragment, depends only on the local delay *workdelay* as defined by 1. Therefore, fragments that enter the *work* state complete it in finite time. Therefore, it is clear, that the order by which the fragment's neighbors enter the *work* state does not affect the order by which it enters the *work* state. This proves that the sequence of events between every pair of neighboring fragments in the graph is predetermined, given the nodes have different identities. Therefore, the sequence of events between all the fragments in the graph is predetermined and cannot be changed throughout the execution of the algorithm.

Proof of Theorem 5 In order to prove the Theorem, we use the following Lemmas and properties.

Property 4. During the execution of the algorithm, nodes within a fragment send messages only while in the *work* state.

Lemma 5. *While in the* work *state, the number of messages sent in a fragment is at most* $3 \cdot k$, *where k is the number of nodes within the fragment.*

Proof of Lemma 5 While in the *work* state, each node can send either one of three messages: FEEDBACK, ACTION and INFO (in this order). Every message is sent only once, from the PIF properties. Therefore, the number of messages sent in a fragment of size k is bounded by $3 \cdot k$.

Lemma 6. *Let l be the number of times a cluster of nodes, initially a fragment, entered state* work. *Then:*

$$l = \frac{lg(n) - lg(1 + X)}{lg(\frac{X+1}{X})} + 1$$

Proof of Lemma 6 A fragment of an arbitrary size k, may join a fragment of size $\frac{1}{X} \cdot k + 1$. Therefore, $\forall l$, the minimal growth rate is of the form: $k_l = k_{l-1} + \frac{1}{X} \cdot k_{l-1} + 1 = \frac{X+1}{X} \cdot k_{l-1} + 1$, where $k_0 = 0$.
Let us define the following:

$$k_l = a \cdot k_{l-1} + 1; \quad a = \frac{X+1}{X}; \quad \sum_{l=1}^{\infty} k_l \cdot Z^l = k(Z)$$

By using the Z transform as defined above, it follows that:

$$k_l = a \cdot \sum_{l=1}^{\infty} k_{l-1} \cdot Z^l = a \cdot Z \cdot \sum_{l=1}^{\infty} k_{l-1} \cdot Z^{l-1} = a \cdot Z \cdot k(Z)$$

Since $k_0 = 0$ and $\forall Z < 1, \sum_{l=0}^{\infty} Z^l = \frac{1}{1-Z}$, we obtain that:

$$k(Z) = a \cdot Z \cdot k(Z) + \frac{1}{1-Z} \quad \Rightarrow \quad k(Z) = \frac{1}{(1-Z) \cdot (1 - a \cdot Z)}$$

By separation of variables we get:

$$k(Z) = \frac{X+1}{1-a \cdot Z} - \frac{X}{1-Z}$$

Therefore:

$$\sum_{l=1}^{\infty} k_l \cdot Z^l = (X+1) \cdot \sum_{l=1}^{\infty} (a \cdot l)^l - X \cdot \sum_{l=1}^{\infty} Z^l = \sum_{l=1}^{\infty} [(X+1) \cdot a^l - X] \cdot Z^l$$

Since by definition $a > 1$, we get: $k_l = (X+1) \cdot a^l - X \geq a^l + X \cdot a^l - X \geq a^{l-1} + X \cdot a^{l-1} = (1+X) \cdot a^{l-1}$. We require that: $(1+X) \cdot a^{l-1} = n$, where n is the number of nodes in the graph. By taking the logarithm of both sides, we obtain:

$$l = \frac{lg(n) - lg(1+X)}{lg(\frac{X+1}{X})} + 1$$

Now we may proceed to prove the message complexity:
From Property 4 it is clear that every fragment sends messages only while it is in the *work* state. Lemma 5 shows that in the *work* state, the maximal number of messages sent within a fragment of size k is $3 \cdot k$. From Lemma 6 and the above we obtain that the message complexity is:

$$(\frac{lg(n) - lg(1+X)}{lg(\frac{X+1}{X})} + 1) \cdot n \; ; \quad X > 1$$

The Arrow Distributed Directory Protocol

Michael J. Demmer[1] and Maurice P. Herlihy[2]*

[1] Tera Computer Company, Seattle WA 98102, miked@tera.com
[2] Computer Science Department, Brown University, Providence, RI 02912
herlihy@cs.brown.edu

Abstract. Most practical techniques for locating remote objects in a distributed system suffer from problems of scalability and locality of reference. We have devised the *Arrow distributed directory protocol*, a scalable and local mechanism for ensuring mutually exclusive access to mobile objects. This directory has communication complexity optimal within a factor of $(1 + MST\text{-}stretch(G))/2$, where $MST\text{-}stretch(G)$ is the "minimum spanning tree stretch" of the underlying network.

1 Introduction

Many distributed systems support some concept of *mobile objects*. A mobile object could be a file, a process, or any other data structure. For an object to be mobile, we require only that it can be transmitted over a network from one node to another. A mobile object "lives" on only one node at a time, and it moves from one node to another in response to explicit requests by *client* nodes. A *directory* service allows nodes to keep track of mobile objects. A directory must provide the ability to locate a mobile object (*navigation*), as well as the ability to ensure mutual exclusion in the presence of concurrent requests (*synchronization*).

This paper describes the *arrow distributed directory protocol*, a novel directory protocol being implemented as part of the Aleph toolkit [10], an distributed shared object system currently under development at Brown. The arrow directory protocol is designed to avoid scalability problems inherent in many directory services currently used in distributed shared memory systems. In this paper, we focus on proving the correctness of the protocol, and on analyzing its communication complexity. The service's data structures and protocols are extremely simple, and yet its communication complexity compares well to more complicated asymptotic schemes in the literature.

2 Motivation

Perhaps the simplest way to implement a directory service is to have each node broadcast each access request, and await the response from the node currently holding the object. Indeed, this approach is common in bus-based multiprocessor systems (e.g., [9]), where broadcasting can be accomplished efficiently. In

---

* Supported by AFOSR agreement F30602-96-0228 DARPA OD885.

distributed systems, however, broadcast is impractical, so a directory structure must provide a way to navigate and synchronize by point-to-point communication. It is equally impractical to have each node store each object's current location, since all nodes must be notified when an object moves. Additionally, since requests occur simultaneously, maintaining consistency in such schemes becomes difficult.

The most common directory protocol used in existing distributed shared memory systems is a *home-based* structure. Each mobile object is associated with a fixed node, termed that object's "home". The home keeps track of the object's location and status (e.g., busy or idle). When a client node requests an object, it sends a message to the object's home. The home sends a message to the client currently holding the object, and that client forwards the object to the requesting client node. The home can also enforce the necessary synchronization, by queuing concurrent requests. Home-based schemes are simple and easy to implement, and they have been observed to work well for small-to-medium scale systems. Nevertheless, such schemes suffer from problems of scalability and locality. As the number of nodes grows, or if an object is a "hot spot", that object's home is likely to become a synchronization bottleneck, since it must mediate all access to that object. Moreover, if a client is far from an object's home, then it must incur the cost of communicating with the home, even if the node currently holding the object is nearby.

One way to alleviate these problems is to allow an object's home to move. For example, Li and Hudak [15] proposed a protocol in which each object is initially associated with a particular node, but as an object is moved around, it leaves a virtual trail of *forwarding pointers*, starting from the original home. A limitation of this approach is that many requests for an object may still go through the original home, or end up chasing an arbitrarily long sequence of pointers. Additionally, if the object is close but the home is far, the client may still have to incur the large communication costs.

Our approach is also based on the idea of a trail of pointers, although we use them in a different way. Objects have no fixed homes, and synchronization and navigation are integrated into a single simple protocol. When a client requests an object from another client, all messages are sent through direct or nearly-direct paths, preserving locality, and permitting us to give explicit worst-case bounds on the protocol's communication complexity.

3   The Directory Structure

In this section, we give an informal definition of the arrow directory protocol, together with examples illustrating the interesting aspects of its behavior. A more formal treatment appears in Section 4.

For brevity, we consider a directory that tracks the location of a single object. We model a distributed system in the usual way, as a connected graph $G = (V, E)$, where $|V| = n$. Each vertex models a node, and each edge a two-way reliable communication link. A node can send messages directly to its neighbors, and indirectly to non-neighbors along a path. Each edge is weighted with a communication *cost*. The cost of sending a message from one node to another along a particular path is just the sum of that path's edge costs. The *distance* $d_G(x, y)$ is the cost of the shortest path from x to y in G. The network is *asynchronous* (steps are interleaved in an arbitrary order) but *reliable* (every node eventually takes a step and every message is eventually delivered). We assume the network provides a *routing service* [7, 21] that allows node v to send a message to node u with cost $d_G(u, v)$.

The *arrow directory* is given by a minimum spanning tree T for G. Each node v stores a directory entry $link(v)$, which is either a neighbor of v in T, or v itself. The meaning of the link is essentially the following: if $link(v) = v$, then the object either resides at v, or will soon reside at v. Otherwise, the object currently resides in the component of the spanning tree containing $link(v)$. Informally, except for the node that currently holds an object, a node knows only in which "direction" that object lies. If T has maximum degree Δ, then the directory requires $n \cdot \log(\Delta)$ bits of memory to track the object (some techniques for memory reduction are discussed below).

The entire directory protocol can be described in a single paragraph. The directory tree is initialized so that following the links from any node leads to the node where the object resides. When a node v wants to acquire exclusive access to the object, it sends a *find*(v) message to $u_1 = link(v)$ and sets $link(v)$ to v. When node u_i receives a *find*(v) message from node u_{i-1}, where $u_{i+1} = link(u_i)$, it immediately "flips" $link(u_i)$ to u_{i-1}. If $u_{i+1} \neq u_i$, then u_i forwards the message to u_{i+1}. Otherwise, u_i buffers the request until it is ready to release the object to v. Node u_i releases the object by sending a *move*(v) message containing the object directly to v, without further interaction with the directory.

Despite the protocol's simplicity, it has a number of non-trivial properties that we believe to be of both practical and theoretical interest. Before analyzing this behavior, it is helpful to review some simple examples. Figure 1 shows a properly initialized directory, where directed edges correspond to the directory links. The object resides at node u (indicated by a square). When node v requests the object, it sends a *find*(v) message to $u_1 = link(v)$, and then sets $link(v)$ to v. When u_1 receives the message from v, it forwards it to $u_2 = link(u_1)$, and sets $link(u_1)$ to v. Continuing in this way, each vertex thus "flips" the link to point in the direction from which the *find*(v) message arrived. Figure 2 illustrates the directory state after three steps. Links changed by the protocol are shown in gray: v's link points to itself, u_1 points to v and u_2 points to u_1.

As shown in Figure 3, the *find*(v) message continues to flip links until it arrives at u, where the object resides (marked by $link(u) = u$). When u receives the *find*(v) message, it responds by sending the object in a *move*$((v)$ message directly to v. This response takes the shortest path, and does not affect the directory structure. As illustrated in Figure 4, after v has received the object, all links in the graph again lead to the object's new location, so any subsequent *find* messages will be directed there. The cost of acquiring access to the object is

$$d_T(u, v) + d_G(v, u).$$

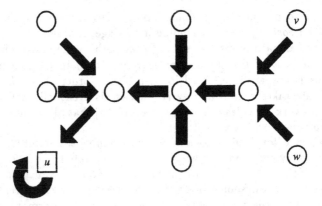

Fig. 1. Initial Directory State

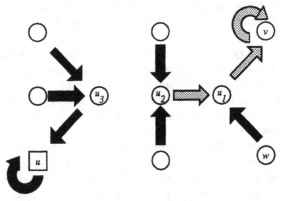

Fig. 2. Threee steps after u issues $find(u)$ message

The term $d_T(u, v)$ is the cost of sending the $find(v)$ message from u to v through the directory tree, and the term $d_G(v, u)$ is the cost of sending the $move(v)$ message directly through the network. Notice the locality of this interaction: the message traffic affects only the nodes between u and v in the directory tree and network.

We now turn our attention to a concurrent example in which multiple nodes try to acquire the object at the same time. As described above, as a *find* message traverses the directory tree, it flips each link to point back to the neighbor from which the *find* originated. If two *find* messages are issued at about the same time, one will eventually cross the other's path, and be "diverted" away from the object and toward its competitor. Figure 2 illustrates this behavior. If any of the nodes on the right half of the tree requests the object, then its *find* message will follow the links to v, whereas nodes on the left half of the tree will follow the links to u.

For example, suppose w requests the object while v's *find* is still in progress.

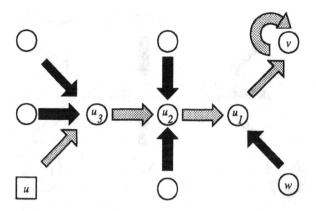

Fig. 3. Find message received

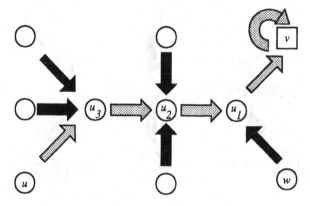

Fig. 4. Move message received

This second *find* will be diverted to v. When v receives w's message, it will not respond until it is has received the object and is ready to release it. This directory state is illustrated in Figure 5, where w's request is blocked at v.

Now suppose that node z issues a *find* which arrives at u, where it is buffered (u is not finished with the object). The *find* message from v is then diverted to z, as illustrated in Figure 6. This example illustrates how the arrow directory integrates synchronization and navigation in a natural way. In a quiescent state (when no messages are in transit), the directory imposes a distributed queue structure on blocked *find* requests. When z completes its *find*, after flipping its links, it blocks at u. Similarly, v blocks at z, and w at v. These blocked requests create a distributed queue where each *find* is buffered at its predecessor's node. When u releases the object, it goes directly to z, then v, then w. This distributed queue structure is valuable from a practical perspective, for several reasons. First, it ensures that no single node becomes a synchronization bottleneck. Second, if there is high contention for an object, then each time that

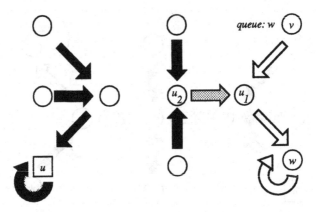

Fig. 5. w's request blocked at v

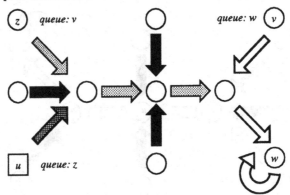

Fig. 6. Deflected find

object is released, that node will already have a buffered *find* request. In the limit, the cost of delivering *find* messages is hidden by the local computation times, and the protocol's performance approaches optimal (repeated local computation followed by direct object delivery). Third, the queue structure ensures locality: each *find* message takes a direct path through the spanning tree to its predecessor's node, with no detour to a home node.

The communication complexity of the concurrent execution in which the object goes from u to z to v to w is

$$(d_T(z, u) + d_G(u, z)) + (d_T(v, z) + d_G(z, v)) + (d_T(w, v) + d_G(v, w)).$$

The first expression in each parenthesized term is the cost of sending the *find* message from each node to its predecessor via the directory tree, and the second is the cost of sending the *move* message directly from each node to its successor. There are two important points to notice about this communication cost. First, there is no synchronization overhead: the communication cost is the same as a serial execution in which each node issues its *find* only after its predecessor is ready to release the object. Second, the inherent cost of the transfer from u to z is $d_G(z, u) + d_G(u, z)$, the inherent cost of delivering matching *find* and *move* messages. The arrow directory replaces the first term with $d_T(z, u)$, suggesting that the navigation cost of the arrow directory approaches optimality to the degree that $d_T(z, u)$ approaches $d_G(z, u)$. We elaborate on these observations in the next section.

4 Analysis

In this section, we describe the algorithm using a simplified version of the I/O automaton formalism of Lynch and Tuttle [17], we sketch safety and liveness issues, and evaluate the algorithm's cost.

4.1 Description

Recall that the network is a connected graph $G = (V, E)$, where $|V| = n$. There are two kinds of messages: node v issues a *find*(v) message to request access to an object, and *move*(u) to transfer ownership to u. Each node v has following attributes: *link*(v) is a node, *queue*(v) is either a node or $\perp$, and *owner*(v) is a boolean. Each pair of nodes (u, v) has a an associated *pending*(u, v), which is a set of messages that have been sent but not delivered (i.e., in transit, or queued at the sender or receiver).

A node v or link *link*(v) is *terminal* if *link*(v) = v. The directory is initialized so that there is exactly one node v_0 such that v_0 is terminal and *owner*(v_0) is true, the remaining non-terminal *link* pointers form an oriented tree, and all *pending*(u, v) sets are empty. Message delivery is reliable, but not necessarily FIFO. A node initiates a *find* operation by sending a *find* message to itself For brevity, we assume that a node w has only one *find*(w) message in the network at a time.

We use T to denote the undirected tree, and L to denote the directed graph induced by non-terminal links. The algorithm has the property that T does not change, but L does. The algorithm is defined by a number of transitions. The first part of each transition is a precondition that must be satisfied for the transition to occur, and the second part describes the state of the directory after the transition. A primed component indicates how a component's state changes after the transition.

Several transitions require a node atomically to remove a message from a network link, undergo an internal transition, and insert the message in another link. In practice, this atomicity is realized simply by requiring each node to finish processing one message before it starts processing the next.

The first transition says that when *find*(w) is sent from node u to a non-terminal node v, v flips its *link* pointer to u and forwards the message to its old link.

pre: $find(w) \in pending(u, v)$
         $link(v) \neq v$
post: $pending'(u, v) = pending(u, v) - \{find(w)\}$
         $pending'(v, link(v)) = pending(v, link(v)) \cup \{find(w)\}$
         $link'(v) = u$

If, however, v is a terminal node, then w is enqueued behind v.

pre: $find(w) \in pending(u, v)$
         $link(v) = v$
post: $pending'(u, v) = pending(u, v) - \{find(w)\}$
         $link'(v) = u$
         $queue'(v) = w$

We do not explicitly model whether the object is actively in use. Instead, we treat the owner's receipt of a *find* and its corresponding *move* as distinct events, separated by an arbitrary but finite delay. If the current owner's queue is non-empty, then it may relinquish ownership and move the object directly to the waiting node.

pre: $owner(v) = true$
         $queue(v) \neq \bot$
post: $pending'(v, queue(v)) = pending(v, queue(v)) \cup \{move(queue(v))\}$
         $owner'(v) = false$
         $queue'(v) = \bot$

When a waiting node receives the object, that node becomes the new owner.

pre: $move(v) \in pending(u, v)$
post: $owner'(v) = true$
         $pending'(u, v) = pending(u, v) - \{move(v)\}$

4.2   Safety

Our proof of the directory's safety properties is an invariance argument. At all times, we show that there exists a well-defined *path* in L from any node that leads either to the object's current owner, or to another node that has requested the object. Because *find* messages follow these paths, any message that reaches the end of a path will either acquire ownership of the object, or join the queue waiting for the object.

First, we need to check that such paths exist.

Lemma 1. *The following property is invariant:*

$$find(w) \in pending(u, v) \Rightarrow link(u) \neq v \wedge link(v) \neq u. \tag{1}$$

Proof. Initially, the property holds vacuously, because no messages are in transit. Consider the first transition to violate the property. There are two cases to consider. In the first case, suppose the directory enters a state where

$$find(w) \in pending'(u, v) \wedge link'(u) = v.$$

Immediately before this transition, we claim that

$$find(w) \in pending(v, u) \wedge link(u) = v,$$

so the property was already violated. First, $find(w)$ is in $pending(v, u)$, because otherwise $link'(u)$ would not be set to v. Second, $link(u)$ must be v, because otherwise the message would not be forwarded to v.

In the second case, suppose the directory enters a state where

$$find(w) \in pending'(u, v) \wedge link'(v) = u.$$

Immediately before this transition, we claim that

$$find(w) \in pending(v, u) \wedge link(v) = u,$$

so the property was already violated. First, $find(w)$ is in $pending(v, u)$, because otherwise $link'(u)$ would not be set to v. Second, $link(v)$ must be u, because the transition does not change $link(v)$.

Lemma 2. *The directed graph L induced by the non-terminal links is always acyclic.*

Proof. Because T is a tree, it suffices to show the directory cannot enter a state where $link(u) = v$ and $link(v) = u$ for distinct nodes u and v. Consider the first transition that sets $link'(v) = u$ while $link(u) = v$. Any such transition is enabled only if $find(w) \in pending(u, v)$ and $link(u) = v$, which is impossible by Lemma 1.

Definition 3. The *path* from a node is the directed path in L from that node to a terminal node.

Definition 4. The *target* of v, denoted $target(v)$, is the terminal node at the end of its path. If $find(w)$ is a message in $pending(u, v)$, then that message's target is $target(v)$.

Lemma 2 guarantees that these notions are well-defined. A node is a *waiter* if it has requested an object, but has not yet become the owner of that object.

We are now ready to prove our principal safety result:

Theorem 5. *The path from any node always leads either to the current owner or a waiter.*

Proof. Any node v partitions the set of nodes G into A_v and B_v, where A_v consists of nodes whose paths include v, and B_v consists of the rest. For every u in A_v, $target(u) = target(v)$.

Consider the directory state immediately before a transition "flipping" $link(v)$ to u. By Lemma 2, $u \in B_v$. After the transition, for every w in B_v, $target'(w) = target(w)$, so $target(w)$ remains an owner or a waiter. For every z in A_v (including v itself), $target'(z) = target'(u) = target(u)$, so $target(z)$ remains an owner or a waiter.

4.3 Liveness

Liveness is also based on invariance arguments. Liveness requires that transitions occur *fairly*: any transition whose precondition remains true will eventually occur. (For example, any message in $pending(u, v)$ will eventually be removed.) We will show that when a *find* message is in transit, that message "traps" its target in a component L_1 of the link graph L: other *find* and *move* messages can move the target within L_1, but the target cannot leave L_1. Each transition that advances the *find* message shrinks L_1 by at least one node, so after at most n advances, L_1 consists of a single node, and the *find* message must reach its target.

Theorem 6. *Each find(w) message will be delivered to its target in n steps or fewer.*

Proof. Suppose $find(w)$ is in $pending(u, v)$. Deleting the edge (u, v) from the undirected tree T splits T into two disjoint trees, $before(w)$ (containing u) and $after(w)$ (containing v). Lemma 1 states that as long as $find(w)$ is in $pending(u, v)$, then $link(v) \neq u$ and $link(u) \neq v$, so the message's target will remain in $after(w)$. (Other *find* requests may still move the target within $after(w)$.)

If a transition delivers $find(w)$ to its target, we are done. A transition that moves the message from $pending(u, v)$ to $pending'(v, link(v))$ induces a new partition $before'(w)$ and $after'(w)$, where $v \notin after'(w)$. Because each $after'(w)$ is strictly smaller than $after(w)$, the $find(w)$ message will arrive at its target after at most n steps.

4.4 Complexity

How should we evaluate the communication cost of this protocol? Following Peleg [20], it is natural to compare our communication complexity to that of an *optimal* directory for which synchronization and navigation are free. The *optimal* directory accepts only serial schedules (so it pays nothing for synchronization), and delivers each *find* and *move* message directly (so it pays nothing for navigation).

An *execution* is a sequence of atomic node steps, message sends, and message receipts. An execution is *complete* if every *find* message has a matching *move*. and an execution is *serial* if the receipt of the i-th *move* message precedes the sending of each $(i + 1)$-st *find*. The next lemma states that we can restrict our attention to complete serial executions.

Lemma 7. *If E is any complete concurrent execution of the arrow directory protocol, then there exists a complete serial execution E' that serializes requests in the same order, sends the same messages, and leaves the directory in the same state.*

Define the *MST-stretch* of G, denoted *MST-stretch*(G), to be

$$\max_{u,v \in V} \frac{d_T(u, v)}{d_G(u, v)}.$$

This quantity measures how far from optimal a path through the minimum spanning tree can be. The MST-stretch can be n in the worst case (a ring), but is likely to be much smaller in realistic networks (such as LANs, or the Internet).

Consider a serial execution in which $v_0, \ldots, v_\ell$ successively acquire the object. In the arrow directory, each *find* message traverses the spanning tree T, with cost $d_T(v_i, v_{i+1})$, while in the optimal directory, the message goes directly from v_i to v_{i+1}, with cost $d_G(v_i, v_{i+1})$. The ratio of these quantities is no more than *MST-stretch(G)*. In both the arrow and optimal directories, the *move* message incurs cost $d_G(v_i, v_{i+1})$, so this ratio is 1. (From a practical perspective, it is worth emphasizing that we are not hiding any constants: these bounds really are *MST-stretch(G)* and 1, not $O(MST\text{-}stretch(G))$ or $O(1)$.)

As a result, for any complete serial execution, the ratio of communication costs for the arrow directory and the optimal directory is bounded by

$$\frac{1 + MST\text{-}stretch(G)}{2}.$$

The lower the network's MST-stretch, the closer the communication cost of the arrow directory is to optimal.

5 Discussion

Our discussion so far has focused on the safety, liveness, and communication cost of an idealized directory scheme. We now briefly address other issues of practical interest.

One sensible way to reduce the directory's memory consumption and message traffic is to organize the directory as a two-level structure. The network is partitioned into neighborhoods of small diameter, where the arrow directory is maintained at a per-neighborhood granularity, and a home-based directory is used within each individual neighborhood. (For example, the neighborhood could be a local subnetwork, and the node its gateway.) The resulting hybrid scheme trades communication cost against memory consumption and directory tree traffic. As discussed below, Peleg [20] and Awerbuch and Peleg [3] have also proposed multi-level directory structures.

Note that only *find* messages go through the directory tree — the network's routing service handles all other traffic, such as *move* messages, remote procedure calls, etc. *Find* messages for different objects that arrive together can be combined before forwarding.

We have assumed for simplicity that every node is initialized with a directory entry for each object. It is more practical to initialize an object's directory links in the following "lazy" manner. Before a node can request an object, it must first acquire that object's name. When a node u receives a message from v containing the name of an unfamiliar object, it sends a message through the directory tree to v initializing the intermediate missing links. This lazy strategy preserves locality: if all references to an object are localized within the directory tree, then the other nodes need never create a directory entry for that object.

So far, we have considered only exclusive access to objects. Many applications would benefit from support for shared (read-only) access as well. We now outline a simple extension of the arrow directory protocol to support read-only replication. When multiple read-only copies exist, one is designated the *primary*. Each directory entry consists of a *primary link* pointing toward the primary copy, and a set of *secondary links*, each pointing toward one or more copies. When a node requests a read-only copy of an object, it follows any secondary link from each vertex, creating a new secondary link pointing back to itself at each node it visits. When a node requests exclusive access to the object, it first follows the primary links, flipping each primary link toward itself. When the node has acquired exclusive access to the primary, it *invalidates* the read-only copies by following, flipping, and consolidating the secondary links. When all invalidations are complete, the node has acquired the object. This protocol is *linearizable* [11]. More efficient protocols might be achieved by replacing linearizability with weaker notions of correctness [1].

We have not addressed the issue of fault-tolerance. Distributed mutual exclusion algorithms address the problem by "token regeneration", effectively electing a node to hold the new token. Here, the problem is different, since we cannot elect a new object, but we do need to recover navigational information that may be lost following a crash.

6 Related Work

Distributed directory management is closely related to the problem of distributed mutual exclusion. Naïmi, Tréhel, and Arnold [18] describe a distributed mutual exclusion algorithm (the *NTA* algorithm) also based on a dynamically changing distributed directed graph. In the NTA algorithm, when a node receives a message, it flips its edge to point to the node from which the request originated. In our algorithm, however, the node flips its edge to point to the immediate source of the message. As a result, our graph is always a directed subgraph of a fixed minimal spanning tree, while the NTA graph is more fluid.

The safety and liveness arguments for NTA and for our algorithm are similar, (though not identical), but the complexity models are quite different. The complexity analysis given in [18] is based on a model in which the underlying network is a clique, with unit cost to send a message from any node to any other. All nodes are assumed equally likely to request the token, and requests are assumed to occur sequentially. Under these assumptions, NTA shows that the average number of messages sent over a long period converges to $O(\log n)$. (Ginat [8] gives an amortized analysis of the NTA algorithm and some variants.) Our analysis, by contrast, models the underlying network as a weighted graph, where the end-to-end cost of sending a message is the sum of weights along its path. Instead of taking an average over a presumed uniform distribution, we compete against a directory with perfect instantaneous knowledge of the object's current location and no synchronization costs. The complexity analysis of Naïmi *et al.* does not apply to our algorithm, nor ours to theirs.

The NTA complexity model is appropriate for the general problem of distributed mutual exclusion, while ours is intended for the more specific problem of managing distributed directories in the Internet. Each link in our spanning tree is intended to represent a direct network link between routers, which is why our algorithm does not flip edges to point to arbitrarily distant network nodes (even though the routing service renders any pair of nodes "adjacent" for communication). The NTA complexity model, while mathematically quite elegant, does not seem well-suited for distributed Internet directory management, because point-to-point communication cost is not uniform in real networks, and access requests to distributed objects are typically not generated uniformly at random, but often have strong locality properties. For these reasons, a competitive complexity model seems more appropriate for our purposes.

Another mutual exclusion protocol employing path reversal is attributed to Schönhage by Lynch and Tuttle [16]. In this protocol, the directory is a directed acyclic graph. *Users* residing at leaf nodes request the object, and requests are granted by *arbiters* residing at internal nodes. Edges change labels and orientation to reflect the object's current status and location.

The arrow directory protocol was motivated by emerging *active network* technology [14], in which programmable network switches are used to implement customized protocols, such as application-specific packet routing. Active networks are intended to ensure that the cost of routing messages through the directory tree is comparable to the cost of routing messages directly through the network.

Small-scale multiprocessors (e.g., [9]) typically rely on broadcast-based protocols to locate objects in a distributed system of caches. Existing large-scale multiprocessors and existing distributed shared memory systems are either home-based, or use a combination of home-based and forwarding pointers [4, 5, 6, 12, 13, 15, 19].

Plaxton et al. [22] give a randomized directory scheme for read-only objects. Peleg [20] and Awerbuch and Peleg [3] describe directory services organized as a hierarchical system of subdirectories based on sparse network covers [2]. The earlier paper [20] proposed the notion of *stretch* to evaluate the performance of distributed directory services. In the worst case, these directories use per-object memory logarithmic in n, while ours is linear. (As described above, we believe we can avoid worst-case memory consumption in practice.) Strictly speaking, the asymptotic communication complexities are incomparable. Their notion of an optimal concurrent *find* execution is less conservative than ours, but for simplicity we will treat them as equivalent. The ratio of their concurrent *find* and *move* operations to their notion of an optimal protocol is polylogarithmic in n, while the ratio of our concurrent *find* and *move* operations to our (more conservative) notion of an optimal protocol is $(1 + MST\text{-}stretch(G))/2$. The arrow directory has lower asymptotic communication complexity when the MST-stretch of the network is less than some polylogarithm in n. Nevertheless, we feel the most important distinction is that the arrow directory protocol is much simpler than any of the hierarchical protocols, because it is explicitly designed to be implemented. We plan to report experimental results in the near future.

References

1. S.V. Adve and K. Gharachorloo. Shared memory consistency models: A tutorial. Technical Report ECE TR 9512 and Western Research Laboratory Research Report 95/7, Rice University ECE, Houston, TX, September 1995. A version of this paper appears in IEEE Computer, December 1996, 66-7.

2. B. Awerbuch, B. Berger, L. Cowen, and D. Peleg. Fast distributed network decompositions and covers. *Journal of Parallel and Distributed Computing*, 39(2):105–114, 15 December 1996.

3. B. Awerbuch and D. Peleg. Online tracking of mobile users. *Journal of the ACM*, 42(5):1021–1058, September 1995.

4. B. Bershad, M. Zekauskas, and W.A. Sawdon. The Midway distributed shared memory system. In *Proceedings of 38th IEEE Computer Society International Conference*, pages 528–537, February 1993.

5. J.B. Carter, J.K. Bennet, and W. Zwaenepoel. Implementation and performance of Munin. In *Proceedings of the 13th Symposium on Operating Systems Principles*, pages 152–164, October 1991.

6. D. Chaiken, J. Kubiatowicz, and A. Agarwal. LimitLESS directories: A scalable cache coherence scheme. In *Proceedings Of The 4th International Conference on Architectural Support for Programming Langauges and Operating Systems*, pages 224–234. ACM, April 1991.

7. P. Fraigniaud and C. Gavoille. Memory requirement for universal routing schemes. In *Proceedings of the 13th Annual ACM Symposium on Principles of Distributed Computing*, pages 223–243. acm, August 1995.

8. D. Ginat. Adaptive ordering of condending processes in distributed systems. Technical Report CS-TR-2335, University of Maryland, Computer Science, October 89.

9. G. Graunke and S. Thakkar. Synchronization algorithms for shared-memory multiprocessors. *IEEE Computer*, 23(6):60–70, June 1990.

10. M.P. Herlihy. The Aleph toolkit: Platform-independent distributed shared memory (preliminary report). www.cs.brown.edu/~mph/aleph.

11. M.P. Herlihy and J.M. Wing. Linearizability: A correctness condition for concurrent objects. *ACM Transactions On Programming Languages and Systems*, 12(3):463–492, July 1990.

12. K. L. Johnson, M. F. Kaashoek, and D. A. Wallach. CRL: High-Performance All-Software Distributed Shared Memory. In *Proc. of the 15th ACM Symp. on Operating Systems Principles*, pages 213–228, December 1995.

13. P. Keleher, S. Dwarkadas, A. L. Cox, and W. Zwaenepoel. TreadMarks: Distributed Shared Memory on Standard Workstations and Operating Systems. In *Proc. of the Winter 1994 USENIX Conference*, pages 115–131, January 1994.

14. U. Legedza, D. Wetherhall, and J. Guttag. Improving the performance of distributed applications using active networks. Submitted to IEEE INFOCOMM, San Francisco, April 1998.

15. K. Li and P. Hudak. Memory coherence in shared virtual memory systems. *ACM Transactions on Computer Systems*, 7(4):321–359, November 1987.

16. N.A. Lynch and M.R. Tuttle. Hierarchical correctness proofs for distributed algorithms. Technical Report MIT/LCS/TM-387, MIT Laboratory For Computer Science, April 1987.

17. N.A. Lynch and M.R. Tuttle. An introduction to input/output automata. Technical Report MIT/LCS/TM-373, MIT Laboratory For Computer Science, November 1988.

18. M. Naïmi, M. Tréhel, and A. Arnold. A log(n) distributed mutual exclusion algorithm based on path reveral. *Journal of Parallel and Distributed Computing*, 34:1–13, 1996.

19. R. S. Nikhil. Cid: A Parallel, "Shared Memory" C for Distributed-Memory Machines. In *Proc. of the 7th Int'l Workshop on Languages and Compilers for Parallel Computing*, August 1994.

20. D. Peleg. Distance-dependent distributed directories. *Information and Computation*, 103(2):270–298, April 1993.

21. D. Peleg and E. Upfal. A trade-off between space and efficiency for routing tables. *Journal of the ACM*, 36:43–52, July 1989.

22. C.G. Plaxton, R. Rajaman, and A.W. Richa. Accessing nearby copies of replicated objects in a distributed environment. In *Proceedings of the 9th Annual ACM Symposium on Parallel Algorithms and Architectures*, pages 311–321, June 1997.

Efficient Byzantine Agreement
Secure Against General Adversaries *

(Extended Abstract)

Matthias Fitzi and Ueli Maurer

Department of Computer Science
Swiss Federal Institute of Technology (ETH), Zurich
CH-8092 Zurich, Switzerland,
{fitzi,maurer}@inf.ethz.ch

Abstract. This paper presents protocols for Byzantine agreement, i.e. for reliable broadcast, among a set of n players, some of which may be controlled by an adversary. It is well-known that Byzantine agreement is possible if and only if the number of cheaters is less than $n/3$. In this paper we consider a general adversary that is specified by a set of subsets of the player set (the adversary structure), and any one of these subsets may be corrupted by the adversary. The only condition we need is that no three of these subsets cover the full player set. A result of Hirt and Maurer implies that this condition is necessary and sufficient for the existence of a Byzantine agreement protocol, but the complexity of their protocols is generally exponential in the number of players. The purpose of this paper is to present the first protocol with polynomial message and computation complexity for any (even exponentially large) specification of the adversary structure. This closes a gap in a recent result of Cramer, Damgård and Maurer on applying span programs to secure multi-party computation.

Key words. Broadcast, Byzantine agreement, general adversary, multi-party computation, fault detection.

1 Introduction

1.1 Byzantine Agreement

In this paper, we focus on unconditionally secure protocols for Byzantine agreement, i.e. the security does not rely on any computational assumptions. We consider the standard model of a complete (fully connected) synchronous network among a set P of n players with pairwise authenticated communication channels.

---

* Research supported by the Swiss National Science Foundation (SNF), SPP project no. 5003-045293

With respect to this model, the goal of a broadcast (or Byzantine agreement) protocol is to let some specific player, the dealer, reliably distribute some value to all other players. Even in the presence of an adversary that corrupts certain players the protocol must satisfy the conditions given in Definition 1. In the sequel, corrupted players are called *faulty* whereas uncorrupted players are called *correct*.

Definition 1. *A protocol* achieves Byzantine agreement *(or is a broadcast protocol) if and only if the following conditions are satisfied:*

1. Termination: *After a finite number of rounds, every correct player decides on a value, i.e. the protocol terminates for all correct players.*
2. Agreement: *All correct players decide on the same value.*
3. Validity: *If the dealer is correct then all correct players decide on the dealer's original value.*

A broadcast protocol secure against an adversary who can corrupt up to arbitrary t of the involved players is called t-*resilient*.

Pease, Shostak and Lamport proved in [PSL80,LSP82] that the condition $t < n/3$ is a tight bound for the existence of a Byzantine agreement protocol. The protocol they proposed requires exponential message complexity and hence is not practical. However, their protocol is round-optimal, as Fischer and Lynch proved in [FL82] that the lower bound on the number of rounds for any perfectly secure Byzantine agreement protocol with t corrupted players is $t + 1$. Efficient protocols for Byzantine agreement with resilience $t < n/3$ have been proposed in [DFF$^+$82,BDDS87,FM88,BGP89]. Finally Garay and Moses [GM93] presented the first protocol that is both efficient and round-optimal.

1.2 General Adversaries

Ben-Or, Goldwasser and Wigderson [BGW88] and independently Chaum, Crépeau and Damgård [CCD88] proved that, in a threshold setting where up to t arbitrary players can be corrupted by an adversary, secure multi-party computation among a set of n players is possible for any function if and only if less than a third of the players are actively corrupted ($t < n/3$). Hirt and Maurer [HM97] extended this result to general (rather than threshold) adversary structures. An adversary structure is a monotone set of subsets of the player set. A similar concept was proposed independently by Malkhi and Reiter in [MR97] in the context of quorum systems. As a strict generalization of the threshold setting, any player subset of the adversary structure may be corrupted in the general adversary setting. The threshold setting ($t < n/3$) is a special case of the general setting where the adversary structure consists of all player subsets of cardinality at most t. As proven in [HM97], multi-party computation secure against a general adversary is possible for any function if and only if no three elements (player subsets) of the adversary structure cover the full player set — this is also a tight bound for the existence of a broadcast protocol as immediately follows by the optimality proof in [LSP82].

Example 1. In order to see that it is useful to handle the general adversary model for multi-party computation (or for broadcast in particular) consider, for example, the player set $P = \{d, e, f, g, h, i\}$.[1] As defined later in the text, we describe an adversary structure $\mathcal{A}$ by its basis $\overline{\mathcal{A}}$ where only all maximal player subsets of $\mathcal{A}$ are contained.

In the threshold setting, according to the condition $t < n/3$, at most one of the players in P can be tolerated to be corrupted by the adversary. Hence the (maximal) adversary structure tolerated by a threshold protocol is defined by the basis

$$\overline{\mathcal{A}} = \{\{d\}, \{e\}, \{f\}, \{g\}, \{h\}, \{i\}\}.$$

In contrast, by considering general adversaries, strictly more corruptions can be tolerated. Consider the adversary structure defined by the basis

$$\overline{\mathcal{A}} = \{\{d, e, f\}, \{d, g\}, \{e, h\}, \{e, i\}, \{f, g\}\}.$$

No three elements of $\mathcal{A}$ cover the full player set. Hence, by the result in [HM97], there is a multi-party computation for every function that tolerates any player subset in $\mathcal{A}$ to be corrupted. Besides several player pairs that are tolerated to be corrupted, the protocol is even resilient against a player triplet ($\{d, e, f\}$). Note that for every single player there is at least one second player that can be tolerated to be corrupted at the same time.

1.3 Contributions of this Paper

Broadcast protocols have been studied extensively for the threshold setting but not for the general adversary setting introduced in [HM97]. Broadcast is a special case of multi-party computation. Hence, the protocol of [HM97] for general multi-party computation can be directly used to implement broadcast. A different such broadcast protocol is described in [MR97]. However, the computation and message complexities of these protocols are generally exponential in the number of players.

Efficient broadcast is an important primitive used as a subprotocol in various applications such as secure multi-party computation. For example, the results of Cramer, Damgård and Maurer in [CDM98] rely on the existence of a broadcast protocol, secure against a general adversary, with computation and message complexity polynomial in the number of players — without giving a solution for this problem. This paper closes this gap by proposing an algorithm to construct a secure broadcast protocol for any general adversary structure satisfying that no three elements of the structure cover the full player set. The resulting protocols have communication complexity polynomial in the number n of players. The computation complexity is polynomial in n assuming only that there exists an algorithm polynomial in n for deciding whether a given subset of the players is an element of $\mathcal{A}$.

---

[1] Throughout we denote the players with single letters and start enumerating them by d. In the context of broadcast d will be used to name the dealer.

Finally, some techniques for extending threshold protocols to the general adversary setting proposed in this paper are generic and can also be applied to other broadcast protocols designed for the threshold setting.

1.4 Definitions

The set of players involved in the broadcast protocol is denoted by P. An *adversary structure* $\mathcal{A}$ over the player set P is a monotone set of subsets of P, i.e.

$$\mathcal{A} \subseteq 2^P \text{ with } A \in \mathcal{A} \Longrightarrow \forall A' \subseteq A : A' \in \mathcal{A}.$$

An element $A \in \mathcal{A}$ is called an *adversary set*. For an adversary structure $\mathcal{A}$, $\overline{\mathcal{A}}$ denotes the *basis* of $\mathcal{A}$, i.e. the set of all maximal elements of $\mathcal{A}$:

$$\overline{\mathcal{A}} := \{ A \in \mathcal{A} \mid \not\exists A' \in \mathcal{A} : A \subset A' \}.$$

The meaning of an adversary structure $\mathcal{A}$ is that the players of exactly one element of $\mathcal{A}$ may be corrupted by the adversary.

Definition 2. *A broadcast protocol that, according to Definition 1, is secure against a general adversary that corrupts the players of an arbitrary element of a structure $\mathcal{A}$ is called $\mathcal{A}$-resilient.*

Later we will consider the properties of subsets $S \subset P$ rather than of the whole player set P. In particular, we will be interested in the properties of the structure $\mathcal{A}$ when *restricted* to some player subset $S \subset P$, i.e. by reducing all adversary sets $A \in \mathcal{A}$ to the players in S:

$$\mathcal{A}|_S := \{ A \cap S \mid A \in \mathcal{A} \}.$$

Definition 3. *An adversary structure $\mathcal{A}$ over a player set P satisfies the predicate $Q^k(P, \mathcal{A})$ if no k sets in $\mathcal{A}$ cover the full player set:*

$$Q^k(P, \mathcal{A}) \quad :\Longleftrightarrow \quad \forall A_{i_1}, A_{i_2}, ..., A_{i_k} \in \mathcal{A} : \bigcup_{j=1}^{k} A_{i_j} \neq P.$$

We will mostly be interested in these predicates applied to subsets $S \subset P$ rather than to P. Instead of writing $Q^k(S, \mathcal{A}|_S)$ for "no k adversary sets (restricted to S) cover the player subset S" we will use the shorthand notation $Q^k(S, \mathcal{A})$ or even $Q^k(S)$ if $\mathcal{A}$ is evident from the context.

1.5 Outline

In Section 2 simple but inefficient broadcast protocols secure against general adversaries are discussed, more precisely, for any given player set P and adversary structure $\mathcal{A}$ satisfying $Q^3(P, \mathcal{A})$ we describe an $\mathcal{A}$-resilient protocol — we refer to a particular protocol of this kind as a *basic protocol*. A basic protocol is obtained by modifying the "exponential" threshold protocol of [BDDS87]. Section 3 describes efficient broadcast protocols based on the basic protocols of Section 2, i.e. for any given player set P and adversary structure $\mathcal{A}$ satisfying $Q^3(P, \mathcal{A})$ we describe an $\mathcal{A}$-resilient protocol with communication and computation complexity polynomial in the number of players — a particular protocol of this kind will be referred to as an *efficient protocol*. The paper ends with some conclusions in Section 4.

2 The Basic Broadcast Protocol

Using the terminology of [BDDS87], the basic protocol proceeds in two subsequent phases, *information gathering (IG)* and *data conversion (DC)*. The information gathering phase consists of a fixed number of communication rounds among the players. Whenever a player p is expected to send a message to some other player q but fails to do so, then q decides for the default value 0 to be his received value. In the data conversion phase, every player locally computes his result (i.e. the broadcast value he decides on) with no further communication. For the sequel, let P be the player set with cardinality $|P| = n$ and let d be the dealer. The remaining players will be enumerated by the letters e, f, etc.

2.1 Information Gathering

Every player maintains a local tree called *information gathering* tree or *IG-tree* for short which is used to keep track of all messages received during information gathering. The structure of this tree is exactly the same for every player. Every node of the IG-tree corresponds to a player $p \in P$. The nodes are labelled by a list α of players — the list of all players corresponding to the nodes in the path from the root to the node itself, i.e. the last element of this list is the node's corresponding player.

Throughout this paper, players are denoted by small Roman letters whereas lists of players are denoted by small Greek letters (or by strings if their elements are mentioned explicitly). For a node αp, player p is called the *corresponding player* of αp and, conversely, we call αp a *corresponding node* of player p. The set of all players corresponding to a node α or to one of its predecessor nodes are called the *corresponding players of α's message path*. Let the *height* of a node α in the IG-tree be defined as its number of predecessors in the tree and let the *tree level* of a node α be $level(\alpha) = height(\alpha) + 1$ (hence the root node is of level 1).

The root node of the IG-tree corresponds to the dealer d. Every node α of some tree level k is either a leaf or an internal node with $n - k$ children — one child αp for each player $p \in P$ that does not occur in α. A node α is defined to be an internal node exactly if there exists an adversary set $A \in \mathcal{A}$ that contains all players in α, else the node is defined to be a leaf. Hence every path from the root to a leaf consists of a sequence of internal nodes that correspond to the

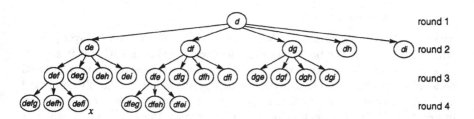

Fig. 1. IG-Tree for Example 1

players of an adversary set $A \in \mathcal{A}$ and finally of a leaf corresponding to a player $p \notin A$. There is no adversary set $\mathcal{A}'$ containing all players corresponding to the nodes in the path ($\nexists \mathcal{A}' : \mathcal{A}' \supseteq A \cup \{p\}$). Note that the height of the IG-tree is by one greater than the cardinality of an adversary set $A \in \mathcal{A}$ of maximal size (and hence at most n since $P \notin \mathcal{A}$). Figure 1 illustrates this construction for the adversary structure $\mathcal{A}$ over the player set $P = \{d, e, f, g, h, i\}$ of Example 1 (defined by the basis $\overline{\mathcal{A}} = \{\{d, e, f\}, \{d, g\}, \{e, h\}, \{e, i\}, \{f, g\}\}$).

The IG-tree describes the local view of the message flow during information gathering by the individual players. The nodes of the tree are used to store the received messages whereas the edges of the tree describe the dependencies of these messages on each other. Every message received during round k is stored in exactly one node of level k. The local tree of player p is denoted by $tree_p$. The value that player p stores at the node α of his IG-tree is denoted by $tree_p(\alpha)$.

In the first communication round of information gathering, the dealer d distributes his original value (i.e. the value to be broadcast) to every other player and decides on this value as his result of the broadcast. The dealer will not be involved in any subsequent communication round. Every player p stores the value received by the dealer at the root node d of his IG-tree. According to the structure of the IG-tree, in the k-th round ($k > 1$) of the protocol every player p distributes to every other player the value $tree_p(\alpha)$ for each node α of level $k - 1$ that has a child node αp and a receiver r stores this message at this node αp of his IG-tree.[2]

Hence, any message received by a player p originates from the dealer and is passed on step by step through some specific message path involving other players[3], and such a message is stored in the node that is labelled by the string corresponding to its message path (excluding the receiver). For example assume the IG-tree in Figure 1 to be $tree_g$. Then the meaning of the value $tree_g(defi) = x$ stored by player g is that "player i told g that player f told i that player e told f that the dealer d told e that x was his original value".

---

[2] Actually, messages must consist of a value and additional information about the node of the IG-tree which is referred to by the message. In the sequel we just assume a message to consist of this value and we neglect this additional information.

[3] Note that faulty intermediary players may alter the contents of the message.

2.2 Data Conversion

After information gathering, in the data conversion phase, every player p computes his result (i.e. the broadcast value he decides on) on his IG-tree in a "bottom up manner" by starting with the leaves and recursively, for every internal node, computing a value that is determined by the values previously computed for its child nodes. The function to perform this computation is called *resolve*. In order to define the function *resolve*, we introduce the new value $\perp$ which is defined to be outside the domain of the value to be broadcast. $\perp$ will only result for nodes with its corresponding player being faulty, i.e. it is used to indicate "severe" inconsistencies for such a node. Indication of inconsistencies is only needed for the efficient protocol in Section 3 and the resolve-function could in fact be simplified for the basic protocol discussed here.

Definition 4. *The set of all players corresponding to the children of a node α of the IG-tree is denoted by $C(\alpha)$. The subset of all correct players among the players corresponding to the children nodes of α is denoted by $C_c(\alpha)$.*

The resolve function takes a node of the IG-tree as an input and outputs the value to be assigned as the resolved value for the given node (described here for the local tree of player p):

$$resolve_p(\alpha) := \begin{cases} tree_p(\alpha) & \text{if } \alpha \text{ is a leaf,} \\ v & \exists!\ v \neq \perp \colon Q^1(\{c \in C(\alpha) \mid resolve_p(\alpha c) = v\}), \\ 0 & \text{else if } \alpha = d, \\ \perp & \text{else.} \end{cases}$$

In other words, an internal node α is resolved to the value v if there is a unique value v such that the children of α resolving to v are covered by an adversary set $A \in \mathcal{A}$ (more precisely, if the set of their corresponding players satisfies Q^1) — else the default value $\perp$ (or 0) is assigned. The distinction between the last two cases in the definition of the resolve function is only needed for the correctness of the efficient protocol in Section 3 (besides this, we want the broadcast value to be in the original domain).

Since $\perp$ is not in the domain of the broadcast, a correct player is not to distribute $\perp$ during information gathering. If, for some node, a correct player receives any value outside the domain during information gathering he will store the default value 0 instead.

2.3 Protocol Analysis

Definition 5. *A node α of the IG-tree is common with value v if every correct player computes the same value v for α in the data conversion phase. The subtree rooted at node α has a common frontier if every path from α to a leaf contains at least one common node.*

Lemma 1. *For any adversary structure $\mathcal{A}$ over a player subset $S \subseteq P$ satisfying $Q^k(S, \mathcal{A})$ and any adversary set $A \in \mathcal{A}$, the restricted adversary structure $\mathcal{A}|_{(S \backslash A)}$ satisfies $Q^{k-1}(S \backslash A, \mathcal{A}|_{(S \backslash A)})$.*

Proof. Let $A \in \mathcal{A}$ be an adversary set. Then $Q^k(S, \mathcal{A})$ implies $\nexists A_{i_1}, \cdots, A_{i_{k-1}} :$ $A \cup A_{i_1} \cup \cdots \cup A_{i_{k-1}} = P$ and hence $\nexists A_{i_1}, \cdots, A_{i_{k-1}} : A_{i_1} \cup \cdots \cup A_{i_{k-1}} = P \backslash A$ which implies $Q^{k-1}(S \backslash A, \mathcal{A}|_{(S \backslash A)})$.

Corollary 1. *If the adversary structure $\mathcal{A}$ over the player set P satisfies $Q^k(P, \mathcal{A})$ then for every internal node α of the IG-tree, $\mathcal{A}|_{C(\alpha)}$ satisfies $Q^{k-1}(C(\alpha), \mathcal{A}|_{C(\alpha)})$.*

Proof. By construction, for every internal node α there is an adversary set $A \in \mathcal{A}$ that contains exactly the players corresponding to α's message path, and $C(\alpha) = P \backslash A$. Hence, by Lemma 1, we have $Q^{k-1}(C(\alpha), \mathcal{A}|_{C(\alpha)})$.

Lemma 2. *All nodes $\alpha = \beta r$ that correspond to a correct player r are common with the value $tree_r(\beta) = v$.*

Proof. Let p and r be correct players. We have to show that $resolve_p(\alpha) = tree_p(\alpha) = tree_r(\beta)$ for player p. Since r is correct, he distributes the same value $tree_r(\beta) = v$ to all other players, and hence $tree_p(\alpha) = tree_r(\beta) = v$.

It remains to prove that $resolve_p(\alpha) = tree_p(\alpha)$. If α is a leaf then by definition $resolve\ resolve_p(\alpha) = tree_p(\alpha)$. Assume the lemma holds for all nodes of level k of the IG-tree and let $\alpha = \beta r$ be a node of level $k - 1$. By condition $Q^3(P)$ and by Corollary 1 we have $Q^2(C(\alpha))$. The adversary corrupts the players of exactly one adversary set $A \in \mathcal{A}$. But by discounting any such adversary set A from the children player set $C(\alpha)$, the set $C_c(\alpha) = C(\alpha) \backslash A$ of all correct players in $C(\alpha)$ still satisfies $Q^1(C_c(\alpha))$ (by Corollary 1). Since these players are correct their corresponding nodes (of level k) are common with value v by induction, and hence $Q^1(\{c \in C(\alpha) \mid resolve_p(\alpha c) = v\})$. On the other hand, for at most all players $a \in A$ of one adversary set $A \in \mathcal{A}$, $resolve_p(\alpha a) \neq v$ and hence $\neg Q^1(\{c \in C(\alpha) \mid resolve_p(\alpha c) \neq v\})$. Hence by the definition of the resolve function, since v is unique, player p computes $resolve_p(\alpha) = v$.

Lemma 3. *Let α be a node of the IG-tree. If there is a common frontier in the subtree rooted in α then α is common.*

Proof. A leaf node has a common frontier exactly if it is common, hence the lemma holds for all leaves. It remains to prove the lemma for internal nodes. For the sake of contradiction, assume an internal node α not to be common but to have a common frontier. Since α is not common there must be a non-common child of α — otherwise, every correct player would compute the same value for α during data conversion and α would be common. This argument holds for such a non-common node as well, and can be recursively applied down to the leaves of the IG-tree. Thus there is a path from α to one of the leaves of its subtree that contains no common node and hence α has no common frontier. This contradicts the assumption.

Theorem 1. *For any player set P and adversary structure $\mathcal{A}$ satisfying $Q^3(P)$ the basic protocol is $\mathcal{A}$-resilient.*

Proof. By the construction of the IG-tree, for every path from the root d to a leaf node there exists no adversary set $A \in \mathcal{A}$ that contains all players that correspond to the nodes in this path. Hence, on every such path there is a correct player, so by Lemma 2 the root has a common frontier and by Lemma 3 the root is common. Finally, if the dealer is correct, then by Lemma 2, the root node is common with the original value of the dealer.

3 The Efficient Broadcast Protocol

It is evident that for any adversary structure $\mathcal{A}$ with exponential size in $|P|$ the basic protocol is not efficient since the number of messages to be sent is of size $\Omega(|\mathcal{A}|)$ (the size of the IG-tree). In order to make the basic broadcast protocol efficient, we generalize and apply the shifting technique introduced in [BDDS87].

We fix some protocol parameter b with $4 \leq b < n$. The original IG-tree is reduced by pruning all nodes of level $l > b$. This reduced tree defines a protocol with b communication rounds which is called *reduced protocol*. In the reduced protocol, information gathering consists of exactly that subset of messages of the basic protocol for which there exists a node in the reduced tree to store the received message. Data conversion is defined in the same way as for the basic protocol. In the sequel we assume that the original IG-tree is of height $h > b$ and that hence the reduced IG-tree is not identical to the original IG-tree of the basic protocol. In the other case we define the efficient protocol to be equal to the basic protocol (since we do not need the protocol extensions described in this section).

3.1 Protocol Overview

The efficient protocol consists of executing the reduced protocol in sequence for $\left\lceil \frac{n-3}{b-3} \right\rceil + 1$ runs as follows[4]: The first run of the reduced protocol proceeds in the same way as the basic protocol (with the difference that it only proceeds for b communication rounds). In every subsequent run (say the m-th run) of the reduced protocol the first communication round of the protocol is omitted. Instead of receiving a value from the dealer, every player p assigns the resolved root value computed at the end of the previous run to the root node of his reduced IG-tree:

$$tree_p^{(m)}(d) := resolve_p^{(m-1)}(d) .$$

Apart from this the subsequent runs proceed in the same way as the first one.

The reason for pruning the IG-tree to obtain the reduced protocol is to reduce the communication complexity of the protocol to polynomial in the number of players. However, as a consequence, there is not necessarily a common frontier for the root node when the reduced protocol is run and hence the root node is

---

[4] Note the difference between the terms *round* and *run*. The term *round* refers to a single communication round of a protocol whereas *run* refers to an execution of the reduced protocol which consists of several communication rounds.

not necessarily common. This problem can be solved by repeating the reduced protocol for a sufficient number of times. The following important properties will be proven:

- If the dealer is correct then the root node is common with his original value after the first run of the reduced protocol (this directly follows since the node d has a common frontier).
- If after some run m of the reduced protocol the root node of the IG-tree is common with some value v then the root node will be common with value v for every subsequent run $m' > m$, i.e. the agreed value will remain persistent.
- There is a method for detecting faulty players such that if after m runs of the reduced protocol the root node is not common, then there are $m(b-3)+1$ players that are globally detected (i.e. detected by all correct players) to be faulty.[5]

Finally, after $\left\lceil \frac{n-3}{b-3} \right\rceil + 1$ runs, either all faulty players have been globally detected or Byzantine agreement has been achieved. If we let every correct player replace all messages from detected players by the default value 0, then Byzantine agreement is also achieved in the former case because all globally detected players are treated like consistently distributing the default value in the last round.

We now describe additional details of the efficient protocol.

3.2 Fault Handling

Every player p maintains a player list L_p and adds to it in each round all players he reliably detects to be faulty. This list of detected players will never contain any correct player.

Let p be a correct player. In order to find conditions for the detection of faulty players by p, we first derive a condition that must be satisfied for every internal node of the IG-tree corresponding to a correct player. Let αr be an internal node corresponding to a correct player r. During information gathering, r distributes the same value $tree_r(\alpha) = v$ for his node α to every player. Accordingly, in the following round, only a faulty player q may send to p a distinct value $w \neq v$ for his node αr. Hence there exists an adversary set $A \in \mathcal{A}$ and a unique value v such that all players q with $tree_p(\alpha r q) \neq v$ are covered by A. Moreover, the set of already detected players L_p must be a subset of such an A, i.e. the condition

$$\exists v : \exists A \in \mathcal{A} : A \supseteq (\{c \in C(\alpha r) \mid tree_p(\alpha r c) \neq v\} \cup L_p)$$

is satisfied. Hence player r can be reliably detected to be faulty by player p if there is no such value v.

This rule can be applied during information gathering: player p adds player r to L_p if there is no such value v. By Lemma 2, this even holds for the converted values of αr's child nodes. Hence we can apply the same rule for the resolved

---

[5] A player does not necessarily know which of the players he detected are globally detected and which are not.

values as well and we obtain the following fault detection rules to be applied by player p for every internal node αr:

Fault detection during information gathering (FD1):

$$L_p := L_p \cup \{r\} \quad \text{if } \not\exists v : \neg Q^1(\{c \in C(\alpha r) \mid tree_p(\alpha rc) \neq v\} \cup L_p).$$

Fault detection during data conversion (FD2):

$$L_p := L_p \cup \{r\} \quad \text{if } \not\exists v : \neg Q^1(\{c \in C(\alpha r) \mid resolve_p(\alpha rc) \neq v\} \cup L_p).$$

Fault Masking:
After a player r has been added to the list L_p by player p in some communication round k, then every message by player r in round k and any subsequent round is replaced by the default value 0. Once a player has been globally detected (by all correct players), he will be masked to send the same values to all correct players. Thus, every node αr for which a value is received after player r's global detection will be common.

We are ready to summarize the complete protocol (the description is given for the view by player p).

Efficient Protocol:

1. Dealer distributes original value to all players.
2. FOR $i := 1$ TO $\left\lceil \frac{n-3}{b-3} \right\rceil + 1$
3.   Information gathering with fault detection FD1 and fault masking for $b - 1$ rounds.
4.   Local data conversion with fault detection FD2 by every player p.
5. $tree_p(d) := resolve_p(d)$.
6. END.
7. Decide on $tree_p(d)$ for the broadcast result and halt.

3.3 Protocol Analysis

We first show that if in any run (FOR-loop in the above protocol) Byzantine agreement is achieved, then the agreement remains persistent (with the same value) for any following run. The following lemma follows immediately by Lemma 2.

Lemma 4. *If all correct players store the same value at the root of the IG-tree at the beginning of information gathering (i.e. before step 3 of some run of the reduced protocol) then the root will be common with this value after data conversion.*

The following lemmas will be needed to argue about global detections of faulty players.

Lemma 5. *Let α be an internal node. If all players corresponding to α's message path are faulty, then the subset $C_c(\alpha) \subseteq C(\alpha)$ of all correct players among the players corresponding to the children of α satisfies $Q^2(C_c(\alpha))$.*

Proof. By construction, $C(\alpha)$ consists of all players except for the players corresponding to α's message path. Let $A \in \mathcal{A}$ contain all players that correspond to α's message path and let A be the corrupted adversary set. Then $C_c(\alpha) = C(\alpha) \backslash A = P \backslash A$ holds and by Lemma 1 we have $Q^2(P \backslash A)$ and hence $Q^2(C_c(\alpha))$.

Lemma 6. *Let p and q be correct players and let αr be an internal node of the IG-tree but not the root node. Assume all players corresponding to αr's message path to be faulty. If p and q obtain different values for αr after data conversion neither of which is $\bot$, then $r \in L_p \cap L_q$.*

Proof. For any value v let $C_v \subseteq C_c(\alpha r)$ denote the set of correct players c for which $tree_p(\alpha rc) = v$ and let $C_{\overline{v}} = C_c(\alpha r) \backslash C_v$.

Suppose that $r \notin L_p$ after data conversion. According to the fault detection rule FD1, since p has not detected r to be faulty, there is a value v such that $\neg Q^1(\{c \in C(\alpha r) \mid tree_p(\alpha rc) \neq v\} \cup L_p)$. This still holds when restricted to all correct players in $C(\alpha r)$: $\neg Q^1(C_{\overline{v}} \cup L_p)$.

By Lemma 5 the correct children of αr satisfy $Q^2(C_c(\alpha r))$. Since there is an adversary set $A \in \mathcal{A}$ with $C_{\overline{v}} \subseteq A$, we obtain $Q^1(C_v)$ for $C_v = C_c(\alpha r) \backslash C_{\overline{v}}$ by Lemma 1.

The correct children of αr are common due to Lemma 2 and hence all correct players will resolve value v for the children nodes corresponding to the players in C_v:

$$Q^1(\{c \in C_c(\alpha r) \mid resolve_p(\alpha rc) = resolve_q(\alpha rc) = v\}).$$

By the uniqueness condition in the definition of the *resolve* function it follows that $resolve_q(\alpha r) \in \{v, \bot\}$. This contradicts the assumption.

Lemma 7. *Let αr be an internal node of the IG-tree, but not the parent of a leaf. If all players corresponding to the path of αr are faulty and there is a correct player p who does not detect r to be faulty by either of the fault detection rules, then αr is common.*

Proof. Since p does not detect r during data conversion, there is a value v with $resolve_p(\alpha r) = v$ and

$$\neg Q^1(\{c \in C(\alpha r) \mid resolve_p(\alpha rc) \neq v\} \cup L_p).$$

Let q be any other correct player and let $s \notin L_p$ be a player with $resolve_p(\alpha rs) = v$. By Lemma 6 $resolve_q(\alpha rs) \in \{v, \bot\}$ (in fact v by Lemma 2 if s is correct), and hence for any $w \notin \{v, \bot\}$, the subset of the children of αr for which w is resolved by player q satisfies

$$\{c \in C(\alpha r) \mid resolve_q(\alpha rc) = w\} \subseteq \{c \in C(\alpha r) \mid resolve_p(\alpha rc) \neq v\} \cup L_p.$$

Therefore for all values $w \notin \{v, \bot\}$ we have

$$\forall w, w \notin \{v, \bot\} : \neg Q^1(\{c \in C(\alpha r) \mid resolve_q(\alpha rc) = w\}).$$

On the other hand, by Lemma 5 we have $Q^2(C_c(\alpha r))$ and hence $Q^1(\{c \in C_c(\alpha r) \mid resolve_p(\alpha rc) = v\})$ for all correct children for which player p resolves v. These children are common by Lemma 2. Hence q computes $resolve_q(\alpha r) = v$ because v is a unique value according to the definition of the resolve function.

Due to Lemma 7, after the initial run of the reduced protocol of $b \geq 4$ rounds, either the root is common or at least $b - 2$ faulty players have been globally detected: If the root is not common then there is no common frontier and hence, by Lemma 2, there is a path from the root to a leaf in the IG-tree that contains only non-common nodes (corresponding to faulty players). All of these corresponding players are globally detected — except for the leaf and its parent node which are not necessarily detected.

In every subsequent run, if Byzantine agreement is not achieved, then further $b - 3$ players are globally detected. Nodes that correspond to players that have been globally detected will be common since fault masking guarantees that all correct players consistently store the default value at such nodes. Hence it is guaranteed that the detections of a new run correspond to players that have not been detected before. On the other hand, the dealer does not distribute any values after the first run of the basic protocol because the values for the root node are locally computed by the players. Hence, there is no masking for the dealer and the dealer will be redetected in every subsequent run not achieving Byzantine agreement. This is the reason why only $b - 3$ further global detections are guaranteed in the subsequent runs.

Theorem 2. *For any player set P and adversary structure $\mathcal{A}$ satisfying $Q^3(P)$ the efficient protocol achieves Byzantine agreement. The algorithm has message complexity polynomial in the size n of the player set and round complexity less than $2n$. Assuming an algorithm polynomial in n for deciding whether a given player set is an element of $\mathcal{A}$, the computation complexity is polynomial in n.*

Proof. Suppose that Byzantine agreement has not been achieved after the given protocol has terminated. According to Lemma 4, agreement was not achieved in any previous round, i.e. the root of the IG-tree has never been common. Hence, due to Lemma 7, $b - 2$ faulty players have been detected in the first run and for every subsequent run, another $b - 3$ players have been globally detected. Hence the number k of globally detected players is

$$k = (b - 2) + \left\lceil \frac{n - 3}{b - 3} \right\rceil (b - 3) \geq (b - 2) + (n - 3) \geq n - 1.$$

Since at least $n - 1$ players have been globally detected, there is at most one single correct player. Hence, by definition, all nodes of the IG-tree are common (for all correct players), contradicting the assumption.

The message and computation complexities follow immediately from the construction of the protocol. The round complexity is $r = b + (b - 1) \left\lceil \frac{n - 3}{b - 3} \right\rceil < 2n$.

3.4 Optimizations

The efficient protocol can be optimized. For simplicity the protocol was described in a way that (except for the dealer) every message that is distributed, must be distributed to every player. In fact this is not necessary. If a player p must distribute a value $tree_p(\alpha)$ of his IG-tree then it suffices that he distributes this value only to those players that are not corresponding to α or any of its predecessor nodes. In other words, the IG-tree of a player p will contain no node $\alpha = \beta p \gamma$ with $|\gamma| > 0$. The efficient protocol can further be optimized by analyzing the concrete structure of the given adversary set which can yield a protocol that needs less runs of the basic protocol than described above.

4 Conclusions

For any adversary structure $\mathcal{A}$ for a player set P for which no three elements of $\mathcal{A}$ cover the full player set we have given an $\mathcal{A}$-resilient broadcast protocol with communication complexity polynomial in the cardinality $n = |P|$ of the player set. The computation complexity is polynomial in n assuming only the existence of an algorithm polynomial in n for deciding whether a given subset of the players is an element of $\mathcal{A}$. Moreover, our methods for generalizing the threshold protocol of [BDDS87] are universal and we expect them to be directly applicable for other broadcast protocols such as those of [FM88,GM93].

5 Acknowledgments

The authors would like to thank Ronald Cramer, Ivan Damgård, Juan Garay and Martin Hirt for helpful hints and interesting discussions.

References

[BDDS87] A. Bar-Noy, D. Dolev, C. Dwork, and H. R. Strong. Shifting gears: Changing algorithms on the fly to expedite Byzantine agreement. In *Proceedings of the Sixth Annual ACM Symposium on Principles of Distributed Computing*, pages 42–51, 1987.

[BGP89] P. Berman, J. A. Garay, and K. J. Perry. Towards optimal distributed consensus (extended abstract). In *30th Annual Symposium on Foundations of Computer Science*, pages 410–415. IEEE, 1989.

[BGW88] M. Ben-Or, S. Goldwasser, and A. Wigderson. Completeness theorems for non-cryptographic fault-tolerant distributed computation. In *Proc. 20th ACM Symposium on the Theory of Computing (STOC)*, pages 1–10, 1988.

[CCD88] D. Chaum, C. Crépeau, and I. Damgård. Multiparty unconditionally secure protocols (extended abstract). In *Proc. 20th ACM Symposium on the Theory of Computing (STOC)*, pages 11–19, 1988.

[CDM98] R. Cramer, I. Damgård, and U. Maurer. Span programs and general secure multi-party computation, Manuscript, 1998.

[DFF+82] D. Dolev, M. J. Fischer, R. Fowler, N. A. Lynch, and H. R. Strong. An efficient algorithm for Byzantine agreement without authentication. *Information and Control*, 52(3):257–274, March 1982.

[FL82] M. J. Fischer and N. A. Lynch. A lower bound on the time to assure interactive consistency. *Information Processing Letters*, 14(4):183–186, 1982.

[FM88] P. Feldman and S. Micali. Optimal algorithms for Byzantine agreement. In *Proc. 20th ACM Symposium on the Theory of Computing (STOC)*, pages 148–161, 1988.

[GM93] J. A. Garay and Y. Moses. Fully polynomial Byzantine agreement in $t + 1$ rounds (extended abstract). In *Proceedings of the Twenty-Fifth Annual ACM Symposium on Theory of Computing*, pages 31–41, 1993.

[HM97] M. Hirt and U. Maurer. Complete characterization of adversaries tolerable in secure multi-party computation. In *Proc. 16th ACM Symposium on Principles of Distributed Computing (PODC)*, pages 25–34, August 1997.

[LSP82] L. Lamport, R. Shostak, and M. Pease. The Byzantine generals problem. *ACM Transactions on Programming Languages and Systems*, 4(3):382–401, July 1982.

[MR97] D. Malkhi and M. Reiter. Byzantine quorum systems. In *Proceedings of the Twenty-Ninth Annual ACM Symposium on Theory of Computing*, pages 569–578, 1997.

[PSL80] M. Pease, R. Shostak, and L. Lamport. Reaching agreement in the presence of faults. *Journal of the ACM*, 27(2):228–234, April 1980.

Long-Lived, Fast, Waitfree Renaming with Optimal Name Space and High Throughput (Extended Abstract)

Wayne Eberly,[*] Lisa Higham,[**] and Jolanta Warpechowska-Gruca[***]

Department of Computer Science, The University of Calgary, Canada
{eberly | higham | jolanta}@cpsc.ucalgary.ca

Abstract. The (n, k, l)-renaming problem requires that names from the set $\{1, \ldots, l\}$ are assigned to processes from a set of size n, provided that no more than $k \leq l$ processes are simultaneously either holding or trying to acquire a name. A solution to this problem supplies a renaming object supporting both ACQUIRE and RELEASE operations so that no two processes ever simultaneously hold the same name. The protocol is *waitfree* if each participant successfully completes either operation in a bounded number of its own steps regardless of the speed of other processes; it is *long-lived* if it there is no bound on the number of operations that can be applied to the object; it is *fast* if the number of steps taken by any process before it completes an operation is independent of n; and it is *name-space-optimal* if $l = k$.

This paper presents the first renaming algorithm for atomic read/write registers that is waitfree, long-lived, fast, and name-space-optimal. Since optimal name space is impossible for deterministic renaming algorithms, our algorithm is randomized. The maximum number (over schedulers and processes) of the expected number (over coin flips) of accesses to read/write registers required to complete either an ACQUIRE or RELEASE operation is $\Theta(k^2)$.

We also define a notion of amortized expected complexity that measures the throughput of a system. The amortized expected step complexity of the new renaming algorithm is $\Theta(k \log k)$, which is a substantial improvement, in this amortized sense, over any preceding long-lived renaming algorithm for read/write registers (whether name-space-optimal or not). The notion of amortized complexity of waitfree protocols may be of independent interest since it seems to suggest that waitfreedom may not be as impractical as is sometimes suspected.

[*] Research was supported in part by Natural Sciences and Engineering Research Council of Canada grant OGP0089756.

[**] Research was supported in part by Natural Sciences and Engineering Research Council of Canada grant OGP0041900.

[***] Research was supported in part by Natural Sciences and Engineering Research Council of Canada grant dOGP0041900 and DeVry Institute of Technology, Calgary, Canada.

1 Introduction

In a distributed system, the maximum allowable contention (henceforth, k) for a particular system resource is typically much smaller than the total number of processes (henceforth, n) in the system. However, several protocols for resource management have complexity that depends on the size of the original name space of all processes that use the resource. Thus we are motivated to temporarily rename processes, so that they have distinct names from a smaller name space before they access a resource. This is a primary application of renaming protocols as first introduced by Attiya et. al. [4]. The (n, k, l)-renaming problem requires that names from $\{1, \ldots, l\}$ are assigned to processes from a set of size n, provided that no more than $k \leq l$ processes are simultaneously either holding or trying to acquire a name. A solution to this problem supplies a renaming object that supports the operations ACQUIRE and RELEASE and ensures that no two processes ever simultaneously hold the same name.

Several desirable properties have been proposed for renaming protocols. In a multiprocessor system, the likelihood of some machine malfunctioning so that it becomes inactive or very slow increases with the size of the system to the point where, with systems of even moderate size, this likelihood is significant. When such a local slow-down or failure occurs on a process that holds a lock or is otherwise involved in a synchronization event, the system performance will be seriously degraded or come to a standstill. This phenomenon has motivated the development of *waitfree* protocols [10], which guarantee that each process successfully completes any operation in a bounded number of its own steps, regardless of the rate of progress (or stop failures) of other processes. All algorithms mentioned in this paper are waitfree.

Anderson and Moir [3] pointed out that, given the intended use, processes should be able to repeatedly ACQUIRE and RELEASE names, and defined a renaming object to be *long-lived* if there is no bound on the number of operations applied to the object. Long-lived renaming protocols have been designed by Moir and Anderson [2], Buhrman et. al. [7], and Moir and Garay [13].

Moir and Anderson also observed that if a (n, k, l)-renaming protocol has complexity that is dependent on n, then it has the same shortcoming that renaming is intended to circumvent, that is, it has complexity determined by the original size of the name space. They defined a renaming protocol to be *fast* if any process, applying any operation, completes the operation in a number of its own steps that is independent of n. Recently, Attiya and Fouren [5] extended the notion of a fast renaming protocol to one that is *adaptive*, where the worst case step complexity depends only on the number $\hat{k}$ of processes that are active, rather than on the upper bound k for this quantity. They presented an $(n, k, 6k - 1)$ adaptive renaming algorithm with worst-case step complexity in $O(\hat{k} \log \hat{k})$. Unfortunately, their protocol is not long-lived, and it is not currently known whether an adaptive long-lived protocol for renaming exists.

Some applications might benefit from having one resource for each contender, with each resource corresponding to a name. Thus, another goal is that the size of the new name space is exactly the contention bound, and many researchers have focused on reducing the size of the new name space as a function of k. Several renaming algorithms with $l = 2k - 1$ have been proposed, including those of Borowski and Gafni [6], Anderson and Moir [2], and Moir and Garay [13]. However, Herlihy and Shavit [11] and, independently, Burns and Peterson [8] proved that no deterministic waitfree solution using only atomic registers can have a name space size below $2k - 1$. It remained to overcome this lower bound by using either stronger objects or randomization. Say that an (n, k, l)-renaming protocol is *name-space-optimal* if $l = k$. Anderson and Moir [2] used stronger objects called *set-first-zero* objects to achieve name-space-optimality. Since a version of these objects can be implemented with test-and-set objects, which in turn have a randomized implementation using shared variables [1], their algorithm can be converted into a randomized long-lived (n, k, k)-renaming algorithm for atomic registers, with worst-case expected step complexity $O(k \log n)$. Further massaging, using ideas similar to those in this paper, can be used to make this solution fast, with worst-case expected step complexity $\Theta(k^2)$. However, after these changes, the amortized expected step complexity, as discussed shortly, is also $\Theta(k^2)$. Panconesi et.al. [14] use randomization to solve the related *naming* problem for anonymous systems. That problem differs from renaming because there are no process identifiers to exploit, and no emphasis on the attributes desired of renaming. If their solution is used for name-space-optimal renaming, it is neither fast nor long-lived. A summary of the contribution of the most recent advances in renaming appears in Table 1.

Table 1. Waitfree renaming algorithms for the shared memory atomic registers model.

Deterministic Renaming

Algorithm	Name Space	Worst Case Complexity	Amortized Complexity	Fast	Long Lived
Borowski, Gafni [6]	$2k - 1$	$O(nk^2)$	N/A	No	No
Anderson, Moir [2]	$\frac{k(k+1)}{2}$	$O(k)$	N/A	Yes	No
Anderson, Moir [2]	$2k - 1$	$O(k^4)$	N/A	Yes	No
Attiya, Fouren [5]	$6k - 1$	$O(\hat{k} \log \hat{k})$	N/A	Yes	No
Anderson, Moir [2]	$\frac{k(k+1)}{2}$	$O(nk)$	$O(nk)$	No	Yes
Moir, Garay [13]	$\frac{k(k+1)}{2}$	$O(k^2)$	$O(k^2)$	Yes	Yes
Moir, Garay [13]	$2k - 1$	$O(k^4)$	$O(k^4)$	Yes	Yes

Randomized Renaming

Algorithm	Name Space	Expected Worst Case Complexity	Expected Amortized Complexity	Fast	Long Lived
Panconesi et. al. [14]	$(1 + \epsilon)k$, $\epsilon > 0$	$O(n \log^2 k)$	N/A	No	No
This Paper	$\frac{3k^2 + k}{2}$	$O(k^2)$	$O(k)$	Yes	Yes
This Paper	k	$O(k^2)$	$O(k \log k)$	Yes	Yes

This paper presents the first waitfree, long-lived, fast, name-space-optimal renaming algorithm for atomic read/write registers. Since name-space-optimal deterministic renaming is impossible, our algorithm is randomized. In the worst case over all schedulers and processes, the expected number (over coin flips) of accesses to read/write registers required to complete either an ACQUIRE or RELEASE operation is $\Theta(k^2)$. We also define a notion of amortized complexity that measures throughput for a long-lived protocol. The amortized expected step complexity of the new renaming algorithm is $\Theta(k \log k)$, which is a substantial improvement, in this amortized sense, over preceding long-lived renaming algorithms for read/write registers (whether name-space-optimal or not). On the way to our final protocol, we also derive a renaming algorithm that achieves $\Theta(k)$ amortized expected step complexity at the expense of a much large name space (with size approximately $(3/2)k^2$).

This notion of amortized complexity of waitfree protocols may be generally useful. As a correctness condition, waitfreedom can be extremely advantageous for the smooth operation of a distributed system. Yet a waitfree solution may be dismissed because, by the traditional worst case cost measure, it is too expensive. It is possible, however, that there is a waitfree solution such that the worst case cost for a process is realized only when the remaining processes are especially efficient. In this case, throughput is guaranteed to be high even though worst case complexity is unappealing. This is the situation with the renaming protocols in this paper. With high probability, the only way that the scheduler can force one process to use the maximum number of steps to complete an ACQUIRE operation is by allowing many other ACQUIRE operations to complete quickly. In the full version on this paper [9] we prove that none of the other existing long-lived renaming algorithms achieve this feature; all have amortized step complexity asymptotically equal to their worst case complexity. For any application that can tolerate the occasional slow (but bounded) operation provided that many other operations complete during the same interval, the traditional notion of complexity may be inappropriate while amortized complexity can provide a reasonable performance measure.

The model of computation, the proposed complexity measures and the renaming problem are defined in the following section of the paper. Our new algorithm is presented in section 3, proved to be correct in section 4, and analyzed in section 5. It has been necessary to abridge some proofs in this version of the paper; a more complete version of the paper, with full proofs, is available from the authors.

2 Definitions

2.1 Model of Computation

We assume an *(asynchronous) shared memory* system, which is a set of n processes with distinct identifiers, together with a globally shared memory composed of randomly accessible (multi-reader/multi-writer) read/write registers. Each register may be either read or written by a process in one atomic step.

A protocol can be regarded as a shared object. Each process can (repeatedly) access the object by applying an operation to it. A data object is *long-lived* if there is no limit on the number of applications of operations to it.

The execution of a shared memory system is determined by a *scheduler*, which determines the operation to be performed by each process (consistently with the semantics of the object) and decides after each step which process will execute the next step. We assume a *strong, adaptive* scheduler that has full knowledge of the past, but cannot predict or bias future random choices.

A shared object is *waitfree* (respectively, *expected waitfree*) if the number (respectively, expected number) of its own steps required by any process to apply any operation to the object is bounded, under any scheduler.

Let S denote the set of all schedulers. For any application α of an operation under a scheduler S, let $\mathrm{cost}(\alpha, S)$ be the number of steps taken by the process applying α to complete it. If the protocol is deterministic, then $\mathrm{cost}(\alpha, S)$ is an integer; if the protocol is randomized, then $\mathrm{cost}(\alpha, S)$ is a random variable with the probability space defined by the random choices made by processes.

Definition 1. For any deterministic protocol, the *worst case step complexity* is the supremum, over all schedulers $S \in S$ and applications α, of $\mathrm{cost}(\alpha, S)$.

Definition 2. For any randomized protocol, the *worst case expected step complexity* is the supremum, over all schedulers $S \in S$ and applications α, of $\mathrm{E}\left[\mathrm{cost}(\alpha, S)\right]$.

Now let $\alpha_1, \alpha_2, \alpha_3, \ldots$ be the sequence of applications of operations under S, ordered by initiation. (This sequence is a random variable, if the protocol is randomized.)

Definition 3. For any deterministic protocol, the *amortized step complexity* is the supremum over all schedulers $S \in S$ of

$$\lim_{m \to \infty} \sum_{i=1}^{m} \mathrm{cost}(\alpha_i, S)/m.$$

Definition 4. For any randomized protocol, the *amortized expected step complexity* is the supremum over all schedulers $S \in S$ of

$$\lim_{m \to \infty} \sum_{i=1}^{m} \mathrm{E}\left[\mathrm{cost}(\alpha_i, S)\right]/m.$$

A deterministic (respectively, randomized) protocol is *fast* if the worst case step complexity (respectively, expected step complexity) is independent of n.

2.2 Renaming

If $l \geq k$ then a (n, k, l)-*renaming object*, Rename, is an abstract data object with name space $\{1, \ldots, l\}$ where each name is in state "used" or "unused". It can be accessed by any of n processes where each access is either an ACQUIRE or a RELEASE. Each participating process continuously cycles through four phases (in order):

1. It executes ACQUIRE which returns a name, say i.
2. It is in its "use" phase.
3. It executes RELEASE(i).
4. It is in its "remainder" phase.

A process is *active* unless it is in the "remainder" phase. The collection of all ACQUIRE and RELEASE operations performed on this object must be linearizable[4] and must satisfy the following *renaming condition*: Provided that each name in $\{1, \ldots, l\}$ is initially marked "unused" and at most k processes are ever active simultaneously,

- ACQUIRE returns exactly one unused name, say $i \in \{1 \ldots, l\}$, and marks i used.
- RELEASE(i) marks i as unused.

We wish to construct a waitfree, long-lived, fast (n, k, k)-renaming object for an asynchronous shared memory system of n processes. That is, algorithms for ACQUIRE and for RELEASE are required such that the above renaming condition for an (n, k, k)-renaming object is satisfied for any set of ACQUIRE and RELEASE operations under any scheduler that ensures that processes behave as described.

3 The New Renaming Algorithms

We first describe three components that are used in our (n, k, k)-renaming algorithm. In these descriptions, and in the sequel, we say that an operation on a data object is applied *in isolation* if the time interval between the beginning and the end of the operation does not overlap with the time interval for any other operation on the same object.

3.1 Components

The k-Large Object: This is the renaming object of Moir and Garay [13]. They prove that k-Large is a deterministic, waitfree, long-lived $(n, k, k(k + 1)/2)$-renaming object, and that the worst case step complexity of any operation supported by k-Large is at most $5k^2$. Denote the ACQUIRE and RELEASE operations of this protocol by ACQ and REL respectively.

The k-Small Object: This object, which we extract from the more complicated object k-Large, is the first component of the triangular array of components that make up k-Large. We state its properties here and give details of its construction elsewhere ([9]). Object k-Small is not a renaming object, since it is not guaranteed to return a name; it may return "failure"

---

[4] See Herlihy and Wing [12].

instead. Specifically, any k-Small object Q is in state either "used" or "unused" and can be accessed by any of n processes where each access is either ACQUIRE-SMALL or RELEASE-SMALL. The collection of all ACQUIRE-SMALL and RELEASE-SMALL operations performed on Q are linearizable and satisfy the following *small object condition*: Provided that initially Q is in state "unused" and at most k processes simultaneously access Q,

- If Q is unused and ACQUIRE-SMALL is applied to Q in isolation, then this ACQUIRE-SMALL operation returns "success" and Q becomes used.
- If Q is unused and ACQUIRE-SMALL is applied to Q but not in isolation, then either all overlapping ACQUIRE-SMALL operations return "failure" and Q remains unused, or at most one ACQUIRE-SMALL operation among the overlapping ones returns "success," all others return "failure," and Q becomes used.
- If Q is used and ACQUIRE-SMALL is applied to Q then "failure" is returned, and Q remains used.
- RELEASE-SMALL, when executed by the last process that successfully applied ACQUIRE-SMALL to Q, sets the state of Q to "unused".

Objects of type k-Small are deterministic, waitfree and long-lived. The worst case step complexity of ACQUIRE-SMALL and RELEASE-SMALL are each at most $5k$.

The m-T&S Object: Object m-T&S is a test-and-set object, which is either in state "set" or "unset" and supports the operations TEST&SET and UNSET, for processes with distinct names from the name space $\{1, \ldots, m\}$. The collection of all TEST&SET and UNSET operations performed on m-T&S is linearizable where the linearized sequence, say L, of TEST&SET and UNSET operations satisfies the following *test-and-set object condition*:

- If m-T&S is unset, then the next TEST&SET in L returns "success" and changes the state of m-T&S to set,
- If m-T&S is set, then TEST&SET returns "failure".
- UNSET, applied to m-T&S by the process that most recently set it, changes its state to unset.

Although it is impossible to construct a deterministic, waitfree, long-lived m-T&S object from read/write registers, a randomized waitfree, long-lived solution due to Afek et. al. [1], does exist, and has worst case expected complexity of both TEST&SET and UNSET in $\Theta(\log m)$.

Objects of types k-Small, k-Large and m-T&S are used to construct our randomized, long-lived, fast renaming object called Rename-1.

3.2 New Renaming Algorithms

The Rename-1 Object: Rename-1 is constructed from k^2 copies of k-Small, called k-Small$_1, \ldots, k$-Small$_{k^2}$, with associated names $1, \ldots, k^2$ respectively, as well as one copy of k-Large and k copies, numbered 1 through k, of m-T&S objects, for $m = k^2 + k(k+1)/2$. Let ACQUIRE-1 and RELEASE-1 denote the acquire and release operations for Rename-1.

To execute ACQUIRE-1, a process first chooses a number, say j, uniformly, independently and randomly from $\{1, \ldots, k^2\}$, and then executes ACQUIRE-SMALL on k-Small$_j$. If it succeeds then it temporarily acquires the name j. Otherwise, it executes ACQ on the k-Large object, and this object returns a name $r \in \{1, \ldots, k(k+1)/2\}$ with certainty; the process then temporarily acquires the name $r + k^2$. Denote the name in $\{1, \ldots, m\}$ acquired so far by tmp. Next, participating with name tmp, and incrementing i (initialized to 1), the process applies TEST&SET to m-T&S$_i$ until it achieves success. The final name acquired by the process is the final value of i.

A process with name j, and which had temporary name tmp, executes the operation RELEASE-1 by first applying UNSET to m-T&S$_j$ and then either by applying RELEASE-SMALL to k-Small$_{tmp}$ if $tmp \leq k^2$, or by applying REL($tmp - k^2$) to the k-Large object if $tmp > k^2$.

The Rename-2 Object: Another renaming object, which can be useful if it is critical to minimize the amortized step complexity, can be immediately derived from Rename-1. Denote by Rename-2 the renaming object that consists of only the k-Small objects and the k-Large object in Rename-1, and let ACQUIRE-2 and RELEASE-2 be its acquire and release operations. Operation ACQUIRE-2 is just the first part of the operation ACQUIRE-1, which returns the name tmp in the set $\{1, \ldots, k^2 + k(k+1)/2\}$ as the final name. Similarly, RELEASE-2 is just the last part of operation RELEASE-1 consisting of applying RELEASE-SMALL on k-Small$_{tmp}$ if $tmp \leq k^2$, or by applying REL($tmp - k^2$) on the k-Large object if $tmp > k^2$.

4 Correctness

Claim 5. *Rename-2 is a waitfree long-lived $(n, k, k(3k+1)/2)$-renaming object.*

Proof. It follows from the properties of k-Large and k-Small that as long as at most k processes are active, a process either acquires a unique name i from k-Small$_i$ for some $1 \leq i \leq k^2$, or it acquires a unique name in $\{1, \ldots, k(k+1)/2\}$ from k-Large. Adding k^2 to the name in this second case ensures that all acquired names are unique and belong to $\{1, \ldots, m\}$ where $m = k^2 + k(k+1)/2 = k(3k+1)/2$. The waitfree and long-lived properties are both inherited from the k-Large and k-Small objects comprising Rename-2.

Claim 6. *Rename-1 is an expected waitfree long-lived (n, k, k)-renaming object.*

Proof. By Claim 5, ACQUIRE-2 returns a unique name tmp in $L = \{1, \ldots, m\}$ where $m = k(3k+1)/2$. By the properties of m-T&S, each m-T&S$_i$ can be set by at most one process with a name from L at any time. Also, by Claim 5 and by the properties of m-T&S, each access has bounded expected time. The long-lived property of object Rename-1 is inherited from its components. In the full paper [9] it is proved, by a straightforward induction on k, that any process that sequentially applies TEST&SET to m-T&S$_i$ for increasing i (from 1 to k) necessarily receives success from one of these objects, as long as at most k processes are ever active simultaneously.

5 Analysis

We first give the analysis for **Rename-2** and then extend it to **Rename-1**. Consider an execution consisting of a sequence of accesses to **Rename-2** by a collection of n processes such that at most k processes are active at any one time. Since there are no more applications of RELEASE-2 than applications of ACQUIRE-2, and each uses no more steps than the corresponding ACQUIRE-2 application, it suffices to bound the cost of the ACQUIRE-2 applications in the sequence in order to obtain a bound on asymptotic performance. Each ACQUIRE-2 application on **Rename-2** either returns the name of a randomly chosen k-Small object or, failing this, a name acquired from the object k-Large. We will overcharge for ACQUIRE-2 applications by assuming that if the chosen k-Small object is not accessed in isolation, then ACQUIRE-SMALL will be unsuccessful and $\Theta(k^2)$ steps will be used by the process to acquire its name. We will show, however, that for the overwhelming majority of accesses, the scheduler cannot prevent a process from applying ACQUIRE-2 to a k-Small object in isolation, in which case the access uses only $\Theta(k)$ steps.

At any time, some *selecting* processes are executing ACQUIRE-SMALL, each on its randomly chosen k-Small object. If there are k selecting processes at some time, then the scheduler must run one or more of the existing selecting processes until a process acquires a name and releases it before another ACQUIRE-2 application can begin. If there are fewer than k processes executing ACQUIRE-2 then the scheduler may choose either to introduce a new selecting process, or to have a process that is already participating in ACQUIRE-2 take its next step.

An application of an operation on a data object is involved in a *collision* if it is not performed in isolation. A scheduler can only cause an application of ACQUIRE-2 to use more than $5k$ steps if this application is involved in a collision on some k-Small object.

We define an "amortized cost" (called $\text{acost}(C_{i-1}, l_i)$ below) for applications of ACQUIRE-SMALL such that for every scheduler's strategy and for every sequence of coin-flip outcomes the (actual) total number of steps taken by processes to complete the first m ACQUIRE-SMALL applications is not more than the sum of the amortized costs associated with them, provided that no additional applications are initiated before these are completed. That is, under these circumstances

$$\sum_{i=1}^{m} \text{cost}(\alpha, S) \leq \sum_{i=1}^{m} \text{acost}(C_{i-l}, l_i) \ .$$

More generally, the total actual cost could exceed the total amortized cost for these applications of operations, but never by more than $5k^2(k-1)$, because at most k of the first m applications are involved in collisions with later applications but with none of the first m.

Consider the i-th application of ACQUIRE-SMALL. If it is not involved in a collision on a k-Small object, we will set its amortized cost to be $5k$. On the other hand, if the application of ACQUIRE-SMALL is involved in a collision on a k-Small object, then (as formalized below), all but the first of the applications involved in the collision are assigned an amortized cost that is at least twice the real cost to acquire a name, while the first may receive an amortized cost that is smaller than the real one. Since at least as many applications of operations are (at least doubly) overcharged as are undercharged, the sum of real costs cannot exceed the sum of the amortized costs.

We represent the state of an execution over time as a sequence of sets $(C_0, C_1, \ldots)$, each of size at most $k - 1$, where C_i represents the state of the execution just before the start of the $(i + 1)$-st application of ACQUIRE-SMALL: For every i, C_i is a subset of $K = \{1, \ldots, k^2\}$ containing names of the k-Small objects chosen by selecting processes. If $(l_1, l_2, \ldots)$ is a sequence of random selections of names made by our algorithm, then C_0 is the empty set, C_i is a subset of $C_{i-1} \cup \{l_i\}$, and the amortized cost for the i-th application of ACQUIRE-SMALL is

$$\mathrm{acost}(C_{i-1}, l_i) = \begin{cases} 5k & \text{if } l_i \notin C_{i-1} \\ 11k^2 & \text{if } l_i \in C_{i-1} \end{cases}$$

Let $K = \{1, \ldots, k^2\}$, and let Ω_m be the probability space of sequences $F = (l_1, \ldots, l_m)$ such that each $l_i \in F$ is chosen uniformly, independently, and randomly from K. Then $\Pr[l_i = t] = 1/k^2$ for all $t \in \{1, \ldots, k^2\}$ and for all $i \in \{1, \ldots, m\}$.

Theorem 7. *The amortized expected step complexity of* ACQUIRE-2 *is* $\Theta(k)$.

Proof. By the above argument, the definition of amortized expected complexity, and linearity of expectation, the amortized expected step complexity of ACQUIRE-2 is at most

$$\begin{aligned} B &= \lim_{m \to \infty} \left(\mathrm{E}\left[\frac{\sum_{i=1}^m \mathrm{acost}(C_{i-1}, l_i)}{m} \right] + 5k^2(k-1) \right) \\ &= \lim_{m \to \infty} \frac{1}{m} \sum_{i=1}^m \mathrm{E}\left[\mathrm{acost}(C_{i-1}, l_i) \right] + \lim_{m \to \infty} 5k^2(k-1) \\ &= \lim_{m \to \infty} \frac{1}{m} \sum_{i=1}^m (5k \cdot \Pr\left[l_i \notin C_{i-1} \right] + 11k^2 \cdot \Pr\left[l_i \in C_{i-1} \right]) + 0 \\ &\leq \lim_{m \to \infty} \frac{1}{m} \sum_{i=1}^m (5k + 11k^2 \cdot \Pr\left[l_i \in C_{i-1} \right]) \\ &= 5k + 11k^2 \lim_{m \to \infty} \frac{1}{m} \sum_{i=1}^m (\Pr\left[l_i \in C_{i-1} \right]). \end{aligned}$$

For all i, $\Pr\left[l_i \in C_{i-1} \right] = |C_{i-1}| / k^2 \leq (k-1)/k^2 < 1/k$. This implies that

$$B \leq 5k + 11k^2 \lim_{m \to \infty} \frac{1}{m} \sum_{1}^m \Pr\left[l_i \in C_{i-1} \right] < 5k + 11k^2 \lim_{m \to \infty} \frac{1}{m} \cdot m \cdot 1/k \in \Theta(k). \quad \Box$$

Rename-1 achieves (n, k, k)-renaming with an amortized cost that is increased by a logarithmic factor. Again, since there are no more RELEASE-1 applications than ACQUIRE-1 applications and each uses no more steps than the corresponding ACQUIRE-1 application, it suffices to bound the cost of the applications of ACQUIRE-1 in the sequence in order to bound asymptotic performance.

Theorem 8. *The amortized expected step complexity of* ACQUIRE-1 *is* $O(k \log k)$.

Proof. By Theorem 7 the amortized expected step complexity of the first stage of ACQUIRE-1 is $O(k)$. In the second stage, processes attempt to set up to k randomized test-and-set objects in sequence after receiving names from a name space of size $O(k^2)$. Each of these test-and-set objects can be implemented using a tournament tree with $O(k^2)$ leaves and with depth $O(\log k)$ — and the worst case expected number of steps required by a process to climb each level of the tree is bounded by a constant (see Afek et. al. [1]). It follows by linearity of expectation that the worst case expected number of steps required to try to set each one of these objects is in $O(\log k)$ and that the worst case expected number of steps required for a process to perform the entire second stage of the algorithm is in $O(k \log k)$. Since the amortized expected step complexity cannot be more than the worst case expected step complexity, the amortized step complexity of the second stage of ACQUIRE-1, and the amortized step complexity for the entire algorithm, is $O(k \log k)$ as well.

The previous two theorems confirm that both our algorithms achieve a substantial improvement over previous renaming algorithms in terms of amortized complexity. The worst-case expected step complexity of both our algorithms, Rename-1 and Rename-2, is easily shown to be dominated by the worst case complexity of the component k-Large, and hence is $\Theta(k^2)$. The space complexity of both our algorithms is $\Theta(k^3)$, but it exceeds by a constant factor (3 in the case of ACQUIRE-2, and 6 in the case of ACQUIRE-1) the space complexity of the deterministic algorithm of Moir and Garay. Reducing the working space is a subject of further research.

References

1. Y. Afek, E. Gafni, J. Tromp, and P. Vitanyi. Wait-free test-and-set. In *Proceedings of the 6th International Workshop, WDAG'92; LNCS No. 647; Springer-Verlag*, 1992.
2. J. Anderson and M. Moir. Fast, long-lived renaming. In *Proceedings of the 8th International Workshop, WDAG'94; LNCS No. 857; Springer-Verlag*, pages 141–155, 1994.
3. M. Anderson, J. amd Moir. Using k-exclusion to implement resilient, scalable shared objects. In *Proceedings of the Thirteenth Annual ACM Symposium on Principles of Distributed Computing*, pages 141–150, 1994.
4. H. Attiya, A. Bar-Noy, D. Dolev, D. Peleg, and R. Reischuk. Renaming in an asynchronous environment. *Journal of the Association for Computing Machinery*, 37(3):524–548, 1990.

5. H. Attiya and A. Fouren. Adaptive wait-free algorithms for lattice agreement and renaming. Technical Report 0931, Computer Science Department, Technion - Israel Institute of Technology, April 1998. Extended Abstract to appear in PODC'98.

6. E. Borowsky and E. Gafni. Immediate atomic snapshots and fast renaming. In *Proceedings of the Twelveth Annual ACM Symposium on Principles of Distributed Computing*, pages 41–52, 1993.

7. H. Buhrman, J. Garay, J.-H. Hoepman, and M. Moir. Long-lived remaning made fast. In *Proceedings of the Fourteenth Annual ACM Symposium on Principles of Distributed Computing*, 1995.

8. J. Burns and G. Peterson. The ambiguity of choosing. In *Proceedings of the Eighth Annual ACM Symposium on Principles of Distributed Computing*, 1989.

9. W. Eberly, L. Higham, and J. Warpechowska-Gruca. Long-lived, fast, waitfree renaming with optimal name space and high throughput. (In preparation), 1998.

10. M. Herlihy. Wait-free synchronization. *ACM Transactions on Programming Languages and Systems*, 11(1):124–149, 1991.

11. M. Herlihy and N. Shavit. The asynchronous computability theorem for t-resilient tasks. In *Proceedings of the 25th Annual ACM Symposium on the Theory of Computing*, pages 111–120, 1993.

12. M. Herlihy and J. Wing. Linerizability: A correctness condition for concurrent objects. *ACM Transactions on Programming Languages and Systems*, 12(3):463–491, 1990.

13. M. Moir and J. Garay. Fast, long-lived renaming improved and simplified. In *Proceedings of the 10th International Workshop, WDAG'96*, 1996.

14. A. Panconesi, M. Papatriantafilou, P. Tsigas, and P. Vitanyi. Randomized waitfree naming. In *ISAAC'94, LNCS No. 834*, pages 83–91, 1994.

The Compactness of Interval Routing for Almost All Graphs

Cyril Gavoille[1] and David Peleg[2]

[1] LaBRI, Université Bordeaux I, 351, cours de la Libération, 33405 Talence Cedex, France. E-mail: gavoille@labri.u-bordeaux.fr.

[2] Department of Applied Mathematics and Computer Science, The Weizmann Institute of Science, Rehovot, 76100 Israel. E-mail: peleg@wisdom.weizmann.ac.il.
Supported in part by grants from the Israel Science Foundation and from the Israel Ministry of Science and Art.

Abstract. Interval routing is a compact way for representing routing tables on a graph. It is based on grouping together, in each node, destination addresses that use the same outgoing edge in the routing table. Such groups of addresses are represented by some intervals of consecutive integers. We show that almost all the graphs, i.e., a fraction of at least $1 - 1/n^2$ of all the n-node graphs, support a shortest path interval routing with at most *three* intervals per outgoing edge, even if the addresses of the nodes are arbitrarily fixed in advance and cannot be chosen by the designer of the routing scheme. In case the addresses are initialized randomly, we show that *two* intervals per outgoing edge suffice, and conversely, that two intervals are required, for almost all graphs. Finally, if the node addresses can be chosen as desired, we show how to design in polynomial time a shortest path interval routing with a *single* interval per outgoing edge, for all but at most $O(\log^3 n)$ outgoing edges in each node. It follows that almost all graphs support a shortest path routing scheme which requires at most $n + O(\log^4 n)$ bits of routing information per node, improving on the previous upper bound.

1 Introduction

1.1 Background

A *universal routing strategy* is an algorithm which generates a routing scheme for every given network. One type of trivial universal routing strategy is based on schemes that keep in each node a full routing table which specifies an output port for every destination. Though this strategy can guarantee routing along shortest paths, each router has to store locally $\Theta(n \log d)$ bits of memory, where d is the degree of the router (i.e., the number of output ports) and n is the number of nodes in the network.

The *interval routing scheme* [9, 10] is a compact routing scheme, i.e., a routing scheme that needs to keep only a small amount of information in each node to route messages correctly through the network. The idea of this scheme is to label the n nodes of the network with unique integers from $\{1, \ldots, n\}$, and to label the outgoing arcs in every node with a set of intervals forming a partition of the name range. The routing process sends a message on the unique outgoing arc labeled by an interval that contains the destination label. While the preprocessing stage of such a routing scheme (which is performed once in the initialization of the network) might be complex, the delivery protocol consists of simple decision functions which can be implemented with $O(kd \log n)$ bits in each node of degree d, where k is the maximum number of intervals assigned to an arc. Such a routing scheme supports a compact implementation whenever k is small in comparison with n or d.

In [8], it is showed that there is no universal routing strategy that can guarantees a shortest path routing scheme with less than $\Omega(n \log d)$ bits per node for all the n-node networks of maximum degree d. This result means that there is some worst-case network where for any shortest path routing function, the number of bits required to be stored in a router is not significantly smaller than the size of a routing table, whatever the node labeling[1] and the shortest paths are. Fortunately, such a problematic situation where the routing tables cannot be compressed occurs for a limited number of worst-case networks only.

In particular, in [3], it is shown that for almost all the n-node networks the size of the routing tables can be reduced to $O(n)$ bits per node. More precisely, it is shown that all networks but a $1/n^3$ fraction, can be routed with a scheme that uses $3n + o(n)$ bits of memory, under the assumption that nodes are arbitrary labeled in the range $\{1, \ldots, n\}$, and that every node knows its neighbors for "free". Moreover, if during the initialization process of the network, nodes can be relabeled with binary string of length $O(\log^2 n)$ bits, then $O(\log^2 n)$ bits per node suffice to route along the shortest paths for almost all networks.

1.2 Definitions and Results

In this paper we consider shortest path routing schemes only. An undirected graph $G = (V, E)$ represents the classic model of the underlying topology of the network. An n-node graph G with the nodes labeled in the set $\{1, \ldots, n\}$ *supports a k-interval routing scheme* (*k*-IRS for short) if there exists an interval routing scheme $\mathcal{R}$ for G with the property that for every (directed) edge e, the set of node labels to which $\mathcal{R}$ routes messages via e is composed of at most k intervals. (An interval means a set of consecutive integers taken from $\{1, \ldots, n\}$, where n and 1 are considered to be consecutive.)

Our goal is to find a labeling of the nodes and a shortest paths system in order to minimize the maximum number of intervals assigned to the edges of the graph. We distinguish three models depending on the freedom we have in labeling the nodes.

1. [**Adversary**]: labels are fixed in advance (by an adversary) and cannot be permuted;
2. [**Random**]: labels are randomly permuted;

---

[1] from the range $\{1, \ldots, n\}$.

3. [**Designer**]: labels can be chosen (by the routing designer) in order to achieve the smallest possible number of intervals.

In all three models, the routing designer has the freedom of selecting the shortest paths to be used.

Corresponding to these three models, we introduce the following three parameters. We denote by $IRS_A(G)$ the smallest integer k such that G supports a k-IRS in the adversary model (namely, for every arbitrary labeling of the nodes). We denote by $IRS_R(G)$ the smallest k such that G supports a k-IRS in the random model (namely, given a random labeling of the nodes of G) with high probability. Finally, we denote by $IRS(G)$ the smallest k such that G supports a k-IRS in the designer model (namely, under some specifically chosen node labeling of G). Clearly, $IRS(G) \leq IRS_R(G) \leq IRS_A(G)$, for every graph G.

The parameter $IRS(G)$ has been computed for many classes of graphs (see [6] for a recent overview). Notably, in [7] it is shown that for every G, $IRS_R(G) < n/4 + o(n)$, whereas there exists some worst-case G_0 such that $IRS(G_0) > n/4 - o(n)$. However, as shown in this paper, the situation is considerably better for the "average" case. Specifically, we will see that $IRS(G) \leq 2$ for a fraction of at least $1 - 1/n^2$ of all the n-node labeled graphs.

Technically, we use random graphs instead of the Kolmogorov random graphs used in [3]. A discussion about the relationships between random and Kolmogorov random graphs can be found in [4]. The class $\mathcal{G}_{n,p}$ denotes the classic model of n-node labeled random graphs, where $0 \leq p \leq 1$ represents the probability of having an edge between any two nodes. Interval routing on random graphs has been first investigated in [5], where some lower bounds are given for $IRS(G)$ for $G \in \mathcal{G}_{n,p}$. More precisely, it is shown therein that for $p = n^{-1+1/s}$ for integer $s > 0$, such that there exists a ε satisfying $(\ln^{1+\varepsilon} n)/n < p < n^{-1/2-\varepsilon}$, a graph $G \in \mathcal{G}_{n,p}$ satisfies

$$IRS(G) \geq \frac{1}{10} n^{1-6/\ln(np)-\ln(np)/\ln n} \tag{1}$$

with high probability. It is also shown that for some $p = n^{-1+1/\Theta(\sqrt{\log n})}$, a graph $G \in \mathcal{G}_{n,p}$ satisfies $IRS(G) = \Omega(n^{1-1/\Theta(\sqrt{\log n})})$ with high probability. In this paper we investigate the case where p is a fixed constant, e.g. $p = 1/2$, in order to establish some average results on the total space of n-node graphs. (Note that for constant p, Eq. (1) cannot be used since in this case p lies outside the validity range.)

The following table presents our results for each model. The results of the table are proved for a fraction of at least $1 - 1/n^2$ of all the n-node graphs.

Label select	Designer	Random	Adversary
Upper bound	$IRS \leq 2$	$IRS_R \leq 2$	$IRS_A \leq 3$
Lower bound	$IRS \geq 1$	$IRS_R \geq 2$	$IRS_A \geq 2$

At this time, we are still unable to decide whether $IRS(G) = 1$ or 2 for almost every graph G, if node labels and shortest paths system can be chosen in advance by the designer. However, we present a polynomial time algorithm to design a 2-IRS for all graphs but a $1/n$ fraction, such that for every node, all its outgoing edges are labeled with a single interval, except for up to $O(\log^3 n)$ edges where 2 intervals are required. It follows that almost every graph supports a shortest path routing scheme that can be implemented with $n + O(\log^4 n)$ bits, improving on the best known result (cf. [3]). Note that our result is stated without the assumption that nodes know theirs neighbors.

2 Randomly Assigned Node Labels

In this section we show that in the random model, almost every graph G satisfies $\text{IRS}_R(G) = 2$. This implies, in particular, that almost every graph G satisfies $\text{IRS}(G) \leq 2$. This is done by showing that, with probability at least $1 - 1/n^2$, a random graph G from $\mathcal{G}_{n,1/2}$ satisfies $\text{IRS}_R(G) = 2$. Actually, we show that the result holds for the class $\mathcal{G}_{n,p}$ of random graphs for each fixed probability $0 < p < 1$.

2.1 Upper Bound

In this subsection we shall prove that $\text{IRS}_R(G) \leq 2$.

Assume the node labels $\{1, \ldots, n\}$ are assigned randomly for the graph G. In that case, given that G is a random graph in $\mathcal{G}_{n,p}$, we may assume that the nodes are first marked by the labels 1 through n, and only then do we draw the edges randomly and uniformly with probability p.

For random graphs selected from $\mathcal{G}_{n,p}$ we have the following simple bounds. (We state a variant of the bounds suitable to our needs, and make no attempt to optimize them; see [2] for sharper statements.) We denote by $\Gamma(v)$ the set composed of v and of its neighbors.

Lemma 1. *With probability at least $1 - 1/n^3$, and for every fixed p, $0 < p < 1$, a random graph $G \in \mathcal{G}_{n,p}$ is of diameter 2, and for every node $v \in V$,*

$$np - 3\sqrt{n \ln n} \leq |\Gamma(v)| \leq np + 3\sqrt{n \ln n} .$$

Let $\mathcal{E}_A$ denote the event that the random graph at hand does not satisfy the properties asserted in Lemma 1. Henceforth we ignore that possibility, and restrict our attention to $\bar{\mathcal{E}}_A$.

For notational convenience we identify nodes with their labels, i.e., denote $V = \{1, \ldots, n\}$.

Consider a node $v_0 \in V$. We need to argue that with high probability, the edges of v_0 can be labeled with at most two intervals per edge so that for every possible destination $v_d \in V$, the selected edge is along a shortest path from v_0 to v_d.

Let $A = \Gamma(v_0) \setminus \{v_0\}$ and $B = V \setminus \Gamma(v_0)$. Since G satisfies the event $\bar{\mathcal{E}}_A$,

$$np - 3\sqrt{n \ln n} \leq |A|, |B| \leq np + 3\sqrt{n \ln n} .$$

Let
$$C = \{v \in B \mid v+1 \in A \text{ and } (v, v+1) \in E\}.$$

Lemma 2. *With probability at least* $1 - 1/n^3$, *the size of the set* C *is bounded by*
$$np^3 - 6\sqrt{n \ln n} \leq |C| \leq np^3 + 6\sqrt{n \ln n}.$$

Proof. Consider a vertex $v \in B$, and let I_v denote the event that $v \in C$. This event happens precisely if $v+1 \in A$ and $(v, v+1) \in E$. These two sub-events are independent and both occur with probability p, hence $\mathbb{P}(I_v) = p^2$. Note also that the events I_v for $v \in B$ are mutually independent. Let Z be a random variable denoting the size of $|C|$. Then $Z = \sum_{v \in B} z_v$, where z_v is the characteristic random variable of the event I_v. Hence Z is the sum of $|B|$ mutually independent Bernoulli variables, and its expected value is $\mathbb{E}(Z) = |B|p^2$, and hence applying Chernoff's bound (cf. [1]) we get,

$$\mathbb{P}\left(Z > np^3 + 6\sqrt{n \ln n}\right) < \mathbb{P}\left(Z > \left(1 + \frac{3}{p^2}\sqrt{\frac{\ln n}{n}}\right)\mathbb{E}(Z)\right)$$

$$< \exp\left(-\frac{9 \ln n}{3np^4}\,\mathbb{E}(Z)\right)$$

$$< \exp\left(-\frac{3}{p}\ln n + o(1)\right)$$

$$< \frac{1}{n^3}$$

and
$$\mathbb{P}\left(Z < np^3 - 6\sqrt{n \ln n}\right) < \frac{1}{n^3}$$

and the lemma follows. □

Let $\mathcal{E}_B$ denote the event that the random graph at hand does not satisfy the property asserted in Lemma 2 for *some* node v_0. Note that the probability for this event is bounded above by $1/n^3$. Henceforth we ignore that possibility, and restrict our attention to $\bar{\mathcal{E}}_B$.

Let us now define one interval per emanating edge of v_0 to take care of routing to the nodes in $A \cup C$. For every node $w \in A$, mark the edge (v_0, w) by the interval $[w-1, w]$ if $w-1 \in C$, and by the interval $[w]$ if $w-1 \notin C$.

It is thus left to show how the remaining interval per edge of v_0 can be used to route optimally towards the nodes in $X = B \setminus C$. This is done as follows. Let $X = \{x_1, \ldots, x_m\}$. Note that since G satisfies the events $\bar{\mathcal{E}}_A$ and $\bar{\mathcal{E}}_B$,

$$np(1-p^2) - 9\sqrt{n \ln n} \leq m \leq np(1-p^2) + 9\sqrt{n \ln n}.$$

We will now describe a process for selecting a subset of A, denoted $Y = \{y_1, \ldots, y_m\} \subseteq A$, such that there is an edge $(x_i, y_i) \in E$ for every $1 \leq i \leq m$. Once this is done, we mark each edge (v_0, y_i) by the interval $[x_i]$, thus completing our task.

The selection process is a straightforward greedy one. Let $Q = A$. Having already selected $y_1, \ldots, y_{i-1}$, the ith step consists of selecting y_i to be some arbitrary neighbor of x_i in Q, and discarding y_i from Q. If, at any stage, the node x_i considered by the process has no neighbors in the remaining set Q, then the process fails and we abort our attempt to provide a 2-IRS for G.

We need to argue that with very high probability, the process does not fail. Let F_i be the event that the process fails in the ith step. Note that at the beginning of step i, the current set Q is of size

$$|Q| = |A| - i + 1 \geq |A| - m \geq np - np(1 - p^2) - 12\sqrt{n \ln n} > \frac{np^3}{2}$$

for sufficiently large n.

Event F_i occurs only if x_i is not connected to any node of Q. This is the intersection of $|Q|$ independent events of probability $1 - p$ each, hence

$$\mathbb{P}(F_i) \leq (1 - p)^{np^3/2} = \left((1 - p)^{p^3/2}\right)^n < c^{-n}$$

For constant $c > 1$. Letting $\mathcal{E}_F(v_0)$ denote the event that the process fails for v_0, i.e., $\mathcal{E}_F(v_0) = \bigcup_i F_i$, we have $\mathbb{P}(\mathcal{E}_F(v_0)) < m \, c^{-n}$. It follows that for a sufficiently large n, the event $\mathcal{E}_F = \bigcup_{v_0} \mathcal{E}_F(v_0)$ has probability $\mathbb{P}(\mathcal{E}_F) \leq 1/n^3$.

Combining all possible failure events (namely, $\mathcal{E}_A \cup \mathcal{E}_B \cup \mathcal{E}_F$), we get that for sufficiently large n, the probability that our process fails to generate an interval routing scheme for the graph with two intervals per edge is bounded from above by $1/n^2$.

Theorem 1. *For sufficiently large n, with probability at least $1 - 1/n^2$, and for every fixed p, $0 < p < 1$, a random graph $G \in \mathcal{G}_{n,p}$ satisfies $\mathrm{IRS}_R(G) \leq 2$.* $\quad\square$

2.2 Lower Bound

In this subsection we shall prove that $\mathrm{IRS}_R(G) \geq 2$ for almost every graph G, for a random assignment of node labels.

Again, we assume the node labels $\{1, \ldots, n\}$ are assigned randomly for the graph G, so given that G is a random graph in $\mathcal{G}_{n,p}$, for p fixed, we may assume that the nodes are first labeled 1 through n and the edges are randomly drawn only later. As in the previous subsection, we assume the event $\bar{\mathcal{E}}_A$.

We need to show that with high probability, a single interval per edge will not be sufficient for producing shortest paths.

Consider a node $x \in \{1, \ldots, n\}$. Suppose that x is connected to $x + 1$ and $x + 3$, and that $x + 2$ is not connected to any node from $\{x, x + 1, x + 3\}$. Let $I(x, u)$ be the interval assigned to the edge (x, u) that contains $x + 2$. Since the diameter of G is 2, it follows that $u \notin \{x + 1, x + 2, x + 3\}$. $I(x, u)$ must contain u and $x + 2$, but neither $x + 1$ nor $x + 3$ which are connected to x. A contradiction for the fact that $I(x, u)$ is composed of a single interval.

Let $x_i = 4i - 3$, for every $i \in \{1, \ldots, m\}$, with $m = \lfloor n/4 \rfloor$. Let K_i denote the event x_i is in the previous configuration, and let $\mathcal{E}_K$ denote the event that there exists an event K_{i_0} that occurs. Note that from the above discussion, the probability of $\text{IRS}_R(G) > 1$ (under the event $\bar{\mathcal{E}}_A$) is lower bounded by $\mathbb{P}(\mathcal{E}_K)$.

Let Z_i be the characteristic random variable of the event K_i, and $Z = \sum_{i=1}^{m} Z_i$. The events K_i are independent, and each one occurs with probability p^5. So, $\mathbb{P}(Z = 0) = (1 - p^5)^m < 1/n^3$, for a sufficiently large n. It follows that $\mathbb{P}(\mathcal{E}_K) \geq 1 - 1/n^3$.

Theorem 2. *For sufficiently large n, with probability at least $1 - 1/n^2$, and for every fixed p, $0 < p < 1$, a random graph $G \in \mathcal{G}_{n,p}$ satisfies $\text{IRS}_R(G) \geq 2$.* $\qquad \Box$

3 Adversely Assigned Labels

We next assume the adversary model, in which the assignment of the node labels $\{1, \ldots, n\}$ to vertices is done by an adversary, aiming to cause the routing scheme to use the maximum number of intervals.

In this case, the lower bound of Section 2.2 remains unchanged, but the only upper bound we can prove is that $\text{IRS}_A(G) \leq 3$ for almost every graph G. Actually, we show that the result holds for the class $\mathcal{G}_{n,p}$ of random graphs for each fixed probability p, $0 < p < 1$.

Once again, by Lemma 1, we are allowed to restrict our attention to the event $\bar{\mathcal{E}}_A$, and assume the graph $G = (V, E)$ at hand is of diameter 2, and such that for every node $v \in V$, $np - 3\sqrt{n \ln n} \leq |\Gamma(v)| \leq np + 3\sqrt{n \ln n}$.

Consider a node $v_0 \in V$. We need to argue that with high probability, the edges of v_0 can be labeled with at most three intervals per edge so that for every possible destination $v_d \in V$, the selected edge is along a shortest path from v_0 to v_d.

Let $A = \Gamma(v_0) \setminus \{v_0\}$ and $B = V \setminus \Gamma(v_0)$. Let us first define one interval per emanating edge of v_0 to take care of routing to the nodes of A. Namely, for every node $w \in A$, mark the edge (v_0, w) by the interval $[w]$. It is left to show how the remaining two intervals per edge of v_0 can be used to route optimally towards the nodes of B. This is done as follows. Let $B = \{b_1, \ldots, b_m\}$. Recall that

$$np - 3\sqrt{n \ln n} \leq |A|, |B| \leq np + 3\sqrt{n \ln n}.$$

We will now describe a process for selecting an intermediate node $a_i \in A$ for every $1 \leq i \leq m$, such that the routing from v_0 to b_i will go through a_i. For this, we need to ensure that there is an edge $(a_i, b_i) \in E$ for every $1 \leq i \leq m$. Once this is done, we mark each edge (v_0, a_i) by the interval $[b_i]$, thus completing our task.

The selection process is similar to the greedy process of Section 2.1. Let $Q = A$, and define a counter $C(a)$ for each node $a \in A$, initially setting all counters to zero. Having already selected $a_1, \ldots, a_{i-1}$, the ith step consists of selecting a_i to be some arbitrary neighbor of b_i in Q, increasing the counter $C(a_i)$ by one, and discarding a_i from Q if the counter has reached two. If, at any stage, the node b_i considered by the process has no neighbors in the remaining set Q, then the process fails and we abort our attempt to provide a 3-IRS for G.

We need to argue that with very high probability, the process does not fail. Let F_i be the event that the process fails in the ith step. Note that at the beginning of step i, the counters sum up to $i - 1$, hence at most $\lfloor (i-1)/2 \rfloor$ nodes were discarded from Q, so the current set Q is of size

$$|Q| \geq |A| - \left\lceil \frac{i-1}{2} \right\rceil \geq |A| - \frac{m}{2} \geq np - \frac{np}{2} - 6\sqrt{n \ln n} \geq \frac{np}{3}$$

for sufficiently large n.

Event F_i occurs only if b_i is not connected to any node of Q. This is the intersection of $|Q|$ independent events of probability $1 - p$ each, hence $\mathbb{P}(F_i) < c^{-n}$, for constant $c > 1$. Letting $\mathcal{E}_F(v_0)$ denote the event that the process fails for v_0, i.e., $\mathcal{E}_F(v_0) = \bigcup_i F_i$, we have $\mathbb{P}(\mathcal{E}_F(v_0)) \leq m\, c^{-n}$. It follows that for a sufficiently large n, the event $\mathcal{E}_F = \bigcup_{v_0} \mathcal{E}_F(v_0)$ has probability $\mathbb{P}(\mathcal{E}_F) \leq 1/n^3$.

Combining all possible failure events (namely, $\mathcal{E}_A \cup \mathcal{E}_F$), we get that the probability that our process fails to generate an interval routing scheme for the graph with three intervals per edge is bounded from above by $1/n^2$.

Theorem 3. *For sufficiently large n, with probability at least $1 - 1/n^2$, and for every fixed p, $0 < p < 1$, a random graph $G \in \mathcal{G}_{n,p}$ satisfies $\mathrm{IRS}_A(G) \leq 3$.* □

4 Designer Chosen Labels

We next assume the designer model, in which the assignment of the node labels $\{1, \ldots, n\}$ to vertices is done be the designer of the routing scheme, aiming to minimize the number of intervals used by the routing scheme.

In this case, the only lower bound we have at the moment is the trivial $\mathrm{IRS}(G) \geq 1$ for every graph G. In the opposite direction, we are also unable so far to prove an upper bound of 1 on the maximum number of intervals per edge.

However, we will show that it is possible to assign the node labels in such a way that, while some edges might still require two intervals, the number of such violations will be very small, and more specifically, bounded by $O(\log^3 n)$ with high probability. In this section we restrict our attention to the case $p = 1/2$, so $G \in \mathcal{G}_{n,1/2}$.

The idea behind the selection process is the following. Suppose that the vertex set of the given random graph is partitioned into cliques $V = C_1 \cup \ldots \cup C_m$. Label the nodes of V according to this partition, so that the nodes of each clique C_i are numbered consecutively. Now use this partition to define the routing scheme as follows. Consider a sender v_0. Suppose that $v_0 \in C_J$, and consider some other clique C_I. The central property we rely upon is that if v_0 is adjacent to *some* of the nodes of C_I, then all the vertices of C_I can be provided for using a single interval on each edge going from v_0 to the nodes of C_I, as follows. Let $C_I = \{p, p+1, \ldots, q\}$. If v_0 has a unique neighbor ℓ in C_I, then mark the edge from v_0 to ℓ by the interval $[p, q]$. Otherwise, suppose v_0 has neighbors $\ell_1 < \ell_2 < \ldots < \ell_k$ in C_I. Then the edges $e_j = (v_0, \ell_j)$ leading from v_0 to these nodes can be labeled by intervals $I(e_j)$ as follows.

$$I(e_j) = \begin{cases} [p, \dots, \ell_2 - 1], & j = 1, \\ [\ell_j, \dots, \ell_{j+1} - 1], & 1 < j < k, \\ [\ell_k, \dots, q], & j = k. \end{cases}$$

(Note that this choice of intervals takes care also of the special case of $C_I = C_J$ itself, where every node other than v_0 itself is a neighbor of v_0.)

Thus we are left only with the need of handling the cliques C_i none of whose vertices are adjacent to v_0. Call these cliques the "remote" cliques. The nodes of these remote cliques must be reached through vertices of other cliques, potentially using additional intervals, and at worst, using a unique new interval for each node. It is thus required to bound from above the maximum number of nodes in the remote cliques. Towards this goal, we rely intuitively on the fact that large cliques are unlikely to be remote. More precisely, the probability that a clique of size k is remote is roughly $1/2^k$. It thus becomes necessary to explore the distribution of clique sizes in a clique partition of random graphs, or at least generate partitions with favorable size distributions.

We make use of the following two properties of random graphs. (In the following the function log denotes the logarithm in base 2.) First, regarding the size of the maximum clique, we have (cf. Chapt. XI.1 of [2])

Lemma 3. *With probability at least $1 - 1/n^{\log \log n}$, the maximum clique in a random graph $G \in \mathcal{G}_{n,1/2}$ is of size at most $2 \log n$.*

Let $\mathcal{E}_C$ denote the event that the random graph at hand does not satisfy the property asserted in Lemma 3. Henceforth we ignore that possibility, and restrict our attention to $\bar{\mathcal{E}}_C$. As before, we also restrict ourselves to $\bar{\mathcal{E}}_A$.

Secondly, we make use of a natural technique for generating a clique partition of a given graph. This technique is the "mirror image" of the greedy algorithm often used to generate a legal coloring for a graph. This simple algorithm operates as follows. Start by ordering the vertices arbitrarily, numbering them as $1, 2, \dots, n$. Assign the vertices to cliques $C_1, C_2, \dots, C_n$ one by one, assigning each node to the smallest-indexed admissible clique. Vertex 1 is thus assigned to C_1, vertex 2 is assigned to C_1 if it is a neighbor of vertex 1, otherwise it is assigned to C_2, and so on. It is known (cf. Chapt. XI.3 of [2]) that with high probability this process will pack the vertices of the given random graph G in fewer than $n/\log n$ cliques. Moreover, analyzing the process in more detail, we will derive bounds on the number of small cliques generated. Specifically, there will be no more than $2^k \log n$ cliques of size k, with high probability. Coupled with Lemma 3, this can be used to show that the total number of nodes in remote cliques is bounded (with high probability) by about

$$\sum_{k=1}^{2 \log n} k \cdot \frac{1}{2^k} \cdot 2^k \log n = O(\log^3 n).$$

The problem that makes formalizing this argument somewhat more difficult is that once the partition is calculated, the graph can no longer be treated as random, as the fact, say, that v_0 is not in the clique C_i, bears some implications on the probability that v_0 is connected to some node of C_i, and prevents us from assuming that all the events considered in the analysis are independent. Nevertheless, the dependencies can be bounded and turn to have but little effect on the resulting probabilities.

Let us fix our attention on a vertex v_0, belonging to the clique C_J, and on another clique C_I. We would like to bound the probability that v_0 is not connected to any node of C_I.

For every clique C_i and vertex $v \in V$, partition C_i into $C_i = A_i(v) \cup B_i(v)$, where $A_i(v)$ consists of all the vertices that entered C_i before v was considered by the algorithm, namely, $A_i(v) = \{w \in C_i \mid w < v\}$, and $B_i(v) = C_i \setminus A_i(v)$, the vertices added to C_i after v was added to some clique. Let $\alpha_i(v) = |A_i(v)|$ and $\beta_i(v) = |B_i(v)|$. In particular, let $A = A_I(v_0)$, $B = B_I(v_0)$, $\alpha = \alpha_I(v_0)$ and $\beta = \beta_I(v_0)$.

Lemma 4. *If $I < J$ then the probability that C_I is remote from v_0 is $1/2^{|C_I|-1}$.*

Proof. We will actually prove the somewhat stronger claim that if $I < J$ then the probability that v_0 is not connected to any vertex in C_I is $\frac{1}{2^\beta(2^\alpha-1)}$.

Since $I < J$, when the greedy algorithm considered v_0 it had to examine (and reject) the possibility of adding it to C_I, before actually adding it to C_J. The fact that v_0 was not added to C_I implies that there is some node in A that does not neighbor v_0. However, of all 2^α possible connection configurations between v_0 and the nodes of A, the event $\mathcal{E}_N = $ "v_0 has a non-neighbor in A" only excludes the possibility that v_0 neighbors all nodes of A, and leaves us with $2^\alpha - 1$ other possibilities. Hence conditioned on $\mathcal{E}_N$, we have

$$\mathbb{P}(v_0 \text{ has no neighbors in } A) = \frac{1}{2^\alpha - 1}.$$

As for the nodes of B, each such node v was added to C_I after v_0 was considered, and since $I < J$, the decision to add v into C_I was reached before considering clique C_J, hence it was independent of the existence (or nonexistence) of the edge (v, v_0). Hence

$$\mathbb{P}(v_0 \text{ has no neighbors in } B) = \frac{1}{2^\beta}.$$

The lemma follows. $\qquad\qquad\qquad\qquad\qquad\qquad\qquad\qquad\qquad\qquad\qquad\square$

Lemma 5. *If $I > J$ then the probability that C_I is remote from v_0 is*

$$\frac{1}{2^\alpha} \cdot \prod_{v \in B} \frac{2^{\alpha_J(v)-1}}{2^{\alpha_J(v)} - 1}.$$

Proof. Since $I > J$, when the greedy algorithm considered each node v of C_I it had to first examine (and reject) the possibility of adding it to C_J. For $v \in A$, the decision not to add v to C_I was clearly independent of the edge (v, v_0). Hence

$$\mathbb{P}(v_0 \text{ has no neighbors in } A) = \frac{1}{2^\alpha}.$$

It remains to consider nodes $v \in \mathcal{B}$.

The fact that a node $v \in \mathcal{B}$ was not added to C_J implies that there exists a node in $\mathcal{A}_J(v)$ that does not neighbor v. But again, of all $2^{\alpha_J(v)}$ possible connection configurations between v and the nodes of $\mathcal{A}_J(v)$, the event $\mathcal{E}_N(v) =$ "v has a non-neighbor in $\mathcal{A}_J(v)$" only excludes the possibility that v neighbors all nodes of $\mathcal{A}_J(v)$, and leaves us with $2^{\alpha_J(v)} - 1$ other possibilities. Of those, v neighbors v_0 in exactly $2^{\alpha_J(v)-1}$ possibilities. Hence conditioned on $\mathcal{E}_N(v)$, the probability that v does not neighbor v_0 is $\frac{2^{\alpha_J(v)-1}}{2^{\alpha_J(v)}-1}$. Hence

$$\mathbb{P}(v_0 \text{ has no neighbors in } \mathcal{B}) = \prod_{v \in \mathcal{B}} \frac{2^{\alpha_J(v)-1}}{2^{\alpha_J(v)} - 1}.$$

The lemma follows. □

The product appearing in the bound of Lemma 5 is small only when the values $\alpha_J(v)$ involved in it are sufficiently large. Fortunately, there cannot be too many nodes v with small $\alpha_J(v)$ values, as we prove next.

For integer $k \geq 1$, let $X_J(k)$ denote the set of vertices v that were considered by the algorithm during the period when C_J contained exactly k nodes, and were rejected from C_J. In particular, we are interested in the collection of such vertices for small values of k, i.e., $\hat{X} = \bigcup_{k=1}^{\log \log n} X_J(k)$.

Corollary 1. *Suppose that the clique C_I, $I > J$, contains no vertex from $\hat{X}$. Then the probability that v_0 is not connected to any vertex in C_I is at most $\gamma/2^{|C_I|}$, for some fixed constant $\gamma > 0$.*

Proof. Under the assumption of the corollary, $\alpha_J(v) > \log \log n$ for every $v \in \mathcal{B}$. Therefore

$$\frac{2^{\alpha_J(v)-1}}{2^{\alpha_J(v)} - 1} = \frac{1}{2}\left(1 + \frac{1}{2^{\alpha_J(v)} - 1}\right) \leq \frac{1}{2}\left(1 + \frac{1}{2^{\log \log n + 1} - 1}\right) \leq \frac{1}{2}\left(1 + \frac{1}{\log n}\right).$$

The bound of Lemma 5 thus becomes

$$\frac{1}{2^\alpha} \cdot \left(\frac{1}{2}\left(1 + \frac{1}{\log n}\right)\right)^\beta.$$

As the size of the maximum clique in a random graph is at most $2 \log n$ (with probability at least $1 - 1/n^{\log \log n}$), this bound is no greater than

$$\frac{1}{2^\alpha} \cdot \frac{1}{2^\beta}\left(1 + \frac{1}{\log n}\right)^{2 \log n} \leq \frac{1}{2^{\alpha+\beta}} \cdot e^2,$$

and the claim follows. □

Lemma 6. *With probability at least $1 - 1/n^3$, the set $X_J(k)$ is of size $|X_J(k)| \leq 2^{k+2} \ln n$ for every $k \geq 1$.*

172

Proof. Suppose that $|X_J(k)| > 2^{k+2} \ln n$. For every $v \in X_J(k)$, the probability for v not joining C_J (on account of a missing edge from v to some node in C_J) is $1/2^k$. Thus the probability of all of those vertices being rejected from C_J is

$$\left(\frac{1}{2^k}\right)^{|X_J(k)|} < \left(\frac{1}{2^k}\right)^{2^{k+2} \ln n} \le e^{-4 \ln n} = \frac{1}{n^4}.$$

Summing these probabilities over all k yields the desired claim. $\qquad\square$

Let $\mathcal{E}_D$ denote the event that the random graph at hand does not satisfy the property asserted in Lemma 6. Henceforth we ignore that possibility, and restrict our attention to $\bar{\mathcal{E}}_D$. Under this restriction, the size of the set $\hat{X}$ is bounded above by

$$|\hat{X}| \le \sum_{k=1}^{\log\log n} 2^{k+2} \ln n = O(\log^2 n).$$

It remains to bound the number of remote cliques C_I (that have no neighbor of v_0). Let $f(k)$ denote the number of cliques of size k.

Lemma 7. *With probability at least $1 - 1/n^2$, $f(k) \le 2^{k+2} \ln n$ for every $k \ge 1$.*

Proof. Let us bound the probability of the event that there are more than $2^{k+1} \log n$ cliques of size k, $C_{i_1}, \ldots, C_{i_{f(k)}}$. Let $m = 2^{k+2} \ln n$ and consider the time when clique C_{i_m} was formed by the greedy algorithm (for the purpose of hosting the currently inspected vertex v'). For any vertex v considered after v', the probability that it could not have joined the clique C_{i_j} is

$$1 - \frac{1}{2^{\alpha_{i_j}(v)}} \le 1 - \frac{1}{2^k}.$$

Hence the probability that v could not have joined any of those m cliques is at most

$$\left(1 - \frac{1}{2^k}\right)^m \le \left(1 - \frac{1}{2^k}\right)^{2^{k+2} \ln n} \le e^{-4 \ln n} = \frac{1}{n^4}.$$

Consequently, the probability that any of the remaining vertices to be considered by the algorithm after v' could not join an existing clique, and a new clique must be formed, is at most $1/n^3$. Summing these probabilities for every k, the lemma follows. $\qquad\square$

Let $\mathcal{E}_H$ denote the event that the random graph at hand does not satisfy the property asserted in Lemma 7. Henceforth we ignore that possibility, and restrict our attention to $\bar{\mathcal{E}}_H$.

Lemma 8. *The number of remote cliques is at most $O(\log^2 n)$, with probability $1 - 1/n^2$.*

Proof. Assuming event $\bar{\mathcal{E}}_D$, the total number of remote cliques that contain a vertex of $\hat{X}$ is at most $O(\log^2 n)$. It remains to count the remote cliques among the cliques that do not contain any vertex of $\hat{X}$. The probability of such a clique

C_I being remote is bounded, in Lemma 4 and Corollary 1, by $\delta/2^{|C_I|}$ for some constant $\delta > 1$.

For every clique C_i of size k, let R_i be the event that C_i is remote. Let R be a random variable representing the number of remote cliques of size k, and let $f_R(k)$ denote its expectation. Since R is the sum of $f(k)$ Bernoulli random variables R_i, each with probability $\delta/2^k$, $f_R(k)$ is at most $\delta f(k)/2^k$. Assuming event $\bar{\mathcal{E}}_H$, we have

$$f_R(k) \leq \frac{\delta 2^{k+2} \ln n}{2^k} = 4\delta \ln n.$$

Applying Chernoff's bound, we get that

$$\mathbb{P}(R \geq 8\delta \ln n) < \exp(-2\delta \ln n) = n^{-2\delta} < \frac{1}{n^2}.$$

Hence for the cliques not containing any vertices from $\hat{X}$, with probability at least $1 - 1/n^2$, the total number of remote cliques of any size k is bounded (recalling Lemma 3) by $O(\log^2 n)$.

Combining both clique types together, we get the claim of the lemma. □

It follows that for every v_0, the number of "problematic" vertices (namely, those of remote cliques) that need to be assigned an individual interval is bounded by $O(\log^3 n)$, with probability $1 - 1/n$.

Combining all possible failure events (namely, $\mathcal{E}_A \cup \mathcal{E}_C \cup \mathcal{E}_D \cup \mathcal{E}_H$), we get that for a random graph in $\mathcal{G}_{n,1/2}$, with probability at least $1 - 1/n$, it is possible to assign node labels and design an interval routing scheme in such a way that for every node v_0, there is a single interval on every edge except at most $O(\log^3 n)$ edges with two intervals each. (Spreading the problematic nodes so that each adds an interval to a different edge - is done by a greedy process similar to those of sections 2.1 and 3.)

Theorem 4. *For sufficiently large n, with probability at least $1 - 1/n$, a random graph $G \in \mathcal{G}_{n,1/2}$ can be given an assignment of node labels and a shortest path interval routing scheme (polynomial time constructible) using a single interval per edge, except for at most $O(\log^3 n)$ edges per vertex where two intervals must be used.* □

Corollary 2. *For almost every n-node graph G there exists an assignment of node labels from the set $\{1, \ldots, n\}$, and a shortest path routing scheme using at most $n + O(\log^4 n)$ bits of memory per vertex. Moreover the routing scheme is constructible in polynomial time.*

Proof. Assume G satisfies Theorem 4. The interval routing scheme on G can be implemented in each vertex by a table of $O(\log^3 n)$ integers, and a binary vector of n bits. Indeed, every 1-IRS can be implemented in each vertex in $n + O(\log n)$ bits (cf. [6]). Note that the $O(\log^3 n)$ problematic nodes contribute for at most $O(\log^3 n)$ single intervals, each one composed of exactly one node label. We store in a table of $O(\log^3 n)$ entries the label of these nodes, and the output port number that makes an overhead of $O(\log^4 n)$ bits in total. These nodes are treated as exceptions, and checked first in the routing process. So, the label of these nodes can be merged to the remaining intervals in order to simulate a 1-IRS. □

References

1. N. ALON AND J. H. SPENCER, *The Probabilistic Method*, John Wiley & Sons, 1992.
2. B. BOLLOBÁS, *Random Graphs*, Academic Press, New York, 1975.
3. H. BUHRMAN, J.-H. HOEPMAN, AND P. VITÁNYI, *Optimal routing tables*, in 15th Annual ACM Symposium on Principles of Distributed Computing (PODC), May 1996.
4. H. BUHRMAN, M. LI, AND P. VITÁNYI, *Kolmogorov random graphs and the incompressibility method*, in IEEE Conference on Compression and Complexity of Sequences, IEEE Comp. Soc. Press, 1997.
5. M. FLAMMINI, J. VAN LEEUWEN, AND A. MARCHETTI-SPACCAMELA, *The complexity of interval routing on random graphs*, in 20th International Symposium on Mathematical Foundations of Computer Sciences (MFCS), J. Wiederman and P. Hájek, eds., vol. 969 of Lecture Notes in Computer Science, Springer-Verlag, Aug. 1995, pp. 37–49.
6. C. GAVOILLE, *A survey on interval routing scheme*, Research Report RR-1182-97, LaBRI, University of Bordeaux, 351, cours de la Libération, 33405 Talence Cedex, France, Oct. 1997. Submitted for publication.
7. C. GAVOILLE AND D. PELEG, *The compactness of interval routing*, Research Report RR-1176-97, LaBRI, University of Bordeaux, 351, cours de la Libération, 33405 Talence Cedex, France, Sept. 1997. Submitted for publication.
8. C. GAVOILLE AND S. PÉRENNÈS, *Memory requirement for routing in distributed networks*, in 15th Annual ACM Symposium on Principles of Distributed Computing (PODC), ACM PRESS, ed., May 1996, pp. 125–133.
9. N. SANTORO AND R. KHATIB, *Labelling and implicit routing in networks*, The Computer Journal, 28 (1985), pp. 5–8.
10. J. VAN LEEUWEN AND R. B. TAN, *Interval routing*, The Computer Journal, 30 (1987), pp. 298–307.

A Wait-Free Classification of Loop Agreement Tasks

(Extended Abstract)[*]

Maurice Herlihy[1] and Sergio Rajsbaum[2]

[1] Computer Science Department, Brown University, Providence RI 02912, USA,
herlihy@cs.brown.edu
[2] Instituto de Matemáticas, U.N.A.M., Ciudad Universitaria, D.F. 04510, México,
rajsbaum@math.unam.mx

Abstract. Loop agreement is a family of wait-free tasks that includes set agreement and approximate agreement tasks. This paper presents a complete classification of loop agreement tasks. Each loop agreement task can be assigned an *algebraic signature* consisting of a finitely-presented group G and a distinguished element g in G. This signature completely characterizes the task's computational power. If $\mathcal{G}$ and $\mathcal{H}$ are loop agreement tasks with respective signatures $\langle G, g \rangle$ and $\langle H, h \rangle$, then $\mathcal{G}$ implements $\mathcal{H}$ if and only if there exists a group homomorphism $\phi : G \to H$ carrying g to h.

1 Introduction

A *task* is a distributed coordination problem in which each process starts with a private input value taken from a finite set, communicates with the other processes by applying operations to shared objects, and eventually halts with a private output value, also taken from a finite set. Examples of tasks include *consensus* [9], *renaming* [2], and *set agreement* [6]. A *protocol* is a program that solves a task. A protocol is *wait-free* if it tolerates failures or delays by n out of $n + 1$ processes. One task *implements* another if one can transform (as described below) any protocol for one into a protocol for the other.

Informally, a *classification* of a set of tasks $\mathcal{T}$ is a way of partitioning $\mathcal{T}$ into disjoint *classes* $\mathcal{C}_0, \mathcal{C}_1, \ldots$ so that tasks in the same class share some interesting property. A classification is *complete* if all tasks in a class are computationally equivalent: each task in a class implements any other task in that class. Computational equivalence is an equivalence relation in the ordinary sense.

Loop agreement is a family of tasks that includes set agreement [6] and approximate agreement [8] tasks. This paper presents the first complete classification of loop agreement tasks. Each loop agreement task can be assigned an *algebraic signature* consisting of a finitely-presented group G and a distinguished element g in G. Remarkably, this signature completely characterizes the

---

[*] This work has been supported by a Conacyt-NSF grant.

task's computational power. If task $\mathcal{G}$ has signature $\langle G, g \rangle$ and $\mathcal{H}$ has signature $\langle H, h \rangle$, then $\mathcal{G}$ implements $\mathcal{H}$ if and only if there exists a group homomorphism $\phi : G \to H$ carrying g to h. In short, the discrete, algorithmic problem of determining how to implement one loop agreement task in terms of another reduces to a problem of abstract algebra.

We believe these results are interesting for several reasons. First, loop agreement tasks are interesting in themselves, as they generalize a number of well-known problems (see Section 4) and they have a rich combinatorial structure. They already proved to be essential in obtaining a variety of results concerning the decidability of distributed tasks [15]. Second, the techniques introduced here differ in important ways from earlier approaches to understanding the computational power of wait-free tasks. Much recent work on task composition and robustness has focused on proving that two tasks are inequivalent by constructing specific counterexamples for which equivalence fails. Although the resulting constructions are often ingenious, we would like to replace the search for counterexamples with a more systematic method of analysis. We identify specific (algebraic) properties of tasks that, in a sense, capture their relative power. Evaluating whether one task is stronger, weaker, or incomparable to another reduces to the problem of analyzing certain group homomorphisms. Finally, while most earlier applications of topological techniques focused on impossibility results, we have been able to identify general *sufficient* topological conditions for one task to implement another.

We are hopeful that the techniques introduced here can be used to derive more general classification results. Moreover, because any more general classification scheme must encompass the algebraic structure described here, these results suggest to us that algebraic and topological techniques remain the most promising approach toward classifying tasks in general.

As an application of this classification, we show that loop agreement protocols can be divided into *torsion classes* which also have a nice mathematical structure. This is a coarser partition which still shows how rich the structure of a task classification can be, but is defined in terms of simpler algebraic properties.

2   Related Work

Perhaps the first paper to investigate the solvability of distributed tasks was the landmark 1985 paper of Fischer, Lynch, and Paterson [9] which showed that *consensus*, then considered an abstraction of the database commitment problem, had no 1-resilient message-passing solution. Other tasks that attracted attention include *approximate agreement* [8], *renaming* [2, 14, 16] and *set agreement* [4, 6, 13, 14, 16, 25].

Herlihy and Shavit [16, 17] introduced the use of homology theory to show certain impossibility results for set agreement and renaming. (The set agreement results were shown independently by Borowsky and Gafni [4] and Saks and Zaharoglou [25] using different techniques.) More recently, Herlihy and Rajsbaum used homology theory to derive further impossibility results for set agreement

[12, 13], and to unify a variety of known impossibility results in terms of the theory of chain maps and chain complexes [14].

A novel aspect of the work described here is the extensive use of the fundamental group; that is, homotopy instead of homology theory. Gafni and Koutsoupias [10] were the first to use the fundamental group to analyze distributed tasks, showing that it is undecidable whether certain wait-free read-write tasks have a protocol. Herlihy and Rajsbaum [12] used the fundamental group to prove undecidability results in a variety of other models.

It should be emphasized that our results apply to short-lived *tasks*, not to long-lived objects. Classifying objects raises the complex question of *robustness*: the question whether one can combine "weak" objects to derive "strong" objects. Jayanti [18] was the first to raise the question of robustness with respect to the consensus hierarchy [11]. Since then, a variety of researchers have contributed a variety of ingenious counterexamples showing that different restrictions of the consensus hierarchy are not robust [5, 19, 21, 24, 26]. Neiger et al. [23] and Borowsky et al. [7] claim that the consensus hierarchy is robust for objects having deterministic sequential specifications.

3 Background

3.1 Distributed Computing

A model *of computation* is characterized by a set of $n + 1$ processes, a set of objects shared by the processes, and a set of assumptions about timing and failures. Examples of shared objects include message-passing channels, read/write memory, or read/write memory augmented by more powerful synchronization primitives, such as *test-and-set* or *compare-and-swap* variables. All models considered in this paper are *asynchronous*: there is no bound on relative process speed.

A *protocol* is a program that solves a task in a particular model of computation. A protocol is *wait-free* if it tolerates failures by n out of $n + 1$ processes. All protocols considered in this paper are wait-free.

An initial (or final) local state of a process is modeled as a *vertex* $v = \langle P, v \rangle$, a pair consisting of a process id P and an input (or output) value v. We speak of the vertex as being *colored* with the process id. A set of $d+1$ mutually compatible initial (or final) local states is modeled as a *d-dimensional simplex* (or *d*-simplex) $S^d = (s_0, \ldots, s_d)$.

The complete set of possible initial (or final) states of a protocol is represented by a set of simplexes, closed under containment, called a *simplicial complex* (or complex) $\mathcal{K}$. A map $\mu : \mathcal{K} \to \mathcal{L}$ carrying vertexes to vertexes is *simplicial* if it also carries simplexes to simplexes. If vertexes of $\mathcal{K}$ and $\mathcal{L}$ are labeled with process ids, then μ is *color-preserving* if $id(v) = id(\mu(v))$.

A *task* specification for $n + 1$ processes is given by an *input complex* $\mathcal{I}$, an *output complex* $\mathcal{O}$, and a recursive relation Δ carrying each m-simplex of $\mathcal{I}$ to a set of m-simplexes of $\mathcal{O}$, for each $0 \leq m \leq n$. Informally, Δ has the following interpretation: if the $(m+1)$ processes named in S^m start with the designated input values, and only they participate, then each simplex in $\Delta(S^m)$ designates a legal final set of values.

Any protocol has an associated *protocol complex* $\mathcal{P}$, in which each vertex is labeled with a process id and that process's final state (called its *view*). Each simplex thus corresponds to an equivalence class of executions that "look the same" to the processes at its vertexes. The protocol complex corresponding to executions starting from a fixed simplex S^m is denoted $\mathcal{P}(S^m)$. A protocol *solves* a task if there exists a a simplicial *decision map* $\delta : \mathcal{P} \to \mathcal{O}$ such that for each simplex $R^m \in \mathcal{P}(S^m)$, $\delta(R^m) \in \Delta(S^m)$.

Task $\mathcal{L}$ *implements* task $\mathcal{K}$ if one can construct a wait-free protocol for $\mathcal{K}$ by interleaving calls to any number of instances of protocols for $\mathcal{L}$ with operations on any number of read-write registers. In this paper we concentrate on the following, more restricted, implementation notion. An *instance* of $\mathcal{L}$ implements $\mathcal{K}$ if one can construct a protocol for $\mathcal{K}$ by interleaving a call to a single instance of a protocol for $\mathcal{L}$ with any number of operations of read-write registers. Two tasks are *equivalent* if each implements the other, and a task is *universal* for some set of tasks if it implements any task in that set.

3.2 Algebraic Topology

We now informally review a number of undergraduate level notions from algebraic topology; more complete descriptions can be found in any standard topology text (such as [1, 20, 22]).

Let $\mathcal{C}$ be a connected simplicial complex. The union of the simplexes which make up the complex can be regarded as a subset of Euclidean space, called the *polyhedron*, $|\mathcal{C}|$. The *barycentric subdivision* [1, p.125], is i..ductively obtained by introducing a new vertex at the barycenter (center of mass) of each i-simplex, and then introducing all simplexes of dimension $\leq i$ determined by the additional vertices. The *ℓ-skeleton skel$^\ell(\mathcal{C})$* of $\mathcal{C}$ is the subcomplex consisting of simplexes of $\mathcal{C}$ of dimension ℓ or less.

Consider a point $x_0 \in |\mathcal{C}|$. We call x_0 the *base point*. A *loop* α in $\mathcal{C}$ with base point x_0 is a continuous map from the unit interval $I = [0,1]$ to $|\mathcal{C}|$:

$$\alpha : I \to |\mathcal{C}|$$

such that $\alpha(0) = \alpha(1) = x_0$. A loop is *simple* if $\alpha(t)$ is unique for all $0 \leq t < 1$. Two loops α and β with base point x_0 are *homotopic* if one can be continuously deformed to the other while leaving the base point fixed. More precisely, there exists a continuous map $h : I \times I \to |\mathcal{C}|$, called a *homotopy*, such that $h(s,0) = \alpha(s)$, $h(s,1) = \beta(s)$, and $h(0,t) = h(1,t) = x_0$ for all $s, t \in [0,1]$. Homotopy is an equivalence relation. Let $[\alpha]$ denote the equivalence class of loops homotopic to α.

The *fundamental group* [1, p.87] $\pi_1(\mathcal{C}, x_0)$ of $\mathcal{C}$ is defined as follows. The elements of the group are equivalence classes under homotopy of loops with base point x_0. The group operation on these equivalence classes is defined as follows. For loops α and β, $\alpha * \beta$ is the loop obtained by traversing first α and then β:

$$\alpha * \beta(s) = \begin{cases} \alpha(2s) & \text{for } 0 \leq s \leq \frac{1}{2} \\ \beta(2s - 1) & \text{for } \frac{1}{2} \leq s \leq 1 \end{cases}$$

Define $[\alpha] \cdot [\beta] = [\alpha * \beta]$. It is easy to check that this defines a group, with the equivalence class of the constant loop $\alpha(s) = x_0$ as the identity, and for an arbitrary loop α based at x_0, $[\alpha]^{-1} = [\alpha^{-1}]$, where α^{-1} is obtained by traversing α in the opposite direction. The identity element consists of the loops that can be continuously deformed to the point x_0, called *null-homotopic*, or *contractible*.

Since we are assuming that $\mathcal{C}$ is connected, the fundamental group is independent of the base point, so we simply write $\pi_1(\mathcal{C})$. To simplify notation, we sometimes write α instead of $[\alpha]$, relying on context to distinguish between a loop and its equivalence class.

Let $f : |\mathcal{K}| \to |\mathcal{L}|$ be a continuous map. Notice that if α is a loop in $|\mathcal{K}|$ then $f \cdot \alpha$ is a loop in $|\mathcal{L}|$. We can define the *homomorphism induced* by f, $f_* : \pi_1(\mathcal{K}) \to \pi_1(\mathcal{L})$, by $f_*(\langle\alpha\rangle) = \langle f \cdot \alpha\rangle$.

The group $\pi_1(\mathcal{C})$ can also be defined combinatorially, in terms of the *edge loops* of $\mathcal{C}$. An edge loop κ is a sequence of vertices such that each two consecutive vertices span a 1-simplex of $\mathcal{C}$, and the initial is equal to the final vertex. Every loop whose base point is a vertex is homotopic to an edge loop, so we can go back and forth between loops and edge loops at will.

4 Loop Agreement

Let $\mathcal{K}$ be a finite (uncolored) 2-dimensional simplicial complex, κ a simple loop of $\mathcal{K}$, and k_0, k_1, k_2 three *distinguished* vertexes in κ. For distinct i, j, and k, let κ_{ij} be the subpath of κ linking k_i to k_j without passing through k_k.

Define the $(\mathcal{K}, \kappa)$-*loop agreement* task as follows. Each of $n + 1$ processes has an input value in $\{0, 1, 2\}$. Let S^n be an input simplex with input values $vals(S^n)$.

$$\text{If } vals(S^n) = \begin{cases} \{i\} & \text{every process chooses } k_i \\ \{i, j\} & \text{all vertexes chosen span a simplex that lies in } \kappa_{ij} \\ \{0, 1, 2\} & \text{all vertexes chosen span a simplex in } \mathcal{K}. \end{cases}$$

(1)

In other words, the processes converge on a simplex in $\mathcal{K}$. If all processes have the same input vertex, they converge on it (Figure 1). If the processes have only two distinct input vertexes, they converge on some simplex along the path linking them (Figure 2). Finally, if the processes have all three input vertexes, they converge to any simplex of $\mathcal{K}$ (Figure 3).

We now present some examples of interesting loop agreement tasks. Let S^2 be the 2-simplex (s_0, s_1, s_2), and $\mathcal{S}^2$ is the complex constructed from S^2 and its faces.

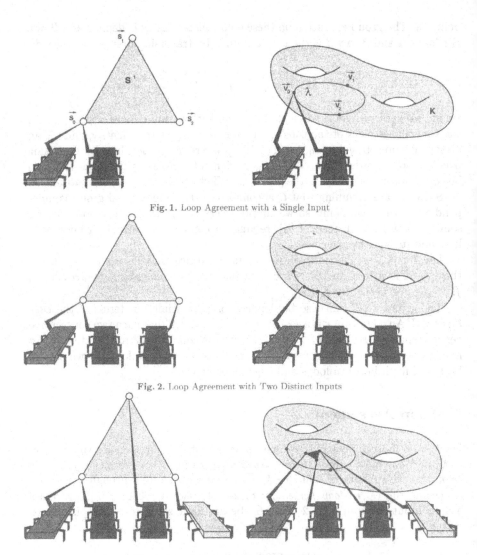

Fig. 1. Loop Agreement with a Single Input

Fig. 2. Loop Agreement with Two Distinct Inputs

Fig. 3. Loop Agreement with Three Distinct Inputs

- In the $(3,2)$-*set agreement* task [6], each of $n + 1$ processes has an input taken from a set of 3 possible values, and each chooses an output value such that (1) each output is some process's input, and (2) no more than 2 distinct values are chosen. This task is the loop agreement task $(skel^1(\mathcal{S}^2), \zeta)$, where ζ is the edge loop $(s_0, s_1), (s_1, s_2), (s_2, s_0)$.
- Let $\sigma(\mathcal{S}^2)$ be an arbitrary subdivision of $\mathcal{S}^2$. In the 2-dimensional *uncolored simplex agreement* task, each process starts with a vertex in $\mathcal{S}^2$. If $S \in \mathcal{S}^2$ is the face spanned by the starting vertexes, then the processes converge on a simplex in $\sigma(S)$. (This task is the uncolored version of simplex agreement [17].) This task is the loop agreement $(\sigma(\mathcal{S}^2), \sigma(\zeta))$, where ζ is the loop described above.
- The 2-dimensional N-*barycentric agreement* task is uncolored simplex agreement for the N-th iterated barycentric subdivision. Notice that 0-barycentric agreement is just the trivial loop agreement task $(\mathcal{S}^2, \zeta)$ where a process with input i can directly decide s_i.
- In the 2-dimensional ϵ-*agreement* task [3], input values are vertexes of a simplex S of $\mathcal{S}^2$, and output values are points of $|S|$ that lie within $\epsilon > 0$ of one another in the convex hull of the input values. It is easily seen that this task can be solved by a protocol for N-barycentric agreement, for suitably large N.
- In the 1-dimensional *approximate agreement* task [8] input values are taken from the set $\{0, 1\}$, and output values are real numbers that lie within $\epsilon > 0$ of one another in the convex hull of the input values. It is easily seen that this task can be solved by a 2-dimensional ϵ-agreement protocol.
- A *torus loop agreement* task can be defined by taking a triangulation of a torus, $\mathcal{K}^2$, and a loop κ.
- A *projective plane loop agreement* task can be defined by taking a triangulation of a 2-dimensional disk, and considering the boundary loop. Identify opposite points on the boundary to obtain a projective plane $\mathcal{K}$, and the resulting loop κ.

5 Algebraic Signatures

Consider the $(\mathcal{K}, \kappa)$-loop agreement task, and another loop agreement task $(\mathcal{L}, \lambda)$ with distinguished vertices ℓ_i. The loop κ represents an element $[\kappa]$ of $\pi_1(\mathcal{K})$.

Definition 1. *The signature of a loop agreement task* $(\mathcal{K}, \kappa)$ *is the pair* $(\pi_1(\mathcal{K}), [\kappa])$.

We use the notation

$$\phi : (\pi_1(\mathcal{K}), [\kappa]) \to (\pi_1(\mathcal{L}), [\lambda])$$

to denote a group homomorphism from $\pi_1(\mathcal{K})$ to $\pi_1(\mathcal{L})$ that carries $[\kappa]$ to $[\lambda]$, i.e., with $\phi([\kappa]) = [\lambda]$. Similarly, we use the notation

$$f : (\mathcal{K}, \kappa) \to (\mathcal{L}, \lambda).$$

to indicate a continuous (sometimes simplicial) map from $|\mathcal{K}|$ to $|\mathcal{L}|$ carrying each k_i to ℓ_i and each κ_{ij} to λ_{ij}.

We are now ready to present the paper's principal technical result: the ability of one loop agreement task to implement another is completely determined by its algebraic signature.

Theorem 1. *A single instance of* $(\mathcal{K}, \kappa)$ *implements* $(\mathcal{L}, \lambda)$ *if and only if there exists a group homomorphism* $\phi : (\pi_1(\mathcal{K}), [\kappa]) \to (\pi_1(\mathcal{L}), [\lambda])$.

Before discussing the proof, we give a few applications. We start with a known ([4, 16, 25]) result, but which illustrates the power of the theorem.

Proposition 1. $(3, 2)$-*set agreement cannot be implemented wait-free.*

Proof. Recall that (3,2)-set agreement is $(skel^1(\mathcal{S}^2), \zeta)$, where ζ is the loop (s_0, s_1, s_2). It is a standard result that $\pi_1(skel^1(\mathcal{S}^2))$ is infinite cyclic with generator ζ. Implementing (3, 2)-set agreement wait-free is the same as implementing it with 0-barycentric agreement $(\mathcal{S}^2, \zeta)$. Because $\pi_1(\mathcal{S}^2)$ is trivial, the only homomorphism $\phi : (\mathcal{S}^2, \zeta) \to (skel^1(\mathcal{S}^2), \zeta)$ is the trivial one that carries ζ to the identity element of the group, and not to ζ.

It is now easy to identify the most powerful and least powerful tasks in this lattice.

Proposition 2. $(3, 2)$-*set agreement is* universal *among loop agreement tasks: it implements any loop agreement task whatsoever.*

Proof. Recall that (3,2)-set agreement is $(skel^1(\mathcal{S}^2), \zeta)$, where ζ is the loop (s_0, s_1, s_2). It is a standard result [1, p.136] that $\pi_1(skel^1(\mathcal{S}^2))$ is the infinite cyclic group $\mathbf{Z}$ with generator ζ. To implement any $(\mathcal{L}, \lambda)$, let $\phi(\zeta) = \lambda$.

Proposition 3. *Uncolored simplex agreement is implemented by any loop agreement task.*

Proof. The complex for uncolored simplex agreement has trivial fundamental group [1, p.96], because it is a subdivided simplex, and hence its poliyhedron is a convex subset of Euclidean space. To implement this task with any $(\mathcal{L}, \lambda)$, let ϕ of every element be 0.

The remainder of this section gives an informal overview of the proof. Recall that a single-instance implementation is allowed to use read/write registers at will. We first check that algebraic signatures are invariant under such compositions. Two algebraic signatures (G, g) and (H, h) are *isomorphic* if there exists an isomorphism between G and H carrying g to h.

Lemma 1. *If* $(\mathcal{K}', \kappa')$ *is a protocol constructed from a single instance of* $(\mathcal{K}, \kappa)$ *and operations on read/write registers, then their signatures are isomorphic.*

It is now easy to obtain the necessary part of Theorem 1. Let $(\mathcal{K}', \kappa')$ be any protocol constructed by composing a protocol for $(\mathcal{K}, \kappa)$ with read/write operations. By Lemma 1, $\pi_1(\mathcal{K}) = \pi_1(\mathcal{K}')$ and $[\kappa] = [\kappa']$. If a single instance of

$(\mathcal{K}, \kappa)$ implements $(\mathcal{L}, \lambda)$, then the decision map $\delta : (\mathcal{K}', \kappa') \to (\mathcal{L}, \lambda)$ induces the desired homomorphism $(\pi_1(\mathcal{K}), [\kappa]) \to (\pi_1(\mathcal{L}), [\lambda])$.

The other direction requires more work. We proceed in three steps. First, we show that the conditions of the theorem suffice to guarantee a *continuous* map

$$f : (\mathcal{K}, \kappa) \to (\mathcal{L}, \lambda).$$

Second, we show how to make this continuous map simplicial. Third, we show how to get the protocol which solves $(\mathcal{L}, \lambda)$.

Assume we have

$$\phi : (\pi_1(\mathcal{K}), [\kappa]) \to (\pi_1(\mathcal{L}), [\lambda]). \tag{2}$$

We need to prove the following lemma.

Lemma 2. *If $\mathcal{K}$ and $\mathcal{L}$ are 2-dimensional simplicial complexes with a homomorphism $\phi : (\pi_1(\mathcal{K}), [\kappa]) \to (\pi_1(\mathcal{L}), [\lambda])$, then there exists a continuous map $f : (|\mathcal{K}|, \kappa) \to (|\mathcal{L}|, \lambda)$.*

We make use of the following standard result:

Lemma 3. *If $\mathcal{K}$ and $\mathcal{L}$ are 2-dimensional simplicial complexes, then every homomorphism $\phi : \pi_1(\mathcal{K}) \to \pi_1(\mathcal{L})$ is induced by some continuous map $f : |\mathcal{K}| \to |\mathcal{L}|$.*

This lemma is not quite enough to prove Lemma 2, because f is constrained only to carry certain equivalence classes of loops to others, while Lemma 2 requires f to carry specific paths and vertexes to others. Nevertheless, in the full paper, we show how to adapt the standard proof of Lemma 3 to prove Lemma 2.

Once we have established the existence of a continuous map $f : (|\mathcal{K}|, \kappa) \to (|\mathcal{L}|, \lambda)$, it remains to be shown that this map can be transformed into a simplicial map. The classical Simplicial Approximation Theorem [1, p.128] guarantees that for sufficiently large $N > 0$, f can be "approximated" by a simplicial map

$$F : (bary^N(\mathcal{K}), \kappa) \to (\mathcal{L}, \lambda).$$

Once we have this map it is a simple matter to obtain a protocol for $(\mathcal{L}, \lambda)$ by running N rounds of barycentric agreement ([15]). This completes the proof of Theorem 1.

6 Application: Torsion Classes

The *torsion number* of $(\mathcal{K}, \kappa)$ is the least positive integer k such that $[\kappa]^k$ is the identity element of $\pi_1(\mathcal{K})$ (related notions appear, for example, in [1, p.178] or [22, p. 22]). If no such k exists, then the order is infinite. Every loop agreement protocol has a well-defined torsion number. Define *torsion class k* to be the tasks with torsion number k.

How much information does a task's torsion number convey? The following properties follow directly from Theorem 1.

- If a task in class k (finite) implements a task in class ℓ, then $\ell|k$ (ℓ divides k).
- Each torsion class includes a *universal* task that solves any loop agreement task in that class.
- The universal task for class k (finite) is also universal for any class ℓ where $\ell|k$.
- The universal task for class k (finite) does not implement any task in class ℓ if ℓ does not divide k.
- The universal task for class ∞ is universal for any class k.

Torsion classes form a coarser partitioning than our complete classification, but they are defined in terms of simpler algebraic properties, and they have an interesting combinatorial structure.

Acknowledgments

We are grateful to Tom Goodwillie of the Brown Mathematics Department for drawing our attention to Lemma 3.

References

1. M.A. Armstrong. *Basic Topology*. Undergraduate Texts In Mathematics. Springer-Verlag, New York, 1983.
2. H. Attiya, A. Bar-Noy, D. Dolev, D. Peleg, and R. Reischuk. Renaming in an asynchronous environment. *Journal of the ACM*, 37(3):524–548, July 1990.
3. E. Borowsky and E. Gafni. Consensus as a form of resilience. private communication.
4. E. Borowsky and E. Gafni. Generalized FLP impossibility result for t-resilient asynchronous computations. In *Proceedings of the 1993 ACM Symposium on Theory of Computing*, pages 91–100, May 1993.
5. T. Chandra, V. Hadzilacos, P. Jayanti, and S. Toueg. Wait-freedom vs. t-resiliency and the robustness of the wait-free hierarchies. In *Proceedings of the 13th Annual ACM Symposium on Principles of Distributed Computing*, pages 334–343, 1994.
6. S. Chaudhuri. Agreement is harder than consensus: Set consensus problems in totally asynchronous systems. In *Proceedings Of The Ninth Annual ACM Symposium On Principles of Distributed Computing*, pages 311–234, August 1990.
7. Y. Afek E. Borowsky, E. Gafni. Consensus power makes (some) sense! In *Proceedings of the 13th Annual ACM Symposium on Principles of Distributed Computing*, pages 363–372, August 1994.
8. A. Fekete. Asymptotically optimal algorithms for approximate agreement. In *Proceedings of the 5th Annual ACM Symposium on Principles of Distributed Computing*, pages 73–87, August 1986.
9. M. Fischer, N.A. Lynch, and M.S. Paterson. Impossibility of distributed commit with one faulty process. *Journal of the ACM*, 32(2):374–382, April 1985.
10. E. Gafni and E. Koutsoupias. Three-processor tasks are undecidable. http://daphne.cs.ucla.edu/eli/undec.ps, 1996.
11. M.P. Herlihy. Wait-free synchronization. *ACM Transactions On Programming Languages And Systems*, 13(1):123–149, January 1991.

12. M.P. Herlihy and S. Rajsbaum. Set consensus using arbitrary objects. Full version of 1994 Herlihy and Rajsbaum PODC paper *op. cit.*

13. M.P. Herlihy and S. Rajsbaum. Set consensus using arbitrary objects. In *Proceedings of the 13th Annual ACM Symposium on Principles of Distributed Computing*, pages 324–333, August 1994.

14. M.P. Herlihy and S. Rajsbaum. Algebraic spans. In *Proceedings of the 14th Annual ACM Symposium on Principles of Distributed Computing*, pages 90–99. ACM, August 1995.

15. M.P. Herlihy and S. Rajsbaum. The decidability of distributed decision task. In *Proceedings of the 1997 ACM Symposium on Theory of Computing*, pages 589–598, May 1997. Brief announcement in PODC 1996.

16. M.P. Herlihy and N. Shavit. The asynchronous computability theorem for t-resilient tasks. In *Proceedings of the 1993 ACM Symposium on Theory of Computing*, pages 111–120, May 1993.

17. M.P. Herlihy and N. Shavit. A simple constructive computability theorem for wait-free computation. In *Proceedings of the 1994 ACM Symposium on Theory of Computing*, pages 243–252, May 1994.

18. P. Jayanti. On the robustness of herlihy's hierarchy. In *Proceedings of the 12th Annual ACM Symposium on Principles of Distributed Computing*, pages 145–158, 1993.

19. W-K. Lo and V. Hadzilacos. All of us are smarter than any of us: more on the robustness of the consensus hierarchy. In *Proceedings of the 1997 ACM Symposium on Theory of Computing*, pages 579–588, 1997.

20. W.S. Massey. *Algebraic Topology: An Introduction*. Graduate Texts In Mathematics. Springer-Verlag, New York, 1977.

21. S. Moran and L. Rappoport. On the robustness of h_m^r. In *Proceedings of the 10th International Workshop on Distributed Algorithms*, pages 344–361. ACM, 1996.

22. J.R. Munkres. *Elements Of Algebraic Topology*. Addison Wesley, Reading MA, 1984. ISBN 0-201-04586-9.

23. G.L. Peterson, R. A. Bazzi, and G. Neiger. A gap theorem for consensus types. In *Proceedings of the 13th Annual ACM Symposium on Principles of Distributed Computing*, pages 344–353, 1994.

24. O. Rachman. Anomalies in the wait-free hierarchy. In *Proceedings of the 8th International Workshop on Distributed Algorithms*, pages 156–163, 1994.

25. M. Saks and F. Zaharoglou. Wait-free k-set agreement is impossible: The topology of public knowledge. In *Proceedings of the 1993 ACM Symposium on Theory of Computing*, pages 101–110, May 1993.

26. Eric Schenk. *Computability and Complexity Results for agreement problems in shared memory systems*. PhD thesis, University of Toronto, 1996.

A Stabilizing Repair Timer

Ted Herman*

University of Iowa, Department of Computer Science
herman@cs.uiowa.edu

Abstract. Certain types of system faults, notably data errors due to transient faults, can be repaired by software. The repair consists of identifying faulty variables and then rewriting data to correct the fault. If fault identification is imprecise, repair procedures can contaminate non faulty processes from data originating at faulty processes. This contamination danger is resolved by delaying data correction for a sufficiently long period. In order to delay correction, processes use a repair timer. This paper considers the problem of how asynchronous processes can implement a repair timer that is itself subject to faults. The main results are requirement specifications for a distributed repair timer and a repair timer algorithm. The algorithm self-stabilizes in $O(\mathcal{D})$ rounds, where $\mathcal{D}$ is the diameter of the network, and provides reliable timing from k-faulty configurations within $O(k)$ rounds.

1 Introduction

Perfectly efficient repair requires precise knowledge of the minimal set of objects requiring some repair action. Several papers [7, 6, 12] have presented examples showing, for transient data faults, that a process cannot ascertain whether it is faulty itself or whether the fault is due to data corruption at a neighboring process. If the algorithm of a correct process trusts values from a faulty process, then the effect of even one initial fault could contaminate previously correct variables.

Some of the challenges of managing repair actions stem from conflicting priorities for fault tolerance. We would ideally like to have self-stabilization, which tolerates worst-case transient faults, and procedures that do not contaminate correct data during repair. Efficiency is also a consideration, so we strive for optimal stabilization times and the local sensitivity called time adaptivity in [12], where k process faults can be repaired in $O(f)$ time.

One way to overcome the danger of contamination is to use an optimistic or conditional approach to repair. New values for variables suspected of being faulty are computed, but not immediately installed. Instead, the repair procedure calculates tentative values and delays the installation of these values. The length of the delay could be given *a priori* by an optimistic bound related to the

---

* This work is supported by NSF CAREER award CCR-9733541.

suspected severity of a fault (using self-stabilization as a fall-back repair strategy), or the delay length could be dynamically set by procedures that verify the legitimacy of tentative values before they are installed.

Algorithms [9, 12] have used the tactic of delay to accommodate limited transient fault scenarios. Typical of this research is the classification of process variables into *output* variables, which are visible to protocol users, and internal variables. The term *output stabilization* is used in [12] to denote the final correction of output variables from an initially faulty state, whereas *state stabilization* refers to the correction of all variables. The delay tactic can be used to delay correction to output variables and can also be used to delay correction of certain internal "backup" variables. The latter is advantageous because output variables can be speculatively (or optimistically) corrected, leading to rapid output stabilization in certain cases, while the backup variables are corrected by a more conservative approach based on delay.

We propose the use of an asynchronous repair timer to provide adequate delay for optimistic repair layered upon self-stabilization. A repair timer can also be used to monitor and control optimistic repair; for instance if a repair procedure should complete in time $t \cdot f$ from an initial state with at most k faults, and if a fault condition persists after $t \cdot f$ time units, then a fall back repair is triggered.

Informally, the requirements of a repair timer are (i) it provides some means to count rounds (the asynchronous measure of time), (ii) it is time adaptive, providing each process a guaranteed number of "ticks" from any k-faulty initial state, (iii) it is efficiently self-stabilizing, and (iv) the timer provides interfaces so that processes can start the repair timer and inspect the elapsed time since repair initiation.

Measuring time in an asynchronous sense is the subject of many investigations, however few of these papers consider transient fault tolerance in an asynchronous system. Research on synchronizers, phase-synchronizers, and integer-valued clocks [2, 5, 8, 11, 13, 1] are the most closely related works to the repair timer of this paper. The only paper considering all cases of transient faults for a synchronizer in the asynchronous model is [3], but the algorithm presented there does not satisfy fault-locality properties in all cases. The algorithm presented in this paper follows the techniques of previous work, and is a small variation on the synchronizer theme. The contributions of this paper lie in the isolation of the requirements, the interfaces, and in a construction for the read/write atomicity model. As more researchers are investigating fault-local optimizations to self-stabilization, the explicit focus on repair timer abstractions is motivated.

2 System Model

The system consists of n processes communicating through link registers with read/write atomicity. The communication network is represented by an undirected, connected graph: for any pair of processes (p, q) there exists a pair of registers $(\mathsf{Register}_{pq}, \mathsf{Register}_{qp})$ if and only if there is an edge between p and q in the communication graph. If (p, q) is an edge in the graph, then we say p and q are neighbors. Process p is the only writer of Register_{pq} and q is the only reader of Register_{pq}.

Let $\mathcal{D}$ denote the diameter of the communication graph. The distance between any pair (p, q) in the graph is denoted by $dist_{pq}$. To denote that p and q are neighbors, we use the notation $p \in \mathcal{N}_q$ and $q \in \mathcal{N}_p$. In the sequel, the term *region* refers to a connected component with a particular property.

A global state is given by the states of all registers and the local states of all process variables and program counters. A process step is either a register operation (and advancement of the program counter) or some modification of internal and output variables (and program counter) of that process. A computation is an infinite sequence of states so that each consecutive pair of states corresponds to a process step and the sequence of states includes an infinite number of steps of each process (computations are fair). The program of each process specifies a *cycle*, which consists of three parts: (i) a process reads one register written by each of its neighbors, (ii) the process assigns values to variables, and (iii) the process writes registers for each of its neighbors.

The system is designed to satisfy some task, and a global state σ is called *legitimate* if the task is satisfied in state σ and any process step from state σ results in a legitimate state. This definition of legitimacy is recursive, and invariants are used to characterize legitimate states of programs. The state predicate $\mathcal{L}$ characterizes legitimacy: state σ satisfies $\mathcal{L}$ iff σ is legitimate. Another state predicate $\mathcal{O}$ characterizes output legitimacy. A global state σ is called *output legitimate* iff $\mathcal{O}$ holds in state σ. If $\mathcal{O}$ is defined, then $\mathcal{L} \Rightarrow \mathcal{O}$, but the converse may not hold.

A state is k-faulty if it can be obtained from a legitimate state by modifying variables and write registers of at most k processes. For an k-faulty state, we call those processes faulty whose variables and/or write registers were modified to differ from their legitimate values. A *faulty region* in a state is a connected component of faulty processes.

Because each iteration of a process program specifies a cycle, time is conveniently measured in asynchronous rounds, which are defined inductively. A *round* of a computation, with respect to a start state σ, is a computation segment originating with σ of minimum length containing at least one complete cycle (from reading registers to writing registers) of each process. The first round of a computation consists of a round with respect to the initial state of the computation, and round k of a computation, $k > 1$, consists of a round with respect to the first state following round $k - 1$.

A system is *self stabilizing* if every computation contains a legitimate state (that is, for any initial state, the system eventually reaches a legitimate state). The *stabilization time* is the worst case number of rounds in any computation before a legitimate state occurs. The *output stabilization time* with respect to k faults is the worst case number of rounds in any computation starting from an k-faulty initial state before a suffix obtains so that $\mathcal{O}$ holds at each state in the suffix.

The repair timer will be added to a system that has known worst-case timing properties. From any initial state, the system stabilizes within $g \cdot \mathcal{D}$ rounds, where $g > 0$ is a known constant. For any k-faulty initial state, $k > 0$, the system satisfies two properties. First, for each faulty region X in the k-faulty state, some process p in X detects a faulty condition in the first round[1]. Secondly, the system output stabilizes within $h \cdot k$ rounds, where $h > 0$ is a known constant.

The assumption that self stabilization occurs within $O(\mathcal{D})$ rounds is based on works in the area of self stabilization showing that a large class of algorithms can be made self stabilizing with $O(\mathcal{D})$ stabilization times [4]. Different assumptions about system repair times, for instance $g \cdot \mathcal{D}^2$ stabilization time, would not drastically change the results of this paper. Even a system that is not self stabilizing can benefit from a repair timer. The assumptions of self stabilization, output stabilization, and constants g, h, are made to strengthen requirements given in Section 3 in the interest of generality. The construction presented in Section 4 is thus useful for systems that do not satisfy weaker assumptions, for instance, a system that does not self stabilize and only tolerates limited cases of k-faulty initial states.

3 Repair Timer Design

3.1 Repair Timer Interface

We consider the repair timer to be a subroutine called by each process in each cycle. Certain register fields are reserved for the repair timer; these register fields are read and written in each cycle so that the repair timers of different processes may communicate. The repair timer of each process has three method calls: void start ( ) initiates the repair timer to start the timing of fault repair; boolean doTick ( ) attempts to advance logical time for the repair, returning *true* iff the logical time advanced by the doTick call; and int getTime ( ) returns the current "repair time" since the most recent start call.

A typical scenario for fault detection and repair for each process p using these methods is the following. In each cycle, p examines variables and register fields to check for a faulty condition. If p's examination reveals a faulty condition, p then calls start to ensure that the repair timer is active (note that p can observe a faulty condition for many successive cycles until the repair is finally complete; in such a case, p will call start in each of these successive cycles). After calling start, or if p does not call start, p invokes doTick to give the repair timer the opportunity to advance logical repair time.

If an invocation of doTick returns *true*, then that call is said to have generated a *tick*. Although p may not locally detect a faulty condition and invoke the start method, ticks can occur at p because fault repair has been initiated elsewhere in the system.

---

[1] For certain applications to contain the effects of corrupted data, it may be necessary to require that each non-faulty process neighboring X detect a faulty condition immediately so that erroneous values do not spread during computation.

3.2 Timing Properties

The repair clock provides ticks so that processes can monitor the progress of distributed repair procedures. Ticks must be related to rounds, which are the asynchronous unit of time measurement for computational progress (and repair). On one hand, a repair timer must produce sufficiently many ticks to be adequate for the worst-case repair times (specified by constants g and h in Section 2), but on the other hand the timer need not continue to produce ticks after repair is complete. The requirements given in this section formalize these two constraints. After the repair timer is added to a system, the resulting system should also be self-stabilizing. This entails that the repair timer itself be self-stabilizing. Note that the stabilization time of the repair timer can exceed the original system stabilization time of $g \cdot \mathcal{D}$ assumed in Section 2, so that adding a repair timer to a system may increase the system's stabilization time.

The essential requirement for a repair timer is that if process p observes ℓ ticks in some computation segment, one can infer that a process q at distance d from p has observed at least $C(d, \ell)$ ticks, where C is some function locally computable by p. A process can thereby count ticks to determine the accuracy of values communicated by neighboring processes in the course of distributed repair. The following constraints for a function C form the basis for designing the repair timer. Let C be a function satisfying

$$C(x+1, y) < C(x, y) \quad \wedge \quad C(x, y+1) > C(x, y) \quad \wedge \quad C(x, y) = \Theta(y)$$

These constraints state that C satisfies monotonicity properties with respect to its arguments and that C is a linear function with respect to the second argument. Assume that C is globally known, that is, C can be calculated by any process. For a fixed value $s \in [0, \mathcal{D}]$, define $C_s(y) = C(s, y)$ and let C_s^{-1} denote the inverse of C_s (which is well defined since C_s is a monotonically increasing function). Suppose also that C_s^{-1} can be calculated by any process.

Requirement 1 For any computation B starting from a k-faulty initial state, if t ticks occur at any process p, then for every q satisfying $dist_{pq} = d$, process q completed at least $C(d, t)$ cycles in computation B.

Requirement 2 In any computation B starting from a k-faulty initial state, $k > 0$, each non-faulty process neighboring a faulty process observes at least $C_k^{-1}(h \cdot k)$ ticks within $O(k)$ rounds.

Requirement 3 In any computation starting from a k-faulty initial state, $k > 0$, each process observes at least $C_{\mathcal{D}}^{-1}(g \cdot \mathcal{D})$ ticks within $O(\mathcal{D})$ rounds.

Requirements 1–3 specify what is needed, at a minimum, for a repair timer. These requirements allow allow considerable latitude in an implementation. For example, many choices for a suitable function C may be possible; and Requirements 2–3 do not specify whether or not the repair timer should continue to generate ticks beyond some threshold. Inevitably, various design choices influence the form that a repair timer takes. For this paper, the design choice is to equip the repair timer with a $clock_p$ variable, which enables each process p to monitor the progress of data repair (by the getTime method call mentioned in Section 3.1). Every tick returned by the repair timer corresponds to a change in the timer's clock variable.

Using a clock variable is a natural choice, given that counters are used in several distributed phase synchronization algorithms. Repair timers are differentiated from phase synchronization algorithms not only by the specifics of Requirements 1–3, but also by another design choice: the counter variables remain unchanged after repair completes (whereas in synchronization algorithms, counters continue to increment throughout computation). Define the constant $\mathcal{T}$ to be the "resting point" of the repair timer's counters.

Requirement 4 Every computation self-stabilizes to $(\forall p : clock_p = \mathcal{T})$ within $O(\mathcal{D})$ rounds.

Part of the motivation for choosing a counter that eventually stops changing is an efficiency consideration. The repair timers of neighboring processes communicate the values of their clock variables via shared registers. Generally, most system computation lies outside a period of repair, and there is no need for activity by the repair timer during such times. If the clock values remain unchanged, then communication of clock values between processes can be greatly reduced (for instance, compressed to a single bit) for the value $\mathcal{T}$.

Requirement 4 suggests a convenient indicator of legitimacy for clock variables (e.g., the condition $clock_p = \mathcal{T}$ can be tested in program statements). Fixing $\mathcal{T}$ as a resting point for the clock variables also makes it easy to start a sequence of ticks for the required timespan (see Requirement 2), and the start call amounts to assigning $clock_p \leftarrow 0$.

Observe that if the system is in a legitimate state and a fault event occurs, then the state resulting from the fault event satisfies $clock_p = \mathcal{T}$ for any non-faulty process p. This fact can be the key to fault containment and correct repair, since to contain faults it is enough that non-faulty processes refrain from changing variables until faulty processes complete their own repairs.

The decision to use clock variables to count ticks also suggests a useful alternative to Requirement 1. A process p can examine $clock_p$ to determine the progress of fault repair. The following requirement presumes a known factor ξ_k, determined by the implementation of the repair timer, that satisfies $\xi_k = O(k)$ for an initially k-faulty state.

Requirement 5 In any computation B starting from a k-faulty initial state, if $clock_p = t$ holds for a non-faulty process p, where $\xi_k < t < \mathcal{T}$, then for any process q such that $dist_{pq} = d$, process q completed at least $\mathcal{C}(d, t) - \xi_k$ cycles in computation B.

For Requirement 5 to be useful, ξ_k should be small enough so that the timings specified in Requirements 2 and 3 can be inferred from clock values. The construction in Section 4 provides an example.

4 Repair Timer Construction

Requirement 1 motivates a construction based on a synchronizer [2, 14]. The algorithmic observation of this paper is that Requirement 4 simplifies the synchronization task. Figure 1 shows code for the repair timer methods. For the code of Figure 1, let $\mathcal{T} \stackrel{\text{def}}{=} (g+3)\mathcal{D}$ and $\mathcal{C}(x, y) \stackrel{\text{def}}{=} y - 2x$. The latter definition satisfies the monotonicity and linearity constraints for $\mathcal{C}$, and the inverse $\mathcal{C}_x^{-1}(z) = z + 2x$ is simple to calculate. Also define ξ_k for a k-faulty initial state of a computation by $\xi_k \stackrel{\text{def}}{=} \min(k, \mathcal{D}) + 3$.

```
boolean doTick ( ):
    for  (q ∈ N_p)  x_p[q] ← read(Register_qp)
    tick_p ← false
    oldclock_p ← clock_p
    if  (∃q : q ∈ N_p : |clock_p − x_p[q]| > 1)  then clock_p ← 0
    else if  (clock_p < T ∧ (∀q : q ∈ N_p : x_p[q] ≥ clock_p))  then
            clock_p ← clock_p + 1
    if  (oldclock_p + 1) = clock_p  then  tick_p ← true
    for  (q ∈ N_p)  write(Register_pq ← clock_p)
    return tick_p

void start ( ):
    if  clock_p ≥ T − D  then  clock_p ← 0
    return
```

Fig. 1. repair timer methods for process p

The program of Figure 1 makes no provision for the case $\text{clock}_p > \mathcal{T}$, as it is assumed that the domain of variable clock_p is $[0, \mathcal{T}]$ (the program can be easily enhanced to assign $\text{clock}_p \leftarrow 0$ in case clock_p is found to be out of the intended range). The doTick method in Figure 1 shows **read** and **write** operations to emphasize that the doTick method is called in each process cycle. When these repair timer methods are integrated into a system, the **read** and **write** operations could be moved outside the doTick method.

Theorem 1. (1) The repair timer construction of Figure 1 satisfies Requirements 4 and 5; (2) For any computation in which some clock resets in the first three rounds, a state ρ occurs within $\mathcal{D} + 3$ rounds such that the computation beginning at state ρ satisfies Requirements 1 and 3; (3) For any computation starting at a k-faulty initial state such that some clock resets in the first three rounds, a state σ occurs within $3 + \min(\mathcal{D}, k)$ rounds such that the computation beginning at state σ satisfies Requirement 1 and satisfies Requirement 2 provided $k \leq \mathcal{D}$ and $g > 2h + 7$.

Proof. Section 5 is devoted to the proof of this theorem. Requirement 4 is proved by Lemma 8. Requirement 1 is addressed by Lemma 18. Lemma 19 verifies that

Requirements 1 and 3 are jointly satisfied within $\mathcal{D} + 3$ rounds. Lemma 21 derives the stated conditions for which Requirement 2 holds. Requirement 5 is not explicitly proven by a lemma, but follows from the lemmas that address Requirements 2 and 3. □

The condition $g > 2h + 7$ is essentially a bound on $\mathcal{T}$, which needs to be large enough to guarantee sufficiently many ticks from a k-faulty initial state. The restriction $k < \mathcal{D}$ is for convenience in the derivation of Lemma 21, however it is also reasonable to propose $k < \mathcal{D}$ for optimistic repair, since Requirement 4 provides the fall back mechanism of self stabilization.

5 Verification

To prove Theorem 1, a sequence of lemmas build up invariants and time dependent properties of the construction in computations that start from a k-faulty initial state. To simplify the verification, most of this section considers the repair timer construction as an isolated system; the program for each system process is thus:

do forever: call doTick ( )

and a fault in this case is a change to variables (and/or program counter) in the doTick method of Figure 1. After proving Theorem 1 with this limited case of a fault and limited application of the repair timer, Section 5.4 considers integrating the repair timer into a system with repair procedures and fault detection procedures that invoke the start and doTick methods as set forth in Section 3.1. Due to space limitations, a number of proofs sketch arguments presented in [10].

Definition 1. A global state σ is a *final state* of the repair timer algorithm iff σ satisfies the weakest invariant F such that $F \Rightarrow (\forall p : \text{clock}_p = \mathcal{T})$.

Definition 2. $timediff_p \overset{\text{def}}{=} (\exists q : q \in \mathcal{N}_p : |\text{clock}_p - \text{clock}_q| > 1)$

Definition 3. A global state σ is a *smooth state* of the stop-clock algorithm iff σ satisfies the weakest invariant G such that $G \Rightarrow (\forall p : \neg timediff_p)$.

Definition 4. A global state σ is a *bumpy state* iff σ satisfies the weakest invariant H such that H implies

$$(\forall p, q : q \in \mathcal{N}_p \wedge |\text{clock}_q - \text{clock}_p| > 1 : \text{clock}_p \in \{\mathcal{T}, 0\} \wedge \text{clock}_q \in \{\mathcal{T}, 0\})$$

Bumpiness thus defines a predicate where the only exception to smoothness is a situation where the clock value $\mathcal{T}$ neighbors a clock value of zero.

Definition 5. A connected component B of the network is a *smooth region* iff

$$(\forall p, q : p \in B \wedge q \in \mathcal{N}_p : |\text{clock}_p - \text{clock}_q| \leq 1 \Rightarrow q \in B)$$

This definition partitions the set of processes into equivalence classes, where each equivalence class is a smooth region.

Definition 6. A *safe region* is a smooth region B satisfying

$$(\forall p, q : p \in B \wedge q \in \mathcal{N}_p : |\text{clock}_p - \text{clock}_q| > 1 \Rightarrow \text{clock}_p = 0)$$

In a cycle, if process p executes $\text{clock}_p \leftarrow 0$, then call that cycle a *clock reset cycle* of p. If process p changes its clock to a non zero value, then call that cycle a *clock increment cycle.*.

5.1 Self-Stabilization

Lemma 1. Let p and q be any processes satisfying $q \in \mathcal{N}_p$, and let $x_p[q]$ be p's internal copy of clock_q. After the second round of any computation, at each state,

$$\text{clock}_q \in \{x_p[q], x_p[q] + 1, 0, \text{clock}_p, \text{clock}_p + 1\} \vee \text{clock}_p = 0$$

Proof. After one round in any computation, every process computes a value for its clock variable and writes that value into all its registers. After the second round, each x variable has therefore been assigned some value previously written from a clock variable. The conclusion can be shown following the second round by considering neighbors p and q and four cases for subsequent computation: (*1*) no step changes clock_p; (*2*) no step writes clock_p to Register_{pq}, but $\text{clock}_p \neq \text{Register}_{pq}$ becomes true by assigning zero to clock_p; (*3*) no step writes clock_p to Register_{pq}, but $\text{clock}_p \neq \text{Register}_{pq}$ becomes true by incrementing clock_p; or (*4*) clock_p increments and is written to Register_{pq}. A straightforward analysis of these four cases verifies the lemma's conclusion. □

Lemma 1 can be used in simple arguments to prove the following pair of lemmas.

Lemma 2. In any computation, there exists a safe region after three rounds.

Lemma 3. In any computation B following round two and any consecutive pair of states (σ, σ') in B, if processes p and q belong to a common safe region at σ, then they belong to a common safe region at σ'.

Lemma 4. If p belongs to a safe region and $q \in \mathcal{N}_p$ does not belong to that region at some state following round two of a computation, then after one additional round, both p and q belong to a common safe region.

Proof. A simple argument by contradiction establishes the result. □

Lemma 5. In any computation, after at most $2 + \mathcal{D}$ rounds, a smooth state is obtained.

Proof. If all processes belong to a common safe region, then the state is smooth. A variant function can be constructed as an n-tuple, sorted in descending order, of the diameters of all safe regions in a given state (padding with zeros in the tuple if there are fewer than n safe regions). Tuples are lexicographically compared to define the variant ordering. Lemma 3 implies that regions do not shrink by any step; and Lemma 4 shows that the variant increases so long as the state is not smooth, since safe regions either grow in diameter or merge with other safe regions in each round, until the maximum of the variant function is obtained (one region of diameter $\mathcal{D}$). Finally, Lemma 2 shows that by round 3, the global state has at least one safe region. Therefore, after $3 + (\mathcal{D} - 1)$ rounds, the global state is smooth. □

Lemma 6. For any computation B containing a smooth (bumpy) state σ in round three or higher, all states following σ in B are smooth (bumpy) states. [Smoothness and bumpiness are invariants.]

Proof. Invariance of smoothness and bumpiness can be verified by straightforward inspection of the code, based on Lemma 1. □

Lemma 7. Starting from an initially smooth state, the clock algorithm stabilizes to a final state within $\mathcal{T}$ rounds.

Proof. Consider a smooth state σ for which the minimum clock value is $t < \mathcal{T}$. After one round the minimum clock value exceeds t; at most $\mathcal{T}$ increments to a clock are possible before reaching the value $\mathcal{T}$. □

Lemma 8. The repair timer construction satisfies Requirement 4.

Proof. Lemma 5 establishes that each system computation contains a smooth state after at most $2 + \mathcal{D}$ rounds; therefore, using Lemma 7, it follows that each system computation stabilizes to a final state within $2 + \mathcal{D} + \mathcal{T}$ rounds. □

5.2 Synchronization Properties

To simplify the statements of upcoming results, suppose in this subsection that all computations start with round three, that is, the conclusion of Lemma 1 holds throughout computation B in each of the following lemmas.

Lemma 9. Let B be a prefix of an arbitrary computation such that there exists a subsequence A of B and a value j for which the sequence of $clock_p$ values in A is $j, (j+1), (j+2), \ldots, (j+\ell)$. Then, for $0 \le d < \ell/2$, for every process q satisfying $dist_{pq} = d$, there exists a subsequence A' of B and a value i for which the sequence of $clock_q$ values in A' is $i, (i+1), (i+2), \ldots, (i+\ell-2d)$.

Proof. The proof is an induction on d. If $d = 0$, then $q = p$ and the lemma holds trivially by the choice $i = j$. By hypothesis, suppose the lemma holds for $d \le m$ and consider some process q such that $dist_{pq} = (m+1)$. Let r be a neighbor to q satisfying $dist_{pr} = m$. The only possible increase to $clock_r$ is by a clock increment cycle, and a precondition of a clock increment cycle is that every clock value neighboring $clock_r$ is equal or one greater than $clock_r$, which can be used to complete the induction. □

Lemma 10. Let B be a prefix of an arbitrary computation such that there exists a subsequence of B and a value j for which the sequence of $clock_p$ values is $j, (j+1), (j+2), \ldots, (j+\ell)$. Then B contains at least $\ell - 2d$ clock increment cycles for every process q satisfying $dist_{pq} = d$, $d < \ell/2$.

Proof. Lemma 9 shows that for each q at distance d from p, provided $d < \ell/2$, that q witnesses $clock_q$ values of $i, (i+1), (i+2), \ldots, (i+\ell-2d)$. Thus q increases the value of $clock_q$ at least $\ell - 2d$ times in computation B. Since the only possible increase for a clock variable is a clock increment cycle, computation B has $\ell - 2d$ clock increment cycles for process q. □

Lemma 11. For any computation B starting from a non-smooth initial state,

$$(\forall p : (\exists \sigma : \sigma \in B : clock_p \leq \mathcal{D} \text{ at state } \sigma))$$

Proof. If the initial state of B is not smooth, then in the first round some process assigns its clock variable to zero. Lemma 7 guarantees that the repair timer algorithm stabilizes with every clock equal to $\mathcal{T}$. Let q be the *last* process to assign its clock variable zero in computation B, and let C be the suffix of B beginning after q's assignment $clock_q \leftarrow 0$. An induction based on distance from q shows that any process s satisfying $dist_{qs} = d$ satisfies $clock_s \leq d$ at some state in computation C. Since $d \leq \mathcal{D}$ by definition of diameter, the lemma holds. □

Lemma 12. In any computation starting from a non-smooth initial state, every process observes at least $\mathcal{T} - \mathcal{D}$ ticks.

Proof. Lemmas 11 and Lemma 7 imply the result. □

Lemma 13. Let B be a computation starting from a smooth initial state σ, and let t be the minimum clock value at state σ. Then for any process p with $s = clock_p$ at σ, within ℓ rounds of computation B, process p observes at least $\min(\mathcal{T} - s, \ell - (s - t))$ ticks.

Proof. The proof is based on a variant function, using a potential res_p for a process p to increment its clock a certain number of times within ℓ rounds. At state σ, let $res_p = \min(\mathcal{T} - s, \ell - (s - t))$. For other states in B, res_p is defined by the following procedure: so long as $res_p > 0$, each increment to $clock_p$ decrements res_p by 1. Also, define for each state $\delta \in B$ the function div_p to be the difference between $clock_p$ and the minimum clock value in the system at state δ. The variant function for the proof is the tuple $\langle res_p, div_p \rangle$, and reduction in this variant is defined by lexicographic comparison of tuples.

Lemma 6 establishes the invariance of smoothness, and no clock variable decreases from a smooth state. In each round, the minimum clock value increments at least once, which implies that div_p decreases in a round for which $clock_p \neq \mathcal{T}$ and $clock_p$ does not increment. Therefore in each round, so long as $clock_p \neq \mathcal{T}$, the variant $\langle res_p, div_p \rangle$ reduces. These ℓ reductions in the variant are due to increments of $clock_p$ except for the initial difference $div_p = s - t$, present at state σ. That is, process p may increment its clock to increase div_p, but if $\ell > s - t$, then p must increment at least $\ell - (s - t)$ times (unless $clock_p$ attains the value $\mathcal{T}$). □

Lemma 14. Let B be a computation starting from a bumpy initial state σ, and let t be the minimum clock value at state σ. Then for any process p with $s = clock_p \neq \mathcal{T}$ at σ, within ℓ rounds of computation B, process p observes at least $\min(\mathcal{T} - s, \lfloor \ell/2 \rfloor - (s - t))$ ticks.

Proof. Lemma 6 establishes the invariance of bumpiness. If after $\ell' < \ell$ rounds, a smooth state σ' is obtained, appeal to Lemma 13 for that part of the computation following round ℓ'. Therefore consider only the case where each state of B during the first ℓ rounds is bumpy, but not smooth, and there is at least one safe region S that has border processes. The remainder of the proof has three claims: *(0)* define $bdist_p$ for $p \in S$ to be the smallest distance from p to a border process in S; then after one round, $bdist_p$ increases (this can be shown by contradiction); *(1)* let P be the set of all border processes of S, that is, $(\forall r : r \in P : \mathsf{clock}_p = 0)$ at state σ; if each process in P increments its clock at least $\lfloor \ell/2 \rfloor$ times within ℓ rounds, then for each $p \in S$, the value of clock_p increments at least $\lfloor \ell/2 \rfloor - s_p$ times within ℓ rounds, where s_p denotes the value of clock_p at state σ (the claim follows essentially from the same argument given for the proof of Lemma 13); *(2)* each border process of S increments its clock at least $\lfloor \ell/2 \rfloor$ times within ℓ rounds (this can be shown by induction). □

Lemma 15. Let B be a computation of bumpy states. If at any state $\sigma \in B$, process p satisfies $\mathsf{clock}_p < \mathcal{T}$, and p observes ℓ ticks following σ, each process q observes at least $\ell - 2\,dist_{pq}$ ticks.

Proof. The lemma can be shown by induction on distance, and for a given distance nested induction on ℓ is used. □

Lemma 16. Let B be a computation and let p be a process in a safe region at the initial state of B. If at any state $\sigma \in B$, process p satisfies $\mathsf{clock}_p < \mathcal{T}$, and p observes ℓ ticks following σ, each process q observes at least $\ell - 2\,dist_{pq}$ ticks.

Proof. The proof is the same as that for Lemma 15, joining to the induction the fact that safe regions grow at each round, or merge with other safe regions as observed in Lemmas 3 and 4. □

5.3 Output Stabilization

Lemma 17. Every computation originating from a k-faulty state contains a bumpy state within $3 + \min(\mathcal{D}, k)$ rounds.

Proof. If $k \geq \mathcal{D}-1$, then Lemma 5 implies the result; therefore suppose $k < \mathcal{D}-1$. Recall that in a k-faulty state, each non-faulty process p has $\mathsf{clock}_p = \mathcal{T}$ initially, so the first change to clock_p is a reset to zero. After two rounds, the computation satisfies the neighbor relations of Lemma 1. After the third round, any process observing a difference in clock values greater than 1 resets its clock. Once a clock is assigned zero, it remains in some safe region throughout the computation.

It is easy to show that if no faulty process resets its clock, a final state is obtained within $2 + k$ rounds. However if any faulty process resets its clock in the computation, the claim is that some process p resets its clock by round three, and p is either initially faulty or a neighbor of a faulty process. These arguments apply independently to each faulty region in the initial state, so each faulty region either converges to a final value (i.e., the clock reaches $\mathcal{T}$ for each process), or some process neighboring to or within the faulty region resets its clock by the end of round three. Once a zero-valued clock exists, processes in the faulty region join a common safe region at the rate of at least one diameter unit per round, and therefore after k additional rounds, all initially faulty processes are in a safe region. $\qquad\square$

Lemma 18. The repair timer construction satisfies Requirement 1 within $3 + \min(\mathcal{D}, k)$ rounds for any computation starting from a k-faulty initial state.

Proof. Lemmas 17 and 15 imply the result. $\qquad\square$

Lemma 19. Let B be a computation starting from a k-faulty initial state, $k > 0$. Within $3 + \min(\mathcal{D}, k)$ rounds of B there is a state σ such that Requirement 1 holds for the remainder of B, and following σ each process observes at least $C_{\mathcal{D}}^{-1}(g \cdot \mathcal{D})$ ticks within $O(\mathcal{D})$ rounds, thus satisfying Requirement 3.

Proof. Lemma 17 identifies σ, and the proof of Lemma 17 applies to the case $k = n$, which is the worst-case faulty initial state. So σ is obtained within $3 + \mathcal{D}$ rounds, even for $k < n$. Also, the proof of Lemma 17 is based on the assumption that some process resets its clock in the first three rounds, thereafter remains in a safe region, and that this region grows at the rate of one process per round. When the safe region grows to cover the network, a smooth state σ is obtained with $\mathcal{D}$ as the maximum clock value. By Lemma 15 subsequent computation satisfies Requirement 1. To guarantee that each process observes at least $C_{\mathcal{D}}^{-1}(g \cdot \mathcal{D})$ ticks, it is enough to establish that $\mathcal{T} - \mathcal{D} \geq C_{\mathcal{D}}^{-1}(g \cdot \mathcal{D})$, since all clock variables increment to the target value of $\mathcal{T}$ within $O(\mathcal{D})$ rounds by Lemma 8. This inequality is directly verified by substitution of the definitions of $\mathcal{T}$ and C. $\qquad\square$

Lemma 20. Let B be a computation starting from a k-faulty initial state σ, and let X be a faulty region at state σ. If any process $p \in X$ resets $clock_p$ in the first three rounds of B, then within the first $3 + \min(\mathcal{D}, k)$ rounds of B there is a safe state where each process $q \in X$ satisfies $clock_q \leq 2k$.

Proof. The proof of Lemma 17 has an argument showing that if some process in a faulty region resets its clock, then within $3 + k$ rounds there exists a state where each initially faulty process is in a safe region. The claim needed here is that once process p resets its clock, it does not increase $clock_p$ beyond the value k until p is contained in a safe region of diameter at least k — such a safe region of diameter at least k contains X and by the definition of a safe region, each clock in X is at most $2k$. $\qquad\square$

Lemma 21. Let B be a computation starting from a k-faulty initial state σ and let X be a faulty region at state σ, and let Y be the smallest region containing X such that each non-faulty process in Y is neighbor to a process in X. If any process $p \in X$ resets $clock_p$ in the first three rounds of B, then within $3 + \min(\mathcal{D}, k)$ rounds there exists a state $\delta \in B$ with the following properties. For the suffix computation C beginning at δ, for each process $q \in Y$, Requirement 1 holds for q throughout C; also, for each faulty process q in Y, $\mathsf{clock}_q \leq 2k$ at state δ, and for each non-faulty process q in Y, either $\mathsf{clock}_q \leq 2k$ or $\mathsf{clock}_q = \mathcal{T}$ at state δ. Finally, within $1 + 2(h+4)k$ rounds of C, each process $q \in Y$ observes at least $C_k^{-1}(h \cdot k)$ ticks, provided $k \leq \mathcal{D}$ and $g > 2h + 7$.

Proof. Lemma 20 provides the starting point for the proof by establishing that within $3 + \min(\mathcal{D}, k)$ rounds there is a state δ such that all processes in X belong to a common safe region with clock at most $2k$. Lemma 17 states that by the end of round $3 + \min(\mathcal{D}, k)$ the state is bumpy. This implies that either δ is bumpy or some state γ occurring later in the round is bumpy. Although some clock in Y may exceed $2k$ when state γ is reached, arguments based on γ will obtain a conservative estimate on the number of additional rounds needed for the lemma's conclusion.

Lemma 14 states that each process in X observes at least $\min(\mathcal{T} - s, \lfloor \ell/2 \rfloor - (s - t))$ ticks within ℓ rounds, where s and t refer to current and minimal clock values at state γ. To obtain a rough bound, suppose $t = 0$ and $s = 2k$. Then to require a process of X to observe $C_k^{-1}(h \cdot k) = h \cdot k + 2k$ ticks,

$$\min(\mathcal{T} - 2k, \lfloor \ell/2 \rfloor - 2k) \geq h \cdot k + 2k \; \Rightarrow \; \ell > 2(h + 4)k$$

The remaining question to complete the proof is to verify that $\mathcal{T} - 2k$, the number of ticks that a faulty process observes following state γ, is sufficient for the required $2(h + 4)k$ bound. Observe that $\mathcal{T} - 2k > 2(h + 4)k$ reduces to $g > 2h + 7$ if $k \leq \mathcal{D}$ is assumed, which establishes the result. $\square$

5.4 Integrating Repair Timer Methods

Results proven to this point depend on some clock variables being reset early in a computation; for instance Theorem 1 and Lemma 20 use the condition that a faulty clock resets within the first three rounds of a computation (also sufficient would be a faulty clock initially zero). Two questions arise when integrating the repair timer into the fault model described in Section 2. First, it should be that some clock does reset early enough in a computation to support the conditions of Theorem 1. Secondly, it should not be that clock variables continue to reset indefinitely.

The model of fault behavior described in Section 2 specifies that in the first round of any computation, for any faulty region X, some process p in X detects a fault condition and calls **start**, which ensures $\mathsf{clock}_p < \mathcal{T} - \mathcal{D}$. If calling **start** makes X smooth, then some non-faulty neighbor will reset in the next round, and if X is non-smooth, some process of X will reset in the next round.

After some clock resets within a faulty region X, a safe region is established, which grows in diameter at each round — provided no other clock resets interfere. However any additional **start** calls fall into two possible cases: either the **start** call occurs within a safe region established (and enlarged) from a clock reset in the first two rounds, or the **start** call occurs at some process of X that had not previously detected a fault condition. If the latter case resets a clock, it also contributes to progress toward the condition that all clock values are at most $2k$ within the first $3 + \min(\mathcal{D}, k)$ rounds (see Lemma 20). Within $O(k)$ rounds, all clock values are at most $2k$ within X and X is a safe region. Any start calls after this point do not change clock values, so long as start calls cease before clock variables increment to $\mathcal{T} - \mathcal{D}$. Repairs complete within $h \cdot k$ rounds, so if at least $h \cdot k$ rounds elapse before clock values reach $\mathcal{T} - \mathcal{D}$, then additional start calls do not occur. The condition to verify is therefore: $(\mathcal{T} - \mathcal{D}) - 2k \geq h \cdot k$, which is $(g + 2)\mathcal{D} \geq (h + 2)k$. Theorem 1 specifies $k \leq \mathcal{D}$, so all that is needed is $g \geq h$, which is conveniently also implied by Theorem 1's conditions.

References

1. A Arora, S Dolev, and MG Gouda. Maintaining digital clocks in step. *Parallel Processing Letters*, 1:11–18, 1991.
2. B Awerbuch. Complexity of network synchronization. *Journal of the ACM*, 32:804–823, 1985.
3. JM Couvreur, N Francez, and MG Gouda. Asynchronous unison. In *ICDCS92 Proceedings of the 12th International Conference on Distributed Computing Systems*, pages 486–493, 1992.
4. S Dolev. Optimal time self-stabilization in dynamic systems. In *WDAG93 Distributed Algorithms 7th International Workshop Proceedings, Springer-Verlag LNCS:725*, pages 160–173, 1993.
5. S Even and S Rajsbaum. Unison, canon and sluggish clocks in networks controlled by a synchronizer. *Mathematical Systems Theory*, 28:421–435, 1995.
6. S Ghosh, A Gupta, T Herman, and SV Pemmaraju. Fault-containing self-stabilizing algorithms. In *PODC96 Proceedings of the Fifteenth Annual ACM Symposium on Principles of Distributed Computing*, pages 45–54, 1996.
7. S Ghosh, A Gupta, and SV Pemmaraju. A fault-containing self-stabilizing algorithm for spanning trees. *Journal of Computing and Information*, 2:322–338, 1996.
8. MG Gouda and T Herman. Stabilizing unison. *Information Processing Letters*, 35:171–175, 1990.
9. T Herman. Superstabilizing mutual exclusion. In *Proceedings of the International Conference on Parallel and Distributed Processing Techniques and Applications (PDPTA'95)*, pages 31–40, 1995.
10. T Herman. Distributed repair timers. Technical Report TR 98-05, University of Iowa Department of Computer Science, 1998.
11. T Herman and S Ghosh. Stabilizing phase-clocks. *Information Processing Letters*, 54:259–265, 1995.
12. S Kutten and B Patt-Shamir. Time-adaptive self stabilization. In *PODC97 Proceedings of the Sixteenth Annual ACM Symposium on Principles of Distributed Computing*, pages 149–158, 1997.
13. C Lin and J Simon. Possibility and impossibility results for self-stabilizing phase clocks on synchronous rings. In *Proceedings of the Second Workshop on Self-Stabilizing Systems*, pages 10.1–10.15, 1995.
14. J Misra. Phase synchronization. *Information Processing Letters*, 38:101–105, 1991.

Java: Memory Consistency and Process Coordination* (Extended Abstract)

Lisa Higham and Jalal Kawash

Department of Computer Science, The University of Calgary, Canada

http://www.cpsc.ucalgary.ca/~{higham|kawash}

{higham|kawash}@cpsc.ucalgary.ca

Abstract

In Java, some memory updates are necessarily visible to some threads but never to others. A definition of Java memory consistency must take this fact into consideration to capture the semantics of non-terminating systems, such as a Java operating system. This paper presents a programmer-centered formal definition of Java memory behavior that captures those semantics.

Our definition is employed to prove that it is impossible to provide fundamental process coordination in Java, such as critical sections and producer/consumer coordination, without the use of the synchronized and volatile constructs. However, we introduce a form of synchronization that is weaker than volatiles and would suffice to solve some of these problems in Java.

keywords: Java, Java Virtual Machine, memory consistency models, process coordination, critical section problem, producer/consumer problem, non-terminating systems.

1 Introduction

The Java Virtual Machine (JVM) [16] provides a global shared memory and a local memory for each Java thread. Because intricate rules [16] determine the communication between these memories, and because much of this communication is optional (at the discretion of the implementor), the possible behaviors of multi-threaded Java programs are complicated. For instance, memory accesses can be visible to some threads but not to others [16, 8] (henceforth called the *invisibility* phenomenon.) These complicated interactions of threads and memories make it imperative to provide programmers with a formal and precise definition of the memory behavior of JVM. The definition should be given in the programmer's terms, by specifying the constraints that Java imposes on the outcomes of the read and write operations used by the programmer.

---

*This work was supported in part by research grant OGP0041900 and a post-graduate scholarship both from the Natural Sciences and Engineering Research Council of Canada.

Previous work by Gontmakher and Schuster [5, 6] provides such a definition (henceforth denoted Java$_1$) of Java memory consistency (Section 4.1). Java$_1$ captures the possible outcomes of any terminating Java computation. However, as will be seen, for terminating computations it is possible to circumvent dealing explicitly with the invisibility phenomenon. We show (Section 4.2) that Java$_1$ is not correct for non-terminating computations such as those of a Java operating system. Section 4.3 extends and adjusts Java$_1$ to our new definition, Java$_\infty$, which does deal with invisibility and which is correct for both terminating and non-terminating Java computations. We also provide a precise and short operational definition of the memory behavior of JVM (Section 3) that captures all the Java ordering constraints.

Existing definitions of weak memory consistency models ([15, 7, 1, 3, 12]) apply to terminating computations. However, process coordination is required in non-terminating systems, such as distributed operating systems, and interesting subtilities arise when extending from terminating to potentially non-terminating computations. Section 4.2 examines and formalizes what is required for a non-terminating computation to satisfy a given memory consistency condition. Later, this formalism is used to show that although Java is coherent when restricted to terminating computations (as proved by Gontmakher and Schuster), non-terminating Java is not (Section 5.1). Java consistency is also compared with SPARC's total store ordering, partial store ordering, and weak ordering in Section 5.2.

Section 6 shows that Java cannot support solutions to fundamental process coordination problems, such as the critical section and producer/consumer problems, without the use of expensive synchronization constructs such as `volatile` variables or `locks`. However, Section 7 shows that a form of "in-between" synchronization would suffice for some process coordination in Java.

Because of space limits, all the proofs have been omitted from this extended abstract. They can be found in the full version of the paper [10] available at the web cite http://www.cpsc.ucalgary.ca/~kawash. Before proceeding with the technical results, we need the definitions of Section 2.

2 Preliminaries

2.1 Memory consistency framework

A multiprocessor machine consists of a collection of processors together with various memory components and communication channels between these components. The behavior of such a machine can be described by specifying the sequence of events that the machine executes when implementing a given program instruction. Alternatively, it can be described by precisely specifying the constraints on the perceived outcomes and orderings of the instructions that can result from an execution. Given a particular machine architecture, our goal is to formulate these constraints on computations. This subsection overviews our general framework for specifying a memory consistency model, and for modeling the corresponding machine architecture. Various memory consistency models that are used in this paper are defined in the next subsection. A comprehensive treatment appears elsewhere [12, 11].

We model a multiprocess system as a collection of processes operating via *actions* on a collection of shared data *objects*. In general, these objects may be of any type, but in this paper it suffices to consider only read(p,x,v) (process p reads value v from register x) and write(p,x,v) (process p writes value v to register x) actions.

A *process* is a sequence of invocations of actions, and the *process computation* is the sequence of actions created by augmenting each invocation in the process with its matching outcome. A *(multiprocess) system*, (P,J), is a collection P of processes and a collection J of objects, such that the actions of each process in P are applied to objects in J. A *system computation* is a collection of process computations, one for each p in P.

Let (P,J) be a multiprocess system, and O be all the (read and write) actions in a computation of this system. $O|p$ denotes all the actions that are in the process computation of p in P. $O|x$ are all the actions that are applied to object x in J. Let O_w denote the set of actions with write semantics and O_r denote the set of actions with read semantics.

A sequence of read and write actions to the same object is *valid* if each read returns the value of the most recent preceding write. A *linearization* of a collection of read and write actions O, is a linear order[1] $(O,<_L)$ such that for each x, the subsequence $(O|x,<_L)$ of $(O,<_L)$ is valid for x.

A *(memory) consistency model* is a set of constraints on system computations. These constraints are given in terms of partial order requirements on the actions O of a computation. Several partial orders are used in the definitions of memory consistency models. One common partial order is $(O,\xrightarrow{prog})$, called *program order*, which is defined by $o_1 \xrightarrow{prog} o_2$, if and only if o_2 follows o_1 in the computation of some process p.

A computation satisfies some consistency model D if the computation meets all the constraints of D. A system provides memory consistency D if every computation that can arise from the system satisfies the consistency model D.

A multiprocessor machine *implements an action* by proceeding through a sequence of *events* that depend on the particular machine and that occur at the various components of the machine. The events in this sequence and the action that is implemented by them are said to *correspond*. A processor of a machine *implements a process* by initiating, in program order, the implementation of the actions corresponding to the action-invocations of the process. A multiprocessor machine *implements a system* (P,J) by having each processor implement a process in P. A *machine execution* is described by the sequence of resulting machine events.[2]

2.2 Memory consistency models

Following are the definitions for sequential consistency (SC) [15], coherence [7], Pipelined-RAM (P-RAM) [17, 1], Goodman's processor consistency (PC-G) [7], weak

---

[1] A linear order is an anti-reflexive partial order (S,R) such that $\forall x, y \in S \; x \neq y$, either xRy or yRx.

[2] Events in a multiprocessor can be simultaneous. For example, two different working memories may be simultaneously updated. However, because the same outcome would arise if these simultaneous events were ordered one after the other in arbitrary order, we can assume that the outcome of a machine execution arises from a *sequence* of events.

ordering (WO) [3], coherent weak ordering ($WO_{coherent}$), SPARC total store ordering (TSO) and partial store ordering (PSO) [19, 12].

Define the partial order $(O, \overset{weak-prog}{\longrightarrow})$, called *weak program order*, by: Action $o_1 \overset{weak-prog}{\longrightarrow} o_2$ if $o_1 \overset{prog}{\longrightarrow} o_2$ and either

1. at least one of $\{o_1, o_2\}$ is a synchronization action, or

2. $\exists o'$ such that o' is a synchronization action and $o_1 \overset{prog}{\longrightarrow} o' \overset{prog}{\longrightarrow} o_2$, or

3. o_1 and o_2 are to the same object.

Let O be all the actions of a computation C of the multiprocess system (P, J). Then C is:

SC if there is a linearization $(O, <_L)$ satisfying $(O, \overset{prog}{\longrightarrow}) \subseteq (O, <_L)$.

coherent if for each object $x \in J$ there is a linearization $(O|x, <_{L_x})$ satisfying $(O|x, \overset{prog}{\longrightarrow})$ $\subseteq (O|x, <_{L_x})$.

P-RAM if for each process $p \in P$ there is a linearization $(O|p \cup O_w, <_{L_p})$ satisfying $(O|p \cup O_w, \overset{prog}{\longrightarrow}) \subseteq (O|p \cup O_w, <_{L_p})$.

PC-G if for each process $p \in P$ there is a linearization $(O|p \cup O_w, <_{L_p})$ satisfying

1. $(O|p \cup O_w, \overset{prog}{\longrightarrow}) \subseteq (O|p \cup O_w, <_{L_p})$, and
2. $\forall q \in P$ and $\forall x \in J$ $(O_w \cap O|x, <_{L_p}) = (O_w \cap O|x, <_{L_q})$.

WO if for each process $p \in P$ there is some linearization $(O|p \cup O_w, <_{L_p})$ satisfying

1. $(O|p \cup O_w, \overset{weak-prog}{\longrightarrow}) \subseteq (O|p \cup O_w, <_{L_p})$, and
2. $\forall q \in P$ $(O_w \cap O_{synch}, <_{L_p}) = (O_w \cap O_{synch}, <_{L_q})$.

$WO_{coherent}$ if for each process $p \in P$ there is some linearization $(O|p \cup O_w, <_{L_p})$ satisfying the two conditions of WO and $\forall q \in P$ and $\forall x \in J$ $(O_w|x, <_{L_p}) = (O_w|x, <_{L_q})$.

In the following, $(A \uplus B)$ denotes the disjoint union of sets A and B, and if $x \in A \cap B$ then the copy of x in A is denoted x_A and the copy of x in B is denoted x_B. Let O_a denote the set of swap atomic actions and O_{sb} denote the set of store barrier actions provided by the SPARC architecture [19]. Then, $O_w \cap O_r = O_a$.

TSO if there exists a total order $(O_w, \overset{writes}{\longrightarrow})$ such that $(O_w, \overset{prog}{\longrightarrow}) \subseteq (O_w, \overset{writes}{\longrightarrow})$ and $\forall p \in P$ there is a total order $(O|p \uplus O_w, \overset{merge_p}{\longrightarrow})$, satisfying:

1. $(O|p, \overset{prog}{\longrightarrow}) = (O|p, \overset{merge_p}{\longrightarrow})$, and
2. $(O_w, \overset{writes}{\longrightarrow}) = (O_w, \overset{merge_p}{\longrightarrow})$, and
3. if $w \in (O|p \cap O_w)$ then $w_{O|p} \overset{merge_p}{\longrightarrow} w_{O_w}$, and

4. $((O|p \uplus O_w) \backslash (O_{invisible_p} \cup O_{memwrites_p}), \overset{merge_p}{\longrightarrow})$ is a linearization, where

$O_{invisible_p} = \{w \mid w \in (O_w \backslash O|p) \cap O|x \wedge \exists w' \in O|x \cap O|p \cap O_w \wedge w'_{O|p} \overset{merge_p}{\longrightarrow}$

$w \overset{merge_p}{\longrightarrow} w'_{O_w}\}$

$O_{memwrites_p} = \{w_{O_w} \mid w \in O|p \cap O_w\}$, and

5. let $w \in (O|p \cap O_w)$ and $a \in (O|p \cap O_a)$, if $w \overset{prog}{\longrightarrow} a$, then $w_{O_w} \overset{merge_p}{\longrightarrow} a$, and if $a \overset{prog}{\longrightarrow} w$, then $a \overset{merge_p}{\longrightarrow} w_{O|p}$

PSO if there exists a total order $(O_w, \overset{writes}{\longrightarrow})$ such that $\forall x, (O_w \cap O|x, \overset{prog}{\longrightarrow}) \subseteq (O_w \cap O|x, \overset{writes}{\longrightarrow})$ and $\forall p \in P$ there is a total order $(O|p \uplus O_w, \overset{merge_p}{\longrightarrow})$, satisfying items 1 through 4 of TSO and (5) if $sb \in (O|p \cap O_{sb})$ and $w, u \in (O|p \cap O_w)$ and $w \overset{prog}{\longrightarrow} sb \overset{prog}{\longrightarrow} u$, then $w_{O_w} \overset{merge_p}{\longrightarrow} u_{O_w}$.

3 Java Virtual Machine

The Java Virtual Machine (JVM) [16] is an abstract machine introduced by SUN to support the Java programming language [8]. Its behavior is specified in the Java manuals [8, 16]. This section provides a simple, precise alternative but equivalent description; the proof is elsewhere [14].

The components and events of JVM are depicted in Figure 1(a) for a two-thread machine. A component called the *waiting area* is introduced to model the delay between stores and writes and between reads and loads. For memory consistency concerns in Java, a thread is considered to be a sequence of prog-read and prog-write actions, which are implemented in the JVM machine as shown in Figure 1(b) where t is a thread, x an object, and v a value (choice $\{f\}$ designates a non-deterministic choice to perform f or not.)

A Java program S is a collection of threads. Any Java machine execution E of S is a sequence of events of the types $\{\text{assign, use, store, load, write, read}\}$[3] satisfying the additional constraints that follow. Let o_1 and o_2 be actions in $\{\text{prog-read}, \text{prog-write}\}$, e_1, e_2, and e be events, and let $e_1 \overset{E}{\longrightarrow} e_2$ denote e_1 precedes e_2 in E.

1. If $o_1 \overset{prog}{\longrightarrow} o_2$ and e_1 (respectively, e_2) is the use or assign corresponding to o_1 (respectively, o_2), then $e_1 \overset{E}{\longrightarrow} e_2$.

2. If $\text{assign}(t,x,v) \overset{E}{\longrightarrow} \text{load}(t,x,u)$, then there is a $\text{store}(t,x,v)$ satisfying $\text{assign}(t,x,v) \overset{E}{\longrightarrow} \text{store}(t,x,v) \overset{E}{\longrightarrow} \text{load}(t,x,u)$.

3. Let $e \in \{ \text{store}(t,x,v), \text{load}(t,x,v) \}$. If $e \overset{E}{\longrightarrow} \text{store}(t,x,u)$, then there exists an $\text{assign}(t,x,u)$ satisfying $e \overset{E}{\longrightarrow} \text{assign}(t,x,u) \overset{E}{\longrightarrow} \text{store}(t,x,u)$.

---

[3] Main memory is also accessible by lock and unlock events. This paper does not deal in detail with these events since we are interested in the memory consistency of Java in the context of ordinary reads and writes.

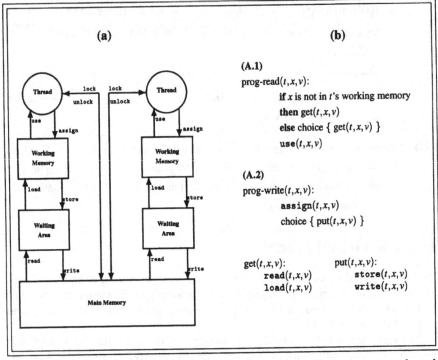

Figure 1: (a) A two-thread JVM architecture (b) Implementing program reads and writes by JVM events

4. Let o_1 and $o_2 \in O|x \cap O|p$ and $o_1 \xrightarrow{prog} o_2$ and let e_1 and e_2 be any events corresponding to o_1 and o_2 respectively, then $e_1 \xrightarrow{E} e_2$.

It is easily confirmed that the consistency model arising from this description is equivalent to that of an even simpler machine where each get and put of Figure 1(b) are atomic events [14], and that these models are unchanged from that arising from the original set of rules describing JVM [14].

For the rest of the paper, we use the term *process* to refer to a Java *thread*.

4 Java Memory Consistency Model

The rules of Java that determine the interaction between working memories and main memory permit a process's write action to be invisible to another process. This is highlighted by the appearance of the choice function in algorithms A.1 and A.2 for prog-read and prog-write. We distinguish two kinds of invisibilities. First, certain stores are optional, which makes some assigns visible to the process that issued them, but invisible to others. We use the term *covert* to refer to this kind of invisibility. Second, a load is optional when a process already has a value for the required variable recorded in its working memory, which can cause a *use* to retrieve a stale value rather than seeing a newly written value. We use the term *fixate* for this kind of invisibility.

To define the memory consistency model of Java, the obstacles that arise from covert and fixate invisibilities can be cleanly and elegantly finessed as long as computations are finite [5, 6] as shown in Section 4.1. Those ideas, however, do not suffice for non-terminating Java computations. After resolving exactly what is meant by a consistency condition for a non-terminating system in Section 4.2, we provide a new definition of consistency that is correct for both terminating and non-terminating Java computations (Section 4.3).

4.1 Consistency of terminating Java computations

Gontmakher and Schuster [5, 6] gave non-operational definitions for Java memory behavior. We use Java$_1$ for their "programmer's view" characterization, after translation to our framework. Given two actions o_1 and o_2 both in $O|p$ for some $p \in P$, the *Java partial program order*, denoted ($\xrightarrow{jpo}$), is defined by: $o_1 \xrightarrow{jpo} o_2$ if $o_1 \xrightarrow{prog} o_2$ and one of the following holds:

1. $o_1, o_2 \in O|x$, or

2. $o_1 \in O_r$, $o_2 \in O_w$, and o_1 returns the value written by o' where $o' \in O_w|q$ $q \neq p$, or

3. there exists o' such that $o_1 \xrightarrow{jpo} o'$ and $o' \xrightarrow{jpo} o_2$.

Definition 4.1 *[5] Let O be all the actions of a computation C of the multiprocess system (P, J). Then C is Java$_1$ if there is some linearization $(O, <_L)$ satisfying $(O, \xrightarrow{jpo}) \subseteq (O, <_L)$.*

Notice that this definition requires one linearization for all actions. Gontmakher and Schuster [5, 6] prove that their definition does capture exactly all terminating Java computations. There are two essential ideas in forming the linearization:

- certain covert writes can be moved to the end of the linearization so that these writes are never read by any other process and hence do not negate validity.

- fixate reads could be moved earlier in the linearization to precede the writes that are invisible to the reader so that the stale value returned is valid.

Furthermore, Java partial program order is just enough to permit these writes and reads to move as described.

A problem arises with Definition 4.1 when a system is non-terminating because the end of the computation is not defined.

4.2 Consistency models for non-terminating systems

Consider Computation 1, where process p continues to read 0 for x even though q at some point writes 1 to x. This could arise as a Java computation either 1) from a fixate invisibility of p to the updated value of x because (after its first load) none of p's uses is preceded by a matching load, or 2) from a covert invisibility of x because q's assign was not succeeded by a store.

Computation 1 $\begin{cases} p : [r(x)0], [r(x)0], [r(x)0], [r(x)0], \ldots \\ q : w(x)1 \end{cases}$

Does Computation 1 satisfy Definition 4.1? Certainly for any finite prefix of p's computation, say after i reads by p, it is Java$_1$, since the linearization $[r(x)0]^i w(x)1$ satisfies the definition. However the linearization(s) required by a consistency model are meant to capture each system component's "view" of the computation. For Java, the given linearization means that $[r(x)0]^i w(x)1$ is consistent with each process's view. We expect that, as the computation continues, processes extend their respective views, but do not "change their minds" about what happened earlier. We will return to this example after we capture what it means for a non-terminating system to satisfy a given consistency condition.

Let O be all actions of some finite computation C of a system (P, J), and let D be a memory consistency model. To establish that C satisfies consistency model D, we provide a set of sequences S, each composed of actions in O, that satisfy the constraints of D. Each sequence is meant to capture a component's "view" of the computation, or some kind of agreement between such views. Call such an S a set of *satisfying sequences* for (C, D).

For the definition D to hold for a non-terminating computation, C, we (informally) have two requirements. First, if C is paused, then the prefix, say $\hat{C}$, that has been realized so far, should have satisfying sequences for $(\hat{C}, D)$. Second, if C is resumed and paused again later, say at $\tilde{C}$, then there are satisfying sequences for $(\tilde{C}, D)$ that are "extensions" of the satisfying sequences for $(\hat{C}, D)$. That is, we do not want to allow a component to reconstruct its view of what the computation did in the past. We formalize this intuition as follows.

A sequence s *extends* $\hat{s}$ if $\hat{s}$ is a prefix of s. A set of sequences $S = \{s_1, \ldots, s_n\}$ *extends* a set of sequences $\hat{S} = \{\hat{s}_1, \ldots, \hat{s}_n\}$ if for each i, s_i extends $\hat{s}_i$.

Definition 4.2 *Let D be a memory consistency model for finite computations. A non-terminating computation $C = \bigcup_{p \in P} \{C_p\}$ satisfies D if $\forall p \in P$ and for every finite prefix $\hat{C}_p$ of C_p, there is a finite prefix $\hat{C}_q$ of $C_q \, \forall q \neq p$, such that*

1. *$\hat{C} = \bigcup_{q \in P} \{\hat{C}_q\}$ satisfies D, and*

2. *for any finite $\tilde{C}_p$ that extends $\hat{C}_p$ and is a prefix of C_p, there is a finite prefix $\tilde{C}_q$ of $C_q \, \forall q \neq p$, such that*

   - *$\tilde{C} = \bigcup_{q \in P} \{\tilde{C}_q\}$ extends $\hat{C}$, and*
   - *$\tilde{C}$ satisfies D, and*

- *the satisfying sequences $\tilde{S}$ for $(\tilde{C}, D)$ extend the satisfying sequences $\hat{S}$ for $(\hat{C}, D)$.*

If we apply Definition 4.2 to Definition 4.1, Computation 1 is not Java$_1$. That is, any linearization of a finite prefix of the computation that contains q's write and satisfies Definition 4.1 cannot be extended to a linearization for a longer prefix of the computation that still satisfies the definition. (Instead, the write action by q would have to be moved to the new end of the linearization.) We need a definition of Java that is equivalent to Definition 4.1 for finite computations but that preserves semantic commitments in the course of non-terminating computations.

4.3 Java consistency

We first define Java$_2$, which is equivalent to Java$_1$ but is described from the point of view of processes.

Definition 4.3 *Let O be all the actions of a computation C of the multiprocess system (P, J). Then C is Java$_2$ if there is a total order $(O_w, \overset{writes}{\longrightarrow})$ satisfying $\forall p \in P$:*

1. *there is a linearization $(O|p \cup O_w, <_{L_p})$ such that $(O|p \cup O_w, \overset{jpo}{\longrightarrow}) \subseteq (O|p \cup O_w, <_{L_p})$, and*

2. $(O_w, <_{L_p}) = (O_w, \overset{writes}{\longrightarrow})$.

Claim 4.4 *Java$_1$ is equivalent to Java$_2$.*

We further adjust Definition 4.3 to cope with invisibility and hence capture both terminating and non-terminating Java computations.

Definition 4.5 *Let O be all the actions of a computation C of the multiprocess system (P, J). Then C is Java$_\infty$ if there is some total order $(O_w, \overset{writes}{\longrightarrow})$ and $\forall p \in P$ there is a subset O_{vis_p} of O_w satisfying:*

1. *there is a linearization $(O|p \cup O_{vis_p}, <_{L_p})$ such that $(O|p \cup O_{vis_p}, \overset{jpo}{\longrightarrow}) \subseteq (O|p \cup O_{vis_p}, <_{L_p})$, and*

2. $(O_{vis_p}, <_{L_p}) = (O_{vis_p}, \overset{writes}{\longrightarrow})$.

Notice that the set O_{vis_p} in Definition 4.5 is the set of writes that "so far" are visible to process p. Notice also that Computation 1 does satisfy Definition 4.5. For any prefix of i reads by p, $(O_w, \overset{writes}{\longrightarrow}) = w(x)1$, $O_{vis_p} = \emptyset$, and $O_{vis_q} = O_w = w(x)1$. So, $(O|p \cup O_{vis_p}, <_{L_p}) = [r(x)0]^i$ and $(O|q \cup O_{vis_q}, <_{L_q}) = w(x)1$. Also, for each i these satisfying sequences are extensions of the satisfying sequences for $i-1$. The revised definition captures exactly what "happened" in the sense that $w(x)1$ took place from q's view but not from p's.

Theorem 4.6 *For finite computations, Java$_\infty$ is equivalent to Java$_2$.*

For the remainder of this paper, Java and Java$_\infty$ are used interchangeably.

5 Comparing Java with Various Consistency Models

5.1 Java versus coherence

Gontmakher and Schuster [5, 6] argue that Java is Coherent. Their proof relies on the regular language R, which is an elegant distillation of the rules for a single Java process.

$$R \begin{cases} \text{Order = (load-block | store-block)}^* \\ \text{load-block = load(use)}^* \\ \text{store-block = assign(use | assign)}^* \text{ store(use)}^* \end{cases}$$

They claim that the events corresponding to the actions of a single process to a fixed variable satisfy R. In fact, if an $\text{assign}(t,x,v)$ is not followed by a $\text{load}(t,x,u)$, then a subsequent store is optional. A modification of R to $\hat{R}$ captures this more general situation (λ denotes the empty string.)

$$\hat{R} \begin{cases} \text{Order = (load-block | store-block)}^* \text{ tail-block} \\ \text{load-block = load(use)}^* \\ \text{store-block = assign(use | assign)}^* \text{ store(use)}^* \\ \text{tail-block = assign(use | assign)}^* \text{ | } \lambda \end{cases}$$

Coherence still holds for any computation such that for each variable, and for each process, the events corresponding to the actions of that process on that variable satisfy $\hat{R}$. Their proof requires only a slight modification so that in the linearization each tail-block follows every load-block and store-block. Thus we can conclude that all finite Java computations are coherent.

Unfortunately, non-terminating Java computations are not necessarily coherent. When there is only one variable, notice that Java_1 and coherence are the same. Computation 1 is Java_∞ but it is not Java_1. Since it uses only one variable, it cannot be coherent. One important consequence of this is that Java_∞ cannot support solutions to the nonterminating coordination problem $P_1 C_1$-queue (see Section 6) even though it has been shown [9, 13] that coherence suffices to solve this problem. The following computation [5] is coherent but not Java.

Computation 2 $\begin{cases} p : r(x)1 \; w(y)1 \\ q : r(y)1 \; w(x)1 \end{cases}$

Hence, Java and coherence are not comparable (except for finite computations.)

5.2 Java versus other consistency models

Gontmakher and Schuster [5, 6] show by examples that:

- Java and P-RAM are incomparable.

- Java and PC-G are incomparable.

Since their examples are finite, these same conclusions apply to Java$_\infty$.

It is easily verified that Computation 2 is WO$_{coherent}$, and (the non-terminating) Computation 1 is not WO$_{coherent}$. Therefore, Java and WO$_{coherent}$ (consequently WO) are incomparable.

To see that PSO [19, 12] is stronger than Java, imagine a situation in which the working memory in JVM mimics the behavior of the store buffer in PSO. Specifically, (1) every assign is paired with a store and (2) every use that follows a store by the same process on the same variable is paired with a load that follows the store. The following claim formalizes this intuition.

Claim 5.1 *PSO (consequently, TSO) is stronger than Java.*

Since TSO and PSO are stronger than coherence [11, 12], Computation 1 is not possible in either PSO or TSO.

The following table summarizes these observations.

M :	coherence	P-RAM	PC-G	WO$_{coherent}$	WO	TSO	PSO
Java $\Rightarrow M$	NO	NO [6]	NO [6]	NO	NO	NO	NO
$M \Rightarrow$ Java	NO [6]	NO [6]	NO [6]	NO	NO	YES	YES

6   Coordination Impossibilities

This section confirms that without the synchronized or volatile constructs, fixate and covert invisibilities make Java too weak to support solutions to coordination problems such as the critical section problem (CSP) [18] or the producer/consumer problem (PCP) [2]. Note that solutions to these problems are assumed to be long-lived; that is, there is no bound on the number of times the protocols are invoked.

6.1   Critical section problem

Given that each process executes:

> **repeat**
> > *<remainder>*
> > *<entry>*
> > *<critical section>*
> > *<exit>*
>
> **until** *false*

a solution to CSP must satisfy[4]:

- **Mutual Exclusion:** At any time there is at most one process in its *<critical section>*.

---

[4]Note that we are not listing fairness as a property. In fact, none of our impossibility results depend on fairness.

- **Progress:** If at least one process is in $<entry>$, then eventually one will be in $<critical\ section>$.

  If $p \in P$ is in $<entry>$, then p will eventually be in $<critical\ section>$.

Theorem 6.1 *There is no Java$_1$ algorithm that solves CSP even for two processes.*

Since Java$_1$ is stronger than Java the following corollary is immediate.

Corollary 6.2 *There is no Java algorithm using only ordinary actions that solves CSP even for two processes.*

6.2 Producer/consumer problems

Producers and consumers are assumed to have the following forms:

producer:	*consumer:*
repeat	**repeat**
$<entry>$	$<entry>$
$<producing>$	$<consuming>$
$<exit>$	$<exit>$
until *false*	**until** *false*

We denote the producer/consumer queue problem as P_mC_n-queue where m and n are respectively the number of producer and consumer processes. A solution to P_mC_n-queue must satisfy the following:

- **Safety:** There is a one-to-one correspondence between produced and consumed items.

- **Progress:** If a producer (respectively consumer) is in $<entry>$, then it will eventually be in $<producing>$ ((respectively $<consuming>$) and subsequently in $<exit>$.

- **Order:** items are consumed in an order consistent with that in which they were produced[5].

P_mC_n-set denotes the producer/consumer set problem. A solution for P_mC_n-set must satisfy Safety and Progress only.

The fixate or covert invisibility makes consumers (respectively, producers) unaware of actions of production (respectively, consumption).

Theorem 6.3 *There is no Java algorithm using only ordinary actions that solves P_mC_n-queue or P_mC_n-set even for $n = m = 1$.*

Even Java$_1$ is too weak to support a solution for general cases of P_mC_n-queue. The solutions for P_1C_1-queue and P_mC_n-set previously presented [9, 13] are correct for any coherent system. Thus, they are correct for Java$_1$.

Theorem 6.4 *There is no Java$_1$ algorithm that solves P_1C_n-queue or P_mC_1-queue even for $n = 2$ or $m = 2$.*

Corollary 6.5 *There is no Java$_1$ algorithm that solves P_mC_n-queue for $m + n \geq 3$.*

---

[5]Item A precedes item B if the production of item A completes before the production of item B begins.

7 Coordination Possibilities

Solving CSP or PCP is trivial with the use of volatile and synchronized constructs. However, synchronized methods and volatile variables are expensive in execution time; volatiles guarantee sequential consistency (SC) [5], which is not a necessary requirement to solve coordination problems. For example, PC-G suffices to solve CSP [1].

This section shows that a significant weakening of the constraints on volatiles, which we call "read-volatile", suffices to support solutions to some common coordination problems. Define a *read-volatile* variable to be one that only satisfies the following rule of those for volatile variables [16, 8]:

> "A *use* operation by T on V is permitted only if the previous operation by T on V was *load*, and a *load* operation by T on V is permitted only if the next operation by T on V is *use*. The *use* operation is said to be "associated" with the *read* operation that corresponds to the *load*."

We suspect that read-volatiles would allow more parallelism than Java's volatile variables for many applications.

Figure 2 presents a multi-writer P_1C_1-queue algorithm, ALG_M, that is correct for coherence[6] [9, 13]. If every read of ALG_M is a read-volatile, the algorithm solves P_1C_1-queue in Java.

```
class ProducerConsumer {
item[] Q = new item[n+1]; (initialized to ⊥)

void producer() {                    void consumer() {
    int in;                              int out;
    item it_p;                           item it_c;

    in = 1;                              out = 1;
    do {                                 do {
        while (Q[in] ≠ ⊥) nothing;           while (Q[out] = ⊥) nothing;
        ... produce it_p;                    it_c = Q[out];
        Q[in] = it_p;                        Q[out] = ⊥;
        in = in + 1 mod n+1;                 out = out + 1 mod n+1;
    } while true;                            ... consume it_c;
}                                        } while true;
                                     }

}
```

Figure 2: ALG_M, a multi-writer P_1C_1-queue algorithm

Claim 7.1 *Read-volatiles are sufficient to solve P_1C_1-queue in Java.*

---

[6]The algorithm even works for P-RAM and WO with only ordinary reads and writes.

Since we have shown previously how to exploit a solution for P_1C_1-queue to build a solution for P_mC_n-set [9, 13], we have the following corollary.

Corollary 7.2 *Read-volatiles are sufficient to solve P_mC_n-set in Java.*

Acknowledgements

We thank Alan Covington for suggesting the problem of Java consistency.

References

[1] M. Ahamad, R. Bazzi, R. John, P. Kohli, and G. Neiger. The power of processor consistency. In *Proc. 5th ACM Symp. on Parallel Algorithms and Architectures*, pages 251–260, June 1993. Also available as College of Computing, Georgia Institute of Technology technical report GIT-CC-92/34.

[2] E. W. Dijkstra. Cooperating sequential processes. Technical Report EWD-123, Technological University, Eindhoven, the Netherlands, 1965. Reprinted in [4].

[3] M. Dubois, C. Scheurich, and F. Briggs. Memory access buffering in multiprocessors. *Proc. of the 13th Annual Int'l Symp. on Computer Architecture*, pages 434–442, June 1986.

[4] F. Genuys, editor. *Programming Languages*. Academic Press, 1968.

[5] A. Gontmakher and A. Schuster. Java consistency: Non-operational characterizations of Java memory behavior. Technical Report CS0922, Computer Science Department, Technion, November 1997.

[6] A. Gontmakher and A. Schuster. Characterizations of Java memory behavior. In *Proc. of the 12th Int'l Parallel Processing Symp.*, April 1998.

[7] J. Goodman. Cache consistency and sequential consistency. Technical Report 61, IEEE Scalable Coherent Interface Working Group, March 1989.

[8] J. Gosling, B. Joy, and G. Steele. *The Java Language Specifications*. Addison-Wesley, 1996.

[9] L. Higham and J. Kawash. Critical sections and producer/consumer queues in weak memory systems. In *Proc. of the 1997 Int'l Symp. on Parallel Architectures, Algorithms, and Networks*, pages 56–63, December 1997.

[10] L. Higham and J. Kawash. Java: Memory consistency and process coordination. Technical Report 98/622/13, Department of Computer Science, The University of Calgary, April 1998.

[11] L. Higham, J. Kawash, and N. Verwaal. Defining and comparing memory consistency models. In *Proc. of the 10th Int'l Conf. on Parallel and Distributed Computing Systems*, pages 349–356, October 1997.

[12] L. Higham, J. Kawash, and N. Verwaal. Weak memory consistency models part I: Definitions and comparisons. Technical Report 98/612/03, Department of Computer Science, The University of Calgary, January 1998. Submitted for publication.

[13] L. Higham, J. Kawash, and N. Verwaal. Weak memory consistency models part II: Process coordination problems. Technical Report 98/613/04, Department of Computer Science, The University of Calgary, January 1998. Submitted for publication.

[14] J. Kawash. Process coordination issues in systems with weak memory consistency. Ph.D. dissertation draft, The University of Calgary.

[15] L. Lamport. How to make a multiprocessor computer that correctly executes multiprocess programs. *IEEE Trans. on Computers*, C-28(9):690–691, September 1979.

[16] T. Lindholm and F. Yellin. *The Java Virtual Machine Specification*. Addison-Wesley, 1996.

[17] R. J. Lipton and J. S. Sandberg. PRAM: A scalable shared memory. Technical Report 180-88, Department of Computer Science, Princeton University, September 1988.

[18] M. Raynal. *Algorithms for Mutual Exclusion*. The MIT Press, 1986.

[19] D. L. Weaver and T. Germond, editors. *The SPARC Architecture Manual version 9*. Prentice-Hall, 1994.

A Complete and Constant Time Wait-Free Implementation of CAS from LL/SC and Vice Versa*

PRASAD JAYANTI

Dartmouth College, Hanover, NH 03755, USA

Abstract. We consider three popular types of shared memory that support one of the following sets of operations: {CAS, read, write}, {LL, SC, VL, read, write}, or {RLL, RSC, read, write}. We present algorithms that, together with Moir's [Moi97], efficiently implement each shared memory above from any of the other two. Our implementations are wait-free and have constant time and space complexity. Thus, concurrent programs developed for one of the above memories can be ported to any other without incurring any increase in time complexity. Further, since our implementations are wait-free, a wait-free concurrent program remains wait-free even after porting.

This work is similar in spirit to [IR94, AM95, Moi97]. The main difference is that in these earlier works the write operation is not included in the set of implemented operations. Specifically, earlier works implement {CAS, read} from {LL, SC} and vice versa, but to our knowledge there are no existing implementations of either of {CAS, read, write} and {LL, SC, VL, read, write} from the other. Consequently, it is not possible to port concurrent programs between systems supporting {CAS, read, write} and {LL, SC, VL, read, write}. The implementations in this paper help overcome this drawback.

At first glance, adding *write* to the set of implemented operations might appear easy. However, there is ample evidence to suggest that simple modifications to earlier implementations do not work. Our implementations are therefore quite different from the ones in earlier works.

1 Introduction

This paper concerns asynchronous shared memory multiprocess systems. In such systems, processes execute their programs at arbitrary rates and communicate with each other by applying operations on shared memory. In general, the set of operations supported by shared memory varies from one system to another. Consequently, porting multiprocess applications is a nontrivial problem. Specifically, consider a multiprocess application developed for systems whose shared memory supports a set S_1 of operations. Suppose that we wish to port this application to another system whose shared memory supports a different set S_2 of operations.

* This work is partially supported by NSF RIA grant CCR-9410421.

Clearly, this is possible if (and only if) each operation in S_1 can be simulated using the operations in S_2. Thus, portability of programs from the first system to the second requires that we implement shared memory supporting operations in S_1 from shared memory supporting operations in S_2.

Henceforth the term S-*memory* denotes shared memory that supports operations in set S. An *implementation of S_1-memory from S_2-memory* specifies a set of procedures, one for each operation in S_1. To execute an operation $op \in S_1$ on the implemented S_1-memory, a process simply executes the procedure specified by the implementation for op. The procedure simulates op using operations in S_2. The value returned by the procedure is considered to be the response for op. We require the implementation to satisfy two properties:

1. Linearizability: If operations on the underlying S_2-memory are atomic, then operations on the implemented S_1-memory also appear to be atomic. That is, each operation on the implemented S_1-memory appears to take effect instantaneously at some point between its invocation and completion [HW90].

2. Wait-freedom: When a process p calls and executes any implementation procedure, the procedure terminates after a finite number of p's steps, regardless of whether remaining processes are fast, slow, or have crashed [Lam77, Her91].

The second property (wait-freedom) implies that, unlike in lock-based implementations, slow or crashed processes cannot impede the progress of faster processes. Further, suppose P is a wait-free protocol designed for systems with S_1-memory. If P is ported to a system with S_2-memory (using an implementation of S_1-memory from S_2-memory), the second property ensures that P remains a wait-free protocol even after porting.

The *time complexity* of an implementation is the number of steps that a process executes, in the worst-case, in order to return from an implementation procedure. The *space complexity* of an implementation of S_1-memory from S_2-memory is the number of words of S_2-memory needed to implement one word of S_1-memory. In general, the time or the space complexity of an implementation depends on n, the maximum number of processes that can concurrently access the implementation. We say the time or space complexity is *constant* if it is independent of n. The implementations in this paper have constant time and space complexity.

Shared memory types considered: We consider three common types of shared memory, described in the following. Our goal is to efficiently implement each type of shared memory from any other.

1. {CAS, read, write}-memory (CAS is an abbreviation for Compare-And-Swap.)

Figure 1 describes the effect of these operations (by convention, the first argument of an operation is the process invoking the operation and the last argument is the object, *i.e.* the memory word, on which the operation is invoked). $CAS(p_i, u, v, O)$ checks if O's value is u. If so, it changes O' value to v and returns *true*; otherwise it leaves O's value unchanged at u and returns *false*. CAS is supported by Pentium and SPARC architectures.

$$\frac{\text{Read}(p_i, O)}{\text{return value}(O)}$$

$$\frac{\text{Write}(p_i, v, O)}{\text{value}(O) = v}$$

$$\frac{\text{CAS}(p_i, old, new, O)}{\text{if value}(O) = old}$$
$$\text{value}(O) := v$$
$$\text{return } true$$
$$\text{else return } false$$

Fig. 1. Specification of {CAS, Read, Write} object O

$$\frac{\text{LL}(p_i, O)}{\text{Pset}(O) := \text{Pset}(O) \cup \{p_i\}}$$
$$\text{return value}(O)$$

$$\frac{\text{VL}(p_i, O)}{\text{return } p_i \in \text{Pset}(O)}$$

$$\frac{\text{SC}(p_i, v, O)}{\text{if } p_i \in \text{Pset}(O)}$$
$$\text{value}(O) := v$$
$$\text{Pset}(O) := \emptyset$$
$$\text{return } true$$
$$\text{else return } false$$

$$\frac{\text{read}(p_i, O)}{\text{return value}(O)}$$

$$\frac{\text{write}(p_i, v, O)}{\text{value}(O) := v}$$
$$\text{Pset}(O) := \emptyset$$

Fig. 2. Specification of {LL, SC, VL, read, write} object O

2. {LL, SC, VL, read, write}-memory

In this type of shared memory, the state of a memory word O is described by two quantities, $value(O)$ and $Pset(O)$. For each operation, its response and its effect on the state of the memory word are specified in Figure 1. Informally, $Pset(O)$ is the set of processes that have performed LL since the time O was last modified. A write operation modifies the object's value and causes Pset to become empty. Like a read operation, LL returns the value of the object; in addition, the process performing LL is added to Pset. An SC either acts like a write operation or has no effect on the state of the object. Specifically, when p_i performs $SC(p_i, v, O)$, if p_i is in $Pset(O)$, SC changes O's value to v, causes $Pset(O)$ to become empty, and returns $true$; otherwise it returns $false$ without affecting O's state (correspondingly, we say SC succeeds or fails). Thus, process p_i's SC on O succeeds if no process modified O (by performing a successful SC or write) since the most recent time p_i performed LL on O. VL by p_i returns true if p_i is in Pset, *i.e.*, if no process modified O since the most recent time p_i performed LL on O.

These operations, as defined above, are not supported by any real multiprocessor. However, many recent wait-free algorithms are designed for a shared memory that supports these operations. Further, these operations are very flexible and often facilitate simple and efficient solutions to process synchronization. Thus, it is important to be able to port programs that are based on this shared memory to real machines supporting other types of shared memory.

3. {RLL, RSC, read, write}-memory

RLL and RSC are weaker versions of LL and SC operations. Their specification is not relevant to understanding the results in this paper. So we omit their specification, but it can be found in [Moi97].

These operations, first proposed in [JHB87], are supported by MIPS-II [Kan89], DEC Alpha [Sit92], and IBM PowerPC [IBM94].

The result and its significance: This paper presents two implementations:
1. {CAS, read, write} from {LL, SC, VL}.
2. {LL, SC, VL, read, write} from {LL, SC, VL}.

These implementations are presented in Sections 2 and 3 and have constant time and space complexity. The following two implementations are due to Moir [Moi97]:
1. {LL, SC, VL} from {CAS}.
2. {CAS} from {RLL, RSC}.

The first implementation has constant time complexity, and the second has constant time complexity provided that RSC does not experience spurious failures (see [AM95, Moi97] for a description of spurious failures). Both implementations have constant space complexity.

Composing our implementations with Moir's, each of the three types of shared memory described in the previous subsection has a constant time and space complexity implementation from any of the other two types of shared memory. It follows that any concurrent program designed for one type of shared memory can be ported to others without affecting its time complexity (the slowdown is only by a constant factor).

Previous work: Israeli and Rappoport implement {LL, SC, VL} from {CAS, read} [IR94]. Their implementation makes an unreasonable assumption that the shared objects used in the implementation have $\Omega(n)$ bits, where n is the number of processes that may concurrently access the implemented memory. Anderson and Moir implement {LL, SC, VL} from {CAS, read} and vice versa [AM95]. Moir implements {LL, SC, VL} from {CAS}, and {CAS} from {RLL, RSC} [Moi97]. The above implementations in [AM95] and [Moi97] have constant time and space complexity.

Bridging a gap in the previous work: In all of the previous works cited above, notice that the *write* operation is not included in the set of implemented operations. This is the conceptual gap that this paper fills.

Most existing concurrent programs that rely on LL/SC for synchronization seem to apply LL and SC on some memory words, and read and write on other memory words. In particular, it seems uncommon to come across programs in which all of LL, SC, read and write are applied on the same memory word. This pattern of operation usage is, however, not universal. For instance, in a snapshot algorithm that we are developing all of LL, SC, *and* write are applied on the same memory word. The same is true of another algorithm—a read-parallel universal construction—that we are developing. To port these and other such programs to a system supporting {CAS, read, write}-memory, we will need an implementation of {LL, SC, VL, write}-memory from {CAS, read, write}-memory, such as the one presented in this paper. In particular, such porting is not possible using the implementations in [AM95, Moi97] since these works implement an object that supports LL and SC, but not an object that supports LL, SC, and write.

We close this section with two remarks. First, each of {CAS, read, write}-memory and {LL, SC, VL, write}-memory can be implemented from the other using existing universal constructions (for instance, the constructions in [HS93, Moi97]). This approach is not satisfactory because the time complexity of the resulting implementation is not constant (the time complexity is $O(n)$, where n is the number of processes that can concurrently access the implementation).

Our second remark concerns the conceptual difficulty of the implementations designed in this paper. At first glance, it might *appear* that it should be fairly straightforward to include the write operation in the set of implemented operations. In fact, after implementing {CAS, read} from {LL, SC}, Anderson and Moir state that a write operation is straightforward to incorporate into their construction and give a two line algorithm to implement the write operation (see lines 6-10 after Theorem 2 on page 186 of [AM95]). We believe that their statement is incorrect: in [Jay98], we point out why their construction is incorrect. We emphasize that this is a very minor aspect of their paper and does not affect the main results of that paper. Nevertheless, it points out that implementing read and write operations in addition to other operations (such as CAS, LL, SC etc.) is subtler than it appears. In fact, in an expanded version of this paper [Jay98] we present ample evidence to suggest that this problem is nontrivial.

2 {CAS, read, write} from {LL, SC, VL}

In this section, we present a constant time and space implementation of an object that supports CAS, Read, and Write operations from objects that support LL, SC, and VL operations. The implementation is designed in two steps. First, we define a new object that we call *dual stream LL/SC/VL object*, and implement it from a {LL, SC, VL} object. Second, we implement a {CAS, read, write} object from dual stream LL/SC/VL objects. Composing these two implementations, we obtain {CAS, read, write} from {LL, SC, VL}.

2.1 Definition of Dual Stream LL/SC/VL

A *dual stream LL/SC/VL object* supports two versions of LL, SC, and VL operations: LL_0, VL_0, SC_0, LL_1, VL_1, and SC_1. The operation SC_j by a process p succeeds if and only if no process performed a successful SC_0 or SC_1 since process p's latest LL_j. The important point is that the success of SC_j does *not* depend on when p performed $LL_{\bar{j}}$.

Formally, the state of an object O supporting these operations is described by $value(O)$, $Pset_0(O)$, and $Pset_1(O)$. Figure 3 gives a precise definition of the operations.

$LL_j(p_i, O)$	$SC_j(p_i, v, O)$	$VL_j(p_i, O)$
$Pset_j(O) := Pset_j(O) \cup \{p_i\}$	**if** $p_i \in Pset_j(O)$	**return** $p_i \in Pset_j(O)$
return $value(O)$	$\quad value(O) := v$	
	$\quad Pset_0(O) := \emptyset$	
	$\quad Pset_1(O) := \emptyset$	
	$\quad$ **return** *true*	
	else return *false*	

Fig. 3. Specification of a dual stream LL/SC/VL object O

To illustrate the definition, consider an execution in which operations are applied in the following order: $LL_1(p_0, O)$, $LL_0(p_1, O)$, $SC_0(p_1, u, O)$, $LL_0(p_0, O)$, $SC_1(p_0, v, O)$, $SC_0(p_0, w, O)$. In this sequence, SC_0 by p_1 succeeds and causes SC_1 by p_0 to fail. The SC_0 by p_0 succeeds because there is no successful SC_0 or successful SC_1 since p_0's latest LL_0.

2.2 Implementing a dual stream LL/SC/VL object

We implement a dual stream LL/SC/VL object $\mathcal{O}$ from an object O that supports LL, SC, and VL operations. To understand the issues involved in getting this implementation right, consider the naive (and incorrect) implementation that works as follows: to implement $LL_j(p_i, \mathcal{O})$, p_i simply performs LL on O; to implement $SC_j(p_i, v, \mathcal{O})$, p_i simply performs $SC(p_i, v, O)$; and to implement $VL_j(p_i, \mathcal{O})$, p_i simply performs VL on O. To see that this implementation is incorrect, consider a run in which the following sequence of operations are applied on $\mathcal{O}$: $LL_1(p_0, \mathcal{O})$, $LL_0(p_1, \mathcal{O})$, $SC_0(p_1, u, \mathcal{O})$, $LL_0(p_0, \mathcal{O})$, $SC_1(p_0, v, \mathcal{O})$. Clearly, by the specification of a dual stream object, SC_1 by p_0 (the last operation in the sequence) should fail. However, with the above implementation, this operation succeeds; this is because $LL(p_0, O)$, performed in implementing $LL_0(p_0, \mathcal{O})$ (the next to last operation in the above sequence), causes $SC(p_0, v, O)$, performed in implementing $SC_1(p_0, v, \mathcal{O})$ (the last operation in the sequence), to succeed.

The above exercise suggests the principal feature that any correct implementation must possess: the application of LL_j on $\mathcal{O}$ (for any $j \in \{0, 1\}$) by a process p_i should *not* cause a subsequent $SC_{\bar{j}}$ by p_i, that should otherwise fail, to succeed. We present such an implementation in Figure 4. Below, we provide intuition for how this implementation works.

Each process p_i maintains three local variables: $value_i$, $ActiveLL(i, 0)$, and $ActiveLL(i, 1)$. Informally, $value_i$ is the value of $\mathcal{O}$ that p_i obtained in its most recent LL operation (*i.e.*, LL_0 or LL_1) on $\mathcal{O}$. $ActiveLL(i, j)$ is a boolean variable. If $ActiveLL(i, j)$ is false, it means that p_i is sure that some process performed a successful SC on $\mathcal{O}$ after its (p_i's) most recent LL_j on $\mathcal{O}$. If $ActiveLL(i, j)$ is true, it means that p_i has no evidence that a successful SC happened after p_i's most recent LL_j. Now we describe how LL_j, VL_j, and SC_j operations on $\mathcal{O}$ are implemented.

O: {LL, SC, VL}-object
Initially, value(O) = value($\mathcal{O}$) and Pset(O) = $\emptyset$.

Local variables of each p_i:
$\overline{ActiveLL(i,j)}$ $(j \in \{0,1\})$: boolean, initialized to *false*
$value_i$: arbitrarily initialized

$LL_j(p_i, \mathcal{O})$	$VL_j(p_i, \mathcal{O})$	$SC_j(p_i, \mathcal{O})$
1. **if** $\neg ActiveLL(i,\bar{j})$	**if** $ActiveLL(i,j)$	**if** $ActiveLL(i,j)$
2. $value_i := LL(p_i, O)$	**return** $VL(p_i, O)$	**return** $SC(p_i, O)$
3. **else if** $\neg VL(p_i, O)$	**else return** *false*	**else return** *false*
4. $ActiveLL(i,\bar{j}) := false$		
5. $value_i := LL(p_i, O)$		
6. $ActiveLL(i,j) := true$		
7. **return** $value_i$		

Fig. 4. Implementing dual stream LL/SC/VL object $\mathcal{O}$ from {LL, SC, VL}-object O

To perform LL_j on the implemented object $\mathcal{O}$, a process p_i proceeds as follows. It checks the value of $ActiveLL(i,\bar{j})$. There are two cases, depending on the value of $ActiveLL(i,\bar{j})$, described as follows.

<u>Case 1</u>: Suppose $ActiveLL(i,\bar{j})$ is false. This means that p_i already knows that some process performed a successful SC on $\mathcal{O}$ after p_i's most recent $LL_{\bar{j}}$. Thus, p_i has enough information in its local variable $ActiveLL(i,\bar{j})$ to know that it should fail a subsequent $SC_{\bar{j}}$ or $VL_{\bar{j}}$. In particular, to implement the current LL_j operation on $\mathcal{O}$, it is safe to perform an LL on the base object O. So it performs LL on O and stores the response in $value_i$ (Line 2), sets the local variable $ActiveLL(i,j)$ to *true* (since it has just performed LL_j on $\mathcal{O}$ and has no evidence that any process has since performed a successful SC on $\mathcal{O}$) (Line 6), and returns $value_i$ (Line 7).

<u>Case 2</u>: Suppose, on Line 1, $ActiveLL(i,\bar{j})$ is true. This means that p_i has so far no evidence that a successful SC operation happened after p_i's latest $LL_{\bar{j}}$ on $\mathcal{O}$. To determine if such a successful SC happened, p_i performs VL on O (Line 3). There are two subcases, depending on whether VL returns true or false, and are described as follows.

<u>Subcase 2 (i)</u>: Suppose VL returns false. This means that a successful SC happened after p_i's latest $LL_{\bar{j}}$. So p_i sets $ActiveLL(i,\bar{j})$ to *false* (Line 4). This ensures that p_i has enough information in its local variable $ActiveLL(i,\bar{j})$ to know that it should fail a subsequent $SC_{\bar{j}}$ or $VL_{\bar{j}}$. Thus, it is now safe to implement the current LL_j on $\mathcal{O}$ by performing an LL on O. So p_i performs LL on O and stores the response in $value_i$ (Line 5), sets the local variable $ActiveLL(i,j)$ to *true* (Line 6), and returns $value_i$ (Line 7).

<u>Subcase 2 (ii)</u>: Suppose VL (on Line 3) returns true. This means that no process

performed a successful SC on $\mathcal{O}$ between time τ when p_i performed its latest $LL_{\bar{j}}$ on $\mathcal{O}$ and time τ' when VL is performed on Line 3. Then, p_i can pretend that its current LL_j takes effect at τ', the time when it performs VL on Line 3. Further, since there is no successful SC on $\mathcal{O}$ during the interval (τ, τ'), the value of $\mathcal{O}$ at τ' is the same as its value at τ, which is already present in the local variable $value_i$. Thus, there is no need for p_i to perform LL on O (in fact, as described in the next paragraph, the implementation would be incorrect if p_i performs an LL on O). So p_i sets the local variable $ActiveLL(i,j)$ to $true$ (Line 6), and returns $value_i$ (Line 7).

As mentioned above, in Subcase 2 (ii), it is important that p_i does not perform LL on O. To see this, suppose that it does. That is, after VL returns true (on Line 3) at time τ', p_i performs LL on O in its next step, say, at time τ''. Suppose that a different process p_k performs a successful SC (SC_0 or SC_1) on $\mathcal{O}$ after τ' and before τ''. If p_i performs $SC_{\bar{j}}$ at a later time, it should fail by the specification of a dual stream object. However, because of the LL on O at time τ'', it will succeed. This is why p_i does not perform LL on O in our implementation. This completes the discussion of how p_i performs LL_j on $\mathcal{O}$.

To perform VL_j on the implemented object $\mathcal{O}$, p_i proceeds as follows. If the local variable $ActiveLL(i,j)$ is false, then some successful SC on $\mathcal{O}$ occurred after p_i's latest LL_j operation; so p_i returns false. Otherwise, p_i performs VL on O to determine if a successful SC occurred on $\mathcal{O}$ since its latest LL_j, and returns the response from O. (As an optimization, if VL returns false, p_i could set its local variables $ActiveLL(i,0)$ and $ActiveLL(i,1)$ to false. But, in the interest of brevity of the algorithm, we did not include these extra lines. They do not affect the correctness.)

To perform SC_j on $\mathcal{O}$, p_i proceeds similarly. If $ActiveLL(i,j)$ is false, then some successful SC on $\mathcal{O}$ occurred after p_i's latest LL_j operation; so p_i returns false. Otherwise, p_i performs SC on O and returns the response from O. (An optimization similar to the one mentioned above for the VL_j implementation is also possible here, but we have omitted it in the interest of brevity.)

Theorem 1. *There is a constant time complexity implementation of a dual stream LL/SC/VL object from a single object supporting LL, SC, and VL operations.*

2.3 Implementing {CAS, Read, Write}

In this section, we implement a {CAS, Read, Write} object $\mathcal{O}$ using a dual stream LL/SC/VL object O and a normal {LL, SC, VL} object R. In the following, we first describe the key ideas incorporated into the algorithm and then provide an informal description of the procedures implementing CAS, Read, and Write operations. The implementation is presented in Figure 5.

The key ideas: The following are the main ideas and conventions incorporated into the algorithm.

1. The value of the implemented object $\mathcal{O}$ is maintained in the base object O at all times.

2. The zeroth stream of O's operations (specifically, LL_0 and SC_0) are used to implement the CAS operation on $\mathcal{O}$. The first stream of O's operations (specifically, LL_1 and SC_1) are used to implement Read and Write operations on $\mathcal{O}$.

3. When a process wants to write a value V in the implemented object $\mathcal{O}$, it first "announces" its intent by attempting to get the value V into the base object R. We use LL and SC operations to ensure that if several processes attempt to announce concurrently, only one will succeed. For example, suppose W and W' are concurrent write operations on $\mathcal{O}$ that both attempt to announce their write values in R. Suppose W's announcement succeeds and W''s fails. After this, both W and W' proceed to install in O the write value announced in R. (Thus, after a Write operation attempts to announce its write value, regardless of whether its announcement is successful, it proceeds to help install in O whatever value was successfully announced in R.) Once a Write operation transfers the value in R to O, it clears the object R (by making its value $\perp$), thus making it possible for another Write operation to announce its write value.

Continuing with the above example, suppose that W and W' have together transferred W's announced value (which is in R) to O. We linearize W at the point where W's write value is transferred to O. As for W', it is linearized immediately before W (this amounts to pretending that W overwrites W' just after W' takes effect.) In other words, W' can be sure that it has taken effect as soon as it helps W take effect. This, in fact, is the incentive for W' to help install W's announced value (even though W''s announcement has failed).

4. Processes use LL_1 and SC_1 operations on O in order to transfer a value from R to O. Further, a process that is attempting to transfer a value V from R to O exercises the following caution: after performing LL_1 on O the process performs $SC_1(V)$ on O if and only if O's value is not already V. Such care is necessary for two reasons: (1) to ensure that at most one successful SC_1 operation is performed (by all helping processes together) on behalf of any Write operation, and (2) to prevent a frivolous Write (*i.e.*, a Write operation that writes the same value as what the object already has) from erroneously causing a CAS to fail (this is explained in detail in the expanded version [Jay98]).

5. When a process p_i wants to apply $CAS(p_i, old, new, \mathcal{O})$, it first obtains O's value by performing LL_0 on O. If O's value is different from old, p_i terminates its CAS returning *false*. On the other hand, if O's value is the same as old and if $old = new$, p_i pretends that its CAS changed O's value from old to old, and terminates returning *true*. If the above cases do not apply, it follows that O's value (as read by p_i's LL) is the same as old and $old \neq new$.

At this point, one strategy would be to have p_i perform an SC on O, attempting to change O's value to new. However, with such a strategy, successive CAS operations can repeatedly succeed, making it impossible for Write operations on $\mathcal{O}$ to take effect.

To prevent such starvation of Write operations, we adopt a different strategy in which p_i helps any pending Write operation on $\mathcal{O}$ before performing SC on

---

O: Dual stream LL/SC object supporting LL_0, SC_0, LL_1, SC_1.
Initially, $value(O) = value(\mathcal{O})$ and $Pset_0(O) = Pset_1(O) = \emptyset$.
R: {LL, SC, VL} object
Initially, $value(R) = \bot$ and $Pset(R) = \emptyset$

Read($p_i, \mathcal{O}$)		InstallWrite(p_i)	
1.	return $LL_1(p_i, O)$	1.	$[val, phase] := LL(p_i, R)$
		2.	if $val = \bot$ return
		3.	if $phase = 0$
Write($p_i, v, \mathcal{O}$)		4.	$val' := LL_1(p_i, O)$
1.	InstallWrite(p_i)	5.	if $val' = val$
2.	$[val, phase] := LL(p_i, R)$	6.	$SC(p_i, [\bot, 0], R)$
3.	if $val = \bot$	7.	else $SC(p_i, [val, 1], R)$
4.	$SC(p_i, [v, 0], R)$	8.	$[val, phase] := LL(p_i, R)$
5.	InstallWrite(p_i)	9.	if $phase = 0$ return
		10.	$val' := LL_1(p_i, O)$
		11.	if $\neg VL(p_i, R)$ return
CAS($p_i, old, new, \mathcal{O}$)		12.	if $val' \neq val$
1.	$val := LL_0(p_i, O)$	13.	if $\neg SC_1(p_i, val, O)$
2.	if $val \neq old$ return $false$	14.	$val' := LL_1(p_i, O)$
3.	if $old = new$ return $true$	15.	if $\neg VL(p_i, R)$ return
4.	InstallWrite(p_i)	16.	if $val' \neq val$
5.	return $SC_0(p_i, new, O)$	17.	$SC_1(p_i, val, O)$
		18.	$SC(p_i, [\bot, 0], R)$

Fig. 5. Implementing object $\mathcal{O}$ that supports CAS, Read, and Write

---

O and completing its CAS operation. Specifically, p_i determines if there is a pending Write operation on $\mathcal{O}$ by checking if R has a non-$\bot$ value. If there is a pending Write operation W, p_i helps complete W by transferring the value in R to O (and then clearing R). After this, p_i completes its CAS operation by performing SC on O.

6. R consists of two fields: a *value* field and a *phase* field. The phase field has either 0 or 1. When there is no pending Write on $\mathcal{O}$, R contains $[\bot, 0]$ (*i.e.*, $R \cdot value = \bot$ and $R \cdot phase = 0$). A Write operation W on $\mathcal{O}$ announces its write value v in R by changing R's state from $[\bot, 0]$ to $[v, 0]$. While helping W, a process p_j changes R's state from $[v, 0]$ to either $[v, 1]$ or $[\bot, 0]$, as described below. While attempting to transfer R's value v to O, p_j first reads O. If O's value is v (this can happen either because some other process has already transferred v from R to O or because the previous value of O is v), then there is no need to change O. In this case, p_j attempts to clear R by swinging its value from $[v, 0]$ to $[\bot, 0]$. On the other hand, if p_j reads a value other than v in O, then p_j believes that v should be written to O to help W take effect. To communicate its belief to other processes, p_j attempts to swing R from $[v, 0]$ to $[v, 1]$ (thus, a value of 1 in the phase field indicates that some process observed in O a value different from v after v was announced in R). Later, after v is transferred to O (by p_j or some other helper), R is swung from $[v, 1]$ to $[\bot, 0]$.

Informal description of procedures: We now describe the procedures implementing Read, Write, and CAS operations, and the auxiliary procedure InstallWrite.

Read($p_i, \mathcal{O}$) procedure: Since $\mathcal{O}$'s value is always contained in O, the implementation of Read($p_i, \mathcal{O}$) is simple: p_i performs LL_1 on O and returns the value obtained.

InstallWrite procedure: The implementations of both Write and CAS operations call the auxiliary procedure InstallWrite. This procedure helps any pending Write operation to run to completion. Below we explain how this is accomplished.

A process p_i executes InstallWrite as follows. It begins by reading R into $[val, phase]$ (Line 1). If val is $\perp$, then there is no pending Write on $\mathcal{O}$; so p_i returns (Line 2). Otherwise, there is a pending Write operation on $\mathcal{O}$. Let W denote this pending Write. In the rest of the procedure, the sole objective of p_i is to help W run to completion.

Suppose *phase* is 0. Then, p_i reads O (Line 4). If O's value is the same as val (the write value announced by W in R), then even without modifying O one can pretend that W has taken effect. So, to effect the completion of W, p_i attempts to swing R from $[val, 0]$ to $[\perp, 0]$ (Line 6). On the other hand, if O's value is different from val, then to make W take effect it is necessary to modify O's value to val. To communicate to other processes the need to modify O, p_i attempts to swing R from $[val, 0]$ to $[val, 1]$ (Line 7). Just after p_i completes executing the if-then-else statement on Lines 5-7, p_i can be certain that either W has completed or R's phase is currently 1. So it reads R again into $[val, phase]$ (Line 8). If *phase* is 0, it deduces that W has completed; since p_i's only goal is to help W run to completion, p_i returns from the procedure. On the other hand, if *phase* is 1, then some Write operation is pending; this pending write may be W or some subsequent write operation W'. In any case, if *phase* is 1, p_i cannot be certain that W has completed and so it cannot return yet from the procedure.

When p_i reaches Line 10, it is certain that when it last read R into $[val, phase]$ (on Line 1 or on Line 8), some Write operation W' was pending and *phase* was 1. (Notice that W' is either W or another Write that followed W.) Since *phase* is 1, it means that some process had noticed O's value to be different from val. So p_i prepares to transfer R's value to O. To do this, p_i performs LL_1 to read O's value into val' (Line 10) and then validates R (Line 11). If VL returns false on Line 11, it means that R was modified since the time p_i performed LL on R. It follows that some process changed R's value from $[val, 1]$ to $[\perp, 0]$ since the time p_i performed LL on R. It follows that W', and therefore W, have completed. So p_i returns from the procedure.

Suppose, on Line 11, VL returns true. Then, p_i knows that W' has not completed (but it may have taken effect). If $val' = val$ (on Line 12), p_i deduces that either some process already installed W''s write value in O or O's value is val even without any process installing W''s write value in O. In the former case, W' took effect. In the latter case, it is possible to pretend that W' took effect (overwriting *val* with *val*). Hence, p_i attempts to mark the completion of W' by swinging R from $[val, 1]$ to $[\perp, 0]$ (Line 18).

Suppose $val' \neq val$ (on Line 12). Then p_i deduces that W' has not taken effect. So it attempts to write *val* to O by performing SC_1 (Line 13). If this SC succeeds, then W' has taken effect, so it proceeds to Line 18 to clear R. Otherwise, some other process performed a successful SC either on behalf of W' or on behalf of a CAS operation. If the latter is the case, then p_i must try again to install W''s write value in O. So it performs LL_1 on O (Line 14), and then on Lines 15-17 performs the same actions as it did on Lines 11-13 (for the same reasons). Clearly, if SC_1 succeeds on Line 17, p_i can be certain that W' has taken effect. Interestingly, the same conclusion (that W' has taken effect) can be drawn even if SC_1 fails on Line 17. This is because the CAS operation is implemented in such a way that, while a Write on O is pending, at most one CAS succeeds. Thus, if SC_1 fails on Line 13 and on Line 17, p_i can be certain that some other process installed W''s write value in O. So it proceeds to Line 18 to clear R.

Write(p_i, v, O) procedure: To implement Write(p_i, v, O), process p_i proceeds as follows. First, p_i executes InstallWrite (Line 1), thereby helping any pending Write operation to complete and R to clear. Next p_i attempts to announce its write value in R (Lines 2-4). At the end of Line 4, either p_i's Write or some other process' Write announced a value in R. Let W denote the Write that successfully announced in R. By executing InstallWrite on Line 5, p_i helps W run to completion. After Line 5, p_i can be certain that its own Write (which may or may not be W) has taken effect. This is justified as follows. If p_i's Write is W, then it has taken effect (because of Line 5). Otherwise, p_i's Write is concurrent with W. Since W has taken effect, p_i's Write can be linearized just before W.

CAS(p_i, old, new, O) procedure: To implement CAS(p_i, old, new, O), process p_i proceeds as follows. First, it reads O's value into a local variable *val* by performing LL on O (Line 1). If $val \neq old$, p_i fails CAS (Line 2). If $val = old = new$, then there is no need to modify O; p_i simply pretends that its CAS succeeded (Line 3). Otherwise, p_i helps any pending Write to run to completion (without such help, Write operations will starve). Finally, p_i attempts to swing the value in O from *old* to *new* by performing SC_0 on O (Line 5). If the SC succeeds, it is obvious that p_i's CAS succeeded, so p_i returns *true*. If the SC fails, it is legitimate for p_i to fail its CAS. The justification is as follows. If p_i's SC fails on Line 5, it follows that some process performed either a write or a successful SC on O sometime between p_i's LL on Line 1 and p_i's SC on Line 5. Further, since O's value was *old* (when p_i performed Line 1) and in our algorithm each successful SC on O changes O's value, p_i can be certain that at some point between p_i's Line 1 and Line 5 O's value was different from *old*. Since p_i's CAS can be linearized at that point, it is legitimate for p_i to fail its CAS.

The theorem below follows from the above implementation and Theorem 1.

Theorem 2. *There is a constant time complexity implementation of an object supporting CAS, read, and write operations from two objects supporting LL, SC, and VL operations.*

3 {LL, SC, VL, Read, Write} from {LL, SC, VL}

In this section, we implement an object $\mathcal{O}$ that supports LL, SC, VL, Read, and Write operations using a dual stream LL/SC/VL object O and a normal {LL, SC, VL} object R. This implementation is presented in Figure 6. There are many similarities, yet significant differences, between this implementation and the one in the previous section. Below, we describe the main ideas on which the implementation is based:

1. O has two fields: a *value* field and a *tag* field. The value of the implemented object $\mathcal{O}$ is maintained in O's value field at all times. When an SC operation on $\mathcal{O}$ modifies O, it writes 2 in O's tag field. When a Write operation on $\mathcal{O}$ modifies O, it writes either 0 or 1 in O's tag field.

2. We ensure $\mathrm{Pset}(\mathcal{O}) = \mathrm{Pset}(O)$.

3. The zeroth stream of O's operations are used to implement the LL, SC, and VL operations on $\mathcal{O}$. The first stream of O's operations are used to implement Read and Write operations on $\mathcal{O}$.

4. As in the previous implementation, R is the object where a Write operation on $\mathcal{O}$ attempts to announce its write value. R has two fields: a *value* field and a *tag* field. When there is no pending Write operation on $\mathcal{O}$, R's value field has $\perp$. A Write operation attempts to announce its write value V by swinging R from $[\perp, tag]$ to $[V, \overline{tag}]$. Subsequently, when clearing R, processes swing R from $[V, \overline{tag}]$ to $[\perp, \overline{tag}]$. Thus, R's tag alternates between 0 and 1 with each successive announcement.

5. The tag fields of O and R make it possible for a process to determine whether or not the announced value in R was already transferred to O. In particular, the implementation has the following key property: If R's value is not $\perp$ (*i.e.*, there is a pending Write), then O's tag and R's tag are equal if and only if the announced value in R has already been applied to O (*i.e.*, the pending Write has already taken effect).

6. Consider a Write operation W that has announced its write value in R. Although many processes may help W run to completion by attempting to transfer its announced value from R to O, the implementation ensures that exactly one process performs a successful SC on O on behalf of W. In particular, even if O's value is V and W's write value is also V, the implementation makes sure that a successful SC is performed on O (by some process) on behalf of W. (This is in sharp contrast to the previous implementation of {CAS, Read, Write} where we took great care to avoid applying a Write operation if it does not change O's value.) In the current implementation, a successful SC is performed on O on behalf of every Write in order to ensure the invariant $\mathrm{Pset}(\mathcal{O}) = \mathrm{Pset}(O)$ (to see this, note that a Write operation on $\mathcal{O}$ should cause $\mathrm{Pset}(\mathcal{O})$ to become empty.

O: Dual stream LL/SC/VL object
Initially, $\text{value}(O) = [\text{value}(\mathcal{O}), 0]$ and $\text{Pset}_0(O) = \text{Pset}_1(O) = \emptyset$.
R: {LL, SC, VL} object
Initially, $\text{value}(R) = [\bot, 0]$ and $\text{Pset}(R) = \emptyset$

$LL(p_i, \mathcal{O})$
return $LL_0(p_i, O)$

$Read(p_i, \mathcal{O})$
return $LL_1(p_i, O)$

$SC(p_i, v, \mathcal{O})$
$\overline{\text{InstallWrite}(p_i)}$
return $SC_0(p_i, [v, 2], O)$

InstallWrite(p_i)
1. $[val, tag] := LL(p_i, R)$
2. if $val = \bot$ return
3. $[val', tag'] := LL_1(p_i, O)$

$VL(p_i, \mathcal{O})$
$\overline{\text{return } VL_0(p_i, O)}$
4. if $\neg VL(p_i, R)$ return
5. if $tag' \neq tag$
6.   if $\neg SC_1(p_i, [val, tag], O)$

$\text{Write}(p_i, v, \mathcal{O})$
1. $\overline{\text{InstallWrite}(p_i)}$
2. $[val, tag] := LL(p_i, R)$
3. if $val = \bot$
4. $SC(p_i, [v, \overline{tag}], R)$
5. InstallWrite(p_i)

7. $[val', tag'] := LL_1(p_i, O)$
8.   if $\neg VL(p_i, R)$ return
9.   if $tag' \neq tag$
10. $SC_1(p_i, [val, tag], O)$
11. $SC(p_i, [\bot, tag], R)$

Fig. 6. Implementing object $\mathcal{O}$ that supports LL, SC, VL, Read, and Write

---

This, together with the need to maintain the invariant $\text{Pset}(\mathcal{O}) = \text{Pset}(O)$, implies that a successful SC must be performed on O on behalf of every write on $\mathcal{O}$).

With the above concepts, it is fairly easy to understand the implementation. The procedures for LL, VL, and Read operations on $\mathcal{O}$ are self-explanatory.

The auxiliary procedure InstallWrite helps any pending Write operation to run to completion. A process p_i executes this procedure as follows. It performs LL on R (Line 1). If R's value field has $\bot$, then no Write is pending, so p_i returns (Line 2). Otherwise, let W denote the pending Write operation. On Line 3, p_i reads O's value by performing LL_1. If VL on R returns false, it means that some process cleared R since the time p_i LL'd it on Line 1; this implies W completed, so p_i returns (Line 4). If $tag' = tag$ (Line 5), it means that some process has already transferred W's announced value from R to O; so p_i proceeds to Line 11 to clear R. If $tag' \neq tag$ (Line 5), it means that W has not yet taken effect. So p_i applies SC_1 on O, attempting to install in O the value and the tag that W announced in R (Line 6). If this attempt fails, p_i tries again (Lines 7-10), taking the same precautions that it took on Lines 3-6. Regardless of whether its SC succeeds or fails on Line 10, p_i can be certain that W's announcement has been successfully transferred to O by some process (the justification for this conclusion is similar to the one provided in the previous implementation). So, it attempts to clear R (Line 11).

The write operation on $\mathcal{O}$ works exactly as in the previous implementation with one exception: when announcing in R, it flips the tag bit of R.

To implement SC operation on $\mathcal{O}$, p_i first helps any pending Write (Line 1). (If it were not for this line, InstallWrite's assumption—that the pending Write operation that InstallWrite is helping to complete would have taken effect even if InstallWrite's SC failed both on Line 6 and on Line 10— would be incorrect). Having helped any pending Write, p_i performs an SC operation on O in order to effect its SC operation on the implemented object $\mathcal{O}$ (Line 2).

The theorem below follows from the above implementation and Theorem 1.

Theorem 3. *There is a constant time complexity implementation of an object supporting LL, SC, VL, Read, and Write operations from two objects supporting LL, SC, and VL operations.*

Acknowledgement: I thank the DISC '98 referees for their helpful comments.

References

[AM95] J. Anderson and M. Moir. Universal constructions for multi-object operations. In *Proceedings of the 14th Annual ACM Symposium on Principles of Distributed Computing*, pages 184–194, August 1995.

[Her91] M.P. Herlihy. Wait-free synchronization. *ACM TOPLAS*, 13(1):124–149, 1991.

[HS93] M. P. Herlihy and N. Shavit. The asynchronous computability theorem for t-resilient tasks. In *Proceedings of the 25th ACM Symposium on Theory of Computing*, pages 111–120, 1993.

[HW90] M.P. Herlihy and J.M. Wing. Linearizability: A correctness condition for concurrent objects. *ACM TOPLAS*, 12(3):463–492, 1990.

[IBM94] IBM. *The Power PC Architecture: A specification for a new family of RISC processors*. Morgan-Kaufmann, 1994.

[IR94] A. Israeli and L. Rappoport. Disjoint-Access-Parallel implementations of strong shared-memory primitives. In *Proceedings of the 13th Annual ACM Symposium on Principles of Distributed Computing*, pages 151–160, August 1994.

[Jay98] P. Jayanti, 1998. See http://www.cs.dartmouth.edu/~prasad.

[JHB87] E. Jensen, G. Hagensen, and J. Broughton. A new approach to exclusive data access in shared-memory multiprocessors. Technical Report Technical Report UCRL-97663, Lawrence Livermore National Laboratory, 1987.

[Kan89] G. Kane. *MIPS RISC Architecture*. Prentice-Hall, Englewood Cliffs, N.J., 1989.

[Lam77] L. Lamport. Concurrent reading and writing. *Communications of the ACM*, 20(11):806–811, 1977.

[Moi97] M. Moir. Practical implementations of non-blocking synchronization primitives. In *Proceedings of the 16th Annual ACM Symposium on Principles of Distributed Computing*, pages 219–228, August 1997.

[Sit92] R. Site. *Alpha Architecture Reference Manual*. Digital Equipment Corporation, 1992.

Failure Detection and Consensus
in the Crash-Recovery Model*

Marcos Kawazoe Aguilera   Wei Chen   Sam Toueg

Cornell University, Computer Science Department, Ithaca NY 14853-7501, USA
aguilera,weichen,sam@cs.cornell.edu

Abstract. We study the problems of failure detection and consensus in asynchronous systems in which processes may crash and recover, and links may lose messages. We first propose new failure detectors that are particularly suitable to the crash-recovery model. We next determine under what conditions stable storage is necessary to solve consensus in this model. Using the new failure detectors, we give two consensus algorithms that match these conditions: one requires stable storage and the other does not. Both algorithms tolerate link failures and are particularly efficient in the runs that are most likely in practice — those with no failures or failure detector mistakes. In such runs, consensus is achieved within 3δ time and with $4n$ messages, where δ is the maximum message delay and n is the number of processes in the system.

1 Introduction

The problem of solving consensus in asynchronous systems with unreliable failure detectors (i.e., failure detectors that make mistakes) was first investigated in [4,3]. But these works only considered systems where process crashes are *permanent* and links are reliable (i.e., they do not lose messages). In real systems, however, processes may *recover* after crashing and links may lose messages. In this paper, we focus on solving consensus with failure detectors in such systems, a problem that was first considered in [5,9,7] (a brief comparison with these works is in Section 1.3).

Solving consensus in a system where process may recover after crashing raises two new problems; one regards the need for stable storage and the other is about the failure detection requirements:

- *Stable Storage:* When a process crashes, it loses all its local state. One way to deal with this problem is to assume that parts of the local state are recorded into stable storage, and can be restored after each recovery. However, stable storage operations are slow and expensive, and must be avoided as much as possible. Is stable storage always necessary when solving consensus? If not, under which condition(s) can it be completely avoided?
- *Failure Detection:* In the crash-recovery model, a process may keep on crashing and recovering indefinitely (such a process is called *unstable*). How should a failure detector view unstable processes? Note that an unstable process may be as useless to an application as one that permanently crashes (and in fact it could be even more disruptive). For example, an unstable process can be up just long enough to be considered operational by the failure detector, and then crash before "helping"

---

* Research partially supported by NSF grant CCR-9402896 and CCR-9711403, by ARPA/ONR grant N00014-96-1-1014, and by an Olin Fellowship.

the application, and this could go on repeatedly. Thus, it is natural to require that a failure detector satisfies the following *completeness* property: Eventually every unstable process is permanently suspected.[1]

But implementing such a failure detector is inherently problematic *even in a perfectly synchronous system*. Intuitively, this is because, at any given point in time, no implementation can predict the future behavior of a process p that has crashed in the past but is currently "up". Will p continue to repeatedly crash and recover? Or will it stop crashing?

In summary, our goal here is to solve consensus in the crash-recovery model (with lossy links). As a crucial part of this problem, we first need to find reasonable failure detectors that can be used for this task. We also need to determine if and when stable-storage is necessary.

1.1 Failure Detectors for the Crash-Recovery Model

We first focus on the problem of failure detection in the crash-recovery model. Previous solutions require unstable processes to be eventually suspected forever [9, 7].[2] We first prove that this requirement has a serious drawback: it forces failure detector implementations to have undesirable behaviors even in perfectly synchronous systems. More precisely, consider a synchronous round-based system with no message losses,[3] where up to n_u processes may be unstable. In this system, *every* implementation of a failure detector with the above requirement has runs with the following undesirable behavior: there is round after which (a) *all* processes are permanently up, but (b) the failure detector incorrectly suspects n_u of them forever (see Theorem 1). Note that these permanent mistakes are *not* due to the usual causes, namely, slow processes or message delays. Instead, they are entirely due to the requirement on unstable processes (which involves predicting the future).

To avoid the above problem, we propose *a new type of failure detector* that is well-suited to the crash-recovery model. This failure detector does not output lists of processes suspected to be crashed or unstable. Instead, it outputs a list of processes deemed to be currently up, with an associated *epoch number* for each such process. If a process is on this list we say it is *trusted*.

The epoch number of a process is a rough estimate of the number of times it crashed and recovered in the past. We distinguish two types of processes: *bad* ones are those that are unstable or crash permanently, and *good* ones are those that never crash or eventually remain up. We first propose a simple failure detector, denoted $\Diamond S_e$, with the following two properties. Roughly speaking (precise definitions are in Section 3):

- *Completeness:* For every bad process b, at every good process there is a time after which either b is never trusted or the epoch number of b keeps on increasing.
- *Accuracy:* Some good process is eventually trusted forever by all good processes, and its epoch number stops changing.

---

[1] In fact, this property is assumed in [9, 7].

[2] In [5], crash-recovery is regarded as a special case of omission failures, and the algorithm is not designed to handle unstable processes that can send and receive messages to and from good processes.

[3] In such a system, processes execute in synchronized rounds, and all messages are received in the round they are sent.

Note that the completeness property of $\Diamond S_e$ does not require predicting the future (to determine if a process is unstable), and so it does not force implementations to have anomalous behaviors. To illustrate this, in [2] we give an implementation of $\Diamond S_e$ for some models of partial synchrony: this implementation ensures that if all processes are eventually up forever they will be eventually trusted forever.

Failure detector $\Diamond S_e$, however, does not put *any* restriction on how the bad processes view the system. In particular, the accuracy property allows unstable processes to repeatedly "suspect" *all* processes.[4] This is problematic because, in contrast to processes that permanently crash, unstable processes may continue to take steps, and so their incorrect suspicions may prevent the progress of some algorithms. For example, in the rotating coordinator consensus algorithms of [4, 5, 7] if a process kept suspecting all processes then consensus would never be reached.

From the above it is clear that sometimes it is better to have a failure detector with:

– *Strong Accuracy:* Some good process is eventually trusted forever by all good *and unstable* processes, and its epoch number stops changing.

Such a failure detector is denoted $\Diamond S_u$. In [2], we show how to transform any $\Diamond S_e$ to $\Diamond S_u$ in an asynchronous system provided that a majority of processes are good.

1.2 On the Necessity of Stable Storage in the Crash-Recovery Model

Can consensus be solved in the crash-recovery model *without stable storage*, and if so, how? Suppose that during each execution of consensus, at least n_a processes are guaranteed to remain up. Clearly, if $n_a < 1$ then consensus cannot be solved: it is possible that *all* processes crash and recover during execution, and the entire state of the system (including previous proposals and possible decisions) can be lost forever.

On the other hand, if $n_a > n/2$, i.e., a majority of processes are guaranteed to remain up, then solving consensus is easy: If a process crashes we exclude it from participating in the algorithm even if it recovers (except that we allow it to receive the decision value). This essentially reduces the problem to the case where process crashes are permanent and a majority of processes do not crash (and then an algorithm such as the one in [4] can be used).

Is it possible to solve consensus without stable storage if $1 \leq n_a \leq n/2$? To answer this question, assume that in every execution of consensus at most n_b processes are bad. We show that:

– If $n_a \leq n_b$ then consensus *cannot be solved without stable storage* even using $\Diamond P$ (the *eventually perfect failure detector* defined in Section 5).
– If $n_a > n_b$ then consensus *can be solved without stable storage* using $\Diamond S_e$ (which is weaker than $\Diamond P$).

This last result is somewhat surprising because with $n_a > n_b$, *a majority of processes may crash and completely lose their state* (including the consensus values they may have previously proposed and/or decided). To illustrate this with a concrete example, suppose $n = 10$, $n_a = 3$ and $n_b = 2$. In this case, up to 7 processes — more than half of the processes — may crash and lose their state, and yet consensus is solvable with a failure detector that is weaker than $\Diamond P$. *Prima facie*, this seems to contradict the fact that if a majority of processes may crash then consensus cannot be solved even with $\Diamond P$ [4]. There is no contradiction, however, since [4] assumes that all process crashes are

---

[4] An unstable process may fail to receive "I am alive" messages sent by other processes since all messages that "arrive" at a process while it is down are lost.

permanent, while in our case some of the processes that crash do recover: even though they completely lost their state, they can still provide some help.

What if stable storage *is* available? In this case, we show that consensus can be solved with $\Diamond S_u$, provided that a majority of processes are good (this requirement is weaker than $n_a > n_b$).[5]

In addition to crashes and recoveries, the two consensus algorithms that we give (with and without stable storage) also tolerate *message losses*, provided that links are fair lossy, i.e., if p sends messages to a good process q infinitely often, then q receives messages from p infinitely often.

1.3 Related Work

The problem of solving consensus with failure detectors in systems where processes may recover from crashes was first addressed in [5] (with crash-recovery as a form of omission failures) and more recently studied in [9,7].

In [5,7,9], the question of whether stable storage is always necessary is not addressed, and all the algorithms use stable storage: in [5,9], the entire state of the algorithm is recorded into stable storage at every state transition; in [7], only a small part of the state is recorded, and writing to stable storage is done at most once per round. In this paper, we determine when stable storage is necessary, and give two matching consensus algorithms — with and without stable storage. In the one that uses stable storage, only a small part of the state is recorded and this occurs twice per round.

The algorithms in [9,7] use failure detectors that require that unstable processes be eventually suspected forever. The algorithm in [5] is not designed to deal with unstable processes which may intermittently communicate with good ones.

1.4 Summary of Results

We study the problems of failure detection and consensus in asynchronous systems with process crashes and recoveries, and lossy links.

1. We show that the failure detectors that have been previously proposed for the crash-recovery model with unstable processes have inherent drawbacks: Their completeness requirement force implementations to have anomalous behaviors even in synchronous systems.
2. We propose new failure detectors that avoid the above drawbacks.
3. We determine under what conditions stable storage is necessary to solve consensus in the crash-recovery model.
4. We give two consensus algorithms that match these conditions, one uses stable storage and the other does not. Both algorithms tolerate message losses, and are particularly efficient in the runs that are most likely in practice — those with no failures or failure detector mistakes, and message delays are bounded. In such runs, consensus is achieved within 3δ time and with $4n$ messages, where δ is the maximum message delay and n is the number of processes in the system.

---

[5] If the good processes are not a majority, a simple partitioning argument as the one in [4] shows that consensus cannot be solved even with $\Diamond P$.

1.5 Roadmap

The paper is organized as follows. Our model is given in Section 2. In Section 3 we show that existing failure detectors for the crash-recovery model have limitations, and then introduce our new failure detectors, namely $\Diamond S_e$ and $\Diamond S_u$. We define the Consensus problem in Section 4. In Section 5, we determine under what conditions consensus requires stable storage. We then give two matching consensus algorithms: one does not require stable storage (Section 6), and the other uses stable storage (Section 7). In Section 8, we briefly consider the performance of these algorithms.

Due to space limitations, all proofs are ommitted here (they are given in [2]).

2 Model

We consider asynchronous message-passing distributed systems. We assume that every process is connected with every other process through a communication link. Links can fail by intermittently dropping messages. A process can fail by crashing and it may subsequently recover. When a process crashes it loses all of its state. However, it may use local stable storage to save (and later retrieve) parts of its state.

We assume the existence of a discrete global clock — this is merely a fictional device to simplify the presentation and processes do not have access to it. We take the range T of the clock's ticks to be the set of natural numbers.

2.1 Processes and Process Failures

The system consists of a set of n processes, $\Pi = \{1, 2, \ldots, n\}$. Processes can crash and may subsequently recover. A *failure pattern* F is a function from T to 2^{Π}. Intuitively, $F(t)$ denotes the set of processes that are not functioning at time t. We say process p is *up at time t (in F)* if $p \notin F(t)$ and p is *down at time t (in F)* if $p \in F(t)$. We say that p *crashes at time t* if p is up at time $t-1$ and p is down at time t.[6] We say that p *recovers* at time $t \geq 1$ if p is down at time $t-1$ and p is up at time t. A process p can be classified (according to F) as *always-up, eventually-up, eventually-down* and *unstable* as follows:

Always-up: Process p never crashes.

Eventually-up: Process p crashes at least once, but there is a time after which p is permanently up.

Eventually-down: There is a time after which process p is permanently down.

Unstable: Process p crashes and recovers infinitely many times.

A process is *good (in F)* if it is either always-up or eventually-up. A process is *bad (in F)* if it is not good (it is either eventually-down or unstable). We denote by $good(F)$, $bad(F)$ and $unstable(F)$ the set of good, bad and unstable processes in F, respectively. Henceforth, we consider only failure patterns with at least one good process.

2.2 Failure Detectors

Each process has access to a local failure detector module that provides (possibly incorrect) information about the failure pattern that occurs in an execution. A process can query its local failure detector module at any time. A *failure detector history H with range $\mathcal{R}$* is a function from $\Pi \times T$ to $\mathcal{R}$. $H(p, t)$ is the output value of the failure detector module of process p at time t. A *failure detector $\mathcal{D}$* is a function that maps each failure pattern F to a set of failure detector histories with range $\mathcal{R}_{\mathcal{D}}$ (where $\mathcal{R}_{\mathcal{D}}$ denotes the range of the failure detector output of $\mathcal{D}$). $\mathcal{D}(F)$ denotes the set of possible failure detector histories permitted by $\mathcal{D}$ for the failure pattern F.

---

[6] We say that p crashes at time $t = 0$ if p is down at time 0.

2.3 Stable Storage

When a process crashes, it loses all its volatile state, but we assume that when it recovers, it knows that it is recovering from a crash. Moreover, a process may use a stable storage device to store and retrieve a set of variables. These two stable storage operations cannot be executed atomically with certain other actions. For example, a process cannot store a variable in stable storage and then send a message or issue an external output, in a single atomic step.

2.4 Link Properties

We consider links that do not create messages, or duplicate messages infinitely often. More precisely, we assume that for all processes p and q:

- *No Creation*: If q receives a message m from p at time t, then p sent m to q before time t.
- *Finite Duplication*: If p sends a message m to q only a finite number of times, then q receives m from p only a finite number of times.

Links may intermittently drop messages, but they must satisfy the following fairness property:

- *Fair Loss*: If p sends messages to a good process q an infinite number of times, then q receives messages from p an infinite number of times.

3 Failure Detectors for the Crash-Recovery Model

In this section, we first consider the failure detectors that were previously proposed for solving consensus in the crash-recovery model, and then propose a new type of failure detector for this model.

3.1 Limitations of Existing Failure Detectors

To solve consensus in the crash-recovery model, Hurfin *et al.* [7] and Oliveira *et al.* [9] assume that processes have failure detectors that output lists of processes suspected to be bad, and that these failure detectors satisfy the following property:

- *Strong Completeness*: Eventually every bad process is permanently suspected by all good processes.

Since bad processes include unstable ones, enforcing this requirement is problematic even in *synchronous* systems, as we now explain. Consider a system S in which processes take steps at perfectly synchronized rounds. In each round, a process is either up, in which case it sends a message to every process, or down, in which case it does nothing in the round. In S at most n_u process are unstable, i.e., alternate between being up and down infinitely often. Links do not lose messages, and all messages sent in a round are received at the end of that round. In system S, it is trivial to implement a failure detector that is almost perfect: by suspecting every process from which no message was received in the current round, each process suspects exactly every process that was down in this round.

Now suppose we want to implement in S a failure detector that satisfies Strong Completeness (and possibly *only* this property). In the following theorem, we show that any such implementation has undesirable behaviors: in some executions where *all* processes are good, some of them will eventually be suspected forever. Note that these mistakes are entirely due to the above requirement on *unstable* processes, not to the lack of synchrony.

Theorem 1. *Let $\mathcal{I}$ be any implementation of a failure detector that satisfies Strong Completeness in S. For every set of processes G of size at most n_u, there is a run of $\mathcal{I}$ in S such that (a) all processes are good, but (b) eventually all processes in G are permanently suspected by all processes in $\Pi \setminus G$.*

3.2 Failure Detectors with Epoch Numbers

Theorem 1 shows that if we require Strong Completeness then incorrect suspicions are inevitable even in synchronous systems. Although many algorithms are designed to tolerate such failure detector mistakes, the erroneous suspicions of some good processes may hurt the performance of these algorithms. For example, the erroneous suspicions of good coordinators can delay the termination of the consensus algorithms in [4, 5, 7, 9]. Thus, requiring Strong Completeness should be avoided if possible.

In this section, we propose a new type of failure detectors that are well-suited to the crash-recovery model: Although they do not require unstable processes to be eventually suspected forever, they do provide enough information to cope with unstable processes.

At each process p, the output of such a failure detector consists of two items, $\langle trustlist, epoch \rangle$, where *trustlist* is a set of processes and *epoch* is a vector of integers indexed by the elements of *trustlist*. Intuitively, $q \in trustlist$ if p believes that q is currently up, and $epoch[q]$ is p's rough estimate of how many times q crashed and recovered so far (it is called the *epoch number of q at p*). Let $H(p, t)$ denote the output of p's failure detector module at time t. If $q \in H(p, t).trustlist$, we say that p *trusts* q *at time t*, otherwise we say that p *suspects* q *at time t*.

We first define $\Diamond S_e$ to be the class of failure detectors $\mathcal{D}$ that satisfy the following properties (the formal definitions of these properties are given in [2]):

- *Monotonicity*: At every good process, eventually the epoch numbers are nondecreasing[7].
- *Completeness*: For every bad process b and for every good process g, either eventually g permanently suspects b or b's epoch number at g is unbounded.
- *Accuracy*: For some good process K and for every good process g, eventually g permanently trusts K and K's epoch number at g stops changing.

Note that $\Diamond S_e$ imposes requirements only on the failure detector modules of good processes. In particular, the accuracy property of $\Diamond S_e$ allows *unstable* processes to suspect all good processes. This is problematic because unstable processes can continue to take steps, and their incorrect suspicions may hinder the progress of some algorithms. Thus, we extend the accuracy property so that it also applies to unstable processes, as follows:

- *Strong Accuracy*: For some good process K: (a) for every good process g, eventually g permanently trusts K and K's epoch number at g stops changing; and (b) for every unstable process u, eventually whenever u is up, u trusts K and K's epoch number at u stops changing.

The class of failure detectors that satisfy Monotonicity, Completeness, and Strong Accuracy is denoted $\Diamond S_u$. For convenience, we sometimes use $\Diamond S_e$ or $\Diamond S_u$ to refer to an arbitrary member of the corresponding class.

$\Diamond S_e$ and $\Diamond S_u$ are closely related: In [2] we show that one can transform $\Diamond S_e$ into $\Diamond S_u$ provided that a majority of processes are good (this transformation does not require stable storage).

---

[7] We require the monotonicity of epoch numbers to hold only *eventually* and only at *good* processes so that the failure detector can be implemented *without* stable storage.

4   Consensus with Crash-Recovery

With consensus, each process proposes a value and processes must reach a unanimous decision on one of the proposed values. The following properties must be satisfied:
- *Uniform Validity*: If a process decides v then some process previously proposed v.
- *Agreement*: Good processes do not decide different values.
- *Termination*: If all good processes propose a value, then they all eventually decide.

A stronger version of consensus, called *uniform consensus* [8], requires:
- *Uniform Agreement*: Processes do not decide different values.

The above specification allows a process to decide more than once. However, with Agreement, a good process cannot decide two different values. Similarly, with Uniform Agreement, no process (whether good or bad) can decide two different values.

The algorithms that we provide solve uniform consensus, and the lower bounds that we prove hold even for consensus.

When processes have access to stable storage, a process proposes v, or decides v, by writing v into corresponding local stable storage locations. By checking these locations, a process that recovers from a crash can determine whether it previously proposed (or decided) a value.

When processes do not have access to stable storage, proposing and deciding v occur via an external input and output containing v, and so when a process recovers it cannot determine whether it has previously proposed or decided a value. Thus it is clear that if stable storage is not available and *all* processes may crash and recover, consensus cannot be solved. In many systems, however, it is reasonable to assume that in each execution of consensus there is a minimum number of processes that do not crash. In such systems, consensus *is* solvable without stable storage provided certain conditions are met, as we will see next.

5   On the Necessity of Stable Storage for Consensus

In this section, we determine some necessary conditions for solving consensus without stable storage. Consider a system in which at least n_a processes are always-up and at most n_b are bad. Our first result is that if $n_a \leq n_b$ then it is impossible to solve consensus without stable storage, even in systems where there are no unstable processes, links are reliable, and processes can use an *eventually perfect failure detector* $\Diamond \mathcal{P}$. Informally, for the crash-recovery model, $\Diamond \mathcal{P}$ outputs a tag $\in \{AU, EU, UN, ED\}$ for each process such that:
- There is a time after which at each process the tag of every process p is AU, EU, UN, or ED iff p is always-up, eventually-up, unstable, or eventually-down, respectively.

Note that $\Diamond \mathcal{P}$ is stronger than the other failure detectors in this paper and in [9, 7].

Theorem 2. *If $n_a \leq n_b$ consensus cannot be solved without stable storage even in systems where there are no unstable processes, links do not lose messages, and processes can use $\Diamond \mathcal{P}$.*

This result is tight in the sense that if $n_a > n_b$ then we *can* solve consensus without stable storage using a failure detector that is weaker than $\Diamond \mathcal{P}$ (see Section 6).

The impossibility result of Theorem 2 assumes that processes do not use any stable storage at all. Thus, if a process crashes it cannot "remember" its previous proposal and/or decision value. Suppose stable storage is available, but to minimize the cost of accessing it, we want to use it *only* for storing (and retrieving) the proposed and decision values. Is $n_a > n_b$ still necessary to solve consensus? It turns out that if $n_b > 2$, the answer is yes:

Theorem 3. *Suppose that each process can use stable storage only for storing and retrieving its proposed and decision values. If $n_a \leq n_b$ and $n_b > 2$ then consensus cannot be solved even in systems where there are no unstable processes, links do not lose messages, and processes can use $\diamond \mathcal{P}$.*

6 Solving Consensus without Stable Storage

It turns out that if $n_a > n_b$, consensus can be solved without stable storage using $\diamond \mathcal{S}_e$. This is somewhat surprising since $n_a > n_b$ allows a majority of processes to crash (and thus lose all their states). Note that the requirement of $n_a > n_b$ is "tight": in the previous section, we proved that if $n_a \leq n_b$ consensus cannot be solved without stable storage even with $\diamond \mathcal{P}$, a failure detector that is stronger than $\diamond \mathcal{S}_e$.

The consensus algorithm that uses $\diamond \mathcal{S}_e$ is given in [2]. In this paper, we present a more efficient algorithm that uses a minor variant of $\diamond \mathcal{S}_e$, denoted $\diamond \mathcal{S}'_e$. The only difference between $\diamond \mathcal{S}_e$ and $\diamond \mathcal{S}'_e$ is that while the accuracy property of $\diamond \mathcal{S}_e$ requires that K be a *good* process (see Section 3.2), the accuracy property of $\diamond \mathcal{S}'_e$ additionally requires that K be an *always-up* process if such a process exists. It is worth noting that the implementation of $\diamond \mathcal{S}_e$ in [2] also implements $\diamond \mathcal{S}'_e$.

The consensus algorithm that we give here always satisfies the Uniform Agreement and Validity properties of uniform consensus for any choice of n_a and n_b, and if $n_a > n_b$ then it also satisfies the Termination property.

This algorithm, shown in Fig. 1, is based on the rotating coordinator paradigm [4] and uses $\diamond \mathcal{S}'_e$. It must deal with unstable processes and link failures. More importantly, since more than half of the processes may crash and completely lose their states, and then recover, it must use new mechanisms to ensure the "locking" of the decision value (so that successive coordinators do not decide differently).[8] We first explain how the algorithm deals with unstable processes and link failures, and then describe the algorithm and the new mechanisms for locking the decision value.

How does a rotating coordinator algorithm cope with an unstable coordinator? In [7,9] the burden is entirely on the failure detector: it is postulated that every unstable process is eventually suspected forever. In our algorithm, the failure detector is not required to suspect unstable processes: they can be trusted as long as their epoch number increases from time to time — a requirement that is easy to enforce. If the epoch number of the current coordinator increases at a process, this process simply abandons this coordinator and goes to another one.

To deal with the message loss problem, each process p has a task *retransmit* that periodically retransmits the last message sent to each process (only the last message really matters, just as in [5–7]). This task is terminated once p decides.

We now describe the algorithm in more detail. When a process recovers from a crash, it stops participating in the algorithm, except that it periodically broadcasts a RECOVERED message until it receives the decision value. When a process p receives a RECOVERED message from q, it adds q to a set R_p of processes known to have recovered.

Processes proceed in asynchronous rounds, each one consisting of two stages. In the first stage, processes send a WAKEUP message to the coordinator c so that c can start

---

[8] The standard technique for locking a value is to ensure that a majority of processes "adopt" that value. This will not work here: a majority of processes may crash and recover, and so *all* the processes that adopted a value may later forget the value they adopted.

For process p:

1   **Initialization:**
2      $R_p \leftarrow \emptyset$; $decisionvalue_p \leftarrow \bot$; for all $q \in \Pi \setminus \{p\}$ do $xmitmsg[q] \leftarrow \bot$

3   **To s-send m to q:**
4   if $q \neq p$ then $xmitmsg[q] \leftarrow m$; send m to q else simulate receive m from p

5   **Task** *retransmit*:
6   **repeat forever**
7   for all $q \in \Pi \setminus \{p\}$ do if $xmitmsg[q] \neq \bot$ then send $xmitmsg[q]$ to q

8   **upon receive** m from q **do**
9   If m = RECOVERED then $R_p \leftarrow R_p \cup \{q\}$
10   If m = ($decisionvalue$, DECIDE) and $decisionvalue_p = \bot$ then
11       $decisionvalue_p \leftarrow decisionvalue$; decide($decisionvalue_p$)
12   terminate task $\{skip\_round, 4phases, participant, coordinator, retransmit\}$
13   If $m \neq (-, \text{DECIDE})$ and $decisionvalue_p \neq \bot$ then send ($decisionvalue_p$, DECIDE) to q

14   **upon** propose(v_p): $\{p$ proposes v_p via an external input containing $v_p\}$
15      $(r_p, estimate_p, ts_p) \leftarrow (1, v_p, 0)$; fork task $\{4phases, retransmit\}$

16   **Task** *4phases*:
17      $c_p \leftarrow (r_p \bmod n) + 1$; fork task $\{skip\_round, participant\}$
18   If $p = c_p$ then fork task *coordinator*

19 **Task** *coordinator*:
20    $\{$Stage 1: Phase NEWROUND$\}$
21    $c\_seq_p \leftarrow 0$
22   **repeat**
23      $PrevR_p \leftarrow R_p$; $c\_seq_p \leftarrow c\_seq_p + 1$
24   s-send $(r_p, c\_seq_p, \text{NEWROUND})$ to all
25   **wait until** [received $(r_p, c\_seq_p, estimate_q,$
26   ts_q, ESTIMATE) from
27        $\max(n_b + 1, n - n_b - |R_p|)$ processes]
28   **until** $R_p = PrevR_p$
29    $t \leftarrow$ largest ts_q such that p received
30      $(r_p, c\_seq_p, estimate_q, ts_q, \text{ESTIMATE})$
31    $estimate_p \leftarrow$ select one $estimate_q$ such that
32   p received $(r_p, c\_seq_p, estimate_q, t, \text{ESTIMATE})$
33    $ts_p \leftarrow r_p$
34    $\{$Stage 2: Phase NEWESTIMATE$\}$
35    $c\_seq_p \leftarrow 0$
36   **repeat**
37      $PrevR_p \leftarrow R_p$; $c\_seq_p \leftarrow c\_seq_p + 1$
38   s-send $(r_p, c\_seq_p, estimate_p,$
39   NEWESTIMATE) to all
40   **wait until** [received $(r_p, c\_seq_p, \text{ACK})$ from
41        $\max(n_b + 1, n - n_b - |R_p|)$ processes]
42   **until** $R_p = PrevR_p$
43   s-send $(estimate_p, \text{DECIDE})$ to all

44 **Task** *participant*:
45    $\{$Stage 1: Phase ESTIMATE$\}$
46   s-send (r_p, WAKEUP) to c_p
47    $max\_seq_p \leftarrow 0$
48   **repeat**
49   if received $(r_p, seq, \text{NEWROUND})$ from c_p
50   for some $seq > max\_seq_p$ then
51   s-send $(r_p, seq, estimate_p, ts_p,$
52   ESTIMATE) to c_p
53        $max\_seq_p \leftarrow seq$
54   **until** [received $(r_p, seq, estimate_{c_p},$
55   NEWESTIMATE) from c_p for some seq]
56   if $p \neq c_p$ then
57      $(estimate_p, ts_p) \leftarrow (estimate_{c_p}, r_p)$
58    $\{$Stage 2: Phase ACK$\}$
59    $max\_seq_p \leftarrow 0$
60   **repeat forever**
61   if received $(r_p, seq, estimate_{c_p},$
62   NEWESTIMATE) from c_p for some
63      $seq > max\_seq_p$ then
64   s-send (r_p, seq, ACK) to c_p
65        $max\_seq_p \leftarrow seq$

66 **Task** *skip_round*:
67    $d \leftarrow \mathcal{D}_p$ $\{$query $\diamond \mathcal{S}'_e\}$
68   If $c_p \in d.trustlist \setminus R_p$ then
69   **repeat** $d' \leftarrow \mathcal{D}_p$ $\{$query $\diamond \mathcal{S}'_c\}$
70   **until** [$c_p \notin d'.trustlist \setminus R_p$ or $d.epoch[c_p] < d'.epoch[c_p]$
71   or received some message $(r, \ldots)$ such that $r > r_p)$]
72   terminate task $\{4phases, participant, coordinator\}$ $\{$abort current round$\}$
73   **repeat** $d \leftarrow \mathcal{D}_p$ until $d.trustlist \setminus R_p \neq \emptyset$ $\{$query $\diamond \mathcal{S}'_e\}$
74    $r_p \leftarrow$ the smallest $r > r_p$ such that $[(r \bmod n) + 1] \in d.trustlist \setminus R_p$ and
75      $r \geq \max\{r' | p$ received $(r', \ldots)\}$
76   fork task *4phases* $\{$go to a higher round$\}$

77 **upon recovery:**
78    $decisionvalue_p \leftarrow \bot$; for all $q \in \Pi \setminus \{p\}$ do $xmitmsg[q] \leftarrow \bot$; fork task *retransmit*
79   s-send RECOVERED to all

Fig. 1. Solving Consensus without Stable Storage using $\diamond \mathcal{S}'_e$

the current round (if it has not done so yet). The coordinator c broadcasts a NEWROUND message to announce a new round, and each process sends its current estimate of the decision value — together with a timestamp indicating in which round it was obtained — to c. Then c waits for estimates from $\max(n_b + 1, n - n_b - |R_c|)$ processes — this is the maximum number of estimates that c can wait for without fear of blocking forever, because more than n_b processes are always-up and respond, and at most $n_b + |R_c|$ processes have crashed and do not respond. Then c checks whether during the collection of estimates it detected the recovery of a process that never recovered before ($R_c \neq PrevR_c$). If so, c restarts the first stage from scratch.[9] Otherwise, c chooses the estimate with the largest timestamp as its new estimate and proceeds to the second stage.

In the second stage, c broadcasts its new estimate; when a process receives this estimate, it changes its own estimate and sends an ACK to c. Process c waits for ACK messages from $\max(n_b + 1, n - n_b - |R_c|)$ processes. As before, c restarts this stage from scratch if during the collection of ACKs it detected the recovery of a process that never recovered before ($R_c \neq PrevR_c$). Finally c broadcasts its estimate as the decision value and decides accordingly. Once a process decides, it enters a passive state in which, upon receipt of a message, the process responds with the decision value.

A round r can be interrupted by task *skip_round* (which runs in parallel with tasks *coordinator* and *participant*): a process p aborts its execution of round r if (1) it suspects the coordinator c of round r, or (2) it trusts c but detects an increase in the epoch number of c, or (3) it detects a recovery of c, or (4) it receives a message from a round $r' > r$. When p aborts round r, it jumps to the lowest round $r' > r$ such that (1) p trusts the coordinator c' of round r', (2) p has not detected a recovery of c' ($c' \notin R_p$) and (3) p has not (yet) received any message with a round number higher than r'.

The code in lines 31–33 is executed atomically, i.e., it cannot be interrupted, except by a crash. As an obvious optimization, the coordinator of round 1 can skip phase NEW-ROUND and simply set its estimate to its own proposed value. We omit this optimization from the code.

The correctness of the algorithm relies on the following crucial property: if the coordinator sends a decision for v in some round, then value v has previously been "locked", i.e., in any later round, a coordinator can only choose v as its new estimate. This property is ensured by two mechanisms: (1) the coordinator uses $\max(n_b + 1, n - n_b - |R_p|)$ as a threshold to collect estimates and ACKs, and (2) the coordinator restarts the collection of estimates and ACKs from scratch if it detects a new recovery ($R_c \neq PrevR_c$).

The importance of mechanism (2) is illustrated in Fig. 2: it shows a bad scenario (a violation of the crucial property above) that could occur if this mechanism is omitted. The system consists of four processes $\{c, p, p', c'\}$. Assume that $n_b = 1$ and there are at least $n_a = 2$ processes that are always up. At point A, the coordinator c of round r sends its estimate 0 to all, and at B, it receives ACKs from itself and p. At F, p' recovers from a crash and sends a RECOVERED message to all. At G, c has received one RECOVERED message from p' (so $|R_c| = 1$) and two ACKs. Since $\max(n_b + 1, n - n_b - |R_c|) = 2$, c completes its collection of ACKs (this is the maximum number of ACKs that c can wait for without fear of blocking), and c sends a decision for 0 to all in round r. Meanwhile, at C, p recovers from a crash and sends a RECOVERED message to all, and c' receives this message before D. At D, c' becomes the coordinator of round $r' > r$ and sends a NEWROUND message to all. At E, c' has received two estimates for 1, one from

---

[9] An obvious optimization is for c to check *during the collection of estimates* whether $R_c \neq PrevR_c$. If so it can restart the first stage right away.

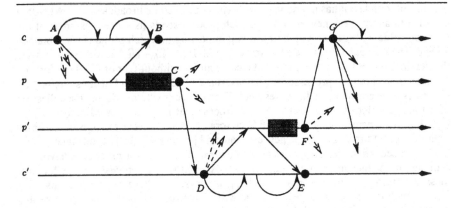

Remarks:
- c is the coordinator in round r; c' is the coordinator in round $r' > r$
- A: c sends $(r, 0, \text{NEWESTIMATE})$ to all
- B: c received (r, ACK) from c and p
- C: p sends RECOVERED to all
- D: c' sends $(r', \text{NEWROUND})$ to all
- E: c' received $(r', 1, ts, \text{ESTIMATE})$ from c' and p', and c' selects 1 as the new estimate
- F: p' sends RECOVERED to all
- G: c sends $(0, \text{DECIDE})$ to all

Legend:

——————▶   - - - - - -▷   ——————▬▬▬————▶

message sent and received   message sent but delayed for a long time   process is down

Fig. 2. A bad scenario that can occur if mechanism (2) is not used.

itself and one from p'. Since it has also received one RECOVERED message from p, c' completes its collection of estimates, and chooses 1 as its new estimate for round r' — even though c sends a decision for 0 in an earlier round.

The proof of the algorithm shows that mechanism (2) prevents this and other similar bad scenarios. In this example, if c had used mechanism (2), then at G it would have restarted the collection of ACKs from scratch because $PrevR_c = \emptyset \neq \{p'\} = R_c$.[10]

Theorem 4. *The algorithm of Fig. 1 satisfies the Uniform Validity and Uniform Agreement properties of uniform consensus. If at most n_b processes are bad, and more than n_b processes are always up, then it also satisfies the Termination property.*

7 Solving Consensus with Stable Storage

We now present a consensus algorithm that uses stable storage and $\Diamond S_u$. It requires a majority of good processes and works in systems with lossy links.

The basic structure of the algorithm (given in Fig. 3) is as in [4,5] and consists of rounds of 4 phases each (task *4phases*). In each round r, initially the coordinator c

---

[10] It is not sufficient to use the restarting mechanism only for collecting ACKs: a symmetric example shows that this mechanism must also be used for collecting estimates.

For every process p:

1 **Initialization:**
2   **for all** $q \in \Pi \setminus \{p\}$ **do** $xmitmsg[q] \leftarrow \perp$
3 **To s-send** m **to** q:
4   **if** $q \neq p$ **then** $xmitmsg[q] \leftarrow m$; send m to q **else** simulate receive m from p
5 **Task** *retransmit*:
6   **repeat forever**
7   **for all** $q \in \Pi \setminus \{p\}$ **do if** $xmitmsg[q] \neq \perp$ **then** send $xmitmsg[q]$ to q
8 **upon propose**(v_p):   {p proposes v_p, by writing it into stable storage}
9    $(r_p, estimate_p, ts_p) \leftarrow (1, v_p, 0)$
10   **fork task** {*4phases, retransmit*}
11 **Task** *4phases*:
12   **store** $\{r_p\}$; $c_p \leftarrow (r_p \bmod n) + 1$; **fork task** {*skip_round, participant*}
13   **if** $p = c_p$ **then fork task** *coordinator*

14 **Task** *coordinator*:
15   {Phase NEWROUND}
16   **if** $ts_p \neq r_p$ **then**
17   s-send $(r_p, \text{NEWROUND})$ to all
18   **wait until** [received $(r_p, estimate_q, ts_q,$
19   ESTIMATE) from $\lceil (n+1)/2 \rceil$ processes]
20     $t \leftarrow$ largest ts_q such that p received
21     $(r_p, estimate_q, ts_q, \text{ESTIMATE})$
22     $estimate_p \leftarrow$ select one $estimate_q$ such that
23   p received $(r_p, estimate_q, t, \text{ESTIMATE})$
24     $ts_p \leftarrow r_p$
25   **store** $\{estimate_p, ts_p\}$
26   {Phase NEWESTIMATE}
27   s-send $(r_p, estimate_p, \text{NEWESTIMATE})$ to all
28   **wait until** [received (r_p, ACK) from
29   $\lceil (n+1)/2 \rceil$ processes]
30   s-send $(estimate_p, \text{DECIDE})$ to all

31 **Task** *participant*:
32   {Phase ESTIMATE}
33   **if** $ts_p \neq r_p$ **then**
34   s-send $(r_p, estimate_p, ts_p, \text{ESTIMATE})$ to c_p
35   **wait until** [received $(r_p, estimate_{c_p},$
36   NEWESTIMATE) from c_p]
37   **if** $p \neq c_p$ **then**
38     $(estimate_p, ts_p) \leftarrow (estimate_{c_p}, r_p)$
39   **store** $\{estimate_p, ts_p\}$
40   {Phase ACK}
41   s-send (r_p, ACK) to c_p

42 **Task** *skip_round*:
43   $d \leftarrow \mathcal{D}_p$ {query $\Diamond \mathcal{S}_u$}
44   **if** $c_p \in d.trustlist$ **then**
45   **repeat** $d' \leftarrow \mathcal{D}_p$ {query $\Diamond \mathcal{S}_u$}
46   **until** [$c_p \notin d'.trustlist$ or $d.epoch[c_p] < d'.epoch[c_p]$
47   or received some message $(r, \ldots)$ such that $r > r_p$]
48   **terminate task** {*4phases, participant, coordinator*}   {abort current round}
49   **repeat** $d \leftarrow \mathcal{D}_p$ **until** $d.trustlist \neq \emptyset$ {query $\Diamond \mathcal{S}_u$ to go to a higher round}
50   $r_p \leftarrow$ the smallest $r > r_p$ such that $[(r \bmod n) + 1] \in d.trustlist$ and $r \geq \max\{r' | p \text{ received } (r', \ldots)\}$
51   **fork task** *4phases*

52 **upon receive** m from q **do**
53   **if** $m = (estimate, \text{DECIDE})$ and decide$(-)$ has not occurred **then**   {check stable storage about decide}
54   decide$(estimate)$ {decide is logged into stable storage}
55   **terminate task** {*skip_round, 4phases, participant, coordinator, retransmit*}
56   **if** $m \neq (-, \text{DECIDE})$ and decide$(estimate)$ has occurred **then**   {check stable storage about decide}
57   send $(estimate, \text{DECIDE})$ to q
58 **upon recovery:**
59   **for all** $q \in \Pi \setminus \{p\}$ **do** $xmitmsg[q] \leftarrow \perp$
60   **if** propose(v_p) has occurred **and**   {check stable storage about propose}
61   decide$(-)$ has not occurred **then**   {check stable storage about decide}
62   retrieve $\{r_p, estimate_p, ts_p\}$
63   **if** $r_p = \perp$ **then** $r_p \leftarrow 1$; **if** $estimate_p = \perp$ **then** $(estimate_p, ts_p) \leftarrow (v_p, 0)$
64   **fork task** {*4phases, retransmit*}

Fig. 3. Solving Consensus with Stable Storage using $\Diamond \mathcal{S}_u$

broadcasts a NEWROUND message to announce a new round, and each process sends its current estimate of the decision value — together with a timestamp indicating in which round it was obtained — to c; c waits until it obtains estimates from a majority of processes; it selects one with the largest timestamp and sends it to all processes; every process that receives this new estimate updates its estimate and timestamp accordingly, and sends an acknowledgement to c; when c receives this acknowledgement from a majority of processes, it sends its estimate as the decision to all processes and then it decides. Once a process decides, it stops tasks *4phases* and *retransmit*, and enters a passive state in which, upon receipt of a message, the process responds with the decision value.

A round r can be interrupted by task *skip_round* (which runs in parallel with tasks *coordinator* and *participant*): a process p aborts its execution of round r if (1) it suspects the coordinator c of round r, or (2) it trusts c but detects an increase in the epoch number of c, or (3) it receives a message from a round $r' > r$. When p aborts round r, it jumps to the lowest round $r' > r$ such that p trusts the coordinator of round r' and p has not (yet) received any message with a round number higher than r'.

In each round, a process p accesses the stable storage twice: first to store the current round number, and later to store the new estimate and its corresponding timestamp. Upon recovery, p reads the stable storage to restore its round number, estimate, and timestamp, and then restarts task *4phases* with these values.

Note that in round 1, the coordinator c can simply set its estimate to its *own* proposed value and skip the phase used to select a new estimate (Phase NEWROUND). It is also easy to see that the coordinator does not have to store its round number in stable storage in this case. We omit these obvious optimizations from the code.

The following regions of code are executed atomically: lines 22–25 and 38–39.

Theorem 5. *The algorithm of Fig. 3 satisfies the Uniform Validity and Uniform Agreement properties of uniform consensus. If a majority of processes are good then it also satisfies the Termination property.*

8 Performance of the Consensus Algorithms

8.1 Time and Message Complexity in Nice Runs

In most executions of consensus in practice, no process crashes or recovers, no message is lost, the failure detector does not make mistakes, and message delay is bounded by some known δ (including the message processing times). In such "nice" executions, our two algorithms (with and without stable storage) achieve consensus within 3δ:[11] it takes one δ for the coordinator to broadcast NEWESTIMATE messages, one δ for processes to respond with ACKs, and another δ for the coordinator to broadcast DECIDE messages. By adding appropriate delays in the *retransmit* task, so that a message is retransmitted only 2δ time units after it is sent, processes send a total of $4(n-1)$ messages: in the first algorithm, there are $n-1$ messages for each of the types ESTIMATE, NEWESTIMATE, ACK, and DECIDE; in the second algorithm, there are $n-1$ messages for each of WAKEUP, NEWESTIMATE, ACK, and DECIDE. In contrast, in nice executions the consensus algorithms of [7, 9] reach decision within 2δ and with $O(n^2)$ messages.

---

[11] This is with the round 1 optimization in which the coordinator chooses its own estimate and sends it without waiting for estimates from other processes.

8.2 Quiescence

An algorithm is *quiescent* if eventually all processes stop sending messages [1]. It is clear that no consensus algorithm can be quiescent in the presence of unstable processes (each time such a process recovers, it must be sent the decision value, at which point it may crash again and lose this message; this scenario can be repeated infinitely often). If no process is unstable, our consensus algorithms are quiescent despite process crashes and message losses (provided all good processes propose a value).

Remark The full version of this paper [2] contains the following additional material: a consensus algorithm that does not require stable storage and uses $\Diamond S_e$ (rather than $\Diamond S_e'$), an implementation of $\Diamond S_e$ and $\Diamond S_e'$ in some models of partial synchrony, an algorithm that transforms $\Diamond S_e$ into $\Diamond S_u$, a discussion on how to do repeated consensus, the formal definition of the failure detector properties, and all the proofs.

Acknowlegments We would like to thank Rachid Guerraoui, Michel Raynal and André Schiper for introducing us to the problem of consensus in the crash-recovery model, and for explaining their own work on this problem. We would also like to thank Borislav Deianov for his helpful comments on an earlier draft.

References

1. M. K. Aguilera, W. Chen, and S. Toueg. Heartbeat: a timeout-free failure detector for quiescent reliable communication. In *Proceedings of the 11th International Workshop on Distributed Algorithms*, Lecture Notes on Computer Science. Springer-Verlag, Sept. 1997. A full version is also available as Technical Report 97-1631, Computer Science Department, Cornell University, Ithaca, New York, May 1997.

2. M. K. Aguilera, W. Chen, and S. Toueg. Failure detection and consensus in the crash-recovery model. Technical Report 98-1676, Department of Computer Science, Cornell University, April 1998.

3. T. D. Chandra, V. Hadzilacos, and S. Toueg. The weakest failure detector for solving consensus. *Journal of the ACM*, 43(4):685–722, July 1996.

4. T. D. Chandra and S. Toueg. Unreliable failure detectors for reliable distributed systems. *Journal of the ACM*, 43(2):225–267, March 1996.

5. D. Dolev, R. Friedman, I. Keidar, and D. Malkhi. Failure detectors in omission failure environments. Technical Report 96-1608, Department of Computer Science, Cornell University, Ithaca, New York, Sept. 1996.

6. R. Guerraoui, R. Oliveira, and A. Schiper. Stubborn communication channels. Technical report, Département d'Informatique, Ecole Polytechnique Fédérale, Lausanne, Switzerland, Dec. 1996.

7. M. Hurfin, A. Mostefaoui, and M. Raynal. Consensus in asynchronous systems where processes can crash and recover. Technical Report 1144, Institut de Recherche en Informatique et Systèmes Aléatoires, Université de Rennes, Nov. 1997.

8. G. Neiger and S. Toueg. Automatically increasing the fault-tolerance of distributed algorithms. *Journal of Algorithms*, 11(3):374–419, 1990.

9. R. Oliveira, R. Guerraoui, and A. Schiper. Consensus in the crash-recover model. Technical Report 97-239, Département d'Informatique, Ecole Polytechnique Fédérale, Lausanne, Switzerland, Aug. 1997.

A More Committed Quorum-Based Three Phase Commit Protocol

Tim Kempster*, Colin Stirling and Peter Thanisch

Department of Computer Science,
University of Edinburgh,
Edinburgh EH9 3JZ, Scotland,
email: {tdk,cps,pt}@dcs.ed.ac.uk

Abstract. In the original quorum-based three phase commit (Q3PC) protocol, a quorum of sites may form after failure, yet those sites remain blocked. Recently, Keidar and Dolev introduced the Enhanced 3PC (E3PC) protocol, in which a quorum never blocks. However E3PC tends to decide to abort transactions in many of those quorate failure sequences where Q3PC would block. We use the concept of "views" to analyse protocols. This allows us to construct an improved version of E3PC which can make progress towards committing a transaction during recovery in circumstances where E3PC would abort. Our new protocol shares with E3PC the property that a quorum never blocks.

1 Introduction

As computing equipment is getting increasingly reliable, distributed transaction processing environments e.g. mobile computing, Internet commerce and replication, are becoming increasingly unreliable. At the same time, the notion of a transaction is gaining wider currency, as it is now recognised that in unreliable distributed environments, transaction semantics simplify the programmer's task of ensuring the atomicity of a set of actions. These computing trends have created fresh challenges to the designers of atomic commit protocols.

A protocol solves Atomic Commit if in all possible runs the following hold.

- **AC1** No two sites that decide, do so differently.
- **AC2** A site cannot reverse its decision once it has reached one.
- **AC3** If any site decides commit then all sites voted yes.
- **AC4** If all participants vote yes and no failures occur, then the decision will be commit.
- **AC5** At any point in the execution of the protocol, if all existing failures are repaired and no new failures occur for sufficiently long then all sites will reach a decision.

---

* This research was supported by EPSRC grant GR/L74798.

In the *two-phase commit* (2PC) protocol, a coordinator collects votes on whether or not participants can commit a transaction and broadcasts whether or not there is unanimity for commit (i.e. make the changes durable). Problems arise with 2PC when site and/or network failures occur. Some working sites may become 'blocked': they want to commit the transaction, but they are unable to proceed until a failure at another site has been repaired. The blocked site must hold resources on behalf of the stalled transaction, preventing other transactions from proceeding. Skeen [6] recognised this problem and developed a *quorum-based, three-phase commit* (Q3PC) protocol. If a single network failure occurs leaving a quorum of sites, Q3PC ensures they will not block.

In Q3PC, it is possible that, after cascading network failures, a quorum of sites may form, yet those sites remain blocked. However the Enhanced 3PC (E3PC) protocol [5] uses two counters ensures that a quorum never blocks. One drawback of E3PC is that it tends to abort transactions in many of those failure sequences where it can proceed, yet Q3PC would block. We describe a framework in which to reason about these protocols and then derive an improved version of E3PC called X3PC in which a coordinator can use the distributed knowledge within a quorum to detect situations where it is possible to make progress towards committing a transaction. Like E3PC, in X3PC a connected quorum of sites never blocks, but X3PC will decide commit more often than E3PC and in no more attempts. E3PC, Q3PC and X3PC all have the same message-passing pattern, but differ in the amount of state information that is exchanged in a message.

2 The Model of Distributed Computation

In our model of distributed computation there is a set of n processes $\mathcal{P} = \{p_1, \ldots, p_n\}$; each process independently takes steps. A step consists of reading a message, changing state (depending on messages read, current state, and any failures detected) and then sending possibly many messages. By writing current state to stable storage before sending messages a process can ensure a step is atomic even if site failure occurs.

After a coordinator has been elected, messages are always exchanged between a coordinator and its participant. Whenever a participant (coordinator) changes state it sends a message to its coordinator (participants) reporting this state change.

Each process has a *view* of the internal state of a remote process. This view is constructed from information it receives from the remote processes in the form of messages. We say,

$$q.s = \lhd \mathbf{x}$$

holds at process p if the most up to date [1] message p received from q informed p that q *was* in state $\mathbf{x}$. Message passing is asynchronous and messages may

---

[1] Message sequence numbers allow a receiving process to determine if a message is stale

be lost during network failure. Each site detects failure using a *perfect failure detector* [2] [1]. It is important to note that if q is in state **x** (which we write as $q.s = $ **x**) then this does not imply that at q's coordinator $q.s = \lhd$**x** will ever hold as the message although sent by q reporting this state change may be lost.

Fig. 1 describes the complete state held at each process p. This includes its external state, e.g. $p.s = $ **c** means p is commited. We utilize the two counters le and la of [5]: $p.le = m$ means that p's last elected counter is m. Our extension of E3PC employs a new component $p.h$ which captures the history of those attempts to move to the pre-abort (**pa**) state: its details are discussed later. Processes have views about the state of other processes. This includes the external state, for p, $q.s = \lhd$**pc** means that p believes q is in state **pc**. For p, $q.la = \lhd m$ means that p believes q's last attempt counter is m.

We say $q.s = \underline{\lhd}$**x** holds at p if $q.s = \lhd$**x** $\wedge$ $q.le = \lhd p.le$ $\wedge$ $q.c = \lhd p.c$ hold at p and $q.s = *$**x** holds at p if $q.s = \underline{\lhd}$**x** $\wedge$ $q.la = \lhd p.la$ hold at p. A view can be updated locally in the same way local process state is updated. Updates to views change local state but do not produce messages. A process always has an up to date view of its own state so $p.s = $ **x** implies that $p.s = \lhd$**x** holds at p. All messages sent are stamped with the senders id, the last elected and last attempt counters and the current senders coordinator and may contain other state information.

$p.s \in \{$**pa, pc, q, w, a, c**$\}$	The external state of a process
$p.c \in \mathcal{P}$	the coordinator according to process p
$p.le$	$p's$ last elected counter
$p.la$	$p's$ last attempt counter
$p.r \in \{true, false\}$	Has p entered the recovery phase?
$p.i \in \{yes, no\}$	$p's$ voting intention
$p.f \in \{true, false\}$	Coordinator is collecting, participants' state
$p.h$	history of attempts to move to **pa**

Figure 1. **a**, **c**, represent the abort and commit decision states. **q** is the initial state before a process has voted, **w** is entered after a yes vote. **pc** and **pa** are entered during attempts to commit and abort respectively.

We model a communication network which may fail and divide $\mathcal{P}$ arbitrarily using the equivalence classes Par, which satisfy

- $Par(p) = \{q \in \mathcal{P} \mid q \text{ can communicate with } p\}$
- $\forall p \in \mathcal{P}, p \in Par(p)$
- $\forall p \in \mathcal{P}, \text{ if } p \in Par(q) \text{ then } Par(p) = Par(q)$

It follows from this definition that if $p \notin Par(q)$ then $Par(p) \cap Par(q) = \varnothing$.

In our notation the E3PC predicate *isMaxAttemptCommitable IMAC(P)* over $P \subseteq Par(p)$ is true at coordinator p where $ma = max\{m \mid \exists r \in P, r.la = $

$\preceq m\}$ if

$$\forall q \in \mathcal{P}, \ q.la = \preceq ma \Rightarrow q.s = \preceq \mathbf{pc}$$

I.e., p believes no member of P with the greatest last attempt number is in a state other than **pc**.

The protocols we consider make use of *quorums*. A quorum is a predicate Q over subsets of $\mathcal{P}$ which has the property

$$\forall P, P' \subseteq \mathcal{P} \ if \ Q(P) \wedge Q(P') \ then \ P \cap P' \neq \oslash$$

The simplest quorum is $Q(P')$ if P' is a *majority* of sites.

Par may change at any time, modelling a network failure. All sites affected elect coordinators in each new component. During the election a coordinator can compute the maximum *last elected* counter *me*, within the group. When a participant adopts a new coordinator it updates its *last elected* counter to be $me + 1$ and begins the protocol's recovery phase, sending its internal state to the coordinator. Once c has been elected within a group:

$$c.f := true \ \wedge \ \forall p \in Par(c), \ p.r := true \ \wedge \ p.le := me + 1 \ \wedge \ p.c := c$$

We can assume this event is atomic. If it is interrupted by another network event the leadership election can be restarted [3]. A *configuration* $\mathcal{C}$ is the collection of processes with their internal state together with *Par*.

$$\mathcal{C} = (p_1, \ldots, p_n, Par)$$

A *run* of our protocol is a sequence of configurations $\mathcal{C}_1, \ldots, \mathcal{C}_m, \ldots$ where $\mathcal{C}_{i+1}$ is derived from $\mathcal{C}_i$ by a protocol step or a network event. A *decided* process is one with external state c or a. A deciding configuration has a quorum of decided processes and a deciding run is one which contains a decided configuration. Each protocol step takes the form of a Precondition followed by a Post-action. If the precondition holds then the post-action may happen.

3 E3PC in our Notation

Initially all processes p start in the q state with $\neg p.f$ and their last attempt and last elected counters set to 0 and 1 respectively. All processes are connected and there exists a process which is the coordinator for all processes. We do not constrain the initial voting intention $p.i$. More formally

$$(\forall p, \ p.s = q \wedge p.la = 0 \wedge p.le = 1 \wedge \neg p.f \wedge \neg p.r) \wedge (\exists p' \in \mathcal{P}, \ \forall p \in \mathcal{P}, \ p.c = p')$$

3.1 Steps in the Protocol

The protocol is divided into two phases. The initial phase before any failures are detected, where $\forall p \in \mathcal{P}, \ \neg p.r$ holds and the recovery phase where $\exists p \in \mathcal{P}, \ p.r$ holds. The steps can further be divided into those taken by the coordinator, $p.c = p$, and those taken by a participant, $p.c \neq p$.

A step is applicable to a process if the pre-condition for that step is satisfied at that process. The initial phase of E3PC is described in Figure 2 and the recovery phase in Figure 3.

$\neg p.r \wedge p.c \neq p$	$\neg p.r \wedge p.c = p$
PVY-NR Participant Votes Yes **PRE:** $p.s = q \wedge p.i = yes \wedge p.s \neq w$ **POST:** $p.s := w$	**CPC-NR** Coordinator enters **pc** **PRE:** $p.s = q \wedge p.i = yes \wedge$ $\forall q \neq p,\ q.s = \trianglelefteq w \wedge p.s \neq pc$ **POST:** $p.s := pc \wedge p.la := p.le$
PVN-NR Participant Votes No **PRE:** $p.s = q \wedge p.i = no \wedge p.s \neq a$ **POST:** $p.s := a$	
PPC-NR Participant enters **pc** **PRE:** $p.s \neq pc \wedge (p.c).s = \trianglelefteq pc$ **POST:** $p.s := pc$	
PC-NR Participant decides c **PRE:** $(p.c).s = \trianglelefteq c \wedge p.s \neq c$ **POST:** $p.s := c$	**PPC-NR** Coordinator decides c **PRE:** $p.s = pc \wedge \forall q \neq p,\ q.s = \trianglelefteq pc$ **POST:** $p.s := c$
PA-NR Participant decides a **PRE:** $(p.c).s = \trianglelefteq a \wedge p.s \neq a$ **POST:** $p.s := a$	**CA-NR** Coordinator decides a **PRE:** $p.s = q \wedge$ $(\exists q \neq p,\ q.s = \trianglelefteq a \vee p.i = no)$ **POST:** $p.s := a$

Figure 2. The initial phase of E3PC

3.2 Q3PC: Skeen's Quorum-based 3PC

Using our notation for representing E3PC as a starting point, we can obtain a representation of Q3PC by changing the pre-condition of **CPC-R** and **CPA-R**:

CPC-R PRE: $p.f \wedge \exists q,\ q.s = \trianglelefteq pc \wedge Q(\{r \in Par(p) \mid r.s = \trianglelefteq pc \vee r.s = \trianglelefteq w\})$

CPA-R PRE: $p.f \wedge Q(\{r \in Par(p) \mid r.s = \trianglelefteq pa \vee r.s = \trianglelefteq w\})$

This introduces the possibility of blocking even if a quorum of sites are in the recovery phase, provided cascading failures occur. See the example below.

3.3 The Advantage of E3PC over Q3PC

Example 3.1. See [5], three sites, p_1, p_2 and p_3, initially all connected, carry out E3PC. All sites vote yes and the first coordinator moves to **pc**. A network partition causes p_2 and p_3 to become isolated. They are both in state **w**, and form a quorum. The second coordinator p_2 starts to move to **pa**, updating its last attempt counter. Another network event occurs and now p_2, rejoins p_1. Q3PC would now block, but E3PC can abort. We note that it would have been safe to commit rather than abort in this case, because there is enough information for the coordinator in the last attempt to know the second attempt was unsuccessful and so view p_2's **pa** state as its previous state **w**. This motivates the development of our new protocol.

$p.r \wedge p.c \neq p$	$p.r \wedge p.c = p$
	CCC-R Coordinator propagates c **PRE:** $p.f \wedge \exists q \in Par(p), q.s = \unlhd c$ **POST:** $p.s := c \wedge p.f := false$
	CCA-R Coordinator propagates a **PRE:** $p.f \wedge \exists q \in Par(p), q.s = \unlhd a$ **POST:** $p.s := a \wedge p.f := false$
PPC-R Participant enters pc **PRE:** $(p.c).s = \unlhd pc \wedge p.s \neq pc \wedge$ $(p.c).f = \unlhd false$ **POST:** $p.la := p.le \wedge p.s := pc$	**CPC-R** Coordinator enters pc **PRE:** $p.f \wedge Q(Par(p)) \wedge$ $IMAC(Par(p))$ **POST:** $p.la := p.le \wedge p.s := pc \wedge$ $p.f := false$
PPA-R Participant enters pa **PRE:** $(p.c).s = \unlhd pa \wedge p.s \neq pa \wedge$ $(p.c).f = \unlhd false$ **POST:** $p.la := p.le \wedge p.s := pa$	**CPA-R** Coordinator enters pa **PRE:** $p.f \wedge Q(Par(p)) \wedge$ $\neg IMAC(Par(p))$ **POST:** $p.la := p.le \wedge p.s := pa \wedge$ $p.f := false$
PC-R Participant decides c **PRE:** $(p.c).s = \unlhd c \wedge p.s \neq c$ **POST:** $p.s := c$	**CC-R** Coordinator decides c **PRE:** $\neg p.f \wedge \exists P \subseteq Par(p), Q(P) \wedge$ $(\forall q \in P, q.s = *pc)$ **POST:** $p.s := c$
PA-R Participant decides a **PRE:** $(p.c).s = \unlhd a \wedge p.s \neq a$ **POST:** $p.s := a$	**CA-R** Coordinator decides a **PRE:** $\neg p.f \wedge \exists P \subseteq Par(p), (Q(P) \wedge$ $(\forall q \in P, q.s = *pa)$ **POST:** $p.s := a$

Figure 3. The recovery phase of E3PC

4 Constructing X3PC from E3PC

To derive X3PC from E3PC we change the rule **CPC-R** and add an extra
rule, **CUV-R**, which updates a coordinator's views during the recovery phase
of the protocol. The update view rule allows a coordinator to determine if a
participant's earlier attempt to abort did not result in any site moving to a.
The coordinator might be able to reach this conclusion in two ways. First, if a
site, p, is in state **pa**, with $p.la = i$, and the coordinator, c, for attempt i is also
involved in the current attempt and $c.s \neq$ a [2], then p knows that in attempt
i, no site decided a. We can then view the state and last attempt counter of p
as the value it took prior to attempt i. Secondly, if enough sites in the current
attempt were involved in attempt i, but did not move to **pa** in attempt i then
the coordinator may be able to deduce that a quorum of sites did not move to
pa in attempt i, so the coordinator for attempt i could not have moved to a.

---

[2] In fact if $p.s =$ a then rule **CCA-R** would take precedence over **CPC-R**

We weaken the pre-condition of **CPC-R**: we only require $IMAC$ to hold over a quorate *subset* of $Par(p)$. The new pre-condition is:

PRE: $p.f \land \exists P \subseteq Par(p), Q(P) \land IMAC(P)$

For a coordinator to reason in this way it must acquire extra information from each site at the start of an attempt. Each site keeps a history h. A site updates h when it enters the **pa** state. This history is indexed by last attempt number and contains all of the sites involved in that attempt, $h[i].involved$, the coordinator of the attempt, $h[i].c$ and the process' previous state and last attempt counter before the transition to **pa**, $h[i].s_{prev}$, $h[i].la_{prev}$. When collecting the states of the participating sites a coordinator collects this history from each participant. Initially, at p $\forall i$, $p.h[i] = \oslash$. When a coordinator makes a transition to **pa**, it includes the list of participating sites in the message it sends to each participant: they use this to update their histories.

CUV-R is defined for coordinator p using the notation $m = max\{t \mid \exists r \in Par(p), r.la = \trianglelefteq t \land r.s \neq \trianglelefteq \mathbf{pa}\}$, m is the highest non-pre-abort attempt in the coordinators view. The rule attempts to change p's view of a participant q, if p's view of q's last attempt is greater than or equal to m, and p's view of q's state is **pa**. $L = \trianglelefteq q.h[q.la].involved$ is p's view of q's involved set at attempt $q.la$ and $L' = \{r \in Par(p) \mid r.h[q.la] = \trianglelefteq \oslash\}$ is p's view of the subset of sites in the current attempt which did not move to **pa** in attempt $q.la$. We can write the rule as:

CUV-R Coordinator updates view during recovery

PRE: $\exists q \in Par(p), (q.s = \trianglelefteq \mathbf{pa} \land q.le \neq q.la \land q.la \geq m \land$
$((q.h[q.la].c = \trianglelefteq c' \land c'.s \neq \trianglelefteq \mathbf{a}) \lor \neg Q(L - L')))$
POST: $q.s := \triangleleft(q.h[q.la].s_{prev}) \land q.la := \triangleleft(q.h[q.la].la_{prev})$

The rule "rolls back" the view of q's **pa** state when there is enough information within the current attempt to be sure that the earlier attempt, $q.la$ did not result in any process moving to state **a**. The pre-condition to the rule ensures that either the coordinator of attempt $q.la$ is in the current attempt and this coordinator could not be in state **a** (since otherwise **CCA-R** would apply), or that this coordinator could not have moved to abort because not enough sites involved in attempt $q.la$ moved to **pa**. The rule considers sites with attempt numbers greater than the highest non-pre-abort attempt.

When several rules can be applied at a site we choose amongst them by prioritising them. We prioritise the rules for the coordinator in the recovery phase in descending order as **CCC-R**, **CCA-R**, **CPC-R**, **CUV-R**, **CPA-R**, **CPA-R**.

In Example 3.1, it was the coordinator of the second attempt which returned to form a quorum with the first site. At this point the last coordinator can apply **CUV-R** to view p_2's state as **w** with last attempt 0 and then rule **CPC-R** to enter **pc**, rather than **pa**, allowing a commit decision.

5 X3PC Solves Atomic Commitment

Lemma 5.1. *If a site decides commit (abort) during attempt i then no site will decide abort (commit) during attempts $j > i$.*

Proof. Let us consider the abort case first. Let p decide abort at attempt i. WLOG we can assume p is a coordinator (If not then some coordinator decides abort during this attempt, or an earlier attempt, by the pre-condition of PA-R). The pre-condition to step CA-R means the coordinator must be able to construct a view of a quorum of sites with equal last attempt counters all with external state **pa**.

Either this quorum exists long enough for the protocol to terminate, as participating sites move to **a**, or a network event occurs. If any of the sites which moved to **a** before the network event are present in a new group the outcome will be assured to be abort. We need only consider the case where a quorum forms and process that did not move to **a** are present.

Let us consider the *first* time this happens. One of the sites from P must be present in this new quorum P', call this site p'. p' must have a not smaller last attempt counter than any of the other sites in P'. If not then $\exists p'' \in P'$ with $p''.la > p'.la$, but this means there was an attempt between i and j but j is assumed to be the first such attempt. Clearly since $p'.s = $ **pa** and p' has a maximal attempt number in P' so $IMAC(P')$ does not hold. We could however apply the rule **CUV-R** to change the view of processes in this Quorum. We will show that neither $q.h[n].c = \trianglelefteq c' \wedge c' \in Par(p)$ nor $\neg Q(L - L')$ could hold at this point so the rule **CUV-R** cannot be applied. We know in the earlier attempt i, the coordinator did move to **a** if this coordinator were present in $Par(p)$ then rule **CCA-R** with a higher priority would apply preventing rule **CPC-R**. In the earlier attempt a quorum of sites did move to **pa** updating their histories for this attempt, so we cannot find a subset L', in P' with $\neg Q(L - L')$. In X3PC the pre-condition for **CPC-R** has been weakened to allow P' to be any smaller quorate subset, but because this subset must be quorate there will still exist an intersecting site p', with the properties we require.

An exactly similar argument but slightly easier applies if in attempt i a process decides commit. The intersecting site in any subsequent quorum will be in state **pc**, with a maximal last attempt counter, and no site could be in state **pa** with equal last attempt counter so, $IMAC$ will hold, without the need for any applications of **CUV-R** $\square$.

Theorem 5.2. *X3PC satisfies AC1.*

Proof. Any decision must be the result of a successful attempt during the recovery phase of the protocol or during the initial phase. It is clear that if any site decides abort in the initial phase no site could reach state **pc** and thus all subsequent attempts could never result in commit. Also if any site was to decide c in the initial phase *all* sites must be in state **pc** so in any subsequent attempt $IMAC$ will hold preventing any site from deciding **a**.

In the recovery phase a coordinator can only move to abort (commit) if there exists a quorum of connected sites. [3] Each attempt is strictly ordered by

---

[3] Of course a coordinator may propagate an abort (commit) decision within a non-quorate group but the decision will remain consistent

attempt number and may not occur concurrently, because two quorums may not coexist and attempt numbers are increasing. So by the previous lemma after one successful attempt a decision value is locked for all future attempts □.

Lemma 5.3. *X3PC satisfies AC2.*

Proof. If a site decides commit (abort) this decision is propagated in any invocation of the recovery phase □.

Lemma 5.4. *X3PC satisfies AC3*

Proof. Let p be a process that decides commit in a run of E3PC. There are two cases. Either it is a coordinator or it is not. If it is not then it can decide commit as the consequence of one of the rules PC-R or PC-NR. In either case the pre-condition $(p.c).s = \trianglelefteq c$ must hold. So there must have been a point when $(p.c).s = c$. Thus some coordinator decided commit, either during recovery or during the initial phase. If a coordinator decided commit during the initial phase then all sites must have voted yes. We may restrict our attention to the recovery phase.

Consider the first time a coordinator, q changes state to pc in the recovery phase. Such an event must occur (if not the protocol could never reach a commit decision after entering the recovery phase).

When q sets $q.s = $ pc it must have been because of step **CPC-R** a precondition of which is is $IMAC(P') \land Q(P')$ for some subset P' of the sites connected to q. For $IMAC(P')$ to hold we know that the coordinator must have constructed a view of some $q' \in P'$ where $q = \triangleleft$pc, ie. q' did enter pc in an *earlier* attempt. But by assumption this is the first such attempt in the recovery phase where a process moves to pc. Thus some process must have been in pc in the initial phase. If some process was in state pc in the initial phase all sites must have voted yes □.

Lemma 5.5. *X3PC satisfies AC4.*

Proof. If no failures occur then X3PC does not enter its recovery phase so it behaves as 3PC □.

Lemma 5.6. *X3PC satisfies AC5.*

Proof. If even only a quorate group G becomes connected for sufficiently long they will reach a decision and if any site becomes connected to a decided site it too will decide □.

Theorem 5.7. *If using the rules of E3PC a commit decision is reached during the recovery phase where no more than two quorums have formed then using the rules of Q3PC will also lead to a commit decision.*

Proof. In a commiting run of E3PC there exists a configuration in the initial phase before the first network failure of the form:

$$\overbrace{w\ w\ \ldots\ w\ w}^{n-m}\overbrace{pc\ pc\ \ldots\ pc\ pc}^{m}$$

where $m > 0$, this follows from the proof of Lemma 5.4. Consider the first time a quorum forms after a failure in the the recovery phase. It must either consist of sites all in state **w**, or sites in **pc** and **w**, in the latter case both E3PC and Q3PC will apply rules **CPC-R** in the recovery phase and sites will move to **pc**. In the former case both E3PC and Q3PC will carry out rule **CPA-R** moving sites to **pa**. Let L be the set of sites that move to **pa**, they will have last-attempt counters of 2. From this point another network event must occur, if not this quorum would decide abort. Consider the next quorum to form, by assumption this must be the last quorum to form and must result in a commit decision. So we know rule **CPC-R** must be applicable in E3PC. Clearly no site from L could be present in this quorum as it would have a maximum attempt counter and then $IMAC$ would not hold invalidating the pre-condition of **CPC-R** so the quorum can only consist of sites in **pc** and **w** and at least one site must be in **pc**. We see then that Q3PC can also apply rule **CPC-R** and behave in an identical way to E3PC producing a committing run □.

6 Performance Comparison

To compare the three protocols we considered runs from the point that all participants had voted yes and entered their **w** state and the coordinator had collected these votes and changed state to **pc**. This is the most interesting initial condition because if any site votes no, or if all vote yes but the coordinator does not change to **pc**, before entering the recovery phase then all protocols will abort the transaction.

Each protocol was compared by examining random runs. Between each protocol step a network event could occur with uniform probability γ, causing the network to partition. We only considered network events which resulted in quorums being formed. The same failure pattern was applied to all protocols during each run. Where there was a choice of steps to apply (i.e. more than one site could take a step) one was picked at random. The protocol was deemed to have decided once a quorum of sites decided, or in the case of Q3PC blocked if no process could take a step. The results of 500 runs for seven sites and seven values of γ are presented in Fig 4.

The behaviour of E3PC and Q3PC is similar when the outcome is commit. E3PC will often abort a transaction if it would block in Q3PC for an identical failure pattern. This is not generally true but by Theorem 5.7 holds in the case where less than three quorum forming failures occur. E3PC is far superior to the Q3PC at avoiding blocking, especially when network disruption is high. In our experiments a run of Q3PC was deemed blocked if it could not take a step. The equivalent E3PC run would continue but might have undergone several more network partitions before reaching a decision. Interestingly if Q3PC was allowed to run for as long as E3PC took to reach a decision it would still block in many cases.

X3PC will commit in all runs that E3PC commits. Especially under high network disruption, X3PC will commit many more of the transactions that E3PC aborted. When network disruption is very high both E3PC and X3PC take many attempts to reach a decision. X3PC is more likely to decide to commit under high, rather than medium, disruption. This is because under high disruption more information can be exchanged between sites about unsuccessful attempts to abort. When a period of calm returns X3PC is then in a good position to move towards commit, whereas in E3PC there is a much greater chance that pre-abort attempts dominate.

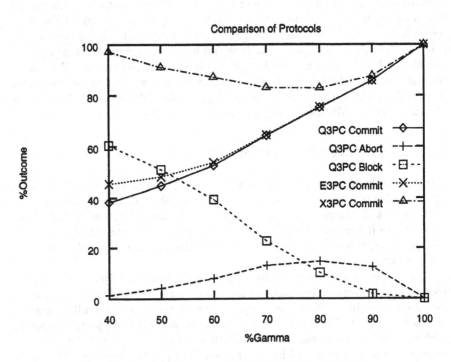

Figure 4. Comparison of E3PC, X3PC and Q3PC

7 Conclusions

It is possible to further optimise X3PC. Sites could store not only their own histories of attempt to pre-abort but also the histories of other processes. Co-ordinators after gathering this information could distribute this information to all participants. This process could go on even in a non quorate component. This would further improve the likelyhood that pre-abort attempt could be rolled back using an update view rule.

The changes to the rules and the addition of **CUV-R** which transform E3PC to X3PC do not make use of the perfect failure detector. By changing AC4 in the problem definition to:

AC4 If all sites voted yes, and no site is ever *suspected* then the decision will be to commit.

X3PC solves this weaker version of Non-blocking Atomic Commit [4] using only an eventually perfect-failure detector [2] [1]. As in E3PC, X3PC will terminate once a quorum of sites become connected and no failures or suspicions occur for sufficiently long.

In a mobile computing or Internet environment where network disruption is common E3PC gives a greater availability of service than Q3PC. As applications use transaction semantics in increasingly varied ways it may become more difficult to restart transactions frequently. X3PC provides a protocol which combines the high availability of E3PC with a much greater chance of committing a transaction even when network disruption is high. Our protocol notation allows a natural style of verification using traditional logical arguments and could form the basis of an automated model checking tool. This notation could also be used for the specification of an implementation and could form the basis of a protocol compiler.

References

1. T.D. Chandra and S. Toueg. Unreliable failure detectors for reliable distributed systems. *Journal of the ACM*, 43(2):225–267, 1996.
2. D. Dolev, R. Friedman, I. Keidar, and D. Malkhi. Failure detectors in omission failure environments. T.R. 96-1608, Dept. of Computer Science, Cornell University, September 1996.
3. H. Garcia-Molina. Elections in a Distributed Computing System. *IEEE Transactions on Computers*, 31(1):48–59, January 1982.
4. R. Guerraoui. Revisiting the relationship between non-blocking atomic commitment and consensus. In J.-M. Helary and M. Raynal, editors, *Proceedings of the 9th International Workshop on Distributed Algorithms*, pages 87–100. Springer Verlag, 1995.
5. I. Keidar and D. Dolev. Increasing the resilience of atomic commit, at no additional cost. In *Proc. of the 14th ACM PoDs*, pages 245–254, May 1995.
6. D. Skeen. A Quorum Based Commit Protocol. *Berkeley Workshop on Distributed Data Management and Computer Networks*, (6):69–80, February 1982.

Multicast Group Communication as a Base for a Load-Balancing Replicated Data Service

Roger Khazan[1], Alan Fekete[2], and Nancy Lynch[1]

[1] MIT LCS, 545 Technology Square, NE43-365, Cambridge, MA 02139, USA.
[2] Basser Dept. of CS, Madsen F09, University of Sydney, NSW 2006, Australia.

Abstract. We give a rigorous account of an algorithm that provides sequentially consistent replicated data on top of the view synchronous group communication service previously specified by Fekete, Lynch and Shvartsman. The algorithm performs updates at all members of a majority view, but rotates the work of queries among the members to equalize the load. The algorithm is presented and verified using I/O automata.

1 Introduction

Multicast group communication services are important building blocks for fault-tolerant applications that require reliable and ordered communication among multiple parties. These services manage their clients as collections of dynamically changing groups and provide strong intra-group multicast primitives. To remedy the existing lack of good specifications for these services and to facilitate consensus on what properties these services should exhibit, Fekete, Lynch and Shvartsman recently gave a simple automaton specification *VS* for a *view-synchronous* group communication service and demonstrated its power by using it to support a totally-ordered broadcast application *TO* [14, 13]. In this paper, we use *VS* to support a second application: a *replicated data service* that *load balances* queries and guarantees *sequential consistency*.

The service maintains a data object replicated at a fixed set of servers in a consistent and transparent fashion and enables the clients to *update* and *query* this object. We assume the underlying network is *asynchronous, strongly-connected*, and subject to processor and communication failures and recoveries involving omission, crashing or delay, but not Byzantine failures. The failures and recoveries may cause the network or its components to partition and merge. The biggest challenge for the service is to cope with network partitioning while preserving correctness and maintaining liveness.

We assume that executed updates cannot be undone, which implies that update operations must be processed in the same order everywhere. To avoid inconsistencies, the algorithm allows updates to occur only in *primary* components. Following the commonly used definition, primary components are defined as those containing a *majority* (or more generally a *quorum*) of all servers. Nonempty intersection of any two majorities (quorums) guarantees the existence of at most one primary at a given time and allows for the necessary flow of information between consecutive primaries. Our service guarantees processing of update requests whenever there is a stable primary component, regardless of the past network perturbations.

On the other hand, processing of queries is not restricted to primary components, and is guaranteed provided the client's component eventually stabilizes. The service uses a round-robin load-balancing strategy to distribute queries to each server evenly within each component. This strategy makes sense in commonly occurring situations when queries take approximately the same amount of time, which is significant. Each query is processed with respect to a data state that is at least as advanced as the last state witnessed by the query's client. The service is arranged in such a way that the servers are always able to process the assigned queries, that is they are not blocked by missing update information.

Architecturally, the service consists of the servers' layer and the communication layer. The servers' layer is symmetric: all servers run identical state-machines. The communication layer consists of two parts, a group communication service satisfying VS, and a collection of individual channels providing reliable reordering point-to-point communication between all pairs of servers. The servers use the group communication service to disseminate update and query requests to the members of their groups and rely on the properties of this service to enforce the formation of identical sequences of update requests at all servers and to schedule query requests correctly. The point-to-point channels are used to send the results of processed queries directly to the original servers.

Related Work

Group communication. A good overview of the rational and usefulness of group communication services is given in [4]. Examples of implemented group communication services are Isis [5], Transis [10], Totem [25], Newtop [12], Relacs [3] and Horus [27]. Different services differ in the way they manage groups and in the specific ordering and delivery properties of their multicast primitives. Even though there is no consensus on what properties these services should provide, a typical requirement is to deliver messages in *total order* and *within a view*.

To be most useful, group communication services have to come with precise descriptions of their behavior. Many specifications have been proposed using a range of different formalisms [3, 6, 8, 11, 15, 24, 26]. Fekete, Lynch, and Shvartsman recently presented the VS specification for a partitionable group communication service. Please refer to [14] for a detailed description and comparison of VS with other specifications.

Several papers have since extended the VS specification. Chockler, Huleihel, and Dolev [7] have used the same style to specify a virtually synchronous FIFO group communication service and to model an adaptive totally-ordered group communication service. De Prisco, Fekete, Lynch and Shvartsman [9] have presented a specification for group communication service that provides a dynamic notion of primary view.

Replication and Load Balancing. The most popular application of group communication services is for maintaining coherent replicated data through applying all operations in the same sequence at all copies. The details of doing this in partitionable systems have been studied by Amir, Dolev, Friedman, Keidar, Melliar-Smith, Moser, and Vaysburd [18, 2, 1, 19, 16, 17].

In his recent book [4, p. 329], Birman points out that process groups are ideally suited for fault-tolerant load-balancing. He suggests two styles of load-balancing algorithms. In the first, more traditional, style, scheduling decisions are made by clients, and tasks are sent directly to the assigned servers. In the second style, tasks are multicast to all servers in the group; each server then applies a deterministic rule to decide on whether to accept each particular task.

In this paper, we use a round-robin strategy originally suggested by Birman [4, p. 329]. According to this strategy, query requests are sent to the servers using totally-ordered multicast; the ith request delivered in a group of n servers is assigned to the server whose rank within this group is ($i \bmod n$). This strategy relies on the fact that all servers receive requests in the same order, and guarantees a uniform distribution of requests among the servers of each group. We extend this strategy with a *fail-over* policy that reissues requests when group membership changes.

Sequential Consistency. There are many different ways in which a collection of replicas may provide the appearance of a single shared data object. The seminal work in defining these precisely is Lamport's concept of sequential consistency [21]. A system provides sequential consistency when for every execution of the system, there is an execution with a single shared object that is indistinguishable to each individual client. A much stronger coherence property is *atomicity*, where a universal observer can't distinguish the execution of the system from one with a single shared object. The algorithm of this paper provides an intermediate condition where the updates are atomic, but queries may see results that are not as up-to-date as those previously seen by other clients.

Contributions of this paper

This paper presents a new algorithm for providing replicated data on top of a partitionable group communication system, in which the work of processing queries is rotated among the group replicas in a round-robin fashion. While the algorithm is based on previous ideas (the load-balancing processing of queries is taken from [4] and the update processing relates to [18, 2, 1, 19]) we are unaware of a previously published account of a way to integrate these. In particular, we show how queries can be processed in minority partitions, and how to ensure that the servers always have sufficiently advanced states to process the queries.

Another important advance in this work is that it shows how a verification can use some of the stronger properties of *VS*. Previous work [14] verified *TO*, an application in which all nodes within a view process messages identically (in a sense, the *TO* application is anonymous, since a node uses its identity only to generate unique labels). The proof in [14] uses the property of agreed message sequence, but it does not pay attention to the identical view of membership at all recipients. In contrast, this paper's load-balancing algorithm (and thus the proof) uses the fact that different recipients have the same membership set when they decide which member will respond to a query.

The rest of the paper is organized as follows. Section 2 introduces basic terminology. Section 3 presents a formal specification for clients' view of the replicated service. Section 4 contains an intermediate specification for the service, the purpose of which is to simplify the proof of correctness. Section 5 presents an I/O automaton for the server's state-machine and outlines the proof of correctness.

2 Mathematical Foundations

We use standard and self-explanatory notation on sets, sequences, total functions ($\rightarrow$), and partial functions ($\hookrightarrow$). Somewhat non-standard is our use of *disjoint unions* (+), which differs from the usual set union ($\cup$) in that each element is *implicitly* tagged with what component it comes from. For simplicity, we use variable name conventions to avoid more formal "injection functions" and "matching constructs." Thus, for example, if *Update* and *Query* are the respective types for update and query requests, then type *Request* = *Update* + *Query* defines a general request type. Furthermore, if *req* $\in$ *Request*, and *u* and *q* are the established variable conventions for *Update* and *Query* types, then "*req* $\leftarrow$ *u*" and "*req* = *q*" are both valid statements.

The modeling is done in the framework of the I/O automaton model of Lynch and Tuttle [23] (without fairness), also described in Chapter 8 of [22]. An I/O automaton is a simple state-machine in which the transitions are associated with named *actions*, which can be either *input, output,* or *internal.* The first two are *externally visible*, and the last two are *locally controlled.* I/O automata are *input-enabled*, i.e., they cannot control their input actions. An automaton is defined by its signature (input, output and internal actions), set of states, set of start states, and a state-transition relation (a cross-product between states, actions, and states). An *execution fragment* is an alternating sequence of states and actions consistent with the transition relation. An *execution* is an execution fragment that begins with a start state. The subsequence of an execution consisting of all the external actions is called a *trace.* The external behavior is captured by the set of traces generated by its executions. Execution fragments can be concatenated. Compatible I/O automata can be *composed* to yield a complex system from individual components. The composition identifies actions with the same name in different component automata. When any component automata performs a step involving action π, so do all component automata that have π in their signatures. The *hiding* operation reclassifies output actions of an automaton as internal.

Invariants of an automaton are properties that are true in all reachable states of that automaton. They are usually proved by induction on the length of the execution sequence. A *refinement mapping* is a single-valued simulation relation. To prove that one automaton implements another in the sense of trace inclusion, it is sufficient to present a refinement mapping from the first to the second. A function is proved to be a refinement mapping by carrying out a *simulation proof,* which usually relies on invariants (see Chapter 8 of [22]).

We describe the transition relation in a *precondition-effect* style (as in [22]), which groups together all the transitions that involve each particular type of action into a single atomic piece of code.

To access components of compound objects we use the *dot* notation. Thus, if *dbs* is a state variable of an automaton, then its instance in a state *s* is expressed as *s.dbs*. Likewise, if *view* is a state variable of a server *p*, then its instance in a state *t* is expressed as $t[p].view$ or as *p.view* if *t* is clear from the discussion.

3 Service Specification *S*

In this section, we formally specify our replicated data service by giving a centralized I/O automaton *S* that defines its allowed behavior. The complete information on basic and derived types, along with a convention for variable usage, is given in Figure 1. The automaton *S* appears in Figure 2.

Fig. 1 Type information

Var	Type	Description
c	C	Finite set of client IDs. (*c.proc* refers to the server of *c*).
db	DB	Database type with a distinguished initial value db_0.
a	Answer	Answer type for queries. Answers for updates are {*ok*}.
u	Update : $DB \to DB$	Updates are functions from database states to database states.
q	Query : $DB \to Answer$	Queries are functions from database states to answers.
r	Request = Update + Query	*Request* is a disjoint union of *Update* and *Query* types.
o	Output = Answer + {ok}	*Output* is a disjoint union of *Answer* and {*ok*} types.

The interface between the service and its blocking clients is typical of a client-server architecture: Clients' requests are delivered to *S* via input actions of the form $\text{request}(r)_c$, representing the submission of request *r* by a client *c*; *S* replies to its clients via actions of the form $\text{reply}(o)_c$, representing the delivery of output value *o* to a client *c*.

If our service were to satisfy *atomicity* (i.e., behave as a non-replicated service), then specification *S* would include a state variable *db* of type *DB* and would apply update and query requests to the latest value of this variable. In the replicated system, this would imply that processing of query requests would have to be restricted to the primary components of the network.

In order to eliminate this restriction and thus increase the availability of the service, we give a slightly weaker specification, which does not require queries to be processed with respect to the latest value of *db*, only with respect to the value that is at least as advanced as the last one witnessed by the queries' client. For this purpose, *S* maintains a history *dbs* of database states and keeps an index *last(c)* to the latest state seen by each client *c*.

Even though our service is not atomic, it still appears to each particular client as a non-replicated one, and thus, satisfies *sequential consistency*. Note that, since the atomicity has been relaxed only for queries, the service is actually stronger than the weakest one allowed by sequential consistency.

The assumption that clients block (i.e., do not submit any new requests until they get replies for their current ones) cannot be expressed within automaton *S* because, as an I/O automaton, it is input-enabled. To express this assumption formally, we *close* *S* by composing it with the automaton $Env = \prod_{c \in C}(C_c)$, where each C_c models a nondeterministic blocking client *c* (see Figure 3); Real blocking clients can be shown to implement this automaton. In the closed automaton $\overline{S}$, the request actions are forced to alternate with the reply actions,

---

Fig. 2 Specification S

Signature:

Input:
$\text{request}(r)_c, r \in Request, c \in C$
Output:
$\text{reply}(o)_c, o \in Output, c \in C$

Internal:
$\text{update}(c, u), c \in C, u \in Update$
$\text{query}(c, q, l), c \in C, q \in Query, l \in \mathcal{N}$

State:

$dbs \in SEQ0\ DB$, initially db_0. Sequence of database states. Indexing from 0 to $|dbs| - 1$.
$map \in C \hookrightarrow (Request + Output)$, initially $\perp$. Buffer for the clients' pending requests or replies.
$last \in C \rightarrow \mathcal{N}$, initially $\{* \rightarrow 0\}$. Index of the last db state witnessed by id.

Transitions:

$\text{request}(r)_c$
  Eff: $map(c) \leftarrow r$

$\text{reply}(o)_c$
  Pre: $map(c) = o$
  Eff: $map(c) \leftarrow \perp$

$\text{update}(c, u)$
  Pre: $u = map(c)$
  Eff: $dbs \leftarrow dbs + u(dbs[|dbs| - 1])$
    $map(c) \leftarrow ok$
    $last(c) \leftarrow |dbs| - 1$

$\text{query}(c, q, l)$
  Pre: $q = map(c)$
    $last(c) \leq l \leq |dbs| - 1$
  Eff: $map(c) \leftarrow q(dbs[l])$
    $last(c) \leftarrow l$

---

which models the assumed behavior. In the rest of the paper, we consider the closed versions of the presented automata, denoting them with a bar (e.g., $\overline{S}$).

Fig. 3 Client Specification C_c

Signature:

Input:
$\text{reply}(o)_c, o \in Output$

Output:
$\text{request}(r)_c, r \in Request$

State: $busy \in Bool$, initially $false$. Status flag. Keeps track of whether there is a pending request.

Transitions:

$\text{request}(r)_c$
  Pre: $busy = false$
  Eff: $busy \leftarrow true$

$\text{reply}(o)_c$
  Eff: $busy \leftarrow false$

---

4 Intermediate Specification D

Action **update** of specification S accomplishes two logical tasks: It updates the centralized database, and it sets client-specific variables, $map(c)$ and $last(c)$, to their new values. In a distributed setting, these two tasks are generally accomplished by two separate transitions. To simplify the refinement mapping between the implementation and the specification, we introduce an intermediate layer D (see Figure 4), in which these tasks are separated. D is formed by splitting

---

Fig. 4 Intermediate Specification D

Signature: Same as in S, with the addition of an internal action $\text{service}(c), c \in C$.
State: Same as in S, with the addition of a state variable $delay \in C \hookrightarrow \mathcal{N}$, initially $\perp$.
Transitions: Same as in S, except update is modified and service is defined.

$\text{update}(c, u)$
  Pre: $u = map(c)$
    $c \notin dom(delay)$
  Eff: $dbs \leftarrow dbs + u(dbs[|dbs| - 1])$
    $delay(c) \leftarrow |dbs| - 1$

$\text{service}(c)$
  Pre: $c \in dom(delay)$
  Eff: $map(c) \leftarrow ok$
    $last(c) \leftarrow delay(c)$
    $delay(c) \leftarrow \perp$

---

each **update** action of S into two, **update** and **service**. The first one extends *dbs* with a new database state, but instead of setting $map(c)$ to "*ok*" and $last(c)$ to its new value as in S, it saves this value (i.e., the index to the most recent database state witnessed by c) in *delay* buffer. The second action sets $map(c)$ to "*ok*" and uses information stored in *delay* to set $last(c)$ to its value.

Lemma 1 *The following function* $DS()$ *is a refinement from* $\overline{D}$ *to* $\overline{S}$ *with respect to reachable states of* $\overline{D}$ *and* $\overline{S}$.[1]

$$
\begin{aligned}
DS(d : \overline{D}) \rightarrow \overline{S} \quad &= \\
s.dbs \quad &\leftarrow d.dbs \\
s.map \quad &\leftarrow overlay(d.map, \{\langle c,\ ok \rangle \mid c \in dom(d.delay)\}) \\
s.last \quad &\leftarrow overlay(d.last, d.delay) \\
s.busy_c \quad &\leftarrow d.busy_c \quad for\ all\ c \in C
\end{aligned}
$$

Transitions of $\overline{D}$ simulate transitions of $\overline{S}$ with the same actions, except for those that involve **service**; these simulate empty transitions. Given this correspondence, the mapping and the proof are straightforward. The lemma implies that $\overline{D}$ implements $\overline{S}$ in the sense of trace inclusion. Later, we prove the same result about implementation $\overline{T}$ and specification $\overline{D}$, which by transitivity of the "implements" relation implies that $\overline{T}$ implements $\overline{S}$ in the sense of trace inclusion.

5 Implementation T

The figure below depicts the major components of the system and their interactions. Set P represents the set of servers. Each server $p \in P$ runs an identical state-machine $VStoD_p$ and serves the clients whose $c.proc = p$.

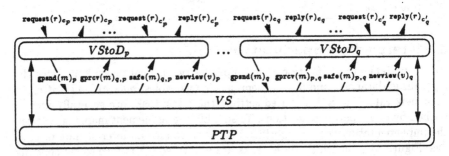

The I/O automaton T for the service implementation is a composition of the servers' layer $I = \prod_{p \in P}(VStoD_p)$ with the group-communication service specification VS [14, see Appendix A] and a collection PTP of reliable reordering point-to-point channels between any pair of servers [22, pages 460-461], with all the output actions of this composition hidden, except for the servers' replies.

$$
T = hide_{out(I \times VS \times PTP) - \{\texttt{reply}(o)_c\}}(I \times VS \times PTP).
$$

---

[1] Given $f, g : X \hookrightarrow Y$, $overlay(f, g)$ is as g over $dom(g)$ and as f elsewhere.

5.1 The Server's State-Machine $VStoD_p$

The additional type and variable-name convention information appears in Figure 5. The I/O code for the $VStoD_p$ state machine is given in Figures 6 and 7.

Fig. 5 Additional Type Declaration

Var	Type	Description
	$\mathcal{Q} \subseteq \mathcal{P}(P)$	Fixed set of quorums. For any $Q \in \mathcal{Q}$ and $Q' \in \mathcal{Q}$, $Q \cap Q' \neq \emptyset$.
g	$\langle G, <_G, g_0 \rangle$	Totally-ordered set of view ids with the smallest element.
v	$V = G \times \mathcal{P}(P)$	An element of this set is called a *view*. Fields: *id* and *set*.
x	$X = G \times (C \times Update)^* \times \mathcal{N}$	Expertise information for exchange process. Fields: xl, us, su.
m	$M = C \times Update+$	Messages sent via VS: Either update requests, query requests,
	$C \times Query \times \mathcal{N} + X$	or expertise information for exchange process.
pkt	$Pkt = C \times Answer \times \mathcal{N} \times G$	Packets sent via PTP. ($\mathcal{N}$ is index of the witnessed *db* state.)

The activity of the server's state-machine can be either normal, marked by *mode* being *normal*, or recovery, marked by *mode* being either *expertise_broadcast* or *expertise_collection*. Normal activity is associated with the server's participation in already established view, while recovery activity — in a newly forming one. We also distinguish whether or not the server is a member of a *primary* view, which is defined as that whose members comprise a quorum (*view.set* $\in \mathcal{Q}$).

Fig. 6 Implementation ($VStoD_p$) : Signature and State Variables

Signature:

Input:
request$(r)_c$, $r \in Request, c \in C, c.proc = p$
gprcv$(m)_{p',p}$, $m \in M, p' \in P$
safe$(m)_{p',p}$, $m \in M, p' \in P$
newview$(v)_p$, $v \in V$
ptprcv$(pkt)_{p',p}$, $pkt \in Pkt, p' \in P$

Output:
reply$(o)_c$, $o \in Output, c \in C, c.proc = p$
gpsnd$(m)_p$, $m \in M$
ptpsnd$(pkt)_{p,p'}$, $pkt \in Pkt, p' \in P$

Internal:
update$(c, u), c \in C, u \in Update$
query$(c, q, l), c \in C, u \in Update$

State:

$db \in DB$, initially db_0.
Local replica. Next state depends on current and action.

$map \in C|_{(c.proc=p)} \hookrightarrow Request + Output$, initially $\perp$.
Buffer that maps clients to their requests or replies.

$pending \in \mathcal{P}(C|_{(c.proc=p)})$, initially $\emptyset$.
Set of clients whose requests are being processed.

$last \in C|_{(c.proc=p)} \to \mathcal{N}$, initially $C|_{(c.proc=p)} \to 0$.
Index of the last db state seen by each client.

$updates \in (C \times Update)^*$, initially $[\,]$.
Sequence of updates. Indexing from 1. Fields: c and u.

$last\_update \in \mathcal{N}$, initially 0.
Index of the last executed element in updates.

$safe\_to\_update \in \mathcal{N}$, initially 0.
Index of the last "safe to update" element in updates.

$queries \in C \hookrightarrow (Query + Answer) \times \mathcal{N}$, initially $\perp$.
Query requests or answers, paired with their last(c).

$query\_counter \in \mathcal{N}$, initially 0.
Number of queries received within current view.

$view \in V$, initially $V_0 = \langle g_0, P \rangle$.
Current view of p. Fields: id and set.

$mode \in \{normal, expertise\_broadcast, expertise\_collection\}$, initially *normal*.
Modes of operation. The last two are for recovery.

$expertise\_level \in G$, initially g_0.
The highest primary view id that p knows of.

$expertise\_max \in X$, initially $\langle g_0, [\,], 0 \rangle$.
Cumulative expertise collected during recovery.

$expert\_counter1 \in \mathcal{N}$, initially 0.
Number of expertise messages received so far.

$expert\_counter2 \in \mathcal{N}$, initially 0.
Number of expertise messages received so far as safe.

Processing of query requests is handled by actions of the type gpsnd$(c, q, l)_p$, gprcv$(c, q, l)_{p',p}$, query$(c, q, l)_p$, ptpsnd$(c, a, l, g)_{p,p'}$, and ptprcv$(c, a, l, g)_{p',p}$. The fact that servers of the same view receive query requests in the same order guarantees that the scheduling function of gprcv$(c, q, l)_{p',p}$ distributes query requests uniformly among the servers of one view.

Fig. 7 Implementation $VStoD_p$: Transitions

Transitions:

$\mathbf{request}(r)_c$
Eff: $map(c) \leftarrow r$

$\mathbf{gpsnd}(c, q, l)_p$
Pre: $mode = normal$
$\quad q = map(c) \wedge c \notin pending$
$\quad l = last(c)$
Eff: $pending \leftarrow pending \cup c$

$\mathbf{gprcv}(c, q, l)_{p', p}$
Eff: $query\_counter \leftarrow query\_counter + 1$
$\quad$ if $(rank(p, view.set) =$
$\qquad query\_counter \mod |view.set|)$
$\quad$ then $queries(c) \leftarrow \langle q, l \rangle$

$\mathbf{query}(c, q, l)$
Pre: $(q, l) \in queries(c)$
$\quad last\_update \geq l$
Eff: $queries(c) \leftarrow \langle q(db), last\_update \rangle$

$\mathbf{ptpsnd}(c, a, l, g)_{p, p'}$
Pre: $c \in dom(queries) \wedge c.proc = p'$
$\quad \langle a, l \rangle \in queries(c)$
$\quad g = view.id$
Eff: $queries(c) \leftarrow \perp$

$\mathbf{ptprcv}(c, a, l, g)_{p', p}$
Eff: if $(g = view.id \wedge c.proc = p)$ then
$\quad pending \leftarrow pending - c$
$\quad map(c) \leftarrow a$
$\quad last(c) \leftarrow l$

$\mathbf{newview}(v)_p$
Eff: $queries \leftarrow \perp;\ query\_counter \leftarrow 0$
$\quad pending \leftarrow pending - \{c \mid (\exists q . \langle c, q \rangle \in map)\}$
$\quad safe\_to\_update \leftarrow \max (safe\_to\_update,$
$\qquad \max\{last(c) \mid c \in C \wedge c.proc = p\})$
$\quad expertise\_max \leftarrow expertise\_max_0$
$\quad expert\_counter1 \leftarrow 0;\ expert\_counter2 \leftarrow 0$
$\quad mode \leftarrow expertise\_broadcast$
$\quad view \leftarrow v$

$\mathbf{gpsnd}(x)_p$
Pre: $mode = expertise\_broadcast$
$\quad x = \langle expertise\_level, updates, safe\_to\_update \rangle$
Eff: $mode \leftarrow expertise\_collection$

$\mathbf{reply}(o)_c$
Pre: $map(c) = o$
Eff: $map(c) \leftarrow \perp$

$\mathbf{gpsnd}(c, u)_p$
Pre: $mode = normal \wedge view.set \in Q$
$\quad u = map(c) \wedge c \notin pending$
Eff: $pending \leftarrow pending \cup c$

$\mathbf{gprcv}(c, u)_{p', p}$
Eff: $updates \leftarrow updates + \langle c, u \rangle$

$\mathbf{safe}(c, u)_{p', p}$
Eff: $safe\_to\_update \leftarrow safe\_to\_update + 1$

$\mathbf{update}(c, u)$
Pre: $last\_update < safe\_to\_update$
$\quad \langle c, u \rangle = updates[last\_update + 1]$
Eff: $last\_update \leftarrow last\_update + 1$
$\quad db \leftarrow u(db)$
$\quad$ if $(c.proc = p)$ then
$\qquad pending \leftarrow pending - c$
$\qquad map(c) \leftarrow ok$
$\qquad last(c) \leftarrow last\_update$

$\mathbf{gprcv}(x)_{p', p}$
Eff: $expertise\_max \leftarrow \max_{\chi}(expertise\_max, x)$
$\quad expert\_counter1 \leftarrow expert\_counter1 + 1$
$\quad$ if $(expert\_counter1 = |view.set|)$ then
$\qquad expertise\_level \leftarrow expertise\_max.xl$
$\qquad updates \leftarrow expertise\_max.us$
$\qquad safe\_to\_update \leftarrow expertise\_max.su$
$\qquad$ if $(view.set \in Q)$ then
$\qquad\quad expertise\_level \leftarrow view.id$

$\mathbf{safe}(x)_{p', p}$
Eff: $expert\_counter2 \leftarrow expert\_counter2 + 1$
$\quad$ if $(expert\_counter2 = |view.set|)$ then
$\qquad$ if $(view.set \in Q)$ then
$\qquad\quad safe\_to\_update \leftarrow |expertise\_max.us|$
$\qquad\quad pending \leftarrow pending -$
$\qquad\qquad \{c \mid c \in pending \wedge$
$\qquad\qquad c \notin updates[(last\_update + 1) ..$
$\qquad\qquad\qquad safe\_to\_update].c\}$
$\qquad mode \leftarrow normal$

Servicing of each query by a background thread $\mathbf{query}(c, q, l)_p$ is allowed only when the current state of the local database is at least as advanced as the last state witnessed by its client. This condition is captured by $last\_update \geq l$. The non-trivial part of this protocol is that the service actually guarantees that the servers always have the sufficiently advanced database states to be able to service the queries that are assigned to them.

When a server learns of its new view, it executes a simple query-related recovery procedure, in which it moves its own pending queries for reprocessing and erases any information pertaining to the queries of others.

Processing of update requests is handled by actions of the type $\mathbf{gpsnd}(c, u)_p$, $\mathbf{gprcv}(c, u)_{p', p}$, $\mathbf{safe}(c, u)_{p', p}$, and $\mathbf{update}(c, u)$. Each server maintains a sequence $updates$ of update requests, the purpose of which is to enforce the order in which updates are applied to the local database replica. The sequence is extended each time an update request is delivered via a $\mathbf{gprcv}$ action. The sequence has two distinguished prefixes $updates[1..safe\_to\_update]$ and $updates[1..last\_update]$, called *safe* and *done*, that mark respectively those update requests that are safe to execute and those that have already been executed. The *safe* prefix is extended to cover a certain update request on *updates* sequence when the server learns that the request has been delivered to all other members of that server's view.[2] The service guarantees that at all times *safe* and *done* prefixes of all servers are consistent (i.e., given any two, one is a prefix of another). Since *done* prefixes mark those update requests that have been applied to database replica, this property implies mutual consistency of database replicas.

When a server learns of its new view, it starts a recovery activity that is handled by actions of the type $\texttt{newview}(v)_p$, $\texttt{gpsnd}(x)_p$, $\texttt{gprcv}(x)_{p',p}$, and $\texttt{safe}(x)_{p',p}$. The query-related part of this activity was described above. For the update-related part, the server has to collaborate with others on ensuring that the states of all the servers of this view are consistent with their and other servers' past execution histories and are suitable for their subsequent normal activity.

For this purpose, each server has to be able to tell how advanced its state is compared to those of others. The most important criterion is the latest primary view of which the server knows. This knowledge may have come directly from personal participation in that view, or indirectly from another server. The server keeps track of this information in its state variable *expertise_level*. Two other criteria are the server's *updates* sequence and its *safe* prefix. The values of these three variables comprise the server's *expertise*.

Definition 1 *The cumulative expertise, $\max_{\chi}(X)$, of a set or a sequence, X, of expertise elements is defined as the following triple*

$$\max_{\chi}(X) = \langle\, \max_{<_G}\{x.xl \mid x \in X\},$$
$$\max_{<_{||}}\{x.us \mid (x \in X) \wedge (x.xl \in \max_{<_G}\{x.xl \mid x \in X\})\},$$
$$\max_{<_N}\{x.su \mid x \in X\}\,\rangle.$$

---

[2] Some of the *optimistic* protocols, such as [16, 17], execute requests as soon as they are delivered by a total order multicast (ABCAST of *Horus*), but may result in inconsistent replicas, in which case they have to undo actions and roll the replicas' states back. On the other hand, *pessimistic* protocols, which implement *strict mutual consistency* among replicas, require additional information before they are able to execute a delivered request. The pessimistic version in [17] allows for a request to be executed only when a server collects a majority of acknowledgments, which have to be multicast by each server once it receives the request. Amir, Dolev, Melliar-Smith, and Moser in [1, 2] eliminate the need for end-to-end acknowledgments by using total order multicast with safe delivery, i.e., a message delivered to one member is guaranteed to be delivered to any other member of the same view provided it does not crash. As pointed out in [14, 13], "A simple 'coordinated attack' argument (as in Chapter 5 of [22]) shows that in a partitionable system, this notion of safe delivery is incompatible with having all recipients in exactly the same view as the sender." As a result, protocols based on this multicast primitive are more complicated than those based on *VS*, which separates message delivery and safe notification events.

As a first step, the server's collaboration with others during recovery activity aims at advancing everyone's expertise to the highest one known to them — their *cumulative* expertise (see Def. 1). Notice that adopting cumulative expertise of other servers can not cause inconsistency among replicas. The first step is completed with a delivery of the last expertise message via action $\text{gprcv}(x)_{p',p}$.

Advancing the server's expertise achieves two purposes. First, it ensures the propagation of update requests to previously inaccessible replicas. Second, it ensures the future ability of servers to process the queries assigned to them.

In addition to advancing their expertise, the servers of primary views have to ensure their ability to process new update requests once they resume their normal activity, which subsumes that they have to start normal activity with identical *updates* sequences, the entire content of which is *safe* and contains as prefixes the *safe* prefixes of all other servers in the system. For this purpose, once the server of a primary view learns that all expertise messages have been delivered to all servers of this view, it extends its *safe* prefix to cover the entire *updates* sequence adopted during the exchange process.

The resultant *safe* prefix acts as a new base that all servers of the future primary views will contain in their *updates* sequences. Attainment of this behavior depends on the intersection property of primary views and the fact that subsequent primary views have higher identifiers.

The established base works as a divider: partially processed update requests that are not included in the base will never find a way to a safe prefix unless they are resubmitted by their original servers. Therefore, once a server of a primary view establishes the base, it moves all pending update requests that are not in this base back for reprocessing. After this step, the server may resume its normal activity, which enables it to process new update and query requests.

5.2   Refinement Mapping from $\overline{T}$ to $\overline{D}$

Automaton $\overline{D}$ has five types of actions. Actions of the types $\text{request}(r)_c$ and $\text{reply}(o)_c$ are simulated when $\overline{T}$ takes the corresponding actions. Actions of the type $\text{query}(c)$ are simulated when $\overline{T}$ executes $\text{ptprcv}(c, a, l, g)_{p',p}$ with $g = p.view.id$. The last two types, $\text{update}(c)$ and $\text{service}(c)$, are both simulated under certain conditions when $\overline{T}$ executes $\text{update}(c, u)_p$. We define actions $\text{update}(c, u)_p$ of $\overline{T}$ as *leading* when $t[p].last\_update = \max_p\{t[p].last\_update\}$, and as *native* when $c.proc = p$. Actions that are just leading simulate $\text{update}(c)$, that are just native simulate $\text{service}(c)$, that are both leading and native simulate "$\text{update}(c), \text{service}(c)$", and that are neither simulate empty transitions. Transitions of $\overline{T}$ with any other actions simulate empty transitions of $\overline{D}$.

Lemma 2 *The following function is a refinement from $\overline{T}$ to $\overline{D}$ with respect to reachable states of $\overline{T}$ and $\overline{D}$.*[3]

---

[3] If s is "$f_1, f_2, \ldots, f_n$" with each $f_i : A \to A$, and if $a \in A$, then $\text{scan}(s) = $ = "$f_1, (f_2 \circ f_1), \ldots, (f_n \circ \ldots \circ f_2 \circ f_1)$" and $\text{map}(s, a) =$ "$f_1(a), f_2(a), \ldots, f_n(a)$".

$$TD(t : \overline{T}) \rightarrow \overline{D} =$$

$let\ t.done =\ t[p].updates[1..t[p].last\_update],\ where\ p \in P\ \ is\ any\ such\ that$
$\qquad\qquad\quad t[p].last\_update = \max_{p \in P}\{t[p].last\_update\}$

$dbs \quad \leftarrow db_0 + map\,(scan(t.done),\, db_0)$

$map \quad \leftarrow \bigcup_{p \in P} t[p].map$

$last \quad \leftarrow \bigcup_{p \in P} t[p].last$

$delay \quad \leftarrow \{(t.done[i].c,\, i) \mid 1 \le i \le |t.done| \wedge t[t.done[i].c.proc].last\_update < i\}$

$busy_c \quad \leftarrow t.busy_c \quad for\ all\ \ c \in C$

An invariant will show that sequences of processed requests at different servers are consistent. In particular, all sequences which have maximum length are the same. $t.done$ is a derived variable that denotes the longest sequence of update requests processed in the system. This sequence corresponds to all modifications done to the database of $\overline{D}$, which explains the way $TD(t).dbs$ is defined. Domain of $TD(t).delay$ consists of ids of update requests that have been processed somewhere (i.e., in $t.done$) but not at their native locations (i.e., the $last\_update$ at their native locations have not yet surpassed these update requests). With each c in this domain we associate its position in sequence $t.done$. This position corresponds to the last database state witnessed by client c, which explains the way $d.delay$ is defined.

Fig. 8 Invariants used in the proof that $TD()$ is a refinement mapping (Lemma 2)

I 1 For each server $p \in P$, $p.last\_update \le p.safe\_to\_update \le |p.updates|$.

I 2 For any two servers p_1 and $p_2 \in P$, if the lengths of their done prefixes are the same, then their done prefixes are the same:

$p_1.last\_update = p_2.last\_update \Rightarrow p_1.updates[1..p_1.last\_update] = p_2.updates[1..p_2.last\_update].$

I 3 Any update request that is safe somewhere but has not been executed at its native location is still reflected in its native map and pending buffers: If $(c, u) = p.updates[i]$ and $c.proc.last\_update < i \le p.safe\_to\_update$, then $(c, u) \in c.proc.map$ and $c \in c.proc.pending$.

I 4 At most one unexecuted update request per each client can appear at that client's server: For any client $c \in C$, there exists at most one index $i \in \mathcal{N}$ such that $i > c.proc.last\_update$ and $c = c.proc.updates[i].c$.

I 5 For all PTP packets $\langle c, a, l, g \rangle$ on a in-transit$_{p',p}$ channel, it follows that $c.proc = p$. Moreover, if $p.view.id = g$ then

    (a) $c \in dom(p.map) \wedge p.map(c) \in Query$ (d) $l \ge p.last(c)$

    (b) $c \in p.pending$ (e) $l \le \max_p\{p.last\_update\}$

    (c) $a = p.map(c)(compose(p.updates[1..l])(db_0))$

The proof of Lemma 2 is straightforward given the five top-level invariants in Figure 8. To prove these invariants assertionally we have developed an interesting approach [20]: One of the fundamental invariants states that *safe* prefixes of *updates* sequences at all servers are consistent. To prove this fact, it is not enough to have properties only about *safe* prefixes — we need invariants that deal also with unsafe portions of *updates* sequences (because the latter become the former during an execution). Invariants that relate *safe* prefixes and *updates* sequences of different servers depend on the servers' *expertise_level*, which may have come to a server directly from the participation in a primary view, or indirectly from someone else. In our proof, we have invented a derived function $\mathcal{X}$ that expresses recursively the highest expertise achieved by each server in each view in terms of servers' expertise in earlier views. In a sense, it presents the law according to which the replication part of the algorithm operates. The recursive nature of this function makes proofs by induction easy: proving an inductive step involves unwinding only one recursive step of the derived function $\mathcal{X}$.

6 Future Work

This paper has dealt with safety properties; future work will consider performance and fault-tolerance properties, stated conditionally to hold in periods of good behavior of the underlying network. In particular, we are planning to compare the response time of this algorithm with others which share query load differently, for example based on recent run-time load reports which are disseminated by multicast.

Other possible extensions to this work involve determining primary views dynamically, using a service such as the one in [9], and integrating the unicast message communication into the group communication layer.

References

1. Y. Amir. *Replication using Group Communication over a Partitioned Network.* PhD thesis, The Hebrew University of Jerusalem, Israel, 1995.
2. Y. Amir, D. Dolev, P. Melliar-Smith, and L. Moser. Robust and efficient replication using group communication. Technical Report 94-20, The Hebrew University of Jerusalem, Israel, 1994.
3. O. Babaoglu, R. Davoli, L. Giachini, and P. Sabattini. The inherent cost of strong-partial view-synchronous communication. *LNCS*, 972:72–86, 1995.
4. K. P. Birman. *Building Secure and Reliable Network Applications.* Manning Publications Co., Greenwich, CT, 1996.
5. K. P. Birman and R. van Renesse, editors. *Reliable Distributed Computing with the Isis Toolkit.* IEEE Computer Society Press, 1994.
6. T. D. Chandra, V. Hadzilacos, S. Toueg, and B. Charron-Bost. On the impossibility of group membership. In *Proceedings of the 15th Annual ACM Symposium on Principles of Distributed Computing*, pages 322–330, New York, USA, May 1996.
7. G. V. Chockler, N. Huleihel, and D. Dolev. An adaptive totally ordered multicast protocol that tolerates partitions. In *Proceedings of the 17h Annual ACM Symposium on Principles of Distributed Computing*, pages 237–246, 1998.
8. F. Cristian. Group, majority, and strict agreement in timed asynchronous distributed systems. In *Proceedings of the Twenty-Sixth International Symposium on Fault-Tolerant Computing*, pages 178–189, Washington, June 25–27, 1996. IEEE.
9. R. De Prisco, A. Fekete, N. Lynch, and A. Shvartsman. A dynamic view-oriented group communication service. In *Proceedings of the 17h Annual ACM Symposium on Principles of Distributed Computing*, pages 227–236, 1998.
10. D. Dolev and D. Malki. The Transis approach to high availability cluster communication. *Communications of the ACM*, 39(4):64–70, Apr. 1996.
11. D. Dolev, D. Malki, and R. Strong. A framework for partitionable membership service. Technical Report TR94-6, Department of Computer Science, Hebrew University, 1994.

12. P. D. Ezhilchelvan, R. A. Macêdo, and S. K. Shrivastava. Newtop: A fault-tolerant group communication protocol. In *Proceedings of the 15th International Conference on Distributed Computing Systems (ICDCS'95)*, pages 296–306, Los Alamitos, CA, USA, May 30 –June 2, 1995. IEEE Computer Society Press.

13. A. Fekete, N. Lynch, and A. Shvartsman. Specifying and using a partionable group communication service. Extended version, http://theory.lcs.mit.edu/tds.

14. A. Fekete, N. Lynch, and A. Shvartsman. Specifying and using a partionable group communication service. In *Proceedings of the Sixteenth Annual ACM Symposium on Principles of Distributed Computing*, pages 53–62, Santa Barbara, California, Aug. 21–24, 1997.

15. R. Friedman and R. van Renesse. Strong and weak virtual synchrony in Horus. Technical Report TR95-1537, Cornell University, Computer Science Department, Aug. 24, 1995.

16. R. Friedman and A. Vaysburd. Implementing replicated state machines over partitionable networks. Technical Report TR96-1581, Cornell University, Computer Science, Apr. 17, 1996.

17. R. Friedman and A. Vaysburd. High-performance replicated distributed objects in partitionable environments. Technical Report TR97-1639, Cornell University, Computer Science, July 16, 1997.

18. I. Keidar. A highly available paradigm for consistent object replication. Master's thesis, Institute of Computer Science, The Hebrew University of Jerusalem, Israel, 1994.

19. I. Keidar and D. Dolev. Efficient message ordering in dynamic networks. In *Proceedings of the 15th Annual ACM Symposium on Principles of Distributed Computing*, pages 68–76, New York, USA, May 1996.

20. R. I. Khazan. Group communication as a base for a load-balancing replicated data service. Master's thesis, Department of Electrical Engineering and Computer Science, Massachusetts Institute of Technology, Cambridge, MA 02139, May 1998.

21. L. Lamport. How to make a multiprocessor computer that correctly executes multiprocess programs. *IEEE Transactions on Computers*, C-28(9):690–691, 1979.

22. N. A. Lynch. *Distributed Algorithms*. Morgan Kaufmann series in data management systems. Morgan Kaufmann Publishers, Los Altos, CA 94022, USA, 1996.

23. N. A. Lynch and M. R. Tuttle. An introduction to input/output automata. *CWI Quarterly*, 2(3):219–246, 1989. Also available as MIT Technical Memo MIT/LCS/TM-373.

24. L. E. Moser, Y. Amir, P. M. Melliar-Smith, and D. A. Agarwal. Extended virtual synchrony. In *Proceedings of the 14th International Conference on Distributed Computing Systems*, pages 56–65, Los Alamitos, CA, USA, June 1994. IEEE Computer Society Press.

25. L. E. Moser, P. M. Melliar-Smith, D. A. Agarwal, R. K. Budhia, and C. A. Lingley-Papadopoulos. Totem: A fault-tolerant multicast group communication system. *Communications of the ACM*, 39(4):54–63, Apr. 1996.

26. A. M. Ricciardi, A. Schiper, and K. P. Birman. Understanding partitions and the "no partition" assumption. Technical Report TR93-1355, Cornell University, Computer Science Department, June 1993.

27. R. van Renesse, K. P. Birman, and S. Maffeis. Horus: A flexible group communication system. *Communications of the ACM*, 39(4):76–83, Apr. 1996.

A The *VS* Specification

The *VS* specification of [14, 13] is reprinted in Figure 9. M denotes a message alphabet and $\langle G, <_G, g_0 \rangle$ is a totally-ordered set of view identifiers with an initial view identifier. An element of the set $V = G \times \mathcal{P}(P)$ is called a *view*. If v is a view, we write $v.id$ and $v.set$ to denote its components.

Fig. 9 *VS-machine*

Signature:

Input:
$gsnd(m)_p$, $m \in M$, $p \in P$
Output:
$gprcv(m)_{p,q}$ hidden g, $m \in M$, $p, q \in P$, $g \in G$
$safe(m)_{p,q}$ hidden v, $m \in M$, $p, q \in P$, $v \in views$
$newview(v)_p$, $v \in views$, $p \in P$, $p \in v.set$

Internal:
$createview(v)$, $v \in views$
$vs\text{-}order(m, p, g)$, $m \in M$, $p \in P$, $g \in G$

State:

$created \subseteq V$, initially $\{\langle g_0, P \rangle\}$
for each $p \in P$:
  $current\_viewid[p] \in G$, initially g_0
for each $g \in G$:
  $queue[g]$, a finite sequence of $M \times P$,
             initially empty

for each $p \in P$, $g \in G$:
  $pending[p, g]$, a finite sequence of M,
            initially empty
  $next[p, g] \in \mathcal{N}^{>0}$, initially 1
  $next\_safe[p, g] \in \mathcal{N}^{>0}$, initially 1

Transitions:

$createview(v)$
  Pre: $v.id > max(g : \exists S, \langle g, S \rangle \in created)$
  Eff: $created \leftarrow created \cup \{v\}$

$newview(v)_p$
  Pre: $v \in created$
     $v.id > current\_viewid[p]$
  Eff: $current\_viewid[p] \leftarrow v.id$

$gsnd(m)_p$
  Eff: append m to $pending[p, current\_viewid[p]]$

$vs\text{-}order(m, p, g)$
  Pre: m is head of $pending[p, g]$
  Eff: remove head of $pending[p, g]$
     append $\langle m, p \rangle$ to $queue[g]$

$gprcv(m)_{p,q}$, hidden g
  Pre: $g = current\_viewid[q]$
     $queue[g](next[q, g]) = \langle m, p \rangle$
  Eff: $next[q, g] \leftarrow next[q, g] + 1$

$safe(m)_{p,q}$, hidden g, S
  Pre: $g = current\_viewid[q]$
     $\langle g, S \rangle \in created$
     $queue[g](next\_safe[q, g]) = \langle m, p \rangle$
     for all $r \in S$:
       $next[r, g] > next\_safe[q, g]$
  Eff: $next\_safe[q, g] \leftarrow next\_safe[q, g] + 1$

VS specifies a partitionable service in which, at any moment of time, every client has precise knowledge of its current view. *VS* does not require clients to learn about every view of which they are members, nor does it place any consistency restrictions on the membership of concurrent views held by different clients. Its only view-related requirement is that views are presented to each client according to the total order on view identifiers. *VS* provides a multicast service that imposes a total order on messages submitted within each view, and delivers them according to this order, with no omissions, and strictly within a view. In other words, the sequence of messages received by each client while in a certain view is a prefix of the total order on messages associated with that view. Separately from the multicast service, *VS* provides a "safe" notification once a message has been delivered to all members of the view.

Efficient Deadlock-Free
Multi-dimensional Interval Routing
in Interconnection Networks[*]

Rastislav Královič, Branislav Rovan, Peter Ružička, Daniel Štefankovič

Department of Computer Science
Faculty of Mathematics and Physics
Comenius University, Bratislava
Slovak Republic

Abstract: We present deadlock-free packet (wormhole) routing algorithms based on multi-dimensional interval schemes for certain multiprocessor interconnection networks and give their analysis in terms of the compactness and the size (the maximum number of buffers per node (per link)). The issue of a simultaneous reduction of the compactness and the size is fundamental, worth to investigate and of practical importance, as interval routing and wormhole routing have been realized in INMOS Transputer C104 Router chips.

In this paper we give an evidence that for some well-known interconnection networks there are efficient deadlock-free multidimensional interval routing schemes (DFMIRS) despite of a provable nonexistence of efficient deterministic shortest path interval routing schemes (IRS). For d-dimensional butterflies we give a d-dimensional DFMIRS with constant compactness and size, while each shortest path IRS is of the compactness at least $2^{d/2}$. For d-dimensional cube connected cycles we show a d-dimensional DFMIRS with compactness and size polynomial in d, while each shortest path IRS needs compactness at least $2^{d/2}$. For d-dimensional hypercubes (tori) we present a d-dimensional DFMIRS of compactness 1 and size 2 (4), while for shortest path IRS we can achieve the reduction to 2 (5) buffers with compactness 2^{d-1} ($O(n^{d-1})$).

We also present a nonconstant lower bound (in the form $\sqrt{d}$) on the size of deadlock-free packet routing (based on acyclic orientation covering) for a special set of routing paths on d-dimensional hypercubes.

1 Introduction

Interval routing is an attractive space-efficient routing method for communication networks which has found industrial applications in INMOS T9000 transputer design. Survey of principal theoretical results about interval routing can be found in [14, 6].

Interval routing is based on compact routing tables, where the set of nodes reachable via outgoing links is represented by intervals. The space efficiency can be measured by *compactness*, i.e. the maximum number of intervals per link.

---
[*] This research has been partially supported by the Slovak Research Grant VEGA 1/4315/97.

Previous work mostly concentrated on *shortest path* interval routing schemes (IRS). Shortest path IRS of compactness 1 are known to exist for a number of well-known interconnection networks including trees, rings, complete bipartite graphs, meshes, and tori. There are however networks that are known to have no shortest path IRS even for large compactness, which include shuffle-exchange, cube-connected cycles, butterfly, and star graphs. Several generalizations of IRS were therefore proposed.

Multidimensional interval routing schemes (MIRS) were introduced in [5] and were used to represent all the shortest paths information. MIRS with low memory requirements were proposed for hypercubes, grids, tori and certain types of chordal rings [5].

Another interesting aspect of the routing problem is related to deadlocks. A deadlock refers to a situation in which a set of messages is blocked forever because each message in the set occupies buffer in a node or on a link which is also required by another message. Deadlock-free routing is relevant in the framework of packet and wormhole routing protocols [2, 3, 8, 12, 13]. The first study dealing with deadlock-free IRS appeared in [11]. Further results were presented in [10, 15, 16]. We follow the model of buffered deadlock-free IRS introduced in [4] based on the notion of acyclic orientation covering. An s-buffered deadlock-free IRS with compactness k is denoted as (k, s)-DFIRS. Some results were already presented in [4]. For d-dimensional tori there exists a shortest path $(2, 2d + 1)$-DFIRS; the reduction to 5 buffers can be achieved with compactness $O(n^{d-1})$. For d-dimensional hypercubes there is a shortest path $(1, d + 1)$-DFIRS; the reduction to 2 buffers can be achieved with compactness 2^{d-1}.

We extend the model in [4] to buffered deadlock-free multi-dimensional interval routing (MIRS). We show that for some interconnection networks there are efficient deadlock-free MIRS even in the case when there does not exist efficient shortest path IRS. For butterflies of order d we give a deadlock-free d-dimensional MIRS with constant compactness and size, while each shortest path IRS needs compactness at least $2^{d/2}$. For cube connected cycles of order d we present a deadlock-free d-dimensional MIRS with compactness and size polynomial in d, while each shortest path IRS needs compactness at least $2^{d/2}$. For d-dimensional hypercubes we give a deadlock-free d-dimensional MIRS of compactnes 1 and size 2. And for d-dimensional tori we show a deadlock-free d-dimensional MIRS of compactness 1 and size 4.

There exist only few lower bounds on the size of deadlock-free packet routing, even for those based on specific strategies. The best lower bound is 3 (see [2]). We give the first nonconstant lower bound (in the form $\sqrt{d}$) on the size of deadlock-free packet routing (based on acyclic orientation covering) for a special set of routing paths on d-dimensional hypercubes. As a consequence, the set of routing paths induced by 1-IRS on the hypercube proposed in [1] is not suitable for the efficient deadlock-free packet routing based on acyclic orientation covering concept.

2 Definitions

An interconnection network is modeled by an undirected graph $G = (V, A)$, where V is a set of nodes and A is a set of links of the network. Assume $|V| = n$. Each node has a finite set of buffers for temporarily storing messages. The set of all buffers in the network G is denoted as B.

A *communication request* is a pair of nodes in G. A *communication pattern* $\mathcal{R}$ is a set of communication requests. We will consider certain significant communication patterns in G. A *static one-to-all* communication pattern is a set $\{(v, w) \mid w \in V\}$ for a given source node v. A *dynamic one-to-all* communication pattern is a set $\{(v, w) \mid w \in V\}$ for some (not given in advance) source node v. An *all-to-all* communication pattern is a set $\{(v, w) \mid v, w \in V\}$. A collection $\mathcal{P}$ of paths in G *satisfies* the communication pattern $\mathcal{R}$ if there is at least one path in G beginning in u and ending in v for each communication request $(u, v) \in \mathcal{R}$.

The *routing problem* for a network G and a communication pattern $\mathcal{R}$ is a problem of specifying a path collection $\mathcal{P}$ satisfying $\mathcal{R}$. A path collection is simple if no path contains the same link more than once, and it is a shortest path collection if for each $(u, v) \in \mathcal{R}$ only shortest paths from u to v in G are considered. Satisfying a communication request consists of routing a message along a corresponding path in $\mathcal{P}$. In this paper, the routing problem is solved by a path collection induced by interval routing schemes. In what follows we shall consider all-to-all communication patterns only unless otherwise specified.

An *Interval Labeling Scheme* (ILS) is given by labeling each node in a graph G by a unique integer from the set $\{1, 2, ..., n\}$ and each link by an interval $[a, b]$, where $a, b \in \{1, 2, ..., n\}$. We allow cyclic intervals $[a, b]$ such that $[a, b] = \{a, a+1, ..., n, 1, ..., b\}$ for $a > b$. The set of all intervals associated with the links incident with a node must form a partition of the set $\{1, 2, ..., n\}$. Messages to a destination node having a label l are routed via the link labeled by the interval $[a, b]$ such that $l \in [a, b]$. An ILS is valid if the set of paths specified by this ILS satisfies the all-to-all communication pattern. (Thus, if, for all nodes u and v in G, messages sent from u to v reach v correctly, not necessarily via shortest paths.) A valid ILS is also called an *Interval Routing Scheme* (IRS). An IRS thus specifies for each pair of distinct nodes u and v in G a (unique) path from u to v.

In a k-ILS each link is labeled with up to k intervals, always under the assumption that at every node, all intervals associated with links outgoing from the node form a partition of $\{1, ..., n\}$. At any given node a message with destination node labeled l is routed via the link labeled by the interval containing l. If k-ILS does not use cyclic intervals, the k-ILS is called *linear* or simply k-LILS. Valid k-ILS and k-LILS are called k-IRS and k-LIRS respectively. A k-IRS (k-LIRS) is said to be *optimal* if it represents a shortest path collection containing exactly one shortest path between any pair of nodes.

Multi-dimensional interval routing schemes (MIRS for short) are an extention of interval routing schemes. In (k,d)-MIRS every node is labeled by a unique d-tuple $(l_1, ..., l_d)$, where each l_i is from the set $\{1, ..., n_i\}$ ($1 \leq n_i \leq n$). Each link is labeled by up to k d-tuples of cyclic intervals $(I_{1,1}, ..., I_{d,1}), ..., (I_{1,k}, ..., I_{d,k})$.

In any node a message with destination $(l_1, ..., l_d)$ is routed along any outgoing link containing a d-tuple of cyclic intervals $(I_1, ..., I_d)$ such that $l_i \in I_i$ for all i. In this case, multiple paths are represented by the scheme, so the intervals on the links of a given node may overlap, i.e. they do not form a partition of the nodes in V.

We intend to model the packet routing, i.e. the so called store-and-forward message passing in which the message from u to v passing via w has to be stored at the node w before it is sent further towards v. We shall assume each node contains a finite number of *buffers*. For a message to pass via a link (x, y) it means, that it has to be moved from a buffer at node x to a buffer at node y. This assumes the existence of an available (i.e., empty) buffer at y.

We follow the notions introduced in [4]. In packet routing, each message is represented by its source-destination pair. For a given message $m = (u, v)$ and a buffer b containing m, a controller $C : V \times V \times B \mapsto 2^B$ specifies the subset $C(u, v, b)$ of buffers which can contain m in the next step along the path to its destination v. We say that a controller C is deadlock-free if it does not yield any deadlock configuration. This property can be guaranteed if the resulting buffer dependencies graph is acyclic. In *buffer dependencies graph* [8], each node represents a buffer and there is a directed edge between b_i and b_j if there is at least one message $m = (u, v)$ such that $b_j \in C(u, v, b_i)$.

Let us by s_u denote the number of buffers used by a controller C at the node u. For a network $G = (V, A)$ and a controller C for G, we define the *size* s of C as $s = max_{u \in V}(s_u)$.

Assume a path $\pi = v_1, ..., v_r$ connecting v_1 to v_r. We say that the controller C *covers* π if there exist r buffers $b_1, ..., b_r$ such that for each i, $1 \leq i \leq r$, b_i belongs to v_i and for each i, $1 \leq i \leq r - 1$, $b_{i+1} \in C(v_1, v_r, b_i)$.

We need to extend the standard k-IRS to deadlock-free k-IRS. Notice that each k-IRS uniquely induces the set of simple paths, one for each pair of nodes in G. A (k, s)-DFIRS (*deadlock-free IRS*) for a graph G is a k-IRS for G together with a deadlock-free routing controller of size s for G which covers the set of paths represented by the k-IRS. The (k, s)-DFIRS is optimal if the k-IRS is optimal.

All controllers considered in this paper are based on the concept of an acyclic orientation covering. An *acyclic orientation* of a graph $G = (V, A)$ is an acyclic directed graph $DG = (V, DA)$ obtained by orienting all links in A. Let $\mathcal{G} = \langle DG_1, ..., DG_s \rangle$ be a sequence of (not necessarily distinct) acyclic orientations of a graph G and let $\pi = v_1, ..., v_r$ be a simple path in G. We say that $\mathcal{G}$ *covers* π if there exists a sequence of positive integers $j_1, ..., j_{r-1}$ such that $1 \leq j_1 \leq ... \leq j_{r-1} \leq s$ and for every i, $1 \leq i \leq r - 1$, (v_i, v_{i+1}) belongs to DG_{j_i}.

Note that a path π need not be covered by $\mathcal{G}$ in a unique way. There could be different sequences $k_1, ..., k_{r-1}$ such that (v_i, v_{i+1}) belongs to DG_{k_i}. But there exists a unique sequence such that the corresponding $(r - 1)$-tuple $(k_1, ..., k_{r-1})$ is minimal (w.r.t. the lexicographical ordering). We assume that the deadlock-free controller based on $\mathcal{G}$ works with minimal tuples. Such a controller is called *greedy*.

Let $\mathcal{P}$ be a set of simple paths connecting every pair of nodes in G. A sequence of orientations $\mathcal{G} = \langle DG_1, ..., DG_s \rangle$ is said to be an *acyclic orientation covering* for $\mathcal{P}$ of size s if $\mathcal{G}$ covers at least one path $\pi \in \mathcal{P}$ for each pair of nodes in G. A $((k, d), s) - DFMIRS$ (*deadlock-free MIRS*) for a graph G is a $(k, d) - MIRS$ for G together with a deadlock-free controller of size s for G which covers the set of paths induced by the $(k, d) - MIRS$.

The main problem covered is to design the deterministic packet routing protocol based on a possibly nondeterministic $(k, d) - MIRS$ with a deadlock-free routing controller (based on acyclic orientation covering $\mathcal{G} = \langle DG_1, ..., DG_s \rangle$) of size s for G. In this paper we solve this problem by applying the greedy mode. At the source node, the message destined for the node labeled l is routed via a link e having the interval containing l and satisfying $e \in DG_1$. Only if such a possibility does not exist it chooses the next orientation DG_2. Generally, at an arbitrary node, the protocol first chooses a link in the current orientation DG_j according to $(k, d) - MIRS$ and only if such a link does not exist, it switches to the next acyclic orientation DG_{j+1} in $\mathcal{G}$. We call this strategy a greedy one. All $((k, d), s) - DFMIRS$ in this paper are working with the greedy strategy.

The importance of acyclic orientation coverings is stated by the following classical result (see [11]) formulated for all-to-all communication patterns: given a network G and a set of simple paths $\mathcal{P}$ connecting all pairs of nodes in G, if an acyclic orientation covering of size s for $\mathcal{P}$ exists, then there exists a deadlock-free packet routing controller of size s for G which covers $\mathcal{P}$.

3 Results

The size of deadlock-free controllers for the optimal (shortest paths) packet routing on arbitrary networks strongly depends on the structure of communication patterns. The following fact for all-to-all communication patterns can be found e.g. in [11]: for any network G and a set of $n.(n - 1)$ shortest paths connecting every pair of nodes in G, there is a deadlock-free controller (based on an acyclic orientation covering) of size $D + 1$, where D is the diameter of G. The best lower bound on the size of deadlock-free controllers is 3 [2].

Considering all-to-all communication patterns on arbitrary networks, the problem is to determine nonconstant lower bound on the size of a deadlock-free controller (based on acyclic orientation covering concept) necessary for the optimal packet routing.

However, if we assume static one-to-all communication patterns, the requirements for the size of deadlock-free controllers are much lower. Namely, for any network G and a set of $n-1$ shortest paths connecting a node with all other nodes in G, there is a deadlock-free controller (based on acyclic orientation covering) of size 1.

For other types of communication patterns the problems are again unsolved. What is the number of buffers sufficient to realize dynamic one-to-all or permutation communication patterns? Can we do better than $D + 1$ buffers per node?

We shall concentrate on specific networks. We shall study the relationship between the size and the compactness of deadlock-free packet routing, based on interval routing schemes, for certain interconnection networks including hypercubes, tori, butterflies and cube connecting cycles.

3.1 Hypercubes

A d-dimensional hypercube H_d is the cartesian product of d complete graphs K_2.

Lemma 1. *There exists a deadlock-free controller of size 2 for the optimal packet routing on a d-dimensional hypercube.*

Proof. A hypercube H_d is a node symmetric graph, so we can fix an arbitrary node as the initiator of H_d and assign it the string 0^d. Let the unique string of the nodes in H_d be from $\{0,1\}^d$ such that two nodes are neighbors if and only if their strings differ in exactly one bit. Define the acyclic orientation covering $\mathcal{G} = \langle DH_1, DH_2 \rangle$ of a hypercube such that in DH_1 all links are oriented from all the nodes towards the initiator and in DH_2 the orientation is opposite.

It is easy to verify that $\mathcal{G}$ forms a greedy deadlock-free controller of size 2 for H_d. There exists a collection of shortest paths between all pairs of vertices in H_d, covered by $\mathcal{G}$. Given any two nodes u and v in H_d with corresponding strings α and β, a shortest path from u to v follows

- in the first place links (in arbitrary order) changing bit 1 to 0 in all positions in which α has 1 and β has 0, and
- later on links (in arbitrary order) changing bit 0 to 1 in all positions in which α has 0 and β has 1.

□

When we consider dynamic one-to-all communication patterns instead of all-to-all communication patterns, we get the following consequence of the previous lemma.

Corollary 2. *There exists a deadlock-free controller of size 2 for the optimal packet routing on a d-dimensional hypercube with dynamic one-to-all communication patterns.*

The next two results are from [4]. When we consider linear interval routing schemes, the size $d + 1$ can be obtained with compactness 1, and the reduction to the size 2 can be achieved with the compactness 2^{d-1}.

Lemma 3. *For every i $(1 \leq i \leq d)$ there exists a $(2^{i-1}, \lceil d/i \rceil + 1) - DFLIRS$ for a d-dimensional hypercube.*

Corollary 4. *There exists a $(1, d+1) - DFLIRS$ on a d-dimensional hypercube.*

We now show that using d-dimensional interval routing schemes (see [5]) the size 2 can be achieved with compactness just 1.

Theorem 5. *For every i $(1 \leq i \leq d)$ there exists a $((2^{i-1}, \lceil d/i \rceil), 2) - DFMIRS$ for a d-dimensional hypercube.*

Proof. Consider a d-dimensional hypercube $H_d = (V, A)$, given as the product of $\lfloor d/i \rfloor$ subcubes of dimension i and a subcube of dimension $d \bmod i$. For simplicity, assume $d \bmod i = 0$. Observe that each of these d/i subcubes $H_i^{(j)} = (V_j, A_j)$, $1 \leq j \leq d/i$, of dimensions i admits a $(\lceil 2^{i-1}/i \rceil, 1)$-MIRS.

We label each node in V by the d-tuple

$$(l_{1,1}, ..., l_{1,i}, l_{2,1}, ..., l_{2,i}, ..., l_{d/i,1}, ..., l_{d/i,i})$$

$(l_{p,q} \in \{0,1\}, 1 \leq p \leq d/i, 1 \leq q \leq i)$ where for each j, $(l_{j,1}, ..., l_{j,i})$ is the label of a node in V_j in the $(\lceil 2^{i-1}/i \rceil, 1)$-MIRS of $H_i^{(j)}$.

We label each link $e = ((l_1, ..., l_h, ..., l_d), (l_1, ..., \hat{l}_h, ..., l_d))$ in A, $\hat{l}_h = 1 - l_h$, by $\lceil 2^{i-1}/i \rceil$ d/i-tuples

$$(I_{1,1}, ..., I_{1,d/i}), ..., (I_{\lceil 2^{i-1}/i \rceil,1}, ..., I_{\lceil 2^{i-1}/i \rceil,d/i})$$

where $(k-1).i+1 \leq h \leq k.i$ (for some $k \in \{1, ..., d/i\}$), and for each m such that either $m < (k-1).i + 1$ or $m > k.i$, $I_{1,\lceil m/i \rceil} = I_{2,\lceil m/i \rceil} = ... = I_{\lceil 2^{i-1}/i \rceil,\lceil m/i \rceil}$ is the interval containing the $\lceil m/i \rceil$-th dimensional component of all node labels, and $I_{1,\lceil h/i \rceil}, ..., I_{\lceil 2^{i-1}/i \rceil,\lceil h/i \rceil}$ are the $\lceil 2^{i-1}/i \rceil$ intervals associated at the node $(l_1, ..., l_h, ..., l_d)$ to the link $((l_1, ..., l_h, ..., l_d), (l_1, ..., \hat{l}_h, ..., l_d))$ in the $(\lceil 2^{i-1}/i \rceil, 1)$-MIRS for $H_i^{(j)}$, $1 \leq j \leq d/i$.

It is easy to verify that the described scheme correctly transmits messages via shortest paths. At each link the number of intervals is at most $\lceil 2^{i-1}/i \rceil$, hence it can be no worse than 2^{i-1} for each i. The dimension of the product cube H_d is clearly the sum of dimensions of all the subcubes, i.e. d/i. Following the proof of Lemma 1 we get a deadlock-free controller of size 2 working in the greedy mode for the optimal packet routing on H_d. $\square$

Corollary 6. *There is a $((1, d), 2)$-DFMIRS on a d-dimensional hypercube.*

In Lemma 1 we proved that there exists a deadlock-free controller, for packet routing on a hypercube, which uses only two buffers in each node and allows messages to be routed via shortest paths. G. Tel [11] posed the question whether it is possible to obtain the set of the paths used by means of a (linear) interval routing scheme. We argue that there is no $(1, 2)$-DFLIRS (based on acyclic orientation controller) on a d-dimensional hypercube. (It is sufficient to show the nonexistence of $(1, 2) - DFLIRS$ on d-dimensional hypercubes for a small constant dimension.)

There exists an acyclic orientation covering of size $d + 1$ for the set of all shortest paths between all pairs of nodes in H_d. We show that the relevant lower bound is $\sqrt{d}$.

The d-dimensional hypercube has a node set consisting of all binary strings of length d with two nodes being connected if and only if they differ in exactly one bit. Thus every path in the hypercube corresponds to a sequence of changes of some bits. If the bits are changed in order from left to right then the path is called *monotone*.

Theorem 7. *Let $\mathcal{P}$ be a path system of a d-dimensional hypercube such that each path between any node v and its complement $\bar{v}$ in $\mathcal{P}$ is monotone. Every acyclic orientation covering for $\mathcal{P}$ has size at least $\sqrt{d}$.*

Proof. A movement of a message along the monotone path connecting a node v and its complement $\bar{v}$ can be simulated by a device consisting of a tape with d cells and a cursor which can be positioned either between any two neighboring cells or at the two ends of the tape. Initially the tape contains the string v and the cursor is on the left end of the tape. Moving a message along one link of the path corresponds to moving the cursor over one cell to the right and inverting the content of that cell. Reaching the destination is equivalent to reaching the right end of the tape. If we are given some acyclic orientation of the hypercube then we allow the cursor to advance only if the corresponding link is properly oriented in the current orientation.

If a sequence $\langle DG_1, ..., DG_s \rangle$ of acyclic orientations of the hypercube is an acyclic orientation covering for $\mathcal{P}$ then if we start the device on any node v and move the cursor according to $DG_1, ..., DG_s$ (in this order, using the greedy strategy) then the cursor reaches the right end of the tape.

Let us assume we shall start the device on all 2^d nodes simultaneously and consider the positions of cursors following the use of each acyclic orientation. An important observation is that for any acyclic orientation only few cursors can make long movements. For any positions of cursors $a, b \in \{0, ..., d\}$, $a < b$ and any acyclic orientation there are at most $2^d/(b-a+1)$ cursors that move between positions a and b in this orientation. For the sake of contradiction suppose that for some a, b there are more than $2^d/(b-a+1)$ cursors moving between positions a and b. From now on we consider only these cursors and their devices. For each device for each of the $b - a + 1$ cursor positions between a and b the tape of the device has different contents. Therefore there must exist two devices that have the same tape content with both cursors between a and b. Let this content be $w_1 w_2 w_3$, the cursor of the first device being between w_1 and w_2 and the cursor of the second device being between w_2 and w_3. In this orientation the first device will move from $w_1|w_2 w_3$ to $w_1 \overline{w_2}|w_3$ and the second device moved from $w_1|\overline{w_2} w_3$ to $w_1 w_2|w_3$. Therefore there is a cycle in the acyclic orientation between $w_1 w_2 w_3$ and $w_1 \overline{w_2} w_3$ which is a contradiction.

Now we are ready to prove that after the i-th orientation at least $\left(1 - \frac{i}{\sqrt{d}}\right) 2^d$ cursors are at most at position $i\sqrt{d}$. For $i = 0$ the claim holds since at the begining all cursors are at position 0. Let the claim holds after the i-th orientation. Based on the observation above at most $2^d/\sqrt{d}$ cursors can advance more than $\sqrt{d}$ positions to the right in the $i + 1$-st orientation. Thus the claim holds also after the $i + 1$-st orientation. Clearly the claim implies the theorem. $\square$

In the 1-LIRS of the hypercube proposed in [1] every path between node and its complement is monotone. The consequence of the previous theorem is that this 1-LIRS is not suitable for the efficient deadlock-free packet routing (based on acyclic orientation covering).

One can observe that there exists a general deadlock-free controller of constant size covering the set of routing paths $\mathcal{P}$ from Theorem 7.

3.2 Tori

A d-dimensional torus $T_{n_1,...,n_d}$ is the cartesian product of d rings $R_1, ..., R_d$, in which each R_i has n_i nodes.

Lemma 8. *There exists a deadlock-free controller of size 4 for the optimal packet routing on a d-dimensional torus.*

Proof. For simplicity, we will assume the case of 2 dimensions. The case of d dimensions is handled in a similar fashion. Fix an arbitrary node w of an $n \times m$ torus $T_{n,m}$. For simplicity, consider n, m even. Say $w = (n/2, m/2)$. Define the acyclic orientation covering $\mathcal{G} = \langle DT_1, DT_2, DT_1, DT_2 \rangle$ of a 2-dimensional tori $T_{n,m}$ such that in DT_1 the links are oriented from (i,j) to $(i+1,j)$ for $i = 1, 2, ..., n/2 - 2, n/2, ..., n$ and $1 \leq j \leq m$ and from (i,j) to $(i,j+1)$ for $1 \leq i \leq n$, $j = 1, 2, ..., m/2 - 2, m/2, ..., m$ and the links are oriented from $(n/2, j)$ to $(n/2 - 1, j)$ for $1 \leq j \leq m$ and from $(i, m/2)$ to $(i, m/2 - 1)$ for $1 \leq i \leq n$. In DT_2 all links are in opposite orientation. Edges $((n/2 - 1, j), (n/2, j))$ for $1 \leq j \leq m$ and $((i, m/2 - 1), (i, m/2))$ for $1 \leq i \leq n$ form row and column frontiers, respectively.

It is easy to verify that $\mathcal{G}$ forms a deadlock-free controller of size 4 for $T_{n,m}$. There is a collection of shortest paths between all pairs of nodes in $T_{n,m}$ that can be covered by $\mathcal{G}$. Given any two nodes u and v in $T_{n,m}$ with coordinates (i,j) and (k,l), respectively, there exists a shortest path from u to v that can be partitioned into four subpaths (where some of them may be empty) such that these subpaths are contained in coverings DT_1, DT_2, DT_1, DT_2, respectively. If the shortest path from u to v does not cross frontiers, the routing from u to v can be done using DT_1, DT_2. If the shortest path from u to v crosses one or two frontiers, the routing from u can reach frontiers using either DT_1 or DT_1, DT_2, then routing through frontiers can be performed with the next orientation in $\mathcal{G}$ and finally routing to v can be done with the next orientation in $\mathcal{G}$. $\square$

The question remains whether it is possible to induce the set of paths achieved by deadlock-free controllers of size 4 by means of efficient interval routing schemes.

The next two results are from [4]. When we consider linear interval routing schemes, the size $2d + 1$ can be obtained with the compactness 2, and the restriction to the size 5 can be achieved with the compactness $O(n^{d-1})$.

Lemma 9. *There exists a $(2, 2d+1)$-DFLIRS for a d-dimensional torus.*

Lemma 10. *For every n and i $(1 < i < d)$ there exists a $(\lceil n^i/2 \rceil, 2.\lceil d/i \rceil + 1)$-DFLIRS on a d-dimensional torus.*

On the other hand, when using d-dimensional interval routing schemes (see [5]) the size 4 can be achieved with compactness of only 1.

Theorem 11. *For every n and i $(1 \le i \le d)$ there exists a $((n^{i-1}, \lceil d/i \rceil), 4) - DFMIRS$ on a d-dimensional torus.*

Proof. Consider a d-dimensional torus, given as the product of $\lfloor d/i \rfloor$ subtori of dimension i and a subtorus of dimension $d \bmod i$. For simplicity, assume $d \bmod i = 0$. Observe that each of these d/i subtori of dimension i admits $(n^{i-1}, 1)$-MIRS. Now, the proof follows in a similar way as the proof of Theorem 5 for hypercubes. Following the proof of Lemma 8 we get a deadlock-free controller of size 4 working in the greedy mode for the optimal packet routing on d-dimensional tori, based on $(n^{i-1}, \lceil d/i \rceil)$-MIRS. $\square$

Corollary 12. *There exists a $((1, d), 4) - DFMIRS$ on a d-dimensional torus.*

3.3 Butterflies

The d-dimensional butterfly network (BF_d for short) has $(d+1).2^d$ nodes and $d.2^{d+1}$ links. The nodes correspond to pairs (α, p), where $p \in \{0, ..., d\}$ is the position of the node and α is a d-bit binary number. The two nodes (α, p) and (α', p') are connected by a link if and only if $p' = p + 1$ and either α and α' are identical or α and α' differ only in the p'th bit.

Lemma 13. *There exists a deadlock-free controller of size 4 for the optimal packet routing on a d-dimensional butterfly.*

Proof. Let $u = (a_{d-1}...a_0, p)$ and $v = (b_{d-1}...b_0, q)$, $p \ge q$, be two nodes in BF_d. The distance $d(u, v)$ is $d(u, v) = p - q$ if $a_i = b_i$ for $i = 0, 1, ..., d-1$ and $d(u, v) = r_{max} - r_{min} + |p - r_{max}| + |q - r_{min}| + c$, where $c = 0$ for $p > r_{max}$, otherwise $c = 2$, and where $r_{max} = max\{i \mid a_i \ne b_i, 0 \le i \le d-1\}$ and $r_{min} = min\{i \mid a_i \ne b_i, 0 \le i \le d-1\}$. In order to reach the length $d(u, v)$, take the shortest path in BF_d from $(b_{d-1}...b_0, q)$ to $(b_{d-1}...b_0, r_{min})$ following $|r_{min} - q|$ links, then the shortest path from $(b_{d-1}...b_0, r_{min})$ to $(a_{d-1}...a_0, r_{max} + 1)$ following $|r_{max} - r_{min}|$ links and finally the shortest path from $(a_{d-1}...a_0, r_{max} + 1)$ to $(a_{d-1}...a_0, p)$ following $|r_{max} - p| - 1$ links when $p > r_{max}$, and $|r_{max} - p| + 1$ links otherwise.

Now, it is easy to verify that each shortest path between two nodes in BF_d can be partitioned into three subpaths such that each subpath either continuously increases or decreases the position parameter p. Hence, there is a deadlock-free controller of size 4 on BF_d. $\square$

It was shown in [7] that there does not exist efficient IRS for d-dimensional butterflies.

Lemma 14. *Each optimal k-IRS for a d-dimensional butterfly needs $k = \Omega(2^{d/2})$ intervals.*

However, there are efficient MIRS on d-dimensional butterflies, with deadlock-free controllers of size only 4.

Lemma 15. *There is a $((2,3),4)$-DFMIRS on a d-dimensional butterfly.*

Proof. Consider the following machine. It has a working tape $[a_1 a_2...a_i | a_{i+1}...a_d]$ with d cells containing bits "a_i" and a head "$|$" which can be positioned between cells or at any end of the tape. In one step the head moves to the left or to the right and writes 0 or 1 to the cell over which it has passed. The graph with vertices corresponding to states of this machine and links corresponding to steps is exactly the d-dimensional butterfly graph. This allows us to consider nodes of BF_d to be the states of the machine described.

Given BF_d and a node w of the form $[u\alpha|v]$, then there exist shortest paths from w to the nodes

- of the form (A): $[\beta_1|\beta_2]$, $|\beta_1| \geq |u\alpha|$, $u\alpha$ is not a prefix of β_1
- or of the form (B): $[\beta_1|\beta_2 0v]$

starting with the link e corresponding to moving the head to the left and writing 0. These are the only such nodes in BF_d.

We have to show that for BF_d there exists a $(2,3)$-MIRS. Let us label the nodes in the three dimensions as follows:

- 1st dimension: The number written on the tape.
- 2nd dimension: The number written on the tape read backwards.
- 3rd dimension: The position of the head.

For each node w and a link e described above it is possible to select the nodes of the form (A) and (B) using two triples of intervals. The first triple selects the nodes not starting with $u\alpha$ (these form a cyclic interval in the 1st dimension) and not having the head to the left of w's head (these form a cyclic interval in the 3rd dimension). The second triple selects the nodes ending with $0v$ (these form a cyclic interval in the 2nd dimension) and having the head to the left of w's head. The construction is similar for the other types of links.

Define $\mathcal{G} = \langle DBF_1, DBF_2, DBF_1, DBF_2 \rangle$, where in DBF_1 the orientation of links is from $[a_1...a_i|a_{i+1}...a_d]$ to $[a_1...a_{i+1}|a_{i+2}...a_d]$ and from $[a_1...a_i|a_{i+1}...a_d]$ to $[a_1...\hat{a}_{i+1}|a_{i+2}...a_d]$ for $0 \leq i \leq d-1$ (where the head in position 0 means $[|a_1...a_d]$ and $\hat{a} = 1 - a$) and in DBF_2 the orientation is opposite. It is easy to verify that each shortest path induced by a $((2,3),4) - MIRS$ on BF_d can be covered by $\mathcal{G}$. □

3.4 Cube connected cycles

Let $u = (a_0...a_{d-1}, p)$ be a tuple consisting of a binary string and a cursor position from $\{0, ..., d-1\}$. The operations of shifting cursor cyclically to the left and to the right on u are denoted as $L(u)$ and $R(u)$, respectively, and the shuffle operation is defined as $S(u) = (a_0...\hat{a}_p...a_{d-1}, p)$, where $\hat{a}_p = 1 - a_p$.

A d-dimensional cube connected cycles (denoted as CCC_d) is a network (V, A), where $V = \{u \mid u \in \{0, 1\}^d \times \{0, ..., d-1\}\}$ and $A = \{(u, v) \mid R(u) = v \text{ or } L(u) = v \text{ or } S(u) = v\}$.

Lemma 16. *There exists an acyclic orientation covering of size $2d + 6$ for the system of all shortest paths between all pairs of nodes in CCC_d.*

Proof. Consider the following acyclic orientation DC_1: for each binary string $\alpha = a_0...a_{d-1}$ the cycle $(\alpha, 0), ..., (\alpha, d-1)$ is oriented $(\alpha, 0) \to ... \to (\alpha, d-1)$ and $(\alpha, 0) \to (\alpha, d-1)$; the remaining links are oriented arbitrarily provided that the resulting orientation is acyclic. The covering $\mathcal{G}$ consists of an alternating sequence of DC_1 and its opposite DC_2 of length $2d + 6$.

Consider an arbitrary shortest path $\pi = (\alpha_0, p_0), ..., (\alpha_k, p_k)$. It clearly contains at most d S-links (such that $p_i = p_{i+1}$). By cycle segment we mean maximal subpath of π that contains no S-link. If a cycle segment does not contain a link $(\alpha, 0), (\alpha, d-1)$ for some α then the entire segment is covered either by DC_1 or by DC_2. Call this segment as non-zero segment. Each zero segment consists of at most three paths such that each of them is covered either by DC_1 or by DC_2.

Because each shortest path contains at most two vertices $(\alpha_1, p), (\alpha_2, p)$ with the same cursor position p, there are at most two zero segments.

Thus π consists of at most $2d+5$ parts (i.e. d S-links, $d-1$ non-zero segments and two zero segments each of three paths) all of which are covered either by DC_1 or by DC_2. Hence π is covered by $\mathcal{G}$. $\square$

Corollary 17. *There exists a deadlock-free controller of size $2d + 6$ for the optimal packet routing on a d-dimensional cube connected cycles network.*

It was shown in [7] that there does not exist an efficient shortest paths IRS for CCC_d (superpolynomial compactness in d is required !).

Lemma 18. *Each optimal k-IRS for a d-dimensional cube connected cycles network needs $k = \Omega(2^{d/2})$.*

Now we show that there are efficient d-dimensional IRS on CCC_d with compactness and size polynomial in d.

Theorem 19. *There exists a $((2d^3, d), 2d + 6) - DFMIRS$ on CCC_d.*

Proof. Let us define a machine whose state diagram is the d-dimensional cube-connected-cycles graph. Its working tape is a *circular* strip consisting of d cells. The head can be positioned above any cell. Each cell can contain one binary digit. In one step the head can change the content of the cell read or move one position to the left or to the right. Again we consider nodes being the states of the machine described.

Let u, v be two nodes of the CCC_d. Take $u\ XOR\ v$ (the tape is unwinded on the picture):

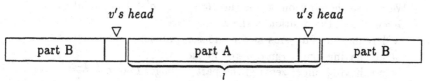

Denote a, b and a' the lengths of the longest runs of consecutive zeros in parts A, B and $A'(= A$ *without the rightmost cell*) respectively and b' the length of the run of consecutive zeros in part B starting immediately to the right of the position of u's head. There exists a shortest path from u to v starting with the left arc e if and only if either:

A: $a' = a$ and $2(l + b - a) \leq d$

or

B: $b' = b$ and $2(l + b - a) \geq d$ and u, v do not differ in the cell scanned by u's head.

The condition for the existence of a shortest path starting with the right arc is symmetric. There exists a shortest path from u to v starting with the shuffle arc if and only if u and v differ in the cell scanned by u's head. Now we briefly describe the $(2d^3, d) - MIRS$ of CCC_d.

The vertices in the i-th dimension ($i \in \{1, ..., d\}$) have numbers $1, ..., d$ according to the following lexicographic ordering:

– the first criterion is the position of the head
– the second criterion is the number written on the tape after the cyclic rotation by i bits to the left

In this labeling the vertices having the same position of the head form a block in each dimension. Another important property of the labeling is that selecting vertices having the head at any given position and containing (resp. not containing) any given binary substring at any given position of the tape can be done using at most two intervals in one block of *one* dimension. The dimension in which intervals are used is determined by the position of the substring.

Let u be any vertex of the CCC_d graph. Labeling the shuffle arc emanating from u is easy, as exactly messages to the vertices having a different symbol at the position of $u's$ head are to be routed along it. As there exists a dimension such that in each of its blocks such vertices form a cyclic interval, we need only d intervals per dimension.

Labeling the left arc is more complicated. We select vertices whose messages are to be routed along this arc for each position of their head independently. If for each given position we need at most q intervals per dimension to select such vertices then in total we need at most dq intervals per dimension.

Vertices satisfying the rule A and having the head at a given position are to be selected as follows:

- We choose the length a' of the longest run of consecutive zeros in the part A' of $u\ XOR\ v$ ($len(A') + 1$ possibilities)
- We choose the position of this run ($len(A') - a' + 1$ possibilities)
- Given a' and the position of the run, vertices
  - having run of a' zeros at the choosen position
  - not having longer run of zeros in the part A
  - not having run of zeros in the part B longer than $a + \frac{d-2l}{2}$

can be selected using two intervals per dimension, because we can fulfill these conditions by selecting the vertices having, or not having certain substrings at different positions.

Vertices satisfying the rule B and having the head at a given position are to be selected as follows:

- We choose the length b' of the run of consecutive zeros in the part B starting immediately to the right of the position of u's head. ($len(B)+1$ possibilities)
- Given b', vertices
  - having run of b' zeros in the part B starting immediately to the right of the position of u's head
  - not having longer run of zeros in the part B
  - not having run of zeros in the part A longer than $b + \frac{2l-d}{2}$
  - not differing from u in the cell scanned by u's head

can be selected using two intervals per dimension, using the same reasoning as in the previous case.

It holds $(len(A') + 1)(len(A') + 1) + len(B) + 1 \le d^2$, therefore we have used in total at most $2d^3$ intervals per dimension which gives us the $(2d^3, d) - MIRS$.
□

4 Conclusions

We have presented efficient deadlock-free MIRSs on hypercubes, tori, butterflies and cube connected cycles. These results can be transformed also to an analogous wormhole routing model (as formulated in [4]). The main question remains whether there are efficient deadlock-free MIRS also for wider classes of graphs, e.g. vertex symmetric graphs, planar graphs etc.

We have also presented a nonconstant lower bound on the size of deadlock-free controllers (based on acyclic orientation covering) for a special set of routing paths in d-dimensional hypercubes. This is the first nontrivial lower bound on specific controllers. Moreover, this set of routing paths can be covered by general deadlock-free controllers of constant size, thus giving the first example of differences between sizes of general and specific controllers. The question is to determine nonconstant lower bounds on the size of deadlock-free controllers for general networks and to give size differences between general and specific deadlock-free controllers.

There are still many unresolved questions concerning DFMIRS (some of them are mentioned in Section 3). It would be nice to have a trade-off between compactness and size for deadlock-free MIRS on general graphs.

References

1. E. Bakker, J. van Leeuwen, R.B. Tan: *Linear interval routing schemes.* Algorithms Review 2, 1991, pp. 45–61.
2. R. Cypher, L. Gravano: *Requirements for Deadlock-Free, Adaptive Packet Routing.* In 14th Annual ACM Symposium on Principles of Distributed Computing (PODC), 1992, pp. 25–33.
3. W.J. Dally, C.L. Seitz: *Deadlock-free message routing in multiprocessor interconnection networks.* IEEE Transactions on Computers, C-36, 1987, pp. 547–553.
4. M. Flammini: *Deadlock-Free Interval Routing Schemes.* In 14th Annual Symposium on Theoretical Aspects of Computer Science (STACS), Lecture Notes in Computer Science 1200, Springer-Verlag, 1997, pp. 351–362.
5. M. Flammini, G. Gambosi, U. Nanni, R. Tan: *Multi-Dimensional Interval Routing Schemes.* In 9th International Workshop on Distributed Algorithms (WDAG), Lecture Notes in Computer Science, Springer-Verlag, 1995. To appear in Theoretical Computer Science.
6. C. Gavoille: *A Survey on Interval Routing Schemes.* Research Report RR-1182-97, LaBRI, Université Bordeaux I, October 1997. Submitted for publication.
7. R. Královič, P. Ružička, D. Štefankovič: *The Complexity of Shortest Path and Dilation Bounded Interval Routing.* In 3rd International Euro-Par Conference, Lecture Notes in Computer Science 1300, Springer-Verlag, August 1997, pp. 258–265. Full version will appear in Theoretical Computer Science.
8. P.M. Merlin, P.J. Schweitzer: *Deadlock avoidance in store-and-forward networks.* IEEE Transactions of Communications, COM-27, 1980, pp. 345–360.
9. P. Ružička, D. Štefankovič: *On the Complexity of Multi-Dimensional Interval Routing Schemes.* Submitted for publication.
10. I. Sakko, L. Mugwaneza, Y. Langue: *Routing with compact tables.* Applications in Parallel and Distributed Computing (APDC), North-Holland, 1994.
11. G. Tel: *Introduction to Distributed Algorithms. (Chapter 5: Deadlock-free Packet Routing).* Cambridge University Press, Cambridge, U.K., 1994.
12. S. Toueg: *Deadlock-free and livelock-free packet switching networks.* In Proceedings of Symposium on Theory of Computing (STOCS), 1980, pp. 94–99.
13. S. Toueg, J. Ullman: *Deadlock-free packet switching networks.* SIAM Journal of Computing 10, 1981, pp. 594–611.
14. J. van Leeuwen, R.B. Tan: *Compact routing methods: A survey.* In 1st International Colloquium on Structural Information and Communication Complexity (SIROCCO), Carleton Press, 1994, pp. 99–110.
15. J. Vounckx, G. Deconinck, R. Lauwereins, J.A. Peperstraete: *Deadlock-free Fault Tolerant Wormhole Routing in Mesh-Based Massively Parallel Systems.* In Technical Committee on Computer Architecture (TCCA) Newsletter, IEEE Computer Society, Summer-Fall issue, 1994, pp. 49–54.
16. J. Vounckx, G. Deconinck, R. Cuyvers, R. Lauwereins: *Minimal Deadlock-free Compact Routing in Wormhole-Switching based Injured Meshes.* In Proceedings of the 2nd Reconfigurable Architectures Workshop, Santa Barbora, Ca, 1995.

A New Protocol for Efficient Cooperative Transversal Web Caching

Jean-Marc Menaud, Valérie Issarny and Michel Banâtre

IRISA/INRIA Rennes Campus Universitaire de Beaulieu 35042 Rennes Cedex, FRANCE
{Jean-Marc.Menaud, Valerie.Issarny, Michel.Banatre}@irisa.fr

Abstract. The bandwidth demands on the World Wide Web continue to grow at an exponential rate. To address this problem, many research activities are focusing on the design of Web caches. Unfortunately, Web caches exhibit poor performance with a hit rate of about 30%. A solution to improve this rate, consists of groups of cooperating caches. In its most general form, a cooperative cache system includes protocols for hierarchical and transversal caching. Although such a system brings better performance, its drawback lies in the resulting network load due to the number of messages that need to be exchanged to locate an object. This paper introduces a new protocol for transversal cooperative caching, which significantly reduces the associated network load compared to that induced by existing systems. ...

1 Introduction

The ever-increasing popularity of the Internet is raising an urgent need for solutions aimed at masking the resulting traffic congestion and hence allowing improved response time. Two types of solutions have been explored: (i) increasing the bandwidth of the network links, which is of limited help due to the associated financial cost and technical problems; (ii) using caches over the Internet for replication of the most frequently accessed data. Although more affordable than the first solution, the actual benefit of caches for improving response time over the Internet still remains negligible [12]. Various approaches have been examined in order to increase the effectiveness of caches. These include the use of large caches and of more efficient cache management techniques. However, such approaches may only have a limited impact since most of the documents are accessed only once [1]. Furthermore, the use of large caches raises financial and technical problems. Other efforts have been focusing on the prefetching of data within caches but the resulting traffic overhead is too costly [7]. In that context, the most promising approach to cache effectiveness is to have a system of cooperating caches. Because that take advantage of network topology, the most popular types of cooperative cache systems are the hierarchical and the transversal ones, which are both implemented by the Squid software [11] from the Harvest project [2].

The hierarchical approach to cache cooperation is among the pioneering one and has been proposed by P. Danzig [3] in the light of a study on the Internet traffic in the USA. Results of this study showed that the Internet traffic can a priori be reduced by 30% through the introduction of a cache on every network node. The hierarchical structure of the cache system then came from the hierarchical organization of national networks. In a hierarchical cache system, a cache gets a missing requested object by issuing a request to the cache at the upper level in the hierarchy. The process is iterated until either the object is found or the root cache is reached, which may ultimately contact the object's server. The object is then copied in all the caches that got contacted when returned to the client. A transversal system enriches the hierarchical one by integrating a set of sibling caches, which are close in terms of latency time, at each level of the hierarchy. Then on a cache miss, a cache not only contacts its ancestor cache but also its siblings.

Hierarchical and transversal cache systems are being evaluated on various national networks such as Renater in France and Janet in the UK. Early results show that hierarchical systems bring actual benefit but there is no significant result for transversal systems. The effectiveness of a transversal system mainly depends on the number of siblings and hence on the number of caches composing the system. But, network administrators voluntarily set this number to 3 or 4 in order to limit the bandwidth overhead caused by the cooperation protocol of the transversal system. This overhead is a direct consequence of how a cache miss is handled in the implementation artifact: a request message is sent to all the siblings, and each of them replies by a hit or miss message, depending on the presence or absence of the requested object. Thus, the number of messages that are exchanged to get a global information about an object within a transversal system is equal to $2 \times (N - 1)$ with N being the number of siblings. This network overhead is far too costly and cannot be reduced since multicast is prohibited due to technical and security problems [11]. Another critical factor of a transversal system is the resulting workload for cache machines: a cache has to handle messages received from its siblings in addition to messages received from its clients. Actually, the workload of a cache in a transversal system is increased by a factor of N in terms of handled requests. Based on the aforementioned evaluation of transversal systems, we have designed a new protocol for transversal cooperation so as to gain the foreseen benefit of such cache systems while having negligible network and machine overhead, and providing a scalable solution.

This paper introduces our protocol for transversal cooperative caching, which we intend to integrate within the Squid software through modification of ICP (*Internet Cache Protocol*) [11], hence using the support of Squid for hierarchical cooperative caching and base cache management. The next section describes the proposed protocol for transversal cooperative caching where we assume an identical bandwidth for all the network links between caches of the transversal system, and homogeneous machines for all the caches. Section 3 then gives an evaluation of our protocol through a comparison with the transversal cooperation protocol of ICP. It is shown that our objective of minimizing both the cache workload and network load induced by transversal cooperation is met. Furthermore, our protocol allows to increase the effectiveness of a transversal cache system by a factor that is proportional to the square root of the number of caches in the system. Finally, Section 4 gives our conclusion.

2 Protocol for Efficient Transversal Cooperation

As previously stated, the workload caused by a transversal cache system results from the cooperation protocol that is used: a cache has to handle the requests issued by its siblings in addition to the ones received from its clients. In the Relais project [9], the way to minimize the number of messages exchanged among siblings is to have local knowledge of the state of the transversal cache system on each cache. Then, on the receipt of an object request, the cache is able to locally identify whether the object is in the transversal cache system based on its knowledge of the system's state. Should the object be within one of the cache's siblings, a request is issued to it in order to get a copy of the object. Local knowledge of the system's state has the advantage of introducing negligible workload for siblings when a cache handles an object request. However, such a local knowledge induces high memory consumption for storing the system state as well as a non negligible network load since messages need to be issued to siblings each time a cache is updated asynchronously or not. In the following, we describe our solution to transversal cooperation based on the idea of having a local knowledge of the system state, while minimizing the resulting memory consumption and network load. Due to our focus on transversal caching, the term *cache system* will be used to mean *transversal cache system* in the remainder.

2.1 Design principles

One way to alleviate the penalty of using local knowledge of the whole system state from the standpoint of memory consumption, is to distribute this knowledge among the caches composing the transversal system. Let us denote by $A(C_i)$, the set of sibling caches for which cache C_i knows locally the content, $A(C_i)$ including C_i. In other words, for each cache C_j of $A(C_i)$, C_i maintains a list, which gives the objects identities that are present on C_j. Let us further denote by S, the set of caches composing the transversal system. Then, to get knowledge of the whole system state and hence to locate an object that is not within a cache of $A(C_i)$, C_i must contact a set of caches, noted $D(C_i)$, as exemplified in Figure 1. The value of $D(C_i)$ should then be such that:

$$A(C_i) \bigcup \cup_{(\forall C_j \in D(C_i), j \neq i)} A(C_j) = S \qquad (1)$$

Thus, a cache C_i in the system can know the state of another cache C_x if C_i maintain locally C_x's list or if one of the caches contacted by C_i, noted C_j ($C_j \in D(C_i)$), maintains C_x's list ($C_x \in A(C_j)$). Note that when $\forall C_i \in S$: $A(C_i) = \{C_i\}$, we are in the presence of a traditional transversal system while when $\forall C_i \in S : \mathcal{A}(C_i) = S$, we are in the presence of a transversal system with local knowledge of the whole system state. Our objective is to find a solution that is a tradeoff between these two alternatives in terms of object retrieval latency, memory consumption, and message exchanges.

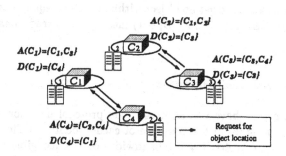

Fig. 1. Exploiting distributed knowledge of the system state

Let us first examine the issue of object retrieval latency in the worst case, where we omit communication between the client and its cache since the associated latency is the same for any cache system. In a traditional transversal system, the object retrieval latency is equal to 4 message exchanges between caches (considering that the time taken to retrieve an object within a cache is negligible compared to the cost of message exchanges): (i) For retrieving an object, a cache C_i sends, in parallel, the object request to its siblings, (ii) each sibling replies by a hit or a miss message depending on whether it holds the object or not, (iii) C_i sends a message to get the object, to one of the caches that replied by a hit, (iv) the object is finally sent to C_i. We observe the same latency using distributed knowledge of the system state. The only difference lies in the achievement of the first two steps: C_i sends messages to every cache C_j of $\mathcal{D}(C_i)$ instead of all the system's caches, each C_j then returns the list of caches that own the object with respect to the state held for the caches of $\mathcal{A}(C_j)$.

Let us now consider the issue of memory consumption. For every cache C_i of S, we want the cardinal of $\mathcal{A}(C_i)$, noted $|\mathcal{A}(C_i)|$, to be much smaller than $|S|$. Furthermore, the scalability criterion requires load balancing, which leads to set an identical value for the cardinal of every $\mathcal{A}(C_i)$.

In the worst case, the number of messages that are sent by a cache upon the treatment of an object request, to locate the object, is equal to $|\mathcal{D}(C_i)|$ and hence we want the cardinal of $\mathcal{D}(C_i)$ to be much smaller than the one of S. Furthermore, as for the cardinals of the $\mathcal{A}(C_i)$s, the cardinals of all the $\mathcal{D}(C_i)$s should be identical for our scalability criterion.

Figure 1 gives an example of a transversal system with distributed knowledge of the system state, for a system composed of 4 caches. Setting such a system depends upon the evaluation of $\mathcal{D}(C_i)$ and $\mathcal{A}(C_i)$ for every cache C_i of S. Furthermore, the value of these sets must satisfy the aforementioned condition of load balancing, and should be such that the number of messages sent for updating the system state on a cache update is minimal.

It can be shown (see appendix) that we have an optimal system meeting our scalability requirement if $|\mathcal{A}(C_i)| = \sqrt{|\mathcal{S}|}$ and $|\mathcal{D}(C_i)| = \sqrt{|\mathcal{S}|} - 1$, the number of exchanged messages on a cache update being then of $\sqrt{|\mathcal{S}|} - 1$. With such values, the network load to get an object within a cache is equal to $3 \times (\sqrt{|\mathcal{S}|} - 1)$ messages, while it is equal to $2 \times (|\mathcal{S}| - 1)$ messages in a traditional transversal system.

2.2 Dealing with cache updates

Up to this point, we have not addressed the protocol used for updating the distributed system state in the presence of cache update. In the following, we introduce an update protocol whose bandwidth cost is negligible.

Let us first consider the addition of an object $\mathcal{O}$ within a cache C_i, C_i must a priori send an update message to every cache C_j whose set $\mathcal{A}(C_j)$ includes C_i. Beforehand, for getting $\mathcal{O}$, C_i already sent messages to caches belonging to $\mathcal{D}(C_i)$[1]. Caches belonging to $\mathcal{D}(C_i)$ can anticipate that $\mathcal{O}$ will be within C_i since C_i requested for it. The two cases where the anticipation is wrong is when either (i) $\mathcal{O}$ no longer exists or (ii) C_i did not get $\mathcal{O}$ due to some failure (e.g. temporary communication failure). The latter case is too rare to have a real incidence on the correctness of anticipation and is thus not considered. The former case can be seen as a special value for the object and is hence cached in place of an actual object value. Thus, whenever a cache C_i is requested on objet $\mathcal{O}$ by a sibling cache C_j, it can anticipate that C_j will hold C_i. Setting further the following *Rule 1*, this allows us to withdraw the network load that was expected for handling the addition of an object within a cache.

Rule 1: for every C_i in $\mathcal{S}$, if C_i is in $\mathcal{D}(C_j)$ then C_j is in $\mathcal{A}(C_i)$.

In other words, a cache C_i that is directly contacted by another cache C_j (i.e. $C_i \in \mathcal{D}(C_j)$) to get an object, C_i maintains the state of this cache (i.e. $C_j \in \mathcal{A}(C_i)$).

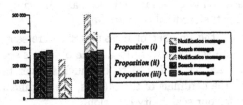

Fig. 2. Number of exchanged messages with different notification policies

---

[1] As will be shown in Subsection 2.2, this is because a cache C_i that searches remotely for an object seeks the object, in parallel, within the caches of both $\mathcal{A}(C_i)$ and $\mathcal{D}(C_i)$.

Let us now examine removal of an object within a cache C_i of the system. Using simulation, achieved in the same framework as simulations detailed in Section 3.2, we have compared three approaches: (i) notification for all object removal, (ii) notification of the object removal to a cache of $\mathcal{D}(C_i)$ when such a cache requests for the object while the object is not present, (iii) absence of notification to caches of $\mathcal{D}(C_i)$ with periodical emission of C_i's state to caches of $\mathcal{D}(C_i)$. Figure 2 gives results obtained by our simulations. It shows that the third solution gives better performance in terms of the overall bandwidth use, which was thus preferred for our protocol.

Figure 3 gives an example of a system composed of 4 caches where the distribution of the system's state is done according to *Rule 1*. As previously, setting such a system depends on the evaluation of $\mathcal{A}(C_i)$ and $\mathcal{D}(C_i)$ for every cache C_i of S, where we recall that the use of anticipation leads to have the following relation: $C_j \in \mathcal{D}(C_i) \Leftrightarrow C_i \in \mathcal{A}(C_j)$ for every C_i of S.

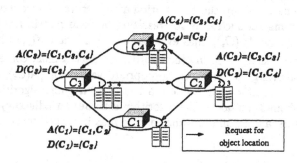

Fig. 3. Distributed knowledge of system state

Let us first address the computation of an optimal cardinal for both $\mathcal{A}(C_i)$ and $\mathcal{D}(C_i)$, under the criterion of scalability. The principle of our protocol lies in the use of a knowledge relation, noted K, where $K(i,j)$ holds if cache C_i knows the state of C_j. For the cache system to be correct, $K(i,j)$ must hold for all the pairs of system caches. Given the proposed distribution of the system state, we are able to set that: for two caches C_i and C_j of S, $K(i,j)$ holds if either $C_j \in \mathcal{A}(C_i)$, or $\exists C_k | C_k \in \mathcal{D}(C_i)$ and $C_j \in \mathcal{A}(C_k)$. Since $C_i \in \mathcal{A}(C_i)$ always holds for any cache C_i of S, we may simplify the above and get that $K(i,j)$ holds if $\exists C_k | C_k \in \mathcal{D}(C_i)$ and $C_j \in \mathcal{A}(C_k)$.

We can now compute the value of $|\mathcal{A}(C_i)|$ for each C_i where we recall that the load balancing condition leads to have $|\mathcal{A}(C_i)| = |\mathcal{A}(C_j)|$ for any two system caches C_i and C_j. The idea consists of distributing the knowledge relations, $K(i,j)$, $\forall C_i \in S$, $\forall C_j \in S$, among the caches of S. Given that $K(i,i)$ always holds, the number of knowledge relations that must be distributed among the system caches is the combination of $|S|$ elements, taken 2 at a time, noted $\binom{|S|}{2}$, which is equal to $(|S| \times (|S| - 1))/2$. We further want all the system caches to manage the same number of relations, leading to have $(|S| - 1)/2$ knowledge relations per cache. We are now able to infer the value of $|\mathcal{A}(C_i)|$ for every C_i of $\mathcal{S}$. Given $|\mathcal{A}(C_i)|$ and by construction of $\mathcal{A}(C_i)$ and $\mathcal{D}(C_i)$, there are $\binom{|\mathcal{A}(C_i)|}{2}$ knowledge relations per cache, which should be equal to $(|\mathcal{S}| - 1)/2$. Hence, we obtain:

$$|\mathcal{A}(C_i)| = \sqrt{|\mathcal{S}| - 3/4} + 1/2, \forall C_i \in \mathcal{S} \tag{2}$$

From the above, we are able to infer $|\mathcal{D}(C_i)|$. By construction, each cache C_j of $\mathcal{D}(C_i)$ knows the state of C_i (i.e. $C_i \in \mathcal{A}(C_j)$) and of some other caches. Thus, when C_i issues a request to a cache $C_j \in \mathcal{D}(C_i)$, only $(|\mathcal{A}(C_j)| - 1)$ cache states known by this cache are significant for C_i to get knowledge of the whole system state. It follows that we should have: $|\mathcal{A}(C_i)| + (|\mathcal{D}(C_i)| \times (|\mathcal{A}(C_j)| - 1)) = |\mathcal{S}|$. Hence, we get:

$$|\mathcal{D}(C_i)| = |\mathcal{A}(C_i)| - 1, \forall C_i \in \mathcal{S} \tag{3}$$

Given the values of $|\mathcal{D}(C_i)|$ and $|\mathcal{A}(C_i)|$ for all the system caches, it is straightforward to map the communication graph used by our protocol over the cache system, leading to set up the cooperation architecture. It amounts to compute an adjacency matrix such that the resulting boolean matrix has $|\mathcal{A}(C_i)|$ rows evaluating to true, $|\mathcal{D}(C_i)|$ lines evaluating to true, and $K(j, k)$ holds for any two caches C_j and C_k of S. In other words, the matrix must contain $\binom{|\mathcal{S}|}{2} + |\mathcal{S}|$ elements evaluating to true with appropriate values for $|\mathcal{A}(C_i)|$ and $|\mathcal{D}(C_i)|$, $\forall C_i \in \mathcal{S}$. The matrix computation is based on a game algorithm using the branch and bound method : The algorithm searches an adjacency matrix with successive tests, and terminates when a valid matrix for our construction criteria is found.

2.3 The complete protocol

The cooperation protocol resulting from the use of a fair distributed knowledge of the system state is depicted in Figure 4. When a cache C_i receives an object request, it checks whether the object is locally present (1). If so, the object is sent to the client. Otherwise, the object is sought within the lists corresponding to the states of the caches belonging to $\mathcal{A}(C_i)$ (2). In parallel, a request for the object is sent to each cache of $\mathcal{D}(C_i)$ (3). A cache C_j receiving such a request updates the list corresponding to the state of C_i (4) (i.e. C_j anticipates the presence of the object within C_i). C_j then searches for the object locally and within the state held for the caches belonging to $\mathcal{A}(C_j)$ (5). If the object is within C_j, C_j sends a hit to C_i while it sends a *miss* to C_i otherwise. Furthermore, for each cache C_k of $\mathcal{A}(C_l)$, $l \in \{i, j\}$, that has (supposedly) the object, C_l sends a request message to C_k (6). Then C_k either replies by a hit or a miss to C_i depending on whether the object is present or absent within the cache (7).

Note that the object retrieval latency in the worst case is now equal to the time taken by 5 message exchanges instead of 4 as discussed in Subsection 2.1. This results from our handling of cache update. The knowledge of the state of the caches in $\mathcal{A}(C_i)$ for any cache C_i is now an approximation of the cache's state. Thus, when a cache C_j of $\mathcal{D}(C_i)$ gets an object request from C_i, it cannot

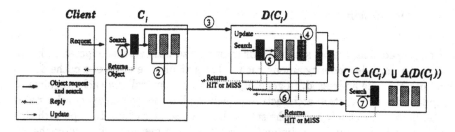

Fig. 4. The cooperation protocol

send a hit or a miss on behalf of the caches in $\mathcal{A}(C_j)$, to C_i. Instead, C_j sends a request message to these caches, which reply directly to C_i. The penalty of one message is negligible from the standpoint of latency since the time taken for message exchanges between sibling caches is in general far less than the one between a cache and the server.

For illustration of the proposed cooperation protocol, let us consider a system composed of 7 caches. Each cache of the system must maintain the states of 3 caches (i.e. $|\mathcal{A}(C_i)| = 3$) and send requests to 2 caches (i.e. $|\mathcal{D}(C_i)| = 2$) to get knowledge of the whole system state. Figure 5 depicts two examples of cache misses in such a system. Let us concentrate on the example on the left hand side of the figure where there is a miss on cache C_1. C_1 seeks the object within the lists it has for the states of C_5 and C_7 (i.e. $\mathcal{A}(C_1) = \{C_1, C_5, C_7\}$), and, in parallel, sends request messages to C_4 and C_2 (i.e. $\mathcal{D}(C_1) = \{C_4, C_2\}$). If C_1 believes that the object is present within either C_5 or C_7, or both, C_1 sends a request message to C_5 and/or C_7. Upon the receipt of the request from C_1, C_i, $i \in \{2, 4\}$, updates the state of C_1 and seeks locally the object. Depending on the presence or absence of the object, C_i either sends a hit or a miss to C_1. In parallel with the local search, C_i seeks the object within the state held for caches of $\mathcal{A}(C_i)$ (i.e. cache C_6 for C_2, and cache C_3 for C_4). If the object is supposed to be within such a cache, a request message is sent to it and the cache will send a hit or a miss to C_1 depending on its actual local state.

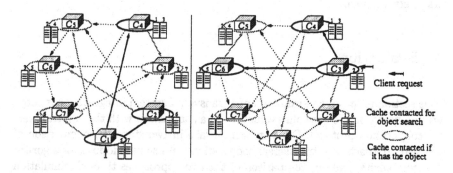

Fig. 5. An example with 7 caches

2.4 Discussion

Unlike traditional cache systems, our approach to transversal cooperation introduces an interdependency among caches. In particular, removal of a cache due to
failure must be addressed. In general, addition or removal of a cache requires to
update the cooperation architecture, which implies the exchange of cache states
(i.e. lists corresponding to cache states) between some caches. To cope with this
issue, we have designed a dynamic reconfiguration method minimizing the resulting network load. The reconfiguration method is computed by one of the
cooperative caches, selected among alive caches.

The proposed reconfiguration method subdivides into two algorithms that
respectively deal with the addition and removal of a cache. In the presence of a
cache addition, the original cooperation architecture is given by the adjacency
matrix of size $|S|$. The reconfiguration computes a valid adjacency matrix (as
defined in Subsection 2.2) of size $(|S| + 1)$ such that the number of cache states
to be exchanged is minimal. The removal of a cache is handled according to the
same principle. A valid adjacency matrix of size $(|S| - 1)$ must be computed
while minimizing the resulting network load. Figure 6 gives the average number
of states (in the link's label) that are exchanged between caches to cope with
the addition and removal of a cache, for a system composed of up to 7 caches.
For instance, adding a cache to a system made of 4 caches requires to exchange
a single cache state.

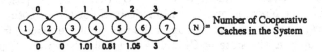

Fig. 6. Reconfiguration cost

The proposed evaluation shows that the bandwidth used for reconfiguration
is negligible (if reconfigurations are rare), compared to the one used by the
transversal system.

3 Evaluation

This section proposes an evaluation of a transversal system integrating our cooperation protocol. We base our evaluation on a comparison with the ICP transversal cooperation protocol. Our comparison falls in two steps: (*i*) comparison of
the two approaches to transversal cooperation from the standpoint of algorithmic complexity, and (*ii*) comparison of the two approaches through simulation
so as to show the benefit of our solution in terms of caching effectiveness.

3.1 Algorithmic complexity

The ICP transversal cooperation protocol requires that a cache issues a request to all its siblings to get knowledge of the whole system state. Thus, the network load is $O(N)$ with N being the number of caches composing the system (i.e. $N = |\mathcal{S}|$). In the same way, the workload for each cache is $O(N)$ since each cache has to handle requests from its siblings, in addition to the requests received from its clients.

Let us consider a centralized system where one of the caches (say C_1) has a local knowledge of the whole system state for cooperation (i.e. $|\mathcal{A}(C_1)| = N = |\mathcal{S}|$). With such a system, the workload for C_1 is $O(N \, Log(N))$ and the network load is $O(1)$ (ignoring state update).

Finally, using our cooperation protocol, the network load is $O(\sqrt{N})$ since the number of requests that are issued to get a global knowledge is equal to $\sqrt{N - \frac{3}{4}} - \frac{1}{2}$ given the value set for $\mathcal{D}(C_i)$ (see § 2.2). Furthermore, the complexity for the workload is $O(\sqrt{N} \, Log(\sqrt{N}))$ since, on an object request, $\sqrt{N}$ caches get contacted and each of them performs a search within $\sqrt{N}$ lists for a cost equal to $O(\sqrt{N})$.

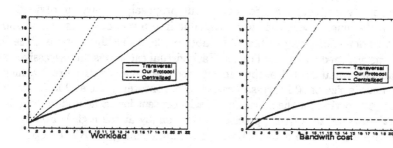

Fig. 7. System comparison in terms of complexity

In addition to the algorithmic complexity, we can evaluate the needs in memory size to have an optimal search time. The search time is optimal if all the lists maintained by a cache are in main memory (to avoid disk accesses). Thus, if we assume that each cache stores 400 000 objects, and that the length of an oject identifier (URL) is of about 50 bytes, the memory consumption per list is equal to 20 MB. Thus, 40MB per cache is required with 7 cooperative caches, 60MB with 13 caches, and 200MB with 111 caches. For comparison, a centralized server, like CRISP [5], requires for the mapping server 140 MB with 7 cooperative caches, 260MB with 13 caches and 2 220MB with 111 caches.

For illustration purpose, Figure 7 gives the bandwidth (resp. workload) cost for each cooperation protocol, for systems whose number of caches ranges from

1 to 21. It can be noticed that for a system composed of 21 caches, 40 messages are exchanged to get knowledge of the whole system state when using the ICP cooperation protocol while only 8 messages are required with our protocol. In general, the efficiency of our solution is proportional to the square root of the number of caches composing the transversal system. Thus, our protocol significantly decreases the bandwidth and workload induced by transversal cooperation. In order to further validate our solution, we have run simulations so as to study the behavior of our system in a real environment.

3.2 Simulation

The proposed simulations were achieved using traces collected on a cache located at the Technical State University of Virginia [10]. These traces are representative of the Web accesses performed by 3 groups of University members, i.e. (*i*) students, (*ii*) professors and (*iii*) students using a Web browser during sessions of a class on multimedia. For our evaluation, we have used the traces corresponding to the accesses performed by the members of the first group. The number of computers used by this group were equal to 31, and traces were collected between April and October 1995, which gives traces over a 185-days period. During this period, 188,674 requests were sent by users and the total size of the objects that were transferred was equal to 2.26 GBytes.

In order to evaluate the efficiency of our proposal, we have subdivided the traces of the single cache that were available into 6 sets of traces. This subdivision was done according to the IP number of client machines, and each set of traces was assigned to a virtual cache. Each virtual cache was further assigned a disk capacity equal to 10% of the capacity required to avoid cache replacement, giving a cache size of 30 Mbytes. Furthermore, concerning the evaluation of our protocol, the period for the emission of cache content for cache update (see Section 2.2), was set to a week (precisely, each sunday at midnight). Finally, the simulations were run on a 100 MHz PC Pentium running the NT 4.0 operating system.

Two kinds of simulations were run: (*i*) one aims at comparing two transversal systems using respectively the protocol of ICP and ours, for a system composed of 6 caches, (*ii*) the other aims at comparing the two aforementioned cache systems from the standpoint of caching effectiveness, i.e., evaluating the hit rate of the two systems for the same bandwidth cost.

Evaluation for a fixed number of cooperating caches: The efficiency of a single cache is measured in terms of its *Hit Rate* and its *Weighted Hit Rate*. The former gives the percentage of requested documents that are present in the cache, and the latter gives the percentage of bytes transferred from the cache to the client.

We have extended the above criteria, relating to a single cache, to a cache system. We have considered the two following criteria for evaluation: (*i*) the *Group Hit Rate* (GHR) that gives the percentage of requested documents that are present in the cache system, (*ii*) the *Group Weighted Hit Rate* (GWHR) that gives the percentage of bytes transferred from the cache system to the client.

Simulations gave identical results for both transversal systems in terms of GHR and GWHR. In the same way, we have evaluated the *Sibling Hit Rate* (resp. *Sibling Weighted Hit Rate*) that gives the proportion of objects (resp. bytes) obtained from a cache over the total number of objects (resp. bytes) obtained from the network (i.e. the remote server and the set of siblings). Similar results were observed for both transversal systems, as shown in table 1.

Table 1. Caching effectiveness for a fixed number of cooperating caches

Results for a fixed number of cooperating caches		Workload	HR	WHR	SHR	SWHR	GHR	GWHR
Mean	ICP	142102	30.93%	18.92%	14.56%	10.61%	40.90%	27.37%
per	Proposition	78087	30.93%	18.92%	14.56%	10.61%	40.90%	27.37%
cache	*Gain*	-45.05%	0%	0%	0%	0%	0%	0%
Bandwith consumption (in number of messages)								
ICP			1322925					
Proposition			553534					
Gain			-58.15%					

The main difference between the two cache systems lies in the bandwidth consumption and workload overhead. For identical results in terms of hit rates, the base transversal system consumes a bandwidth that is 138 % higher than the bandwidth consumed by a system integrating our cooperation protocol[2]. Thus it increases by 82 % the number of request treated by each of the cooperative caches.

Evaluation for a fixed bandwidth cost: Let us now evaluate our system from the standpoint of caching effectiveness for a fixed bandwidth cost. This cost is given in terms of request messages exchanged among caches, which determines the maximal number of cooperating caches. If we set this cost to 4 messages, our protocol enables to have a single transversal system composed of 6 caches while the ICP protocol leads to have 2 transversal systems made of 3 caches. Simulation results showed that the efficiency of the cache system in terms of *Hit Rate* equals 30.93% in the absence of cooperation, 35.77% with transversal cooperation based on the ICP protocol, and 40.90% with transversal cooperation based on our protocol. Table 2 further shows the complete results of the mean caching effectiveness for the two systems. In general, our simulation results about the efficiency of the cache systems showed that the system based on our protocol is in the average 2.12 times more efficient than the other system in terms of *Hit Rate*, and is 2.49 times more efficient in terms of *Weighed Hit Rate*. Depending on the number of caches composing the system and the associated system configuration, the improvement gained by our cache system ranges from 82% to 132%.

---

[2] This follows from the fact that a cache miss leads to send 5 request messages in the base system while only 2 are sent with our system.

Let us notice that to get the proposed results, our system actually increases the bandwidth cost of at most 4%, which is due to the absence of update of the distributed system state on object removal.

Table 2. Caching effectiveness for a fixed bandwith cost

Results for a fixed bandwith cost		Workload	HR	WHR	SHR	SWHR	GHR	GWHR
Mean	ICP	76059	30.93%	18.92%	6.98%	4.97%	35.77%	22.82%
per	Proposition	78087	30.93%	18.92%	14.56%	10.61%	40.90%	27.37%
cache	Gain	2.66%	0%	0%	112.44%	149.73%	14.22%	21.41%
Bandwith consumption (in number of messages)								
	ICP		529170					
	Proposition		553534					
	Gain		4.60%					

The efficiency of our system is a direct consequence of the number of caches composing the transversal system. Even better results could be exhibited with a system composed of 13 or 21 caches. Unfortunately, the traces we have been using to run our experiment were not suited to run the evaluation of such transversal systems. Further experiment will thus be run using our prototype, which is currently under testing. In particular, we will then be able to evaluate and compare the fetching delay associated to our protocol and to the one of ICP.

4 Conclusion

This paper has introduced a new protocol for cooperation among caches composing a *transversal system* so as to reduce both the bandwidth load and the cache workload, which are general induced by such systems. The novelty of our protocol comes from a fair distribution of the whole system state among the cooperating caches, which significantly reduces the load caused by transverse cooperation. As a consequence, this enables to set up transversal systems composed of a larger number of caches compared to existing systems, hence leading to improved cache effectiveness.

Among related work, let us cite Gadde's proposal with CRISP [5], who addresses a solution to the ICP bandwidth overhead problem, by using a centralized mapping server, maintaining a list of all objects present in each system's cache. Thus, for a local cache miss, only 2 requests (central mapping server interrogation and response) are needed to localize an object. However, this solution has several drawbacks: it requires a specialized machine (i.e. the central mapping server) which can easily becomes a bottleneck ; moreover, it needs a synchronous interaction between caches and the central mapping server for the maintenance of the object lists. Many solutions are proposed to address this problems [4] but none of them guarantee to deliver a hit if the requested object is present in the system. There exist other various studies on the improvement of cooperative cache systems. However, we are not aware of a proposal similar to ours. Existing work should rather be considered as complementary to our effort. For instance, let us mention the work of R. Malpani [6] and D. Povey [8] whose contribution lies in reducing the memory consumption of caches by limiting object replication within the system.

We are currently working on the integration of our protocol within the Squid software. In addition, we are examining an enhancement of our protocol in order to cope with heterogeneous architectures of cache systems, including systems composed of caches having different capacities. Another concern is to dynamically compute the cooperation graph underlying the proposed protocol. In particular, this would allow to couple caches that frequently share common objects.

References

1. M. Abrams, C. R. Standridge, G. Abdulla, S. Williams, and E. A. Fox - Caching Proxies: Limitations and Potentials - Proceedings of the 4th International World-Wide Web Conference, Available from http://ei.cs.vt.edu/~succeed/WWW4/WWW4.html – 1995.

2. A. Chantkuthod, P. B. Danzig, C.Neerdaels, M. F. Schwartz and K. J. Worrell - A Hierarchical Internet Object Cache - Technical Report 95-611-University Of Southern California, Boulder – 1996.

3. P. Danzig, R. S. Hall and M. F. Schwartz - A Case for Caching File Object Inside Internetworks - Proceedings of ACM Sigcomm'93, pp.239-248 – 1993.

4. S. Gadde, J. Chase and M. Rabinovich - Directory Structures for Scalable Internet Caches - Technical Report CS-1997-18-Duke University, Durham, North Carolina – Novenber 1997.

5. S.Gadde, M.Rabinovich, and J. Chase - Reduce, Reuse, Recycle: An Approach to Building Large Internet Caches. -The Sixth Workshop on Hot Topics in Operating Systems (HotOS-VI), Available from http://www.cs.duke.edu/ari/cisi/crisp/ – May 1997.

6. R. Malpani, J. Lorch and D. Berger - Making World Wide Web Caching Servers Cooperate - Proceedings of the 4th International World-Wide Web Conference, pp.107-117– 1995.

7. G. C. Mogul - Hinted Caching in the Web - Proceedings of the 7th ACM SIGOPS European Workshop, Available from http://mosquitonet.stanford.edu/sigops96/papers/ – 1996.

8. D. Povey and J. Harrison - A Distributed Internet Cache - Proceedings of the 20th Australian Computer Science Conference, Available from http://www.psy.uq.edu.au/~dean/project/ – 1997.

9. The Relais Group. Relais : cooperative caches for the world wide web. Available from http ://www-sor.inria.fr/projects/relais - 1998

10. Trace Files of WWW Traffic Available from http://www.cs.vt.edu/~chitra/www.html.

11. D. Wessels. - Configuring Hierarchical Squid Caches - Available from http://squid.nlanr.net/ Squid/Hierarchy-Tutorial – 1997.

12. S. Williams, M. Abrams, C. R. Standridge, G. Abdulla and E. A. Fox - Removal policies in network caches for World Wide Web documents - Proceedings of ACM Sigcomm'96, pp.293-305 - 1996.

Appendix

In our system the number of messages sent for an object search depends on the list number maintained by each cache, noted $|\mathcal{A}(C)|$, and is equal to $\frac{|S|-|\mathcal{A}(C)|}{|\mathcal{A}(C)|}$. The number of research mesages sent by a cache is inversely proportional to the number of lists maintained by a cache. In opposition, the number of updating messages is proportional to $|\mathcal{A}(C)|$ and equal to $|\mathcal{A}(C)|$. So, the total number $\mathcal{N}$ of exchanged messages for the object search and fetching is a function which depends on the $|\mathcal{A}(C)|$ and which is egual to $\mathcal{F}(\mathcal{N}) = \frac{|S|-|\mathcal{A}(C)|}{|\mathcal{A}(C)|} + |\mathcal{A}(C)|$.

Finaly, by derivation, we find that the optimal number of list maintained by each cache for minimizing the number of messages exchanged[3], is egual to $|\mathcal{A}(C_i)| = \sqrt{|S|}$.

---

[3] The minimal value for $\mathcal{F}(\mathcal{N})$ is obtain when $\mathcal{F}'(\mathcal{N}) = 0$

Fairness of Shared Objects
(Extended Abstract)

Michael Merritt*   Gadi Taubenfeld**

Abstract. Fairness in concurrent systems can be viewed as an abstraction that bridges low-level timing guarantees and make them available to programmers with a minimal loss of power and a maximal ease of use. We investigate the implementation and power of a range of fairness models that are appropriate to the synchronous, semi-synchronous and asynchronous contexts of various concurrent systems.

1 Introduction

1.1 Motivation

Fairness is a powerful abstraction that has led to fruitful results in the theory of concurrent, distributed and nondeterministic programs. Various notions of fairness can be explained very briefly, but small differences have important consequences on the computability and complexity of concurrent systems. We investigate the implementation and power of a range of fairness models that are appropriate to the synchronous, semi-synchronous and asynchronous contexts of various concurrent systems.

While some previous work has effectively focused on designing algorithms using strong primitives, we try to lay out a more general framework. Consider for example the mutual exclusion problem. Almost all solutions to this problem assume a lower level "hardware" solution to the very problem they are solving. That is, the solutions are based upon an underline assumption of mutually exclusive atomic operations. Hence, as was pointed out by Lamport [17], they are not satisfactory for a fundamental study of this problem. The same can also be said about the fairness requirements. Almost all interprocess communication mechanisms require some underlying fairness in their implementation (usually, starvation-freedom), which may be the same fairness requirement of the problem they are being used to solve. This motivates the question of what can be done when the primitive objects are not assumed to satisfy the same fairness assumptions as the problem to be solved. We address such fairness issues here.

Unlike timing-based models and other fairness requirements which are defined with respect to processes (or schedulers), in this paper fairness is defined with respect to accesses made to distinct shared *objects*. In our framework it is possible

* AT&T Labs, 180 Park Av., Florham Park, NJ 07932-0971. mischu@research.att.com.
** The Open University, 16 Klausner st., P.O.B. 39328, Tel-Aviv 61392, Israel. gadi@cs.openu.ac.il. Part of this work was performed while visiting at AT&T Labs.

to assume that not all shared objects satisfy that same fairness requirement, and that there are no fairness dependencies between objects.

The contribution of the paper is first in focusing on the fairness of the basic shared objects rather than on the fairness of the system as a whole. This gives rise to questions about the power of various objects under a variety of fairness assumptions. In this framework, we prove several new results, show how to express existing results, (including lower and upper bounds), and then generalize and strengthen them by changing the underlying fairness assumptions.

1.2 Definitions

We outline our model of distributed systems and define various notions of fairness. Processes are modeled as (possibly infinite) state-machines communicating via shared objects. A *configuration* of the system includes the state of each process and the state of each shared object. An *event* is either (1) an update of the internal state of a process, (2) a *request* by some process to access some shared object, (3) an update of the internal state of an object on behalf of a process, or (4) a *response* by a shared object to a pending request. We require an access' semantics (updating the object state and determining the value to return) to be the result of one or more internal steps of the object by the requesting process.

As in the standard interleaving semantics, a *run* α of the system is an alternating sequence $s_0 \xrightarrow{e_0} s_1 \xrightarrow{e_1} \cdots$ of configurations s_i and events e_i such that (1) the initial configuration s_0 satisfies appropriate initial conditions, and (2) every configuration s_{i+1} is derived from the previous configuration s_i by executing the event e_i.

We require the occurrence of each event to respect the associated process and/or object semantics. (In particular, we are not concerned with Byzantine failures.)

As noted, we are primarily interested in studying the impact of fairness properties imposed on accesses to shared objects. This study takes place under simple liveness properties imposed on processes: we assume any process that is not blocked by a non-terminating access either takes an infinite number of steps, or has failed (by terminating). Formally, a process p is *correct* in an execution α iff either p takes infinitely many steps in α or the last steps of p in α are of a pending request. (A request is pending if it is not followed by a response.) A process is *faulty* if it is not correct. [3]

We say that an algorithm or object implementation is *fault-free* if it meets its specification assuming all the processes are correct. Such a solution is *fully-resilient* if it works correctly regardless of the number of faulty processes.

Several of the fairness definitions below depend on the notion of a process trying to access an object. Let α be a run in which a process p issues a request

---

[3] We assume that all processes are infinite. That is, if an access is correct and if all its accesses all terminate, it takes an infinite number of steps. For terminating algorithms such as consensus, all but a finite number of those steps may be internal process events.

R to a shared object X. We say that p is *trying to access* X during the interval beginning with the last response to p preceding R from any shared object, or beginning with the initial state if no such response exists, ending with the response to R, or the remainder of α if the response does not exist. That is, we include in the interval in which we consider p to be trying to access X, the local computation by p preceding the explicit request R, and any subsequent steps of the run up to the response. This definition relates local computation time with the time needed to access shared objects. Most timing-based models assume that local computation time is negligible compared to the time it takes to access the shared memory. Although it is very convenient to assume that local computation takes zero time, in our framework it suffices to make this weaker assumption.

Some natural fairness properties for a set of shared objects, O, are defined below. (Each property implies the preceding.)

- *deadlock-freedom:* If a process is trying to access an object in O, then some process (not necessarily the same one) eventually succeeds in accessing some object in O.
- *starvation-freedom:* If a process is trying to access an object in O, then this process eventually succeeds. (Notice that one process can access objects in O arbitrarily many times ahead of another.)
- *bounded-waiting:* O is deadlock-free, and in any run there is a bound r such that whenever a process, p, is trying to access an object in O then no other process successfully accesses objects in O more than r times before p succeeds with its access.
- *r-bounded-waiting:* O is deadlock-free, and if a process is trying to access an object in O then it will succeed before any of the other processes is able to access O $r+1$ times.

We say that a given object X satisfies a fairness property F if the singleton set $\{X\}$ satisfies F, and call X an F object.

Simple Properties: Let O be a set of objects,

1. If each object in O is deadlock-free then O is deadlock-free. (The converse does not hold in general.)
2. Each object in O is starvation-free if and only if O is starvation-free.
3. If O is bounded-waiting then each object in O is bounded-waiting. (The converse does not hold in general.)
4. If O is r-bounded-waiting then each object in O is r-bounded-waiting. (The converse does not hold in general.)

1.3 Summary of results

We assume the reader is familiar with the definitions of mutual exclusion, consensus and leader election problems. A *decision* problem is, informally, a problem that can defined as an input-output relation. Thus, consensus and leader election are decision problems, while mutual exclusion is not. All statements below about mutual exclusion assume a fault-free model. For simplicity, read/write registers are called registers.

Deadlock-freedom: We prove the following,

- There is no deadlock-free mutual exclusion algorithm which uses only deadlock-free objects. [4]
- There is no fault-free solution to the consensus or leader election problems using deadlock-free registers. (There is a trivial fully-resilient solution to these problems using a single deadlock-free read-modify-write register.)
- Let P be a *decision* problem. There is a fully-resilient solution to P using deadlock-free objects of type X if and only if there is a fully-resilient solution to P using starvation-free objects of type X.
- Consensus is universal for deadlock-free objects.

The results show that deadlock-free objects are much weaker than starvation-free objects, and that both in the fault-free and the fault-tolerant models, different deadlock-free objects can have different computational power. The proof of the first result observes that deadlock-free objects are not sufficiently powerful to guarantee the transmission of even a single bit of information from a predefined sender process to a receiver process. The second result is proved by a reduction to known impossibility results for 1-resilient consensus [11, 19]. The proof of the third result relies on the simple structure of decision problems, while the fourth result is proved by a simple modification of the proof that consensus is universal for starvation-free objects [14].

Starvation-freedom: We make an observation which relates different fairness assumptions. It implies that in various cases, algorithms can be designed that perform well under fairness assumptions, but whose correctness (safety properties) are robust when those assumptions are violated.

- An algorithm A satisfies a safety property ϕ only if it does not matter whether the objects it uses are deadlock-free, starvation-free or bounded-waiting.

A similar type of result was proved in [1], showing that asynchronous systems and unknown-delay timing-based systems (see related work) are the same when safety properties are considered.

Bounded-waiting: We prove the following,

---

[4] There is a crucial distinction between a deadlock-free mutual exclusion *algorithm*, where some contending process must enter the critical section, and a deadlock-free mutual exclusion *object*. In the latter case, infinitely many accesses by contenders (accesses which return but deny the contenders the critical section) can satisfy the deadlock-free constraint, while the holder of the critical section hangs forever in its attempt to release it.

- Any deadlock-free mutual exclusion algorithm for n processes using a single bounded-waiting set of registers must use such a set which includes at least n registers.
- Any starvation-free mutual exclusion algorithm for n processes using a single bounded-waiting set of registers and test-and-set bits must use such a set which includes at least n instances of these objects.
- Using an unbounded number of bounded-waiting registers is a necessary and sufficient for construction of a fully-resilient consensus algorithm for an unspecified number of processes.
- Any fully-resilient consensus algorithm using a single bounded-waiting set of registers must use such a set which includes at least $\Omega(\sqrt{n})$ registers.
- Consensus is universal for bounded-waiting objects.

The first two results might suggest that there is not much difference between starvation-free objects and bounded-waiting objects, but the third and fourth results show that this is not the case. The proofs of the first and second results are based on proofs of corresponding results for starvation-free objects [8, 22]. A related lower bound of n starvation-free registers was proved in [21] for the unknown-delay timing-based model. To prove the sufficient condition of the third result, a fully-resilient consensus algorithm is presented. The algorithm is an adaptation of a consensus algorithm for the unknown-delay model using starvation-free registers [1]. The fourth result is also used to prove the necessary condition of the third result. Its proof is based on a construction from [10]. The last result is proved again by a simple modification to the proof in [14].

r-bounded-waiting: We prove that for any positive integer r:

- There is a deadlock-free mutual exclusion algorithm using a single r-bounded-waiting register.
- There is a fully-resilient consensus algorithm using a single r-bounded-waiting register.
- There is a starvation-free mutual exclusion algorithm, for an unspecified number of processes, which uses two r-bounded-waiting test-and-set bits and two starvation-free bits.
- There is a *fast* deadlock-free mutual exclusion algorithm which uses three r-bounded-waiting registers.
- There is a *fast* fully-resilient consensus algorithm which uses a single (3-valued) r-bounded-waiting register, and two deadlock-free bits.

These results demonstrate that, no matter how big r is, r-bounded-waiting objects are much stronger than bounded-waiting objects. The mutual exclusion and consensus algorithms which use a single r-bounded-waiting register are based on a simple timing-based algorithm due to Fischer [18]. The algorithm which is used to prove the third result is based on an algorithm due to Friedberg and Peterson [13], which originally used weak semaphores. (Recall that achieving constant space is not possible using bounded-waiting registers and bounded-waiting test-

and-set bits.) The two algorithms which are used to prove the fourth and fifth results are adaptations of timing-based algorithms from [4].

1.4   Related Work

The text [12] brings together most of the known approaches for proving properties of programs and, in particular, focuses on proving the termination of programs under various fairness assumptions about the processes' behavior (such as unconditional, weak and strong fairness). Our focus in this paper is less on formal verification issues and more on algorithmic issues that arise due to various fairness assumptions on how pending requests are served by shared objects.

In [3, 4, 18, 21, 23], a shared memory model, called the *known-delay* model (also called delay-based), is considered where it is assumed that there is an upper bound on the time required for a single access to shared memory, and that the bound is known to all the processes. This is a powerful model that enables efficient algorithms for various problems, and is similar to a system where *all* shared objects are assumed to be included in one big set which is r-bounded-waiting for some known r. Some of the work for the above timing-based model has been extended to the *unknown-delay* model, where an upper bound exists on the memory-access time, but is not known *a priori* [1]. Such a model is stronger than the asynchronous model, enabling the design of algorithms for problems that are unsolvable in the asynchronous model.

The notion of *finitary fairness* was introduced in [2]. Finitary fairness requires that for every run of a system there is an unknown bound k such that no enabled transition is postponed more than k consecutive times. It is shown in [2], that under finitary fairness formal verification can be simplified and that fully-resilient consensus is solvable (since finitary fairness can replace the timing assumption for the consensus algorithm in [1]). Bounded fairness was also considered in [16], by introducing a new operator into temporal logic. Both systems that satisfy the finitary fairness assumption and unknown-delay timing-based systems are basically the same as systems where *all* shared objects are considered to be one big bounded-waiting set.

The "Archimedean" systems explored in [25, 24] provide an interesting concept for using fairness as abstraction in message passing systems, and has motivated some of the work for shared memory systems mentioned above. In such systems, relative but unknown bounds are assumed on the speeds of network components, and efficient algorithms can be designed that exploit this synchrony assumption. Models slightly stronger than Archimedean systems are studied in [6, 5, 9, 15].

Two common notions used in the literature are those of *non-blocking* and *wait-free* objects [14]. The first corresponds to implementations which are both fully-resilient and deadlock-free, while the second corresponds to implementations which are both fully-resilient and starvation-free. (While wait-freedom requires only that every operation (process) always terminates within a finite number of steps, bounded wait-freedom requires that it terminates within a fixed and pre-determined number of steps [7].) An interesting notion of fairness, called closed schedulers, is explored in [20].

2 Deadlock-freedom

Assuming the fairness assumption is deadlock-freedom, several results are presented. The first result implies that deadlock-free objects are much weaker than starvation-free objects.

Theorem 1. *There is no deadlock-free mutual exclusion algorithm which uses only deadlock-free objects.*

Proof. The proof is based on the observation that deadlock-free objects are not sufficiently powerful to guarantee the transmission of even a single bit of information from a predefined sender process to a receiver process. (Suppose we want to block transmission from process P to Q. Run Q in isolation. There is a deadlock-free run of P and Q in which Q takes the same steps: at any object o touched by both P and Q one of two cases holds. Either Q accesses o a finite number of times, all before P's first access to o, or Q accesses o an infinite number of times, preventing P's first access from terminating.) Consider a mutual exclusion system in which process P holds the critical section and accesses shared variables to release it forever: by this observation, there is a deadlock-free run in which P never succeeds in informing Q that the critical section is available, so Q can never enter it. □

There are many deadlock-free mutual exclusion algorithms using various starvation-free objects, such as, starvation-free registers, test&set, read-modify-write objects. Thus, such objects cannot be implemented using deadlock-free objects, even in a fault-free model.

The next result, together with the observation that there is a trivial, fully-resilient solution to consensus and leader election using a single deadlock-free read-modify-write register, shows that, even in a fault-free model, deadlock-free objects have different computational power. (The trivial solution is that the first process to access the read-modify-write register writes its proposed value, and every other process reads this value and decides on it. Since every correct process stops accessing the object after a single access, in deadlock-free runs every correct process must eventually finish its access.)

Theorem 2. *There is no fault-free solution to the consensus or leader election problems using deadlock-free registers.*

The proof is a reduction to the impossibility of 1-resilient consensus using starvation-free (read/write) registers [11, 19].

Our next theorem shows that, unlike the result of Theorem 1, in the context of decision problems (consensus, leader election, etc.) deadlock-free and starvation-free fairness are interchangeable.

Theorem 3. *Let P be a decision problem. There is a fully-resilient solution to P using deadlock-free objects of type X if and only if there is a fully-resilient solution to P using starvation-free objects of type X.*

(At first glance, using Herlihy's result that consensus is universal [14], Theorem 3 seems to contradict Theorem 1 by implying that deadlock-free objects has the same computational power as starvation-free objects. This problem is resolved by observing that Herlihy's construction makes use of starvation-free registers, and hence holds only for starvation-free objects.)

We say that an object of type T is *universal for deadlock-free objects*, if there is a fully-resilient implementation of any (linearizable) deadlock-free object using any number of objects of type T together with deadlock-free registers. The next result is that any deadlock-free object which can implement consensus for n processes is universal for deadlock-free objects in a system of n (or fewer) processes.

Theorem 4. *Consensus is universal for deadlock-free objects.*

The proof is constructed by replacing starvation-free registers with deadlock-free registers in Herlihy's proof that consensus is universal for starvation-free objects [14].

3   Starvation-freedom

Most algorithms, lower bounds, and impossibility results for the shared memory model assume that the primitive shared objects are starvation-free. We make an observation which relates different fairness assumptions, showing that using deadlock-free, starvation-free or bounded-waiting objects is the same as far as safety properties are concerned. (A property ϕ is a *safety* property if the following holds: an infinite run satisfies ϕ if and only if all finite prefixes of the run satisfy ϕ, that is, a safety property has to be *prefix-closed*.)

Theorem 5. *An algorithm A satisfies a safety property ϕ only if it does not matter whether the objects it uses are deadlock-free, starvation-free or bounded-waiting.*

Proof. To show that it does not matter whether each of the objects being used is deadlock-free or starvation-free, it is enough to observe that the set of (legal) finite runs of A is the same whether each of the objects is deadlock-free or starvation-free. If A satisfies a safety property ϕ with starvation-free objects then, clearly, it satisfies ϕ with bounded objects. To prove the other direction, suppose A does not satisfy ϕ with starvation-free objects. If ϕ is a safety property then there is a finite run which violates ϕ. This run is also possible when using bounded-waiting objects since we can chose the bound to be as big as needed. Thus A does not satisfy ϕ also with bounded objects. □

4 Bounded-waiting

Of all the fairness assumptions covered in this papers, bounded-waiting is probably the most useful one. While bounded-waiting objects abstract from implementation details, they are arguably a better approximation of real shared objects compared to the (usually assumed) starvation-free objects. Furthermore, they enable us to design algorithms for problems that are unsolvable using starvation-free objects.

In the case of starvation-free registers, any deadlock-free mutual exclusion algorithm for n processes must use at least n such registers [8]. Similar result holds also for bounded-waiting registers.

Theorem 6. *Any deadlock-free mutual exclusion algorithm for n processes using a single bounded-waiting set of registers must use such a set which includes at least n registers.*

Proof. To prove the corresponding results for starvation-free registers [8], Burns and Lynch have shown how to construct a finite run which violates mutual exclusion, for any algorithm which uses less than n starvation-free registers. Since any such finite run is a bounded-waiting run (for some bound r), this construction similarly constrains the number of bounded-waiting registers needed. □

The lower bound of a bounded-waiting set of n registers is tight since there exists a deadlock-free mutual exclusion algorithm which uses only n starvation-free bits [8]. While n bounded-waiting registers are needed, the problem can be solved with only one r-bounded-waiting register, no matter how big r is. A related lower bound of n (starvation-free) registers was proved in [21] for the unknown-delay timing-based model.

In the case of starvation-free registers and starvation-free test-and-set bits, any starvation-free mutual exclusion algorithm for n processes must use at least n such objects [22]. Our next result shows that a similar result holds for the bounded-waiting case.

Theorem 7. *Any starvation-free mutual exclusion algorithm for n processes using a single bounded-waiting set of registers and test-and-set bits must use such a set which includes at least n instances of these objects.*

Proof. To prove the result for starvation-free objects [22], Peterson constructs a finite run which violates mutual exclusion. As above, this construction also holds for a set of bounded-waiting registers and test-and-set bits. □

We will see below that the problem can be solved with only a constant number of r-bounded-waiting registers and test-and-set bits, no matter how big r is.

While the last two results seem to suggest that there is not much difference between starvation-free objects and bounded-waiting objects, the next result shows that this is not the case. Recall, that consensus cannot be solved using starvation-free registers only, even in the presence of a single faulty process [11, 19].

Theorem 8. *An unbounded number of bounded-waiting registers is a necessary and sufficient for constructing a fully-resilient consensus algorithm for an unspecified number of processes.*

The sufficient condition is proved by presenting a fully-resilient consensus algorithm using an unbounded number of bounded-waiting registers.

Theorem 9. *There is a consensus algorithm for an unspecified number of processes using an unbounded number of bounded-waiting registers.*

Proof. The algorithm below is an adaptation of the algorithm for the unknown-delay model from [1]. The algorithm is *fast*: in the absence of contention, a process needs to take only a constant number of steps before terminating.

CONSENSUS ALGORITHM: program for process i with input in_i.
out: starvation-free register, initially $\perp$
$x[1..\infty, 0..1]$ array of starvation-free registers, initially 0
$y[1..\infty]$ array of bounded-waiting registers, initially $\perp$
round, v: local registers initially 1 and in_i, resp.

```
1 while out =⊥ do
2     x[round, v] := 1;
3     if y[round] =⊥ then y[round] := v fi;
4     if x[round, v̄] = 0 then out := v
5                 else for j = 1 to round do dummy := y[round] od;
6                      v := y[round];
7                      round := round + 1 fi
8 od;
9 decide(out).
```

Due to lack of space, we only give a brief explanation. The algorithm proceeds in rounds. Each process has a preference for the decision value in each round; initially this preference is the input value of the process. We assumed that all the infinite number of bounded-waiting registers $y[i]$ are r-bounded-waiting for some unknown number r. Once the algorithm reaches round r, it is guaranteed that all processes will move to the next round with the same preference. Once all processes in a round have the same preference, then a decision is reached in that round.[5] □

The next result is a space lower bound for solving consensus, and is also used to prove the necessary condition of Theorem 8.

Theorem 10. *Any fully-resilient consensus algorithm using a single bounded-waiting set of registers must use such a set which includes at least $\Omega(\sqrt{n})$ registers (even if each register has unbounded size).*

---

[5] We can make the algorithm more time efficient by modifying the for-loop as follows: for $j = 1$ to round! do $dummy = y[round]$ od; Let r denotes the unknown bound of the bounded-waiting registers $y[i]$. It can be shown that the step complexity of the algorithm (with r factorial) is $O(r \frac{\log r}{\log \log r})$, and that this bound is tight.

Proof. In [10] Fich, Herlihy and Shavit show that when less than $c\sqrt{n}$ starvation-free registers are used for some sufficiently small constant c, there is a *finite* run in which processes decide on opposite values. This is then used to prove a $\Omega(\sqrt{n})$ lower bound for randomized consensus. This construction holds also assuming the registers are bounded-waiting, since the finite run is a bounded-waiting run.

□

Extensions of the cited theorem noted in [10] also apply in this context: hence a similar bound to that in Theorem 10 holds on the number of swap objects or history-less objects needed to solve consensus. As we noted previously, there are several deadlock-free objects, such as read-modify-write or compare-and-swap, such that consensus can be solved using only one such object. Thus, any implementation of such objects using only swaps and registers requires $\Omega(\sqrt{n})$ swaps and registers.

In a related result [2], it is proved that under finitary fairness, there is no fully-resilient consensus algorithm even for two processes that uses a fixed number of bounded-size registers. This result and Theorem 10 still leave open the question of tight bounds on the number of bounded-waiting registers (some of which must be of unbounded-size) necessary to solve the consensus problem as a function of the number of processes.

An object is *universal for bounded-waiting objects*, if together with bounded-waiting registers it can implement any other bounded object (assuming any number of faults may occur). The next result is that any bounded-waiting object which can implement consensus for n processes is universal for bounded-waiting objects in a system of n (or fewer) processes.

Theorem 11. *Consensus is universal for bounded-waiting objects.*

The proof is constructed by replacing starvation-free registers with bounded-waiting registers in Herlihy's proof that consensus is universal for starvation-free objects [14].

5 r-bounded-waiting

In these section we present several algorithms which make use of r-bounded-waiting objects. The algorithms demonstrate that r-bounded-waiting objects are much stronger than bounded-waiting objects. We start with a very simple observation about r-bounded-waiting registers.

Theorem 12. *For any positive integer r, there is a deadlock-free mutual exclusion algorithm and a fully-resilient consensus algorithm each uses a single r-bounded-waiting register.*

Proof. The simple mutual exclusion algorithm uses a single r-bounded-waiting register and is based on a timing-based algorithm due to Fischer [18]. The register, called x, is initially 0. A process first waits until $x = 0$ and then assigns its *id* to x. Then, it reads x exactly r times. The fact that x is an r-bounded-waiting register ensures that after a process finishes reading, the value of x remains unchanged until some process leaving its critical section sets x back to 0. If x hasn't been changed and hence equals the process id, the process can safely enter its critical section, otherwise it goes to the beginning of its code and repeats this procedure. A consensus algorithm is constructed in a similar way. $\qquad\square$

Theorem 13. *For any positive integer r, there is a starvation-free mutual exclusion algorithm, for an unspecified number of processes, which uses two r-bounded-waiting test-and-set bits and two starvation-free bits.*

Proof. The algorithm presented is based on an algorithm due to Friedberg and Peterson [13], which originally used weak semaphores. Recall that achieving constant space is not possible using bounded-waiting registers and bounded-waiting test-and-set bits (Theorem 7). For luck of space, the algorithm is given without additional explanation. In the code that follows we use **await** *test-and-set(lock)* $= 0$ with the meaning **while** *test-and-set(lock)* $\neq 0$ **do skip od**.

THE ALGORITHM: program of a process.

T_0 and T_1: r-bounded-waiting test-and-set bits, both are initially 0;
queue, empty: starvation-free bits initially 0 and *false*, respectively;
myqueue, otherqueue: local bits;
counter: local register;

```
1   myqueue := queue;                              %remember where to wait
2   await test-and-set(T_myqueue) = 0              %wait to be flushed
3   if queue = myqueue                             %first to enter?
4   then                                           %become the doorkeeper
5       otherqueue := myqueue + 1 (mod 2);
6       await test-and-set(T_otherqueue) = 0;      %take the other bit
7       queue := otherqueue;                       %change queue
8       repeat                                     %flush out waiting processes
9           if empty := false then counter := 0
9           else counter := counter + 1 fi;
9           empty := true;
11          release(T_myqueue);
10          await test-and-set(T_myqueue) = 0;
12       until counter = r;                        % r-boundedness is used
13       Critical Section;
14       release(T_otherqueue);                    %give up the bit
15   else                                          %not a doorkeeper
16       empty := false;
17       Critical Section;
18   fi;
19   release(T_myqueue);                           %give up the original bit
```

The algorithm satisfies mutual exclusion deadlock freedom, and 2-bounded waiting (i.e., a process can enter its critical section ahead of another only twice). □
A mutual exclusion algorithm is *fast* if in the absence of contention, a process can always enter its critical section and exit it in a constant number of steps. I.e., the number of steps in this case does not depend on r. Similarly, a consensus algorithm is *fast* if, in absence of contention, a process can decide after a constant number of steps.

Theorem 14. *For any positive integer r, there is a fast deadlock-free mutual exclusion algorithm which uses three r-bounded-waiting registers.*

Proof. A solution is presented in which, in the absence of contention, a process can always enter its critical section and exit it in a constant number of steps. The solution is an adaptation of a known timing-based algorithm from [4]. For luck of space, the code of the algorithm is given without additional explanation.

A FAST ALGORITHM: **process i's program.**
x, y, z: r-bounded-waiting registers, initially $y = 0$ and $z = 0$.

```
1  start: x := i;
2         await (y = 0);
3         y := i;
4         if x ≠ i then for i = 1 to 2r do
                       dummy := x; dummy := y; dummy := z od;
5                      if y ≠ i then goto start fi;
6                      await (z = 0)
7              else z := 1 fi;
8         critical section;
9         z := 0;
10        if y = i then y := 0 fi;
```

The algorithm satisfies mutual exclusion and deadlock-free. □

Theorem 15. *For any positive integer r, there is a fast fully-resilient consensus algorithm which uses a single (3-valued) r-bounded-waiting register, and two deadlock-free bits.*

Proof. The simple fast algorithm presented below is an adaptation of a known timing-based algorithm from [4].

FAST CONSENSUS: **program for process i with input in_i.**
$x[0]$ and $x[1]$: deadlock-free bits, initially 0
y: r-bounded-waiting register, initially $\perp$

```
1  x[in_i] := 1;
2  if y = ⊥ then y := in_i fi;
3  if x[1 − in_i] = 1 then for i = 1 to r do dummy := y od fi;
4  decide(y).
```

□

Finally, we point out that using r-bounded-waiting registers it is simple to implement r'-bounded-waiting test-and-set bits (with reset) and r'-bounded-waiting compare-and-swap objects, for some r'. These implementations are similar to the corresponding timing-based constructions from [3, 23].

6 Discussion

We have defined fairness with respect to objects. It is possible, however, to define fairness with respect to operations. For example, consider registers which support deadlock-free read operations and starvation-free write operations. With such registers it is possible to solve deadlock-free mutual exclusion and hence such registers are strictly stronger than deadlock-free read/write registers. Also, all our fairness definitions can be generalized to apply also to sets of sets etc. of objects. Let O be the set $\{\{X_1, X_2\}, \{X_3, X_4\}\}$. If X_1, X_2, X_3, X_4 are all bounded-waiting objects then O is starvation-free (but not bounded-waiting).

In the way object fairness is defined, an object bestows the same fairness guarantees to all participating processes. This can be generalize by defining fairness w.r.t. a pair of a process and an object. This would enable the same object to guarantee starvation-freedom to one process and bounded-waiting to another.

There are several other fairness assumptions that can be further explored. For example, our definitions can be generalized to reflect priorities of processes. Yet another interesting direction is to define a weaker version of r-bounded-waiting fairness, by assuming that the r-bounded-waiting requirement may not hold from the beginning of each run, but is guaranteed to hold *eventually*.

References

1. R. Alur, H. Attiya, and G. Taubenfeld. Time-adaptive algorithms for synchronization. *SIAM Journal on Computing*, 26(2):539–556, April 1997.
2. R. Alur and T. Henzinger. Finitary fairness. In *Proc. 9th IEEE Symp. on Logic in Computer Science*, pages 52–61, 1994.
3. R. Alur and G. Taubenfeld. How to share an object: A fast timing-based solution. In *Proceedings of the 5th IEEE Symposium on Parallel and Distributed Processing*, pages 470–477, December 1993.
4. R. Alur and G. Taubenfeld. Fast timing-based algorithms. *Distributed Computing*, 10:1–10, 1996.
5. H. Attiya and T. Djerassi-Shintel. Time bounds for decision problems in the presence of timing uncertainty and failures. *Lecture Notes in Computer Science*, 725, 1993.
6. H. Attiya, C. Dwork, N. Lynch, and L. Stockmeyer. Bounds on the time to reach agreement in the presence of timing uncertainty. In *Proc. 23rd ACM Symp. on Theory of Computing*, pages 359–369, May 1991.
7. H. Brit and S. Moran. Wait-freeom vs. bounded wait-freeom in public data structures. In *Proc. 13th ACM Symp. on Principles of Distributed Computing*, pages 52–60, August 1994.

8. J. N. Burns and N. A. Lynch. Bounds on shared-memory for mutual exclusion. *Information and Computation*, 107(2):171–184, December 1993. (Also, in Proc. of 18th Annual Allerton Conference on Communication, Control and Computing, 1980, pages 833–842.).

9. C. Dwork, N. Lynch, and L. Stockmeyer. Consensus in the presence of partial synchrony. *Journal of the ACM*, 35(2):288–323, 1988.

10. F. Fich, M. Herlihy, and N. Shavit. On the space complexity of randomized synchronization. In *Proc. 12th ACM Symp. on Principles of Distributed Computing*, pages 241–250, August 1993.

11. M. J. Fischer, N. A. Lynch, and M. S. Paterson. Impossibility of distributed consensus with one faulty process. *Journal of the ACM*, 32(2):374–382, April 1985.

12. N. Francez. *Fairness*. Springer-Verlag, 1986.

13. S. A. Friedberg and G. L. Peterson. An efficient solution to the mutual exclusion problem using weak semaphores. *Information Processing Letters*, 25(5):343–347, 1987.

14. M. Herlihy. Wait-free synchronization. *ACM Trans. on Programming Languages and Systems*, 11(1):124–149, January 1991.

15. A. Herzberg and S. Kutten. Efficient detection of message forwarding faults. In *Proc. 8th ACM Symp. on Principles of Distributed Computing*, pages 339–353, 1989.

16. D. N. Jayasimha and N. Dershowitz. Bounded fairness. Technical Report 615, Center for Supercomputing Research and Development, University of Illinois, Urbana, IL, December 1986.

17. L. Lamport. The mutual exclusion problem: Part I – a theory of interprocess communication. *Journal of the ACM*, 33:313–326, 1986.

18. L. Lamport. A fast mutual exclusion algorithm. *ACM Trans. on Computer Systems*, 5(1):1–11, 1987.

19. M. C. Loui and H. Abu-Amara. Memory requirements for agreement among unreliable asynchronous processes. *Advances in Computing Research*, 4:163–183, 1987.

20. R. Lubitch and S. Moran. Closed schedulers: a novel technique for analyzing asynchronous protocols. *Distributed Computing*, 8(4):203–210, 1995.

21. N. Lynch and N. Shavit. Timing-based mutual exclusion. In *Proceedings of the 13th IEEE Real-Time Systems Symposium*, pages 2–11, December 1992.

22. G. L. Peterson. New bounds on mutual exclusion problems. Technical Report TR68, University of Rochester, February 1980 (Corrected, Nov. 1994).

23. S. Ramamurthy, M. Moir, and J. H. Anderson. Real-time object sharing with minimal system support (extended abstract). In *Proceedings of the 15th Annual ACM Symposium on Principles of Distributed Computing*, pages 233–242, May 1996.

24. Paul G. Spirakis and Basil Tampakas. Efficient distributed algorithms by using the Archimedean time assumption. In *5th Annual Symposium on Theoretical Aspects of Computer Science*, volume 294 of *lncs*, pages 248–263. Springer, 1988.

25. Paul M. B. Vitányi. Distributed elections in an Archimedean ring of processors (preliminary version). In *Proceedings of the Sixteenth Annual ACM Symposium on Theory of Computing*, pages 542–547, 1984.

Optimistic Atomic Broadcast*

Fernando Pedone and André Schiper

Département d'Informatique
Ecole Polytechnique Fédérale de Lausanne
1015 Lausanne, Switzerland

Abstract. This paper presents an Optimistic Atomic Broadcast algorithm (OPT-ABcast) that exploits the spontaneous total order message reception property experienced in local area networks, in order to allow fast delivery of messages. The OPT-ABcast algorithm is based on the Optimistic Consensus problem (OPT-Consensus) that allows processes to decide optimistically or conservatively. A process optimistically decides if it knows that the spontaneous total order message reception property holds, otherwise it decides conservatively. We evaluate the efficiency of the OPT-ABcast and the OPT-Consensus algorithms using the notion of latency degree.

1 Introduction

Atomic Broadcast is a useful abstraction for the development of fault tolerant distributed applications. Understanding the conditions under which Atomic Broadcast is solvable is an important theoretical issue that has been investigated extensively. Solving Atomic Broadcast efficiently is also an important and highly relevant pragmatic issue. We consider in this paper an *Optimistic Atomic Broadcast* algorithm (called hereafter OPT-ABcast), derived from the Chandra-Toueg Atomic Broadcast algorithm [4] (called hereafter CT-ABcast), which allows processes, in certain cases, to deliver messages *fast*. The idea of our OPT-ABcast algorithm stems from the observation that, with high probability, messages broadcast in a local area network are received totally ordered. We call this property *spontaneous total order message reception*.[1] Our algorithm exploits this observation: whenever the spontaneous total order reception property holds, the OPT-ABcast algorithm delivers messages fast.

Similarly to Chandra-Toueg Atomic Broadcast algorithm, our OPT-ABcast algorithm is also based on a reduction to the Consensus problem.

---

* Research supported by the EPFL-ETHZ DRAGON project and OFES under contract number 95.0830, as part of the ESPRIT BROADCAST-WG (number 22455).

[1] Spontaneous total order reception occurs for example with very high probability when network broadcast or IP-multicast are used.

However, the classical Consensus problem is not the right abstraction to use in the context of the OPT-ABcast algorithm. This led us to the specification of the *Optimistic Consensus* problem (called hereafter OPT-Consensus). In the OPT-Consensus problem a process can take up to two decisions: (1) an optimistic decision, and (2) a conservative solution. The two decisions are not necessarily the same. A process can decide only optimistically, or both optimistically and conservatively, or only conservatively. The details of the specification of the OPT-Consensus problem are given in Section 5. In our OPT-ABcast algorithm, the consensus decisions are optimistic whenever the spontaneous total order reception property holds, and the run is failure free and suspicion free. The efficiency of our OPT-ABcast algorithm is related to an optimistic decision of the underlying OPT-Consensus problem. We evaluate the *efficiency* of our OPT-ABcast algorithm using the notion of *latency degree* introduced in [13].

The rest of the paper is structured as follows. Section 2 describes some related work. Section 3 is devoted to the system model and to the definition of latency degree. In Section 4 we give an overview of the OPT-ABcast algorithm and of the OPT-Consensus problem. In Section 5 we specify the OPT-Consensus problem and give an algorithm that solves the problem. Section 6 describes the OPT-ABcast algorithm. We conclude in Section 7. Due to space limitations, all proofs have been omitted. They can be found in [12].

2 Related Work

The paper is at the intersection of two issues: (1) Atomic Broadcast algorithms, and (2) *optimistic* algorithms.

The literature on Atomic Broadcast algorithms is abundant (e.g., [1], [3], [4], [5], [6], [8], [11], [14]). However, the multitude of different models (synchronous, asynchronous, etc.) and assumptions needed to prove the correctness of the algorithms renders any fair comparison difficult. We base our solution on the Atomic Broadcast algorithm as presented in [4] because it provides a theoretical framework that permits to develop the correctness proofs under assumptions that are realistic in practical system (i.e., unreliable failure detectors).

Optimistic algorithms have been widely studied in transaction concurrency control ([9,2]). To our knowledge, there has been no attempt, prior to this paper, to introduce optimism in the context of agreement algorithms. The closest to the idea presented in the paper is [7], where the authors reduce the Atomic Commitment problem to Consensus and, in order to have a fast decision, exploit the following property of the Consensus problem: if every process starts Consensus with the same value v, then the decision is v. This paper presents a more general idea, and does not require that all the initial values be equal. Moreover, we have here the trade-off of typical optimistic algorithms: if the optimistic assumption is met, there is a benefit (in efficiency), but if the optimistic assumption is not met, there is a loss (in efficiency).

3 System Model and Definitions

3.1 System Model

We consider an asynchronous system composed of n processes $\Pi = \{p_1, \ldots, p_n\}$. Processes communicate by message passing. A process can only fail by crashing (i.e., we do not consider Byzantine failures). Processes are connected through reliable channels, defined by the two primitives $send(m)$ and $receive(m)$.

We assume causal order delivery for a subset of the messages.[2] We distinguish two types of messages, denoted by $\mathcal{M}$ and $\mathcal{M}_{CO}$. Causal order delivery is ensured only for messages of type $\mathcal{M}_{CO}$. Causal order is defined by the $send(m)$ primitive and the $CO\text{-}deliver(m)$ primitive. If m_1 and m_2 are two messages of type $\mathcal{M}_{CO}$ sent to the same destination process p_i, and $send(m_1) \rightarrow send(m_2)$, then $CO\text{-}deliver(m_1) \rightarrow CO\text{-}deliver(m_2)$, where $\rightarrow$ is the happened before relation [10]. In order to simplify the notation, we rename the $CO\text{-}deliver(m)$ primitive to $receive(m)$. So, if m_1 and m_2 are two messages of type $\mathcal{M}_{CO}$ sent to the same destination process p_i, and $send(m_1) \rightarrow send(m_2)$, we have $receive(m_1) \rightarrow receive(m_2)$.

Each process p has access to a local failure detector module that provides (possibly incorrect) information about the processes that are suspected to have crashed. A failure detector may make mistakes, that is, it may suspect a process that has not failed or never suspect a process that has failed. Failure detectors have been classified according to the mistakes they can make [4]. We consider in the paper the class of Eventually Strong failure detectors, denoted by $\Diamond \mathcal{S}$.

---

[2] Causal order simplifies the presentation of the OPT-ABcast algorithm. However, OPT-ABcast can also be implemented with an algorithm that does not need causal order.

3.2 Reliable Broadcast and Atomic Broadcast

We assume the existence of a *Reliable Broadcast* primitive, defined by *R-broadcast(m)* and *R-deliver(m)*. Reliable Broadcast satisfies the following properties [4]: (i) if a correct process R-broadcasts a message m, then it eventually R-delivers m *(validity)*, (ii) if a correct process R-delivers a message m, then all correct processes eventually R-deliver m *(agreement)*, and (iii) for every message m, every process R-delivers m at most once, and only if m was previously R-broadcast by *sender(m)* *(uniform integrity)*. We assume that the execution of *R-broadcast(m)* results in the execution of *send(m)* to every process p.

Atomic Broadcast is defined by *A-broadcast(m)* and *A-deliver(m)*. In addition to the properties of Reliable Broadcast, Atomic Broadcast satisfies the *total order* property [4]: if two correct processes p and q A-deliver two messages m and m', then p A-delivers m before m' if and only if q A-delivers m before m'.

3.3 Latency Degree

The latency degree has been introduced in [13] as a measure of the efficiency of a distributed algorithm. It has been defined based on a slight variation of Lamport's clocks [10]:

- a *send* event and a *local* event on a process p_i do not modify p_i's local clock;
- let $ts(send(m))$ be the timestamp of the *send(m)* event, and $ts(m)$ the timestamp carried by message m: $ts(m) \stackrel{\text{def}}{=} ts(send(m)) + 1$;
- the timestamp of *receive(m)* on a process p_i is the maximum between $ts(m)$ and p_i's current clock value.

With this definition, the *latency* of a run $\mathcal{R}$ of an algorithm $\mathcal{A}_{\mathcal{P}}$ solving an agreement problem $\mathcal{P}$ is defined as the largest timestamp of all *decide* events (at most one per process) of run $\mathcal{R}$. The *latency degree* of algorithm $\mathcal{A}_{\mathcal{P}}$ is defined as the minimum latency over all the runs that can be generated by the algorithm $\mathcal{A}_{\mathcal{P}}$. The minimal latency is obtained in failure free and suspicion free runs.

We consider in the paper the Atomic Broadcast problem. To define the latency degree of Atomic Broadcast we assume that every process p_i A-broadcasts only one single message, and that A-broadcast is the first event of process p_i.

4 Overview of the Results

4.1 OPT-Consensus Problem

Similarly to the Chandra-Toueg Atomic Broadcast algorithm, our OPT-ABcast algorithm is based on a reduction to the Consensus problem [4]. However, the classical Consensus problem is not adequate here: we need a Consensus that, under certain (problem dependent) conditions, allows processes to decide *fast*, even if without the guarantee that all processes decide on the same value. We call this Consensus the OPT-Consensus problem. We formalise the OPT-Consensus problem by introducing the notion of *optimistic* and *conservative* decisions, where the optimistic decision is the fast one. A process p_i can decide optimistically if it knows that a certain condition is satisfied (evaluating this condition requires the knowledge about the initial values of all processes; however, it does not necessarily require that all the initial values be identical). If a process p_i cannot decide optimistically, then p_i decides conservatively. The optimistic and the conservative decisions can be different, but are related.

The details of the specification of the OPT-Consensus problem are given in Section 5.1.[3] In Section 5.2, we show that the Chandra-Toueg consensus algorithm using $\Diamond \mathcal{S}$ can, with minor modifications, evaluate the condition that allows the fast decision and solve the OPT-Consensus problem.

4.2 OPT-ABcast Algorithm

The Chandra-Toueg Atomic Broadcast algorithm is based on a Reliable Broadcast and on a sequence of consensus problems, where the initial value of each consensus is a *set* of messages (i.e., the decision of each consensus is a *set* of messages). Our OPT-ABcast algorithm is based on a Reliable Broadcast and on a sequence of OPT-Consensus problems, where the initial value of each consensus is a *sequence* of messages (i.e., the decision of each OPT-Consensus problem is a *sequence* of messages). The initial value of process p_i for the OPT-Consensus depends on the order in which the messages that are Atomically Broadcast are received (more precisely, R-delivered) by p_i.

Consider the k-th OPT-Consensus problem, and let v_i^k be the initial value of p_i. The optimistic decision is possible whenever all the sequences

---

[3] The OPT-Consensus problem is defined with the optimistic Atomic Broadcast algorithm in mind, but we believe that it can be used to solve other problems, where assumptions about the values proposed by the processes can be made. For lack of space we do not further develop this statement in the paper.

v_i^k $(1 \leq i \leq n)$ have a non empty common prefix. If a process p_i decides optimistically, the optimistic decision is the longest common prefix. If a process p_j decides conservatively, the conservative decision is an initial value. So, an optimistic decision is a *prefix* of a conservative decision. In other words, the fact that an optimistic decision is different from a conservative decision does not lead to the violation of the properties of Atomic Broadcast.

The performance of our OPT-ABcast algorithm is directly related to an optimistic decision of the OPT-Consensus algorithm, which depends on the order of reception (more precisely, the order of R-delivery) of the messages that are Atomically Broadcast. We show in Section 6.4 that, in failure free and suspicion free runs, if messages are spontaneously R-delivered in the same order at all processes, then all the OPT-Consensus algorithms terminate with an optimistic decision. Furthermore, if the spontaneous ordering property does not hold for a while, then as soon as the property holds again, all OPT-Consensus problems again terminate with an optimistic decision.

4.3 Latency Degree of the OPT-ABcast Algorithm

The latency degree of the OPT-ABcast algorithm is given by $L_{OPT\_AB} = L_{RB} + L_{OPT\_C}$, where L_{RB} is the latency degree of the Reliable Broadcast algorithm and L_{OPT_C} is the latency degree of the OPT-Consensus algorithm.

The OPT-Consensus algorithm given in Section 5.2 is such that the latency of an optimistic decision is equal to 2, and the latency of a conservative decision is at least equal to 4. Therefore, the latency degree of our OPT-ABcast algorithm is equal to $L_{RB} + 2$. By comparison, the Chandra-Toueg Consensus algorithm, using the failure detector $\Diamond S$, has latency degree of 4, but a trivial optimisation leads to a latency degree of 3. This results in a latency degree of $L_{RB} + 3$ for the CT-ABcast algorithm.

The latency degree of the OPT-ABcast algorithm can even be reduced by considering another algorithm for solving OPT-Consensus. If, instead of deriving the OPT-Consensus algorithm from the Chandra-Toueg consensus algorithm, we derive it from the Early Consensus algorithm [13], we get an OPT-Consensus algorithm such that the latency of an optimistic decision is equal to 1, and the latency of a conservative decision is at least equal to 3. So the latency degree of the overall OPT-ABcast algorithm is equal to $L_{RB} + 1$.

5 The Optimistic Consensus Problem

5.1 Problem Definition

The Optimistic Consensus problem is defined in terms of the primitive $propose(v, f_{opt})$ and the primitives $decide(OPT, v)$ and $decide(CSV, v)$. The *propose* primitive has two parameters: an initial value v (the initial value of p_i is denoted by v_i), and a function $f_{opt} : \mathcal{V}^n \to \mathcal{V} \cup \bot$, where $v \in \mathcal{V}$ and $\bot \notin \mathcal{V}$ (the function f_{opt} is the same *for all processes*). The primitive $decide(OPT, v)$ corresponds to an "optimistic" decision, and the primitive $decide(CSV, v)$ corresponds to a "conservative" decision. A process can decide both optimistically *and* conservatively, and the two decisions can be different. The Optimistic Consensus problem is specified as follows.

- *Termination.* Every correct process eventually decides optimistically or conservatively. If a process conservatively decides, then all correct processes also eventually conservatively decide.
- *Uniform Integrity.* No process can optimistically decide more than once and no process can conservatively decide more than once. Moreover, no process can decide optimistically after having decided conservatively.
- *Uniform Validity.* If a process p conservatively decides v then v was proposed by some process. If a process optimistically decides v then $f_{opt}(v_1, \ldots, v_n) \neq \bot$ and $v = f_{opt}(v_1, \ldots, v_n)$.
- *Uniform Conservative Agreement.* No two processes conservatively decide differently.

The *Termination* condition requires that if some process decides conservatively, then every correct process also decides conservatively. This is not true for the optimistic decision: some processes might decide optimistically and others not. So, some processes may decide twice (once optimistically and once conservatively), while other processes decide only once (conservatively). The above specification allows, for example, the following runs: (1) all the correct processes decide optimistically, and no process decides conservatively, or (2) some processes decide optimistically and all correct processes decide conservatively, or (3) no process decides optimistically and all correct processes decide conservatively.

Furthermore, it follows from the *Uniform Validity* condition that no two processes optimistically decide differently. This is because an optimistic decision is computed by the function f_{opt} over *all* proposed values. Thus we have the following result.

Lemma 1. (UNIFORM OPTIMISTIC AGREEMENT). *No two processes optimistically decide differently.*

5.2 The OPT-Consensus Algorithm

Algorithm 1 solves the OPT-Consensus problem using any Eventual Strong failure detector $\mathcal{D} \in \Diamond \mathcal{S}$ and assuming a majority of correct processes. The algorithm is very similar to Chandra-Toueg's Consensus algorithm [4]: the mainly difference is in Phase 2 of the algorithm, and in the task responsible for the decision. However, the advantage of the OPT-Consensus algorithm is that it has a latency degree of 2, whereas the Chandra-Toueg Consensus algorithm has a latency degree of 3. A run with latency 2 happens whenever all processes can decide optimistically and no process decides conservatively. The OPT-Consensus algorithm works as follows:

1. In Phase 2 of the first round, the coordinator waits either (1) for estimates from a majority of participants if some process is suspected, or (2) for the estimates from all participants if no participant is suspected.
2. If all estimates are received, the coordinator applies the function f_{opt} over them. Let tmp_p be the value returned by f_{opt}. If $tmp_p \neq \perp$, then tmp_p is the optimistic decision, and the coordinator R-broadcasts the message $(OPT, -, -, tmp_p, decide)$.
3. A process that R-delivers the message $(OPT, -, -, estimate, decide)$ optimistically decides *estimate*.
4. If not all the estimates are received by the coordinator (item 2 above), the execution proceeds as in Chandra-Toueg's algorithm. In this case, the decision is conservative, and the latency is at least equal to 4.

The messages in the OPT-Consensus algorithm that are issued using the *send* primitive are of type $\mathcal{M}$ (see Section 3.1). The messages in the OPT-Consensus algorithm that are issued using the *R-Broadcast* primitive (*R-Broadcast* of the optimistic or conservative decisions) are of type $\mathcal{M}_{CO}$. We come back to this issue in Section 6.2 when discussing the reduction of Atomic Broadcast to OPT-Consensus.

5.3 Proof of Correctness

Lemma 2. *No process remains blocked forever in the **wait** statement of Phase 2 in the OPT-Consensus algorithm.*

Theorem 1. *If $f < n/2$, the OPT-Consensus algorithm solves the OPT-Consensus problem using a failure detector of class $\Diamond \mathcal{S}$.*

Algorithm 1 OPT-consensus algorithm

---

procedure $propose(v_p, f_{opt})$
  $estimate_p \leftarrow v_p$
  $OPTstate_p \leftarrow undecided$
  $CSVstate_p \leftarrow undecided$
  $r_p \leftarrow 0$
  $ts_p \leftarrow 0$
  while $OPTstate_p = undecided$ **and** $CSVstate_p = undecided$ **do**
    $r_p \leftarrow r_p + 1$
    $c_p \leftarrow (r_p \bmod n) + 1$
    send $(p, r_p, estimate_p, ts_p)$ to c_p *{Phase 1}*
    if $p = c_p$ **then**   *{Phase 2}*
      wait until for $\left\{ \begin{array}{l} \lceil (n+1)/2 \rceil \ q: received(q, r_p, estimate_q, ts_q) \text{ from } q \text{ and} \\ [\ \forall q: received(q, r_p, estimate_q, ts_q) \text{ from } q \text{ or } \mathcal{D}_p \neq \emptyset\ ] \end{array} \right.$
      $msgs_p[r_p] \leftarrow \{(q, r_p, estimate_q, ts_q) \mid p \text{ received } (q, r_p, estimate_q, ts_q) \text{ from } q\}$
      if $\forall q, (q, r_p, estimate_q, ts_q) \in msgs_p[r_p]$ **and** $ts_q = 0$ **then**
        $tmp_p \leftarrow f(\text{all estimates})$
        if $tmp_p \neq \bot$ **then**
          $R\text{-}broadcast(OPT, p, r_p, tmp_p, decide)$
          return from procedure
      $t \leftarrow$ largest ts_q such that $(q, r_p, estimate_q, ts_q) \in msgs_p[r_p]$
      $estimate_p \leftarrow$ select one $estimate_q$ such that $(q, r_p, estimate_q, t) \in msgs_p[r_p]$
      send $(p, r_p, estimate_p)$ to all
    wait until [received $(c_p, r_p, estimate_{c_p})$ from c_p or $c_p \in \mathcal{D}_p$]   *{Phase 3}*
    if [received $(c_p, r_p, estimate_{c_p})$ from c_p] **then**
      $estimate_p \leftarrow estimate_{c_p}$
      $ts_p \leftarrow r_p$
      send (p, r_p, ack) to c_p
    else
      send $(p, r_p, nack)$ to c_p
    if $p = c_p$ **then**   *{Phase 4}*
      wait until [for $\lceil \frac{(n+1)}{2} \rceil$ processes q : received (q, r_p, ack) or $(q, r_p, nack)$]
      if [for $\lceil \frac{(n+1)}{2} \rceil$ processes q : received (q, r_p, ack)] **then**
        $R\text{-}broadcast(CSV, p, r_p, estimate_p, decide)$
    return from procedure

  repeat   *{Decision Task}*
    when $R\text{-}deliver(decision\_type, q, r_q, estimate_q, decide)$
      if $decision\_type = OPT$ **then**
        if $OPTstate_p = undecided$ **and** $CSVstate_p = undecided$ **then**
          $decide(decision\_type, estimate_q)$
          $OPTstate_p \leftarrow decided$
      else
        if $CSVstate_p = undecided$ **then**
          $decide(CSV, estimate_q)$
          $CSVstate_p \leftarrow decided$
    until $decision = CSV$

5.4 Latency Degree of the OPT-Consensus Algorithm

Proposition 1. *If all processes optimistically decide, the latency of the run of the OPT-Consensus algorithm is equal to 2. If the processes conservatively decide, the latency is greater than or equal to 4.*

Proposition 2. *The OPT-Consensus algorithm has latency degree equal to 2.*

6 The Optimistic Atomic Broadcast Algorithm

6.1 Additional Notation

Our OPT-ABcast algorithm handles sequences of messages, and not sets of messages as in the Chandra-Toueg algorithm [4]. We define some terminology that will be used in Section 6.2.

A sequence s of messages is denoted by $s = <m_1, m_2, \ldots>$. We define the operators $\oplus$ and $\ominus$ for concatenation and decomposition of sequences. Let s_i and s_j be two sequences of messages: $s_i \oplus s_j$ is the sequence of all the messages of s_i followed by the sequence of all the messages of s_j that are not in s_i. $s_i \ominus s_j$ is the sequence of all the messages in s_i that are not in s_j. The *prefix* function applied to a set of sequences returns the longest common sequence that is a prefix of all the sequences, or the empty sequence denoted by ϵ.

For example, if $s_i = <m_1, m_2, m_3>$ and $s_j = <m_1, m_2, m_4>$, then $s_i \oplus s_j = <m_1, m_2, m_3, m_4>$, $s_i \ominus s_j = <m_3>$, and the function $prefix(s_i, s_j) = <m_1, m_2>$.

6.2 The OPT-ABcast Algorithm

We give now the reduction of Atomic Broadcast to OPT-Consensus (see Algorithm 2). The reduction has similarities with the reduction proposed by Chandra and Toueg [4], however with some additional complexity to cope with sequences of messages and optimistic and conservative decisions. When process p_i A-broadcasts some message m, then p_i executes *R-broadcast(m)*. Process p_i starts the OPT-Consensus algorithm with its initial value s_i equal to the sequence of messages that it has R-delivered (but not yet A-delivered). An optimistic decision is a non-empty prefix over all the sequences s_i ($1 \leq i \leq n$) of messages proposed by all the processes p_i. The function f_{opt} that defines an optimistic decision is as follows:

$$f_{opt}(s_1, \ldots, s_n) = \begin{cases} prefix(s_1, \ldots, s_n) & \text{if } prefix(s_1, \ldots, s_n) \neq \epsilon \\ \perp & \text{otherwise} \end{cases}$$

A conservative decision is a sequence s_i of messages proposed by some process p_i. Multiple OPT-Consensus executions are disambiguated by processes by tagging all the messages pertaining to the k-th OPT-Consensus execution with the counter k.

All tasks in Algorithm 2 execute concurrently. The algorithm works as follows for any process p.

1. When p wants to A-broadcast a message m, p executes $R\text{-}broadcast(m)$ (Task 1). Message m is R-delivered by Task 2 and included in the sequence $R\_delivered_p$.

2. If the sequence $R\_delivered_p \ominus A\_delivered_p$ is not empty, p executes $propose(k_p, seq, f_{opt})$ in Task 3 with $seq = R\_delivered_p \ominus A\_delivered_p$. Before proceeding to the next OPT-Consensus $k_p + 1$, p waits until a decision (optimistic and/or conservative) for OPT-Consensus k_p is known.

3. Task 4 waits for *decide*. However a process does not know whether there will be one or two decisions for any given execution of the OPT-Consensus algorithm. Therefore if a process executes an optimistic *decide* it also has to expect a conservative one. However, conservative decisions are not mandatory, that is, a process never knows until when it has to wait for a second decision.

   This is handled by Task 4 as follows. Whenever p decides optimistically for OPT-Consensus number k_p, the variable $prev_p^{CSV}$ is set to k_p. Task 4 then waits either a $decide(prev_p^{CSV}, -, -)$ (conservative decision of the previous OPT-Consensus $k_p - 1$) or a $decide(k_p, -, -)$ (optimistic or conservative decision of the current OPT-Consensus k_p). Causal order delivery of messages of type $\mathcal{M}_{CO}$ (see Section 3.1 and 5.2) ensures that a conservative decision of OPT-Consensus $k_p - 1$, if any, occurs before any decision of OPT-Consensus k_p.

   Once a sequence of messages $msgSeq_p^k$ is decided, process p A-delivers sequentially the messages in $msgSeq_p^k$ that it has not A-delivered yet.

6.3 Proof of Correctness

Lemma 3. *For all $l > k$, causal order delivery of the messages of type $\mathcal{M}_{CO}$ ensures that no process executes $decide(l, -, -)$ before executing $decide(k, -, -)$.*

For the following Lemmata we define $A\_delivered_p^k$ as the sequence of messages A-delivered by process p and decided in OPT-Consensus k.

$A\_delivered_p^k$ may contain messages included in optimistic and/or conservative decisions. The sequence $A\_delivered_p^1 \oplus \ldots \oplus A\_delivered_p^k$ contains all the messages delivered by process p until, and including, the messages decided in OPT-Consensus k.

Algorithm 2 OPT-ABcast algorithm

Initialisation:
  $R\_delivered_p \leftarrow \epsilon$
  $A\_delivered_p \leftarrow \epsilon$
  $k_p \leftarrow 0$
  $prev_p^{CSV} \leftarrow 0$

To execute A-$broadcast(m)$:   *{Task 1}*

  R-$broadcast(m)$

A-$deliver(-)$ occurs as follows:

  when R-$deliver(m)$ *{Task 2}*
    $R\_delivered_p \leftarrow R\_delivered_p \oplus \{m\}$

  when $R\_delivered_p \ominus A\_delivered_p \neq \epsilon$ *{Task 3}*
    $k_p \leftarrow k_p + 1$
    $A\_undelivered_p \leftarrow R\_delivered_p \ominus A\_delivered_p$
    $decision_p^{k_p} \leftarrow unknown$
    $propose(k_p, A\_undelivered_p, f_{opt})$
    wait until $decision_p^{k_p} \neq unknown$

  when $decide(k_p, decision\_type, msgSeq_p^{k_p})$ **or**   *{Task 4}*
      $decide(prev_p^{CSV}, decision\_type, msgSeq_p^{prev_p^{CSV}})$
    let $\#c$ be equal to k_p or $prev_p^{CSV}$, according to the decide executed above
    $A\_deliver_p^{\#c} \leftarrow msgSeq_p^{\#c} \ominus A\_delivered_p$
    atomically deliver messages in $A\_deliver_p^{\#c}$ following the order in $A\_deliver_p^{\#c}$
    $A\_delivered_p \leftarrow A\_delivered_p \oplus A\_deliver_p^{\#c}$
    if $decision\_type = OPT$ **then** $prev_p^{CSV} \leftarrow \#c$ {prepare a possible csv decision}
    $decision_p^{\#c} \leftarrow known$

Lemma 4. *For any two processes p and q, and all $k \geq 1$, if*

(a) p and q decide only optimistically for OPT-Consensus k, or
(b) p and q decide only conservatively for OPT-Consensus k, or

(c) p decides optimistically and conservatively, and q decides only conservatively for OPT-Consensus k, or

(d) p and q decide optimistically and conservatively for OPT-Consensus k

then $A\_delivered_q^k = A\_delivered_p^k$.

Lemma 5. *For any two correct processes p and q, and all $k \geq 1$, if p A-delivers the sequence of messages $A\_delivered_p^k$, then q eventually A-delivers the sequence of messages $A\_delivered_q^k$, and $A\_delivered_q^k = A\_delivered_p^k$.*

Theorem 2. *Algorithm 2 reduces Atomic Broadcast to OPT-Consensus.*

6.4   Latency Degree of the OPT-ABcast Algorithm

Proposition 3. *Let L_{RB} be the latency degree of Reliable Broadcast. If every process decides only optimistically, the run of the OPT-ABcast algorithm based on our OPT-Consensus algorithm has latency equal to $L_{RB} + 2$. If the decision is conservative the latency of the run of the OPT-ABcast algorithm is greater than or equal to $L_{RB} + 4$.*

Proposition 4. *The OPT-ABcast algorithm based on OPT-Consensus has latency degree equal to $L_{RB} + 2$.*

It remains to discuss under what conditions the latency degree of $L_{RB} + 2$ is obtained. Proposition 5 states that, if every message is R-delivered in the same order at every process, then every execution of the OPT-Consensus algorithm has only an optimistic decision (i.e., the latency degree is $L_{RB} + 2$). This holds even if processes do not start each OPT-Consensus with the same sequence of messages as initial value (e.g., p starts OPT-Consensus k with the sequence $< m_1, m_2, m_3 >$ and q starts OPT-Consensus k with the $< m_1, m_2 >$).

Proposition 5. *Consider a failure free and suspicion free run, and assume that all the processes R-deliver the messages that are A-Broadcast in the same order. Then for each execution of the OPT-Consensus algorithm, every process decides only optimistically.*

Proposition 6 states that temporary violation of the spontaneous total ordered R-delivery of messages does not prevent future optimistic decisions: after the messages are again spontaneously R-delivered in total order, the decisions are again optimistic.

Proposition 6. *Consider a failure free and suspicion free run, and assume that after R-delivering the k-th message, all processes R-deliver all messages in total order. Then, after all the first k messages are A-delivered, for each execution of the OPT-Consensus every process decides only optimistically.*

7 Conclusion

This work originated from the pragmatic observation that messages broadcast in a local area network are, with high probability, spontaneously totally ordered. Exploiting this observation to develop a *fast* Atomic Broadcast algorithm turned out to be technically more difficult then we initially expected. The difficulty has been overcome by the introduction of the OPT-Consensus problem, with two (possibly different) decisions: an optimistic decision and a conservative decision. The OPT-Consensus problem abstracts the property exploited by our OPT-ABcast algorithm.

The efficiency of the OPT-ABcast algorithm has been quantified using the notion of latency degree, introduced in [13]. The latency degree of the OPT-ABcast algorithm has been shown to be $L_{RB} + 2$, where L_{RB} is the latency degree of Reliable Broadcast. This result has to be compared with the latency of the Chandra-Toueg Atomic Broadcast algorithm, which is equal to $L_{RB} + 3$.

Finally, to the best of our knowledge, the OPT-ABcast algorithm is the first agreement algorithm to exploit an *optimistic* condition: if the conditions are met the efficiency of the algorithm is improved, if the conditions are not met the efficiency of the algorithm deteriorates. We believe that this opens interesting perspectives for revisiting or improving other agreement algorithms.

References

1. Y. Amir, L. Moser, P. Melliar-Smith, D. Agarwal, and P. Ciarfella. Fast Message Ordering and Membership Using a Logical Token-Passing Ring. In *Proceedings of the 13th International Conference on Distributed Computing Systems*, pages 551–560, May 1993.
2. P. Bernstein, V. Hadzilacos, and N. Goodman. *Concurrency Control and Recovery in Database Systems*. Addison-Wesley, 1987.
3. K. Birman, A. Schiper, and P. Stephenson. Lightweight Causal and Atomic Group Multicast. *ACM Transactions on Computer Systems*, 9(3):272–314, August 1991.
4. T. D. Chandra and S. Toueg. Unreliable failure detectors for reliable distributed systems. *Journal of the ACM*, 43(2):225–267, March 1996.
5. J. M. Chang and N. Maxemchuck. Reliable Broadcast Protocols. *ACM Transactions on Computer Systems*, 2(3):251–273, August 1984.

6. H. Garcia-Molina and A. Spauster. Ordered and Reliable Multicast Communication. *ACM Transactions on Computer Systems*, 9(3):242–271, August 1991.
7. R. Guerraoui, M. Larrea, and A. Schiper. Reducing the cost for non-blocking in atomic commitment. In *Proceedings of the 16th International Conference on Distributed Computing Systems*, pages 692–697, May 1996.
8. P. Jalote. Efficient ordered broadcasting in reliable csma/cd networks. In *Proceedings of the 18th International Conference on Distributed Computing Systems*, pages 112–119, May 1998.
9. H. T. Kung and J. T. Robinson. On optimistic methods for concurrency control. *ACM Transactions on Database Systems*, 6(2):213–226, June 1981.
10. L. Lamport. Time, clocks, and the ordering of events in a distributed system. *Communications of the ACM*, 21(7):558–565, July 1978.
11. S. W. Luan and V. D. Gligor. A Fault-Tolerant Protocol for Atomic Broadcast. *IEEE Trans. Parallel & Distributed Syst.*, 1(3):271–285, July 90.
12. F. Pedone and A. Schiper. Optimistic atomic broadcast. Technical Report TR-98/280, EPFL, Computer Science Department, 1998.
13. A. Schiper. Early consensus in an asynchronous system with a weak failure detector. *Distributed Computing*, 10(3):149–157, 1997.
14. U. Wilhelm and A. Schiper. A Hierarchy of Totally Ordered Multicasts. In *Proceedings of the 14th IEEE Symp. on Reliable Distributed Systems*, pages 106–115, September 1995.

Approximate Agreement with Mixed Mode Faults: Algorithm and Lower Bound

Richard Plunkett, Alan Fekete

University of Sydney, Australia

Abstract. Approximate agreement is a building block for fault-tolerant distributed systems. It is a formalisation for the basic operation of choosing a single real value (representing say speed) for use in later computation, reflecting the different approximations to this value reported from a number of possibly-faulty processors or sensors. We study the approximate agreement problem in distributed systems where processor failures are characterised depending on their severity. We develope a new algorithm that can tolerate up to b byzantine faults, s symmetric ones, and o send-omission faults. We analyse the convergence attained by this algorithm, and also give a universal bound on the convergence available to any algorithm no matter how complicated.

1 Introduction

Fault-tolerance is an important property for distributed systems. Distribution makes fault-tolerance possible, becausse if some processors fail, there are others which can continue with the computation. Distribution also makes fault-tolerance necessary, since as we increase the number of sites involved in a computation , we increase the likelihood that some will fail during the execution.

There are many different ways in which parts of a distributed system can misbehave during a computation. In general, a fault-tolerant system will be able to produce an appropriate answer in the face of some situations, but others will be so severe that the whole computation is corrupted. To study fault-tolerance more carefully, we describe a system in terms of a *fault model*, which describes the sorts of erroneous behaviour that can be overcome. It is clear that more severe forms of behaviour will require more sophisticated algorithms to tolerate them. In the theoretical literature, the most studied failure is *byzantine*, which covers a processor changing its state and sending messages arbitrarily. Clearly any algorithm that can overcome such arbitrary faults will be very useful, since almost any imaginable situation will be covered. However, some famous impossibility results [6, 9, 7] show that byzantine failures are very difficult to overcome. Other work has proposed a model with less severe faults, called *omission faults*, in which a faulty processor may neglect to send some messages, but whenever it does send, the transmitted data is valid. This is an abstraction of the common situation where transmission errors cause identifiable corruption (detected for example by a checksum). It is common in the theoretical literature to present an algorithm that tolerates a bounded number of a certain kind of fault; for example, one might work whenever at most t omission errors occur in any execution.

Since it seems reasonable that the number of very severe errors will be low but not zero, some of the more practical researchers have examined algorithms that are designed to operate in an environment with more than one class of faults. These are described as mixed-mode fault models. For example, Thambidurai and Park [10] divided Byzantine faults as symmetric or asymmetric, depending on whether the *same* incorrect value was sent to all processors in a round of broadcast transmission; they also considered *benign* faults which are detectable by all recipients (and so correspond to universal omission).

The most famous abstract formulation of a fault-tolerance problem is *agreement* [9], in which each processor has an initial value (representing its state so far), and the processors exchange messages in an attempt to reach a consistent basis for continued computation. It has been shown that solving this, even with very restricted fault types, requires some fault-free executions to run for a long time: at least $t + 1$ rounds of message exchange.

In order to see what could be done with faster response times, Dolev Lynch Pinter Stark and Weihl [2] introduced the problem of approximate agreement, where each processor has an initial real value (say representing a sensor reading), and communication is used to try to give each processor a new value which more accurately reflects the true sensor value. This is formalised by requiring that the final value at any non-faulty processor must be within the range of initial values among the non-faulty processors (the "Validity" condition). The success of such an algorithm is measured by its *convergence*, symbolised by K, defined as the ratio between the spread of final values of non-faulty processors to the spread among initial values of non-faulty processors. This definition means that a small value of K is desirable. Following [2], most work has assumed a single round of message exchange in the algorithm; if extra time is available, one can simply iterate the protocol, reducing the spread of values by a factor of K in each round.

While most of the emphasis in the literature on Approximate Agreement has been on presenting algorithms and analysing their convergence, it is also crucial to understand the theoretical limitations on what any algorithm can do, no matter how cleverly written. Thus we need to find lower bounds on the values of K that are possible for different fault models.

In this paper, we use a model with three significant classes of faults. Byzantine faults are the most general, covering arbitrary changes of state and messages that are individually corrupted in arbitrary, non-detectable ways. Omission faults result in messages that are corrupted in ways that can be detected by the recipient: formally we represent this as the faulty node failing to send a message which is required by the protocol. Symmetric faults are not detectable, but act identically on all the messages sent by the faulty node in a round of communication. (The fourth possibility, of messages corrupted in identical detectable ways, is what has previously been called a benign fault. Since it is equivalent to a node that never does anything, we will simply ignore such nodes from the whole problem.) The justification for this model comes from separating the processor into two logical sections from which faults can emerge. The numerical calculations and data source being one section and the communication unit being the other. A fault in the numerical unit will provide an incorrect value to the communication unit which it may the distribute correctly. These are symmetric faults. Similarly the numerical unit may provide a correct value, but have the communications unit fail to send one or more of the required messages. These are omissive faults. A byzantine fault is usually the failure of both, or a severe failure (undetectably) by the communications unit.

We give an algorithm for approximate agreement that works among N processors, whenever there are at most b byzantine faults, at most o omission ones, and at most s symmetric faults. We analyse the convergence of this algorithm, and show that

$$K \leq \left(\left\lceil \frac{N - 2b - 2s - o}{b + o/2} \right\rceil \right)^{-1}$$

We also prove that every algorithm for this problem (involving a single round of message exchange) must attain convergence that satisfies

$$K \geq \left(2 \left\lceil \frac{N - 2b - 2s - o}{2b + o} \right\rceil \right)^{-1}$$

As can be seen our algorithm comes asymptotically close to this bound.

There have been five main papers dealing with approximate agreement. The problem was defined in [2], which gives an algorithm for systems with synchronous (time-constrained) communication and at most b byzantine failures. This algorithm is found to have performance $K \leq (\lceil \frac{N-2b}{b} \rceil)^{-1}$ and a matching lower bound is proved. Fekete [4] examines the problem for systems with only omission failures, and gives an algorithm with $K \leq \frac{o}{2N-2o}$; he also proves a lower bound $K \geq \frac{o}{2N+3o}$ Kieckhafer and Azadmanesh [8] use the model with byzantine and symmetric faults, and give an algorithm with $K \leq (\lceil \frac{N-2b-2s}{b} \rceil)^{-1}$.

The problem has also been considered for systems with asynchronous (unlimited delay) communication. Algorithms are found for byzantine faults [2], omission faults [5] and mixed byzantine and symmetric faults [1].

None of these papers includes a lower bound for any mixed mode model; our technique for dealing with this is a major contribution of our work. The rest of this paper is as follows. In section 2 we present the formal fault model, and also give the important facts about multisets and operations on them, used in the algorithm and its analysis. Section 3 gives the algorithm and the analysis of its convergence rate. Section 4 gives the lower bound. Section 5 concludes.

2 The Model and Preliminaries

2.1 Multisets and Some Associated Functions

Approximate agreement requires the manipulation of multisets containing real values and the null value($\perp$). A multiset is a collection of values similar to a set, except multiple occurrences of the same are permitted. The number of times a value occurs in a multiset is referred to as its multiplicity.

There are several representations of these multisets. Let $\Re^+$ be the set of real number plus the null value $\perp$. A multiset may be represented as a mapping $V : \Re^+ \to N$. For each value r from $\Re^+$, $V(r)$ is defined as the multiplicity of r in V, hence $|V| = \sum_{r \in \Re^+} V(r)$.

Another useful representation of the multiset is as a monotonically increasing sequence. So $V = \langle v_0, v_1, \ldots, v_{|V|-1} \rangle$, ordered such that $v_i \leq v_{i+1}$, for convenience of notation we consider the null value to be greater than any real value. These two representations are equivalent, though each is best suited to different styles of manipulation. When we refer to the ith element of V as v_i we are using the ordered sequence representation.

There are a number of useful functions we need to define on multisets.

- $min(V)$ = the smallest non-null value in V.
- $max(V)$ = the largest non-null value in V.
- $\delta(V) = max(V) - min(V)$ is called the diametre of V.
- $mean(V) = \frac{1}{|V|} \left(\sum_{r \in \Re} V(r) \cdot r \right)$ = the arithmetic mean of the non-null values of V
- Union If $U = V \cup W$ then $\forall r \in \Re^+$ $U(r) = max(V(r), W(r))$
- Intersection If $U = V \cap W$ then $\forall r \in \Re^+$ $U(r) = min(V(r), W(r))$
- Sum If $U = V + W$ then $\forall r \in \Re^+$ $U(r) = (V(r) + W(r))$
- Difference If $U = V - W$ then $\forall r \in \Re^+$ $U(r) = max(V(r) - W(r), 0)$
- $redS(V) = V - min(V)$
- $redL(V) = V - max(V)$
- $reduce(V) = redS(redL(V)) = V$ with the largest and smallest values removed.

The function $redS$, $redL$, and $reduce$ can be applied recursively to remove more than one extremal values from V. A superscript identifies how many applications are needed. So $reduce^k(V)$ is the set that would remain if the k smallest and k largest values were removed from V.

We also use $|V|$ to represent the number of elements in V and V^* to represent the multiset of non-null values in V.

A simple approach to approximate agreement is to reduce the set of values received in the message exchange, by removing extreme values which might have come from faulty processors, and then average the remaining values. More highly tuned algorithms take elements from the reduced set at regular spacing, and average these. Formally, we define $select_d(v)$ is a subsequence of the multiset V obtained by selecting the first and every subsequent dth element of V. So for $V = \langle v_0, \ldots, v_{|V|-1} \rangle$ we have $select_d(V) = \langle v_o, v_d, v_{2d}, \ldots, v_{jd} \rangle$ where $j = \lfloor \frac{|V|-1}{d} \rfloor$.

2.2 Three Fault Model

We consider algorithms where there are N processors. In any execution, a non-faulty processor must follow its protocol precisely. Since we are considering a single-round of communication in a synchronous communication system, this protocol involves sending the processors initial value to all others (for simplicity we include the processor itself among the destinations), and then after the period of one message delay, the processor will collect a multiset of values received in messages: if a processor does not send to it, we place the special null value $\perp$ in the multiset to represent the omission. Different protocols are described by indicating how the final value is to be calculated from the multiset of received data. This approach is called a full-information model of a protocol.

A processor with a symmetric fault will send the same possibly incorrect value to all other nodes. A processor with an omission fault may send its correct value to some destinations, and it may omit sending to others, but it can't send an incorrect value. A processor with a byzantine fault may send arbitrary messages to any nodes. Since symmetric faults represent numerical/data faults we will require they distribute a possibly incorrect real value, so any nodes which produces only $\perp$ values must be ommisively or byzantinely faulty. We will throughout assume that there are at most b byzantine faults, at most o omission faults, and at most s symmetric faults, in any execution of our algorithms.

Notice that our model subsumes those previously considered. For example, the byzantine model of [2] corresponds to $s = o = 0$, the omission model of [4] is $b = s = 0$, and the mixed-fault model of [8] is $o = 0$.

2.3 Variance

In analysing our new algorithm, we will make extensive use of a new measure of similarity between multisets, which we call *variance*. To define $variance(V, W)$ we will require V and W be two multisets containing the same number of entries and $V(\perp) = W(\perp) = 0$. A matching $P_{V,W}$ of these multisets is a pairing of each element in V with a separate element from W. This is most easily thought about using the monotonically increasing sequence representation for multisets. The function $match(P_{V,W}, v_i)$ refers to an element of the other set (w_j of W) to which v_i is matched in $P_{V,W}$. $D_=(P_{V,W})$ is the number of pairings in $P_{V,W}$ which have the element from V equal to the element from W. Similarly, $D_<(P_{V,W})$ is the number of pairings in which the element from V is smaller than the element from W and $D_>(P_{V,W})$ is the number of pairing in which the element from V is larger. We define $D(P_{V,W}) = max(D_<(P_{V,W}), D_>(P_{V,W}))$. We define the $variance(V, W)$ to be the minimum value d for which a matching $P_{V,W}$ exists that satisfies $D(P_{V,W}) \leq d$. To prove $variance(V, W) \leq d$, we need only provide an example matching $P_{V,W}$ for which $D(P_{V,W}) \leq d$. While actual variance of two sets is difficult to find, calculating an upper limit on the possible value of the variance is easily done using the following lemmas.

These lemmas assume unless otherwise specified $|V| = |W| = |X| = m$ and $V = < v_0, ..., v_{m-1} >$, $W = < w_0, ..., w_{m-1} >$ and $X = < x_0, ..., x_{m-1} >$.

Lemma 1. $variance(V, W) \leq |V - W|$.

Proof. Any matching $P_{V,W}$ of the elements from V to W which matches as many equal values as possible will leave only $|V - W|$ non-equal pairs, thus

$D_<(P_{V,W}) + D_>(P_V,w) = |V - W|$ thus $D(P_{V,W}) \leq |V - W|$ so $variance(V, W) \leq |V - W|$.

Lemma 2. $variance(reduce^k(V), reduce^k(W)) \leq variance(V, W)$.

Lemma 3. $variance(V, W) \leq variance(V, X) + variance(X, W)$

Lemma 4. *Suppose C is a multiset, and $|C|$ mod $2 = 0$. Then*

$$variance(V, reduce^{\frac{|C|}{2}}(V + C)) \leq \frac{|C|}{2}$$

Proof. Let $V' = reduce^{\frac{|C|}{2}}(V + C)$. Divide C into two sets C_1 (containing the $\frac{|C|}{2}$ smallest elements of C) and C_2 (containing the $\frac{|C|}{2}$ largest elements of C). Note V' now equals $reduce^{\frac{|C|}{2}}(V + C_1 + C_2)$. Consider the following matching $P_{V,V'}$. Match all elements of V that are retained in V' to themselves, since $reduce^{\frac{|C|}{2}}(V + C_1 + C_2)$ removes only $|C|$ elements from $V + C_1 + C_2$ at least $|V| - |C|$ elements of V are retained. Now consider the effect of the reduce function. Firstly it will remove the $\frac{|C|}{2}$ smallest elements, which must be in V and/or C_1. Let cv_1 be the number of those smallest elements found in V and cc_1 be the number found in C_1. Now we have that $cv_1 + cc_1 = \frac{|C|}{2}$ and $\frac{|C|}{2} - cc_1 = cv_1$ elements of C_1 will be found in $reduce^{\frac{|C|}{2}}(V + C_1 + C_2)$. Match those cv_1 elements from C_1 to the cv_1 elements of V which are removed as being in the $\frac{|C|}{2}$ smallest of $V + C_1 + C_2$. Each of these matching has the element in V smaller than or equal to the elements it is matched to in V' since the removed element were smaller than or equal to any of the remaining elements in V and C_1 by definition of reduce. Similarly for the top half, $\frac{|C|}{2}$ elements will be removed from either V and/or C_2, let cv_2 be the number of those elements which are from V. So cv_2 elements from C_2 will then be found in $reduce^{\frac{|C|}{2}}(V + C_1 + c2)$. Match those elements to the elements of V that were removed as being in the largest $\frac{|C|}{2}$ elements of $V + C_1 + C_2$. These matchings all have the elements from V being greater than or equal to the elements it is matched to in V' since the removed elements were greater than or equal to any of the remaining elements.

So the matching $P_{V,V'}$ has $D_<(P_{V,V'}) \leq \frac{|C|}{2}$ and $D_>(P_{V,V'}) \leq \frac{|C|}{2}$ which guarantees $variance(V, V') \leq \frac{|C|}{2}$.

Lemma 5. *If $variance(V, W) \leq d$ then $v_i \leq w_{i+d}$ and $w_i \leq v_{i+d}$.*

Proof. By contradiction, assume $v_i > w_{i+d}$. Then consider a matching $P_{V,W}$ for which $D(P_{V,W}) = variance(V, W) \leq d$. Look at which values of V the first $i + d + 1$ elements of W are matched to. At most i can be matched to elements smaller than v_i ($\langle v_0, ..., v_{i-1} \rangle$) and as such may be equal or less than the element from V they are matched to. This leaves at least $d + 1$ elements less than or equal to w_{i+d} which must be matched to elements of V greater than or equal to v_i. If $v_i > w_{i+d}$ then all of these matchings are the greater than type matchings, leaving $D_>(P_{V,W}) \geq d+1$, $D_>(P_{V,W}) > d$ for that matching. However, $D_>(P_{V,W}) \leq D(P_{V,W}) = d$ so $D_>(P_{V,W}) \ngtr d$ so $v_i \ngtr w_{i+d}$. So $v_i \leq w_{i+d}$. By a symmetric argument $w_i \leq v_{i+d}$.

Lemma 6. *If variance$(V, W) \leq d$ then*

$$mean(select_d(V)) - mean(select(W)) \leq \delta(V \cup W) \cdot \frac{1}{\lceil \frac{m}{d} \rceil}$$

Proof. The select function produces sets $X = \langle v_0, v_d, v_{2d}, ..., v_{jd} \rangle$ and $Y = \langle w_0, w_d, w_{2d}, ..., w_{jd} \rangle$ where $j = \lfloor \frac{m-1}{d} \rfloor$, so $|X| = |Y| = \lceil \frac{m}{d} \rceil$. Let X also be labelled $\langle x_0, ...x_j \rangle$ and Y also be labelled $\langle y_0, ...y_j \rangle$. From Lemma 5 we know that $v_{id} \leq w_{(i+1)d}$ and $w_{id} \leq v_{(i+1)d}$ so $x_i \leq y_{i+1}$ and $y_i \leq x_{i+1}$. Wlog assume $\sum X \geq \sum Y$. $\sum X - \sum Y = (x_0 - y_0) + (x_1 - y_1) + ... + (x_j - y_j) = -y_0 + (x_0 - y_1) + (x_1 - y_2) + ... + (x_{j-1} - y_j) + x_j$. Since all the middle terms are guaranteed to be less than or equal to zero, maximising the equation has them set to zero, leaving $\sum X - \sum Y \leq x_j - y_0 \leq \delta(V \cup W)$. Thus $mean(select(V)) - mean(select(W)) \leq \delta(V \cup W) \cdot \frac{1}{\lceil \frac{m}{d} \rceil}$

3 The New Algorithm *BSO*

Here is the algorithm, which we call *BSO*, to be followed by a processor m, once it has sent its initial value to all processors, and received the values they sent.

1. Collect multiset M_1 of n values, one from each processor. Processes from which values aren't received are assumed to have sent $\perp$.
2. If there are more than o elements of value $\perp$ in M_1, replace the excess elements by a default real value (eg zero). More formally, let M_2 denote the multiset defined by $M_2(\perp) = min(M_1(\perp), o)$, $M_2(0) = M_1(0) + max(0, M_1(\perp) - o)$, and $\forall x \notin \{0, \perp\} : M_2(x) = M_1(x)$.
3. Remove the highest and lowest $b + s$ values from the multiset. Formally, let $M_3 = reduce^{b+s}(M_2)$
4. Let j_m be the number of $\perp$ values in M_3 and apply the double operator to the multiset. Thus $j_m = M_3(\perp)$, and $M_4 = double(M_3)$.
5. Remove all $2j_m$ elements of value $\perp$ from the multiset. Thus $M_5(\perp) = 0$ and $\forall x \neq \perp: M_5(x) = M_4(x)$. For brevity, we will write $M_5 = M_4^*$ to denote this.
6. Again we remove extreme values, to make the multiset have a fixed size of $2N - 4b - 4s - 2o$. Formally, let $M_6 := reduce^{o-j_m}(M_5)$.
7. We use a tuned averaging function to collapse the remaining multiset to a single value. $Result := Mean(Select_{2b+o}(M_6))$

3.1 Analysis of Convergence

We are going to analyse the convergence of this algorithm, by taking two processors in an arbitrary execution, and calculating the difference between their final values, using intermediate analysis showing variance between the multisets produced in the steps of the calculation. To begin, we show that we can restrict our attention to executions where every processor sees at most o missing messages (represented by $\perp$ in its multiset). In essence, there is no advantage to the fault source, in making a byzantine node omit a message.

Lemma 7. *If the convergence rate of BSO is bounded above by K for all executions in which at every processor p_i $M_1(\perp) \leq o$, then its convergence rate is bounded above by K for all executions.*

Now we can prove a bound on the convergence of BSO

Theorem 8. *For any execution of BSO algorithm, we have*

$$K \leq \left(\left\lceil \frac{N - 2b - 2s - o}{b + o/2} \right\rceil \right)^{-1}$$

Proof. The following argument on the convergence of the algorithm hinges on analysing the variance that can develop between the sets held at to processors p_v and p_w at each step. Let V_1 be the multiset received at processor p_v and W_1 be the multiset received at processor p_w. Similarly we use V_j to denote the multiset computed as M_j by p_v at stage j of the calculation done after all values are received. Of course, W_j is used similarly.

The result of the above Lemma 7 is we can assume for our following analysis that the number of omissions received at p_v and p_w are less than o. Without loss of generality, we will assume that $V_1(\perp) \leq W_1(\perp)$.

Consider an execution, from the perspective of processors p_v and p_w. Nodes in the network can behave correctly towards both of them or omissively or byzantinely. Byzantine faulty processors may also behave omissively. For analysis we will count the number of each types of behaviour that occurs during this execution. Thus we denote by b_0 the number of processors from which p_v and p_w receive different incorrect values (of course, the algorithm can't determine this internally; it is an artifact in our analysis). For brevity we represent an incorrect value as x, so we write $(x1, x2) : b_0$ to indicate that there are b_0 such cases. Similarly, we use g for a correct value and $\perp$ for a missing value, giving a complete catalogue of cases which can be written as follows:

$(x1, x2)$	b_0
$(x1, \perp)$	b_1
$(\perp, x2)$	b_2
$(\perp, \perp)$	o_0
$(g, \perp)$	o_1
$(\perp, g)$	o_2
$(x1, x1)$	s_0
(g, g)	g_0

Notice that a processor need not suffer a symmetric fault, as defined in the fault model, in order to be counted under s_0, all that is needed is that it behave symmetrically to the two processors of interest. However, every symmetric fault will be counted under s_0 or o_0 or g_0.

For convenience we collect in Table 1 the exact sizes and bounds of the sets involved. In the following, we give names to important combinations of the counts: let $bo_1 = b_1 + o_1$, $bo_2 = b_2 + o_2$ and $bo_3 = bo_1 - bo_2$. Here are brief explanations for the values stated.

In Step 1 we gather V_1 and W_1. At this point V_1 can have $b_0 + max((b_1 + o_1), (b_2 + o_2))$ additional elements compared with $V_1 \cap W_1$, and since we assumed that V_1 had more $\perp$ entries than W_1, we see that $max((b_1 + o_1), (b_2 + o_2))$ is $(b_1 + o_1)$. W_1 will contain the same number of elements not in the intersection, however $(b_1 + o_1) - (b_2 + o_2)$ of these will be the value $\perp$.

In step 2, excess $\perp$ entries are replaced by defaults. Because we have assumed no processor has excess $\perp$ entries, we have $V_2 = V_1$ and $W_2 = W_1$.

In step 3, we remove extremal (potentially illegal) values from V and W leaving them with the same or fewer different values.

Step 4 calculates the number of $\perp$ entries in each case. Thus $j_v = bo_2 + o_0$, and $j_w = bo_1 + o_0$.

In step 5 the remaining $\perp$ entries are removed so V_5 contains $2bo_3$ elements more than W_5. Break V_5 into 2 new sets for analysis, X and V_c by placing $|W_5|$ elements of V_5 into X giving preference to the elements of V_5 present in $W_5 \cap V_5$; then we place the remaining $2bo_3$ elements into V_c. Now $|V_x| = |W_5|$ and $|W_5 - X| \leq 2b_0 + 2bo_2$, and $|X - W_5| \leq 2b_0 + 2bo_2$. By lemma 1 $variance(X, W_5) \leq 2b_0 + 2bo_2$.

Table 1. Key values at different steps in the Algorithm

Step	$|V_i|$	$|W_i|$	$|V_i^*|$
1,2	N	N	$N - bo_2 - o_0$
3	$N - 2(b + s)$	$N - 2(b + s)$	$N - 2(b + s) - bo_2 - o_0$
4	$2N - 4(b + s)$	$2N - 4(b + s)$	$2N - 4(b + s) - 2bo_2 - 2o_0$
5	$2N - 4(b + s) - 2bo_2 - 2o_0$	$2N - 4(b + s) - 2bo_1 - 2o_0$	$2N - 4(b + s) - 2bo_2 - 2o_0$

Step	$|W_i^*|$	$|V_i^*| - |W_i^*|$	bound on $|V_i - W_i|$	bound on $|W_i^* - V_i^*|$
1,2	$N - bo_1 - o_0$	bo_3	$b_0 + bo_1$	$b_0 + bo_2$
3	$N - 2(b + s) - bo_1 - o_0$	bo_3	$b_0 + bo_1$	$b_0 + bo_2$
4	$2N - 4(b + s) - 2bo_1 - 2o_0$	$2bo_3$	$2b_0 + 2bo_1$	$2b_0 + 2bo_2$
5	$2N - 4(b + s) - 2bo_1 - 2o_0$	$2bo_3$	$2b_0 + 2bo_1$	$2b_0 + 2bo_2$

Now we can complete the proof of our theorem. Note $|X| = |W_5|$, and thus $j_x = j_w$. We see that $variance(X, W_5) \leq 2b_0 + 2bo_2$. If we form X' from X just as M_6 is formed from M_5, we have $X' = reduce^{o - j_w}(X)$. Since $W_6 = reduce^{o - j_w}(W_5)$, by lemma 2, we see $variance(X', W_6) \leq variance(X, W_5)$. Thus $variance(X', W_6) \leq 2b_0 + 2bo_2$.

Now consider the relative behaviour of V and X. Step 6 does $V_6 = reduce^{o-jv}(V_5)$, where $jv = bo_2 + o_0$, so that $o - jv = o - o_0 - bo_2 = o - o_0 - bo_1 + bo_3$. Also $V_5 = X + V_c$. So, $V_6 = reduce^{o-jv}(V_5) = reduce^{o-o_0-bo_1+bo_3}(X + V_c) = reduce^{o-o_0-bo_1}(reduce^{bo_3}(X + V_c))$. Let $V_5' = reduce^{bo_3}(X + V_c)$. By Lemma 4, noting $|V_5'| = 2bo_3$, we have $variance(V_5', X) \le bo_3$. Also $X' = reduce^{o-o_0-bo_1}(X)$, $V_6 = reduce^{o-o_0-bo_1}(V_5')$ so $variance(X', V_6) \le bo_3$, by Lemma 2. From above $variance(W_6, X') \le 2b_0 + 2bo_2$, so by Lemma 3 we have

$$variance(V_6, W_6) \le 2b_0 + 2bo_2 + bo_3 = 2b_0 + bo_1 + bo_2 = 2b_0 + b_1 + b_2 + o_1 + o_2 \le 2b + o$$

Note $|V_6| = 2N - 4b - 4s - 2o$. Since $variance(V_6, W_6) \le 2b + o$ by lemma 6 we see $mean(select_{2b+o}(V)) - mean(select_{2b+o}(w)) \le \delta(V \cup W)/\lceil \frac{2N-4b-4s-2o}{2b+o} \rceil$. So the guaranteed convergence rate of the algorithm is

$$K = \left(\left\lceil \frac{N - 2b - 2s - o}{b + o/2} \right\rceil \right)^{-1}$$

4 Lower Bound on Convergence of Arbitrary Algorithm

Any algorithm can be represented as a full information protocol, in which values are exchanged and then some protocol-specific function is applied to the collected messages to determine the final value. Thus we define a view as the vector of values received at each processor after the communication step. It contains a list of values and the processor they came from. Typically only the values are used, the vector being converted immediately into a multiset. Consider an execution E in this fault model. It may be described by the starting value of each node and stating which nodes have which fault types, and how those faulty nodes behave. During E not all nodes need receive the same data vector (view) due to faulty behaviour of some nodes as specified in E. We say that two views V and W are directly compatible ($V \approx W$) if there can exist an execution E in which V can be received at one correct processor and W be received at another correct processor. In this situation we say that E produces V and W ($E \Rightarrow (V, W)$).

A valid approximation function for this model is one that takes any view/multiset and produces a new approximation guaranteed to be in the range of correct values. If there are b byzantine and s symmetric faults then the $(b + s)$ smallest and the $(b + s)$ largest values received are suspect. Thus a valid approximation function must always choose a value in the range of the $(b + s + 1)$th smallest to $(b + s + 1)$th largest elements received.

In our lower bound we will use a simple counting argument, expressed in the following result.

Lemma 9. *Let f be any valid approximation function. Suppose that $V_0, V_1, \ldots, V_c$ is a chain of views such that $V_i \approx V_{i+1}$ and where $f(V_0) = 0$ and $f(V_c) = 1$. There exists an i ($0 \le i < c$) such that*

$$|f(V_i) - f(V_{i+1})| \ge \frac{1}{c}$$

Proof. We argue by contradiction, and let $S = \langle s_1, s_2, \ldots, s_c \rangle$ where $s_i = f(V_i) - f(V_{i-1})$.

$$\sum_{i=1}^{c} s_i = (f(V_1) - f(V_0)) + (f(V_2) - f(V_1)) + \cdots + (f(V_c) - f(V_{c-1})) = f(V_c) - f(V_0) = 1$$

However, if $s_i < \frac{1}{c}$ for all i then $\sum_{i=1}^{c} s_i < c * \frac{1}{c} < 1$, which, since $\sum_{i=1}^{c} s_i = 1$, isn't true. So for some $i : s_i \geq \frac{1}{c}$

We can now use the lemma to establish our lower bound

Theorem 10. *If A is any algorithm that solves Approximate Agreement in all executions of a distributed systems with at most b byzantine faults, s symmetric ones and o omission failures, then the convergence of A is bounded below by*

$$K \geq \left(2 \left\lceil \frac{N - 2b - 2s - o}{2b + o} \right\rceil \right)^{-1}$$

Proof. We will produce a chain of views of length c, such that every consecutive pair are directly compatible, the final value produced from the first must be 0, the final value produced from the last must be 1, and every one contains only entries of 0, 1 or $\perp$. The lemma above will then show that one execution exists in which two neighbouring views are produced, where the final values differ by at least $\frac{1}{c}$. In this execution, all initial values are 0 or 1, showing that the interval of values is reduced to no less than $1/c$; that is, the convergence is no less than $1/c$.

We will now complete the lower bound by providing a specification of a chain of executions $E_0, \ldots, E_{c-1}$ which produces a chain of views $V_0, \ldots, V_c$ ($E_i \Rightarrow (V_i, V_{i+1})$) which satisfies the above conditions. The precise characterisation is given below, but we offer a diagram that may make things more clear. The chain starts with all entries being 0 except for some nulls and ones, whose total number is less than the maximum faults; thus the decision value must be 0, since possibly all non-zero values came from faulty processors and so were not initial values of correct ones. Similarly the decision value in the final view must be 1, with all entries (except a few that might be from faulty processors) being 1. In between views in the chain are made by gradually replacing zero-value entries with nulls and 1-value entries, as shown in Figure 1.

Now to make this precise, we indicate exactly what happens in each execution, giving different constrictions for alternating pairs in the chain. In the execution E_i containing nodes $\langle p_0, \ldots, p_{N-1} \rangle$ where $i \bmod 2 = 0$ the nodes behave as follows. (All ranges are inclusive.)

- Nodes p_0 to $p_{(\frac{i}{2}+1)*o-1}$ start with value 1.
- Nodes $p_{N-b*(i+1)-s}$ to p_{N-1} start with value 1.
- The remaining nodes all start with value 0.

In the message exchange, the following is observed

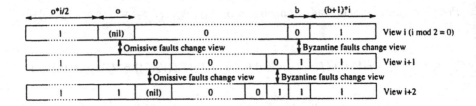

Fig. 1. Construction of the chain of views

- Nodes $p_{\frac{i}{2}*o}$ to $p_{(\frac{i}{2}+1)*o-1}$ are omissively faulty, they contribute $\perp$ to view V_i and 1 to the view V_{i+1}.
- Nodes $p_{N-b*(i+2)-s}$ to $p_{N-b*(i+1)-s-1}$ are byzantine faulty, contributing 0 to view V_i and 1 to the view V_{i+1}.
- The remaining nodes are non-faulty

In execution E_{i+1} where $i \bmod 2 = 0$ the nodes behave as follows.

- Nodes p_0 to $p_{(\frac{i}{2}+1)*o-1}$ start with value 1.
- Nodes $p_{N-b*(i+1)-s}$ to p_{N-1} start with value 1.
- The remaining nodes all start with value 0.

The behaviour in these executions is as follows

- Nodes $p_{(\frac{i}{2}+1)*o}$ to $p_{(\frac{i}{2}+2)*o-1}$ are omissively faulty, they contribute 0 to view V_{i+1} and $\perp$ to the view V_{i+2}.
- Nodes $p_{N-b*(i+3)-s}$ to $p_{N-b*(i+2)-s-1}$ are byzantine faulty, contributing 0 to view V_{i+1} and 1 to the view V_{i+2}.
- The remaining nodes are non-faulty

As can be seen $V_0(1) = b + s$ with the only other values being 0 and $\perp$, so that and valid f will have $f(V_0) = 0$. E_i and E_{i+1} both produce the same thing for V_{i+1}, so for any V_i and V_{i+1} we have $V_i \approx V_{i+1}$ because $(E_i \Rightarrow (V_i, V_{i+1}))$. We now need only show $f(V_c) = 1$ for any f.

Notice that the number of 0's in each view is reducing by $2b + o$ every two steps.$(V_{i+2}(0) = V_i(0) - (2b+0))$. We set $c = \left\lceil \frac{N-2b-2s-o}{2b+o} \right\rceil \times 2$. This is sufficient to ensure $V_c(0) \leq b + s$. Since the only other values in V_c are 1 and $\perp$ it follows that $f(V_c) = 1$ for any valid f.

This completes the construction of the chain, so by Lemma 9 we have for any approximation function f the convergence rate is bound by

$$K \geq \frac{1}{\left\lceil \frac{N-2b-2s-o}{2b+o} \right\rceil \times 2}$$

Since $\left\lceil \frac{N-2b-2s-o}{2b+o} \right\rceil \times 2$ is equal to or one greater than $\left\lceil \frac{N-2b-2s-o}{b+\frac{o}{2}} \right\rceil$. This lower bound demonstrates that Algorithm BSO is optimal or near optimal depending on the choice of b, s, o. Importantly Algorithm BSO is optimal in the maximum robustness cases, that is when $N = 3b + 2d + \frac{3}{2}o + 1$.

Also notice that if we set $c = \left\lceil \frac{N-2b-2s-\frac{o}{2}}{b+\frac{o}{2}} \right\rceil$ in the above chain of executions/views then $V_c(0)$ is still less than $b + s$. Setting $o = 0$ as in fault-model studied in [8] and we get

$$K \geq \left(\left\lceil \frac{N - 2b - 2s}{b} \right\rceil \right)^{-1}$$

This is guarantees exact optimality of our algorithm for that fault model.

5 Conclusion

We have analysed the Approximate Agreement problem for distributed systems subject to at most b byzantine faults, s symmetric ones and o omission failures. We have presented an algorithm, called BSO, and shown that it has convergence given by

$$K \leq \left(\left\lceil \frac{N - 2b - 2s - o}{b + o/2} \right\rceil \right)^{-1}$$

We have proved a lower bound of

$$K \geq \left(2 \left\lceil \frac{N - 2b - 2s - o}{2b + o} \right\rceil \right)^{-1}$$

which is asymptotically matching our algorithm.

In future work we plan to extend our analysis to asynchronous systems, and to the closely related clock synchronisation problem.

References

1. M. Azadmanesh, R. Kieckhafer, "New Hybrid Fault Models for Asynchronous Approximate Agreement" *IEEE Trans on Computers*, 45(4):439–449, (1996).
2. D. Dolev, N. Lynch, S. Pinter, E. Stark, W. Weihl, "Reaching Approximate Agreement in the Presence of Faults", *Journal of the ACM*, 33(3):499–516, (1986).
3. C. Dwork, Y. Moses, "Knowledge and Common Knowledge in a Byzantine Environment: Crash Failures", *Information and Computation*, 88(2):156-186, (1990).
4. A. Fekete, "Asymptotically Optimal Algorithms for Approximate Agreement", *Distributed Computing*, 4:9-29, (1990).
5. A. Fekete, "Asynchronous Approximate Agreement" *Information and Computation* 115(1):95-124, (1994).
6. M. Fischer, N. Lynch, "A Lower Bound for the Time to Assure Interactive Consistency", *Information Processing Letters* 14(4):183-186 (1982).

7. M. Fischer, N. Lynch, M. Patterson, "Impossibility of Distributed Consensus with One Faulty Process", *Journal of the ACM*, **32**(2):374–382 (1985).

8. R. Kieckhafer, M. Azadmanesh, "Reaching Approximate Agreement with Mixed-Mode Faults", *IEEE Trans on Parallel and Distributed Systems*, **5**(1):53–63, (1994).

9. M. Pease, R. Shostak, L. Lamport, "Reaching Agreement in the Presence of Faults", *Journal of the ACM* **27**(2):228–234 (1980).

10. P. Thambidurai, Y. Park, "Interactive Consistency with Multiple Faiilure Modes", in *Proc 7th IEEE Symposium on Reliable Distributed Systems*, (1988).

Using Remote Access Histories for Thread Scheduling in Distributed Shared Memory Systems

Assaf Schuster[1] and Lea Shalev[2]

[1] Computer Science Department, Technion, Haifa, Israel 32000.
assaf@cs.technion.ac.il,
WWW home page: http://www.cs.technion.ac.il/~assaf
[2] IBM R&D Center, Center of Advanced Technologies, Haifa, Israel.
Much of this work was done while this author was still with the Department of
Computer Science at the Technion.

Abstract. We developed the *remote access histories mechanism* (RAHM), a technique that can be used to dynamically, adaptively, and transparently improve the locality of memory references in distributed shared memory systems (DSMs). The RAHM helps the run-time system make correct decisions concerning the redistribution of threads to hosts – operations that typically involve high overhead.

The RAHM is independent of the memory consistency model, and comes into play only when the memory model fails to achieve locality of memory reference. The RAHM piggybacks on existing communication and adds only a negligible overhead. It is designed to work in dynamically changing systems, such as non-dedicated distributed environments.

The RAHM is fully implemented in user-space as part of the MILLIPEDE system, a Virtual Parallel Machine (VPM) designed for non-dedicated NT/PC clusters. The performance evaluation shows a potential for dramatic improvement in the efficiency of shared-memory parallel computations in loosely coupled distributed environments, due to an enhanced hit-ratio for local memory references.

1 Introduction

Improved efficiency of uniprocessor computing systems depends mainly on the principle of locality, which led to the development of memory hierarchies. Applying the same principle to parallel computing in distributed systems involves making performance-critical decisions concerning the migration of data and computation. Unfortunately, it turned out to be a lot more complicated than its uniprocessor counterpart.

Many multiprocessor DSM systems attempt to utilize the principle of locality by bringing a whole page into the local memory of a machine, whenever that page is accessed by a thread which is executed on that machine. However, this may result in the page being sent out promptly, to be used by another thread on a remote machine. Although low-level DSM hacking (such as padding pages, page-in locks, work-split on page boundaries, etc.) enables efficient manual optimization, it requires alot of effort and cannot be expected to solve the problem completely. Automatic methods can simplify this process; however, those available are static, compile-time tools, not capable of dealing with irregular problems on dynamically changing systems such as non-dedicated non-homogeneous distributed environments.

One type of problem caused by the implicit data placement in DSM systems is *false sharing*: two or more logically unrelated data objects that are used by different application components are placed on the same page. These objects may be accessed by different threads that reside in different machines, causing frequent transfer of the page between these machines. A similar situation may occur when several threads share the same data item, in which case threads that are placed at different hosts and attempt to simultaneously access the data can cause repeated transfer of the related page between the hosts, while the hosts are unable to do any useful work. Such frequent page transfer, whether caused by true data sharing or by false sharing, is called *page ping-pong*.

A popular method in DSM systems is to weaken the consistency conditions on the memory behavior. Each of the hosts contending for a memory object may get its own private copy, thus eliminating ping-pong situations. Reduced consistency, however, is not always a satisfactory solution. Sometimes weak memory cannot be applied, or the memory location must be synchronized frequently in order to keep certain variables highly consistent. In fact, frequent synchronization of the same location can cause ping-pong situations similar to those resulting from data sharing in a strong memory consistency model.

In general, weak memory models are a hassle to apply, and verifying the correctness of the resulting program is difficult at best. Some relaxed memory models attempt to assist the programmer by imposing a special programming paradigm, which, assuming the same memory behavior for all of the variables, is translated into efficient memory management. However, programmers (possibly importing already existing code) may find the imposed programming paradigm inadequate for certain tasks, and in particular too restrictive, or too permissive, for their programs or their coding style. Furthermore, because all modified variables are synchronized whether or not this is necessary, many relaxed models involve additional overhead which makes it hard to obtain speedups.

In this work we focus on a different optimization domain which may significantly reduce remote data access in DSM systems. Here the improvement is obtained automatically at run-time by redistributing the threads according to the application *memory access pattern*.

In order to better understand our method, we first consider an optimization problem known as the *multi-way cut*. Suppose that the memory access pattern is known in advance for the application at hand and an unlimited processing time is available. The memory access pattern may be represented by a weighted, bipartite graph, with one side consisting of the threads, the other side consisting of the memory pages, and an arc, weighted w, connecting the ith thread with the jth page, if the ith thread accesses the jth page with (some normalized) frequency w. Minimizing the communication with an optimal distribution of the work and data can be accomplished by finding cuts in the graph that will minimize the sum of the weights of edges crossing all cuts. The resulting optimization problem (called, as we said, multi-way cut) is NP hard (see [11] for 2-approximation algorithms), where the size of its input is typically in the billions.

Although this method is deficient for several reasons, its relation to our own method is instructive. Our method succeeds in circumventing the problems given rise to by the multi-way cut, which does not, for instance, always take the need for some load balancing policy into account, nor consider the fact that load balancing may depend on the dynamically changing and possibly non-homogeneous capabilities of the underlying system. Dynamic changes in the memory access pattern are also not accounted for by this method. Furthermore, the problem is complicated by the fact that most DSM systems use page replication (in either strong or weak consistency models) to decrease DSM-related communication; after replication, what used to be an optimal cut is so no longer. Finally, the information available before run-time may not be complete; the global memory access pattern may be implied, for instance, by the input.

Attempting to avoid the partial information problem by modeling the memory access pattern during run-time raises the following problem. Although the overhead required for recording remote accesses is negligible in comparison to that of the involved communication operation, it is much too high for recording local accesses. Local accesses cannot, therefore, be recorded, and the gathered data remains incomplete.

The method we propose in this paper actually utilizes partial information about data accesses (collected at run-time) to approximate the (possibly dynamically changing) memory access pattern. The method, called RAHM (Remote Access History Mechanism), is an adaptive distributed heuristic that strives to improve the distribution of the threads according to their observed memory access behavior, in order to achieve optimal locality of the DSM data accesses. RAHM collects information about the memory access pattern into a compact data structure which we call *page access history*. At any point in time, this data structure may be viewed as an approximation of the full representation of the application's memory access pattern, containing that part of the information which can be inferred by observing the application's remote memory references up to this point. Decisions about the redistribution of the computation are then made by consulting the accumulated information.

The RAHM can be applied regardless of the strength of the memory consistency model. When memory references are local due to a local copy of an item, the RAHM is inactive and incurs essentially no overhead. This is also the case when, due to relaxation of the memory consistency, there is a single remote access to the item which brings in a copy, so that all subsequent accesses will also be local.

The RAHM itself only records events that require communication and need not know anything about the memory consistency. However, its mechanism ensures that it will only "wake up" when the applied weakening of memory consistency (if applicable and exists) fails, causing remote references to a memory item that are frequent enough to require intervention. This frequency can, in fact, be viewed as the interpolation of all the important parameters: the strength of the memory model, the rate of accesses to the item, and the rate of memory synchronization operations. Thus, for example, the RAHM decision mechanism reacts identically to the case of an item accessed frequently by a thread where the memory model is weak, and to that of an infrequently accessed item in a strong memory consistency model.

The RAHM requires only limited resources and incurs, as we said, only a small overhead. It piggybacks on the network activity that is already taking place, so that the collection and storage of access information is done only when remote memory access occurs. Processing this information and using it to redistribute threads is done only when sending threads is required anyway by the load-balancing algorithm, or when page ping-pong is detected.

The rest of this work is organized as follows. In the rest of this section we give our assumptions about the underlying system on which RAHM is to be implemented and mention related work. Section 2 presents the basic method for choosing among the candidates for migration, when migration is required by some load balancing algorithm. Section 3 discusses ping-pong detection and treatment. Section 4 gives some performance measurements and expected improvements. We conclude the paper in Section 5.

System Requirements

We assume the following type of environment and applications: The system consists of (possibly non-homogeneous, non-dedicated) machines, interconnected by some communication network. In particular, the system may include SMP multiprocessor machines with physically shared memory, each considered here as a single host.

We assume a page-based system: when a remote memory access occurs, the corresponding page may move or is copied into the local memory of the issuing machine. We remark that the method presented in this work is not restricted to this framework and may be described in the more general context of memory objects. Nevertheless, for the sake of uniform terminology, we refer to page-based DSM systems only.

Thread migration. The system is multi-threaded, and a migration module exists, capable of moving threads between the machines. **Slow communication.** Sending messages between machines in the network is relatively slow; it makes sense to add some extra overhead in order to reduce future communication. Additional overhead *must be avoided*, however, for local memory accesses. Of course, applications which stabilize in some steady state in which locality is maximized experience no overhead whatsoever. **Coarse granularity.** The overhead associated with creating a thread and with initiating a remote execution is relatively high. A thread should therefore carry a sufficient amount of computation in order to justify the cost of its creation or migration. Thus, we assume the expected lifetime of a thread to be relatively long. **Unpredictable computation and communication.** Requests for the execution of one or more threads may arrive arbitrarily. No a-priori assumption is made about the memory access patterns of the threads. No previous knowledge is assumed about the relative amounts of communication and computation used by the applications.

Related Work

Most DSM systems do not use memory access pattern information to improve locality of data references. Instead, they concentrate on smart consistency schemes using various replication methods. Few systems attempt to do beyond reducing the consistency, including *Amber* [3], *Locust* [4], *MCRL* [8], *Olden* [1], and *COOL* [2]. Most of these are not fully transparent. A comprehensive comparison is given in the full paper [12].

2 Thread Scheduling

Since it is essential that a DSM system be adaptive to dynamic changes in the environment and to varying needs of the applications, one may use thread migration for sharing the load among the nodes in the system. However, improper placement of threads results in high communication overhead. Therefore, the threads that are chosen to migrate when the load balancing policy is enforced must be selected with care, so as to minimize the resulting remote memory accesses.

In this section we present a general method that can be used by a DSM system for selecting threads that will migrate to another host, while keeping the expected communication to a minimum. We assume that some external module decides that the migration of n threads from one host to another is to take place; this module then invokes the thread migration module. The goal of the migration is load transfer from an overloaded host to an idle or an underloaded one; however, the thread selection strategy is independent of the load balancing policy that is implemented in the algorithm which initiated the migration. Hence, the load balancing algorithm (which is described elsewhere [10]) is not described here; in fact, the RAHM can be incorporated in systems which employ any standard load sharing/balancing algorithm.

The thread selection module is thus concerned only with the problem of optimizing for maximal locality. It collects information concerning remote page accesses, and in this way "learns" the memory access patterns of the threads. However, the information about local accesses is not recorded. Thus, the knowledge about the memory access patterns is incomplete and incorrect decisions may be made. What makes things interesting is that these "poor" decisions can then be utilized for future improvements.

If, for example, all the threads which frequently access the same page occupy the same host, no information is (initially) recorded. Some of these threads may therefore be selected as candidates for migration to another host, a poor decision if the memory consistency is strong and page duplicates are not allowed at this point, or if they are allowed but require rapid memory synchronizations. At the same time, information about the page will also become available, making it possible to correct the decision and improve future decisions based on this information. We proceed in the following subsections to describe the details of this method.

2.1 Choosing Threads for Migration

The thread selection module receives as input both a destination for the migration and the number of threads to migrate. It starts by determining the set of threads that are allowed to migrate. A thread may fail to fit into this category for several reasons. It may have started to perform some location-dependent activities, or be waiting for some synchronization event. Finally, if it migrated recently in an attempt to resolve a page ping-pong, additional migration may cause a *thread ping-pong* instead. This issue is explained in detail in Section 3.

Once the Migration Server determines which threads can migrate, it selects n such threads whose migration is expected to minimize the number of remote DSM references for both the source and the destination hosts. Let L denote the local host and R denote the migration target host. The migration should not increase the number of remote accesses and should reduce it whenever possible. This requirement is easily met if there exist n threads that reside on L and are using only pages that are transferred between L and R, such that these pages are used by no other thread on L. In this case, as a result of migrating these threads, the corresponding pages will become local on R, or at least they will not be accessed from L, while the other pages will not be affected by the migration.

In the general case, the selected set of threads should have the following characteristics.

Maximal frequency of remote references to pages on R. This condition makes it possible to decrease the number of existing page transfers between L and R.

Maximal frequency of any remote references. Since the threads are intended to migrate to a less loaded host, it makes sense to move those with high communication demands. However, this condition should be given less weight than the previous one, as it does not reduce the total amount of communication.

Minimal access frequency of the threads remaining in L to the pages used by the selected threads. This condition attempts to minimize the expected number of accesses to these pages by the remaining threads. If the threads which remain in L do not use these pages at all, the pages may become local on R.

Minimal access frequency to local pages. Since local accesses are not recorded, there is no information regarding the local threads which used the page recently. Sometimes, however, it is possible to know that a thread once used this page, and that the page is local. Thus, the condition is applied only when the corresponding frequency can be inferred from the history of execution on another host. By the principle of locality, the threads that used the page (according to the history) are assumed to continue using it.

These requirements are clearly in conflict, necessitating a tradeoff. Our solution is to let the thread selection algorithm estimate the improvement that can be obtained by migrating each individual thread to the target host. To this end, the thread selection algorithm uses a heuristic function which takes into account the information that is available about the memory access pattern of the candidate thread and the impact of migration on the other threads.

If there is no information concerning remote accesses (i.e., at the beginning of the execution), or if there is more than a single choice, then an additional heuristic is applied: two threads that were created successively have a higher chance of sharing data (See [5]). Accordingly, successively spawned threads are preferred in such cases.

2.2 Page Information

On each host the local history of remote-references is collected using data provided by the DSM mechanism. As explained above, only remote accesses are treated; hence, no information concerning local accesses is available. For each remote access the following are recorded: page id, peer host id, access type, and the id of the accessing thread. This information is collected into three different types of stores, called *histories*: *page history*, *thread access history*, and *reduced history*.

The reason for splitting into different storage types is three-fold. As we will see, this split simplifies the retrieval of the necessary information during decision time. It also protects the system from unstable behavior that may be caused by communication bursts. In such cases, care must be taken to limit the amount of memory that is used to store the histories, while still keeping enough information even when memory constraints do not allow storage of the full history. In addition, out-of-date information should be discarded, lest wrong decisions be made due to past events that no longer characterize the current behavior. Finally, keeping the histories in different stores also helps dealing with page duplicates in systems employing memory models of weak consistency. The details follow.

History of a page is maintained in a certain host for each page P that visits the host, unless P leaves the host and does not return for "a very long time", which is a configurable parameter of time units, denoted T_{epoch}. It includes the following information about a limited number of the most recent paging events:

- Event type: an attempt to access the remote page, receipt of the remote page, or sending the page to another host.
- The remote host id.
- Event's timestamp. The timestamp is used both to discard out-of-date information, and to determine the frequency of references to this page. It is

important to note that the timestamps are strictly local: there is no global clock in the system, nor do we assume any coherency mechanism on the global ordering of the timestamps.

The length of the history is limited for each page; out-of-date information is removed from the history even when there is enough place to store it.

Access history of a thread is maintained for each thread that is currently executing locally; when a thread leaves the host its access history goes with it. The access history includes the following information about a limited number of its most recent remote accesses:

 - page id;
 - timestamp of the access.

An access that occurred more than T_{epoch} time units ago is discarded. If the page resides locally, the thread is assumed to continue using this page (although no remote accesses can be recorded), and the corresponding information is stored in the thread's *reduced access history,* as described below. If access information is discarded because of space limitations, then its "summary" is stored in the thread's reduced access history.

Reduced access history of a thread. An additional data structure, called *reduced access history,* is maintained for each thread. It contains *old* data about remote accesses that occurred a long time ago, but are still relevant because the corresponding page became local, and *reduced-size* data about accesses that occured recently, but cannot be stored in the full history because of space limitations.

The *reduced history* includes at most one entry for each page that is known to be referenced by the thread. The entry describing the page includes:

 - The frequency of remote accesses of the thread to the page, as calculated from the full access history (just before it was discarded), and
 - the timestamp of the thread's most recent access to the page (if it has already been deleted from the full history).

Information concerning pages that became local (i.e., reside at the same host as the thread) remains in the reduced history forever, or, in the case where the pages cease to be local (due to either page or thread migration), for T_{epoch} time units.

Migration of History The history of each page is maintained locally at each host visited by the page. This promotes quick and easy page migration, as the history does not travel with the page. The access histories of a thread (full and reduced) are maintained locally on the host that is currently executing the thread. When a thread migrates to another host, its full access history is translated to the reduced format; that is, reduced information about each page in the full history is extracted and added to the reduced history. The resulting reduced access history migrates together with the thread, and is used by the target host to improve future decisions made by its own migration module.

RAHM **and Memory Behavior** Since the RAHM is independent of the memory model we somehow need to determine how local histories are handled when pages are duplicated, synchronized, discarded, or simply migrated. Fortunately, the division into thread and page histories makes it possible to handle everything in a natural way, and serves to clarify which module is responsible for which actions.

The page history is maintained for the local copy of the page only, and is never synchronized with other histories of copies of this page that are maintained elsewhere. If the page copy moves to another machine, or is discarded, the local history is stored for some time, waiting for another copy of the page. If such a copy fails to arrive, the history is eventually deleted.

As will be explained in Section 3, if the local copy of a page is frequently accessed by remote threads, the threads will sometimes be redistributed in order to improve locality. However, it is left for the DSM to decide whether requests to access the page or requests for its copies are sent to this host or another. The DSM also decides (according to the corresponding consistency protocol) whether to move the page to another machine, to make a copy of it, or to synchronize copies. Once again, the RAHM does not intervene in the DSM decisions regarding these events, unless it detects a ping-pong situation to be resolved. This will be explained in Section 3.

In Section 3.3 we elaborate further on the relationship between the RAHM and the memory behavior, and further explain why the page histories for copies that are maintained on different hosts are never synchronized.

2.3 Thread Selection

We now describe the general method used to select n threads that will migrate from host L to host R. Choosing the best set of n threads is infeasible because of the high computation overhead and incomplete information. Therefore, we suggest a greedy strategy: the best thread is chosen according to some heuristic value calculated at the onset of each thread; the heuristic value for all other threads is then revised to take into account the changes in the memory access pattern that will be caused by migrating the selected thread. The process is repeated iteratively until n threads are chosen.

It seems, however, that a naive "hill-climbing" strategy will not work: if m threads that communicate with each other are located at L (where $m \leq n$), migrating only some of them would be unwise. Therefore, the heuristic function must take into account both the memory access pattern and the number of threads that should be chosen. We suggest the following generic heuristic function, in which the heuristic value will be the additive sum of the contributions by the individual pages, where a page contribution may be either positive or negative, depending on the factors described below.

The contribution of a page to the heuristic value of a thread increases if the page is used by threads on R. This is because the migration of the additional thread to R will bring together all the threads that are using this page, thus improving the locality of accesses to it. For the same reason, any other thread which uses this page and was already selected for migration should increase the contribution. In addition, the contribution correlates with the frequency at which the currently examined thread accesses this page, because the locality of accesses is more important for frequently accessed pages.

The next factor, which is more subtle, can be used to avoid the migration of only part of a set of communicating threads by assigning negative heuristic values, as follows. Each thread that references the page and will definitely stay at L (either because it is immobile or because there are too many threads in L that use this page) should decrease the contribution. When the additive heuristic value becomes negative, the candidate thread will not migrate, thus remaining at the same host with the other threads in the set.

The contribution of a local page is calculated using exactly the same method, according to the information contained in the reduced history. Of course, this information may not be available for some local pages, or may be available for only some of the threads that are using a certain local page. This raises a question concerning the quality of decisions that can be expected from the thread selection algorithm. We discuss this question below.

2.4 Correctness of the Migration Module Decisions

As already mentioned, incorrect decisions concerning migration are inevitable. However, as a consequence of each such wrong decision, more information will become available, because the accesses which have become remote will then be recorded in the histories. Thus, the next time one of the involved hosts transfers its threads, it will do so with improved decision making capability.

The global effect is an initial unstable period when the threads migrate relatively frequently and the system is busy collecting remote access data. Ideally, after some time, the system knows enough about the memory access pattern, so that a series of correct decisions bring it to a stable state in which the locality of page references is optimized with respect to the heuristic value calculations.

Note, however, that in the above scheme the thread selection module is activated externally. For example, it might be invoked only when serious load imbalance is detected. This introduces a new problem: ping-pong situations which are caused by incorrect decisions may appear even when the load is perfectly balanced. Since ping-pong causes high overhead, an additional mechanism for prompt treatment of it is required.

3 Ping-Pong Treatment

As explained in Section 2.4, the optimal (or suboptimal) locality of data accesses cannot be achieved merely by using a "smart" scheduler, because we neither assume a-priori information about the way the threads use the DSM, nor can we obtain complete information about it during run-time. Thus, our algorithm for the selection of migrating threads is bound to make mistakes, which reveal themselves in ping-pong situations. We thus suggest an additional mechanism, the *ping-pong treatment* mechanism, whose role is to *detect* and *correct* wrong decisions made by the thread scheduler.

When a ping-pong situation is detected, the ping-pong treatment module uses the corresponding page history (for the copy which resides in the host sending the alarm) to determine which hosts take part in this ping-pong, i.e., which copies of the application have threads that are rapidly accessing (the same copy of) the page. Then it initiates a protocol that determines which host can accommodate all the threads involved in the ping-pong. If such a host is found, all the threads involved migrate to it. The threads access histories are modified in order to avoid repeating those bad decisions which resulted in the ping-pong. If no such host is found, then other mechanisms are applied in order to reduce overhead and stabilize the system (see full version [12]).

3.1 Ping-Pong Detection

Each time an access to a remote page occurs, the ping-pong treatment module is invoked. Suppose some local thread attempts to use a remote page P. The ping-pong treatment module records the information concerning this access in P's history and in the access history of the thread, and examines the history of previous remote accesses to P. If the total number of entrances and exits of P to/from the host exceeds a certain threshold, then the module checks for a ping-pong situation according to the following general criteria.

Informally, a ping-pong is detected when the following two conditions are met. First, local threads attempt to access the page a short time after it leaves the host, indicating frequent access. Second, the page leaves the host a short time after it arrived, indicating frequent access by remote threads. Obviously, there are many ways to formalize these conditions. In the full paper we describe one of them and its implementation [12].

3.2 Determining Where to Migrate

The objective is to select a target host to which all the threads participating in a detected ping-pong can be transferred. Unfortunately, the selection of the target host cannot be made locally at a host that detects a ping-pong, because the participating hosts have different (local) information and may thus make different decisions regarding the same ping-pong. Furthermore, a host might have incomplete or out-of-date information about the other participants; it also does not know how many threads at the other hosts are using the page. Finally, more than a single page may be involved in a ping-pong, and selecting the same host as the target for all them would adversely affect the load balance. Ping-pongs are thus handled in a centralized manner by the *Ping-Pong Server*, which is in charge of collecting all the necessary information about each ping-pong, resolving them one at a time.

Each host contains a ping-pong treatment module called the *Ping-Pong Client*, which initiates a ping-pong resolution protocol when it detects a ping-pong situation, or when it receives a ping-pong message from the Ping-Pong

Server. When the ping-pong protocol for a page (copy) P is initiated, the Ping-Pong Client examines the page history of P to determine the set of threads that are using it and the corresponding set of hosts. Note that the host may be communicating with only some of the other hosts involved in the ping-pong, and thus the list of participants that is locally available is not necessarily complete. The Ping-Pong Client then sends the Ping-Pong Server a message containing the number of local threads that are using P, a flag indicating whether or not they are migratable, and a list of the hosts known to be participating in the ping-pong.

When the Ping-Pong Server gets the first message concerning a detected ping-pong situation, it sends a query to each host that is mentioned in the message. The Ping-Pong Server continues collecting information until up-to-date information from all the involved hosts has been received. If the number of threads involved is below a certain threshold, then the server selects the target host whose load is low enough to accommodate all of the threads involved. Otherwise, the server may decide to abort the ping-pong treatment in an attempt to keep the load balanced and avoid high migration overhead.

3.3 Relation to the Memory Consistency Revisited

As explained in Section 2.2, the decisions as to which copy of which page is accessed, modified, copied, discarded, etc., are left to the DSM, which implements the desired memory consistency. Since two different histories for two local copies of the same page are never synchronized, these decisions also determine which page copy's history is chosen for modification. This approach, in which the histories are not synchronized, was originally planned to simplify information retrieval, to avoid communication overhead, and to avoid clock synchronization and event ordering issues. As it turned out, this approach is what also enabled the system to adapt to different memory consistency protocols.

Consider, for instance, the case of four hosts with two copies of a single page. One copy is accessed by all the threads on hosts A and B, resulting in a ping-pong between them, and the second copy is accessed by all the threads on hosts C and D, also resulting in a ping-pong. This situation can be a result of several memory configurations and behaviors. It may occur when there is a true sharing of the threads on A and B, a true sharing of those on C and D, and both data items are falsely shared on the same page.

The aforementioned situation could occur if the required memory behavior guarantees *Coherence* (accesses to each variable are globally seen in the same order), but there is no strong connection between the operations on different variables. Suppose, more specifically, that the threads at A and B frequently access the same variable a, and the threads at C and D frequently access another variable b, and a and b share the same page. The DSM decides whether to send requests for the page from A to B and vice versa, or to send them between C and D only; i.e., the underlying shared memory implementation is "smart enough" to propagate modifications only to the places where they are required.

In order to resolve the ping-pong between A and B, only the page history on these hosts should be examined, and likewise for the ping-pong between C and D. Since no communication exists between the copies, the Ping-Pong Server does not try to synchronize all the local histories of the page, but only those of the hosts which take part in the ping-pong.

The memory behavior in the above example was designed to support efficient execution of at least two independent sets of threads which access the page simultaneously at remote locations. However, if *both* page histories were to be consulted, or synchronized at times, the Ping-Pong Server would then try to transfer all the threads from all four hosts to the same location, perhaps exceeding this host's capacity and interfering with the load balancer.

The current approach allows the RAHM to coexist efficiently with different memory behaviors. Of course, if in the above example a machine were hosting threads which access both variables a and b, then the joint page history would mention both of them, and the method, flexible as it is, could not adapt. Further work is required in this direction.

Treating Ping-Pong When Migration is Impossible Transferring all the threads that are using the page P to the same place may cause unstable behavior of the system. We refer the reader to the full version of the paper [12] where we describe mechanisms that can be applied in order to keep the system stable.

4 Implementation and Performance Evaluation

In order to prove that the methods presented in the previous sections can dramatically improve the performance of a DSM system, we used MILLIPEDE – a work-frame for adaptive distributed computation on networks of personal workstations [7,6,9].[1] MILLIPEDE includes a user-level implementation of a DSM and thread-migration mechanisms [10]; it provides a convenient way to execute multi-threaded DSM applications with transparent page- and thread- migration. Based on the ideas described above, MILLIPEDE provides a built-in optimization for data locality.

For lack of space we omit in this extended abstract the details of how MILLIPEDE implements the general method from Sections 2 and 3, they can be found in the full paper [12]. We proceed to present preliminary results of our experiments with the MILLIPEDE system, focusing on the effects of the RAHM on the locality of memory references. A full account of our measurements can be found in the full version [12].

In general, testing the MILLIPEDE system for just one parameter at a time is very hard, sometimes impossible. MILLIPEDE is designed to be very flexible, promptly responding to environmental changes. Thus, when one parameter reaches (or is fixed to) some value that causes the system to handle the situation

---

[1] Currently MILLIPEDE is implemented using the Windows-NT operating system; see also www.cs.technion.ac.il/Labs/Millipede

inefficiently, other parameters adapt their behavior accordingly. In the full paper we give several examples of this phenomenon.

The Traveling Salesman Problem (TSP) is an example of an NP-hard optimization problem in graph theory. The algorithm we use is not the most efficient one can find for this problem. It was selected for its suitability as a simple "platform" for testing the way RAHM handles various memory access patterns.

The basic solution to the TSP problem is to scan a search tree having a node for each partial path of any Hamiltonian path which starts in a given node of the input graph. In the parallel algorithm work is divided among threads, so that the subtree of each node $0 \rightarrow i$ is searched by $n - 2$ threads.

We compared three different variants of the program. In the first variation, denoted *NO-FS*, false sharing is avoided by allocating more memory than necessary, i.e., the allocations are padded to fit precisely into a page. In the two additional variants, the $n - 2$ threads that search the paths starting with $0 \rightarrow i$ store their private data on the same page. The variant called *FS* uses no optimizations, whereas the one called *OPTIMIZED-FS*, uses optimizations for data locality by enabling the RAHM.

As one can see in Figure 1, treating false sharing using our method is about as effective as avoiding false sharing by enlarging the DSM allocations; both improve the performance substantially compared to the case in which false sharing is not treated (in fact, almost to the point of optimal speedup). As expected, the relative improvement resulting from the use of the RAHM becomes higher when the number of hosts increases, because there are more false sharing situations to resolve.

One may ask: why use optimization when it is so simple to avoid false sharing by padding? There are two answers: first, the RAHM also solves the communication caused by true data sharing (which cannot be avoided by padding); and second, in many cases it is impossible to increase the size of all allocations to the size of a virtual page simply because this will overflow the working set.

Table 4 summarizes the results of running the TSP algorithm on six machines with a varying number k of threads sharing the *best-result-until-now* variable (thus contending for the same page). Since the load-balancing mechanism does not know which threads share the same variable, it sends them elsewhere in a non-deterministic fashion (which depends on which under-loaded machine is faster in asking for work). The result is a random placement of the threads in the hosts, which may represent arbitrary initial conditions for many applications with different memory access patterns.

The table shows a dramatic reduction in the network traffic when the RAHM is activated: the number of DSM-related messages, which reflects on the DSM *miss-ratio* (ratio of remote to total number of accesses), drops by a factor of 30 to 40! If the TSP problem involved more cities, this factor would grow exponentially. Note that the number of extra messages that are added by the RAHM itself is negligible compared to the improvement in the number of DSM-related messages.

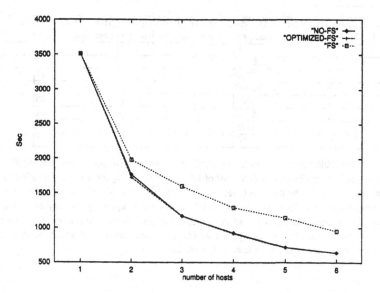

Fig. 1. The effect of the locality optimizations using the RAHM for the TSP. In the NO-FS case false sharing is avoided by aligning all allocations to page size. In the other two cases each page is used by two threads: in FS no optimizations are used, and in OPTIMIZED-FS the history mechanism is enabled.

5   Conclusions and Open issues

The RAHM – a dynamically adaptive, transparent mechanism that can be used to improve decisions concerning thread scheduling in a DSM system was presented. It was shown to have the potential to significantly improve the locality of memory references in such systems. Although the RAHM is described in terms of *pages* and *threads,* the same ideas can be applied in the case of threads which use *Remote Message Invocation* (RMI) in order to access remote *objects.* This will give us a mechanism that will optimize the migration decisions in a distributed environment supporting object oriented programming and concurrent execution.

There are many issues in the paper that clearly require further work. These include the interaction of the RAHM and the load balancing algorithm, the automatic tuning of parameters such as Δ, the ping-pong detection sensitivity, and additional stabilizing mechanisms.

References

1. M.C. Carlisle and A. Rogers. Software caching and computation migration in Olden. In *Proc. of the 5th ACM SIGPLAN Symp. on Principles and Practice of Parallel Programming (PPOPP),* July 1995.

k	Optimization enabled?	Number of DSM-related messages	Number of ping-pong treatment messages	Number of thread migrations	Execution time
2	Yes	5100	290	68	645
2	No	176120	0	23	1020
3	Yes	4080	279	87	620
3	No	160460	0	32	1514
4	Yes	5060	343	99	690
4	No	155540	0	44	1515
5	Yes	6160	443	139	700
5	No	162505	0	55	1442

Table 1. This table contains statistics regarding applying the RAHM to the TSP application with false sharing for different k (number of threads contending for a page). Random placement of the threads in the hosts represents arbitrary initial conditions for many applications with different memory access patterns. In all cases tested, applying locality optimizations dramatically decreases the number of DSM messages (page lookup and transfer). The table shows that the added overhead imposed by the ping-pong treatment mechanism and the increased number of thread migrations is negligible.

2. R. Chandra, A. Gupta, and J.L. Hennessy. Data Locality and Load Balancing in COOL. In *Proc. of the Fourth ACM SIGPLAN Symp. on Principles and Practice of Parallel Programming (PPOPP)*, pages 249–259, May 1993.
3. J. S. Chase, F. G. Amador, E. D. Lazowska, H. M. Levy, and R. J. Littlefield. The Amber System: Parallel Programming on a Network of Multiprocessors. In *Proc. of the 12th ACM Symp. on Operating Systems Principles (SOSP)*, pages 147–158, December 1989.
4. T. Chiueh and M. Verma. A compiler-directed distributed shared memory system. In *Proc. of the Int'l Conf. on Supercomputing*, July 1995.
5. A. Dubrovski, R. Friedman, and A. Schuster. Load Balancing in Distributed Shared Memory Systems. *International Journal of Applied Software Technology*, 3, March 1998.
6. R. Friedman, M. Goldin, A. Itzkovitz, and A. Schuster. Millipede: Easy Parallel Programming in Available Distributed Environments. *Software: Practice & Experience*, 27(8):929–965, August 1997. Preliminary version appeared in Proc. Euro–Par, Lyon, August 1996, pp. 84–87.
7. T. Hershman. Millipede Virtual Parallel Machine. *BYTE*, pages 3–4, May 1998.
8. W.C. Hsieh, M.F. Kaashoek, and W.E. Weihl. Dynamic Computation Migration in DSM systems. In *Proc. of Supercomputing*, November 1996.
9. A. Itzkovitz, A. Schuster, and L. Shalev. Millipede: Supporting Multiple Programming Paradigms on Top of a Single Virtual Parallel Machine. In *Proc. HIPS Workshop*, Geneve, April 1997.
10. A. Itzkovitz, A. Schuster, and L. Shalev. Thread Migration and its Applications in Distributed Shared Memory Systems. *To appear in the Journal of Systems and Software*, 1998. (Also: Technion TR LPCR-#9603).
11. J. Naor and L. Zosin. A 2-Approximation Algorithm for the Directed Multiway Cut Problem. Manuscript (naor@cs.technion.ac.il).
12. A. Schuster and L. Shalev. Using Remote Access Histories for Thread Scheduling in Distributed Shared Memory Systems. In *12th Intl. Symp. on Distributed Computing*, Andros, September 1998. A Technion/LPCR TR-#9701, January 1997.

The *Bancomat* Problem: An Example of Resource Allocation in a Partitionable Asynchronous System

Jeremy Sussman and Keith Marzullo

University of California, San Diego
Department of Computer Science and Engineering
La Jolla, CA 92093–0114
{jsussman,marzullo}@cs.ucsd.edu

Abstract. A partition-aware application is an application that can make progress in multiple connected components. In this paper, we examine a particular partition-aware application to evaluate the properties provided by different partitionable group membership protocols. The application we examine is a simple resource allocation problem that we call the *Bancomat* problem. We define a metric specific to this application, which we call the *cushion*, that captures the effects of the uncertainty of the global state caused from partitioning. We solve the *Bancomat* problem using three different approaches for building partition-aware applications. We compare the different group membership protocols in terms of the cushions they provide when solving the *Bancomat* problem.

1 Introduction

There exist several specifications and protocols for group membership in systems that can suffer partitions [13, 9, 2, 5]. Informally, there is a set of core properties that they all share, but they differ in the exact properties that they provide. These systems are meant to provide a basis for implementation of what has been called *partition-aware* applications, which are applications that are able to make progress in multiple concurrent partitions (that is, in multiple connected components) without blocking [2].

An essential problem confronted when building any distributed system is the uncertainty at any process of the global state. Partition-aware applications are especially sensitive to this problem because actions taken in one connected component cannot be detected by the processes outside of that component. Furthermore, when communication failures cause the system to partition, the processes may not agree at the point in the history that the partition occurred. The first issue must be directly addressed by the application, and partitionable group membership protocols help processes address the second issue.

In this paper, we examine a particular partition-aware application to evaluate the properties provided by different partitionable group membership protocols. The application we examine is a simple resource allocation problem that we call the *Bancomat* problem. We define a metric specific to this application, which we call the *cushion*, that captures the effects of the uncertainty of the global state caused from partitioning. The cushion is not the only interesting metric for the *Bancomat* problem, in that one cannot say that one partitionable group membership protocol is absolutely better than another because it allows a protocol to have a smaller cushion. Other metrics, such as message complexity, message size, and latency are important from a practical point of view. However, the cushion metric does give a measure of how well a given partitionable group membership protocol addresses uncertainty in the global state for the purposes of solving the *Bancomat* problem.

There are three main contributions of this paper. First, this paper specifies and examines a useful partition-aware application. We are not the first to consider this application, but we have not found a specification detailed enough to allow for a comparison of the properties of partitionable group membership protocols. Second, the paper contains such a comparison of partitionable group membership protocols. We believe that this comparison complements more taxonomic ones, such as [11]. Finally, the paper presents three different approaches to writing partition-aware applications: one in which no state is explicitly shared among the processes in the system and the processes take unilateral actions based on their local states; one in which all of the processes in a connected component share the same state and the actions are tightly coordinated in the component; and one in which processes in a connected component share state and a process informs the other processes when it has taken an action.

The paper proceeds as follows. Section 2 defines the *Bancomat* problem and the cushion metric, and gives a lower bound for the cushion metric. Section 3 presents the system model. Section 4 reviews the properties that the group membership protocols that we examine provide. Section 5 presents a solution for the *Bancomat* problem that uses a very weak idea of group membership to provide an upper bound on the cushion metric. Section 6 and Section 7 present two different solutions which require stronger group semantics, one based on a total delivery order and one without a total delivery order, and compare the cushions that result from building these solutions on top of the various group membership protocols. Section 8 summarizes our findings.

2   The *Bancomat* Problem and the *Cushion* Metric

The problem that we consider is loosely based on automatic teller machines, and so we call it the *Bancomat* problem.[1] This problem is a kind of resource allocation problem, where there is a relatively large number of identical resources that can be allocated. A practical example of such a service is a wide-area license service, where a relatively large but bounded number of clients can have a license to

---

[1] *Bancomat* is a common European term for an automatic teller machine. It doesn't suffer from the possible confusion that could arise if we were to name this the *ATM* problem.

use a software package simultaneously. Issuing licenses is implemented using withdrawals, and returning licenses is implemented using deposits.

There are a collection of n processes $A = \{b_1, b_2, \ldots b_n\}$ called *bancomats*. Collectively, the bancomats maintain a balance B of money, initially B_0. A client process can make two kinds of requests to a bancomat: it can ask for d amount of money to be withdrawn and it can ask for d amount of money to be deposited, where in both cases d is a (nonnegative) parameter of the request. When a client requests a bancomat to deposit d, d is added to B and the request terminates. When a client requests a bancomat to withdraw d, the bancomat can give the money to the client in pieces (deducting it from B as it goes), but the request will not terminate until d has been withdrawn.

We assume that bancomats are fully connected by asynchronous point-to-point channels: $c_{i,j}$ is the channel through which b_i sends messages to b_j. If b_i sends a message to b_j when $c_{i,j}$ is not faulty, then b_j will eventually deliver the message. If b_i sends this message when $c_{i,j}$ is faulty, then b_j will never deliver this message. We do not require that $c_{i,j}$ be faulty exactly when $c_{j,i}$ is faulty.

We define a *connected component* C of the bancomats A to be a maximal set of A for which $\forall\, b_i, b_j \in C : c_{i,j}$ and $c_{j,i}$ are not faulty. Each bancomat is in exactly one connected component at any time. The set of connected components can change over time, and components can split, can combine, and can simultaneously do both.

Given a bancomat b_i, we denote with d_i the amount of deposits that have been submitted, r_i the amount of withdrawal requested, and w_i the amount withdrawn at that bancomat. There are two safety properties: $\Box(w_i \leq r_i)$ and $\Box(\sum_{i=1}^{n}(w_i - d_i) \leq B_0)$. The first property states that money is not withdrawn from a bancomat unless it has been requested, and the second states that the balance is never negative.

We don't specify a liveness property for the protocol. We are interested in having solutions for systems that can suffer partitions, and specifying liveness properties for partitionable group membership has proven to be difficult. Instead, we define a metric that we call the *cushion*. Consider an infinite run in which there are no deposits and there have been withdrawal requests sufficient to receive as much money as can be withdrawn. The balance will eventually stabilize on some value, which we call the *final balance*. This balance represents money that the system did not allow to be withdrawn. The *cushion* is defined as the maximum final balance of any run in which every connected component received withdrawal requests for more than the initial balance B_0. A smaller cushion is desirable, since it ensures that the clients will be able to access more of their money.

Formally, consider a protocol Π that implements a bancomat system, and consider the set of runs $\rho \in R_\Pi \subseteq \Pi$ that satisfy the following constraints:

1. ρ is infinite.
2. There are no deposits.
3. Channels that fail remain failed.

4. For any connected component that persists forever, at least one bancomat in that connected component will receive at least B_0 withdrawal requests.

We define the cushion of the protocol Π to be the largest possible final balance: $cushion_\Pi = \max \rho \in R_\Pi : B_\rho$.

In any solution to the *Bancomat* problem for an asychronous system, messages are used to move money, explicitly or implicitly, both into or out of the system and among bancomats. In a partitionable system, any message that transfers money between bancomats is susceptible to the *Two Generals Problem* [10]— there is no way to ensure that both the sender and the receiver will agree on whether the last message sent between them has been successfully received. Since messages transmit money, the transmittor must assume, if given no reason not to, that the money was transferred even though it was not. That is, such money cannot be further used by the transmittor, since it cannot be certain that the receiver did not get the money. If the receiver did not receive the money, it cannot use it either. This money is unavailable for future transactions, and must be accounted for in the cushion. From this point forward, we will refer to this unavailable money as "lost".

In order to bound the amount of money that can be lost in a run, there must be a limit on both the number of messages that can suffer from this problem and the amount that can be lost by an individual message. The former can be addressed by only allowing there to be one message in transit from one bancomat to another, and the latter by specifying a *quantum* value of transfer. To fairly compare the different solutions and group membership protocols, we consider the quantum value a constant q, and impose the restriction of one outstanding message per process per group. A smaller quantum will allow for a smaller cushion, but will increase the message complexity. In this paper, we ignore this trade-off and only consider the cushion metric when comparing protocols.

3 Partitionable Group Membership System Model

We assume a system model that supports the partitionable group membership protocols that we consider. Processes communicate only through sending messages over a network. The network may partition. The exact details of what constitutes a partition have proven difficult to define, and so we rely on whatever abstraction each protocol provides. We do rely on one property that all protocols provide: if the network partitions the processes into a set of components, and then the processes remain in these components forever, then eventually the group membership protocols will detect this condition and form groups equal to these components. Section 4 discusses this property further.

We assume that the network preserves FIFO order, in that if process p sends message m to process p' and then sends message m' to process p', then p' may receive just m, or just m', or m before m', but never m' before m. Note that this is not assumed by the system models of the partitionable group membership protocols we consider, but most of the protocols we consider implement such a FIFO ordering.

Since the system model admits message loss, the Two General's Problem occurs with respect to bancomats adjusting the balance and clients withdrawing or receiving money. [10] We avoid this problem by defining correctness in terms of withdrawals and deposits that have been made at each bancomat.

If bancomats can crash, then the values d_i, r_i and w_i would need to be stored in stable storage and the balance would be defined in terms of the values recorded to stable storage. We avoid this additional complexity by assuming that bancomats do not crash.

Under this system model, and defining the cushion only in terms of runs in which failed links do not recover, one would expect that a reasonable protocol would not have a cushion larger than $n(n-1)q$. This is because no more than q can be lost by the failure of any channel. In [16], we show that a lower bound on the cushion is $\lfloor n/2 \log(n) \rfloor q$.

4 Properties of Partitionable Group Membership Services

We consider six different partitionable group membership protocols:

1. Extended virtual synchrony communication (hereafter EVSC) [13] used by both the *Transis* [7] and *Totem* [1] systems;
2. A protocol that we call asynchronous virtually synchronous communication (hereafter AVSC) that is provided for application use by the *Transis* system; [6]
3. Weak virtually synchronous communication (hereafter WVSC) [9] used by the *Horus* system [15];
4. A protocol that we call Unibo (for the University of Bologna, where it was developed) that was designed specifically for wide-area network based applications [2] [2];
5. Two protocols associated with the specification given by Cristian and Schmuck in [5]. The specification does not include communication properties which are needed to solve the *Bancomat* problem. This specification was meant to be instantiated with one of two sets of communication properties [4]. We call the two resulting protocols CS1 and CS2 (for the initials of the last names of the developers).

Partitionable group memberships provide the abstraction of *teams* and *groups*. A team specifies an abstract set of processes that communicate with each other to provide a service, and a group is a concrete set of processes associated with a team. Processes associated with a team *install* a group, which provides the process with an identifier for the group and a set of process identifiers, called the *membership* of the group. In order to differentiate groups with the same membership, a unique identifier is associated with each group. A group is installed at most once by each process. Once a process installs a group, it is said

---

[2] An earlier version of the specification of this protocol can be found in [3]. In terms of cushions for the *Bancomat* application, the differences are irrelevant.

to be *in* that group until it installs another. If a process p installs a group g and then installs group g', we say that *p regroups from g to g'*. For the purposes of the *Bancomat* problem we need only one team that defines the abstract set of machines.[3]

One can impose a relation on groups based on their installation by a process: g precedes g' if a process p regroups from g to g'. All group membership protocols ensure that this relation is irreflexive and asymmetric. An irreflexive strict partial order can be defined by taking the transitive closure of this relation, and two groups that are not related by this order are said to be *concurrent*.

All of the protocols that we consider in this paper use the group installed at a process to approximate the component to which that process belongs. They differ in the tightness of this approximation. However, all share the property that if the system stabilizes into a permanent set of components, then each process will eventually install a group whose membership is the members of the component and will forever remain in that group.

We denote with $|g|$ the number of processes that are in group g. We say that a group g is *fully formed* when all processes in the membership of g install g. There may be groups that are never fully formed, and a process may not know when a group is fully formed. All protocols ensure that concurrent fully formed groups do not have overlapping memberships.

All protocols allow a process to broadcast a message m to a team of which it is a member. All processes that deliver m must be members of the team to which m was broadcast, and all must be in the same group when they deliver m. This group must contain the sender. However, not all members of the group may deliver the message.

There are two ways that a process can determine which processes received a message. One method is based on *message stability*. A message m is said to be stable within a group when all processes in the group have received m, and a message is stable at a process p when p knows that the message is stable in p's group. A message can become stable only after it has been delivered in a fully formed group. All protocols considered in this paper provide a mechanism for alerting the members of a group when a message becomes stable. Some of the protocols offer an option to not deliver a message until it becomes stable.

The second method for a process to learn which processes received a message is based on regrouping. Suppose a process p regroups from g to g'. Define the *survivor set $SS(g, g')$* to be those processes that installed g, and then installed g' without installing any intermediate groups. All of the protocols guarantee that all of the members of $SS(g, g')$ have delivered the same set of messages while in group g. These members also agree on the stability of these messages: if p in $SS(g, g')$ knows that m became stable in g, then all of $SS(g, g')$ know that m became stable in g.

---

[3] Some protocols use the term *group* to indicate what we refer to here as a team, the term *view* to indicate a group, and the verb *to join* a group to indicate to install a group.

For each process, there is a point when it leaves group g and a later point when it joins the successor group g'. These two points define what we call the *regrouping interval* from g to g'. Group membership protocols differ in how messages are delivered and whether messages can be sent during regrouping intervals. In particular,

- EVSC does not allow messages to be sent during regrouping intervals. Outside of regrouping intervals, if the option to only deliver stable messages is chosen, then at the end of regrouping intervals a block of unstable messages may be delivered.
- CS1 does not allow messages to be sent during regrouping intervals. CS1 only delivers stable messages both outside and during regrouping intervals. Notification can be given when a message is known by all members of the group to be stable.
- WVSC allows messages to be sent during regrouping intervals, but these messages are delivered in the successor group g'. Messages can be delivered at all times, and need not be stable to be delivered.
- AVSC, CS2 and Unibo all allow messages to be sent during regrouping intervals. Their delivery semantics with respect to the stability of messages correspond to EVSC, CS1 and WVSC respectively.

Let g be the group that p has most recently installed when it sends a message m. All group membership protocols guarantee that m, if delivered, will be delivered in a group that does not precede nor is concurrent with g. Group membership protocols EVSC, CS1, WVSC and Unibo further restrict the group in which m is delivered. Specifically,

1. EVSC stipulates that m is delivered in g.
2. CS1 stipulates that if m is delivered, then it is delivered in g. A process p will not deliver m if p does not know that m is stable.
3. WVSC stipulates that if p sends m outside of a regrouping interval, then m will be delivered in g, and if p sends m during a regrouping interval, m will be delivered in the subsequent view g'.
   In addition, during a regrouping interval WVSC provides a sequence of zero or more membership lists $\langle V_1, V_2, \ldots V_\ell \rangle$ that are all supersets of the membership of g'. These membership lists, which are called *suggested views* are nested: $V_1 \supseteq V_2 \supseteq \ldots \supseteq V_\ell$. One could think of these membership lists as defining a sequence of groups, but none of these groups would become fully formed and no messages would be delivered in them. Hence, as is done in [9], we treat them simply as membership lists.
4. Unibo stipulates that if m is sent during a regrouping period, it will be delivered in the group g' that is installed after the regroup concludes. This, combined with the FIFO ordering that is also part of the Unibo specification, ensures that if m was not sent in a regrouping interval, m will either be delivered in g or in g', the next group installed by p.

The group membership protocols provide optional delivery order semantics. Most provide *causal ordering* options, in which messages delivered in the same group are delivered in a manner that respects the causal order defined in [12]. Also, many provide a *total order* option, in which all messages delivered in a group have been assigned a unique order in that group, and a message is delivered by a process only if all of the messages which preceed that message in the group have been delivered.

5   First Approach: No Shared State, Unilateral Actions

The first solution that we examine is formally presented in [2]. Informally, each bancomat maintains a local balance. The initial balance is initially partitioned in some manner among the bancomats. When a bancomat receives a withdrawal request, it will immediately fulfill the request without communication if there are sufficient funds in the local balance. If the local balance is insufficient to fulfill the request, then the bancomat requests a transfer of funds from some other bancomat. If this bancomat cannot transfer sufficient funds, then the original bancomat asks another bancomat for a transfer, and so forth. When the original bancomat receives sufficient funds to fulfill the request, it completes the transaction. Deposits are added to the local balance of the bancomat that receives the deposit request.

5.1   Cushion and Group Membership Requirements

The cushion for this protocol depends on the way a bancomat b_i, with insufficient funds, requests a transfer of funds from b_j. One strategy would have b_i not request a transfer from yet another bancomat b_k until either b_j responds with insufficient funds or b_i regroups into a group without b_j before receiving the response. The other strategy allows b_i to make concurrent transfer requests. With the latter strategy, the cushion is $n(n-1)q/2$. A run that attains this cushion is as follows. Let b_n be the first bancomat to receive withdrawal requests. When b_n has no more money in its local balance, it asks all the other bancomats for transfers. When each of the other bancomats send a quantum to b_n, the communication between that bancomat and b_n fails. This contributes $q(n-1)$ to the final balance. The next bancomat to receive requests, b_{n-1}, performs similarly, and the communication fails similarly, adding $q(n-2)$ to the final balance. Thus, there will be $\sum_{i=1}^{n}(i-1) = n(n-1)/2$ messages lost, resulting in a final balance of $n(n-1)q/2$. This is the worst possible final balance, since if a channel $c_{i,j}$ fails with money in transit, then b_j will never get from b_i a subsequent request for a transfer.

With the former strategy, the cushion is smaller but has the same complexity: as proven in [16] it is $\lfloor n/2 \rfloor \lceil n/2 \rceil q$. The run constructed above can not occur. Bancomat b_n lost the transfer from b_{n-1}, and so b_n sent the transfer request to b_{n-2} while in a group not containing b_{n-1}. Therefore, b_{n-2} must be in a group without b_{n-1} when it delivers the transfer request, and b_{n-1} will therefore not make the transfer request to b_{n-2}.

This solution requires very little from the group membership service. Indeed, for the larger cushion, all that is needed is a mechanism whereby a bancomat decides that another bancomat is disconnected. For the smaller cushion, all that is needed is the simple message delivery property that a message sent in group g is not delivered in a group preceeding or concurrent with g. All group membership protocols that we consider implement this property. Hence, using the weakest partitionable group membership protocol improves the cushion over using *no* protocol, but any further strengthing of group membership is not useful for this approach.

6 Second Approach: Shared State, Unilateral Actions

The second approach for the *Bancomat* problem has the optimal cushion of $n/2 \log(n)q$. We give an informal description of the protocol here; the complete protocol is detailed in [16]. We build the protocol on top of a group membership protocol in which concurrent fully-formed groups are disjoint, messages are delivered in the group in which they are sent, and messages cannot be sent during regrouping intervals. This is equivaluent to EVSC.

The complexity of the protocol arises from withdrawals, and so we temporarily ignore deposits. A client sends a request for a withdrawal to a bancomat. The bancomat waits until it can safely issue a quantum of money to the client, then issues that money, and broadcasts this fact to its group. We say that a message m is *application stable* when all members of the group have delivered m. Once the bancomat knows that its withdrawal request is application stable, it repeats the process until either the request is satisfied or it can no longer safely issue a quantum.

A bancomat can safely issue a quantum when it knows that by doing so the group balance will remain nonnegative. It is possible for all other bancomats in its group to concurrently issue a quantum of money, and so it is safe for a bancomat to issue a quantum only when the group balance is at least the quantum value multiplied by the size of the group.

Suppose bancomat b regroups from group g to group g'. The bancomat computes a final value for the group balance of g, and then contributes its share of this balance towards the group balance of g'. We define the *final group balance* of group g to be the initial value of the group balance of g minus all quanta that were delivered in g. Unfortunately, b may not have delivered all of the withdrawal requests delivered in g, and so it must compute an upper bound on the number of quanta withdrawn.

Recall that a bancomat can send a withdrawal request only after the previous withdrawal request it sent has become application stable. Hence, b knows that each bancomat that was in g but is not in g' may have sent one withdrawal request that b did not deliver. The upper bound on the number of withdrawal requests sent in g is the number that b delivered plus one for each bancomat that left g. Note that this message must be application stable; message stability as defined in Section 4 is not sufficient. A message is application stable when the states of all of the processes in the group reflect that message. A message is stable when all processes in the group are guaranteed to eventually deliver the message or crash. This solution requires the former.

Let b' be a bancomat that left g. If at some later time b' joins a group containing b also, then b can tighten its estimate of the final group balance of g. It does so by b' telling b (using a *state transfer* message) how many quanta it withdrew while in g.

Hence, b computes the group balance for the new group g' as follows. It first computes its share of the final group balance of g. From the properties of the group membership protocol, all bancomats in $SS(g, g')$ compute the same share, and so b includes these shares into the group balance of g'. Then, for each bancomat b' in g' but not in g, b waits for a state transfer message from b' that contains b''s contribution to the group balance of g' and the number of quantum it delivered the last time it was in a group with b. If b installs yet another group without receiving this message from b', b computes the group balance of g without b''s contribution. Since b''s contribution is always nonnegative, omitting this contribution is always safe.[4]

Deposits are implemented as follows. A bancomat b quantizes the deposit amount. b broadcasts the first quantum deposit notification to the group. When b knows that the deposit notification is stable, it broadcasts the next quantum, and so on. Upon delivery of a deposit notification, each bancomat increases the group balance by a quantum. Those that do not deliver the deposit still have a safe estimate of the final group balance. These bancomats will learn of the deposit via a state transfer message if they eventually join a group which b also joins.

6.1 Cushion

In [16] we show that this protocol has a cushion of $\lfloor n \log(n)/2 \rfloor q$. Informally, the worst-case run is constructed as follows. For simplicity, we consider n to be a power of 2. In this run, each connected component of bancomats repeatedly splits into two equal-sized connected components. This continues until there are n connected components, each containing one bancomat. At this point, each connected component receives B_0 withdrawal requests.

When a connected component of size $2k$ splits into two components of size k, then the bancomats in one component must assume that each bancomats in the other component sent a withdrawal request that was lost due to the split. Hence, each component deducts kq from the final balance of the original connected component. Amortized per bancomat, each bancomat contributes $q/2$ to the cushion for each time that bancomat joins a new group. Each bancomat joins $\log(n)$ groups, and so the cushion is $nq \log(n)/2$.

---

[4] If the state transfer message is lost due to the failure of a communications channel, then the amount carried by this message will be added to the final balance. State transfer messages occur only when channels recover, and so runs with state transfers are not considered when the computing the cushion of a protocol. The money is still lost, however. In practice, state transfers should also be quantized.

6.2 Group Membership Requirements

This protocol requires that a message be delivered in the group in which it was sent, and that concurrent fully-formed groups be disjoint. In addition, the protocol was written with no messages sent during regrouping intervals. These are the properties that are provided by EVSC, and so this protocol can be run, as is, on EVSC. CS1 also provides these properties, but in CS1 a message will not be delivered if it does not become stable. Thus, when a bancomat b sends a message m in g, b must rebroadcast m in the subsequent group g' should b not deliver m in g. This does not affect the cushion.

Unlike EVSC and CS1, WVSC allows for messages to be sent during regrouping intervals. A simple way to port the protocol to WVSC is for a bancomat to not send any messages during a regrouping interval, to ignore all suggested views, and to perform the actions that occur due to a regroup event at the end of the regrouping interval. One can modify the protocol, however, to allow bancomats to send messages (in particular, withdrawals) during regrouping intervals.

To do so, b computes a conservative estimate of the initial balance of g': b assumes that it is the only bancomat that brings any funds to the new group. In addition, the current suggested view is a superset of the membership of g'. For b to allow a withdrawal to occur during a regrouping interval, it ensures that its (conservative) share of the conservative balance is sufficient to cover the withdrawal. If so, b sends the withdrawal request; otherwise, b waits for the regrouping interval to complete.

In both cases, no additional messages can be lost over the original protocol, and so the cushion for both versions of the protocol on EVSC have the same optimal cushion as before. The second WVSC protocol may perform better than the original protocol because withdrawal requests are not automatically blocked during regrouping intervals. Since regrouping uses timeouts and is usually based on multiple rounds of communication, the performance improvement may be significant.

Adapting this protocol to run on top of AVSC, CS2, and Unibo is harder because a sending process knows very little about the group in which its message will be delivered. As with WVSC, we use a conservative approach. Before a bancomat b sends a withdrawal request, it first computes a conservative initial group balance for a hypothetical group in which the withdrawal request might be delivered. In order for this group balance to be conservative, b assumes that this group arose by having b first regroup into a group by itself, all bancomats except for b reduce their balances to zero, and then all the bancomats join a group with b. Bancomat b sends a withdrawal request only if this conservative balance is sufficiently large. Thus, if b is in a group of size k and that has a group balance of B, then it can withdraw a quantum only when $(B/k)/n \geq q$.

This protocol has a cushion that is at least $q(n^2 - 1)$. Consider the run in which all bancomats remain connected and all withdrawal requests are sent to b_n. It will continue to allow withdrawals through $B = qn^2$. Once the final quantum is taken, b_n will allow no more withdrawals giving a final balance of $q(n^2 - 1)$.

This is a very conservative protocol, and it is an open question whether there is a less conservative version.

7 Third Approach: Shared State, Coordinated Actions

The third approach has the bancomats in a group share their state. This is provided by totally-ordered group multicast, with stable message notification, as described in Section 4. The protocol is given in [16], and is informally described here.

The protocol is similar to the one of Section 6. The main difference is in how withdrawals and deposits are handled. As before, requests are broken into quanta and handled sequentially. In the earlier protocol, a bancomat will allow a withdrawal of a quantum if its share of the group balance is at least a quantum. In this protocol, a bancomat first broadcasts the request to withdraw a quantum to the team, and does not check for sufficient funds until it delivers this request. For this protocol, "sufficient funds" means that the group balance is at least a quantum. Thus, in this protocol, withdrawal requests can be rejected due to insufficient funds even when the reqesting bancomat had sufficient funds in its local balance when it did the broadcast.

Since the requests are delivered in a total order, each bancomat that delivers a request r will agree on the group balance when r is delivered, and will therefore take the same action. Bancomats other than the sender b of the request r can act on r as soon as they deliver it, but b must wait to act until r becomes stable in the group. By waiting until r becomes stable, b guarantees that all other members of its group will include r in any final balance they compute for the group.

Rebalancing is similar to the protocol of Section 6. The only difference is in the computation of the final balance of a group. Consider a bancomat b in $SS(g, g')$. In the previous protocol, b assumes that any bancomat not in $SS(g, g')$ had sent a withdrawal notification in g that b did not deliver. Hence, b includes such possible notifications when computing the final balance for g. In the protocol of this section, b knows that any withdrawal request from a bancomat b' not in $SS(g, g')$ must be stable at b' before b' performs the withdrawal. Thus, b includes a withdrawal request from b' in the final balance of g only when it has delivered such a request in g. As with the earlier protocol, this is a conservative estimate: r may never have become stable at b'.

7.1 Cushion and Group Membership Requirements

In [16] we show that this protocol has a cushion of $\lfloor n \log(n)/2 \rfloor q$. Informally, the worst-case run is the same as for the protocol of Section 6.

This solution requres the group membership service to provide total ordering of messages and stability notification. All of the protocols that we examine in this paper can supply both. Since these are the only requirements needed for this solution, the stronger group membership protocols may provide more than is needed. Indeed, a protocol such as that suggested in [8] is sufficient for this solution. Total ordering comes at a cost, however, especially in a wide-area network.

8 Discussion

In this paper, we (1) examine a partition-aware problem, (2) discuss three different approaches to solving partition-aware problems, and (3) compare how well different group membership protocols support solutions to this problem. In this section, we make some observations and raise some questions about these three issues.

8.1 Partition-Aware Problems

We were surprised at how hard it was to find a partition-aware problem that was concrete enough to be amenable to formalization. For example, [2] lists four different partition-aware problems, one of which is a version of the *Bancomat* problem. We have tried to formalize the other three, but so far have had only limited success in defining a metric, like the cushion, that captures the value of the properties of different partitionable group membership protocols.

We suspect that there are only a few different kinds of partition-aware applications. If it is the case, then it might be worthwhile to design partitionable group membership protocols with these specific applications in mind.

8.2 Different Approaches for Partition-Aware Problems

We examined three different approaches to solving partition-aware problems: one in which processes act autonomously and communicate as infrequently and with as few processes as possible, one that generalizes the state machine approach [14] to partitionable systems, and one that is an intermediate approach; processes act autonomously but broadcast their actions to their connected component.

The first approach is appealing because it uses very little from the group membership service. We were surprised that one property about message delivery in groups was sufficient to lower the cushion from $qn(n-1)/2$ to $q\lfloor n/2\rfloor\lceil n/2\rceil$. The required property does not appear to be very expensive to provide.

The state-machine-like approach also does not require much from the group membership service, but what it does require is not cheap: total message delivery order within a connected component. A totally-ordered multicast is required before every withdrawal, which implies that the latency for this protocol could be high.

The intermediate approach strikes a balance between these two, but we don't yet know the value of such a balance. Our suspicion is that it should perform better, but we have not yet tested this hypothesis.

8.3 Group Membership Protocols and the *Bancomat* Problem

The differences between the different group membership protocols were most important for the intermediate approach of Section 6. Using a weak partitionable group membership protocol like AVSC, CS2 and Unibo resulted in a large cushion, while the other protocols allow for an optimal cushion. On the other hand, the protocol for the weak membership services is extremely conservative. We are currently trying to design a less conservative version.

It has been suggested that there are a class of applications that require the EVSC-supplied property that a message is delivered in the group in which it was sent. This class of application has been named *group aware* [6]. The *Bancomat* problem is not group aware by this definition, but we suspect that without either at least the WVSC delivery properties or a total ordering on message delivery, it cannot be solved with an optimal cushion.

Our experience with this problem has led us to reconsider how partitionable group membership services should be presented. Many of the differences appear to be irrelevant with respect to implementing at least this partition-aware problem. Instead of concentrating on providing different properties, it might be worthwhile to provide more information to the application concerning the state of the system when communication fails. The fundamental problem we had to confront when designing these protocols was bounding the possible states of the processes in different connected components. Having more information might allow one to further restrict the possible states.

Acknowledgements We would like to thank Özalp Babaoğlu, Karan Bhatia, Idit Keidar, Alberto Montressor and Aleta Ricciardi for their help with this paper.

References

1. Amir, Y.; Moser, L.E.; Melliar-Smith, P.M.; Agarwal, D.A.; et al. The Totem single-ring ordering and membership protocol. In *ACM Transaction on Computer Systems*, 13(4):311-42, November 1995.
2. Ö. Babaoğlu, R. Davoli, A. Montresor and R. Segala. System Support for Partition-Aware Network Applications. Technical Report UBLCS-97-08, Department of Computer Science, University of Bologna, September 1996. A shorter version of this paper appears in: *Operating Systems Review*, 32(1):41-56, January 1998.
3. Ö. Babaoğlu, R. Davoli and A. Montresor. Group Membership and View Synchrony in Partitionable Asynchronous Distributed Systems: Specifications. Technical Report UBLCS-95-18, Department of Computer Science, University of Bologna, September 1996.
4. F. Cristian. Personal communication.
5. F. Cristian and F. Schmuck. Agreeing on processor-group membership in asynchronous distributed systems. Technical Report CSE95-428, UCSD, 1995. Available via anonymous ftp at cs.ucsd.edu as /pub/team/asyncmembership.ps.Z.
6. D. Dolev. Personal communication.

7. D. Dolev, and D. Malki. The Transis approach to high availability cluster communication. In *Communications of the ACM*, vol. 39, (no.4), ACM, April 1996. pages 64–70.

8. A. Fekete, N. A. Lynch, and A. A. Shvartsman. Specifying and using a partitionable group communications service. In *Proceedings of The Sixteenth Conference on Principles of Distributed Computing*, Santa Barbara, CA, 21–24 August 1997, pages 53–62.

9. R. Friedman and R. van Renesse. Strong and weak virtual synchrony in Horus. In *Proceedings 15th Symposium on Reliable Distributed Systems*, Nigara-on-the-Lake, Ont., Canada, 23–25 October 1996, pages 140–9.

10. J. N. Gray. Notes on Data Base Operating Systems. In *Operating Systems: An Advanced Course*, Springer-Verlag Lecture Notes in Computer Science 60:393–481, 1978.

11. M. A. Hiltunen and R. D. Schlichting. Properties of membership services. In *Proceedings of the Second International Symposium on Autonomous Decentralized Systems*, Phoenix, Az., 25–27 April 1995, pages 200–207.

12. L. Lamport. Time, clocks, and the ordering of events in a distributed system. *Communications of the ACM*, July, 1978, pages 558-565.

13. L. E. Moser, Y. Amir, P. M. Melliar-Smith, and D. A. Agarwal. Extended virtual synchrony. In *Proceedings of the 14th International Conference on Distributed Computing Systems*, Pozman, Poland, 21–24 June 1994, pages 56–65.

14. F. B. Schneider. Implementing fault tolerant services using the state machine approach: A tutorial. In *Computing Services*, vol. 22, (no.4), December 1990. pages 299-319.

15. R. van Renesse, K. P. Birman, S. Maffeis. Horus: a flexible group communication system. In *Communications of the ACM*, vol. 39, (no.4), ACM, April 1996. pages 76–83.

16. J. Sussman and K. Marzullo. The *Bancomat* Problem: An Example of Resource Allocation in a Partitionable Asynchronous System. Technical Report CS98-570, Department of Computer Science and Engineering, University of California, San Diego, (revised) July 1998.

Lifetime Based Consistency Protocols
for Distributed Objects[†]

Francisco J. Torres-Rojas[1], Mustaque Ahamad[1] and Michel Raynal[2]

[1]College of Computing
Georgia Institute of Technology, USA
{torres, mustaq}@cc.gatech.edu
[2]IRISA, France
raynal@irisa.fr

Abstract. Techniques such as replication and caching of objects that implement distributed services lead to consistency problems that must be addressed. We explore new consistency protocols based on the notion of object value *lifetimes*. By keeping track of the lifetimes of the values stored in shared objects (i.e., the time interval that goes from the writing of a value until the latest time when this value is known to be valid), it is possible to check the *mutual consistency* of a set of related objects cached at a site. Initially, this technique is presented assuming the presence of physical clocks. Later, these clocks are replaced by *vector* clocks and then by *plausible* clocks. Lifetimes based on such clocks result in weaker consistency but do provide more efficient implementations.

1 Introduction

The popularity of the Internet and WWW has motivated new applications that allow widely distributed users to share and manipulate complex and rich information. For example, applications such as virtual or cyber communities that span large number of geographically distributed users are already being developed. As these applications scale, we get a shared virtual world that can be navigated by users from any part of the world. A system that implements such a virtual world will store and provide access to a huge number of objects that will model the features of the physical world. Other objects will correspond to users who will interact with objects in the virtual world as well as with each other. This application scenario leads to a widely distributed computing system that will store and provide access to a massive number of constantly evolving information objects across widely distributed users. Most of the objects that capture features of the world require just read-only access but others, that model users and active features of the physical world, will change. Furthermore, although a large number of objects may exist in the distributed system, a particular user or group of users will only access a very small fraction of the object space.

In this paper, we address a problem that is motivated by an application and system environment as described above. We assume that a user, modeled as a *computation*,

---

†. This work was supported in part by an INRIA/NSF grant and by NSF grant CDA-9501637 and CCR-9619371.

accesses n objects from an object space that consists of m objects ($n \ll m$). An access to an object may only require the reading of its state (e.g., representation of a graphical object is read for its rendering) or it may also result in an update to the state of the object. To ensure that a user interacts with a coherent view of the virtual world, it is necessary that a computation accesses a *consistent* set of object copies. Such consistency has to be ensured in a system environment where object replication and caching are employed to meet the interactive response time needs of the applications. In particular, a user may cache a local copy of an object to minimize the effects of communication latency on the access time of this object. Such a copy could be received from a number of servers where the object is replicated.

A number of techniques have been previously explored for maintaining the consistency of distributed objects which included ordered group communication [10], replicated data management protocols such as quorum protocols [1], and consistency protocols that have been developed in distributed shared memory systems. We believe that these techniques are inadequate in the application and system environment presented here because of the following reasons:

- Since a user may navigate through a part of virtual space quickly and may not return to it, there is poor locality of access. Thus, the cost of membership operations (to join a group when a user requests an object and delete when its access is complete) may not be amortized over a large number of accesses. If a deletion is not done quickly after the user's focus of attention moves, a user may receive unnecessary updates for objects that will not be locally accessed. Furthermore, although few users may be accessing an object at a given time, the potential number of users can be very large which makes it difficult to manage the data structures (e.g., vector clocks) used in group communication protocols.

- It is reasonable to assume that objects may be owned by certain users and groups who may want to control how and when the objects are modified. Such control can be provided using locks. However, most accesses of non-owner nodes will be read-only. It should be possible to use a nearby copy of an object without acquiring a lock to meet such a request. Many of the distributed shared memory protocols that use synchronization operations to drive consistency operations may not be appropriate when synchronization is not utilized by most object accesses.

- Consistency protocols that require synchronous communication between large number of widely distributed nodes cannot meet the response time needs of interactive applications.

We explore an approach for providing consistent access to related objects to a user[1] in the described environment, that does not suffer from the problems of existing techniques. To motivate our approach, assume that the system has a synchronized global clock T available to all user sites. Consider an operation that assigns value $\mathbf{v}$ to object

---

1. We do not address synchronous interactions across multiple users which are addressed in groupware applications. Thus, our focus is on consistent access to dynamic information for a given user.

X at time t. Furthermore, assume that it is known that object X will be written next at time t'. Thus, along with the new updated value of X, the time interval $[t, t']$ is also stored. This interval is the *lifetime* of the value **v** of object X. If a computation accesses two related objects X and Y, to ensure that values **v** and **w** of these objects are consistent, we require that the lifetime of **v** does not end before the start of the lifetime of **w** and vice versa. This guarantees that the lifetimes of these values overlap and that they coexisted at the same time, and the user is accessing the state of the virtual world at that time. Several problems arise in the implementation of this approach. Although the lifetime is easily known for write-once objects (they are valid until time *infinity* in the future) and for objects that are updated at regular intervals, in general object lifetimes are not known. Secondly, the assumption of a synchronized global clock for recording lifetimes may not be valid. We avoid this problem by using scalable logical clocks instead of real-time clocks in our implementations. We also develop practical techniques for determining lifetimes of objects.

As we present the consistency protocols based on the lifetime approach, it will become evident that our approach is well suited for scalable implementations of object sharing across widely distributed users. First, a site only needs to ensure consistency of objects that are accessed by local computations and does not need to be directly aware of computations at other sites and their access to objects, unless that a cache miss triggers communications with server sites. Second, it permits considerable flexibility in the choice of replication, caching and update propagation policies (e.g., push vs. pull). Thus, we believe that it is an important approach for meeting the object sharing and consistency requirements of future applications.

In Section 2, we define the consistency criteria considered in this paper. We describe the lifetime approach in Section 3. In Section 4, we present an implementation that assumes the presence of synchronized physical clocks. We substitute the physical clocks by vector clocks and analyze the properties of the new scheme in Section 5. In order to obtain a more efficient implementation, we replace the inherently non-scalable vector clocks by *plausible clocks* [21] and present some preliminary performance results of these protocols in Section 6. The paper is concluded in Section 7.

2 Consistency Criteria

The *global history* H of a distributed system is a partially ordered set of all operations occurring at all sites of the system. We assume that all the operations in H are either **read** or **write**, where a **read** operation retrieves the value of an object and a **write** operation updates an object by assigning it a new value. In order to simplify, it is assumed that each value written is unique. The *local history* H_i of site i is the sequence of operations that are executed on this site. If operation **a** occurs before operation **b** in H_i we say that **a** precedes **b** in program order. If D is a set of operations, then S is a *serialization* of D if S is a linear sequence containing exactly all the operations of D such that each **read** operation to a particular object returns the value written by the most recent (in the order of S) **write** operation to that same object.

Sequential Consistency (**SC**) requires that the result of any execution is the same as if the operations of all sites were executed in some sequential order, and the operations of each individual site appear in this sequence in the order specified by its program [15]. Therefore, global history H satisfies SC if there is at least one serialization S of H that respects the program order for each site in the system.

The *causality relation* "$\rightarrow$" for message passing systems as defined in [14] can be modified to order the operations of H. Let $a, b, c \in H$. We say that $a \rightarrow b$, i.e., a causally precedes b, if one of the following holds: (i) a and b are executed at the same site and a is executed before b; (ii) b reads an object value written by a; (iii) $a \rightarrow c$ and $c \rightarrow b$. If none of the above conditions holds between two distinct operations a and b, a and b are "concurrent". We denote this situation as $a \parallel b$.

Let H_{i+w} be the set of all the operations in H_i plus all the **write** operations in H. History H satisfies *Causal Consistency* (**CC**) if for each site i there is a serialization S_i of H_{i+w} that respects causal order "$\rightarrow$" [3]. This is equivalent to saying that if $a, b, c \in H$ are such that a writes value v in object X, c reads the same value v from object X, and b writes value v' in object X, it is never the case that $a \rightarrow b \rightarrow c$. CC requires that all the causally related operations be seen in the same order by all sites, but at the same time allows different sites to perceive concurrent operations in different order. CC has been shown to be sufficient for applications that support asynchronous sharing among distributed users. It has been explored both in message passing systems [5] and in shared memory and object systems [2, 4, 11, 12, 13, 19]. Relations between SC and CC have been studied in [3, 17].

3 Lifetime of Object Values

3.1 General Architecture

We assume a Client/Server architecture where each object has a set of *server* sites that provide long term storage for the object. Other sites must cache a local copy of the object before accessing it. At a given instant, each cache does not contain more than one copy of a given object. Notice, however, that as a result of caching and replication there may exist several different versions of the same object at different sites (either client or server sites) of the system. Each site's cache holds a finite number of object copies. Some kind of replacement algorithm is executed when the cache runs out of room for new objects. Cache misses are solved by communicating with a server site, which either has a copy of the requested object or can obtain it. As it was mentioned before, a **write** operation assigns a particular value to an object copy stored in the local cache. Eventually, this version of the object may be communicated to one or more server sites and from there to other sites in the system.

Let the cache of site i be modeled as a set of objects C_i. In the context of a particular site cache there is at most one copy of any object of the system, thus let X_i denote the version of object X currently stored in C_i. Similarly, when a cache miss occurs at site i while accessing object X, some server s provides a copy of X_s, i.e., its current version of X. Once that this copy is stored in C_i, we denote it X_i.

3.2 Start and Ending Times

The *start time* of X_i, denoted as X_i^{α}, is the time when its corresponding **write** operation occurred. The start time of an object copy allows us to know since when the particular value of the object stored in the cache is valid. The latest time when the value stored in X_i is known to be valid is called its *ending time* and it is denoted as X_i^{ω}. For any object version X_i we have that $X_i^{\alpha} \leq X_i^{\omega}$. The interval $[X_i^{\alpha}, X_i^{\omega}]$ is the *lifetime* of the value stored in X_i.

The concept of lifetime allows us to evaluate the mutual consistency of the object copies stored in a site's cache. Two object copies are mutually consistent if it is possible that their values coexisted at some time in a distributed computation. Thus, the local copies X_i and Y_i are mutually consistent if the lifetime of one object value does not end before the start of the lifetime of the other object value, i.e., if $\mathbf{max}(X_i^{\alpha}, Y_i^{\alpha}) \leq \mathbf{min}(X_i^{\omega}, Y_i^{\omega})$. The cache of site i is consistent if every pair of objects in C_i is mutually consistent, or, equivalently, if the *maximum* start time of any object value in C_i is less than or equal to the *minimum* ending time of any object value in C_i.

3.3 Cache Context Time

In general, the protocols presented in this paper induce the intended level of consistency in the global execution by checking the mutual consistency of the objects stored at each site's cache and by invalidating those objects which do not satisfy the consistency criteria. However, when the number of objects which can be held at a cache is less than the total number of objects in the system, it is not enough just to consider the current state of the cache because we are ignoring the mutual consistency with objects that *have been* in the cache previously [13]. For instance, if we don't take into account the past content of a cache with room for just a few objects or in the extreme case exactly one single object (which is always mutually consistent with itself), we may generate executions where an object value moves back and forth between two or more possible values.

In order to avoid any "flickering" of the object values between present and past values and to guarantee the liveness of our protocols, we associate a timestamp called **Context**$_i$ to C_i. The initial value of this timestamp is 0. When either a copy of object X is brought into C_i (becoming X_i) or when the local version X_i is updated, **Context**$_i$ becomes $\mathbf{max}(X_i^{\alpha}, \textbf{Context}_i)$. In other words, **Context**$_i$ is the latest start time of any object value that is stored or that has been stored in C_i. Whenever **Context**$_i$ is updated all the local copies of objects $Y_i \in C_i$ such that $Y_i^{\omega} < \textbf{Context}_i$ are invalidated. Similarly, it is required that any object X brought from server s into C_i has an ending time not less than Context_i, i.e., $X_s^\omega \geq \text{Context}_i$. If C_i is consistent, then site i is accessing the state of the objects at least at time Context_i.

4 Sequential Consistency Protocol based on Physical Clocks

In this section we explore Protocol **A**, a SC protocol based on the concept of lifetime of object values. This protocol guarantees SC by ensuring that the contents of the caches of every site are always mutually consistent. We presuppose the existence of a perfectly synchronized physical clock T available to all the sites of the system. We say that $T(\mathbf{a})$ is the real time when operation $\mathbf{a}$ is executed. It is assumed that $\forall \mathbf{a}, \mathbf{b} \in H_i$, $\mathbf{a} \neq \mathbf{b} \Rightarrow T(\mathbf{a}) \neq T(\mathbf{b})$.

4.1 General Description

If site i has a cache miss when accessing object X, Protocol **A** executes the following steps:

1. It is requested that a server site s sends back a copy of X_s such that $X_s^\omega \geq \text{Context}_i$. This copy of X_s is inserted in C_i and from now on it is denoted as X_i.

2. Context_i is updated to $\max(X_i^\alpha, \text{Context}_i)$.

3. All the local copies of objects $Y_i \in C_i$ such that $Y_i^\omega < \text{Context}_i$ are invalidated. This implies that all objects $Y_i \in C_i$ such that $(\min(X_i^\omega, Y_i^\omega) < \max(X_i^\alpha, Y_i^\alpha))$ are invalidated.

Since a **write** operation executed at site i establishes a new value for Context_i (see Section 3.3), it is necessary to repeat step **3** on all the objects in C_i after an object value is updated. Notice that it is possible that site i is accessing a consistent state of the virtual world at some point in the past, specifically at time Context_i even when the current time is much later than Context_i (notice that Context_i is never decreased).

If the computation of site i can be modeled as a series of *sessions*, where each one has a well defined set of objects O to be accessed, we may consider an interesting "lazy" variation of Protocol **A**. In this new protocol, we assume the existence of some kind of *begin session* operation that declares the set of objects O associated with the current session. At this point, it is verified that the values of the objects $O \cap C_i$ are consistent, i.e., the set of object values to be accessed by the session that currently reside in the cache must be consistent. Any object $Y_i \in (O \cap C_i)$ such that $Y_i^\omega < \text{Context}_i$ is invalidated. When an object X is brought into the cache, instead of testing it against all the objects $Y_i \in C_i$, we test it just against the objects $Y_i \in (O \cap C_i)$. This protocol can be a more efficient alternative to Protocol **A**, specially if the caches are able to store a large number of objects, many of them unrelated to the current session.

4.2 Estimation of Lifetimes

Let's assume that when a local copy of object X is updated by site i at time t, the time t' when any copy of object X is written next at any site of the system is known beforehand. This knowledge would allow us to establish with precision the lifetime of an object value. For write-once objects, the ending time is trivially known to be *infinity* in the future. Similarly, the ending time for objects that are updated periodically, such as dynamic content web pages with time-to-live (TTL) fields, can be easily estimated. If a site holds a lock with time-out (also known as a fault-tolerant lock or *lease*) on a particular object, the time-out of the lock is a conservative estimate of the ending time of the value of this object.

However, in general, we don't know the lifetime of arbitrary object values. When site i updates object version X_i at time t, we start by assigning t to both X_i^{α} and X_i^{ω}. Thus, site i only knows the lifetime of this object value in an incomplete way. We have to discover as we go that no object copy X_j ($i \neq j$) has been overwritten and use this information to advance X_i^{ω}. For this we need a protocol that determines if the object copy X_i is valid at time $t' > X_i^{\omega}$.

When site i requests that a server s provides a copy of X such that $X_s^{\omega} \geq \mathbf{Context}_i$, it may happen that X_s does not satisfy this condition. In this case, this server communicates with other sites that could potentially have updated X, to determine if X_s is still valid at a time not less than $\mathbf{Context}_i$. If it is, X_s^{ω} is advanced. Otherwise, some client or server site j has a more recent copy of X such that X_j^{ω} is not less than $\mathbf{Context}_i$; in this case X_j is copied into X_s. Eventually, a copy of an appropriate version of X is provided to site i. Notice that with this protocol server s is effectively advancing X_s^{ω} and X_i^{ω}.

It is reasonable to assume that even if many sites read an object, it will only be written by a small number of sites. In the extreme case of a single site that writes an object, communication with this site can be used to advance lifetime. Otherwise, several ways are possible. For instance, server may keep track of last writer, or asynchronous, gossip style communication discovers that an object has not been overwritten and its lifetime is increased.

4.3 Protocol A and Sequential Consistency

If $a \in H_i$, we say that $Context(a)$ is the value of $\mathbf{Context}_i$ when operation a is executed, and that $Pos(a)$ is the relative position of a in the sequence H_i. Let $L(a)$ be a structure of the form <*Time, Position*> where:

If a is a **write** operation then $L(a) = <T(a), 0>$.
If a is a **read** operation then $L(a) = <Context\ (a), Pos(a)>$.

If $a,b \in H$ are such that $L(a) = <Time_a, Position_a>$ and $L(b) = <Time_b, Position_b>$, we say that $L(a) < L(b)$ if:

$(Time_a < Time_b) \vee$

$((Time_a = Time_b) \wedge$

   (a and b are executed at the same site) $\wedge$ ($Position_a < Position_b$)) $\vee$

$((Time_a = Time_b) \wedge$ (b reads the value written by a))

Otherwise, $L(b) < L(a)$.

Theorem 1. *Protocol* **A** *generates execution histories that satisfy* **SC**.

Proof. Let the sequence S be the product of sorting all the operations $a \in H$ by the values of $L(a)$. It is easy to see that S includes all the operations in H and that S respects the program order for all the local histories. Now, we have to prove that each **read** returns the value of the most recent **write** in the order of S.

Let $a,b,c \in H$ be such that **a** writes value **v** in object X, **b** reads the same value **v** from object X and **c** writes value **v'** in object X. Since we assume that each value written is unique, the fact that **b** reads the value that **a** writes implies that $L(a) < L(b)$. If $T(c) < T(a)$, then $L(c) < L(a) < L(b)$, i.e., operation **c** does not affect the value **v** read by operation **b**.

If $T(a) \leq T(c)$, then, assuming that operation **a** is executed at site i, operation **a** assigned a value to X_i^{ω} such that $X_i^{\omega} \leq T(c)$. This implies that $T(a) \leq Context(b) \leq X_i^{\omega} \leq T(c)$ and since **b** does not read the value written by **c**, then $L(a) < L(b) < L(c)$. Once again, **c** does not affect the value **v** read by operation **b**.

Thus, S is a serialization of the global history H that respects the program order for each site in the system and, in conclusion, Protocol **A** generates an execution that satisfies **SC**.   □

If the lifetimes of the object values are estimated incompletely, unnecessary invalidations and communications will occur, reducing the efficiency of the system. In the next sections we consider the relaxation of certain assumptions which lead to weaker consistency models, but with more efficient implementations.

5 Causal Consistency Protocol based on Logical Clocks

The assumption of perfectly synchronized physical clocks made by protocol **A** is not realistic in general, specially if we consider widely distributed systems. Furthermore, as it was mentioned in Section 4, if the ending times of the object values cannot be determined efficiently, the cost of guaranteeing sequential consistency can become high. In this section we consider a protocol that uses logical clocks [18] instead of physical clocks. This change reduces the level of consistency from **SC** to **CC**.

5.1 Background

A *Time Stamping System* (TSS) defines a particular format of timestamp, assigns these timestamps to each operation in H and provides tests for comparing timestamps [21]. Let $a, b \in H$ and let X be an arbitrary TSS. The timestamps of a and b are $X(a)$ and $X(b)$, respectively. X reports the causal relationship (not necessarily correct) between two operations by comparing their assigned timestamps, in this way:

$a \overset{X}{=} b \Leftrightarrow X(a) \overset{X}{=} X(b) \Leftrightarrow X$ "believes" that a and b are the same operation.

$a \overset{X}{\rightarrow} b \Leftrightarrow X(a) \overset{X}{\rightarrow} X(b) \Leftrightarrow X$ "believes" that a causally precedes b.

$a \overset{X}{\leftarrow} b \Leftrightarrow X(a) \overset{X}{\leftarrow} X(b) \Leftrightarrow X$ "believes" that b causally precedes a.

$a \overset{X}{\|} b \Leftrightarrow X(a) \overset{X}{\|} X(b) \Leftrightarrow X$ "believes" that a and b are concurrent.

We define TSS V to be the well known *vector clocks* technique [7, 8, 9, 16, 18]. Each site i keeps an integer vector $\mathbf{V}_i$ of N entries (N is number of sites), where $\mathbf{V}_i[j]$ is the knowledge that site i has of the activity at site j. Entry $\mathbf{V}_i[i]$ is incremented each time that an operation is executed at site i. If site i reads an object value whose start time is the vector clock $\mathbf{W}$, $\mathbf{V}_i$ becomes the component-wise maximum of $\mathbf{V}_i$ and $\mathbf{W}$. $V(a)$ is the value of $\mathbf{V}_i$ when operation a is executed at site i. Given $a, b \in H$, we have the following tests:

$a \overset{V}{=} b \Leftrightarrow V(a) \overset{V}{=} V(b) \Leftrightarrow \forall k\ V(a)[k] = V(b)[k]$

$\qquad V(a) \le V(b) \Leftrightarrow \forall k\ V(a)[k] \le V(b)[k]$

$a \overset{V}{\rightarrow} b \Leftrightarrow V(a) \overset{V}{\rightarrow} V(b) \Leftrightarrow V(a) \le V(b)$ and $\exists k$ such that $V(a)[k] < V(b)[k]$

$a \overset{V}{\|} b \Leftrightarrow V(a) \overset{V}{\|} V(b) \Leftrightarrow \exists k,j$ such that $V(a)[k] < V(b)[k]$ and $V(a)[j] > V(b)[j]$.

Vector clocks characterize completely the causality relation between operations in H [16]. Given vector clocks a and b, we define the functions $\mathbf{max}_V$ and $\mathbf{min}_V$ in this way:

$\mathbf{max}_V(a, b)$ is the vector t such that $\forall k\ t[k] = \mathbf{max}(a[k], b[k])$

$\mathbf{min}_V(a, b)$ is the vector t such that $\forall k\ t[k] = \mathbf{min}(a[k], b[k])$

5.2 Consistency Protocol based on Vector Clocks (Protocol B)

We now propose Protocol **B**, whose purpose is to produce executions that satisfy **CC** by verifying that all the objects stored in a cache are mutually consistent among themselves according to **CC**. This protocol basically follows the same rules of Protocol **A** with the main difference that instead of physical clocks, we use vector clocks (i.e., TSS V) to timestamp the operations and that, since there is not a total order of these timestamps, the tests are modified slightly.

Let **Clock**$_i$ be the current logical time of site i. **Clock**$_i$ is copied to x_i^α and x_i^ω when the local copy x_i is updated. As before, C_i has an associated timestamp called **Context**$_i$. When object copy x_s is brought from server s into C_i (becoming x_i) or when object x_i is updated at site i, **Context**$_i$ becomes $\mathbf{max}_V(x_i^\alpha, \mathbf{Context}_i)$. Several mechanisms, similar to the ones described in Section **4.2**, can be used to update the ending vector time of an object value [12]. Any later start time of a different value of the same object will be after or concurrent with the assigned ending time. For any object copy $x_i \in C_i$ it is true that $(x_i^\alpha \xrightarrow{V} x_i^\omega) \vee (x_i^\alpha \stackrel{V}{=} x_i^\omega)$.

CC allows that for all objects $x_i \in C_i$, x_i^ω advances as the logical time at the site i progresses. Therefore, unlike Protocol **A**, no objects are invalidated as consequence of a local **write** operation. We assume the existence of an asynchronous component responsible for sending updated versions of the objects to the servers. Before sending its copy of x_i back to the server, site i makes $x_i^\omega = \mathbf{max}_V(x_i^\omega, \mathbf{Clock}_i)$. The server updates its own clock with the information provided by x_i^α and updates x_i^ω with this clock.

If site i has a cache miss when accessing object x, Protocol **B** executes the following steps:

1. It is requested that a server s sends back a copy of x_s such that $\neg(x_s^\omega \xrightarrow{} \mathbf{Context}_i)$. This copy of x_s is inserted in C_i and from now on it is denoted as x_i.

2. **Context**$_i$ is updated to $\mathbf{max}_V(x_i^\alpha, \mathbf{Context}_i)$.

3. $y_i^\omega = \mathbf{max}_V(y_i^\omega, \mathbf{Clock}_i)$ for all the local copies of objects $y_i^\omega \in C_i$.

4. All the local copies of objects $y_i \in C_i$ such that $\neg(x_i^\alpha \overset{V}{\parallel} y_i^\alpha) \wedge (\mathbf{min}_V(x_i^\omega, y_i^\omega) \xrightarrow{V} \mathbf{max}_V(x_i^\alpha, y_i^\alpha))$ are invalidated.

5.3 Protocol B and Causal Consistency

Given two object copies $x_i, y_i \in C_i$ such that $x_i^\alpha \overset{V}{\parallel} y_i^\alpha$, it is easy to see that their values are mutually consistent because there exists no operation o such that o alters either x_i or y_i and that $x_i^\alpha \xrightarrow{V} V(o) \xrightarrow{V} y_i^\alpha$ or that $y_i^\alpha \xrightarrow{V} V(o) \xrightarrow{V} x_i^\alpha$.

Now, let two object copies $x_i, y_i \in C_i$ be such that $\neg(x_i^\alpha \overset{V}{\parallel} y_i^\alpha)$, i.e., their start times are causally related. Without loss of generality, let's say that $x_i^\alpha \xrightarrow{V} y_i^\alpha$. If the values stored in x_i and y_i are mutually consistent it has to be the case that $\neg(x_i^\omega \xrightarrow{V} y_i^\alpha)$, and vice versa.

In conclusion, two object copies X_i, $Y_i \in C_i$ are mutually consistent according to Causal Consistency if $(X_i^\alpha \overset{V}{\parallel} Y_i^\alpha) \vee \neg(\min_V(X_\omega, Y_\omega) \overset{V}{\rightarrow} \max_V(X_\alpha, Y_\alpha))$. A cache C_i is consistent if every pair of elements in C_i is mutually consistent. Protocol **B** starts with an empty cache and systematically checks each new cached object against the current contents, invalidating those objects that may compromise the consistency of the cache.

Theorem 2. *Protocol* **B** *generates execution histories that satisfy* **CC**.

Proof. We have to prove that for each site i there is a serialization S_i of H_{i+w} that respects causal order "$\rightarrow$". We start by making $S_i = H_i$. Notice that the sequence H_i respects the causal order "$\rightarrow$".

Let $w \in H$ be a **write** operation not included in H_i such that w assigns value v to an arbitrary object X and that this value is read by operation $a \in H_i$, Protocol **B** guarantees that $V(w) \overset{V}{\rightarrow} V(a)$ and that there cannot exist another **write** operation $w' \in H$ that assigns value v' to object X and $V(w) \overset{V}{\rightarrow} V(w') \overset{V}{\rightarrow} V(a)$, because if this were the case the value v of object X would have been invalidated by step **3** of Protocol **B**. Therefore, w can be inserted into its proper position in S_i, i.e., in the rightmost position in S_i such that there is not operation a in S_i to the left of w such that $V(w) \overset{V}{\rightarrow} V(a)$.

The rest of the **write** operations in H are either concurrent with the operations inserted in S_i or causally related to some other **write** operation already in S_i. In both cases these operations can be inserted into S_i in the rightmost position such that the causal order is not violated and that there is no interference between a **write** and a **read**. $\quad \square$

6 Causal Consistency Protocol based on Plausible Clocks

It is proved in [16] that vector clocks capture completely the causality relation between all the operations in H and therefore they are able to detect all the cases where two operations are concurrent. However, [6] proved that given a distributed system with N sites, causality can only be captured by vector clocks with N entries. If N is large, several problems arise such as growing storage costs, considerable communications overhead and extended processing time. Thus, vector clocks have poor scalability. *Plausible clocks* strive to provide a high level of accuracy in ordering events but they do not guarantee that certain pairs of concurrent events are not ordered. These clocks can be constructed with a constant number of elements independent of the number of sites and yet, under a Client/Server communication pattern, they can decide the causal relationship between arbitrary pairs of operations with an accuracy close to V. Examples of plausible clocks are presented in [20, 21] and it is proved that if TSS P is plausible then $\forall\, a, b \in H$:

$$a \overset{P}{=} b \Leftrightarrow a = b$$
$$a \overset{P}{\to} b \Rightarrow (a \to b) \vee (a \parallel b)$$
$$a \overset{P}{\leftarrow} b \Rightarrow (a \leftarrow b) \vee (a \parallel b)$$
$$a \overset{P}{\parallel} b \Rightarrow a \parallel b$$

In general, if v and w are two timestamps generated by P, we say that timestamp t is $\max_P(v, w)$, if all the following conditions hold [22]:

- $v \overset{P}{\to} t \vee v \overset{P}{=} t$

- $w \overset{P}{\to} t \vee w \overset{P}{=} t$

- There is no timestamp u such that $v \overset{P}{\to} u \wedge w \overset{P}{\to} u \wedge u \overset{P}{\to} t$

Similarly, timestamp $t \in \mathbf{S}$ is $\min_P(v, w)$, if:

- $v \overset{P}{\leftarrow} t \vee v \overset{P}{=} t$

- $w \overset{P}{\leftarrow} t \vee w \overset{P}{=} t$

- There is no timestamp u such that $v \overset{P}{\leftarrow} u \wedge w \overset{P}{\leftarrow} u \wedge u \overset{P}{\leftarrow} t$

We now propose Protocol **C**, which follows exactly the *same rules* of Protocol **B** but, in order to use a logical clock whose size is constant and independent of the number of sites in the system, vector clocks are replaced with a plausible clock P. For instance, if site i has a cache miss when accessing object X, Protocol **C** executes the following steps:

1. It is requested that the server s sends back a copy of X_s such that $\neg(X_s^{\omega} \overset{P}{\to} \text{Context}_i)$. This copy of X_s is inserted in $\boldsymbol{C}_i$ and from now on it is denoted as X_i

2. **Context$_i$** is updated to $\max_P(X_i^{\alpha}, \textbf{Context}_i)$.

3. $Y_i^{\omega} = \max_P(Y_i^{\omega}, \textbf{Clock}_i)$ for all the local copies of objects $Y_i^{\omega} \in \boldsymbol{C}_i$.

4. All the local copies of objects $Y_i \in \boldsymbol{C}_i$ such that $\neg(X_i^{\alpha} \overset{P}{\parallel} Y_i^{\alpha}) \wedge (\min_P(X_i^{\alpha}, Y_i^{\omega}) \overset{P}{\to} \max_P(X_i^{\alpha}, Y_i^{\alpha}))$ are invalidated.

A number of pairs of concurrent timestamps may be reported by P as being ordered, but it can be seen that there is no case where Protocol **C** decides that a set of objects is mutually consistent and that Protocol **B** decides that this same set is *not* mutually consistent. However, for a mutually consistent set, **C** may decide that the set is not consistent and issues unnecessary invalidations of local copies of objects. In any case, since the use of plausible clocks affects only the efficiency of the approach and not its correctness, Protocol **C** induces executions that satisfy Causal Consistency. It is expected that the reduction in the size of the logical clocks and their associated overhead will compensate positively for the unnecessary invalidations and communications with server sites generated by Protocol **C**. Furthermore, under the assumption of a very high number of users sharing a virtual world through the Internet, vector clocks are not feasible.

For purposes of illustration, Table 1 shows some results of a simple simulation of a distributed system where 50 sites sharing 5 objects executed 20 operations each one. We collect the number of messages (either from client to server or vice versa) originated when an object was updated, a cache miss occurred, an object was invalidated or when a server verifies whether an object is still valid up to certain time. The same history was executed under different protocols. The first row shows the results when a sequentially consistent *invalidations scheme* is used (i.e., all the copies of a particular object are invalidated when it is updated at any site). As expected, Protocol **B** generates significantly less messages than Protocol **A**. The number of messages generated by Protocol **C**, which utilizes the plausible clock *REV* [20, 21] with 5 entries per clock, is not much bigger than the number of messages generated by Protocol **B**. However, each one of the 752 messages generated by Protocol **B** must carry a 50 entry vector, i.e., an overhead of 37600 integers, while each one of the 960 messages generated by Protocol **C** must include a 5 entry vector, i.e., an overhead of just 4800 integers.

Table 1. Causal Consistency with Vector Clocks and Plausible Clocks.

	Updates	*Cache Misses*	*Invalidations*	*Validations*	*Total*
Invalidations Scheme	319	1310	1260	0	2890
Protocol **A**	319	1114	771	118	2322
Protocol **B**	319	382	51	0	752
Protocol **C**	319	488	153	0	960

7 Conclusions

We have presented mechanisms to ensure that a set of objects stored in the cache of a site in a distributed system is mutually consistent. The start time of an object value corresponds to the instant when this particular value is written and its ending time indicates the latest time when this value is known to be valid. These two times are updated in such a way that the ending time is always posterior to the start time and previous (or concurrent) to any future update of the object. The lifetime of an object value goes from its start time to its ending time. The basic idea of the presented techniques is to check if the lifetimes of a set of object values overlap, which implies that they are mutually consistent.

Protocol **A** assumes the existence of synchronized physical clocks and generates executions that satisfy Sequential Consistency. Protocol **B** replaces the physical clocks by vector clocks and redefines slightly the rules of Protocol **A**, which requires a less expensive implementation but relaxes the consistency level to Causal Consistency. Finally, Protocol **C** follows exactly the same rules of Protocol **B** but replaces the expensive vector clocks by constant-size plausible clocks, which makes sense if we consider that vector clocks require an entry for each one if the sites in the system. Protocol **C** may execute unnecessary invalidations of local copies of objects, but in the long term this is compensated by the use of shorter timestamps.

Currently we are exploring optimizations to protocols for lifetime estimation and evaluating our mutual consistency techniques under different workloads and applications. At the same time, different families of plausible clocks are being considered. We are interested in characterizing the cases where a "lazy" protocol may be more convenient than guaranteeing the consistency of the complete contents of local caches. This work extends the schemes presented in [2, 4, 12, 13], solving in particular the problem of caches with capacity for just a subset of the shared objects [13] and focusing on implementations with constant-size logical clocks.

References

1 M. Ahamad, M. Ammar and S.Y. Cheung, "Replicated Data Management in Distributed Systems", in *Advances in Distributed Computing: Concepts and Design*, IEEE ComputerSociety Press, T.L. Casavant and M. Singhal eds., 1993.

2 M. Ahamad, F. Torres-Rojas, R. Kordale, J. Singh, S. Smith, "Detecting Mutual Consistency of Shared Objects". Proc. of Intl. Workshop on Mobile Systems and Appl., 1994.

3 M. Ahamad, G. Neiger, J. Burns, P. Kohli and P. Hutto. "Causal memory: definitions, implementation, and programming". Distributed Computing. September 1995.

4 M. Ahamad, S. Bhola, R. Kordale, F. Torres-Rojas. "Scalable Information Sharing in Large Scale Distributed Systems". Proc. of the Seventh SIGOPS Workshop, August 1996.

5 M. Ahamad, M.Raynal, and G. Thiakime, "An adaptive architecture for causally consistent services". Proc. of the 18th IEEE Int. Conf. on Distributed Computer Systems (ICDCS98), pp. 86-95, Amsterdam, 1998.

6 B. Charron-Bost, "Concerning the size of logical clocks in Distributed Systems", Information Processing Letters 39, pp. 11-16. 1991.

7 C.J. Fidge, "Timestamps in message-passing systems that preserve the partial ordering", Proc. 11th Australian Comp.Science Conference, Univ. of Queensland, pp. 55-66, 1988.

8 C.J. Fidge, "Logical Time in Distributed Computing Systems", Computer, vol 24, No. 8, pages 28-33, August 1991.

9 C.J. Fidge, "Fundamentals of Distributed Systems Observation", IEEE Software, vol 13, No. 6, November 1996.

10 U. Friztke, P. Ingels, A. Mostefaoui and M. Raynal, "Fault-Tolerant Total Order Multicast to Asynchronous Groups", Proc. 17th IEEE Symposium on Reliable Distributed Systems (SRDS98), Purdue, October 1998.

11 R. John and M. Ahamad, "Evaluation of Causal Distributed Shared Memory for Data-race-free Programs", Tech. Report, College of Computing, Georgia Institute of Technology, 1991.

12 R. Kordale and M. Ahamad. "A Scalable Technique for Implementing Multiple Consistency Levels for Distributed Objects". Proc. of the 16th. International Conference in Distributed Computing Systems. May 1996.

13 R. Kordale. "System Support for Scalable Services". Ph.D. dissertation, College of Computing, Georgia Institute of Technology. January 1997.

14 L. Lamport, "Time, clocks and the ordering of events in a Distributed System", Communications of the ACM, vol 21, pp. 558-564, July 1978.

15 L. Lamport, "How to make a multiprocessor computer that correctly executes multiprocess programs", IEEE Transactions on Computers, C-28(9), 690-691, 1979.

16 F. Mattern, "Virtual Time and Global States in Distributed Systems", Conf. (Cosnard et al (eds)) Proc. Workshop on Parallel and Distributed Algorithms, Chateau de Bonas, Elsevier, North Holland, pp. 215-226. October 1988.

17 M. Raynal and A. Schiper, "From Causal Consistency to Sequential Consistency in Shared Memory Systems", Proc. 15th Int. Conference FST & TCS (Foundations of Software Technology and Theoretical Computer Science), Springer-Verlag LNCS 1026, pp. 180-194. Bangalore, India, Dec. 1995.

18 M. Raynal and M. Singhal, "Logical Time: Capturing Causality in Distributed Systems", IEEE Computer, Vol. 29, No. 2, Feb., 1996.

19 M. Raynal and M. Ahamad, "Exploiting write semantics in implementing Partially Replicated Causal Objects", Proc. of 6th Euromicro Conference on Parallel and Distributed Systems, pp. 175-164, Madrid, January 1998.

20 F. Torres-Rojas, "Efficient Time Representation in Distributed Systems", MSc. Thesis, College of Computing, Georgia Institute of Technology, 1995.

21 F. Torres-Rojas and Mustaque Ahamad, "Plausible Clocks: Constant Size Logical Clocks for Distributed Systems", Proc. 10th International Workshop on Distributed Algorithms, WDAG'96. Bologna, Italy, October 1996.

22 F. Torres-Rojas and Mustaque Ahamad. "Computing Minimum and Maximum of Plausible Clocks", Technical Report, Georgia Institute of Technology, 1998.

Deriving a Scalable Algorithm for Mutual Exclusion*

Yih-Kuen Tsay

Department of Information Management
National Taiwan University
Taipei 106, TAIWAN
tsay@im.ntu.edu.tw

Abstract. This paper details the design of a scalable algorithm for the mutual exclusion problem. Starting by inserting a redundant assignment into Peterson's algorithm for two processes, we derive another algorithm that uses only local spins, i.e., a process busy-waits only on locally accessible shared variables. The new two-process algorithm is then adapted to serve as a building block of the complete tournament-like algorithm; the adaptation is such that the entire algorithm still uses only local spins, which is crucial for scalability. We consider the simplicity of the algorithm and its derivation to be the main contributions of this paper.

Keywords: local spins, mutual exclusion, read/write atomicity, refinement, scalability.

1 Introduction

New solutions seem never to stop emerging for the mutual exclusion problem, despite its relatively old age.[1] A new solution is proposed either to meet newly conceived criteria or to improve over previous ones with respect to certain tangible or less tangible measures. Simplicity is one of the less tangible measures. This paper presents a solution to the mutual exclusion problem which we believe to be simpler than previous ones that meet the same criteria.

To recapitulate the problem, each of a set of N processes from time to time may wish to execute a special segment of code called its critical section; the execution time of the critical section is assumed to be finite. Two segments of code—the *trying* protocol and the *exit* protocol are needed respectively before and after the critical section of each process such that the following two requirements are satisfied: (a) mutual exclusion—no two processes are in their critical sections at the same time and (b) fairness (starvation-freedom)—a process that is trying to enter the critical section, i.e., executing the trying protocol, will eventually enter the critical section.

---

* This work was supported in part by research awards from the National Science Council, Taiwan (R.O.C.) and College of Management, National Taiwan University.
[1] The mutual exclusion problem has come into existence since 1962, according to Dijkstra [3].

In [10], Yang and Anderson proposed the first (and, to our knowledge, the only previous) scalable solution that assumes only read/write atomicity. Their solution is scalable mainly due to the facts that

1. a process uses only local spins, i.e., it busy-waits only on locally accessible shared variables, and
2. the number of remote read/write operations for each access to the critical section is $O(\log N)$.

It is assumed that a shared variable can be made locally accessible to at most one process. Also, busy-waiting on a remote shared variable implies an unbounded number of remote read operations.

Scalable solutions that assume stronger atomic operations such as fetch&add and compare&swap had been proposed earlier [1, 7]. However, such solutions require special hardware support and may fail to meet the criteria of fairness and portability (across different hardware architectures). Moreover, despite its use of less powerful read/write operations, Yang and Anderson's solution is nearly as efficient as these earlier solutions.

In this paper, we propose a new scalable solution that also assumes only read/write atomicity. The proposed solution is scalable due to the same reasons as described previously for Yang and Anderson's. One distinct feature of our work is that we derive our algorithm through a sequence of refinement steps (rather than give the final solution and then prove its correctness). We justify the refinement steps informally, though a more formal treatment is possible.

The overall structure of our algorithm is based on the idea of a tournament. All tournament-like algorithms, including [9, 4, 6, 10], require a suitable mutual exclusion algorithm for two processes. Near two decades ago, Peterson [8] proposed an elegant solution to the two-process mutual exclusion problem. He argued that his algorithm does not appear out of nowhere, but is derived from combining two simpler algorithms, each solving part of the problem. Peterson's idea inspired us to derive a new two-process algorithm that uses only local spins and has essentially the same simple structure as his algorithm does. We adapt the new two-process algorithm to serve as a building block of our tournament-like algorithm; the adaptation is such that the entire algorithm still uses only local spins.

Another criterion closely related to scalability is adaptiveness. Scalability emphasizes the performance of an algorithm when the number of contending processes is large, while adaptiveness emphasizes the performance when the contention is low. Lamport [5] proposed an algorithm in which only a constant number of operations is required for entering the critical section in the absence of contention. His algorithm is followed by a few more algorithms, in particular Choy and Singh [2], that exhibit better adaptiveness. An existing idea for combining an adaptive algorithm with our scalable algorithm will be discussed.

2 The Two-Process Algorithm

In this section, we derive the basic algorithm for two processes that uses only local spins. The derivation starts by inserting a redundant assignment into the exit protocols of Peterson's two-process algorithm. The redundancy is then exploited to eliminate busy-waitings on remote shared variables.

2.1 Peterson's Algorithm

The celebrated Peterson's two-process algorithm is recreated below.

```
/* shared variables and initial conditions */
shared var Q: array [0..1] of boolean;
            TURN: 0..1;
    initially Q[0..1] = false;
```

```
/* process P₀ */                    /* process P₁ */
while true do                        while true do
    remainder;                           remainder;
    Q[0] := true;                        Q[1] := true;
    TURN := 0;                           TURN := 1;
    await ¬Q[1] ∨ TURN ≠ 0;              await ¬Q[0] ∨ TURN ≠ 1;
    critical section;                    critical section;
    Q[0] := false                        Q[1] := false
od                                   od
```

Peterson pointed out in his paper that the two-process algorithm is derived by combining two simple (but incorrect) algorithms, which we refer to as Primitives A and B⁻, respectively.

```
                        Primitive A:
            ...                          ...
            Q[0] := true;                Q[1] := true;
            await ¬Q[1];                 await ¬Q[0];
            critical section;            critical section;
            Q[0] := false;               Q[1] := false;
            ...                          ...
```

```
                        Primitive B⁻:
            ...                          ...
            TURN := 0;                   TURN := 1;
            await TURN ≠ 0;              await TURN ≠ 1;
            critical section;            critical section;
            ...                          ...
```

Both primitives satisfy the mutual exclusion requirement, but both may deadlock. However, the deadlocks are caused by very different reasons. In Primitive A, deadlock occurs when both processes are trying (and execute the assignments in their trying protocols at about the same time); while, in Primitive B⁻, deadlock occurs when only one process is trying. A "disjunctive" combination of the two primitives avoids the deadlocks, while preserving mutual exclusion.

2.2   Peterson's Algorithm with Redundancy

There are no exit protocols in Primitive B⁻, as they would become redundant in Peterson's algorithm. In Primitive B⁻, one of the two processes will be blocked in the **await** statement even after the other has left its critical section. This suggests that the left-out exit protocols are "$TURN := 0$" for P_0 and "$TURN := 1$" for P_1. Let us put them back to recover the "original" primitive, referred to as Primitive B.

Primitive B:

...	...
$TURN := 0;$	$TURN := 1;$
await $TURN \neq 0;$	**await** $TURN \neq 1;$
critical section;	critical section;
$TURN := 0;$	$TURN := 1;$
...	...

Combining Primitives A and B in the same way as Peterson did, we obtain a variant of Peterson's algorithm with redundancy in the exit protocols, shown below.

...	...
$Q[0] := true;$	$Q[1] := true;$
$TURN := 0;$	$TURN := 1;$
await $\neg Q[1] \vee TURN \neq 0;$	**await** $\neg Q[0] \vee TURN \neq 1;$
critical section;	critical section;
$Q[0] := false;$	$Q[1] := false;$
$TURN := 0;$	$TURN := 1;$
...	...

2.3   First Refinement: Exploiting the Redundancy

The redundancy in the exit protocols provides opportunities for optimizing the trying protocols (with respect to the number of remote operations). Thanks to the assignments to $TURN$ in the exit protocols, the testings of $\neg Q[0]$ and $\neg Q[1]$ in the **await** statements need to be done only once using conditional statements and can be separated from the repeated testings of $TURN \neq 0$ and $TURN \neq 1$. The resulting algorithm is shown in Figure 1.

```
...                                    ...
Q[0] := true;                          Q[1] := true;
TURN := 0;                             TURN := 1;
if Q[1] then                           if Q[0] then
    await TURN ≠ 0                          await TURN ≠ 1
fi;                                    fi;
critical section;                      critical section;
Q[0] := false;                         Q[1] := false;
TURN := 0;                             TURN := 1;
...                                    ...
```

Fig. 1. A two-process algorithm obtained from the first refinement

Remark: In the algorithm above, if P_0 finds $Q[1]$ to be *false* after setting $Q[0]$ to *true*, then it could immediately enter the critical section without setting $TURN$ to 0 and subsequently executing the conditional statement; also, P_0 could set $TURN$ to 0 in the exit protocol only if it finds Q_1 to be *true*. An analogous observation applies to P_1. The algorithm could be further refined as below to make clearer the use of $TURN$. However, to prevent the additional testings of Q from distracting our focus on the elimination of remote busy-waitings, we postpone this refinement till a later stage.

```
...                                    ...
Q[0] := true;                          Q[1] := true;
if Q[1] then                           if Q[0] then
    TURN := 0;                             TURN := 1;
    if Q[1] then                           if Q[0] then
        await TURN ≠ 0                          await TURN ≠ 1
    fi                                     fi
fi;                                    fi;
critical section;                      critical section;
Q[0] := false;                         Q[1] := false;
if Q[1] then                           if Q[0] then
    TURN := 0                              TURN := 1
fi;                                    fi;
...                                    ...
```

2.4 Second and Third Refinements: Localizing Busy-Waitings

We still have one remote busy-waiting in each process after the first refinement. Since the same variable $TURN$ is involved, the only way to go is representing $TURN$ by two separate variables. As the second refinement step, we introduce two new boolean variables $T[0]$ and $T[1]$ to replace $TURN$ and stipulate that $T[0] = T[1]$ if and only if $TURN = 0$. The assignment $TURN := 0$ in P_0 becomes a sequence of two assignments $t := T[1]$ and $T[0] := t$ (t is a private variable), via which P_0 attempts to make $T[0]$ and $T[1]$ equal; while, the statement **await**

$TURN \neq 0$ becomes **await** $T[1] \neq t$, where t can be shown to equal $T[0]$ in the statement. An analogous change is made for P_1 so that P_1 attempts to make $T[0]$ and $T[1]$ unequal and t can be shown to equal $\overline{T[1]}$ (the binary complement of $T[1]$) in the **await** statement. The algorithm becomes as follows; $\bar{t}$ denotes the binary complement of t.

```
/* t is a private variable */          /* t is a private variable */
...                                     ...
Q[0] := true;                           Q[1] := true;
t := T[1];                              t := T[0];
T[0] := t;                              T[1] := t̄;
if Q[1] then                            if Q[0] then
    await T[1] ≠ t                          await T[0] ≠ t
fi;                                     fi;
critical section;                       critical section;
Q[0] := false;                          Q[1] := false;
t := T[1];                              t := T[0];
T[0] := t;                              T[1] := t̄;
...                                     ...
```

If we would allocate $T[0]$ and $T[1]$ in such a way that $T[0]$ is locally accessible to P_1 and $T[1]$ is locally accessible to P_0, then we would have successfully eliminated all remote busy-waitings. However, to make an indexed variable more suggestive of its location, we swap $T[0]$ and $T[1]$ in the third refinement step. The resulting algorithm is shown in Figure 2.

Lemma 1. *The following are true for the algorithm in Figure 2: for P_0, t equals $T[1]$ when (the control of) P_0 is at Statement 5; and, for P_1, t equals $\overline{T[0]}$ when P_1 is at Statement 5.*

Proof. For P_0, since only P_0 may change the value of $T[1]$, Statement 3 makes $T[1]$ equal to t, and Statement 4 does not change t or $T[1]$, it follows that t equals $T[1]$ when P_0 is at Statement 5. An analogous argument applies to P_1. □

Theorem 1. *The algorithm in Figure 2 solves the mutual exclusion problem of two processes. And, the number of remote operations for each access to the critical section is $O(1)$.*

Proof. We prove only one interesting and nontrivial case that, when both processes find $Q[0]$ and $Q[1]$ to be *true*, it is impossible for the processes to pass the **await** statements and end up in the critical section simultaneously. Assume without loss of generality that P_0 passes the **await** statement first. From the preceding lemma, $T[0] \neq T[1]$ when P_0 passes the **await** statement. We need to show that P_1 cannot subsequently find $T[1] \neq t$, i.e., $T[0] = T[1]$ according to the preceding lemma, and pass the **await** statement before P_0 leaves the critical section. We observe that P_1 must have changed the value of $T[0]$ after P_0 reads $T[0]$ for the last time in Statement 2 and before P_0 enters the critical

```
/* shared variables and initial conditions */
shared var Q, T: array [0..1] of boolean;
initially Q[0..1] = false;
```

```
/* process P₀ */                    /* process P₁ */
private var t: boolean;              private var t: boolean;
while true do                        while true do
0:   remainder;                      0:   remainder;
1:   Q[0] := true;                   1:   Q[1] := true;
2:   t := T[0];                      2:   t := T[1];
3:   T[1] := t;                      3:   T[0] := t̄;
4:   if Q[1] then                    4:   if Q[0] then
5:      await T[0] ≠ t               5:      await T[1] ≠ t
     fi;                                  fi;
6:   critical section;               6:   critical section;
7:   Q[0] := false;                  7:   Q[1] := false;
8:   t := T[0];                      8:   t := T[1];
9:   T[1] := t                       9:   T[0] := t̄
od                                   od
```

Fig. 2. A two-process algorithm using only local spins

section; otherwise, P_0 cannot possibly find $T[0] \neq T[1]$ after the execution of Statements 2 and 3, which makes $T[0]$ and $T[1]$ equal. Consider the following three representative scenarios (the private variable t is indexed by the identity of its owner process to avoid confusion) :

```
1: Q[0] := true;
                                ...
2: t₀ := T[0];
                       ...
                     1: Q[1] := true;
                     2: t₁ := T[1];
                     3: T[0] := t̄₁;
3: T[1] := t₀;
4,5: ...
```

In this scenario, P_1 will find $T[0] \neq T[1]$ as P_0 did and be blocked, since the values of $T[0]$ and $T[1]$ have not been changed after P_0 last found $T[0] \neq T[1]$ and passed the **await** statement.

$1: Q[0] := true;$

$\ldots$

$2: t_0 := T[0];$

$\qquad\qquad\ldots$

$\qquad\qquad 8: t_1 := T[1];$

$\qquad\qquad 9: T[0] := \overline{t_1};$

$\qquad\qquad\ldots$

$\qquad\qquad 1: Q[1] := true;$

$\qquad\qquad 2: t_1 := T[1];$

$3: T[1] := t_0;$

$4,5: \ldots$

$\qquad\qquad 3: T[0] := \overline{t_1};$

We observe that, in the above scenario, the execution of Statement 2 by P_1 does not change the value of t_1 and the execution of Statement 3 by P_1 does not change the value of $T[0]$. Like in the first scenario, P_1 will find $T[0] \neq T[1]$ as P_0 did and be blocked, since the values of $T[0]$ and $T[1]$ have not been changed after P_0 last found $T[0] \neq T[1]$ and passed the **await** statement.

$1: Q[0] := true;$

$\qquad\qquad\ldots$

$2: t_0 := T[0];$

$\qquad\qquad\ldots$

$\qquad\qquad 8: t_1 := T[1];$

$\qquad\qquad 9: T[0] := \overline{t_1};$

$\qquad\qquad\ldots$

$\qquad\qquad 1: Q[1] := true;$

$3: T[1] := t_0;$

$4,5: \ldots$

$\qquad\qquad 2: t_1 := T[1];$

$\qquad\qquad 3: T[0] := \overline{t_1};$

In this scenario, the execution of Statements 2 and 3 by P_1 makes $T[0]$ and $T[1]$ unequal. P_1 will be blocked until later P_0 changes the value of $T[1]$ in the exit protocol. $\qquad\qquad\qquad\qquad\qquad\qquad\qquad\qquad\qquad\qquad\qquad\quad\Box$

2.5 Fourth Refinement: Using "$TURN$" Only If Necessary

Having eliminated all remote busy-waitings, we now take the refinement step indicated earlier in the end of Section 2.3. Though $TURN$ has been refined into a pair of boolean variables, the refinement step still applies. This completes our derivation of the two-process algorithm; its final design is shown in Figure 3.

Theorem 2. *The algorithm in Figure 3 solves the mutual exclusion problem of two processes. And, the number of remote operations for each access to the critical section is $O(1)$.*

```
            /* shared variables and initial conditions */
            shared var Q, T: array [0..1] of boolean;
            initially Q[0..1] = false;
```

```
/* process P0 */                    /* process P1 */
private var t: boolean;             private var t: boolean;
while true do                       while true do
    remainder;                          remainder;
    Q[0] := true;                       Q[1] := true;
    if Q[1] then                        if Q[0] then
        t := T[0];                          t := T[1];
        T[1] := t;                          T[0] := t;
        if Q[1] then                        if Q[0] then
            await T[0] ≠ t                      await T[1] ≠ t
        fi                                  fi
    fi;                                 fi;
    critical section;                   critical section;
    Q[0] := false;                      Q[1] := false;
    if Q[1] then                        if Q[0] then
        t := T[0];                          t := T[1];
        T[1] := t                           T[0] := t̄
    fi                                  fi
od                                  od
```

Fig. 3. Final design of the two-process algorithm

3 Adapting the Two-Process Algorithm

The two-process algorithm derived in the previous section provides a mechanism of arbitration between two *predetermined* processes. However, in a tournament-like algorithm for N processes, an arbitration may need to be made between two processes whose identities can be determined only during the execution time. To take into account this dynamic aspect, we consider the following variant of the mutual exclusion problem.

Definition 1. The dynamic two-process mutual exclusion problem: *The set of processes are divided into two groups, represented respectively by two disjoint sets ID_0 and ID_1 of non-negative integers. The terms trying protocol, critical section, and exit protocol as well as the two correctness requirements are as defined before. However, we assume that the processes are well-behaved in the sense that at most one process from each group can be active at any time; a process is said to be active if its control is between the beginning of the trying protocol and the end of the exit protocol.*

We shall adapt the two-process algorithm to solve this problem. The main difficulty is that, since which processes will become active cannot be predetermined, a fixed allocation of $T[0]$ and $T[1]$ will ruin the virtue of "local spins only". The idea is to let the processes supply their own copies of $T[0]$ or $T[1]$. But, this causes a new problem for a process to identify its opponent, i.e., to tell which copy of $T[0]$ or $T[1]$ (depending on its role) it should access. To resolve the problem, we change the type of $Q[0]$ and $Q[1]$ from boolean to the set $\{-1\} \cup ID_0 \cup ID_1$ so that they can be used not only as flags but also for recording the identities of processes. To try to enter its critical section, a process sets the appropriate entry of Q to its identity, which is reset to -1 by the process after leaving the critical section. Testing the truth value of $Q[0]$ or $Q[1]$ in the original algorithm is replaced by testing that of $opp \neq -1$, where opp records the value of $Q[0]$ or $Q[1]$.

Moreover, it is possible for a process in the trying protocol to see a different opponent when it checks the value of $Q[0]$ or $Q[1]$ for the second time. This occurs, for example, when a process p_i, $i \in ID_0$, first reads and checks $Q[1]$ to find that p_j, $j \in ID_1$, is its opponent. Subsequently p_j leaves the critical section and finishes executing the exit protocol. Another process $p_{j'}$, $j' \in ID_1$, may then start to execute the trying protocol, setting $Q[1]$ to j'. At this moment, p_i will find that $Q[1]$ has been changed. We claim that p_i may immediately enter the critical section. This is the case because $p_{j'}$ sees p_i as its opponent and will make $T[i]$ and $T[j']$ unequal and be blocked at the **await** statement until later p_i sees $p_{j'}$ as its opponent in the exit protocol and make $T[i]$ and $T[j']$ equal.

Figure 4 shows the adapted two-process algorithm for process p_i to compete as P_0 and process p_j to compete as P_1.

Theorem 3. *The algorithm in Figure 4 solves the dynamic two-process mutual exclusion problem. And, the number of remote operations for each access to the critical section is $O(1)$.*

4 The N-Process Algorithm

In this section, we utilize the adapted two-process algorithm as a building block to obtain a tournament-like algorithm for N processes. Without loss of generality, we assume that N (≥ 2) is a power of 2 (dummy processes may be added if N is not so) and the processes will be referred to as p_0, p_1, ..., and p_{N-1}.

Consider a tournament tree of N leaves which represent from left to right the N processes p_0, p_1, ..., and p_{N-1}. To enter the critical section, a process (leaf) has to "win" (in the ascending order) the $\log N$ rounds of matches represented by its ancestors. There are totally $N-1$ matches in the tournament tree, which we refer to as Matches 1 through $N-1$ going from top to bottom and left to right. Below is a tournament tree for 8 processes:

```
/* shared variables and initial conditions */
shared var Q: array [0..1] of {-1} ∪ ID₀ ∪ ID₁;
            T: array [ID₀ ∪ ID₁] of boolean;
initially Q[0..1] = -1;
```

```
/* pᵢ, i ∈ ID₀, competing as P₀ */
private var opp: {-1} ∪ ID₀ ∪ ID₁;
            opp': {-1} ∪ ID₀ ∪ ID₁;
            t: boolean;
while true do
    remainder;
    Q[0] := i;
    opp := Q[1];
    if opp ≠ -1 then
        t := T[i];
        T[opp] := t;
        opp' := Q[1];
        if opp' = opp then
            await T[i] ≠ t
    fi
    fi;
    critical section;
    Q[0] := -1;
    opp := Q[1];
    if opp ≠ -1 then
        t := T[i];
        T[opp] := t
    fi
od
```

```
/* pⱼ, j ∈ ID₁, competing as P₁ */
private var opp: {-1} ∪ ID₀ ∪ ID₁;
            opp': {-1} ∪ ID₀ ∪ ID₁;
            t: boolean;
while true do
    remainder;
    Q[1] := j;
    opp := Q[0];
    if opp ≠ -1 then
        t := T[j];
        T[opp] := t̄;
        opp' := Q[0];
        if opp' = opp then
            await T[j] ≠ t
    fi
    fi;
    critical section;
    Q[1] := -1;
    opp := Q[0];
    if opp ≠ -1 then
        t := T[j];
        T[opp] := t̄
    fi
od
```

Fig. 4. The adapted two-process algorithm for the dynamic two-process mutual exclusion problem

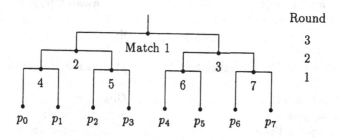

Note that the matches that a process has to win are predetermined, but its opponents in the matches, except in the first round, are not. To enter the critical section, for instance, p_4 has to win Matches 6, 3, and 1 (in this order). The opponent of p_4 in Match 3 may either be p_6 or p_7.

Remark: The tournament here is very different from a real tournament; the analogy is only for an informal explanation of how the algorithm works. In a match here, we allow a loser to become a new winner when the original winner returns at a later time (after executing the critical section) and "turns" the loser into a new winner. A player may also win the same match many times in a row (or many instances of the same match) if its potential opponent never shows up.

4.1 Trying and Exit Protocols for a Match

Our plan is to use an instance of the adapted two-process algorithm for determining the winner of a particular match. We stipulate that the process from the left branch of a match plays the role of P_0, while the process from the right plays P_1. For instance, p_4 should play P_0 and p_5 should play P_1 in match 6, whose winner then should play P_0 in Match 3. Note that the role of a process in each round of match can be predetermined. Below is the adapted two-process algorithm instantiated for process p_i to play Match m in Round r as P_0 and process p_j to play as P_1:

```
/* shared variables involved and their initial conditions */
shared var Q[m, 0], Q[m, 1]: -1..(N - 1);
             T[r, i], T[r, j]: boolean;
initially Q[m, 0..1] = -1;
```

`...`	`...`
`/* entering Round r */`	`/* entering Round r */`
`Q[m, 0] := i;`	`Q[m, 1] := j;`
`opp := Q[m, 1];`	`opp := Q[m, 0];`
`if opp ≠ -1 then`	`if opp ≠ -1 then`
`    t := T[r, i];`	`    t := T[r, j];`
`    T[r, opp] := t;`	`    T[r, opp] := t̄;`
`    opp' := Q[m, 1];`	`    opp' := Q[m, 0];`
`    if opp' = opp then`	`    if opp' = opp then`
`        await T[r, i] ≠ t`	`        await T[r, j] ≠ t`
`    fi`	`    fi`
`fi;`	`fi;`
`...`	`...`
`/* next round or critical section */`	`/* next round or critical section */`
`...`	`...`
`Q[m, 0] := -1;`	`Q[m, 1] := -1;`
`opp := Q[m, 1];`	`opp := Q[m, 0];`
`if opp ≠ -1 then`	`if opp ≠ -1 then`
`    t := T[r, i];`	`    t := T[r, j];`
`    T[r, opp] := t`	`    T[r, opp] := t̄`
`fi;`	`fi;`
`/* leaving Round r */`	`/* leaving Round r */`
`...`	`...`

Parameterizing i (the identity of a process), m, r, and x (the role of a process), we obtain the final trying and exit protocols for a match, shown below.

$$\mathbf{binary\_trying}(i, m, r, x):$$
$$Q[m, x] := i;$$
$$opp := Q[m, \overline{x}];$$
$$\text{if } opp \neq -1 \text{ then}$$
$$\qquad t := T[r, i];$$
$$\qquad T[r, opp] := \overline{x} \cdot t + x \cdot \overline{t};$$
$$\qquad opp' := Q[m, \overline{x}];$$
$$\qquad \text{if } opp' = opp \text{ then}$$
$$\qquad\qquad \text{await } T[r, i] \neq t$$
$$\qquad \mathbf{fi}$$
$$\mathbf{fi};$$

$$\mathbf{binary\_exit}(i, m, r, x):$$
$$Q[m, x] := -1;$$
$$opp := Q[m, \overline{x}];$$
$$\text{if } opp \neq -1 \text{ then}$$
$$\qquad t := T[r, i];$$
$$\qquad T[r, opp] := \overline{x} \cdot t + x \cdot \overline{t}$$
$$\mathbf{fi};$$

4.2   The Complete Algorithm

The derivation is near completion. What remains to be done is appropriate allocation of the shared variables.

Each match m needs a copy of $Q[m, 0..1]$; there are $N - 1$ matches in total. Each process p_i needs to supply a copy of $T[r, i]$ for each round r; there are $\log N$ rounds. The array T should be allocated in such a way that the entries $[1..\log N, i]$ are locally accessible to p_i. How Q should be allocated is not critical. The complete algorithm is shown in Figure 5. In the algorithm, $match(i, r)$ gives the number of the match that p_i should play in Round r, while $role(i, r)$ tells its role. The value of $match(i, r)$ can be computed by $2^{\log N - r} + \lfloor \frac{i}{2^r} \rfloor$ and the value of $role(i, r)$ can be computed by $\lfloor \frac{i}{2^{r-1}} \rfloor \bmod 2$

Theorem 4. *The algorithm in Figure 5 solves the mutual exclusion problem of N processes. And, the number of remote operations for each access to the critical section is $O(\log N)$.*

Proof. We associate with each match an instance of the dynamic two-process mutual exclusion problem (Definition 1) as follows. The processes that may become the players of the match constitute the set of processes in the instance. Those coming from the left branch (according to the tournament tree) of the match form the group ID_0, while those from the right branch form the group ID_1; the two groups are apparently disjoint. The critical section of a process in

```
/* shared variables and initial conditions */
shared var Q: array [1..(N − 1), 0..1] of −1..(N − 1);
         T: array [1..log N, 0..(N − 1)] of boolean;
initially Q[1..(N − 1), 0..1] = −1;

/* process p_i, 0 ≤ i ≤ (N − 1) */
private var opp, opp': −1..(N − 1);
         t: boolean;
while true do
     remainder;
     binary_trying(i, match(i, 1), r, role(i, 1));
     binary_trying(i, match(i, 2), r, role(i, 2));
     ...
     binary_trying(i, match(i, log N), r, role(i, log N));
     critical section;
     binary_exit(i, match(i, log N), r, role(i, log N));
     ...
     binary_exit(i, match(i, 2), r, role(i, 2));
     binary_exit(i, match(i, 1), r, role(i, 1))
od
```

Fig. 5. The N-process algorithm

the problem instance consists of the code between the end of the trying protocol for the match and the beginning of the exit protocol for the same match.

In every problem instance associated with a match of the first round, the processes are well-behaved, since there is exactly one process in each of the two groups of the problem instance. It is easy to see by induction (from bottom to top of the tournament tree) that, in every instance of the dynamic two-process mutual exclusion problem associated with a match, the processes are well-behaved.

In the problem instance associated with Match 1, the execution time of the critical section, which is identical to the critical section as defined in the N-process mutual exclusion problem, is finite by assumption. Again, it is easy to see by induction (from top to bottom of the tournament tree) that, in every instance of the dynamic two-process mutual exclusion problem associated with a match, the execution time of the critical section is finite.

The theorem then follows from Theorem 3.   □

5 Concluding Remarks

In our algorithm, a trying process needs to go through $\log N$ rounds of matches even if there are actually no other processes trying to enter their critical sections. The algorithm can be made fast in the absence of contention, like Yang and Anderson's tournament algorithm [10]. Below is their idea in picture:

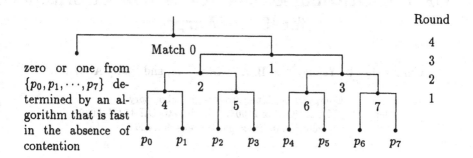

zero or one from $\{p_0, p_1, \cdots, p_7\}$ determined by an algorithm that is fast in the absence of contention

References

1. T.E. Anderson. The performance of spin lock alternatives for shared-memory multiprocessors. *IEEE Transactions on Parallel and Distributed Systems*, 1(1):6–16, January 1990.
2. M. Choy and A.K. Singh. Adaptive solutions to the mutual exclusion problem. *Distributed Computing*, 8(1):1–17, 1994.
3. E.W. Dijkstra. Solution of a problem in concurrent programming control. *Communications of ACM*, 8:569, 1965.
4. J.L.W. Kessels. Arbitration without common modifiable variables. *Acta Informatica*, 17:135–141, 1982.
5. L. Lamport. A fast mutual exclusion algorithm. *ACM Transactions on Computer Systems*, 5(1):1–11, February 1987.
6. N.A. Lynch. *Distributed Algorithms*. Morgan Kaufmann, 1996.
7. J.M. Mellor-Crummey and M.L. Scott. Algorithms for scalable synchronization on shared-memory multiprocessors. *ACM Transactions on Computer Systems*, 9(1):21–65, February 1991.
8. G.L. Peterson. Myths about the mutual exclusion problem. *Information Processing Letters*, 12(3):115–116, June 1981.
9. G.L. Peterson and M.J. Fischer. Economical solutions for the critical section problem in a distributed system. In *Proceedings of the 9th Annual ACM Symposium on Theory of Computing*, pages 91–97, 1977.
10. J.-H. Yang and J.H. Anderson. A fast, scalable mutual exclusion algorithm. *Distributed Computing*, 9(1):51–60, 1995.

OFC: A Distributed Fossil-Collection Algorithm for Time-Warp*

Christopher H. Young, Nael B. Abu-Ghazaleh, and Philip A. Wilsey

Computer Architecture Design Laboratory
Dept. of ECECS, PO Box 210030, Cincinnati, OH 45221–0030
{cyoung,nabughaz,paw}@ececs.uc.edu

Abstract. In the Time-Warp synchronization model, the processes must occasionally interrupt execution in order to reclaim memory space used by state and event histories that are no longer needed (fossil-collection). Traditionally, fossil-collection techniques have required the processes to reach a consensus on the Global Virtual-Time (GVT) — the global progress time. Events with time-stamps less than GVT are guaranteed to have been processed correctly; their histories can be safely collected. This paper presents Optimistic Fossil-Collection (OFC), a new fossil-collection algorithm that is fully distributed. OFC uses a local decision function to estimate the fossilized portion of the histories (and optimistically collects them). Because a global property is estimated using local information only, an erroneous estimate is possible. Accordingly, OFC must also include a recovery mechanism to be feasible. An uncoordinated distributed checkpointing algorithm for Time-Warp that is domino-effect free and lightweight is used. We show that, in addition to eliminating the overhead for GVT estimation, OFC has several desireable memory-management properties.

1 Introduction

The Time-Warp paradigm is an optimistic distributed synchronization model that utilizes *Virtual Time* [6, 7]. In particular, Time-Warp is used to build optimistically synchronized parallel discrete-event simulators (PDES)[1]. Under this paradigm, the simulation model is partitioned across a collection of concurrent simulators called Logical Processes (LPs). Each LP maintains a Local Virtual Time (LVT) and communicates with other LPs by exchanging time-stamped event messages. Each LP operates independently; no explicit synchronization is enforced among the LPs. Instead, each LP enforces causal ordering on local events (by processing them in time-stamp order). Causality errors are tolerated temporarily across different LPs; a rollback mechanism is used upon detection of

---

* This work was partially supported by the Advanced Research Projects Agency and monitored by the Department of Justice under contract number J-FBI-93-116.
[1] While this paper focuses on Time-Warp in a PDES context, the techniques suggested herein generalize to any application of the Time-Warp model.

a causality error to restore a correct state. A causality error is detected when an arriving event message has a time-stamp less than LVT. Such events are called *straggler* events and their arrival forces the LP to halt processing and rolls back the LP to the earlier virtual time of the straggler. Thus, each LP must maintain state and event histories to enable recovery from straggler events.

The progress of the simulation is determined by the smallest time-stamp of an unprocessed event in the simulation (taking into account messages in transit). Since all the LPs have passed that time, messages with time-stamps earlier than that time cannot be generated (events may only schedule other events with a higher time-stamp). Hence, rollbacks to states before the global progress time are not possible. Accordingly, as progress is made by the simulation, some information in the state and event histories is no longer needed for rollback. These history elements are called *fossils* and the reclamation of the memory space occupied by these fossils is called *fossil collection*. Fossil collection is required to free up memory for new history items, and to enhance the memory locality properties of the simulation.

Traditionally, Time Warp simulators have implemented fossil collection by comparing history item time-stamps to the simulation's global progress time, called the *Global Virtual Time* (GVT). Histories with a time-stamp earlier than GVT can be safely fossil collected. The GVT estimation problem has been shown to be similar to the distributed snapshots problem [12] and requires the construction of a causally consistent state in a distributed system without a common global clock. In particular, GVT estimation algorithms require coordination among the distributed set of LPs to reach a consensus on GVT.

This paper presents a new model for fossil collection that does not require coordination among the LPs. This new model, called Optimistic Fossil-Collection (OFC), allows each of the LPs to estimate the fossilized portions of their history queues probabilistically. OFC eliminates the overheads associated with GVT calculation, and allows fossil-collection to be customized by each LP to best match its local behavior. However, as the decision functions use local information only, there is a nonzero probability of an occurance of a rollback to an erroneously fossil-collected state (an *OFC fault*). In order to overcome OFC faults, a recovery mechanism must be incorporated to restore the simulation to a consistent state. Thus, OFC consists of two primary mechanisms: (i) the local decision mechanism; and (ii) the recovery mechanism.

The remainder of this paper is organized as follows. Section 2 reviews Time-Warp memory management and GVT estimation algorithms. OFC is presented in more detail in Section 3. Section 4 examines the decision mechanism, while Section 5 discusses the facets of OFC's recovery mechanism. Section 6 presents our uncoordinated checkpointing algorithm for Time-Warp applications that is free from the domino-effect (traditionally, freedom from domino-effect is guaranteed only by coordinated checkpointing). In Section 7, OFC is emperically compared to traditional Time-Warp fossil collection techniques. Finally, Section 8 presents some concluding remarks.

2 Fossil Collection and GVT estimation

The Time-Warp synchronization paradigm implements causality by recovering from causal errors, rather than preventing them. When an LP discovers a causal violation (a message with a time-stamp *lower* than the LP's LVT is received), a rollback occurs. A rollback: (i) restores the latest state before the straggler message time from the state history queue, and (ii) cancels the messages that were sent out erroneously (due to optimistically executed events). Thus, rollbacks require that each LP store their state after every event is processed[2]. Since memory is bounded, Time Warp simulators must implement a fossil-collection mechanism to scavenge unneeded items from the state and event history queues.

While fossil-collection and GVT estimation are distinct operations, fossil-collection requires a GVT estimate in order to establish a marker, against which fossils can be identified. Fossil-collection occurs either as a "scavenge all fossils" operation [9] or a "scavenge one item" operation (*on-the-fly* fossil collection) [2]. In addition, GVT estimates can be maintained continuously [3, 12] or explicitly requested (usually when memory space is exhausted) [9]. Algorithms that continuously update GVT vary according to the level of aggressiveness in updating GVT. Less aggressive algorithms have a lower overhead but produce a relaxed estimate of GVT [12]. Aggressive algorithms maintain a close estimate of GVT but have a high overhead [3]. Despite the differences in obtaining the GVT estimate, fossil-collection algorithms have two common steps: (i) produce a GVT estimate; (ii) free up (all or a subset of) history items with a time-stamp lower than the estimate. A close estimate of GVT allows tight management of memory, increasing the memory locality properties and improving the range of optimism for models where memory space is constrained. However, tracking GVT aggressively increases the overhead of the GVT estimation algorithm and adversely affects performance.

3 Optimistic Fossil-Collection and Active History

Figure 1 presents a real-time snapshot of LPs in a Time-Warp simulation. Each axis represents a LP in the simulation; a solid square indicates the LP's current virtual time. Viewing the histories as a queue of entries ordered by simulation time-stamp, GVT[3] represents a time-line that separates fossils from *active histories*. Traditional Time-Warp identifies fossils by estimating GVT (using GVT estimation algorithms that calculate a virtual time that true GVT is guaranteed to have passed). Thus, the solid lines on the figure represent the history items that cannot be freed according to this model.

In practice, some items ahead of GVT may also never be needed for rollback purposes. The fact that such items exist is a by-product of the behavior that en-

---

[2] In order to minimize state saving overhead, states may be saved incrementally, or periodically — reducing the cost of state-saving, but requiring an overhead when a rollback occurs [5].

[3] Here GVT refers to the true simulation GVT; by the time GVT estimation algorithms reach a consensus on GVT, true GVT could have further advanced.

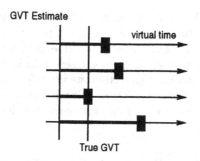

Fig. 1. LPs in a Time-Warp Simulation

ables optimistic synchronization in the first place; if none of the events executed optimistically are correct, then optimistic synchronization cannot succeed. Such events produce history items which will never be needed but are ahead of GVT. Unfortunately, these items cannot be identified at run-time without application information and global state information. Consider the extreme case where the LPs are completely independent — no rollbacks are necessary and the simulation completes correctly even if no state and event histories were maintained. GVT-based fossil-collection requires that each LP maintain history entries back to the current GVT estimate (even if their LVT is far ahead of GVT). Thus, GVT-based fossil-collection techniques maintain a conservative (larger than necessary) set of history information because: (i) the GVT-estimate lags the true GVT value; and (ii) true GVT is an absolute lower bound on fossilized entry times, but does not precisely mark the set of history items that are no longer needed.

Optimistic Fossil-Collection (OFC) is a fully distributed probabilistic fossil-collection technique for Time-Warp simulators. Under a basic OFC implementation, an LP: (i) implements a local decision function to estimate the portion of the history that is fossilized; and (ii) signals other LPs to recover if the LP detects an OFC fault (a rollback to a state that was optimistically collected). Thus, each LP makes its own fossil-collection decisions without the benefit of a GVT estimate. In addition to eliminating the overhead of GVT estimation, OFC allows each LP to customize its memory management to best suit its behavior. Because OFC is maintained optimistically, it can yield a tighter bound on memory than that produced by the GVT-based estimates. The decision function and recovery mechanism aspects of OFC are examined in more detail in the following two sections.

4 The Decision Function

The decision function is a critical component of the OFC technique. If the decision function is too aggressive in collecting fossils, OFC faults will occur frequently and the performance of the simulator drops. On the other hand, if it is too conservative, the memory consumed by history information will be large, causing inefficiencies due to loss of locality properties. It was shown [17], that OFC is safe and live for any decision function that increases its estimate after an OFC fault. Thus, there is greater freedom in implementing the decision function. In the remainder of this section, we identify two general classes of decision functions: one that predicts future rollback distances by statistical analysis of previous rollback behavior and one that converges heuristically to an active history estimate.

4.1 Statistically Bounding the Rollback Distance

This decision function requires that each LP sample event arrival times and create a statistical model of the rollback behavior. Note that, at any given point, the longest rollback distance from the current LVT defines the active history. The sampled rollback behavior is used to estimate a bound on the maximum rollback distance (the active history size). More precisely, an estimated bound X, can be obtained such that the probability of a future rollback of a distance larger than X (an OFC fault) is some pre-specified risk factor, α. Accordingly, history entries with a time-stamp smaller than $LVT - X$ can be optimistically reclaimed. If a smaller risk factor (α) is chosen, the predicted active-history size X, becomes larger, and OFC reclaims histories less aggressively.

The value of X can be expressed as a function of α if an underlying assumption on the rollback behavior is assumed. Consider the case where the length of a rollback is represented by a geometric distribution. Then the probability of a rollback of length l is given by $P(X = l) = p(1 - p)^{l-1}$, where p is the probability of a rollback of length 1. A geometric distribution is a reasonable assumption since studies have shown that short rollbacks occur more frequently than long rollbacks [6]. The probability that a rollback of length X exceeds some distance l is given by $P(X > l) = (1 - p)^{l+1}$. Thus, for a given p (obtained from sampling the rollback distances) and α, solve for l such that $P(X > l) < \alpha$ and $P(X > l - 1) > \alpha$. This analysis can be adapted for other distributions too.

Note that it is not cost effective to verify that the sampled rollback distances conform to the presumed distribution at run time. The discrepancy between the distribution and the actual behavior of rollbacks adversely affects the risk factor. However, it is possible to use the Chebyshev inquality [14] to provide an upper bound on the X for a given α that is independent of the underlying distribution. The Chebyshev inquality provides an upper bound on the probability that a random variable will deviate a given distance from its mean μ. The bound is computed in terms of the variance σ^2 and holds regardless of the original distribution F (provided the variance and mean are finite). The Chebyshev inequality gives the probability of the LVT change exceeding l as

$$P\{|X - \mu| \geq l\} \leq \frac{\sigma^2}{l^2}.$$

The bound is a function of both the variance and the distance from the mean. Once an independent sample of the rollbacks has been gathered, a confidence interval for the mean can be determined via the central limit theorem [14]. Emperical results have shown that the statistical bounds are highly successful for the models that were studied [17].

4.2 Converging on the Active History Heuristically

The liveness proof for OFC required only that the decision function increase its estimate of the active history X when an OFC fault occurs [17]. Starting with an initial estimate of X, heuristic decision functions increase X to $f(X)$, where $f(X)$ is monotonic. An example of such a decision function is to simply double the current estimate of X when an OFC fault occurs. A conservative initial estimate of X will eventually converge on an upper limit for the active history size as it suffers OFC faults.

5 Recovering from OFC faults

Because the decision function estimates a non-local property using only local information, there is a nonzero probability that a history entry that was predicted to be fossilized (and was subsequently collected) will be needed in the future — an OFC fault occurs. When an OFC fault occurs, the simulation cannot overcome the causality error using rollback because the required history information is not available. In order for OFC to be feasible, a recovery mechanism that allows the simulation to return to a causally correct state must be implemented. With the additional level of recovery, OFC-based Time-Warp becomes a two level recovery system; it incorporates: (i) rollbacks to recover from erroneous optimism in computation, and (ii) a recovery mechanism to overcome erroneous optimism in fossil-collection.

The simplest possible recovery mechanism is to restart the simulation from the initial state; all the work invested in the simulation up to the OFC fault has to be discarded. Moreover, in this case guarantees on liveliness can only be provided if the memory is arbitrarily large [17]. In general, recovery can be implemented as a restart from a *globally consistent simulation state*. A globally consistent state is a state that may occur in a legal execution of the simulation [1, 11]. Note that the state of a distributed application consists not only of the local states of the processors, but also of the state of the communication channels between the processors. Thus, as the simulation is progressing, globally consistent checkpoints must be constructed infrequently. A full definition of global snapshot consistency is given by Chandy and Lamport [1].

Constructing globally consistent checkpoints is a well researched problem [4]. Uncoordinated checkpointing does not guarantee freedom from the domino-effect [13]; a globally consistent checkpoint cannot be guaranteed (other than the initial state). It is possible to prevent the domino-effect by performing *co-ordinated* checkpointing [4]; the processes save their local state, and coordinate in saving the state of the communication channels between them to insure that the local snapshots together form a "meaningful" global snapshot [1, 8, 12, 15].

Using coordinated checkpointing to protect from OFC faults presents the following dilemma. GVT algorithms have been shown to be an instance of coordinated distributed snapshot algorithms — What is the point of OFC if it requires coordinated checkpointing to eliminate the equivelant of coordinated checkpointing (GVT estimation)? The answer is: (i) if the decision function is accurate, checkpointing can be carried out infrequenty (since it is required if an OFC fault occurs but not under normal operation). In contrast GVT estimates are on the forward path of operation for traditional Time-Warp simulators and must be invoked frequently if a reasonably memory bound is desired; and (ii) in the next section, we present an uncoordinated distributed checkpointing algorithm for virtual time applications that is domino-effect free and lightweight.

6   Uncoordinated Distributed Checkpointing for Time-Warp

In this section, we present an algorithm for uncoordinated distributed checkpoints using virtual time (the viability of this approach was recognized previously [11]). There are two main advantages for this algorithm: (i) it produces domino-effect free consistent checkpoints without coordination; and (ii) the size of the checkpoint is small; instead of checkpointing all of the input, output, and state queues (as required by a consistent checkpoint in real time), only a minimal subset of the entries is required to be checkpointed for this algorithm. The algorithm is lazy, because it does not enforce consistency of the checkpoints as they are created; instead, the last consistent checkpoint is detected when a failure occurs. The algorithm is described in two parts: (i) *checkpointing*, and (ii) *recovery*.

Checkpointing: As each LP advances its simulation without an OFC fault, it checkpoints itself at pre-negotiated virtual times (similar to *Target Virtual Time* [16]). This feature is the key to the algorithms superiority to coordinated checkpointing algorithms; instead of coordinating *in real time* at a considerable overhead to realize a consistent state, static coordination in virtual time is established. The checkpointing steps are:

- LPs negotiate a simulation checkpoint interval, τ; this step could be carried out off-line, or infrequently.
- A checkpoint is taken independently by each LP as it reaches the preapproved checkpoint simulation time t; the checkpoint is taken at the last state *before* simulation time t. Note that if an LP rolls back past t, it will be checkpointed again when its simulation time reaches t again[4].
- At a checkpoint, each LP saves the state before t and all messages with a *sendtime* $< t$ and a *receivetime* $\geq t$.

---

[4] To minimize repeated checkpointing because of roll-backs, the checkpoint is taken when the checkpoint state is about to be fossil-collected.

Note that no communication occurs other than in the initial set-up step (the algorithm is uncoordinated), and that only one state entry and a subset of the messages in the output queue are saved at each checkpoint (the algorithm is lightweight).

Recovery: In the event of an OFC fault, the recovery mechanism is invoked. Because checkpointing is carried out without coordination, it is first necessary to determine which checkpoint should be used for recovery. The recovery algorithm composes a consistent checkpoint from the individual checkpoints by using the latest checkpoint that has been reached by all LPs (accounting for messages in transit)[5]. Determining the correct recovery checkpoint requires a consensus among the LPs to be reached, in a manner similar to GVT algorithms. The simulation is restarted by having each process discard state and event histories, reload the state information from the checkpoint, and resend the saved messages. Note that the messages in the network must be either drained before restart, or detected and discarded. For space considerations, we do not present proofs that the algorithm produces and detects consistent cuts [17]. Informally, the proof uses the following observations: (i) a set of states occuring at the same virtual time is legal if GVT has passed it (which is ensured by detecting the checkpoint that all LPs have passed) — it is the distributed equivelant of the state produced by sequential simulation; and (ii) the message behavior is preserved by regenerating only the messages that cross the restored snapshot (generated from its past and destined to its future).

Collecting the Checkpoints : Although the checkpoints are stored infrequently, there has to be a method to collect them to free up resources. There are several possibilities for collecting checkpoints, including: (i) invoke a lightweight GVT calculation when a certain number of checkpoints accumulates and free up the ones earlier than GVT; (ii) when an OFC fault occurs, a consistent checkpoint is detected and restored. At every LP, the checkpoints earlier than the one used can be collected (since a more recent checkpoint exists); (iii) a two level checkpointing scheme where checkpoints are maintained in memory. Occasionally, older checkpoints are flushed to disk (freeing up memory space). Although disk space is not infinite, this reduces the frequency at which the checkpoint space needs to be reclaimed.

7 Analysis

In this section, we compare the performance and memory properties of OFC to traditional fossil-collection techniques such as pGVT [3] and Mattern's [12] GVT algorithm. The pGVT algorithm maintains a tight bound on GVT by having the LPs report increments in their LVT to a statically elected LP (which then assumes the role of a GVT manager) periodically. In contrast, Mattern's algorithm

---

[5] Some LPs may have surged ahead with their computation and taken checkpoints that other LPs have not yet reached.

is a lightweight algorithm based on the Chandy-Lamport distributed termination detection algorithm [1]. Mattern's algorithm is less aggressive than pGVT; it has a lower overhead but produces a less accurate estimate of GVT. The three algorithms were implemented in the WARPED Time-Warp simulator [10]. The performance is reported for two simulation models (a RAID disk array model and the P-Hold benchmark) simulating across a network of workstations (4 processors were used for each simulation).

Algorithm	Model	Time (s)	Memory (bytes)	
			Avg.	Max
pGVT	RAID	1110.17	2133403	5400631
Mattern	RAID	1023.19	2180713	6540746
OFC	RAID	955.40	1864138	2013004
pGVT	PHOLD	593.26	1666736	5245655
Mattern	PHOLD	534.14	4118584	15731407
OFC	PHOLD	466.92	1558613	1616748

Table 1. Performance Characteristics of OFC, pGVT, and Mattern's Algorithm

Three simulator configurations were created: two corresponding to the two GVT-based garbage collectors, and one corresponding to an OFC-based garbage collector using the Chebyshev decision model with a low risk factor ($\alpha = 0.999$). For this risk factor, we expect the number of OFC faults to be small, and the memory bound to be conservative. Table 1 shows the performance results obtained for the two models. For both sets of experiments, OFC achieved better execution time and a tighter memory bound (average as well as maximum) than either pGVT or Mattern's algorithms. Recall that Mattern's algorithm is less aggressive than pGVT and, therefore, produces a less accurate memory bound but with a better execution time.

8 Conclusion

In Time-Warp simulations, each logical process (LP) maintains history queues in order to allow recovery from overly optimistic computation. As the global progress time of the simulation advances, older histories are no longer needed (fossilized), and the memory space they occupy must be reclaimed to allow newer histories to be stored. Traditional implementations of Time-Warp estimate the Global Virtual Time (GVT) in order to identify fossils. Estimating GVT involves a significant communication overhead that varies with the GVT estimation algorithm. In addition, because a global overhead is incurred whenever an individual LP requires fossil-collection, the technique is vulnerable to inefficiency from LPs that are memory constrained.

This paper presented Optimistic Fossil-Collection (OFC): a probabilistic distributed model for garbage collection on Time-Warp simulators. OFC eliminates the need for GVT estimates and allows the LPs to tailor their memory usage to their local rollback behavior. Each LP decides which history items are likely to be fossilized using a local decision function and proceeds to collect these items optimistically. A perfect decision function would converge on the *active history* for the LP. The active history is the minimum subset of history items that is sufficient to recover from any rollback that occurs in the future. Note that this limit is bounded by true GVT — a perfect decision mechanism will yield a memory bound superior to the true GVT bound (in fact, it is a minimal memory bound). Even though a perfect decision mechanism is impossible to construct at run-time, there is a potential for OFC to produce memory bounds superior to GVT-based algorithms, especially since the GVT estimate used by these algorithms lags true GVT.

Since history items are collected without global knowledge of the simulation state, there is a nonzero probability that an history item that was collected will be needed in the future — an OFC fault occurs. A recovery mechanism must be implemented to enable recovery from OFC faults. Thus, OFC consists of two, largely decoupled, facets: the decision mechanism and the recovery mechanism. The paper investigated models for both the decision and recovery aspects of OFC. We classified decision functions into statistical and heuristic based functions. The statistical decision functions presume a rollback distribution function (created by sampling local rollbacks) and predict an upper bound on the rollback distance with specified acceptable risk factor (confidence). Because the rollback behavior may not correspond to the presumed distribution, we also presented a limit based on the Chebyshev inequality — this limit is independent of the underlying rollback distribution. The heuristic functions adaptively converge to an active history estimate. Both of these approaches provide good bounds on the maximum rollback distance [17].

For the recovery aspect of OFC, a method for creating on-the-fly consistent checkpoints is required. We presented an algorithm for uncoordinated checkpointing of applications using virtual time. With OFC, Time-Warp simulators become a two-level recovery algorithm: (i) rollback to recover from erroneous optimism in computation, and (ii) the OFC recovery mechanism to overcome erroneous optimism in fossil-collection. We conducted an empirical comparison of OFC with two traditional GVT algorithms: pGVT [3] and Mattern's algorithm [12]. OFC executed faster than pGVT, while producing a tighter memory bound. Conversely, OFC produced a tighter memory bound than that achieved by Mattern's algorithm for the studied models. However, Mattern's algorithm execution time was better than OFC's on SMMP, but worse on RAID. We anticipate that refinement to our decision and recovery algorithms will further enhance the performance of OFC.

References

[1] CHANDY, K. M., AND LAMPORT, L. Distributed snapshots: Determining global states of distributed systems. *ACM Transactions on Computer Systems 3*, 1 (Feb. 1985), 63–75.

[2] DAS, S., FUJIMOTO, R., PANESAR, K., ALLISON, D., AND HYBINETTE, M. GTW: a time warp system for shared memory multiprocessors. In *Proceedings of the 1994 Winter Simulation Conference* (Dec. 1994), J. D. Tew, S. Manivannan, D. A. Sadowski, and A. F. Seila, Eds., pp. 1332–1339.

[3] D'SOUZA, L. M., FAN, X., AND WILSEY, P. A. pGVT: An algorithm for accurate GVT estimation. In *Proc. of the 8th Workshop on Parallel and Distributed Simulation (PADS 94)* (July 1994), Society for Computer Simulation, pp. 102–109.

[4] ELNOZAHY, E., JOHNSON, D., AND WANG, Y. A survey of rollback-recovery protocols in message-passing systems. Tech. Rep. Tech. Rept. CMU-CS-96-181, School of Computer Science, Carnegie Mellon University, Oct. 1996.

[5] FLEISCHMANN, J., AND WILSEY, P. A. Comparative analysis of periodic state saving techniques in time warp simulators. In *Proc. of the 9th Workshop on Parallel and Distributed Simulation (PADS 95)* (June 1995), pp. 50–58.

[6] FUJIMOTO, R. Parallel discrete event simulation. *Communications of the ACM 33*, 10 (Oct. 1990), 30–53.

[7] JEFFERSON, D. Virtual time. *ACM Transactions on Programming Languages and Systems 7*, 3 (July 1985), 405–425.

[8] LAI, T., AND YANG, J. On distributed snapshots. *Information Processing Letters 25* (May 1987), 153–158.

[9] LIN, Y.-B. Memory management algorithms for optimistic parallel simulation. In *6th Workshop on Parallel and Distributed Simulation* (Jan. 1992), Society for Computer Simulation, pp. 43–52.

[10] MARTIN, D. E., MCBRAYER, T. J., AND WILSEY, P. A. WARPED: A time warp simulation kernel for analysis and application development. In *29th Hawaii International Conference on System Sciences (HICSS-29)* (Jan. 1996), H. El-Rewini and B. D. Shriver, Eds., vol. Volume I, pp. 383–386.

[11] MATTERN, F. Virtual time and global states in distributed systems. In *Proc. Workshop on Parallel and Distributed Algorithms* (Oct. 1989), M. Cosnard et al, Ed., pp. 215–226.

[12] MATTERN, F. Efficient algorithms for distributed snapshots and global virtual time approximation. *Journal of Parallel and Distributed Computing 18*, 4 (Aug. 1993), 423–434.

[13] RANDELL, B. System structure for software fault tolerance. *IEEE Trans. on Software Engineering SE-1*, 2 (June 1975), 220–232.

[14] ROSS, S. M. *Introduction to Probability Models*, 4 ed. Academic Press, San Diego, CA, 1989.

[15] SPEZIALETTI, M., AND KEARNS, P. Efficient distributed snapshots. In *Proc. IEEE International Conference on Distributed Computing Systems* (1986), pp. 382–388.

[16] TOMLINSON, A. I., AND GARG, V. K. An algorithm for minimally latent global virtual time. In *Proc of the 7th Workshop on Parallel and Distributed Simulation (PADS)* (July 1993), Society for Computer Simulation, pp. 35–42.

[17] YOUNG, C. *Methods for Optimistic Reclamation of Fossils in Time Warp Simulation*. PhD thesis, University of Cincinnati, June 1997. (Ph.D. proposal).

Author Index

Springer
and the
environment

At Springer we firmly believe that an international science publisher has a special obligation to the environment, and our corporate policies consistently reflect this conviction.
We also expect our business partners – paper mills, printers, packaging manufacturers, etc. – to commit themselves to using materials and production processes that do not harm the environment. The paper in this book is made from low- or no-chlorine pulp and is acid free, in conformance with international standards for paper permanency.

Springer

Lecture Notes in Computer Science

For information about Vols. 1–1415

please contact your bookseller or Springer-Verlag

Vol. 1456: A. Drogoul, M. Tambe, T. Fukuda (Eds.), Collective Robotics. Proceedings, 1998. VII, 161 pages. 1998. (Subseries LNAI).

Vol. 1457: A. Ferreira, J. Rolim, H. Simon, S.-H. Teng (Eds.), Solving Irregularly Structured Problems in Prallel. Proceedings, 1998. X, 408 pages. 1998.

Vol. 1458: V.O. Mittal, H.A. Yanco, J. Aronis, R-. Simpson (Eds.), Assistive Technology in Artificial Intelligence. X, 273 pages. 1998. (Subseries LNAI).

Vol. 1459: D.G. Feitelson, L. Rudolph (Eds.), Job Scheduling Strategies for Parallel Processing. Proceedings, 1998. VII, 257 pages. 1998.

Vol. 1460: G. Quirchmayr, E. Schweighofer, T.J.M. Bench-Capon (Eds.), Database and Expert Systems Applications. Proceedings, 1998. XVI, 905 pages. 1998.

Vol. 1461: G. Bilardi, G.F. Italiano, A. Pietracaprina, G. Pucci (Eds.), Algorithms – ESA'98. Proceedings, 1998. XII, 516 pages. 1998.

Vol. 1462: H. Krawczyk (Ed.), Advances in Cryptology - CRYPTO '98. Proceedings, 1998. XII, 519 pages. 1998.

Vol. 1463: N.E. Fuchs (Ed.), Logic Program Synthesis and Transformation. Proceedings, 1997. X, 343 pages. 1998.

Vol. 1464: H.H.S. Ip, A.W.M. Smeulders (Eds.), Multimedia Information Analysis and Retrieval. Proceedings, 1998. VIII, 264 pages. 1998.

Vol. 1465: R. Hirschfeld (Ed.), Financial Cryptography. Proceedings, 1998. VIII, 311 pages. 1998.

Vol. 1466: D. Sangiorgi, R. de Simone (Eds.), CONCUR'98: Concurrency Theory. Proceedings, 1998. XI, 657 pages. 1998.

Vol. 1467: C. Clack, K. Hammond, T. Davie (Eds.), Implementation of Functional Languages. Proceedings, 1997. X, 375 pages. 1998.

Vol. 1468: P. Husbands, J.-A. Meyer (Eds.), Evolutionary Robotics. Proceedings, 1998. VIII, 247 pages. 1998.

Vol. 1469: R. Puigjaner, N.N. Savino, B. Serra (Eds.), Computer Performance Evaluation. Proceedings, 1998. XIII, 376 pages. 1998.

Vol. 1470: D. Pritchard, J. Reeve (Eds.), Euro-Par'98: Parallel Processing. Proceedings, 1998. XXII, 1157 pages. 1998.

Vol. 1471: J. Dix, L. Moniz Pereira, T.C. Przymusinski (Eds.), Logic Programming and Knowledge Representation. Proceedings, 1997. IX, 246 pages. 1998. (Subseries LNAI).

Vol. 1473: X. Leroy, A. Ohori (Eds.), Types in Compilation. Proceedings, 1998. VIII, 299 pages. 1998.

Vol. 1474: F. Mueller, A. Bestavros (Eds.), Languages, Compilers, and Tools for Embedded Systems. Proceedings, 1998. XIV, 261 pages. 1998.

Vol. 1475: W. Litwin, T. Morzy, G. Vossen (Eds.), Advances in Databases and Information Systems. Proceedings, 1998. XIV, 369 pages. 1998.

Vol. 1476: J. Calmet, J. Plaza (Eds.), Artificial Intelligence and Symbolic Computation. Proceedings, 1998. XI, 309 pages. 1998. (Subseries LNAI).

Vol. 1477: K. Rothermel, F. Hohl (Eds.), Mobile Agents. Proceedings, 1998. VIII, 285 pages. 1998.

Vol. 1478: M. Sipper, D. Mange, A. Pérez-Uribe (Eds.), Evolvable Systems: From Biology to Hardware. Proceedings, 1998. IX, 382 pages. 1998.

Vol. 1479: J. Grundy, M. Newey (Eds.), Theorem Proving in Higher Order Logics. Proceedings, 1998. VIII, 497 pages. 1998.

Vol. 1480: F. Giunchiglia (Ed.), Artificial Intelligence: Methodology, Systems, and Applications. Proceedings, 1998. IX, 502 pages. 1998. (Subseries LNAI).

Vol. 1481: E.V. Munson, C. Nicholas, D. Wood (Eds.), Principles of Digital Document Processing. Proceedings, 1998. VII, 152 pages. 1998.

Vol. 1482: R.W. Hartenstein, A. Keevallik (Eds.), Field-Programmable Logic and Applications. Proceedings, 1998. XI, 533 pages. 1998.

Vol. 1483: T. Plagemann, V. Goebel (Eds.), Interactive Distributed Multimedia Systems and Telecommunication Services. Proceedings, 1998. XV, 326 pages. 1998.

Vol. 1484: H. Coelho (Ed.), Progress in Artificial Intelligence – IBERAMIA 98. Proceedings, 1998. XIII, 421 pages. 1998. (Subseries LNAI).

Vol. 1485: J.-J. Quisquater, Y. Deswarte, C. Meadows, D. Gollmann (Eds.), Computer Security – ESORICS 98. Proceedings, 1998. X, 377 pages. 1998.

Vol. 1486: A.P. Ravn, H. Rischel (Eds.), Formal Techniques in Real-Time and Fault-Tolerant Systems. Proceedings, 1998. VIII, 339 pages. 1998.

Vol. 1487: V. Gruhn (Ed.), Software Process Technology. Proceedings, 1998. VIII, 157 pages. 1998.

Vol. 1488: B. Smyth, P. Cunningham (Eds.), Advances in Case-Based Reasoning. Proceedings, 1998. XI, 482 pages. 1998. (Subseries LNAI).

Vol. 1490: C. Palamidessi, H. Glaser, K. Meinke (Eds.), Principles of Declarative Programming. Proceedings, 1998. XI, 497 pages. 1998.

Vol. 1493: J.P. Bowen, A. Fett, M.G. Hinchey (Eds.), ZUM '98: The Z Formal Specification Notation. Proceedings, 1998. XV, 417 pages. 1998.

Vol. 1495: T. Andreasen, H. Christiansen, H.L. Larsen (Eds.), Flexible Query Answering Systems. IX, 393 pages. 1998. (Subseries LNAI).

Vol. 1497: V. Alexandrov, J. Dongarra (Eds.), Recent Advances in Parallel Virtual Machine and Message Passing Interface. Proceedings, 1998. XII, 412 pages. 1998.

Vol. 1498: A.E. Eiben, T. Bäck, M. Schoenauer, H.-P. Schwefel (Eds.), Parallel Problem Solving from Nature – PPSN V. Proceedings, 1998. XXIII, 1041 pages. 1998.

Vol. 1499: S. Kutten (Ed.), Distributed Computing. Proceedings, 1998. XII, 419 pages. 1998.

Vol. 1501: M.M. Richter, C.H. Smith, R. Wiehagen, T. Zeugmann (Eds.), Algorithmic Learning Theory. Proceedings, 1998. XI, 439 pages. 1998. (Subseries LNAI).

Vol. 1503: G. Levi (Ed.), Static Analysis. Proceedings, 1998. IX, 383 pages. 1998.

Vol. 1504: O. Herzog, A. Günter (Eds.), KI-98: Advances in Artificial Intelligence. Proceedings, 1998. XI, 355 pages. 1998. (Subseries LNAI).

Vol. 1510: J.M. Żytkow, M. Quafafou (Eds.), Principles of Data Mining and Knowledge Discovery. Proceedings, 1998. XI, 482 pages. 1998. (Subseries LNAI).